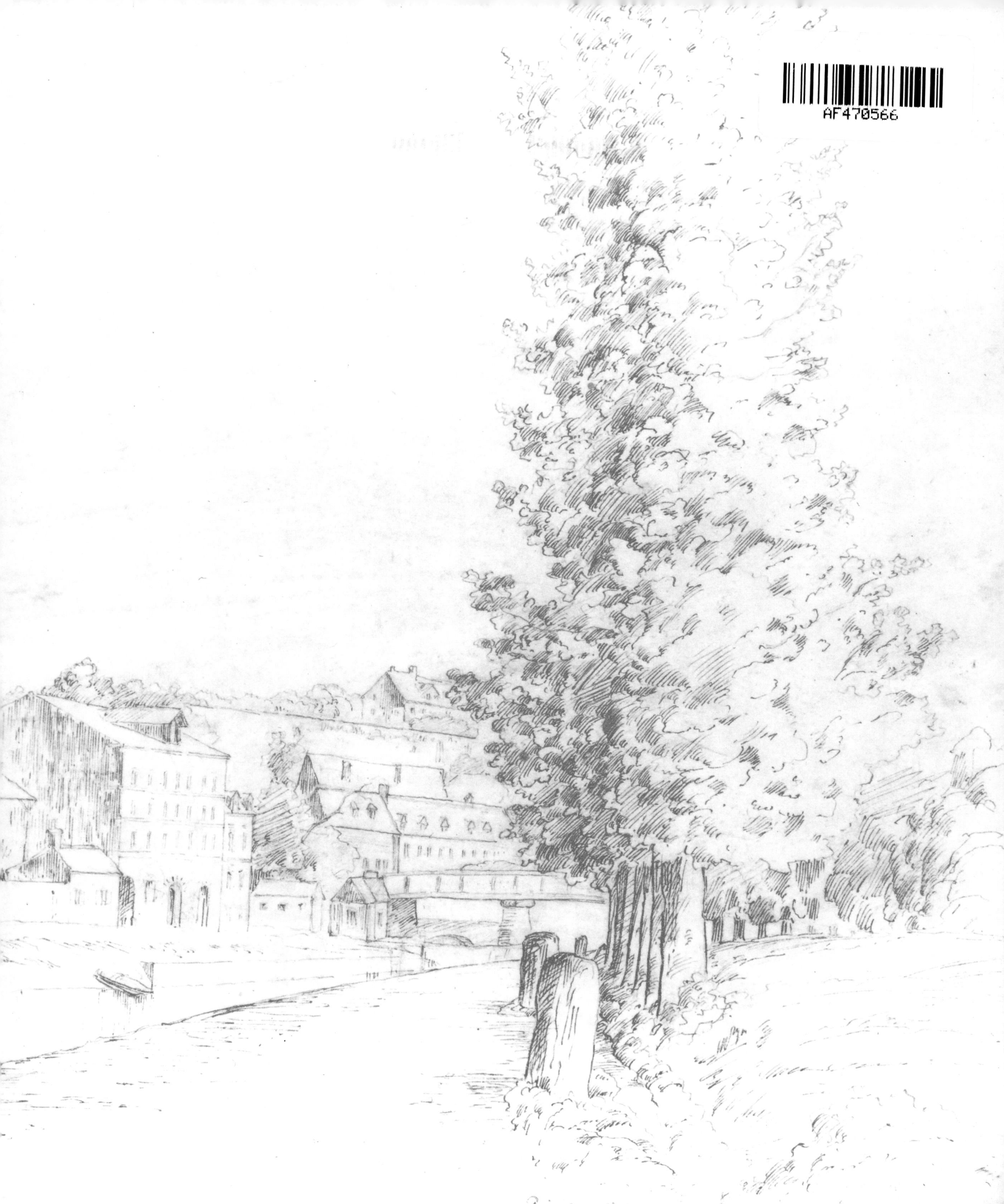
AF470566

Pissarro and Pontoise

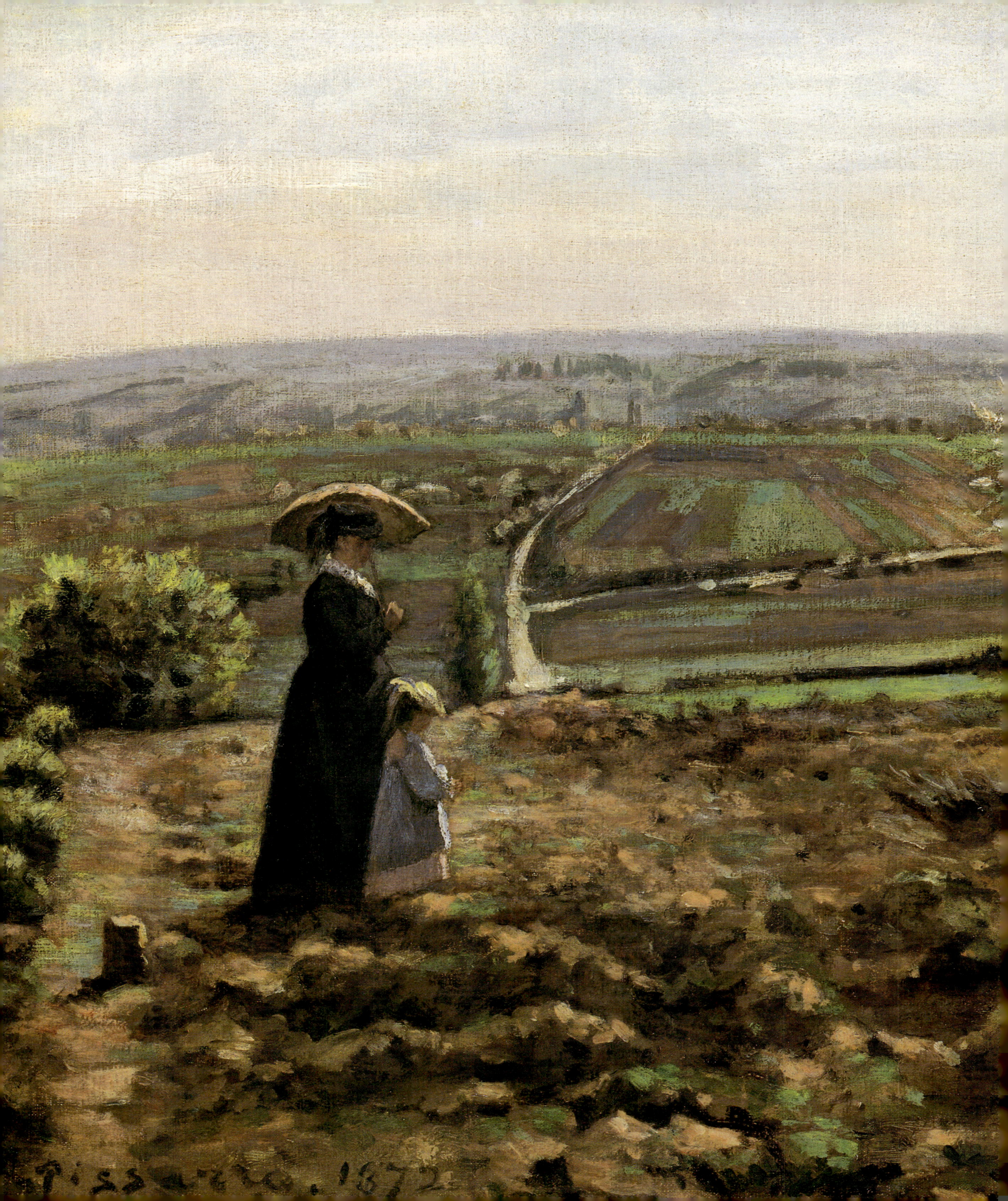

Pissarro. 1872.

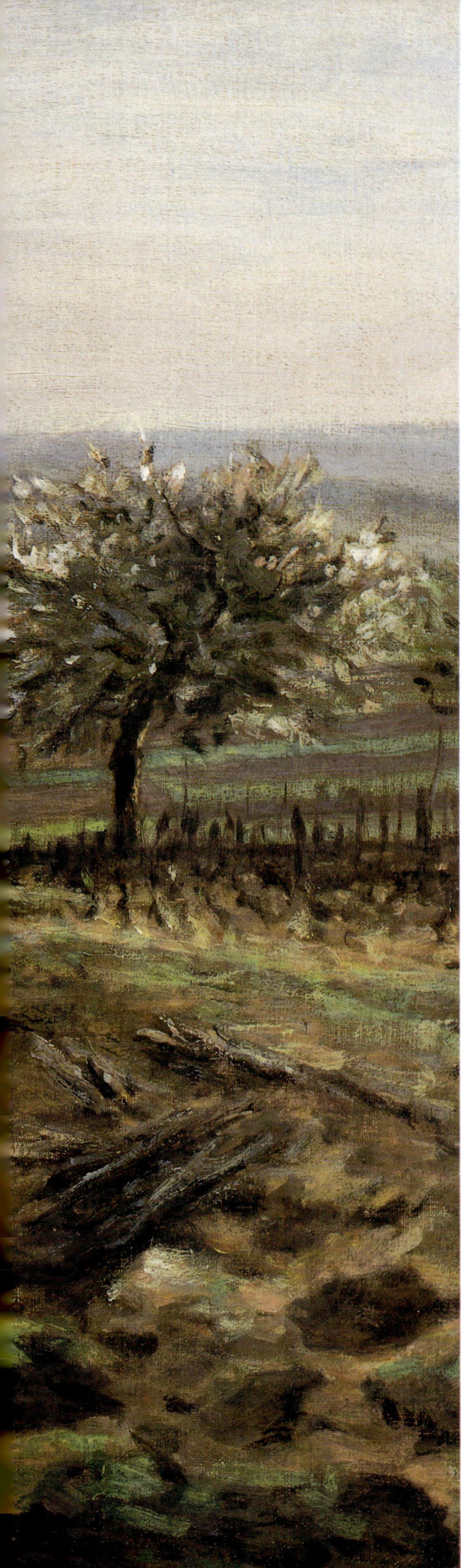

Pissarro
and Pontoise

THE PAINTER IN A LANDSCAPE

RICHARD R. BRETTELL

with assistance from

JOACHIM PISSARRO

GUILD PUBLISHING
LONDON · NEW YORK · SYDNEY · TORONTO

Designed by Gillian Malpass
Typeset in Linotron Bembo by Best-set Typesetter Ltd, Hong Kong
Printed in Spain by Heraclio Fournier S.A., Vitoria

This edition published
1990 by Guild Publishing
by arrangement with
Yale University Press

CN 4400

Frontispiece: Detail of pl. 121.
Endpapers: Detail of pl. 69.

For my teachers

Robert L. Herbert and Anne Coffin Hanson

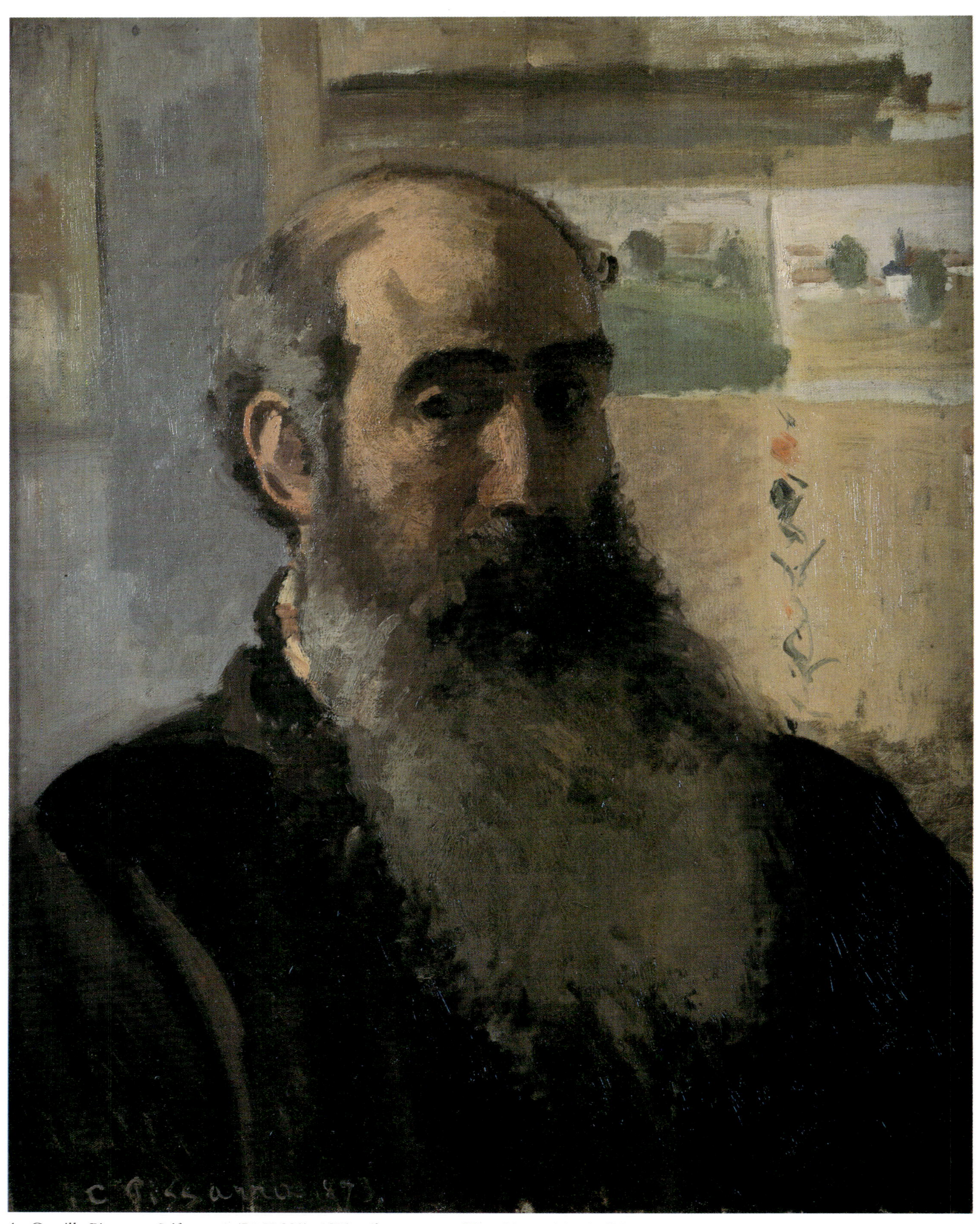

1. Camille Pissarro, *Self-portrait* (P&V 200), 1873, oil on canvas, 55 × 46cm., Musée d'Orsay, Paris.

Contents

Acknowledgments

The author's interest in Impressionism and the theories of "modern" reality was generated and encouraged by Professors Robert L. Herbert and Anne Coffin Hanson at Yale University. Their undergraduate and graduate courses as well as numerous conversations form the conceptual basis for this book. Their combination of the methodologies of the historian of art and the historian of culture has been invaluable. Others at Yale were also important. Professor Peter Gay and his wife, Ruth Gay, provided the author with both intellectual and actual sustenance in New Haven and abroad. Former Master Beekman C. Cannon and the Fellowship of Jonathan Edwards College supported my work in a good many more ways than the financial ones that are recorded in the lists of Jonathan Edwards College Fellowships. Alan Shestack and James Burke, both formerly of the Yale University Art Gallery, and now directors of the Museum of Fine Arts, Boston, and the Saint Louis Art Museum respectively, helped immeasurably by providing a basis for generalizations about art in the examination of actual works of art. Douglas and Roseline Crowley provided good cheer, good conversation, and good advice at several points in the history of this book. My fellow graduate students, especially Barbara Anderson, Pat McNaughton, Ellie Saunders, Melanie Simo, Marilyn Brown, and Thom Kren, were as supportive as fellow graduate students can possibly be, and it would be difficult to imagine having written the dissertation that forms the corpus of this book without the hours of discussion with Eve Blau in New Haven, Paris, London, and Oxford. Finally, the author would like to thank the Yale Graduate School, the Kress Foundation, and the Whiting Foundation for their financial support.

The greatest "scholarly" thanks must go to the author's fellow workers in Pissarro studies. Paula Hays Harper and Barbara Shapiro gave more than generously of their time and conversation. Christopher Lloyd led me through the riches of the Pissarro archives at the Ashmolean Museum and gladly allowed me the honor of a partnership with him in the catalogue of the very large collection of Pissarro drawings housed in that venerated museum. John Rewald has been willing to answer my written queries and to discuss "problems Pissarro" in person. Mark Gerstein shared with me his vast knowledge of French art in the late nineteenth century while we both worked in Paris.

In France, the author's greatest debt of appreciation must go to the people of Pontoise. The staff of the Mairie de Pontoise, the Mairie de Saint-Ouen-l'Aumône, the Société historique et archéologique de Pontoise et du Vexin français, the Archives du Val-d'Oise, and the newly formed Association des amis de Camille Pissarro were generous beyond any expectation. Mme. Edda Maillet of the Musée de Pontoise helped with the intricacies of the bureaucracy of Pontoise and introduced me to many fascinating and informative people. M. Jean Hecquet, a "Pontoisien" by birth and affection and, at present, a resident of Paris, allowed me unlimited access to his huge collection of the "iconographie de Pontoise" and to his enormous personal knowledge of Pontoise's history.

In Paris, thanks must be directed to the staffs of the Bibliothèque d'Art et d'Archéologie of the University of Paris, of the Cabinet des Dessins and the Service de Documentation at the Musée du Louvre, of the Cabinet des Estampes and the Salle de Travail in the Bibliothèque Nationale, and of the Archives Nationales. M. Jean Adhémar and M. Michel Melot were particularly helpful and encouraging. In addition, the photographs of Louveciennes taken in the 1860s and 1870s by Henri Bevan provided by his late granddaughter, Mme. Renée Merle-d'Aubigné, were of enormous help to the progress of the dissertation. Alden Gordon shared with me his experiences and knowledge of France and nineteenth-century French art.

In England, Mr. Michael Kitson of the Courtauld Institute, now director of the Paul Mellon Centre for Studies in British Art, and Ms. Frances Cary of the Department of Prints and Drawings in the British Museum were extremely helpful. The staffs of the Victoria and Albert Museum, the National Gallery, the Tate Gallery, and the British Museum provided a good deal of information and suggestions that would never have occurred to the author himself. The staff of the Ashmolean Museum in Oxford seemed willing to adopt me into their ranks for long periods of time. Particular thanks are due to Mr. David Brown, Mr. John deWitt, and Mr. Kenneth Garlic for their help.

The author would like to extend thanks to the staffs of many museums and private galleries that he visited in France, Switzerland, England, Scotland, Germany, and Italy—too numerous to mention by name.

The warmest thanks are due to the author's former colleagues at the University of Texas at Austin, Eleanor Greenhill, Caroline Houser, Brenda Preyer, Dick Townsend, Don Stadtner, Bill Francis, Terry Grieder, and the chairman, Ken Prescott, who, through the supportive and stimulating environment they provided, own their share in this book. I want to give special thanks to Karen Pope who lent her editorial talents.

It is at once odd—and oddly fitting—that a dissertation completed in Texas should become a book also completed in Texas. My assistant Heidi Bruster, my secretary Liza Skaggs, Linda Ledford, and many other members of the museum staff have contributed to a state of mind compatible with the finishing of this book. The dissertation could not have become a book without the advice, help, persistence, and knowledge of Joachim Pissarro and the wonderful support of his wife, Annabel.

The most profound and personal thanks go to my wife, Carol.

Dallas, September 1989

Maps and Charts

Abbreviations

B&L   Richard R. Brettell and Christopher Lloyd, *Catalogue of the drawings by Camille Pissarro in the Ashmolean Museum*, Oxford, 1980.

D   Loys Delteil, *Le Peintre-graveur illustré (XIXe et XXe siècles)*, vol. 1: *J.F. Millet et al.*, Paris 1906; and vol. 17: *Camille Pissarro, Alfred Sisley, Auguste Renoir*, Paris, 1923.

P&V   Ludovic-Rodo Pissarro and Lionello Venturi, *Camille Pissarro, son art—son oeuvre*, 2 vols., Paris, 1939.

W   Daniel Wildenstein, *Claude Monet: biographie et catalogue raisonné*, 4 vols., Lausanne and Paris, 1974.

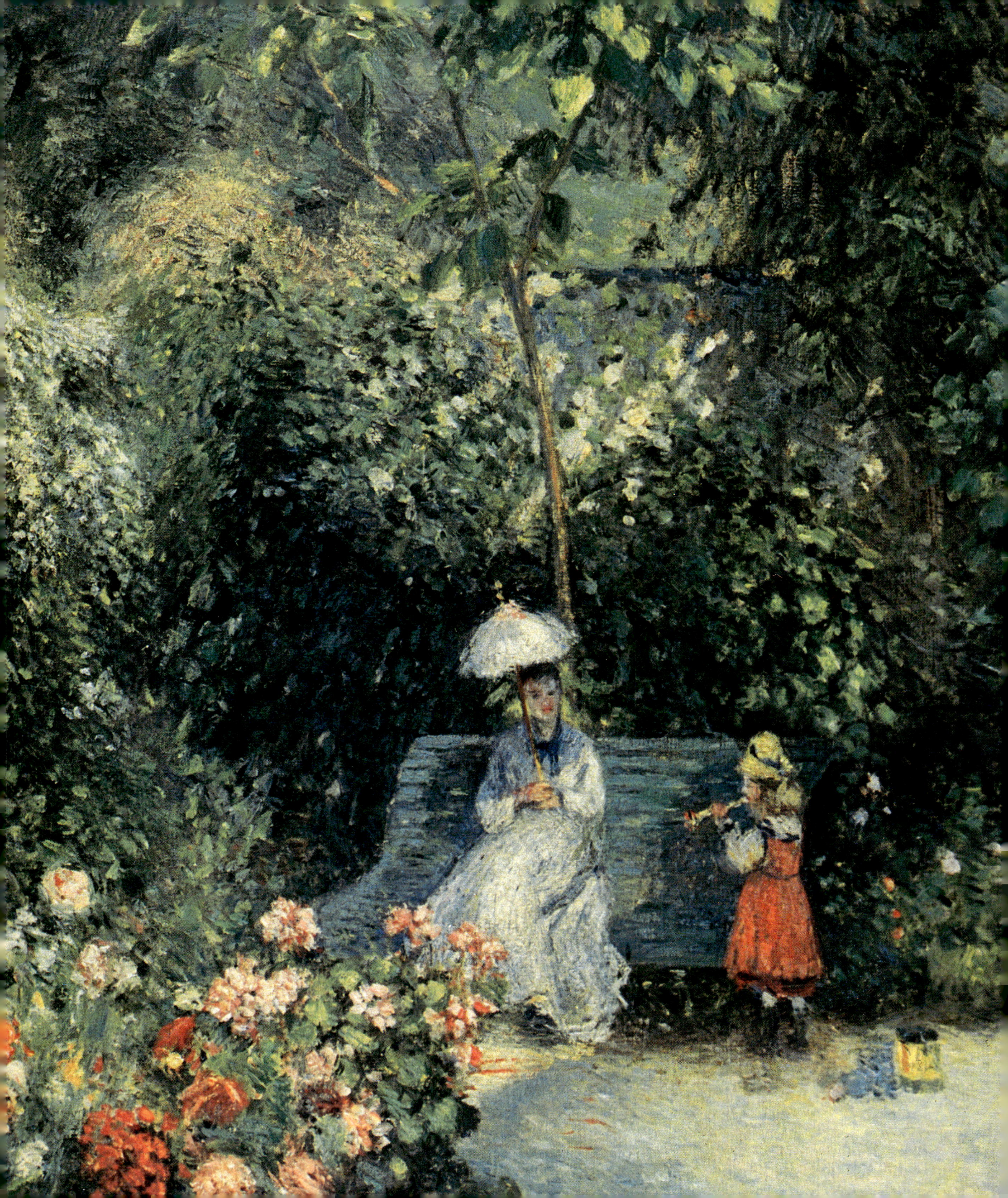

Introduction

Camille Pissarro painted at least three hundred pictures of, in, and around the town of Pontoise between 1866 and 1883. These, together with the prints and the yet uncountable drawings, watercolors, and gouaches representing the same site, form what is probably the most sustained portrait of a place painted by any French landscape painter in the nineteenth century. The number and variety of locative images surpass that of Courbet's Ornans, Chintreuil's Igny, Monet's Argenteuil, and Millet's Barbizon. Pissarro concentrated on Pontoise and its immediate environs with a perseverance and intensity matched only by Cézanne in Aix-en-Provence. The site itself, rather small in surface area when compared with Cézanne's landscape around Aix, possessed a wide variety of motifs or types of nature. It was not the simple rural village in a simple landscape mentioned by so many writers on Pissarro. Both the semi-urban, crowded genre scenes and the views of railroads and factories common in the landscapes of Second Empire tourist illustrators, and the "traditional" or anti-modern aspects of rural life popularized by mid-century Salon landscape painters could be found in and around Pontoise during the period of Pissarro's stay there. In fact, the complexity of Pontoise as a landscape site is remarkable and separates it both from the more purely suburban landscapes of the other Impressionist painters and from the village landscapes of the Barbizon School and their progeny.

The connection between a painter and his site is especially important in the landscape production of the so-called generation of 1830 and their mid-century successors. Fontainebleau, the first and greatest of the famous French "places," is strongly associated with the names of many painters who, in fact, painted in other places as well, and the village of Barbizon was the nominal and physical center for landscape painters as diverse in esthetic temperament as Corot and Théodore Rousseau. The critic Jules Castagnary, in a marvelously contemptuous essay on landscape painting in his Salon of 1866, divided French landscape painters into groups not by style or esthetic persuasion, but by the area of the country in which they painted.[1] Imaginative landscape, composite landscape, and the landscape of fantasy were all but dead by the 1860s, and Castagnary was not alone in emphasizing the territory of the landscape painter as the single most important variable in the definition of that painter's style. The little-known Provençal savant Louis Brès delivered a lecture to the Academy of Marseilles in 1883 with the rather startling title, "Le Paysage Provençal et son influence au point de vue littéraire et artistique."[2] According to Brès, the landscape influenced the painter — sentiments echoed by many other historians of Provençal art in the nineteenth century.[3] Frédéric Henriet, who considered that a more or less mystical-emotional union between the painter and his motif was necessary for the creation of a masterpiece, divided the career of Chintreuil into four parts, each defined by the site in which the painter was working. These distinct stylistic periods were, for Henriet, intimately connected with place, with the kind of nature that the painter depicted. When a painter changed his source of motifs, or so Henriet implied, his style changed accordingly.[4]

2. Detail of pl. 32.

This rather exaggerated idea is of fundamental importance both to an understanding of French landscape painting in the nineteenth century and to an understanding of Pissarro, considered, since Théodore Duret, the archetypal painter of rural life. Nature, for the critics referred to above, is the basis for rather than the mere subject of landscape painting, and, by consequence, form must be found in rather than applied to nature.[5] What all these writers on landscape were attempting to do with this concept of the "geography" of landscape painting was to root art in that most evasive of realms, reality, rather than to place it in the long, glorious, and fundamentally separate tradition of art itself. Indeed, they grounded the artistic process in the very struggle between pictorial and actual realities that enlivened the theory and the production of Renaissance art. The "reality," the *coin de la terre*, chosen by the landscape painter was of vital importance to his career and revealed his esthetic temperament within the landscape tradition as much as a studio painter's copy of a Raphael or a Rembrandt revealed his. Pissarro approached Pontoise at the height of this realist rhetoric and his choice of the modest but ancient provincial city can be analyzed in itself.

When Pissarro arrived in Pontoise in 1866, at the age of thirty-six, France had been significantly pictorialized and therefore "claimed" by landscape painters of various degrees of talent and differing esthetic proclivities. Certain sites or geographical areas evoked the memory of great artists or schools of artists, and, in portraying them, a young painter was either paying homage or trespassing. No one site in France produced more than a generation of landscape painters, or, at least, significant landscape painters. The paintings produced by the followers of the Barbizon School receive as little attention today as Pissarro's lone successor in Pontoise, Gustave Loiseau. Monet, Renoir, and Pissarro went through their rites of passage as landscape painters by visiting and painting in the forest of Fontainebleau in the 1860s, and, of the three, only Pissarro returned to one of the hallowed mid-century sites on his two late trips to Moret in 1901 and 1902. The elderly Sisley, whose frustrated desire for success in later years is difficult to overemphasize, moved to Moret in 1882 in an evident and unsuccessful attempt to reconnect himself with the great mid-century landscape tradition.[6]

In his review of the Salon of 1866, Castagnary placed the young Pissarro into what he called the "division of the Région Parisienne," part of his "great army of landscape painters." With the exception of the artist's short, infrequent trips to England and Belgium, Pissarro remained in that landscape throughout his life. His ties to Paris, the home of his family and the center for the most active art market of the nineteenth century, gave him a choice of sites in a rather crowded landscape. In fact, young landscape painters began to desert the Fontainebleau region in increasing numbers during the 1850s and 1860s, preferring the less established and therefore less burdensome charms of towns in the environs like Cernay-la-Ville, Igny, La Tournelle-Septeuil, Ecouen, Couttes, and Mont-Saint-Père.[7] The hundreds of landscape painters active in the city of Paris during the nineteenth century left the city *en masse* during the season and raged over the landscape of the Région Parisienne. Henriet, the most sympathetic and detailed critic of this movement, was certainly correct in calling the Région Parisienne "the landscape of landscape painters."

It is important to remember that this landscape, described by Henriet in his writings of the 1860s, 1870s, and 1880s, was filled with associations for the young landscape painter. Ville-d'Avray evoked the name of Corot, whose students were so numerous that even he joked about it. Nearby Saint-Cloud was connected with Huet; Mont-Saint-Père, with Lhermitte; Igny, with Chintreuil; Barbizon, with Rousseau; L'Isle-Adam, with Dupré; and Auvers, with Daubigny. It is not uncommon to find the names of landscape painters in the contemporary guide-book descriptions of French towns. The inn at Cernay-la-Ville, filled with paintings and painters, was one of the principal curiosities of the town as the guidebook writer, Adolphe Joanne, described it in 1856 and 1872. Tourists as well as painters were encouraged to think of art and reality at the same time. Most of the painters in this enormous landscape tradition are unknown and unstudied today, but during their lifetime they formed a huge, internally differentiated society who combed the environs of Paris in search of sites.[8] The area around Paris was not a benign and sunkissed source of motifs in which the young painter could or would want to wander freely. It was a well-known, well-documented, and even a rather tired landscape. By 1870, when it had been drawn, sketched, etched, photographed, and painted countless times, the Ile-de-France was the most recorded landscape of the nineteenth century, taking its place with the Roman Campagna as the two greatest landscape sites in the history of western art.[9]

In the decade following his arrival in Paris from Venezuela in 1855, Pissarro was an almost stereotypical landscape painter of the Ile-de-France. He is recorded at Montmorency, La Roche-Guyon, Nanterre, Montmartre, Varenne-Saint-Hilaire, La Tournelle-Septeuil, and Chailly.[10] He probably painted also in other regions with Ludovic Piette, Corot, or any of the many painters with whom he made early alliances. The list above is geographically diverse enough to suggest a great deal of exploration and experimentation with the region as a whole and with the numberous masters who inhabited it. The geographical range of Pissarro's early career is paralleled by the esthetic range observable in his style. All students of the early Pissarro record a mélange or, perhaps more flatteringly, an attempted synthesis of the major landscape styles operating in the Salon or Paris-based landscape-painting world. Champa and Rewald mention Daubigny, Courbet, Corot, and Anton Melbye, and Charles Kunstler and Charles Cogniat both mention the under-studied Chintreuil whom Pissarro knew and with whom he worked at La Tournelle-Septeuil.[11]

Pissarro's eventual choice of Pontoise as "his" landscape can be considered, at least in part, as an indication of his desire to separate himself from the influence of the recognized landscape masters with whom he worked. Pontoise is only six kilometers from Auvers, which was Daubigny's home and the center for his wide-ranging pictorial activity between 1860 and his death in 1878. But Pontoise and its small environs constituted a relatively unrecorded landscape, lacking associations with a painter. It was, insofar as such a thing was possible in 1866, a "virgin" landscape. Its "iconography" is slight and consists, for the most part, of travel images, illustrations from magazines and newspapers, amateur photographs, early postcards and forgettable and forgotten paintings by amateurs.[12] Théodore Rousseau had painted around Pontoise in the 1850s, but his paintings of the site were probably as unknown to Pissarro as they are untraceable by the modern historian of art. Berthe Morisot located herself in a *maison paysanne* in Le Chou near Pontoise during the summer of 1863 and might have told Pissarro or any of a number of mutual friends about the region. Yet, neither Rousseau nor Morisot ever returned to or concentrated on the site.[13]

Pontoise as a site was not visually unique. It was just relatively untouched. Its similarity to other sites of the environs was, in fact, among its principal advantages to a landscape painter so ingrained in the Paris-centered landscape tradition. The Oise was a river among several in the Ile-de-France. Its resemblance to the divided Seine near Bougival is marked, causing Ludovic-Rodo Pissarro and subsequent writers to mistake several river scenes painted in 1871 and 1872 in Bougival for Pontoise pictures.[14] Similar kinds of parallels can be found in the various orchard landscapes painted in Louveciennes and Pontoise during the early 1870s. The hills around Pontoise were not unlike those near the popular region between Cernay-la-Ville and Dampierre. The plateau towns of Vexin, like nearby Ennery, were similar to the Beauce plateau towns, of which Cernay-la-Ville was the most prominent and the most painted example. The cultivated *côtes* near L'Hermitage[15] are comparable to those of Igny and Bièvres where Chintreuil painted in the 1850s and 1860s.

It is clear that, as a site, Pontoise was more associative than original. Pissarro did not seek a new kind of landscape in which he could express his personality in isolation. Such was the motivation for Courbet's choice of sites and, in all probability, for that of Cézanne.[16] The kind of separateness Pissarro sought from the active, even claustrophobic milieu in which he operated, was only partial. In choosing Pontoise, he manifested a desire for independence, but not isolation.

The central concern of this study is the relationship between pictorial and actual realities. Pissarro's paintings during the years 1866 to 1883 will be seen in the context not so much of other works of art, but of the environment they depict and from which they spring. Pontoise and not "nature" itself was the subject of Pissarro's art during the years covered by this study. His landscape titles have an uncanny locative precision and most often convey to the viewer enough information to find the motif in reality without much trouble.[17] Pissarro's very insistence on place names in his titles proves that he was interested in the delicate relationship between perception and representation that so fascinated men of his generation. Indeed, the rooting of art in observation is as important a component of modern esthetics as the idea of *l'art pour l'art* that has provided the intellectual basis for the great majority of critics, connoisseurs, and historians of modern art. Art, for these latter, is best lifted from its context, analyzed either in isolation or in terms of other works of art.

In his charming and often brilliant book of 1876, *Le Paysagiste aux champs*, Frédéric Henriet criticized the "amateurs de Paris" for judging works of pictorial art by comparing them only with other works of art. For Henriet, the sheerly "artful" aspects of art ("l'artifice") are not related to the mental and moral well-being of man, who is, for thinkers like Henriet, rooted in nature.[18] Henriet's sentiments are generalized and might have been advanced more eloquently by Diderot, but they are both compelling and in need of further explication in our post-modernist age in which the work of art has definitively entered the purified realm of the museum. For Henriet and many thinkers of his own and the previous generation, the intimate dialogue between seeing and representing was the crucial element of art. The landscape painter's task was to alter and develop man's perception of and, therefore, relationship with nature by engaging in a protracted experiment in natural representation. The artist, or at least the successful artist, was to devote himself to a new task – "savoir voir." The phrase, which Henriet borrowed ostensibly from Daubigny, is of immense consequence. The artist who devotes himself to "seeing" is decidedly different from the craftsman who devotes himself to "making." When "savoir voir" replaces "savoir faire" as the aim of the artist, the entire meaning of the work of art vis-à-vis both society and other works of art changes.[19] The carefulness and technicality of the craftsman is replaced by the ceaseless experimentation of the representor. Sight itself is subject to continual scrutiny. Seeing, the most "natural" of faculties, is to be learned.

The ramifications of the two words "savoir voir," ascribed to a gentle, unprovoking painter and reported by a minor critic, are of considerable philosophical complexity. By the late nineteenth century in France, seeing and representing had become concepts rather than simple acts, and, as concepts, were continually tested by both viewers and painters of real landscape. Most French landscape paintings dating from the middle and later nineteenth century were painted either within the environs of Paris or in areas within easy reach by train. Any viewer of a landscape painting could have been as familiar with the original landscape as with a particular pictorial version of it. Household libraries contained guidebooks describing the environs of Paris in great detail, and French literature became increasingly concerned with happenings close to a very real Paris. Indeed, the "vision" of the late nineteenth-century Parisian was rather more complicated than the simple term "realism" implies, because "reality" interacted so intensely with various painted or written versions of it. Novels, newspaper articles, guidebooks, prints, photographs, and paintings both defined and altered the educated Parisian's view of the ever-present and ever-changing reality of Paris and its landscape. "Savoir voir" within this context is a richly associationist concept, very far indeed from the workaday dialectic of "illusion" and "reality."

Painters who depict real landscapes derive their flat images from environments of enormous complexity. As they move about in these environments, they are attracted to certain forms and not to others. They observe fortuitous structural parallels between totally different forms viewed from a specific vantage point. They are captivated by certain light qualities which they might never before have perceived. As such, many of the painters' esthetic predilections and pictorial attitudes manifest themselves in their choice of certain sites or motifs within the larger landscape. Settled or stationary landscape painters who "mine" an environment for a number of years are susceptible to rather sophisticated analysis of their painted landscapes.[20] The degree to which they are repetitive or even obsessive in their choice of subjects can be measured. The amount of typological variety within their motifs can be determined. The fullness of their response to the environment can be ascertained. The question as to whether their vision is formally, iconologically, socially, or even psychologically motivated can be asked.

The study of the relationships between pictorial and actual realities is still at a very incipient stage. Historians of art like Leopold Reidemeister, William Seitz, and, more recently, Rewald, have made extensive use of landscape photographs in their efforts to tease out the nature of a painter's transformation of a motif.[21] Yet the results of their studies are often timid and inconclusive. Not only must the veracity of the photograph be questioned by any serious student of pictorial "realities," but also the relationship between the various pictorial media must be thoroughly understood before comparison can be made.

Paul Tucker, whose now famous study *Monet at Argenteuil* (1982) was written somewhat later than the bulk of this text, is a more subtle and patient student of the relationships between real and painted landscapes. Yet, even in his brilliant book, the reader comes away with the feeling that landscape paintings *are* what they represent, and that, if we learn enough about their apparent subjects, we shall be able to understand them. Perhaps because Pissarro was a maddeningly complex artist—more so than Monet—Tucker's methods do not work very well when dealing with Pissarro and Pontoise, and, for that reason, the two books will be independent pendants, whose texts will often appear to contradict each other.

As any student of the "photographic comparative" tradition or any viewer of the photographs of Pontoisian sites published by Reidemeister in *Auf den Spuren der Maler des Ile de France* can easily see, Pissarro's transformations of visual reality were so considerable in the decades of the 1860s and 1870s that comparison with a photograph of a discrete framed view within nature is practically useless. It is, in fact, almost impossible to take a meaningful photograph that will correspond in any full sense to a painting under investigation. Pissarro did not work, as we all

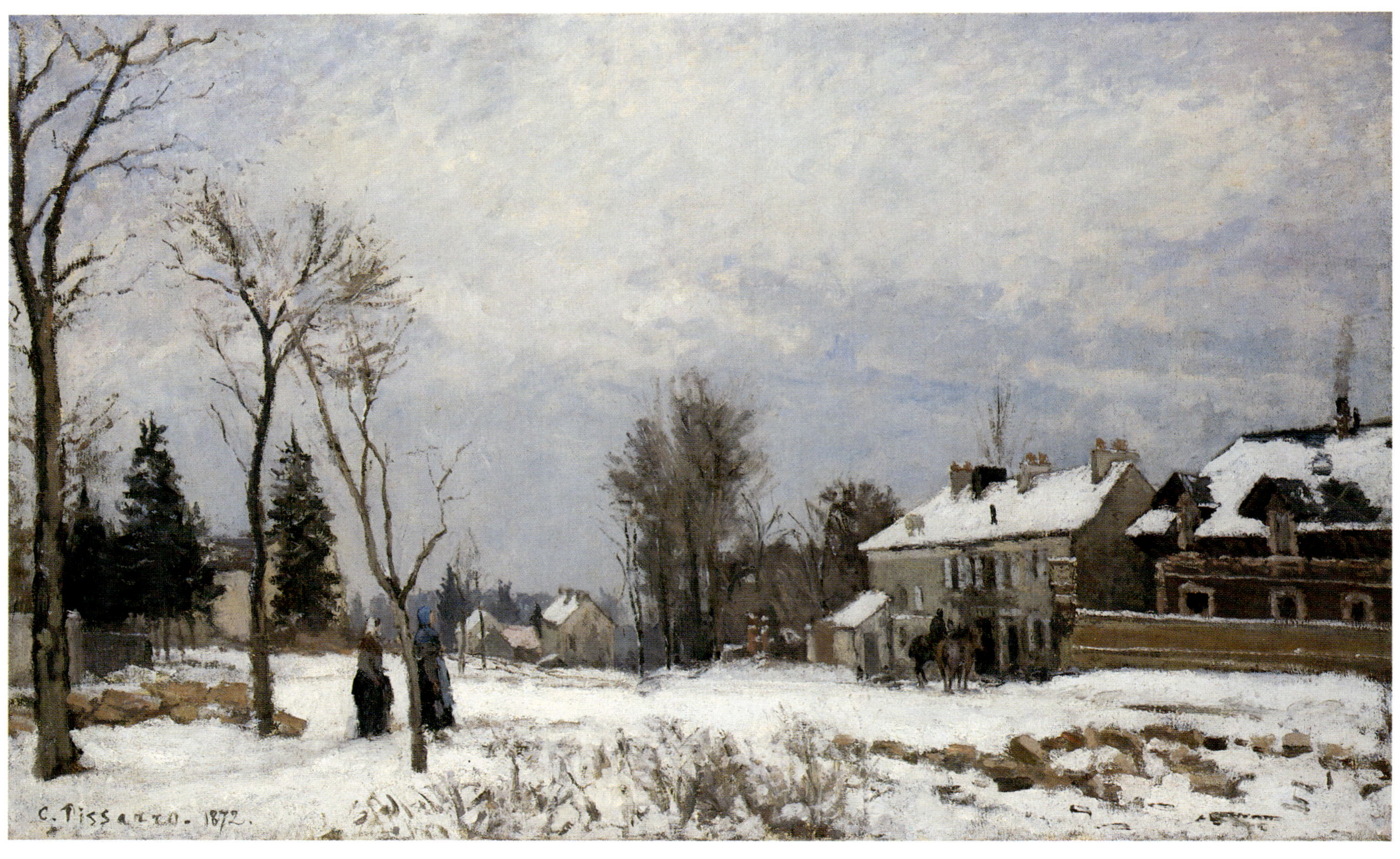

3. Camille Pissarro, *La Route de Versailles à Saint-Germain, Louveciennes, effet de neige* (P&V 130), 1872, oil on canvas, 55 × 91cm., private collection, U.S.A.

know, from photographs. His own perception of the landscape, rooted as it was in the French nineteenth-century landscape tradition, was considerably more complex. A simple examination of his many paintings of the route de Versailles in Louveciennes will show that he altered the size, character, length, and gradient of the street as well as the relative position of the buildings that lined it. One curious pairing of 1872 (pls. 3 and 4) shows an identical winter landscape on the route de Versailles both with and without a large Second Empire country house next to the auberge that Pissarro painted so often. The house existed on the route de Versailles, and still does, but it is at least three hundred yards down the street from the auberge. This simple example is clear evidence that Pissarro did not view nature photographically. In fact, he altered forms within the environment, moved architectural masses with all the glorious freedom available to the landscape painter, and changed the slope and character of the earth's topography. The elasticity of his vision does not permit a ready comparison with the more standardized and inclusive eye of the camera.[22]

Another objection to the photographic comparative method relates to the abstractness and detachment of the photographic image, when compared with human perception. People do not see like cameras, as both perceptual scientists and nineteenth-century critics of photographs readily tell us. The eye moves with a nervous rapidity over the field of vision, and it moves at the service of the psyche. We structure reality as we have been taught to, ignoring bothersome or psychologically painful forms and caressing other forms associated both with cultural concepts and with important phases in our own psychological lives. The

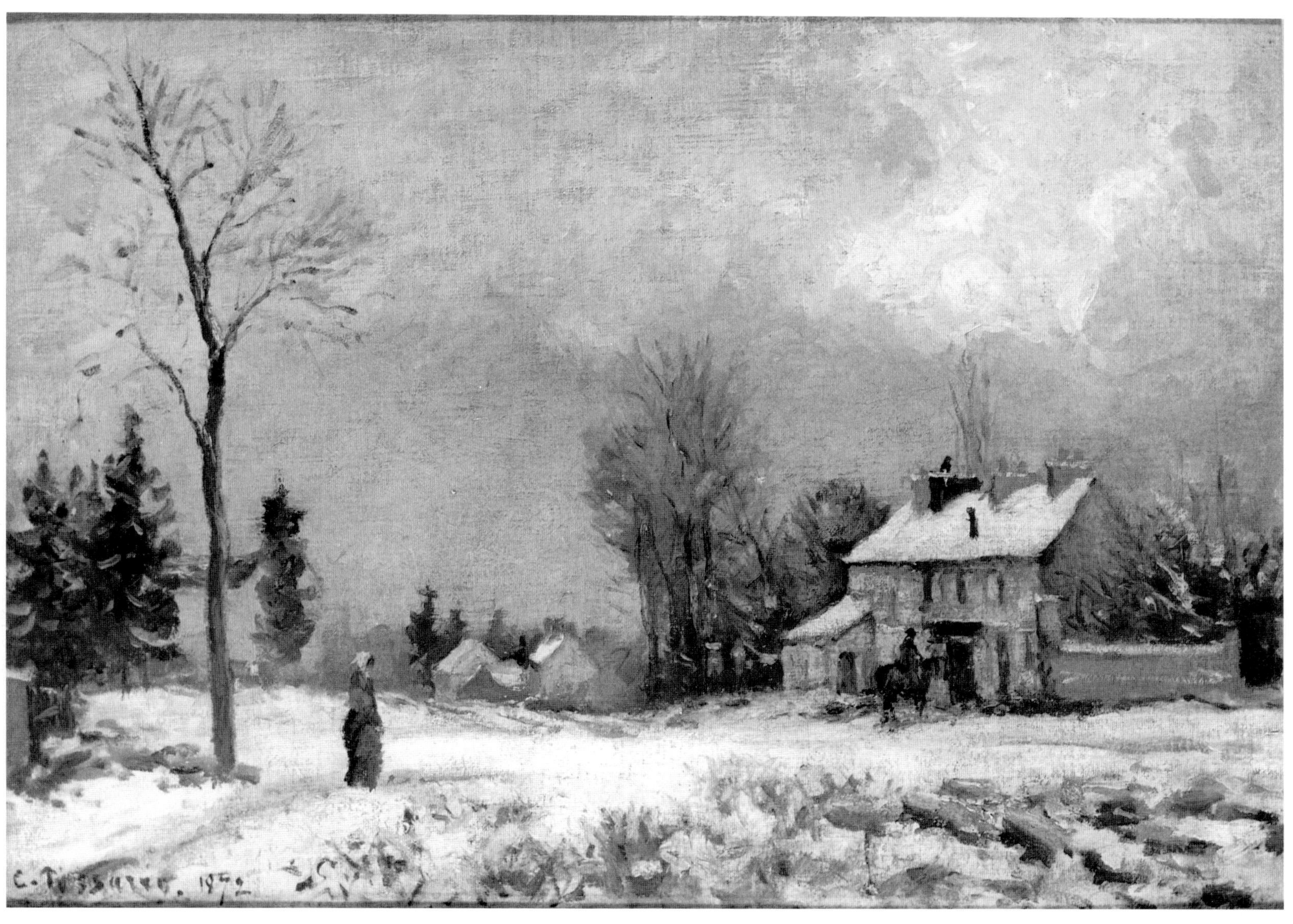

4. Camille Pissarro, *Route de Versailles à Saint-Germain à Louveciennes* (P&V 131), 1872, oil on canvas, 32 × 46cm., private collection.

camera has no such psyche. It neither sees nor interprets reality as does a human being.

Pissarro and Pontoise derives its methodological impetus not only from the history of art, but from literary and cultural historical studies as well. Indeed, the works that stand most forcefully behind this study are Vincent's monumental *George Sand et le Berry*, published in 1934, and the more recent literary scholarship of Geoffrey Hartman. Hartman's detailed investigations of Wordsworth's vision lack the topographical precision that a student of Pissarro must insist upon, but range widely in their analysis of the interstices of vision and the visionary.[23] Recent investigations of Constable's work by British historians of art have been much more sensitive to the various meanings of a place infused into landscape than have contemporary investigations of French painting. Martin Reid, in an article in the *Burlington Magazine*, has applied many of the methods that Reynolds, Parris and Fleming-Williams developed for the study of Constable to Pissarro's landscapes painted in England. Reid makes extensive and intelligent use of maps and cadastral surveys in an effort to "place" the landscapes by Pissarro in the real landscape, but fails, in the final analysis, to draw even tentative conclusions from a very rich body of data.[24]

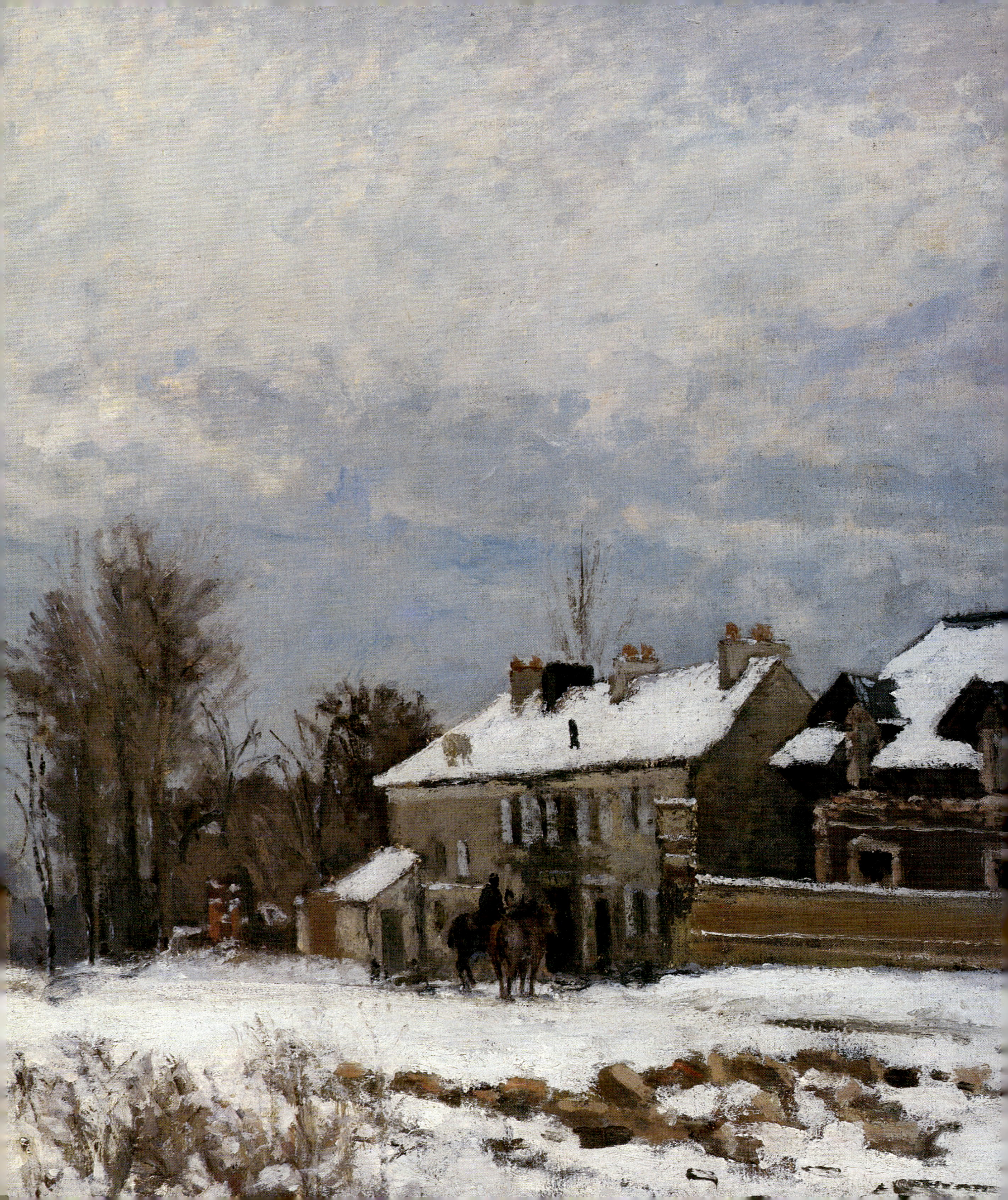

Much more can be learned about the nature of a painter's perception of reality by learning more about the reality he depicted in all its detail. Maps, photographs, historical accounts, guidebook entries, newspaper articles, and statistical tables can aid the modern scholar in his attempts to give flesh to the many realities within the reality portrayed by the painter. Questions of a social and even political nature must be asked when analyzing a painter's response not to a collection of forms, but to an inhabited world with an important resonance.

Although sources and documents related to the history of Pontoise itself are numerous, sources for the study of Pissarro in Pontoise are visual rather than documentary. Few letters survive from this crucial period. Although some of the material appears in other contexts, most of it remained unpublished until Janine Bailly-Herzberg's publication of the first volumes of Pissarro's correspondence.[25] The important correspondence between Pissarro and Piette, who was undoubtedly Pissarro's closest friend before his premature death in 1877, has also been recently published.[26] But even with these two welcome additions to Pissarro's published correspondence, the source material for the 1870s remains rather scarce.

The paucity of source material for this period contrasts dramatically with what is available for the period between 1883 and 1903, for which we have an almost daily account of the life of Pissarro in the two massive correspondences to his sons, Georges and Lucien.[27] Yet, the lack of documentary sources for the 1870s has both advantages and disadvantages. Like the historian of preliterate cultures or the writer on the work of an anonymous painter, the historian of Pissarro's career in Pontoise is essentially undistracted by the biographical concerns that mar so much of the Pissarro literature. The bare outlines of the life are known, but little else interrupts the analysis of the environment and the landscape paintings that depict it. Indeed, Pissarro's art, in all media, is the principal source for the historian of this period of his career. Pontoise itself seems to have hardly noticed him. His name never occurs in the local newspapers, and, since he did not own property, he was not recorded in the accessible communal archives for the period of his stay there. His anonymity seems to have been almost complete. He lived in Pontoise surrounded by his family and paid homage to the town not in documents, not even in friendships, but in paintings, drawings, and prints.

This study is more an interpretation than a definitive treatment of the subject. The many thousands of works of art cannot be treated adequately in a scant two hundred pages of text without overwhelming both the writer and the reader. Therefore, certain key problems related to landscape painting have been chosen for intensive analysis, and several very important works of art will be treated in preference to others. The discussion is focused almost completely on Pissarro himself and on the environment in which he lived. Comparison with contemporary trends in French painting are secondary to the progress of the argument. This decision, while in some respects unfortunate, has certain advantages and responds to certain truths about Pissarro's own artistic interaction with the avant-garde" in the 1870s. The great bulk of correspondence indicates that Pissarro kept abreast of news by letter rather than by personal visits and trips. His journeys to Paris in the early and middle 1870s do not seem to have been either frequent or protracted, and, as a consequence, his knowledge of the contemporary painting of Monet, Manet, and Degas, painting that we know so well today, was more limited than ours. Pissarro did not have a studio in Paris until 1877, and it is not until the latter part of the 1870s that his art becomes truly Impressionist, truly related to the developments of the two artists of his own generation who were most important to him, Monet and Degas.

5. Detail of pl. 3.

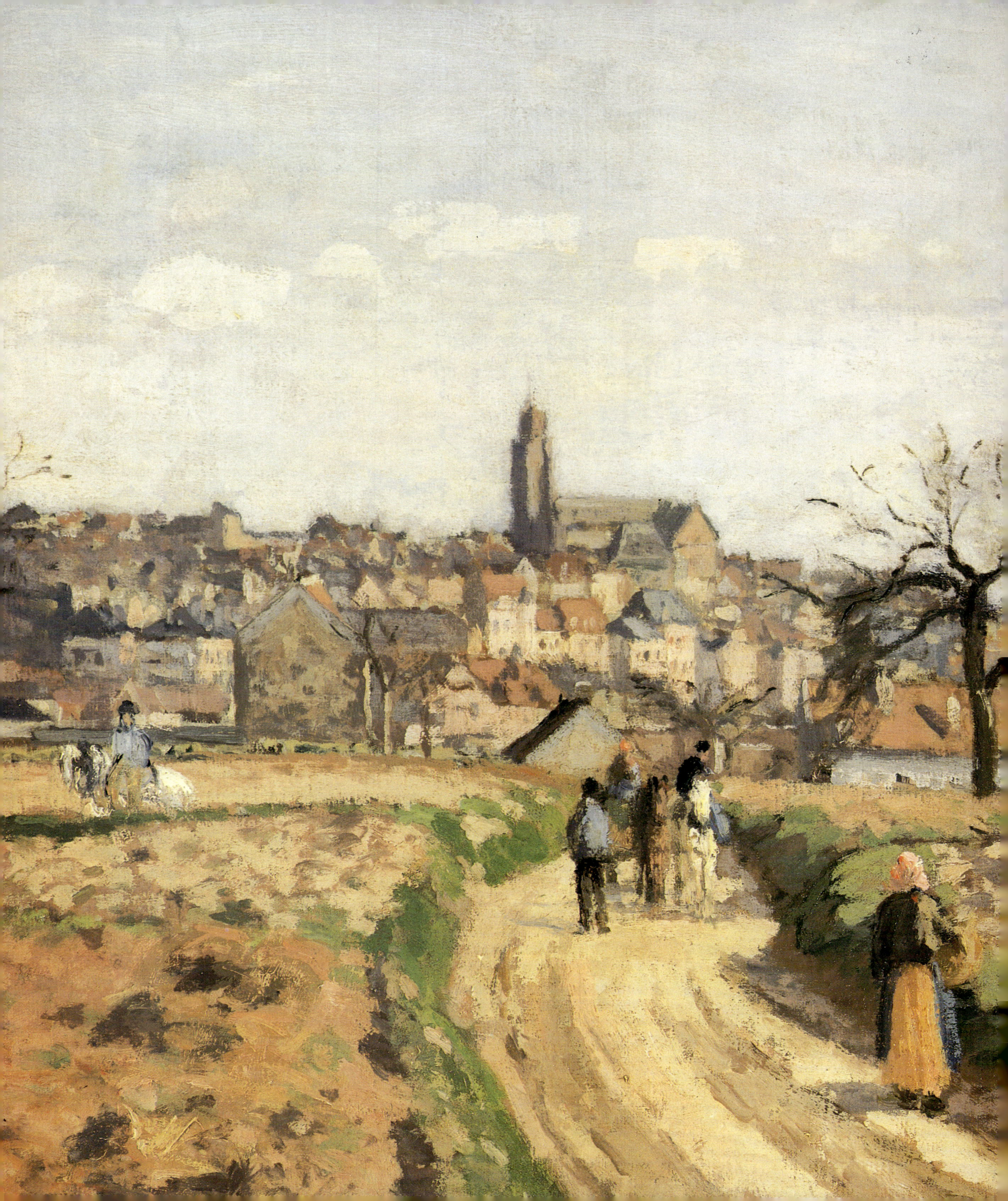

1 Pontoise: The Landscape Itself

The town that Pissarro chose in 1866 as the site for his first significant group of landscape paintings is no ordinary village in the Ile-de-France. Situated strategically on the edge of a plateau above the river Oise, Pontoise commands a view of the vast plain of Montmorency stretching from the Buttes de Cormeilles on the west and the Buttes de Montmorency on the east to the ecclesiastical bastion of Saint-Denis and the center of Paris itself. Possessor of a double character, both port and fortress, Pontoise has been inhabited continuously since the time of the Celts. Its importance within the history of France is far deeper, more complex, and more multi-layered than that of the better-known towns of Versailles, Compiègne, Fontainebleau, or Argenteuil. Of the many towns and villages in the environs of Paris, only a few, like Saint-Denis, Etampes, and Provins, surpass it in the depth and variety of its historical significance.

These claims may seem exaggerated, even extravagant to the modern visitor to Pontoise. The town now spreads sloppily across the river, up the hills, and along the plains of Vexin français. There is little discreteness or urbanity about it. The old section, crowned by the attractive tower of Saint-Maclou, has few buildings of architectural or urban importance except the fifteenth-century Hôtel Tavet, the church of Notre-Dame, and Saint-Maclou itself. It rates no more than a single star in the star-studded Michelin guide to the environs of Paris, a star that acknowledges Pontoise's historical significance more than its present charms. In order to grasp the various meanings of Pontoise in the period of Pissarro's stay there, two aspects of its identity will be examined, its "image," both visually and historically defined, and its actual character and appearance between 1866 and 1885. Both image and appearance are interrelated and equally important in our apprehension of place. For the nineteenth-century tourist visiting Pontoise, guidebook in hand, or even for the permanent inhabitant of the town, imagination and perception would have contributed almost equally to his idea of the place. The modern viewer with his more succinct, less informative guidebooks and what might be called a more literal or photographic vision relies less on his imagination than his nineteenth-century counterpart. His vision is more "accurate," more time-bound, and less romantic. Stories do not spin so readily from forms. Imagination is constrained by a relatively undifferentiated "present," the time of the international tourist.

The historian of Pontoise's image has a plethora of sources. Its inhabitants have produced a formidable body of writing about their town.[1] The Société historique et archéologique de Pontoise et du Vexin français has been the keeper of fact, rumor, and memory since its founding in 1877.[2] Guidebook writers have visited the town and written accounts of it since the eighteenth century; travel artists and photographers have interpreted its appearance to suit the tastes and pocketbooks of several eras. Both outsiders and insiders have gazed long and lovingly at this modest, but proud capital of the ancient region of Vexin français. The appearance or character of Pontoise during the period Pissarro lived there is decidedly more difficult to discern. Sources are spotty and inaccurate. Guidebooks publish con-

6. Detail of pl. 42.

flicting "facts" or, alternatively, perpetuate inaccuracies by basing themselves on earlier inaccurate guidebooks. The official statistics of the department, the arrondissement, and the canton are all too often long lists of names and titles with little solid information about the local economic structure. The picture of Pontoise presented in this chapter is composed from many sources, most of which are far from error-free. It partakes of the partisan splendor of French – indeed of all – local histories.

Most guidebooks, statistical tables, and historical accounts that mention Pontoise begin with geography or with ancient history recounted with an eye toward geography. Earliest habitations were thought to have arisen for geographical reasons, and Pontoise's origins seem clearly related to the characteristics of its site. We learn from various sources that it was founded as a Celtic fortification. Some of these sources give us more information about the nature or precise location of that fortification, but nothing more is needed. Two essential "facts" within the imagistic history of Pontoise are clearly discernible in these origins – its antiquity and its geographical advantages as a protected place. An image of Pontoise is evoked in the two words, Celtic fortification, that is mysterious and older than France herself.

The story then leaps with little effort and no narrative continuity to Pontoise as a Roman city. Its name was Briva Isarae, or bridge on the river Isère. The bridge itself was apparently constructed in Celtic times and acted as a connection between the Veliocasses or people of Vexin and the Parisians. The Romans rebuilt both the bridge and the town or fortification on the hill. The double character of Pontoise, which was to serve as the *raison d'être* of its continued existence, was thus established in Celtic times and reinforced by the Romans. The two great facts of Pontoise – the bridge and the hill, one man-made and the other natural – were stated in the first two sentences of most nineteenth-century guidebooks.

Nineteenth-century histories of Pontoise and guidebooks that treat the town with any fullness begin their evocations of the town with a description of the site. Paul Joanne, the son of the first and greatest writer of popular guidebooks in French, Adolphe Joanne, offers perhaps the most succinct geographical introduction in his monumental *Dictionnaire géographique et administratif de la France* of 1899. Pontoise is situated in "an amphitheatre on top of a hill on the right bank of the river Oise; this river is joined by a brook, most frequently dry, called the brook of the Fond Saint-Antoine, and by a lovely little river, called the Voisne."[3] This description summarizes a century of florid descriptions. It is partially cribbed from his father's guidebook, *Les Environs de Paris*, of 1856, which is in turn derived from J.-B. Richard's earlier *Guide du voyageur aux environs de Paris* and from late eighteenth-century descriptions of Pontoise. The simple juxtaposition of hill and river is made more precise by mention of the natural amphitheatre within the plateau facing the Viosne. The word "amphitheatre" evokes the ancient Romans with a canny precision and was used in virtually every guidebook description of Pontoise, but the word "hill" ("colline") is not quite accurate. In fact, the town of Pontoise rests not on a hill, but on the edge of a long plateau that stretches north in flat agricultural splendor and borders the river Oise with a steep embankment. This embankment is of crucial importance in understanding the history of Pontoise because it formed a natural border between two very ancient and persistent regions of France, Vexin and Parisis. Pontoise, the capital of ancient Vexin français, stands at the edge of the two regions, casting a wary eye on the valley of Montmorency, the basin of Parisian civilization.

The agricultural goods from Vexin descended to the granaries of Pontoise along the small river called the Viosne, and the urban goods and manufactured

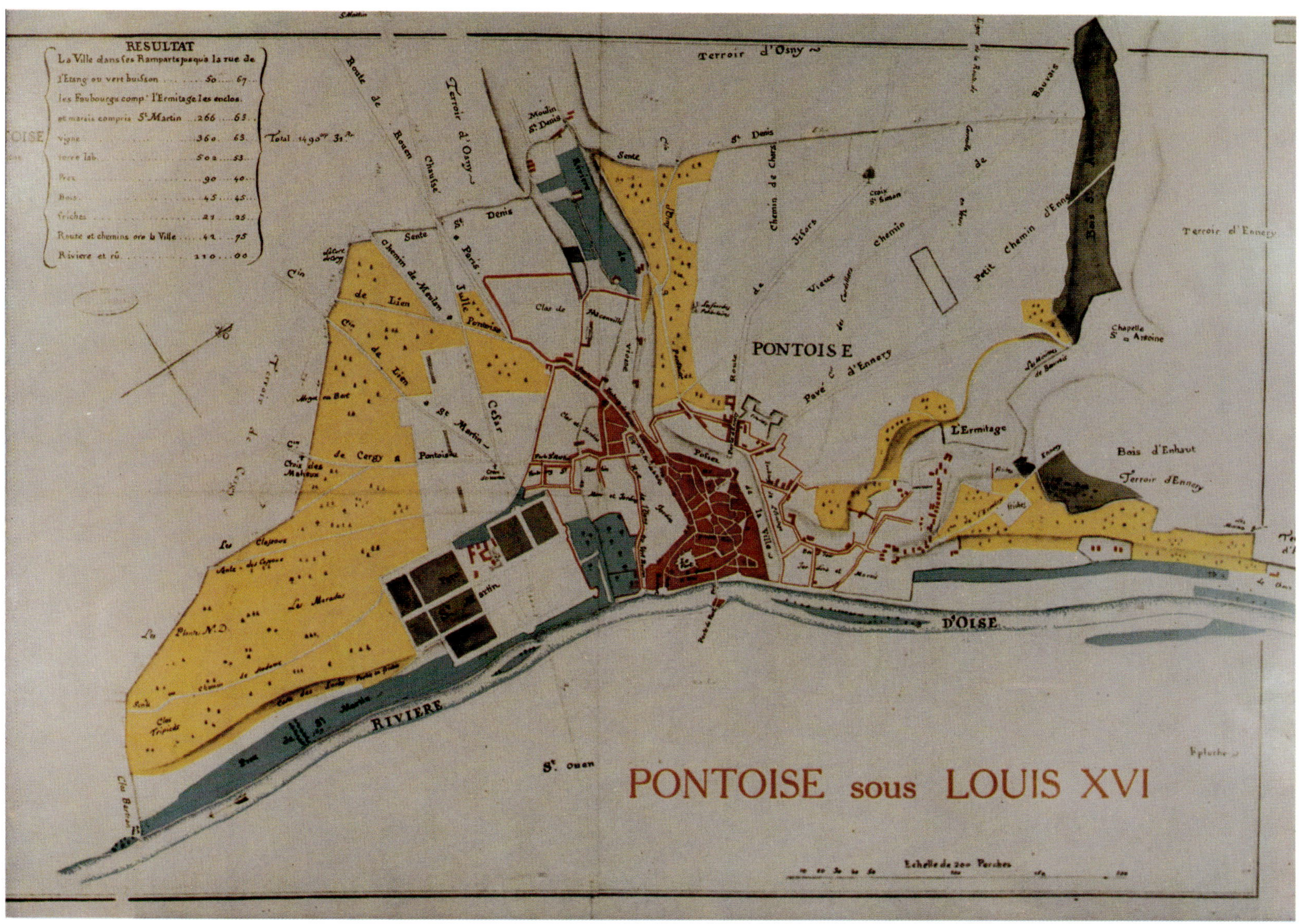

7. Map of Pontoise in the eighteenth century from the Archives départementales des Yvelines, ed. Marcel Lachiver, Meulan, 1968.

products from Pontoise and from Paris were carried along the same route to the rural villages and farms of Vexin (pl. 7). Pontoise is a border capital formed by the complicated interaction of geography and history at a place of maximum strategic and economic importance. The site itself partakes of the nature of all borders – it is various, even contradictory. Plateau meets valley, and tributary joins river. It is a specific site where the characters of two different and internally homogeneous regions intertwine. The simple names of its geographic components give a sense of this complexity – hill, island, river, valley, plateau, plain, stream, cave, canyon – all can be viewed in isolation and combination from a variety of angles and points of view within a ten-minute walk of Saint-Maclou.

History, Revolution, and Memory

For the nineteenth century (and for us today), the most significant aspect of the history of Pontoise was its florescence as a center of power in the Middle Ages. Pontoise, like many towns in the north of France (one thinks immediately of Chinon, Provins, Loches, Fougères, etc.), had had a more glorious, richer, and

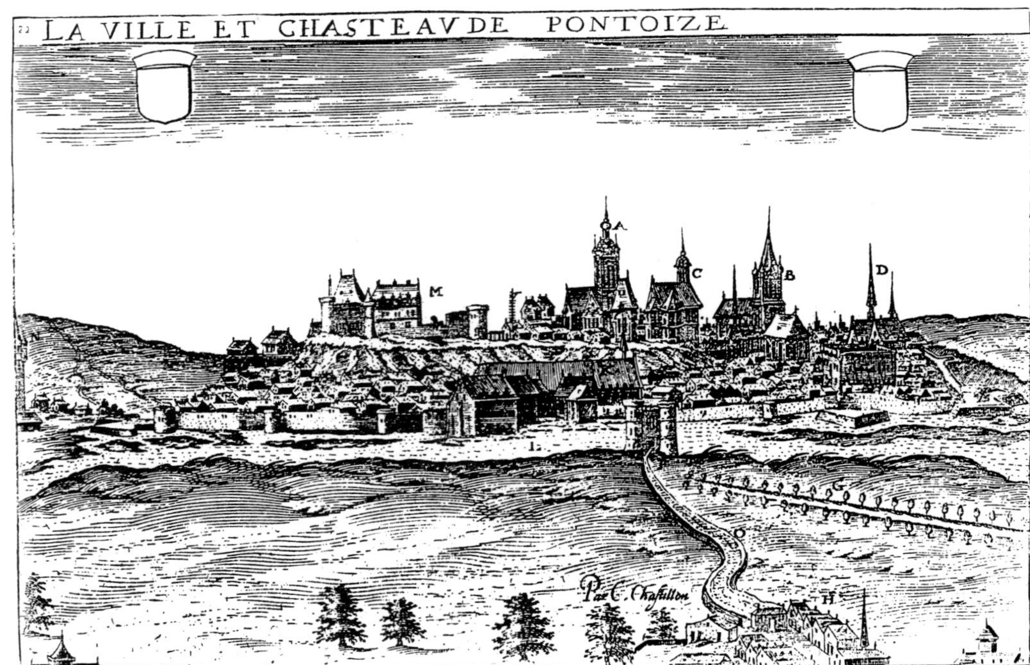

8. Claude Chastillon, *La Ville et le château de Pontoise, c.* 1550, etching, from H. Le Charpentier, *La Ligue à Pontoise et dans le Vexin français*, Pontoise, 1878.

more significant past than present. Demographers estimate its thirteenth-century population at about 12,000, roughly twice the census population of 1861.[4] In fact, Pontoise's "golden age," its period of greatest building activity, population growth, institutional diversification, and, hence, historical significance, occurred in the late Middle Ages. The history of Pontoise during the twelfth and thirteenth centuries constitutes the bulkiest and most crucial paragraphs in guidebook accounts, chapters in the several nineteenth-century local histories, and pages within the publications of the local historical society. One can make a fairly sharp differentiation between guides and descriptions of the eighteenth century and those of the nineteenth by comparing their respective uses of history. The psychological ruptures in modern civilization evidenced in the French Revolution were repaired later in the nineteenth century by a kind of historical perception lacking in the works of pre-revolutionary writers. Monuments and cities became not only expressions but emanations of history: they preserved time.

The Revolution had first destroyed and later reformed the institutional fabric of society, and the lists of officials and tasteful descriptions of the local châteaux that constituted most eighteenth-century descriptions of places were not enough for the reader or writer of the following century. The meaning of Pontoise for the nineteenth-century Frenchman was to be found in its history and not merely in its institutional ties with the government, the church, and the aristocratic classes of France. The justly famous *Description générale et particulière de la France*, begun in the *ancien régime* and published in several editions in the late eighteenth century, pays very little attention to Pontoise.[5] There are no major châteaux there; it was not the seat of a diocese; it was not a major commercial center. The history of the town is not detailed with any care or chronology. Its origins and its Roman name are mentioned, and the anonymous author lists several random events in its history and mentions several of its churches. This weak, insignificant Pontoise described at the end of the institutional age is very different from the "historical" Pontoise so important in the nineteenth century. For the tourist of that century and for the inhabitants of Pontoise during the industrial revolution, place and time formed a vital continuity.

The French Revolution was certainly the most violent and dramatic event in the long history of Pontoise. Most of the town's institutions and, consequently, its significant buildings were monastic, conventual, ecclesiastical, or concerned with the administration of the archdiocese of Vexin. Already somewhat shabby from two centuries of architectural neglect, the ecclesiastical architecture of Pontoise suffered terribly during the Revolution and the Reign of Terror. Abbé Trou, a royalist and violently anti-revolutionary priest, records this destruction with a grim determination in his pioneering *Recherches historiques, archéologiques, et biographiques sur la ville de Pontoise*, published in 1841.[6] He almost relishes the violence and idiocy that he sees as the essential characteristics of Pontoise during the years between 1789 and 1794, His sources are cloudy: some documents, but mostly the memories and oft-told tales of men who looked back on the revolutionary period with a horror equal to his own. Although modern scholars of the same period in Pontoise's history can and have questioned both the slant and the tenor of Abbé Trou's account, there is little doubt that it is essentially correct both in its broad outline and in its recognition of the sweeping changes experienced in Pontoise. Historic Pontoise, the Pontoise of Blanche of Castille, of Saint Louis, and of the rich merchants of the Middle Ages, was essentially destroyed in the Revolution. Trou's list of the buildings that were either badly mutilated or totally demolished during those years contains the names of every important institution in Pontoise except the château, which had already been demolished. Perhaps no small city in France suffered worse destruction. The Hôtel-Dieu, built by Saint Louis, was demolished; the convent of the Carmelites, damaged and abandoned; and the churches of Saint-Mellon, Saint-Pierre, Saint-André, Saint-Maclou, and Notre-Dame were looted and defaced with axes and hammers.

The damage, however, was more than physical. In the sweeping administrative changes that characterized Napoleonic France, Pontoise was removed from its ancient territory, Vexin français, and made the district town (*chef-lieu*) of a smaller area of land, the arrondissement of Pontoise in the huge and Paris-oriented department of Seine-et-Oise. The department's capital was Versailles, and its land circled Paris on three sides. After centuries of struggle, Pontoise was pulled under the administrative control of the environs of Paris. Its ecclesiastical institutions, still connected with Rouen and with Vexin itself, were considerably weakened after the Revolution. The two large abbeys of Saint-Martin and Maubuisson never opened again, and the ruined churches were not rebuilt or replaced. Only the large hospital, the Hôtel-Dieu, was rehoused on a grander scale in a decidedly unecclesiastical building designed by a Pontoisian and a favorite of Napoleon, the architect Pierre-François Fontaine.

An historian of Pontoise would have difficulty finding much continuity between pre- and post-revolutionary Pontoise. The site was the same, but the institutional allegiances and even the buildings were different. However, the historical image of the town lived on in the writings of men such as Abbé Trou, whose two books on Pontoise began a long chain of local historical research that was institutionalized in 1877 in the form of the Société historique et archéologique de Pontoise et du Vexin français. This society, housed during the nineteenth century in the notable fifteenth-century Hôtel Tavet, was an archive of memories, a gathering place of local savants who had little professional historical interest. Its founder, Pierre Séré-Depoin, was a mayor of Pontoise during the Second Empire, and its founding members were among the more important citizens of the town. The great French historian, Marc Bloch, in his early essay-cum-bibliographical survey of the Ile-de-France, wrote with a certain skepticism of such local historical socie-

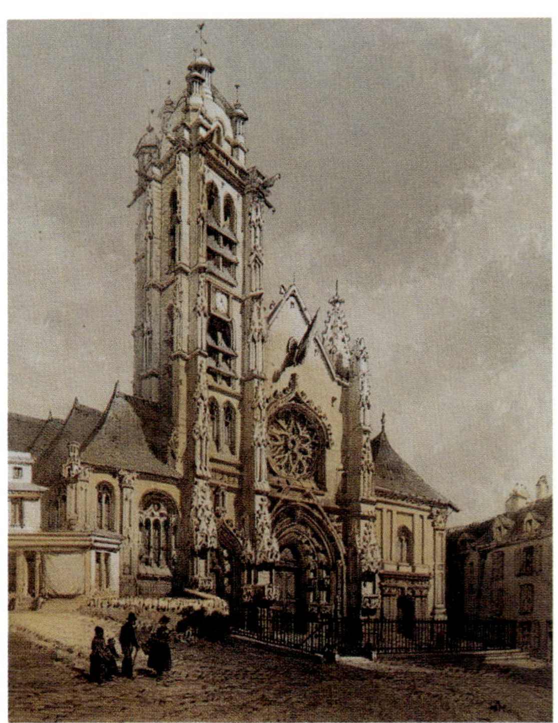

9. Adolphe d'Hastrel, *Eglise paroissiale de Saint-Maclou, c.* 1843, lithograph, Archives départementales du Val d'Oise.

ties, intended more often to enshrine the past than to understand it. Bloch, writing as a modern professional historian, criticized the Société historique et archéologique de Pontoise et du Vexin français for its rather sloppily edited memoires and published archives.[7] Clearly, accuracy and professionalism were not the motivating goals of the Société. The association had a subtler and, in a way, more vital task. It strove to reconnect Pontoise with its past, so few reminders of which existed in the nineteenth century.

"History is the memory of the nations," Abbé Trou had written in 1841; "You know Rome, Athens, Greece, and all their memories. But do you know your own native town? Are you acquainted with your Pontoise?"[8] Trou's ringing and rhetorical questions had a great validity in the 1840s. Although the bibliography of Pontoise published before Trou's history is lengthy and impressive, most, if not all, the books were out of print and known only to a select few. Trou was correct in implying that very few Pontoisians knew much, if anything, about their own town. By the 1870s, however, this was no longer true. *Guides, Annuaires, Descriptions, Histoires,* and collections of statistics abounded. The largest, most important, and oldest of Pontoise's newspapers, *L'Echo Pontoisien,* published articles by local historians about interesting aspects of the town's past. Although the churches and abbeys of ancient Pontoise had been destroyed, late nineteenth-century Pontoisians were almost inundated with historical information about their town. Historical perception was the rule of the day. Knowing was tantamount to seeing.

The Pontoisian discontinuity between "history" and "reality" is difficult to overstress. Guidebook writers and local historians were united in their presentation of two separate Pontoises: an historical Pontoise and an actual or "new" Pontoise. Richard, in his description of the city in the third edition (1840) of his *Guide du voyageur aux environs de Paris dans un rayon de 60 kilomètres,* divides his account into three parts: geography, history, and description.[9] The historical section, brief and enticing, tells us that Pontoise was inhabited by "several" kings of France, that it was conquered and lost by the English in the reign of Charles VII, that the Estates General met there in 1561, and that Parliament was put into exile there "several times." The text is inexact—the rule rather than the exception in early and mid-nineteenth-century guidebooks—and hints tantalizingly at palatial ruins and large institutional structures of great age—in short, at a town of some importance. But the physical description—or the "reality"—hardly coincides with this romantic past. He tells us to visit the church (he means Saint-Maclou; there are, in fact, two churches worth visiting in Pontoise) and the ruins of the château, which he does not recommend in themselves, but for the view they command of the forest of Saint-Germain to the south. Where, we might ask, did the kings live? Why did the Estates General meet here? Where did Parliament assemble? Why would the English want to conquer Pontoise? What remains of the ancient capital of Vexin français? All those questions were to remain unanswered for the nineteenth-century tourist.

Not even Adolphe Joanne's more famous descriptions make much connection between historical and actual Pontoise. His historical account is the fullest and the most interesting of the many guidebook histories.[10] By extracting the vital incidents from his source—Abbé Trou—Joanne writes perhaps the best short narrative of Pontoise's history in print. His efficient guidebook prose is a decided improvement on Trou's halting, even lugubrious narrative, and his confident selection of events reveals the practiced hand of a popular historian. Joanne's account ends quite suddenly and rather dramatically with a single sentence that precedes the briefer account of modern Pontoise: "Up until the Revolution,

16

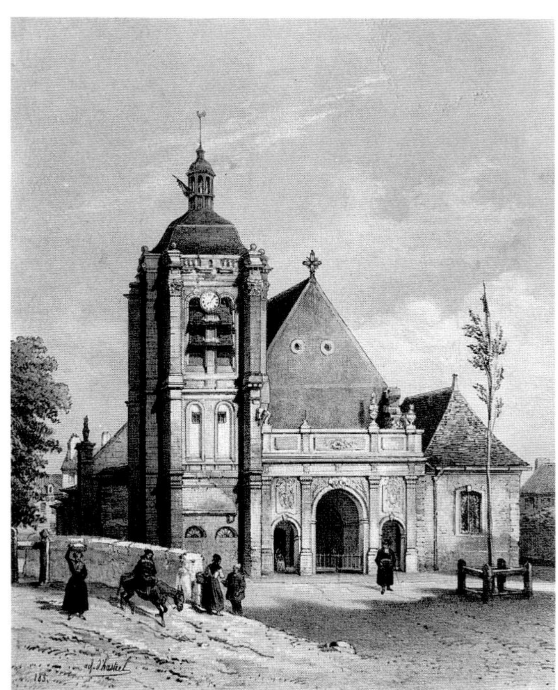

10. Adolphe d'Hastrel, *Façade et place de l'église Notre-Dame, c.* 1843, lithograph, Archives départementales du Val d'Oise.

Pontoise remained a monastic city; numerous churches and convents could then be seen, among all of which only three survive, Saint-Maclou, Notre-Dame, and the convent of the Carmelites.'' The narrator changes abruptly from historian to guide and, functioning in the latter capacity, suggests only two monuments to the visitor, Saint-Maclou and Notre-Dame (pls. 9 and 10).

What is clear from these accounts and from many others written throughout the century is that Pontoise's "tourist attractions" had been destroyed. There was simpiy very little to see in Pontoise. Saint-Maclou was described in loving and lengthy passages by historians and guidebook writers not because it was the most significant monument in the history of Pontoise, but because it was all there was left to describe. It was as difficult for the historically minded tourist to imagine medieval Pontoise as it was for him to imagine the extent of the abbey of Saint-Germain-des-Prés in Paris or the vast ecclesiastical center around the cathedral of Saint-Denis. Pontoise was not a tourist town, nor was it a place of retreat for wealthy businessmen who built "pretty country houses" in Auvers, L'Isle-Adam, Enghien-les-Bains, or Argenteuil.[11] Its population remained surprisingly constant throughout the period, growing slowly and steadily from about 6,000 in 1850 to about 8,000 at the end of the century. Its history during the later part of the century is characterized by a more or less languid expansionism. Agriculture progressed, new streets were added, the barge port was improved, small-scale industry made some inroads, the railroad arrived. There were no dramatic leaps in population, no bursts of progress, no spectacular urban redevelopment or important architectural restorations in an era notable for all these things.

Indeed, Pontoise's significance was still to be found in its history. Even at the end of a century of "progress" and "modernism," Pontoisians "remembered" their town as the ancient capital of Vexin français, as the birthplace of Saint Louis. In his section on Pontoise in *Les Environs de Paris* of 1886, Louis Barron shows us the fragility of Pontoise's historicism:

> The Northern Railway or the Western Railway takes you straight into the remarkable valley. You arrive in Pontoise. The train passes Saint-Ouen-l'Aumône and whistles as it crosses the river Oise, shimmering with reflected light; right in front of you, flooded with light, a wall of rocks and ramparts along the right bank of the river stands like a Norman cliff. Above this wall, which is as white as chalk, rooftops intermingle confusingly, dominated by an enormous and dark spire, crowned with bells. You have a swift and striking vision of a Gothic city, almost oriental-looking. Just as this image is about to vanish, the train stops at the very modern boundary line of a little provincial town. Strange contrast.[12]

A strange contrast indeed! The subject of Pissarro's many paintings of Pontoise is the "little provincial town" and not the evanescent image of a Gothic city evoked by Louis Barron.

Economic Activity, 1840–1880

The nineteenth-century town of Pontoise did not spring fully formed from its monastic ruins. The process of growth was long and involved. Its institutional and economic bases were altered; an increasing emphasis on barge activity, small-scale industry, and various kinds of agriculture is discernible throughout the century. The change in Pontoise's economic base is evidenced in guidebook entries for the town. The description in the *Description générale et particulière de la*

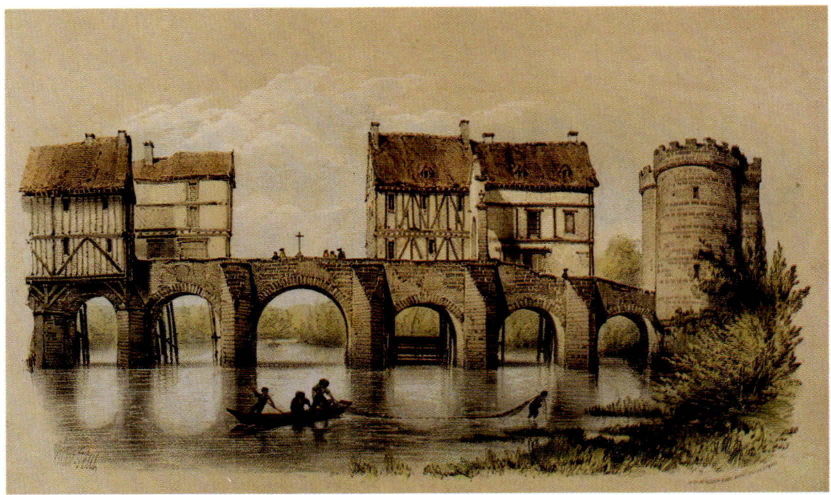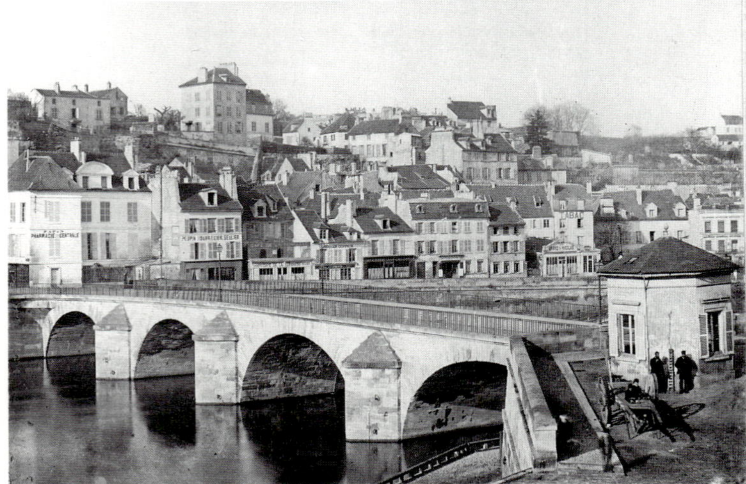

11. Victor Petit, *Vieux pont de Pontoise*, mid-19th century, lithograph, Archives départementales du Val d'Oise.

12. The new bridge in Pontoise, late 19th century, photograph, collection of M. Jean Hecquet, Paris.

France, written before the Revolution, mentions the town's ecclesiastical institutions, a little history, and its geography without any word about industry or the port, and no mention of the major agricultural products. By the 1840s, Richard and most other guidebook writers point to the importance of the granaries and, by implication, to the port which disseminated the grain in a pre-railroad era. Abbé Trou, in his chapters dealing with the post-revolutionary history of Pontoise, treats the port as the principal cause of the wealth and activity of the town in the nineteenth century. He mentions ten million tons of wheat each year and four to five million tons of other cereals. In addition, he lists two "large and beautiful factories" ("usines") on the Viosne.[13] Their works were run by water-powered motors; one was a sugar factory and the other manufactured "sulphur water" ("eau sulphurique"). Both businesses must have been profitable as the houses of their owners are noted in Joanne's 1856 guide as being particularly attractive and imposing residences.[14]

The prosperity of Pontoise's mills and granaries was, of course, related to the town's geographical advantages. The large fields of Vexin were especially suited to the cultivation of grains, which were transported to Pontoise, the nearest port, along the Viosne.[15]

The Oise was commercially navigable by barge throughout the eighteenth and nineteenth centuries. Canalization of northern France significantly increased the importance of the Oise in the nineteenth century. The canal Saint-Quentin was constructed in the late eighteenth century and the important canal du Nord, begun in 1878, connected the Oise valley with a system of canals that extended to Creil, Douai, and the industrial cities of the north of France. The barge traffic in Pontoise was considerable in the nineteenth century and remains so today. Many textiles and raw materials from northern France descended to the Région Parisienne via this network of canals.[16]

The harbor or, perhaps more accurately, the docks of Pontoise were improved and enlarged with the construction of stone quays begun in 1843. The medieval toll bridge, so beloved by a generation of Romantic travel artists and amateur painters who depicted Pontoise in the 1820s and 1830s, was removed and replaced by a large stone bridge completed in 1843 and built on the Parisian model with slight stylistic noddings to its predecessor (pls. 11 and 12). The new bridge, with higher and wider arched openings, was built to facilitate docking activity and to permit larger barges access to canals further upriver. Pontoise was, in the early and middle nineteenth century, the most important barge port on the Oise (pl.

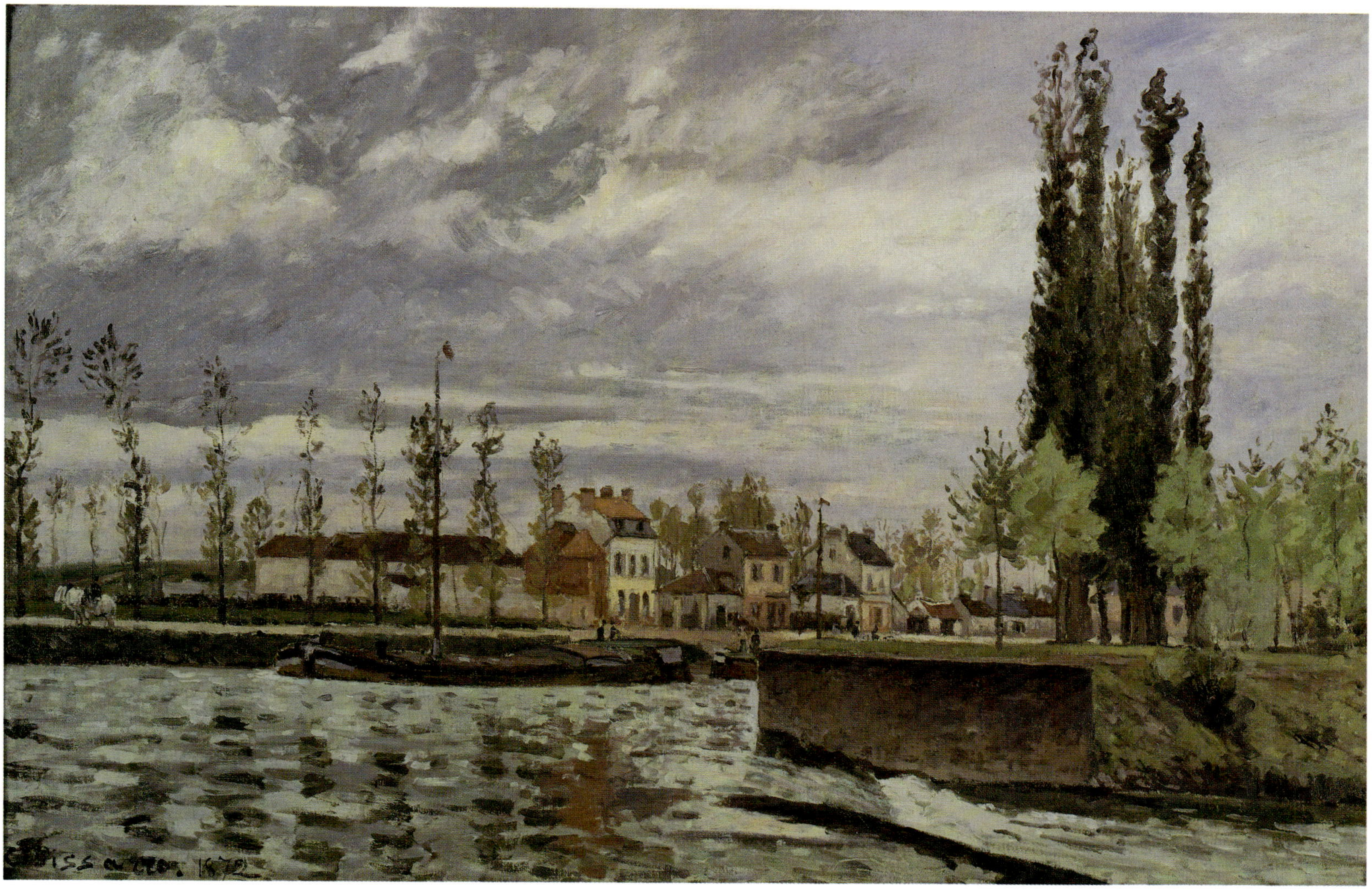

13. Camille Pissarro, *L'Ecluse à Pontoise* (P&V 156), 1872, oil on canvas, 53 × 83cm., The Cleveland Museum of Art; Leonard C. Hanna, Jr. Fund.

14. The Oise at the Ile Saint-Martin, late 19th century, postcard, collection of M. Jean Hecquet, Paris.

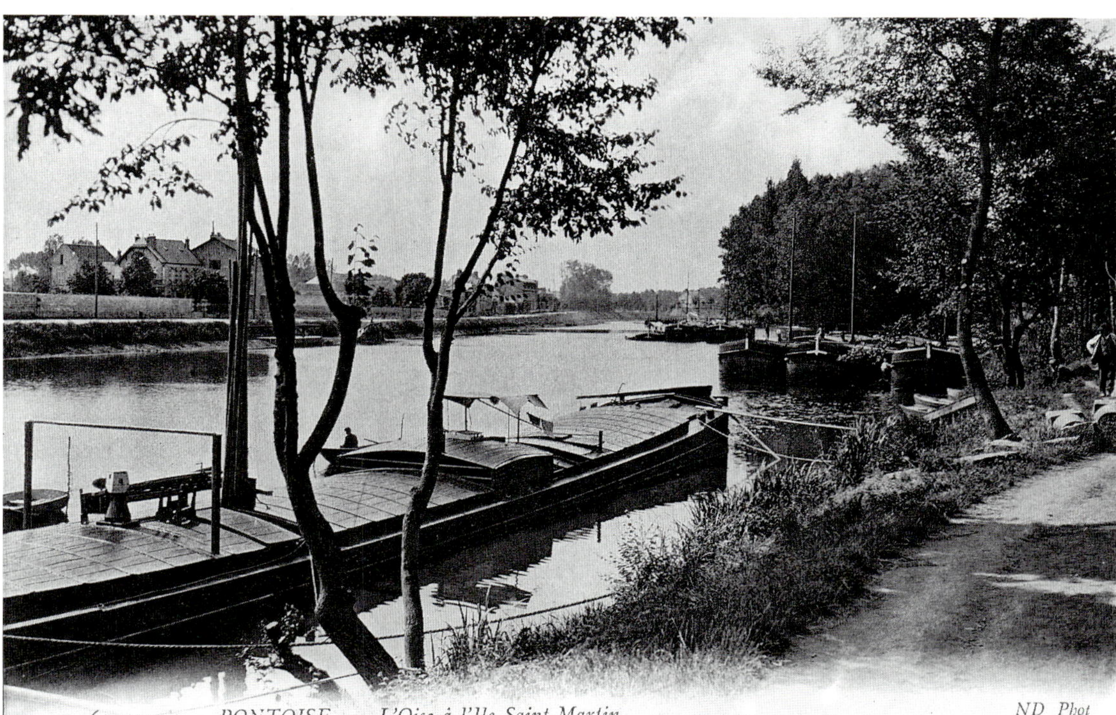

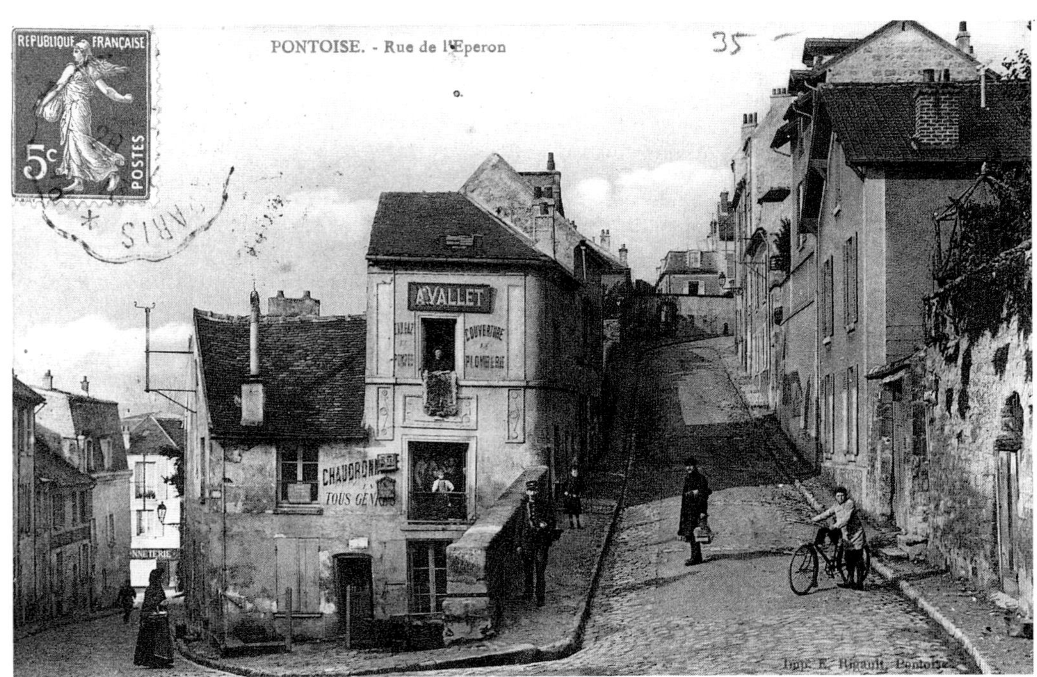

15. Rue de l'Eperon, Pontoise, late 19th century, postcard, collection of M. Jean Hecquet, Paris.

14). As the century continued, the relative importance of the town waned with the industrial florescence of Creil, Compiègne, and Saint-Quentin, and with the increased sophistication of the northern canal system.[17]

The greatest period of construction and civic improvement occurred during the building boom of the Second Empire. The railroad, which had been constructed as far as Saint-Ouen-l'Aumône in 1846, was pushed across the river on a new cast-iron bridge in 1863. The large Pontoise station and the imposing place de la Gare with its characteristic rows of well-pruned trees were opened in the same year. Pontoise was connected both to Rouen and to Paris, and the route of the new railroad was, not accidentally, almost identical with that of the Celtic-Roman road that had given rise to the town.

The town itself was never praised in the nineteenth century for its architectural distinction or urban character. The *Guide pittoresque du voyageur en France, Département de Seine-et-Oise* of 1834 calls the town's streets "narrow and rather steep" and considers them to be more inconvenient than picturesque (pl. 15).[18] Joanne perhaps uses and certainly amplifies this judgment in both editions of *Les Environs de Paris*: "The interior of the town has only steep and twisted streets, lined with houses without style or character."[19] Joanne's image is, of course, antithetical to Second Empire urbanism which popularized the aristocratic grandeur of the French Baroque. The place de la Gare and the park in front of Fontaine's Hôtel-Dieu were the first new open spaces in Pontoise, but both were at the edge of the maze of medieval streets. To correct this deficiency and to penetrate the town itself, the rue Impériale, later called the rue Thiers, was constructed, beginning in 1864, on an axis between Saint-Maclou and the railroad station. Designed on a continuous slope along an implacably straight line, the street interrupted the tortuous continuity of Pontoise's ancient streets and provided a visually symbolic link between the Pontoise of the Middle Ages and the Pontoise of the railroad era. The significance of this street is seen most clearly in a large colored lithograph produced in 1864 at the inception of the project (pl. 16). Although the imaginary bird's-eye view obliterates any sense of topography, the print is in other ways the most accurate and detailed recording of Pontoise ever made. The town dominates

20

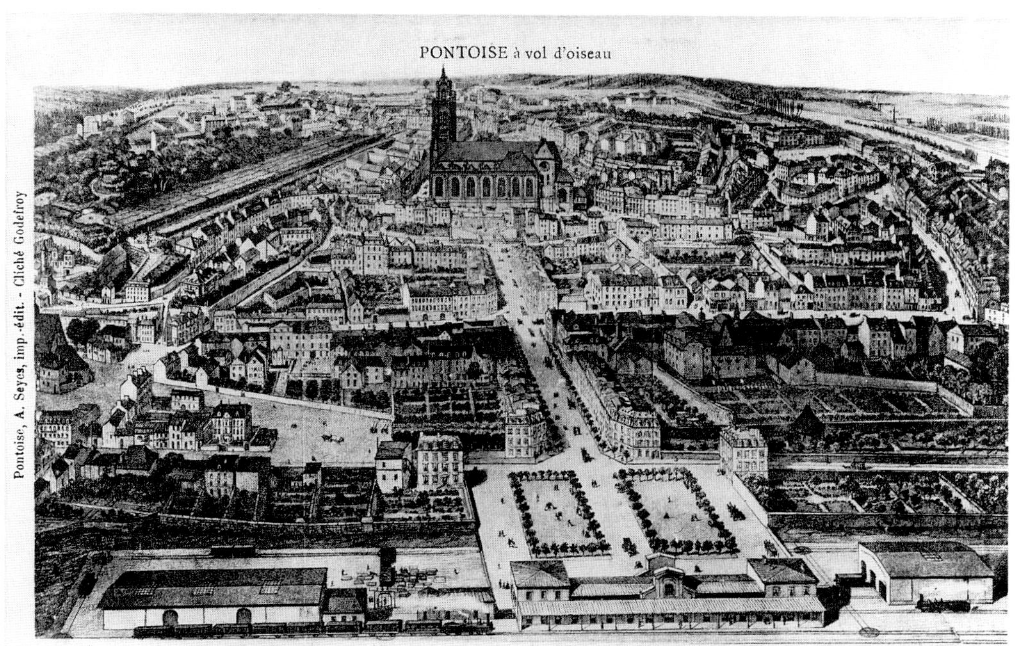

16. *Pontoise à vol d'oiseau*, 1864, Bibliothèque Nationale, Paris, from a postcard in the collection of M. Jean Hecquet, Paris.

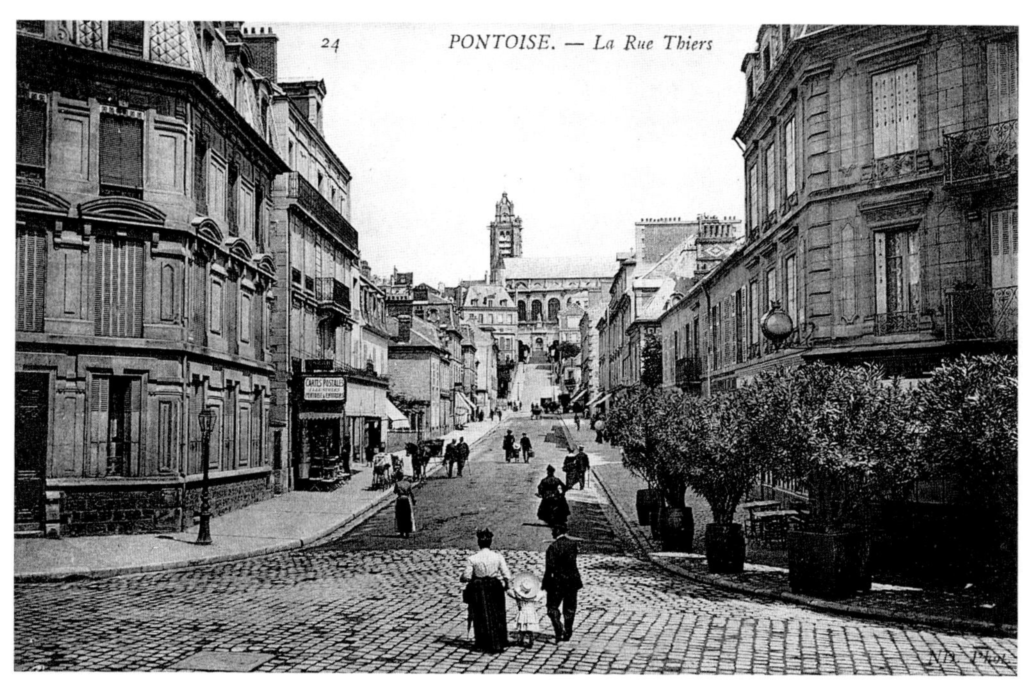

17. Rue Thiers (formerly rue Impériale), Pontoise, late 19th century, postcard, collection of M. Jean Hecquet, Paris.

the landscape, spreading generously beyond the edges of the already copious pictorial space. The bridge and the river, the two components that make up the name of Pontoise and the reasons for its continued prosperity in the nineteenth century, are virtually ignored. The new Pontoise, the Pontoise of the Second Empire, has redefined itself around the railroad. The station acts as the "base" of the town, and the rue Impériale marks an access into the town that for once has no relationship to the Oise. This 1864 view of Pontoise is radical within the history of representations of the town for being the first to turn away from the river and to focus all its attentions on Saint-Maclou, the recently declared symbol of Pontoise's history.

The rue Impériale was built relatively quickly in the middle of the 1860s and was concluded with a monumental staircase connecting the street with Saint-

Maclou. At the top of this staircase, splendidly inaugurated in 1869, was placed a statue of General Leclerc–revolutionary general, son of a wealthy Pontoisian grain merchant, and briefly the brother-in-law of his mentor, Napoleon I (pl. 17).[20] Even Saint-Maclou itself was pared down and restored throughout the late nineteenth century in keeping with its new role as urban symbol. Formerly attached at several points to the town, Saint-Maclou stood in complete isolation by the end of the century. The small stores that huddled at its sides were methodically purchased by the town and demolished, until the church resembled a statue, standing on its base, cut off from the active population around it.

In 1854, the town bought the damaged convent of the Cordeliers for use as the city hall. A program of demolition and reconstruction was commenced in the late 1850s which ended in the clearing of the new place de l'Hôtel de Ville and the creation of an extensive series of gardens in the ruins of the church of the Cordeliers and the adjacent city walls. Other projects accomplished in the late 1850s and the early 1860s were the clearing and construction of the beautiful avenue des Fossés on the site of the ancient *fossés* of the fortifications; the improvement and extension of the avenue Victor-Hugo which connected the town to the hamlet of L'Hermitage, and the creation of a completely new, straight, and attractive rue de L'Hermitage in the same hamlet. These two latter projects brought L'Hermitage more within the realm of Pontoise itself and altered its character from that of a peasant hamlet. The avenue des Fossés formed a long axis of greenery that united the town of Pontoise and the expanding *banlieue* of L'Hermitage.

Industry

The images that crowd the modern mind on hearing the word "industry" have little, if anything, to do with Pontoise in the nineteenth century. There were no enormous factories employing thousands of workers who toiled repetitively. There was no pollution. There were no rows of workers' houses like those of northern England or the real industrial towns of Douai, Creil, and Lyons in the nineteenth century. Although lacking all these, Pontoise was not untouched by industrialism. In fact, industry, in the proper sense of the word, was much older in this area of France than the industrial revolution. The presence of minor industry along the banks of rivers and streams had been a noticeable aspect of European culture since the Middle Ages. Pontoise had been a center of such industry as early as the twelfth century. The small tributary, the Viosne, was the site of the granaries, tanneries, and draperies that began to appear in Pontoise in increasing numbers in the late Middle Ages. These small industries brought in workers from Normandy and even England and created a respectable working-class population in medieval Pontoise. This kind of industry continued to exist in Pontoise throughout the *ancien régime* and even after the Revolution. The *Description générale et particulière de la France* mentions very small factories and industries along the Oise in the late eighteenth century but is not topographically specific enough to give the sites of these industries.[21]

The most complete pictures of industry and the industrial revolution in Pontoise itself can be found in a series of "annuals" published sporadically throughout the late nineteenth century. The first mentions of industry in the arrondissement of Pontoise date from the Napoleonic period. The *Almanach historique de Pontoise*, published in 1803, notes a lack of industry and industrial progress in the area:

> The establishment of a few more manufacturing industries in this district is something to be wished for. Such companies would find there sites that are

manageable and advantageous in many more ways than one. Moreover, everything leads one to think that the manpower necessary for running those industries would be easy to find![22]

The implication that there was a large population of minor landowners or impoverished, unlanded peasants ready to be exploited for industrial expansion
was probably correct. The arrondissement of Pontoise had almost everything it
needed to become an industrial area, but it never did.

The lack of industrial development can be seen very clearly and dramatically
by skipping forward to the *Annuaire administratif, statistique, agricole, industriel et
commercial de Seine-et-Oise* published at the height of the Second Empire in 1865.
This publication, prepared by H. Moser of Versailles, lists all the commercial and
industrial establishments of Pontoise and the surrounding towns. In 1865, only a
manufacturer of "chemical products" stands out from the list of grocers, hair-
dressers, creamers, and other establishments common to any small provincial
town.[23] The mills and granaries remain the dominant industry of the town as they
had been in the Middle Ages and continued to be until the middle of the twentieth
century. Three grain establishments are listed for Pontoise as well as eight *meu-
neries* or grain mills. The former were wholesale dealers in grain and had considerably greater economic importance than the smaller mills along the Viosne.
The mills themselves were not large employers in Pontoise. The *Statistique de la
France; industrie: résultats généraux de l'enquête effectuée dans les années 1861–1865*
mentions 48 mills in the entire arrondissement of Pontoise, employing a total of
127 men and 1 woman, or less than 3 workers per mill. The sulphuric acid
factory, listed under "chemical products" in the same source, employed 25 men.
This factory is probably the same as the "beautiful factory" specializing in
"sulphur water" mentioned by Abbé Trou in 1841 and in 1856 by Joanne.[24] Its
smokestack is clearly visible in postcards and views of Pontoise throughout the
nineteenth century and appears also in several drawings and paintings by Pissarro.
The two local tanneries, one in Pontoise and the other in Saint-Ouen, were the
next largest "industrial" employers of the area. They employed 31 men at the
respectable wage of 3.25 francs per day. Although the tanneries of the Région
Pontoisienne never regained the importance they had had in the Middle Ages, the
large Saint-Ouen firm of Millet et Frères was very profitable throughout the
period of the 1860s, '70s, and '80s and was the only Pontoisian firm to maintain an
office and salesroom in Paris.

The greatest period of industrial expansion in Pontoise was the 1870s and
occurred not in the town itself but in the smaller community of Saint-Ouen-
l'Aumône directly across the Oise from Pontoise. Neither the *Statistique de la
France; industrie* for the period 1861–65, nor the *Annuaire de Seine-et-Oise* of 1865
lists any industrial development in Saint-Ouen-l'Aumône, and the cadastral
records of the town indicate that the industrial development along the Oise was
begun immediately after the disruptions of the Franco-Prussian War and the
Commune. The larger and more important of the two major industries of Saint-
Ouen was the industrial distillery of Chalon et Cie. Its initial development dates
from 1871 and consisted of a small factory called a potato distillery (*féculerie*) built
along the Oise in the Italianate style and screened from the view of Pontoise by
the heavily foliated Ile du Pothuis. The *féculerie* was built by the partnership of
Chalon et Brenot Associés, a firm specializing in the distillation of alcohols and
other unnamed chemicals from potatoes. Very shortly after the completion of the
first small factory (*fabrique*), Chalon et Cie, now separated from the initial partnership, began the construction of a vast and expanding factory (*usine*) imme-

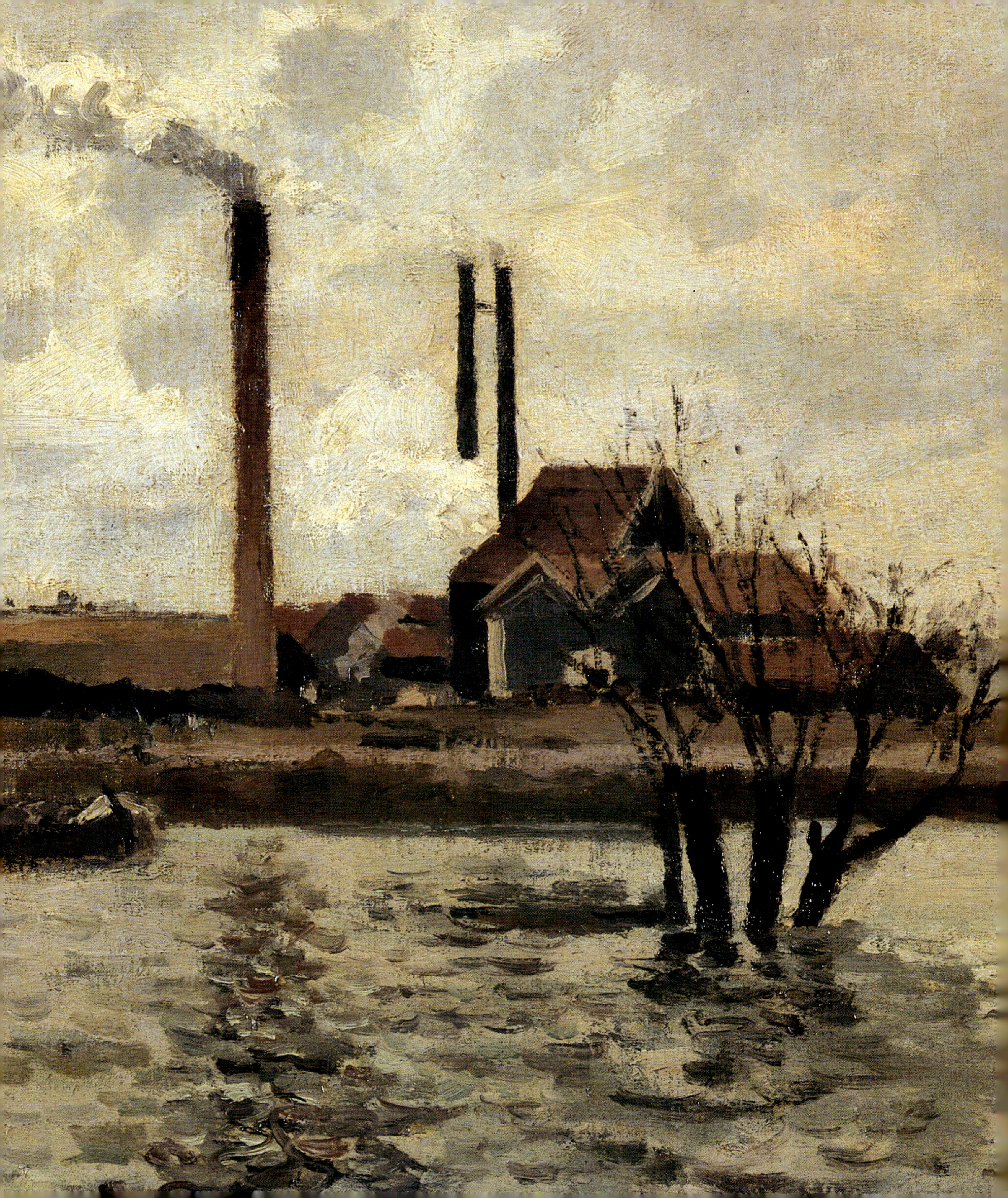

diately adjacent to the older and more traditionally styled *féculerie*. This new enterprise recorded enlargements and new constructions in 1873, 1876, and 1880 in the cadastral improvement records of Saint-Ouen. No employment statistics for the firm during the 1870s and 1880s survive today, but its prosperity is clearly reflected in the amount and regularity of capital construction on the site. In addition, tax records of Saint-Ouen reveal that the company was by far the largest local tax payer throughout the late nineteenth century. The larger and newer factory specialized in the distillation of sugar beet. Although sugar itself was a by-product of the operation, the largest amount of the firm's business involved the manufacture and sale of industrial and commercial alcohols distilled from the beets.[25]

The smaller and more picturesque of the two major industries of Saint-Ouen was a factory specializing in "chemical products" owned by a M. Camille Arneuil. This factory was probably begun one or two years later than M. Chalon's *féculerie* and is first mentioned in the cadastral records in 1873. Like the distillery, M. Arneuil's factory expanded substantially in the decade of the 1870s. Although local records are not more precise in identifying the product made by the firm, it is generally considered to have been commercial wall paints. The physical plant of M. Arneuil was considerably smaller than that of M. Chalon, consisting of several small shed structures and one small smokestack. It clustered informally amidst the large grain fields and pastures bordering the Oise. Its site, further up the river than that of the distillery, was considerably more rural.

These two factories and the much smaller one for the manufacture of sulphuric acid on the Viosne in Pontoise were the only industries of any size established in the region of Pontoise in the nineteenth century. Other industry in this area during the period falls more easily under the category of cottage industry, and there was no factory approaching the size and modernity of the textile mill at Creil.

Although the two large factories belonging to M. Chalon and M. Arneuil were conspicuous additions to the Pontoisian landscape in the nineteenth century, their importance within the economy of Saint-Ouen or Pontoise should not be exaggerated. Together with the cottage industry, granaries, and the small commercial establishments of Pontoise, they acted as stabilizers of the local economy, providing employment for the slightly increased population and arresting or at least restraining the movement of small agriculturalists to Paris and other industrial centers in the north. They certainly did not revolutionize or really modernize the Pontoisian economy, which remained, as I shall show later, an economy of small-scale agricultural production and market exchange, much as it had been in the Middle Ages. In his very full and intelligent "portrait" of Pontoise written in 1899, E. Sagine described the industry of Pontoise as "rather limited" and called for her industrial development in words not all that dissimilar to those used by the writer of the *Almanach historique de Pontoise* in 1803. Indeed, his description of the industry and commerce of Pontoise could have been written a century earlier: "Pontoise's strategical location, royal favour, and commercial activity all contributed to boost the town's prosperity. . . . Now times have changed . . . there are no longer kings, and the trade in Pontoise is rather quiet."[26]

The Market Economy

What Pontoise lacked in the way of advanced industry it made up for with its markets and small-scale commerce. As the *chef-lieu* of a large agricultural area and

18. Detail of pl. 72.

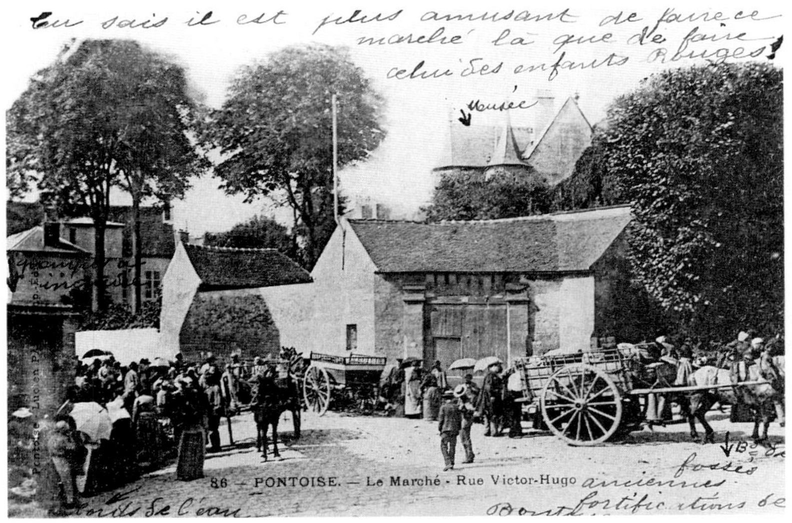

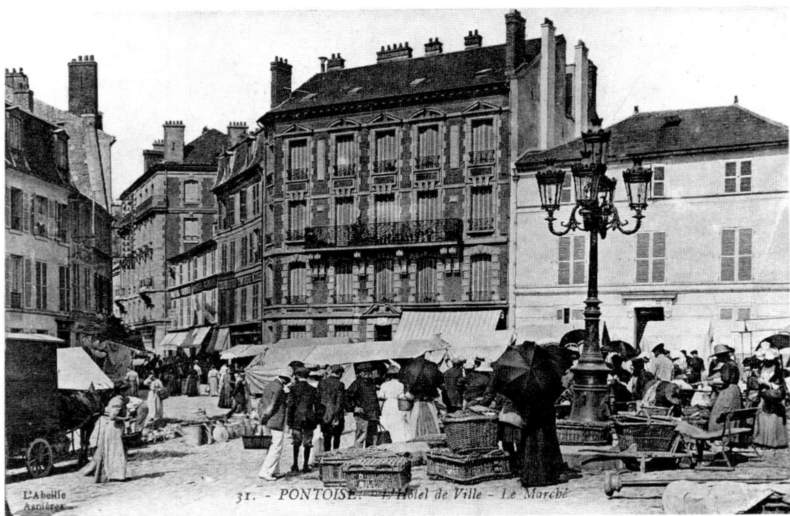

19. The market in rue Victor-Hugo, Pontoise, late 19th century, postcard, private collection.

20. Hôtel de Ville, market, Pontoise, late 19th century, postcard, collection M. Jean Hecquet, Paris.

as the town in old Vexin closest both to Paris and to the network of rivers and canals so important in northern France, Pontoise was the central market of Vexin français. All guidebooks, histories, and statistical tables mention the markets of Pontoise, giving their times and the major products in which they dealt. Their importance increased during the nineteenth century with the expansion of peasant marketing and the introduction of agricultural improvements in southern Normandy.[27] The large market area at the foot of the plateau surrounding the church of Notre-Dame was increased several times in the century, and smaller market areas were cleared in other parts of the town and its hamlets. Market days were active and bustling days of local commerce in which peasants, market gardeners, and more important agriculturalists specializing in grains and livestock sold their goods to local and regional dealers as well as to the better-known marketeers of Les Halles in Paris. Pontoise's markets were known primarily for their grains which constituted the great bulk of Vexin agriculture, but nineteenth-century guides mention the veal and the cabbage of Pontoise as being famous throughout France (pls. 19 and 20).

The size and the importance of the markets were increased rather than diminished by the arrival of the railroad at Saint-Ouen in 1846 and, more significantly, at Pontoise itself in 1863. The railroad brought Pontoise and many of the market towns in the larger environs of Paris into the net of Paris's own market system. This greatly expanded market, as well as the enormous population growth of Paris itself throughout the period, gave extra vitality to agriculture in the larger environs of Paris and created a system of market economy that survived until the arrival of refrigerated vehicles and air transport in the mid-twentieth century.[28]

As far as commercial shops and establishments are concerned, Pontoise was like any small provincial town. H. Moser's list of commercial establishments in Pontoise published in 1865 reveals nothing surprising or spectacular, with the exception of a high number of architects and, perhaps, a coach builder. The reading population of the town must have been large as there were three bookstores and two commercial printers. For their food needs, Pontoisians of the Second Empire had a small group of specialized foodstores for cheese, wine, milk, horsemeat, and candy, but they lacked a butcher, a baker of either bread or cakes, a vegetable and fruit market, and a general store. Most of the buying must have been done at the markets themselves and the bread was undoubtedly provided by non-commercial, domestic establishments. There were few, if any,

21. Camille Pissarro, *Le Marché à la volaille, Pontoise* (P&V 576), 1882, oil on canvas, 81 × 65cm., Norton Simon Museum, Pasadena, Calif.

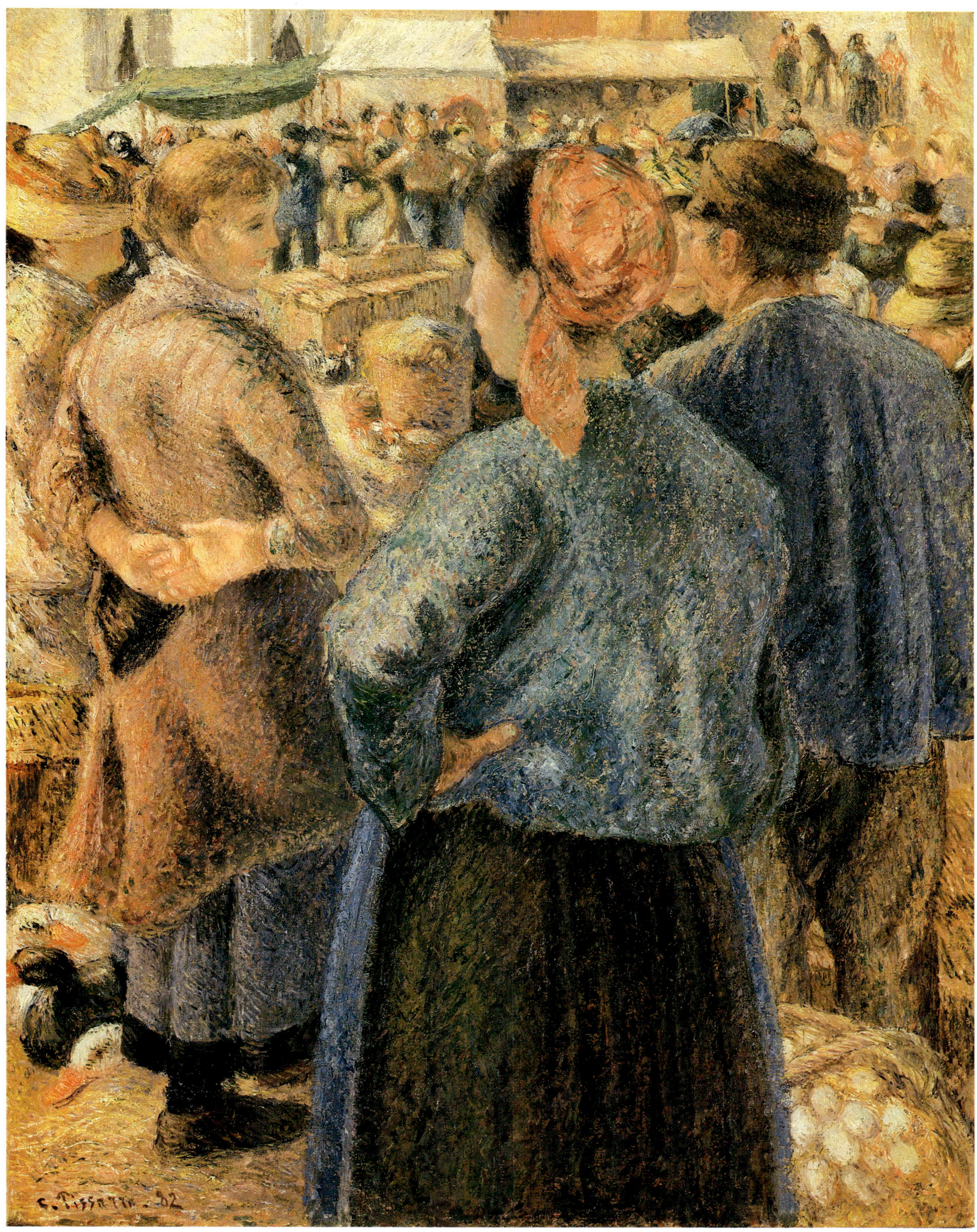

"modern" professions in Pontoise, with the possible exception of a plumber and a watch and clock maker.[29]

Agriculturalists or Workers: The Population of Pontoise

A statistically derived list of professions of men and women in Pontoise during the 1860s and 1870s is curiously incomplete. Taking both Saint-Ouen and Pontoise, which had a combined population in 1861 of 8,087 and in 1881 of 8,814, five or six factory owners, several dozen shop proprietors, and perhaps five hundred workers would be listed. This total of around seven hundred people indicates the tentativeness of the statistics. The question now becomes somewhat more complex and moves beyond the realm of "provable" fact. What did the rest of the people do? How did the nineteenth-century Pontoisian support himself? There were amateur real-estate agents or land dealers, as well as doctors, lawyers, and civil servants who numbered no more than seventy-five; but this still leaves many unaccounted for. The simplest solution to this puzzle is that the other Pontoisians were "peasants," a word of frustrating inexactness and only some applicability to Pontoise inhabitants of the period.[30] Pontoise was not a peasant village in the nineteenth century or, indeed, at any time in its history following its florescence in the Middle Ages. Rather, as has been shown, it was a market town and a commercial center with a large ecclesiastical population to support. Before the sales of nationalised properties after the Revolution (known as the *vente des biens*), the land of Pontoise was owned by small-scale farmers, by various parishes and churches in the area, and by a few large landowners who rented much of their land to the peasant farmers. After the sales, the land was further subdivided into often tiny parcels which crowded the valleys and chequered the hillsides with an agrarian patchwork.[31] Small landowners worked the areas of land adjacent to their houses or in the same district and rented the disparate patches to people who lived closer to them. The agriculture that developed in these areas was distinctly related to peasant polyculture, or agriculture for subsistence and not for specialized market or commercial sales of any magnitude. As the century progressed and as the market for vegetables and fruits increased, the class of agriculturalists who owned, rented, and worked these plots became increasingly specialized. Their production became more varied and "scientific." New crops such as green peas, special cabbages, and greater varieties of fruits were cultivated for the new market, and these peasant subsistence farmers became a class of small market gardeners (*maraîchers*) who worked within an economic system defined by modern, large-scale capitalism.[32]

Perhaps the best term for the group of people that formed the numerical majority of the citizens of Pontoise during the period of Pissarro's stay there is the conjunctive "peasant-proletarian" or, less awkwardly, rural workers. There are, of course, disadvantages to the Marxist term. It implies a steady shift from "traditional" peasant life to "modern" proletarian existence with a transition period called "peasant-proletarian." In fact, the class described by the combinative term has proved extremely hardy and exists throughout rural France even today. Neither Marxist concepts of the proletariat nor the modern sociological and anthropological definitions of the peasantry apply to these people who have survived in France for several centuries, becoming very strong in the eighteenth century, weakening somewhat in the early nineteenth century, and regaining force with the vast internal migrations in France during the middle and late nineteenth century. The group evades statistical classification. Many, if not most

22. Camille Pissarro, *Le Jardin potager à L'Hermitage, Pontoise* (P&V 437), 1878, oil on canvas, 55 × 46cm., Bridgestone Museum of Art, Ishibashi Foundation, Tokyo.

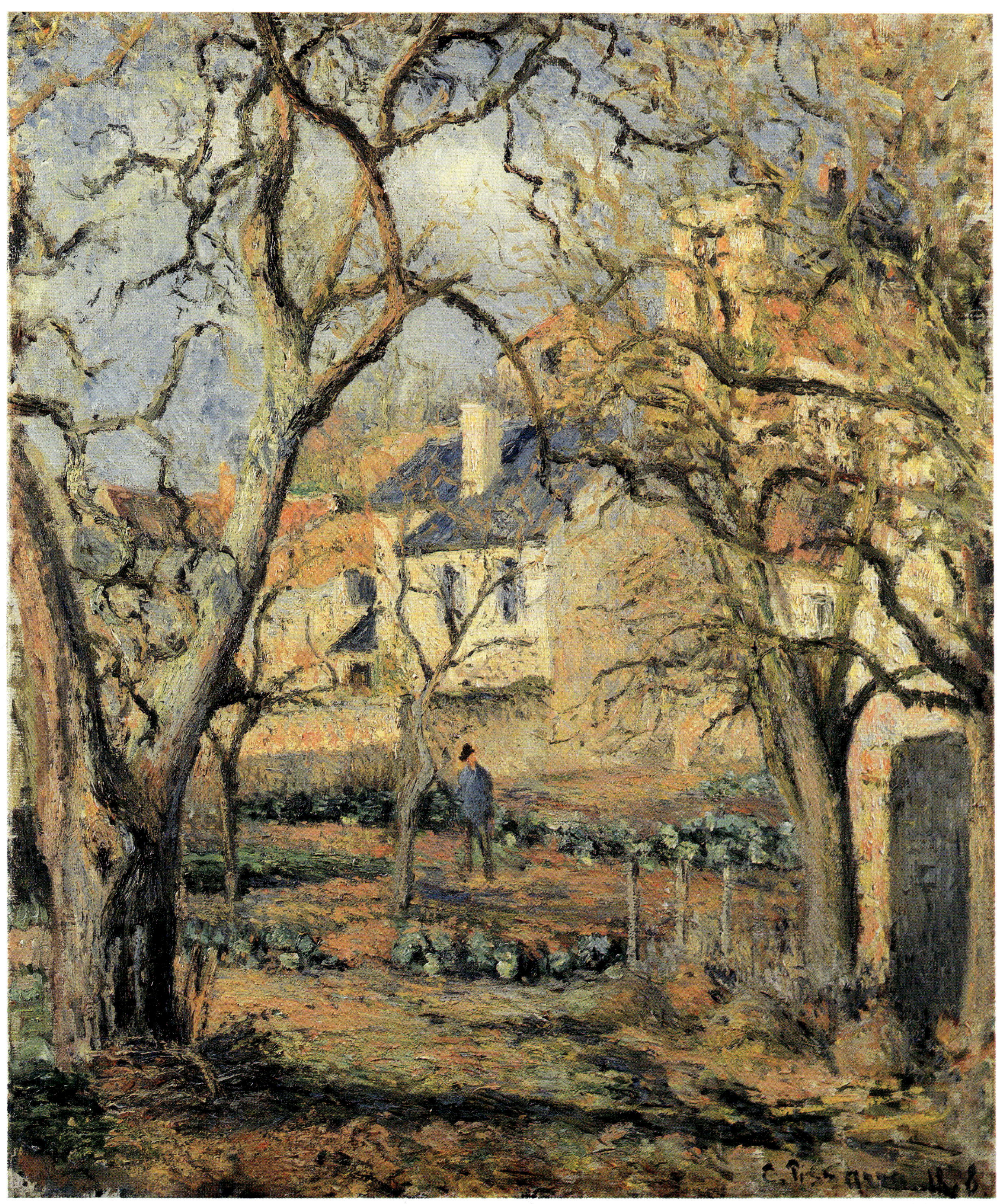
C. Pissarro 1876

of its members did not own land; they worked in both the private and public sectors, gaining income that is not recorded and that was often not subject to taxation. They are people who are inhabitants of the so-called "modern world," but who would never be called modern. Perhaps the most accurate portrayal of this group within the larger population of France can be found in Olwen Hufton's excellent book, *The Poor of Eighteenth-Century France.*[33] Hufton describes the occupations, the movements, and the problems of the poor in the latter part of the *ancien régime.* Although the book attempts to describe the situation for all France, most of its examples and its strongest body of data is from Normandy and is, therefore, extremely useful in understanding the structure of the rural population of Pontoise during the eighteenth and early nineteenth centuries. Hufton portrays a class of people whom she calls simply "the poor" and who lead a hand-to-mouth existence that is quite different from the settled, agrarian life of the traditional peasant. She charts massive internal migrations which were generally seasonal rather than permanent. She defines a complex life of cottage industry, polyculture, begging, prostitution, and other unsavory occupations that were part of a modern and national economic life rather than the subsistence life of a single village or a small region. Families split in ways designed to provide maximum income for the whole, thereby defining the family as an economic rather than a social or religious unit. Hufton's "poor," descendants of the peasant movements and rebellions that characterized the history of the peasantry in France during the sixteenth and seventeenth centuries, are the forefathers of the "peasants" of Pissarro's Pontoise, a group of people who led considerably more comfortable lives than their eighteenth-century ancestors, but lives of equal complexity to and equally removed from those of simple village peasants.[34]

This brief portrayal of the class of agriculturalists who inhabited the Région Pontoisienne in the nineteenth century hints at a very complicated kind of agriculture, one based on familial needs and on market and informal market economies. It suggests a combination of family gardens, market gardens, orchards, and grain fields. The reality of Pontoisian agriculture during the period Pissarro was there seems to coincide with this variegated portrait. Although precise sources discussing local agriculture are not numerous, a very full discussion of the subject in Sagine's 1899 monograph on Pontoise fills many of the gaps in the statistical account from the 1870s and 1880s.

French towns are defined by a legal system very similar to that of the townships of England and New England, combining the governments of "town" and "country" (or county). The "city limits" of Pontoise extended considerably outside the built-up area, and many of the town's inhabitants owned and worked land in the outskirts, which were considered just as much Pontoise as the streets encircling Saint-Maclou. The economy of Pontoise was a mélange of the commercial-industrial and the agricultural. The divisions between or, rather, among these aspects of economic life were blurred and often non-existent. Many shopkeepers owned or rented land in any of several agricultural areas of the town on which they raised grain, grew vegetables either for their own consumption or for sale, or kept animals.[35] Conversely, farmers and landowners of Pontoise often made their income not from the working of their own lands, but from the rental of those lands to various families. Not even families could be classified internally as agricultural or commercial with regard to the source of their active incomes. Shops and small-scale industry often employed both women and children as well as men during the period of Pissarro's stay (for lower wages of course; women earned slightly less than half as much as men, and children, in turn, earned slightly more than half as much as women), and a family could be receiving several different incomes from different types of sources. This complexity of earning patterns was probably the norm rather than the exception among working-class Pontoisians. Very few people had nameable jobs or professions; they merely worked at whatever they could.[36]

Fields or Gardens: The Agricultural Economy of Pontoise

Pontoisian agriculture undoubtedly progressed during the period between 1880 and 1899, when Sagine finished his monograph on the town and its cadastral regions. The large local firm of agricultural merchants specializing in chemical fertilizers, modern metal tools, and farm machinery began business in 1880 and considerably affected the agriculture of the region. Its stocks of seeds and its close relationship with the Société d'agriculture et d'horticulture de Pontoise, a group founded in 1854, placed it in a unique position to infuse new ideas in agriculture into the local milieu. In spite of this modernization, the structure of agricultural production remained nearly identical at the end of the century to what it had been in the period of Pissarro's stay in the region. Of the 367 cultivated hectares within the town, 299 were *cultures alimentaires*, garden produce or home-grown vegetables; 54 were *prairies artificielles* or animal fodder; and 14 were *cultures industrielles*. The latter category included 10 hectares of potatoes harvested for the potato distillery owned by M. Chalon and 4 hectares of sugar beets for the same firm. The major vegetables included peas, beans, potatoes, carrots, and the famous Pontoise cabbages. Over half of the cultivated production was grain, comprising wheat, rye, barley, and lesser-known grains which were sold at the local markets and ground at the local mills. Sagine also emphasized the importance of orchards – mostly of pears and apples, the latter used for making cider – which clustered by the sides of the roads and paths.

Aside from the private vegetable gardens that flourished in the town throughout the nineteenth century and continue to be important today, the agriculture of Pontoise had two major aspects, large-scale grain production and the smaller-scale but equally important cultivation of fruits and vegetables. As has been discussed above, both these agricultures operated within a market economy that extended as far as Paris, and both are mentioned in guidebook descriptions of the town. Grain cultivation was a feature of the large, relatively dry plains of the Vexin plateau bordered Pontoise in the north. The fields of Vexin stretched between isolated farm villages such as Ennery, Osny, and Cergy. This kind of agriculture was extremely susceptible to mechanization, which began slowly in the 1860s and 1870s and had transformed the region by the end of the century. Harvesting machines, reapers, and other equipment were being used by the time of Pissarro's arrival in Pontoise, as were the chemicals and other trappings of "scientific" farming satirized later in the century in Zola's novel, *La Terre*.

Indeed, local interest in progressive agriculture was very great, Many of Pontoise's mayors and leading citizens were cultivators and farmers. The mayor of the city mentioned in the 1865 *annuaire*, a M. Thomassin, was a successful scientific farmer and a chevalier in the Légion d'honneur. The Société d'agriculture et d'horticulture de Pontoise, of which he was a prominent member, published a trimestral bulletin beginning in 1854 with reports on new inventions, fertilizers, seeds, and other products suited to local agriculture. In addition to the bulletin, the Société ran a small experimental garden in the larger garden of the Hôtel de Ville in which it displayed new products and conducted experiments with the local soil.[37]

The importance of this progressive spirit to the agriculture of the area should not be overstressed. Members of the Société tended to be rather large landowners or important cultivators with enough money and time for experimentation. Most of the local farmers and gardeners, however, seem to have been conservative in outlook and suspicious of the Société's ideas. Some of the suspicion seemed well justified. One M. Laroche of Saint-Ouen constructed a modern mechanical thresher in 1868 and demolished it in 1869. The next recorded mechanical thresher in Saint-Ouen was not constructed until 1878. The best local statistics for agricultural mechanization relate to nearby Osny, a mixed-agriculture village specializing in grain, to which the Pissarro family moved in 1882. These statistics suggest a large rise in mechanization in the 1870s: by 1882, there were six mechanical threshers, two mechanical planters, and one harvester. The statistics

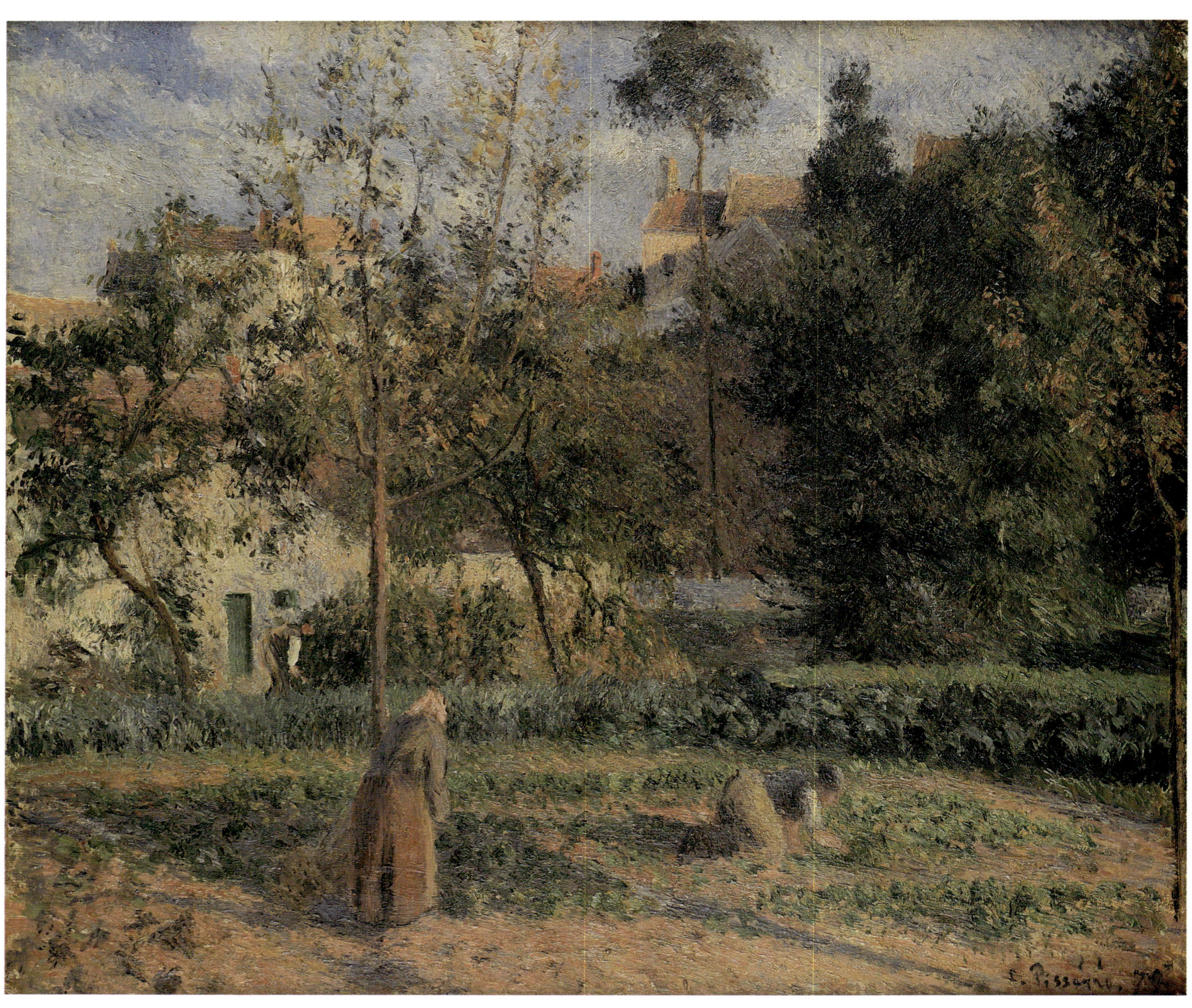

23. Camille Pissarro, *Jardin potager à L'Hermitage* (P&V 496), 1879, oil on canvas, 55 × 65cm., Musée d'Orsay, Paris.

can probably be applied also to the Vexin plateau in general and show a delayed reaction of about twenty years to the suggestions made by the Société d'agriculture et d'horticulture de Pontoise.[38]

The second type of agriculture in the region, market gardening or the *jardin potager*, is easily contrastable to the large-scale wheat agriculture of the plateaux. The gardens were clustered along the Oise and its tributaries. There was additional terracing on the hillsides to trap run-off moisture, and these gardens, in Sagine's rather fanciful description, were "a curiosity in town – they seemed to be hanging, like the famous Babylonian gardens, perched at incredible heights." The small market gardens differed from the grain fields of Vexin in practically every aspect. They were found in areas of denser population and were often adjacent to small houses. They required constant attention. They were, in most ways, unsuited to mechanization, although new developments in pesticides, fertilizers, and specialization did affect them considerably. The economic success and the importance of these gardens undoubtedly increased after the arrival of the railroad at Saint-Ouen in 1846, and they are mentioned in Joanne's guide and many other books on agriculture in Seine-et-Oise.

Pontoise's two agricultures produced two completely different types of cultivators, two different agricultural classes, and two different attitudes toward the land. The plateau grain cultivators lived in large, court-yarded farms grouped into small villages. Each farm consisted of a house, a tool shed, an animal barn, and a large covered shed for the storage of hay. The operation of the farm was large-scale and simple, involving only two major disruptions of the terrain annually: planting and harvesting. The harvests were cooperative, often mechanically aided. By contrast, the *jardiniers* along the Oise and in the small valleys adjacent to it lived in small, detached houses or row houses along a road, stored their tools in sheds near the gardens they tended, used few, if any animals, and generally spaded the earth by hand rather than with the plow. Their gardens clung to the surface of the hills and used all the available loam of the Oise estuary. Many may have been maintained by women in the household and by older men who were unable to do sustained physical labor. The employable men might have done only occasional chores in the gardens and worked, more likely, in nearby granaries, quarries, or small industries, or perhaps as itinerant farm laborers during planting or harvest seasons. The gardens needed constant care throughout the year – planting, weeding, replanting, spading, fertilizing, harvesting, and so on.

Provincial Leisure: Daily Life in Pontoise

In spite of its accessibility to Paris, Pontoise was a slow, archetypally provincial town in the nineteenth century. Local scandal contained in the historical list compiled in 1882 by the historian Henri Le Charpentier consists of one murder in 1844 and a public execution in 1852. The end of the century contributed very little to Le Charpentier's *Calendrier historique de Pontoise, éphémérides quotidiennes de l'histoire de cette ville*, with the exception of the inauguration of the gas works in 1867, the construction of the railroad and of the rue Impériale, the opening of the private Bibliothèque populaire in 1869, a terrible hailstorm in 1875, and a heavy snowfall in 1879. Apart from the occupation of Pontoise by the Prussians in 1870 and their destruction of the two bridges, nothing of historical note occurred in the town during the later part of the century.[39] The provincial sleepiness, the slow, methodical time of a small town is very much reflected in the cultural and intellectual life. The most representative and long-standing of local newspapers, *L'Echo Pontoisien*, published articles on local history written by members of the Société historique, lists of markets and prices, notices on agricultural matters by members of the Société d'agriculture, reports of the meetings of the town council, requests for zoning changes, demands for the continuance of the gas lines to the outlying areas, many advertisements for elixirs and new products, and the like. This newspaper, which was founded in 1820 and exists today, ran unchallenged until the radical feminist and rare woman member of the Freemasons, Maria Desraimes, founded *Le Républicain de Seine-et-Oise* in 1879.[40]

Le Républicain was designed as a thinking-person's newspaper. It covered events throughout the world, virtually ignoring the community of Pontoise itself. Its editorial policy was centrist republican with that odd mixture of socialist leanings and a concern for strong individual rights that characterized Desraimes's politics. The newspaper, in the style of the period, published poetry and fiction as well, including *Le Roman d'un homme brave* by Edmond About, a noted but minor novelist who summered in Osny and who, with Pissarro and Maria Desraimes, constituted Pontoise's population of cultured notables.

Pontoise's cultural life hardly deserved that title. A musical society gave occasional concerts and band performances, and a drama society presented several plays each year – in good years. There was little opportunity for public amusement, aside from the several local fêtes of which only one, the Foire Saint-Martin, held in November, had more than local importance. The promenade on Sunday and on summer evenings became perhaps the major public social event after the construction of the Jardin public, the garden of the Hôtel de Ville, and the enlarged *quai* in front of the Hôtel-Dieu. Pontoisians promenaded in the picturesque areas of their town and visitors took the promenade recommended in the guidebooks or strolled aimlessly along the river.

Indeed, the promenade was the principal form of relaxation and social intercourse in late nineteenth-century France. Associated with bourgeois leisure and the life of the city, it was equally important in the social life of many provincial towns. Guidebook writers would suggest promenades in the towns and throughout the neighboring countryside. For Adolphe Joanne nature or the out-of-doors was just as important as history and its monuments. His guide to the environs of Paris, the standard and most important guidebook of that region in the middle of the nineteenth century and throughout the Impressionist period, suggested many promenades along rivers, up hills, through agricultural villages, and along small rural paths. These walks through the countryside, orchestrated by Joanne, satirized by Daumier, and described by Zola, Renoir, and the Goncourts, were a standard feature of mid-century Parisian life. Even Pontoise, far as it was from the favorite outing spots of Second Empire and Third Republic Parisians, had its rural charms extolled by Joanne.[41]

What emerges from these excursions into the industry, the agriculture, the history, and the society of Pontoise, is a complex, unself-confident provincial town, a town both within and beyond the realm of Paris itself. The historical happenings during the nineteenth century were minimal. Pontoise's golden age had unquestionably been during the late Middle Ages, although the town figures prominently in the voluminous studies of the effect of the French Revolution on the countryside. The continued importance of Pontoise during the nineteenth century was dependent on the railroad. The railroad bridge and not the river became the principal explanation of Pontoise's success. In fact, Pontoise can be compared very easily with the similar towns of Provins and Etampes to the south of Paris. All were ancient capitals of regions that were absorbed into the growing environs of Paris. All three had long histories and collections of local monuments to remind them of these long histories. All three were more or less "middle places," lacking the smallness and charm of real agricultural villages, but also the bustle and consequence of a city or true *chef-lieu*. Pontoise suffered far more physical damage in the French Revolution than either Provins or Etampes, both of which still display fragments of city walls, many small churches, and houses dating from the late Middle Ages. Pontoise had none of this picturesque attractiveness, and yet it had as many memories of and pretensions to past importance as the other two, better-preserved towns. The intellectual community of Pontoise strove to keep the historical flame burning, to continue the vitality and the significance of its town by focusing its attention on its past. This attempt, a generalized outgrowth of Romanticism as well as a specific response to the psychological needs of a small town that had lost more than it gained during the modernist triumph that began in the French Revolution, went hand in hand with another attempt to modernize and industrialize Pontoise, an attempt that failed. Pontoise did everything in a small way during the nineteenth century. It made small civic improvements; it built a small and respectable railroad station; it industrialized to a very limited extent; its agriculture modernized cautiously and carefully; it was, in short, neither a modern town nor a Gothic relic. It lost the distinctiveness that made French places "important" either visually or economically. It was neither beautiful nor prosperous.

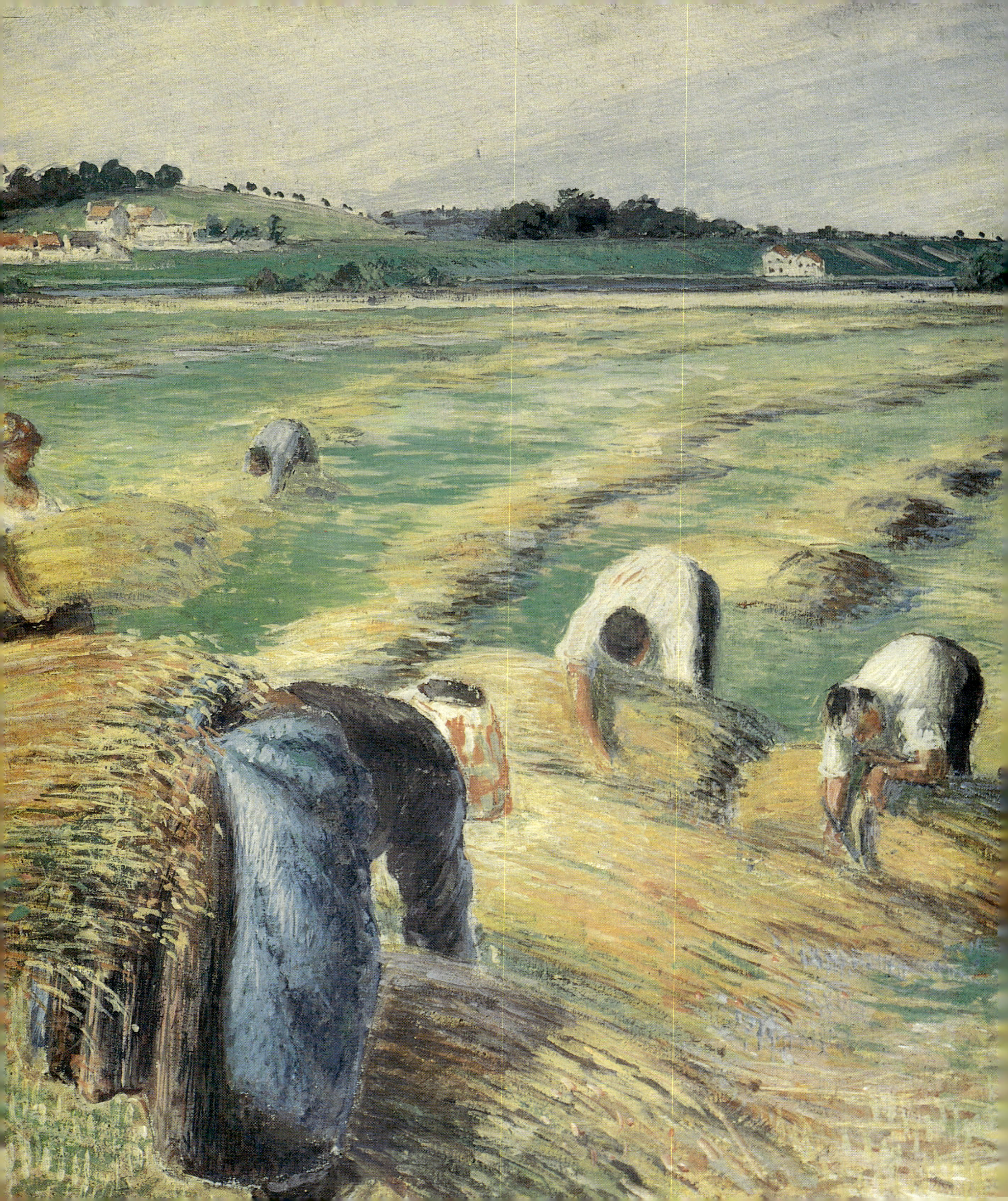

2 Pissarro's Pontoise: Omissions and Admissions

A map of Pontoise marked with each point from which Pissarro painted a single landscape painting (fig. 1) readily shows two characteristic approaches: a concentrated examination of one small region, the hamlet of L'Hermitage; and a broader, more equilibrious study of the entire Pontoisian area. The first of these approaches is the more evident from the map and is, in many ways, the more peculiar to Pissarro. He did not wander persistently through the fields in search of motifs. He was, for the most part, a fixated rather than an exploratory landscape painter. A comparison with other major landscape painters of his generation sets this concentrated aspect of his landscape geography into relief. Monet traveled considerable distances along the Seine at Argenteuil, often with the aid of his boat. Sisley moved in the landscape with a great freedom; indeed, his paintings of the region around Louveciennes, as revealed by Francois Daulte's catalogue raisonné, stand clearly in contrast to those of Pissarro in the same general landscape for their wide-ranging geography. Sisley painted in Louveciennes, Bougival, and Marly-le-Roi, moving easily throughout a large and diverse landscape, while Pissarro, during the same period, clung obsessively to the route de Versailles. Cézanne's motifs in his landscape around Aix-en-Provence are widely spaced and would have required strenuous hikes from any of his various homes or studios.[1] Chintreuil, if we can believe the early commentators, searched widely in his various landscapes for the open fields and empty forests he preferred.[2] No major landscape painter of the nineteenth century was more bounded, less geographically adventurous, than Pissarro. His entire perception of the landscape as an environment that encircled the studio separates him from the many painters who spent a considerable portion of the day looking for the absolutely right pictorial motif or, alternatively, simply returning to an habitual motif. Frédéric Henriet, both in his book of 1876, *Le Paysagiste aux Champs*, and in his many letters to landscape painters, emphasized the importance of protracted site and motif selection, and Théophile Thoré described the days he spent with Théodore Rousseau in long rambles throughout the countryside surrounding Paris.[3] Indeed, a great many images of the landscape painter in the nineteenth century represented hikers or wanderers who walk long distances in a day, searching for meaningful motifs.[4] The map illustrated here demonstrates that Pissarro circumvented this search, in spite of the evidence of Cézanne's marvelous drawing of him as a hiker. Pissarro lived in the landscape that he painted and, in addition, radically restricted its physical extent. His paintings describe, in this way, a personal and home-centered landscape.

The second characteristic of Pissarro's Pontoise is its relative completeness. There are few areas left out altogether. A curator of the Musée de Pontoise designing an exhibition of painted views representing Pontoise could easily choose paintings by Pissarro that would "illustrate" almost every region within the Pontoisian environment. The curator would deemphasize the pictures of L'Hermitage mentioned above and concentrate on those that range more freely in the landscape. In fact, this aspect of Pissarro's "double" perception of the

24. Detail of pl. 55.

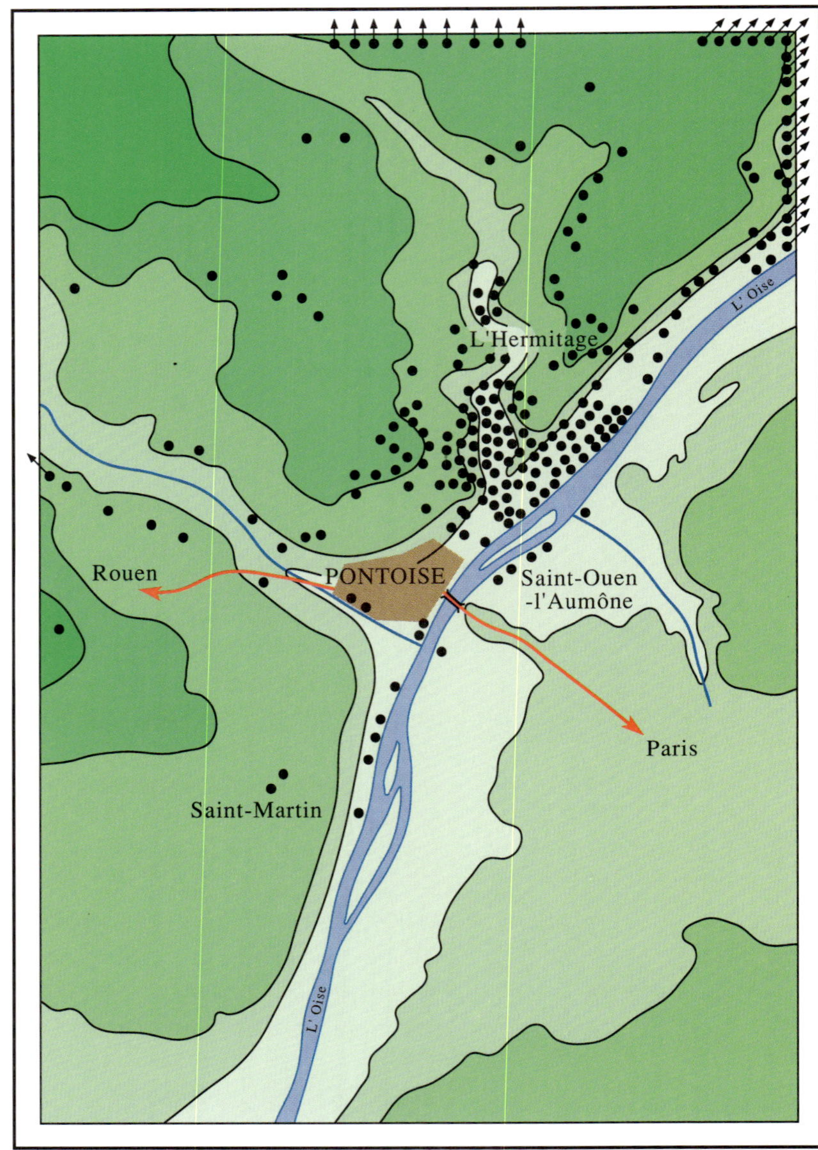

Fig. 1. Map of Pontoise as portrayed by Pissarro, 1866–83.

landscape differentiates his Pontoise from Monet's Argenteuil or Cézanne's Aix-en-Provence as much as does his concentration on a specific neighborhood. Monet and Ceźanne had certain areas or "spots," to use Wordsworth's inelegant but apt word, that they preferred to others and that they depicted many times.[5] A map of Monet's Argenteuil or Cézanne's Aix would lack the stray dots that play as important a part in reconstructing the Pissarro landscape as does the concentration of dots on L'Hermitage.

These two features of Pissarro's pictorial landscape, its range and its depth, are interesting in themselves. They suggest that the painter had a desire to observe and record all aspects of a place. There were, however, many specific forms and at least one important area of the Pontoisian landscape that Pissarro avoided. These "omissions" tell us a great deal about his particular landscape esthetics. Standing in front of a real landscape with a painted version of it in hand is often a startling experience for the student of landscape painting because of the painter's omission or lateration of a large, forceful form, or, alternatively, his exaggeration of a minor or weak element in the same environment. These experiences, not available to the viewer of a painting in the isolated context of a museum or gallery,

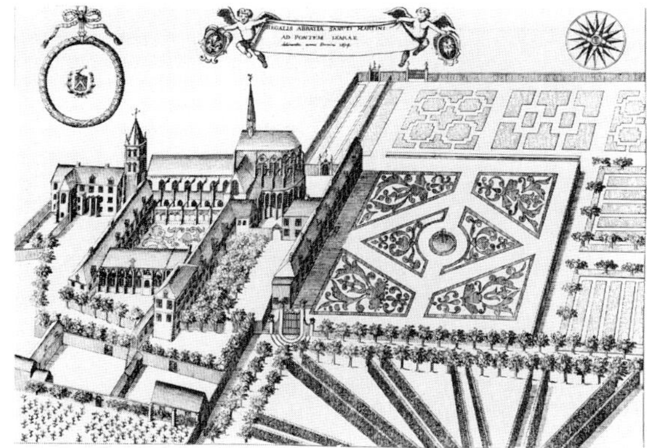

25. *Abbaye de Saint-Martin*, 17th century, engraving, Archives départementales du Val d'Oise.

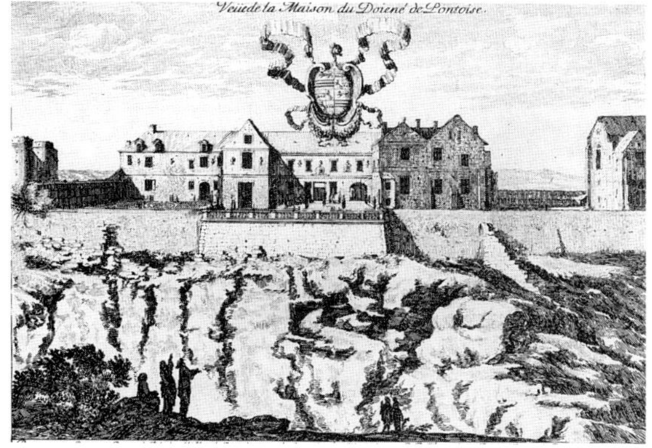

26. Israël Silvestre, *Château de Pontoise*, 17th century, engraving, from H. Le Charpentier, *La Ligue à Pontoise et dans le Vexin français*, Pontoise, 1878.

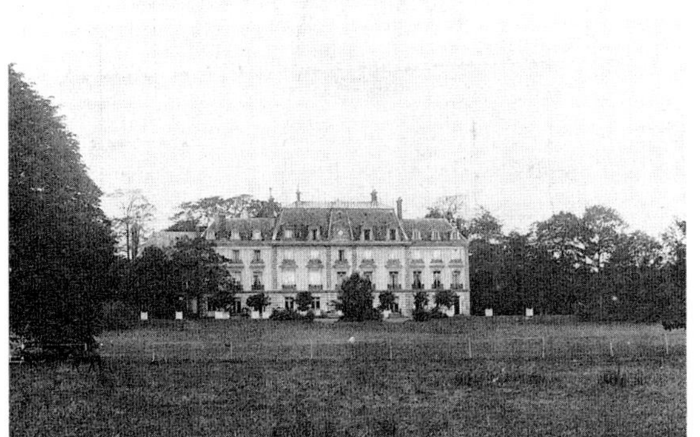

27. Château de Saint-Martin, Pontoise, late 19th century, postcard, collection of M. Jean Hecquet, Paris.

were of primary consequence to the painter and, hence, to a careful student of landscape painting.

Fortunately, Pissarro's omissions have a definite character, helping us, by contrast, to interpret his admissions. In the main, his response to the landscape was political and social as much as pictorial. He avoided images of either wealth or poverty. He deemphasized leisure, while reveling in agricultural work. As for history, whether ecclesiastical or secular, he was uninterested, preferring to lavish all the subtleties of his pictorial language on the enduring aspects of quotidien life. More than anything else, his landscapes are anti-Romantic. Images of ancient forests, picturesque mills, quarries, churches, ruins, and the like are either absent or designified in his landscape paintings, in spite of the fact that, as we have seen, all of them were to be found in the actual landscape around Pontoise.

Omissions

1 Surplus and suffering: the world of the rich and the world of the poor

Pontoise, like all towns and villages of the north of France, had long been divided into *seigneuries*, some owned by aristocrats and others by various ecclesiastical institutions. Sales of these areas to independent farmers and land speculators began as early as the fourteenth century and became the pattern in the eighteenth and nineteenth centuries.[6] By the time of Pissarro's arrival in Pontoise, these large estates were broken up into thousands of tiny plots owned by hundreds of families and rented by hundreds of others. There were, however, four notable châteaux in the environs: the Château de Marcouvilles near the hamlet Les Pâtis; the Château de Saint-Martin (formerly the powerful monastery of Saint-Martin); the Château près de Saint-Martin; and the Château de Maubuisson (formerly the convent of Maubuisson founded by Blanche of Castille, the mother of and regent for Saint Louis).[7] The Château de Maubuisson and the Château de Saint-Martin incorporated the ruins of medieval and baroque conventual buildings, while the other two châteaux were of more recent origins (pls. 25, 26, and 27). All the châteaux of Pontoise had fallen into the hands of wealthy Parisians after the *ventes des biens* in the late eighteenth century. Their owners were no longer the abbots or *seigneurs* of former times, but were absentee landlords with little economic and social relationship to the town itself. The *seigneuries* and abbeys had become *maisons de campagne*. The Château de Maubuisson was owned by the Rothschilds and was one of several large family properties in the environs of Paris. The large Second Empire house of the Château près de Saint-Martin belonged to the founder and the owner of the Parisian department store Printemps. Its site, adjacent to the larger Château de Saint-Martin, as its name implies, was a spectacular, exposed hillside overlooking the Oise near the lock painted several times by Pissarro in 1870 and 1872.

These large houses form an essential part of the "image" of Pontoise, indeed of any town in the environs of Paris during the eighteenth, nineteenth, and even twentieth centuries. Most guidebooks treat the châteaux and the large country houses as absolute characteristics of a place, and popular engravings and other prints from Israël Silvestre until the twentieth century show a dominant—even a predominant—concern with the country residences of both the nobility and the *haute bourgeoisie*.[8] They played a correspondingly important role in the iconography of Impressionism. Sisley and Monet both depicted large estates in their paintings of the 1870s. Sisley's Louveciennes, although it lacks the famous châteaux such as Ledoux's constrained and masterful house built for Mme. du

39

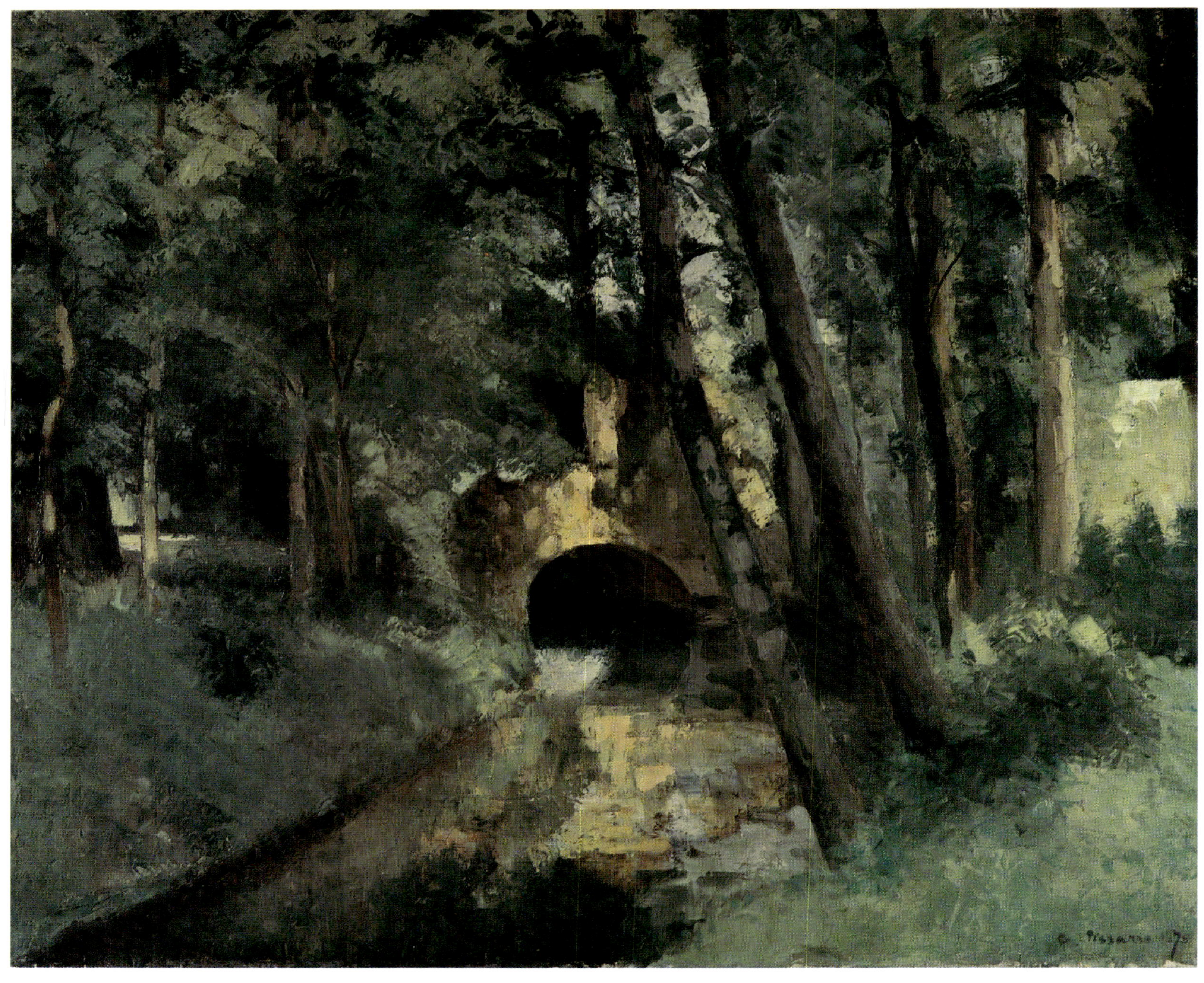

28. Camille Pissarro, *Le Petit pont* (P&V 300), 1875, oil on canvas, 65 × 81cm., Städtische Kunsthalle Mannheim.

Barry, includes less notable but equally capacious houses. Monet's overriding concern with bourgeois leisure permitted him to include many bourgeois gardens and one vast house, the Château de Rottembom, belonging to the Hoschedé family, in his odd, large-scale picture, *Les Dindons*, of 1876 (pl. 31).[9]

Pissarro was considerably more circumspect in his pictorial and social relationships with the *haute bourgeoisie*. His own friendships were confined mostly to artists, small dealers, and writers, and he was certainly rhetorically contemptuous of the commercial bourgeoisie.[10] This almost professional prejudice against the upper classes, either *nouveaux-riches* or *vieilles fortunes*, is clearly related to Pissarro's pictorial prejudice against the residues of wealth in the countryside of both Louveciennes and Pontoise. It is surely no accident that among his several hundred paintings, drawings, and prints of Pontoise, Pissarro never depicted one of the large châteaux. He painted *around* the Château de Saint-Martin and the

40

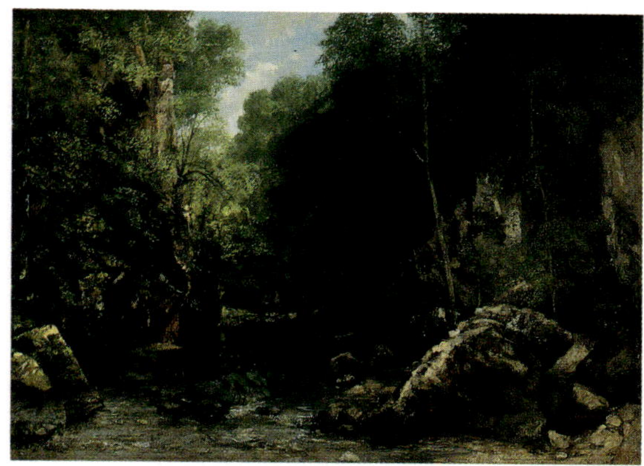

29. Gustave Courbet, *Le Ruisseau couvert* (*Le Ruisseau du Puits noir*), oil on canvas, 94 × 135cm., Musée d'Orsay, Paris.

Château près de Saint-Martin, but never painted the houses themselves. Guidebooks as well as contemporary prints and photographs show us that these châteaux, sited beyond spreading lawns, were clearly visible from the public road in the nineteenth century as they are today. Pissarro painted the road twice (pls. 63 and 141) and the landscape across the river at least four times (pl. 13 and P&V 70, 125, and 157), but not the châteaux themselves.

Yet, Pissarro did venture within the gates of a Pontoisian château at least once in his career. In 1875, he painted the small pont de Marcouville in an evident remaking of Courbet's structural *sous-bois* of the 1860s. The picture, never exhibited in his lifetime and called simply *Le Petit pont* in the catalogue raisonné, is devoid of aristocratic suggestion (pl. 28). No sculpture, no lawn, no outbuildings, no border wall mar the structural regularity of its surface.[11] It gives the illusion of immersion in a forest (very rare in Pissarro's oeuvre), an illusion that does not correspond to the broader, more spacious reality of the park of Marcouville itself. *Le Petit pont* is a testament to the painter's powers of exclusion. By framing an intimate and vegetative section of the château park, Pissarro actually disguised the aristocratic aspects of his real environment.

The question remains, however, why did Pissarro enter the park in the first place? His adoption of the palette knife and his renewed interest in a dark-valued and green palette are strong evidence of a desire to root his landscape esthetic in the art of Courbet. The forested section of the Château de Marcouville was probably the only motif resembling Courbet's *sous-bois* (pl. 29) in the environs of Pontoise. Most of the forests near Pontoise were small, regularly harvested, and hence, of no great age. Only the château park of Marcouville combined a rather older forest and a stream (the Viosne), both essential elements of the Courbet model. In addition, the park of Marcouville was opened to the public, at least on weekends, and Joanne mentioned it in both editions of *Les Environs de Paris*.

Pissarro was a bourgeois – there is no doubt of that – but he believed in a society of equals, an idealized republican society, and not one in which the disparity between rich and poor was so great. His omission of the châteaux of Pontoise can be interpreted in light of these ideas, ideas that were hardly radical, if that word is used in its modern sense, but that show evidence of the clear anti-aristocratic and anti-wealth character of Pissarro's thought. Yet, this omission has a social explanation as well, and one that should not be overlooked too hastily in an eagerness to find precedence for Pissarro's political radicalism. Pissarro was not integrated into Pontoisian society to any notable extent, and his social world would never have included the extremely wealthy, Paris-based owners of the local châteaux. His non-French origins, his profession, his Jewish background, and his income made this kind of social life all but impossible. The world of the châteaux – supper parties, promenades, boating, and evening entertainments – was not the world of Pissarro. Its explicit hedonism was not in keeping with his own life of family traumas and professional sufferings so familiar to students of the lives of nineteenth-century painters.

There are, however, certain important exceptions to Pissarro's omission of the châteaux from his work at Pontoise. The first is *Le Jardin des Mathurins, Pontoise*, painted in 1876 (pl. 152). Its subject is the large pleasure garden of the small Château des Mathurins, situated within a short walk of Pissarro's home. It was owned throughout the 1870s by Maria Desraimes and her sisters and was used by them as a summer house (pl. 30).[12] Why did Pissarro avoid the other châteaux of Pontoise and paint this one? The answer to this question lies with its owner. Maria Desraimes was anything but an ornamental bourgeois woman of the type celebrated by Monet and Renoir. She was a successful realist playwright in the

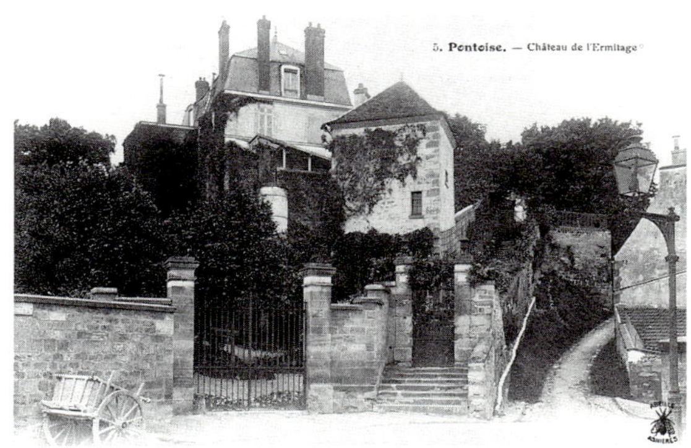

30. Château de L'Hermitage (actually Château des Mathurins), Pontoise, late 19th century, postcard, collection of M. Jean Hecquet, Paris.

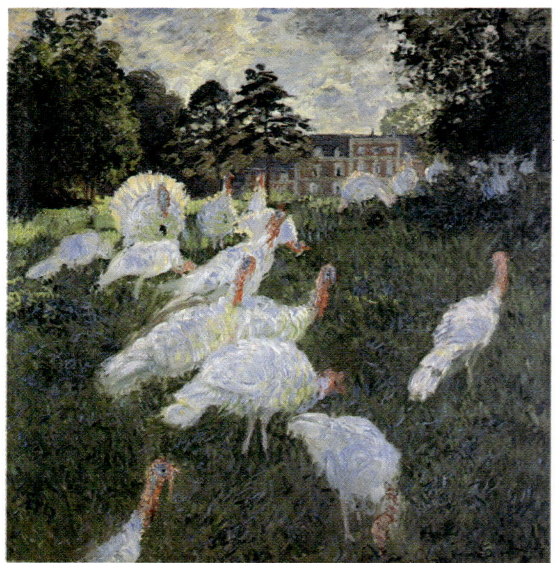

31. Claude Monet, *Les Dindons*, 1876, oil on canvas, 172 × 175cm., Musée d'Orsay, Paris.

32. Camille Pissarro, *Le Jardin à Pontoise* (P&V 394), 1877, oil on canvas, 125 × 165cm., private collection, France.

1860s, a politicized polemicist during the Commune and its aftermath, and an ardent republican in the 1870s. She was a tireless worker, an opinionated and strident woman, whose energy was more remarkable than her insights.[13] She was a friend of the Pissarro family, and the familiar correspondence between the two suggests that the painter was given access to her garden in the late 1870s.[14] It is quite probable that two garden landscapes of 1877, *Le Jardin à Pontoise* (pl. 32) and the smaller and closely related *Un Coin du jardin à L'Hermitage* (P&V 396), were painted in it, and three landscapes (pls. 108 and 109, and P&V 397) include the house and its walls. *Le Jardin des Mathurins* and *Le Jardin à Pontoise*, both large by Pissarro's standards, reveal the leisured life of the wealthy. They take their place with Monet's garden landscapes of the 1860s and 1870s as celebrations of *la vie bourgeoise*. The presence of these pictures in Pissarro's "series" of Pontoise strengthens the social rather than the political or economic explanations for his omission of the larger châteaux. To Pissarro, Maria Desraimes was both an acceptable and an accessible member of the bourgeoisie. Her house was open to the painter, and her ideas, opinionated and confused as they were, probably coincided with many of his own.

The two large gardenscapes and the several small pictures that relate to them must be seen within the overwhelmingly working-class context of Pissarro's other paintings of Pontoise. They exist as exceptional images. Their relationship to Monet's subject matter is undeniable: *Le Jardin des Mathurins* made its debut in the Impressionist exhibition of 1877 in the same room as Monet's unfinished decoration, *Les Dindons* (pl. 31), and its very existence sprung surely not so much from the garden itself, as from Monet's decorative panel, *Le Déjeuner*, which represented his own garden, shown in the Impressionist exhibition of 1876. Thus, the imagery of Pissarro's gardenscapes, although "real," is borrowed: the presence of Monet is everywhere, in the brushstrokes, in the use of well-dressed female figures, in the sunkissed laziness of the motifs.[15] The images were a compromise for Pissarro, departures from his normal subject matter derived from Corot, Courbet, Daubigny, and Chintreuil. With the exception of the garden landscapes painted in 1900 at the country home of Octave Mirbeau, they are the only scenes of the bourgeois garden in Pissarro's output as a landscape painter.

An omission that is perhaps more surprising but no less important relates not to the world of the rich, either aristocratic or bourgeois, but to the world of the poor. There are few, if any, indications of suffering in Pissarro's landscapes, none of homelessness, and none of rural miseries. In a century in which images of picturesque beggars, rural wanderers, and squalid peasants were anything but rarities, Pissarro, once again, avoided "slumming," even in the country. He stuck to the middle road, and, if his rural inhabitants seem to work hard for their living, their painter glories in their work.

Although both contemporary and modern studies of Pissarro refer with great abandon to the "peasant" villages, "peasant" architecture, and "peasants," the realities of Pontoise display a considerably more complex social system, as has been shown above. The rural architecture of the Région Pontoisienne reflected the social changes that had begun to alter the "peasant" populations in the environs of the town. The ruination, the sagging roofs, and the messy barnyards that had characterized rural architecture in fact and in image since the seventeenth century were rapidly disappearing from the actual rural landscape of the improving north of France. Most writers on the rural architecture of Normandy and, more specifically, of the towns around Pontoise, date that architecture not from the Middle Ages or vaguer distant past, as is popularly believed, but from the late eighteenth and the nineteenth centuries.[16] The older houses, dating from the seventeenth and

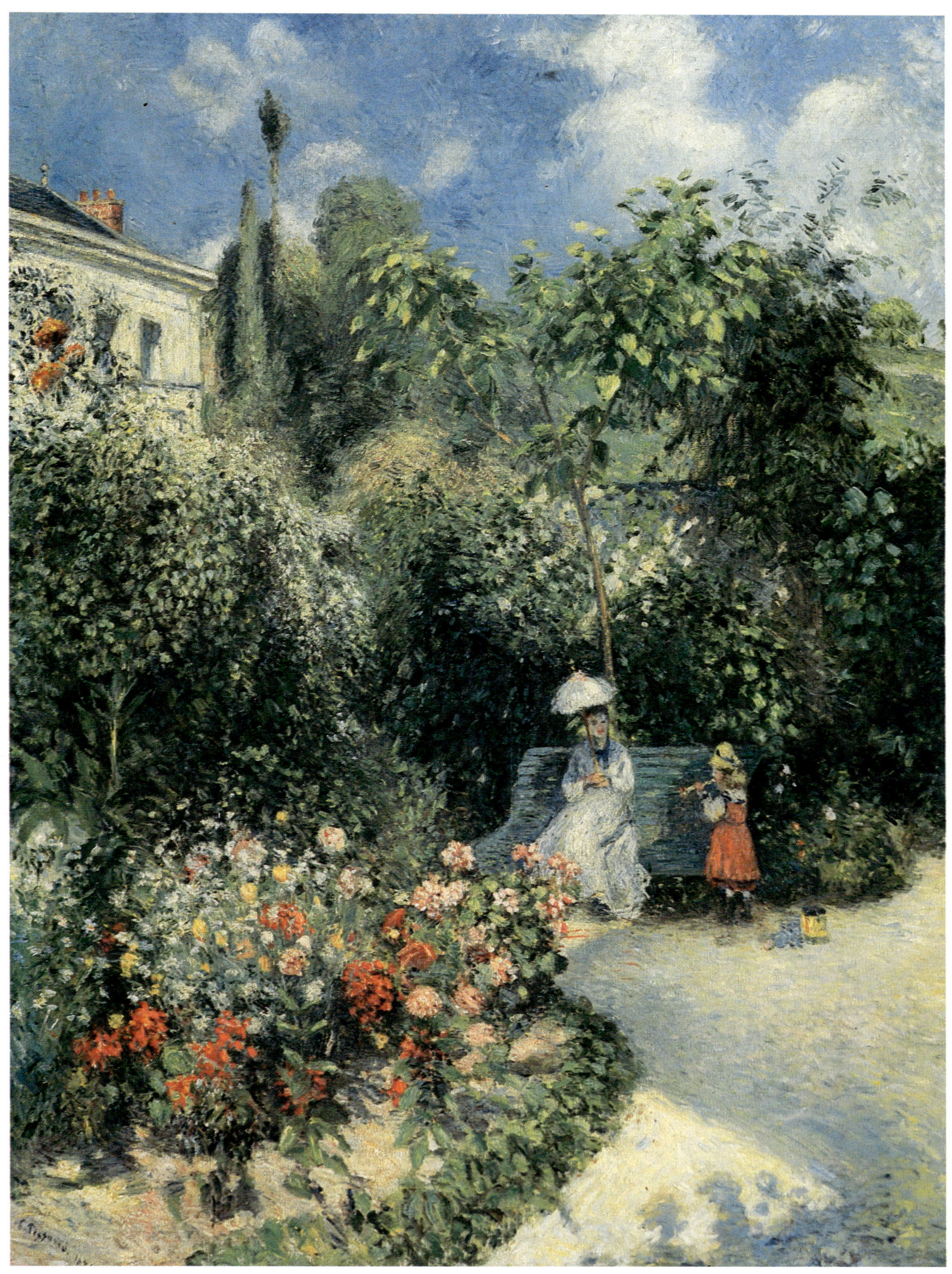

early eighteenth centuries, were built of grey granite and softer slate. Their roofs were most often thatched and, if they were tiled, were a weathered brown color, further naturalized by moss and lichens. These houses merged with the landscape. Their coloration was dull and "natural"—grey, dark brown, and dark green. Their contours were curved, sagged, and bent. Their presence in the landscape was minimal. They were hidden in the environment, disguised as nature.

Only four times, twice in 1873 (P&V 228, 229) and twice in 1880 (pl. 168 and P&V 512) did Pissarro represent the famous *chaumières* or thatched cottages that were to be found in the hamlets around Pontoise. In each of these cases, he emphasized the road, not the houses, preferring to treat the hamlets as aggregate forms rather than to dwell on the thatched cottages for their picturesque appeal. By contrast, the *Rue de L'Hermitage, Pontoise* of 1874 (pl. 103) and the *Paysage à Chaponval* of 1880 (pl. 167) depict neat white-and-cream-colored houses with brightly colored tile roofs and clear geometric proportions. This is not the architecture of a dying peasantry, the architecture of the "sauvages" peasants described by Zola, Balzac, and more hysterical writers of peasant genre.[17] Nor is it the peasant architecture that had dominated the *paysage champêtre* of the eighteenth century and the tourist illustrations of the north of France from the early and middle nineteenth century. Pissarro painted the new, "improved" rural architecture, much of which was as recently finished as the more ostensibly modern *maison bourgeoise* on the rue de L'Hermitage. The tiles for the roofs were available in different colors, most of which were bright, in keeping with the new anti-natural, modernizing tastes of the period. The desire for smooth, finely plastered, and light-colored surfaces was another product of the late eighteenth and the nineteenth centuries. Stone peasant dwellings were plastered with a startling regularity in the period of the Second Empire and the Third Republic. The natural, rough-cut, unquarried stone of these buildings was thought unrefined by a generation of rural workers whose lives were characterized by seasonal migrations, factory jobs, and stints in the cities.

Pissarro's avoidance of rural poverty can be extended to include two other picturesque and impoverished areas of Pontoise, the fishermen's quarter along the Viosne and the cave dwellings that clustered along the route Saint-Antoine and the hillsides of L'Hermitage (pls. 34 and 35). Mentions of the cave dwellings are frequent in nineteenth-century accounts of Pontoise, and several postcards dating from late in the century show what Pissarro chose not to paint. They reveal a population of rural workers, without property, who had set up housekeeping in the abandoned caves and quarry sites throughout the Région Parisienne. The houses and their inhabitants would have enchanted a more traditional painter of rural life than Pissarro; one can imagine depictions by Hervier, Lhermitte, Isabey, or even Cazin. But Pissarro was not attracted to these "natural" dwellings, which were as accessible to his home as any of the motifs he preferred to use. The fishermen's quarter along the Viosne was, it is true, a little further from L'Hermitage, but, if postcards are any indication, the complicated intertwinings of fishermen's sheds, huts, nets, poles, and paraphernalia might have proved as pictorially fascinating as the cave dwellings to artists other than Pissarro.

The sagging, the complex, the rundown rural picturesque was not a subject admired by Pissarro. He was not fascinated by the simple, if miserable, existence of an almost archaic peasantry, as was Lhermitte and, to a lesser extent, Millet. His omission of the fishermen's quarter and of the cave dwellings was an omission of the kind of rural life that had been portrayed by popular artists of the nineteenth century and by famous artists of the eighteenth century. The kind of ruralism that is easily found in the drawings and paintings of Boucher as well

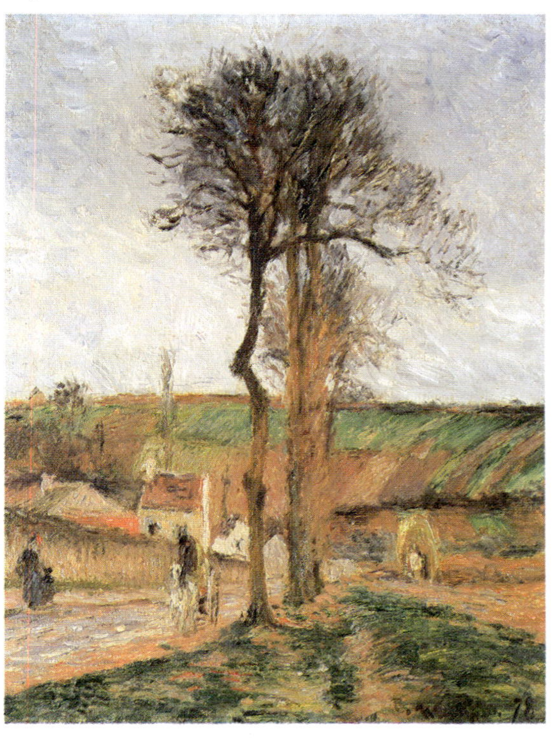

33. Camille Pissarro, *Route d'Ennery à L'Hermitage, environs de Pontoise* (P&V 436), 1878, oil on canvas, 45 × 36cm., Sotheby's, London (29 Nov. 1988, lot 36).

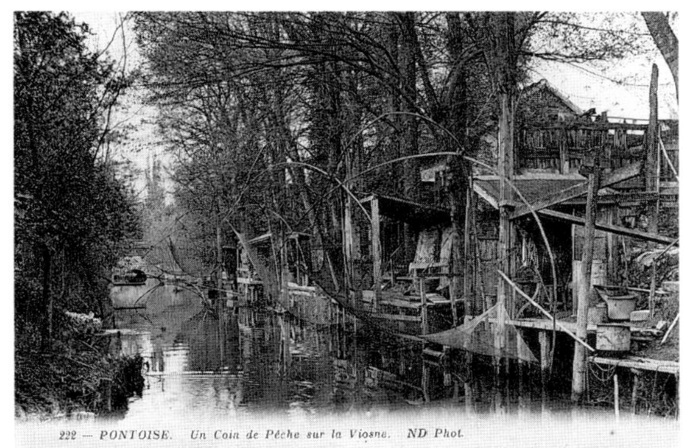

34. Fishermen's quarters on the Viosne, Pontoise, late 19th century, postcard, collection of M. Jean Hecquet, Paris.

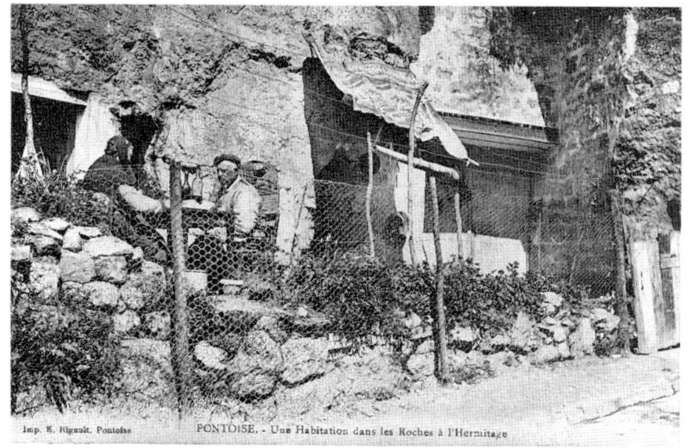

35. A cave dwelling at L'Hermitage, Pontoise, late 19th century, postcard, collection of M. Jean Hecquet, Paris.

as the travel lithographs of countless unknown artists acted as a symbolically "natural" and anti-urban image. This rural life was juxtaposed pictorially with the fashion-conscious, modern, and tasteful world of the archetypal city, Paris. Pissarro's Pontoise, with its omission both of the large châteaux and of the traditionally picturesque ruralism of the local poor, was a pictorial hymn to the rapidly developing rural proletariat. Pissarro's world lacked both suffering and surplus: economic extremes were not permitted.

2   Piety and tradition: the church in the landscape

Another omission, less surprising, but in many ways as significant as the others, was the religious architecture and the religious life of Pontoise. Pissarro lived in a period characterized by an increase in Roman Catholic piety as well as in the general importance of the church, and, more importantly, he lived, during his years in Pontoise, in a provincial religious center.[18] Pontoise's religion and its religious significance were, in many ways, as important to its self-image as its grain markets, railroads, and river port. The vast majority of items in the *iconographie de Pontoise* are portrayals of the churches and convents of the town and its region. The historical stories about Pontoise that had popular currency in the nineteenth century were tales of the devotions of Blanche of Castille; of the visionary piety of Saint Louis, whose boyhood was spent in the town; in short, of matters closely connected with the church. The ecclesiastical institutions, which were the *raison d'être* of the town until the end of the eighteenth century, continued to exercise profound influence in the nineteenth century, in spite of their relative decline. The abbots were important local citizens and savants, and even the tourists' Pontoise, which owed much to the historical writings of Abbé Trou, centered on Saint-Maclou and Notre-Dame.

Pissarro's portrait of the town pays singularly little attention to these matters. Although they appear within the larger context of his rare views of Pontoise itself, the two major churches are never depicted on their own account. Neither the architectural residues of the religious institutions that had always controlled Pontoise, nor the religious festivals and parades that provided evidence of the continuity of religious life concerned Pissarro.

Pissarro's religion has never been discussed in detail.[19] There is some evidence that his parents were practicing Jews, at least to the bare extent that they celebrated Yom Kippur (the Day of Atonement). Pissarro, however, and his family were not. His wife, Julie, was from a traditional, rural Roman Catholic background but had left the church for her husband. Pissarro himself lived according to vigorous atheistic convictions, with a strong tinge of anti-clericalism.[20] His thinking was the exact opposite of the fervor or intense emotionality that led the aging Cézanne back to the Catholic church, and his paintings lack the almost pantheistic quality evident in much of the work of Rousseau, Chintreuil, Courbet, Cézanne, and even Monet. In Pissarro's landscape, men and women work together in a world defined by that work, not by the hand of God.

Pissarro's lack of religiosity and the anti-Catholic and anti-clerical aspects of his social thinking are manifested in his pictures. His depictions of Saint-Maclou and Notre-Dame are distant views, lacking the singularity and immediacy that characterized depictions of the churches by other artists. D'Hastrel, a prominent travel illustrator and painter of the early 1850s, designed three lithographs of Pontoise: a general river view and studies of the two principal churches (pls. 9 and 10). The churches were, for d'Hastrel and for most nineteenth-century visitors

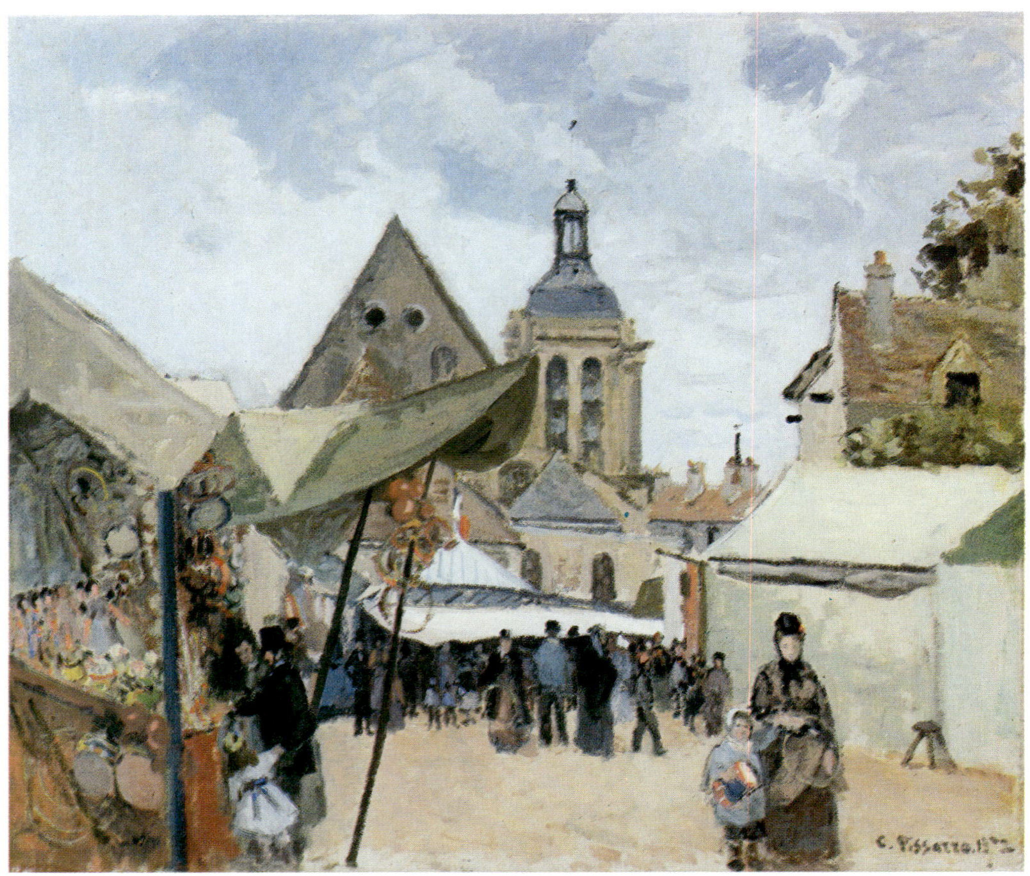

36. Camille Pissarro, *Fête de Septembre, Pontoise* (P&V 188), 1872, oil on canvas, 46 × 55 cm., Sotheby's, New York (9 May 1989, lot 5).

38 (facing page). Camille Pissarro, *Le Parc aux Charrettes, Pontoise* (P&V 442), 1878, oil on canvas, 60 × 73 cm., collection of Mrs. Benjamin Reeves, New York.

37. The apse of the church of Notre-Dame, Pontoise, late 19th century, postcard, collection of M. Jean Hecquet, Paris.

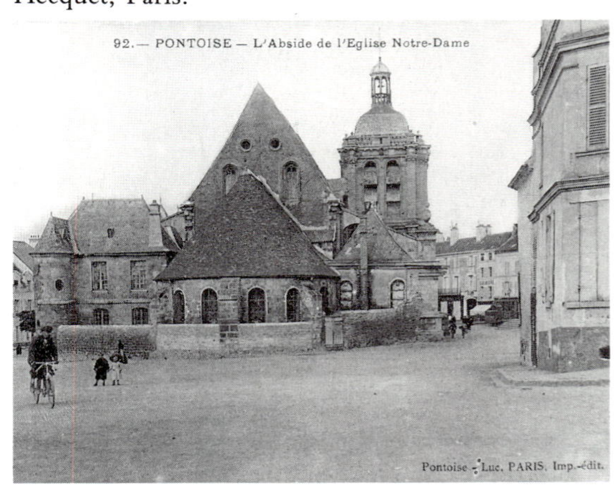

to and inhabitants of Pontoise, the glories of the city. Representations of these buildings, like Monet's later views of the facade of Rouen, are exclusive studies of the form in light. Very little of the architectural ambience of the town is allowed to impinge on the isolated grandeur of these religious images. In Pissarro's depictions of Pontoise, by contrast, the churches are literally overwhelmed by their environment. They are pushed into corners, reduced in size, screened by layers of trees. As if in opposition to the traditional images, their forms are encroached upon and, to a large extent, designified by their context. Notre-Dame becomes the backdrop for an active urban market in the *Fête de Septembre* of 1872 (pls. 36 and 37). Saint-Maclou is actually reduced in scale and in pictorial import- ance in the *Parc aux Charrettes* of 1878 (pl. 38). For this latter picture, Pissarro chose a site in a small transitional square between the place de la Gare and the place aux Marchés with an unlikely name, parc aux Charrettes. The square com- mands an excellent view of the flamboyant Gothic tower of Saint-Maclou with its oddly appropriate Renaissance "crown" by the great Pontoisian architect, Jacques Lemercier. Standing in the square and looking uphill, the tower is the single dominating form. Its uppermost proportions are rather broader and physically taller than they are in the picture, where the tower is of roughly the same size and surface scale as the adult figures and is insignificant compared with the curvilinear activity of the tree. The tree is, in fact, the most active and fascinating form within the composition. It is larger, more potent, and taller than the tower of Saint-Maclou and makes it shrink in relative importance. What Pissarro has done in this tiny, attractive townscape, is to enlarge the natural element of the scene and reduce the architectural. The tree screens a large house on the hill above it and vies for dominance with the more psychologically potent form of the church

46

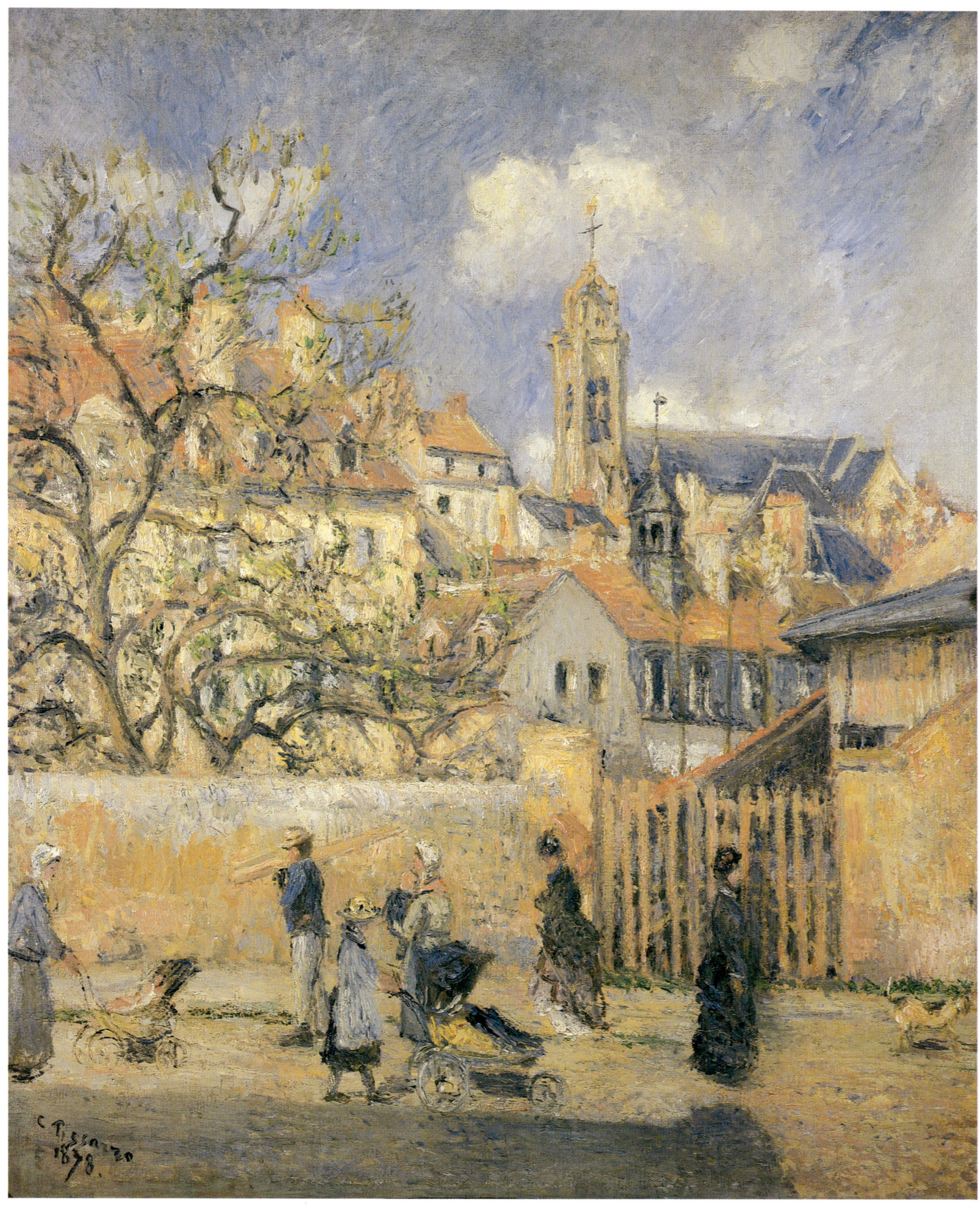

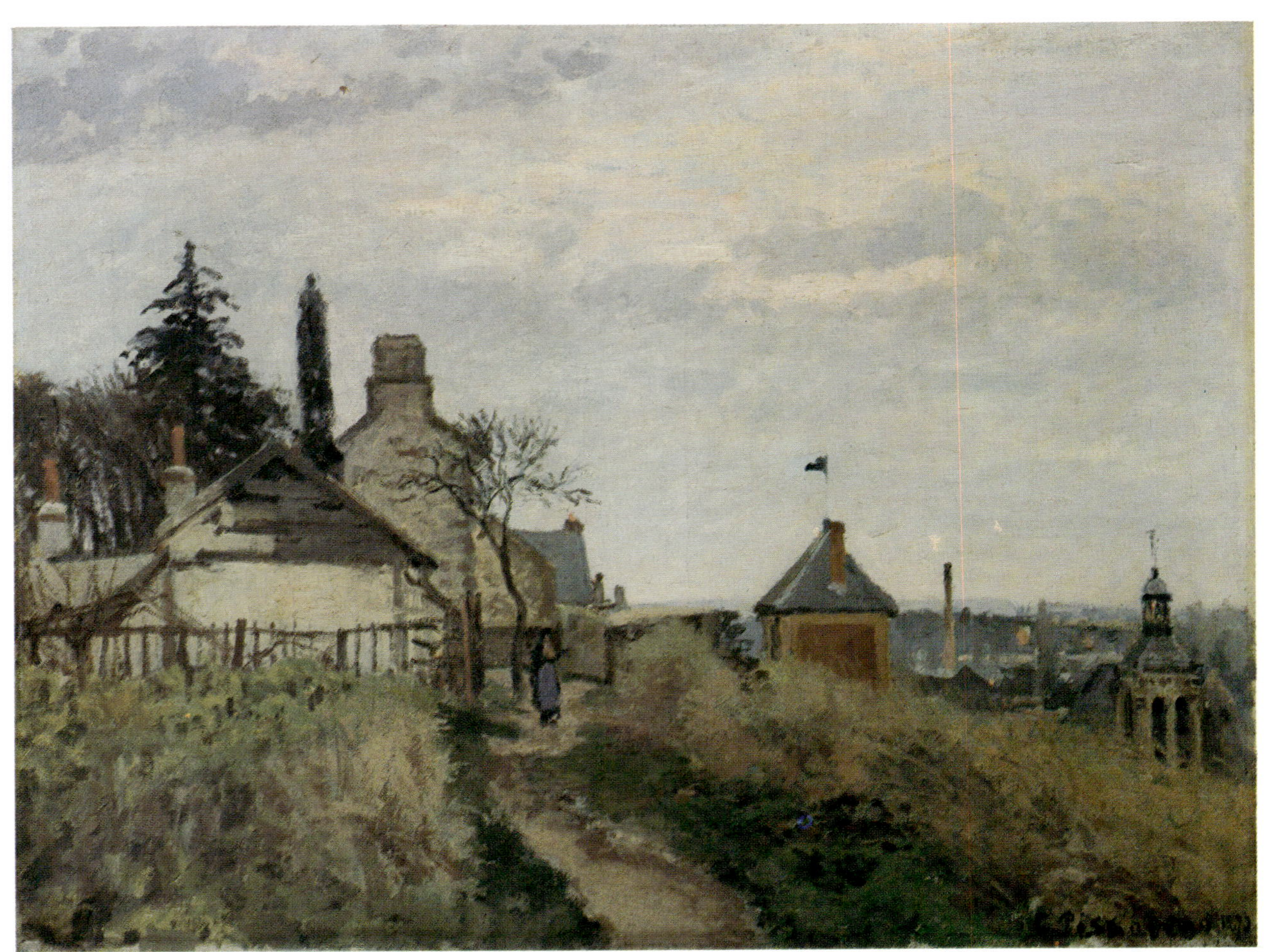

39. Camille Pissarro, *Pontoise* (P&V 172), 1872, oil on canvas, 40 × 53cm., Musée d'Orsay, Paris.

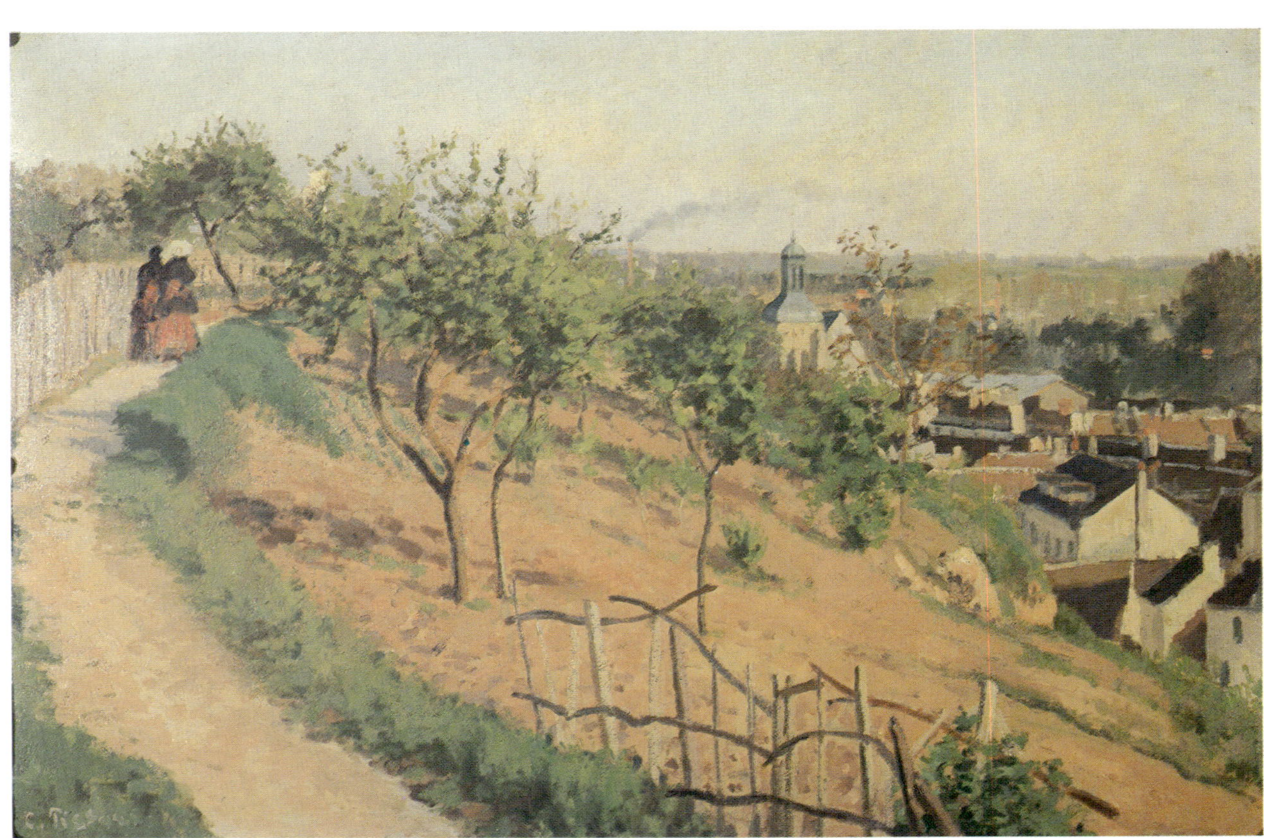

40. Camille Pissarro, *La Sente de Justice, Pontoise,* *c.*1872, oil on canvas, 52 × 81cm., Memphis Brooks Museum of Art; Gift of Mr. and Mrs. Hugo N. Dixon, 53.60.

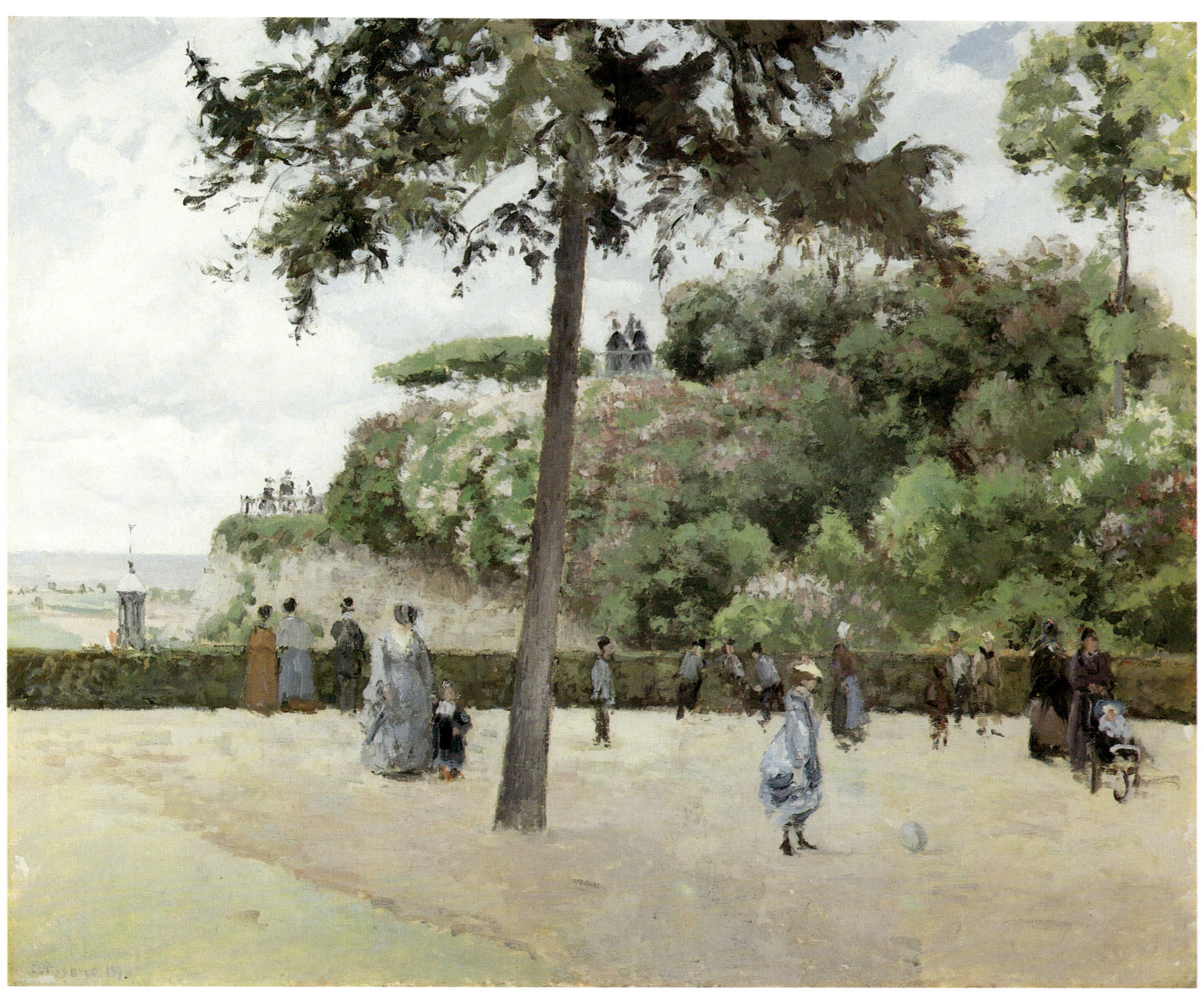

41. Camille Pissarro, *Le Jardin de la Ville, Pontoise* (P&V 257), 1874, oil on canvas, 60 × 73cm., private collection.

itself. And both "nature" and "religion" are put in their place by the passers-by, who walk with little, if any regard for their setting.

The pictorial designification of the important religious structures of Pontoise is the rule rather than the exception in Pissarro's pictures of the town. The tower of Notre-Dame is seen from above and is a relatively insignificant inclusion in the view *Pontoise*, of 1872, as well as in the earlier *La Sente de Justice* (pls. 39 and 40). The same tower is barely included in the large *Jardin de la Ville, Pontoise* (pl. 41).[21] In all these paintings, Pissarro has transformed an obvious motif into a simple element of the landscape. Within the tradition of French landscape painting, this designification is surprising, even radical. Churches almost always anchor landscape compositions. The church of Saint-Lo controls and defines the panoramic *Vue de Saint-Lo* by Corot. In Pissarro's *Pontoise*, Notre-Dame is no more important than the smokestack of the factory and less important than the rather

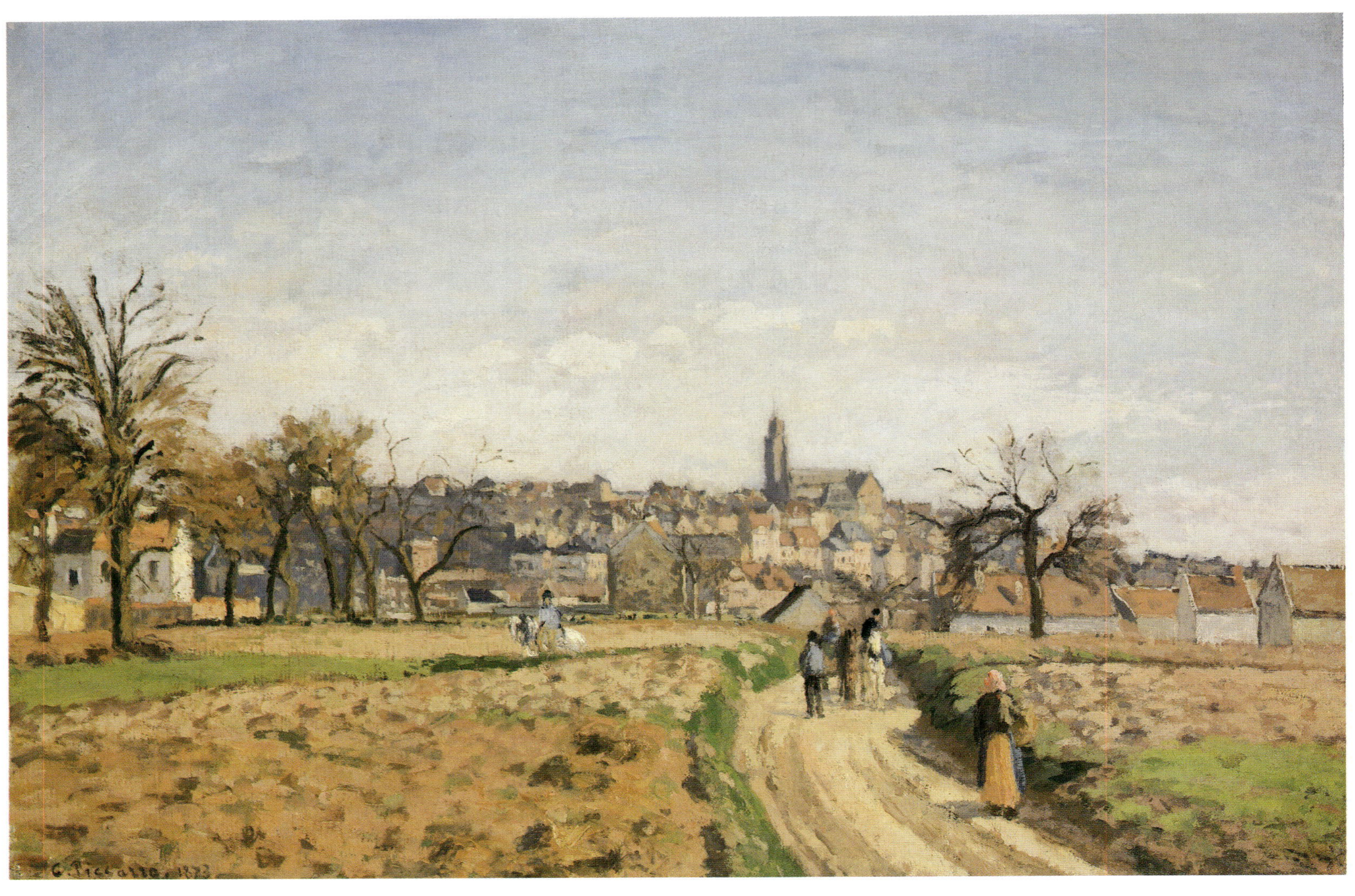

42. Camille Pissarro, *Vue de Pontoise* (P&V 210), 1873, oil on canvas, 53 × 82 cm., private collection, Dallas.

common group of rural houses that dominate the foreground of the picture (pl. 39). Churches are the central motifs of countless canvases by artists as diverse as Corot, Hervier, Millet, Monet, and Van Gogh, but there is only one panorama of Pontoise, *Vue de Pontoise* (pl. 42), of 1873, that is centered on the church of Saint-Maclou. And, even in this picture, the figures on the road and the ordinary houses to the left and right are at once larger and more colorful than the church tower.

Pissarro's own religion, or lack thereof, profoundly altered his perception of the Pontoisian landscape. His view of the city was secular and skeptical. In his rather short-lived stint as a visual historian of Pontoise, he recorded the two major secular events of the year, the Fête de Septembre and the Foire Saint-Martin.[22] He painted the urban leisure of the parks and the broad public walk-ways, and he depicted the life of the harbor and its factories; but he avoided the major religious festivals and the street processions that were, in many ways, more significant local events. His Pontoisians are not the pious peasants of Millet's *Gleaners*, of Breton's first Salon picture, *The Benediction of the Wheat*, or, even, of the ambiguous and provocative *Burial at Ornans* by Courbet. It seems that he was suspicious of the idea of a mystic unity between man and the earth. His own early life, with its evident uprootings and extensive travels, had perhaps made him wary of roots. Indeed, his views of the "traditional" peasantry and of the church were equally suspicious, and he avoided any connection between the two. Pissarro could never have painted Cézanne's *Old Woman with the Rosary* (Venturi 702; 1895–96), even as a genre picture; his women sit or sew rather than pray. He avoided depiction of private as well as public devotion.

3   *Mills and quarries: the functional landscape*

Industrial images are very important in the iconography of Pissarro's Pontoise and warrant separate discussion; yet, the numerous mills and associated grain sheds were avoided by him. As a glance at several maps of the Viosne valley will reveal, the large area adjacent to the railroad station near the Maison Rouge and behind the Château de Marcouville was filled with grain mills. A map of 1778 shows fifteen of these mills, many of which were in operation during the 1870s.[23] While the introduction of mechanized milling operations in Paris had begun to undercut the business of these local water mills, they continued to be extremely important within the Pontoisian economy. Neither the rapid diversification of local agriculture nor the introduction of industry in the late nineteenth century altered the fact that the single most significant element of the Pontoisian economy in 1899, when Sagine wrote his monograph on the town, was still grain. Farmers from the plateau towns between Pontoise and Gisors brought their wheat, rye, and oats to the grain mills and the large grain markets of Pontoise throughout the nineteenth century.

In addition to its economic significance, the mill, powered by either water or wind, plays a crucial role in the iconography of landscape painting and was an important feature of the rural novels of the mid-nineteenth century.[24] One of Pissarro's very few depictions of a mill, *Le Moulin des Pâtis, près Pontoise* (pl. 43), painted in 1868, is as much a repudiation as it is an acceptance of the traditional mill motif. The mill is placed at a great distance from the viewer and none of the obvious features – the picturesque stream, the paddling waterwheel – is shown. It is further deemphasized by its position immediately behind a canted, spindly, and dead tree. The painting is an important and beautiful landscape that assumes its place among the masterpieces of Pissarro's first L'Hermitage period. Yet, to the historian of landscape imagery, it is at once odd and surprising: Pissarro has both

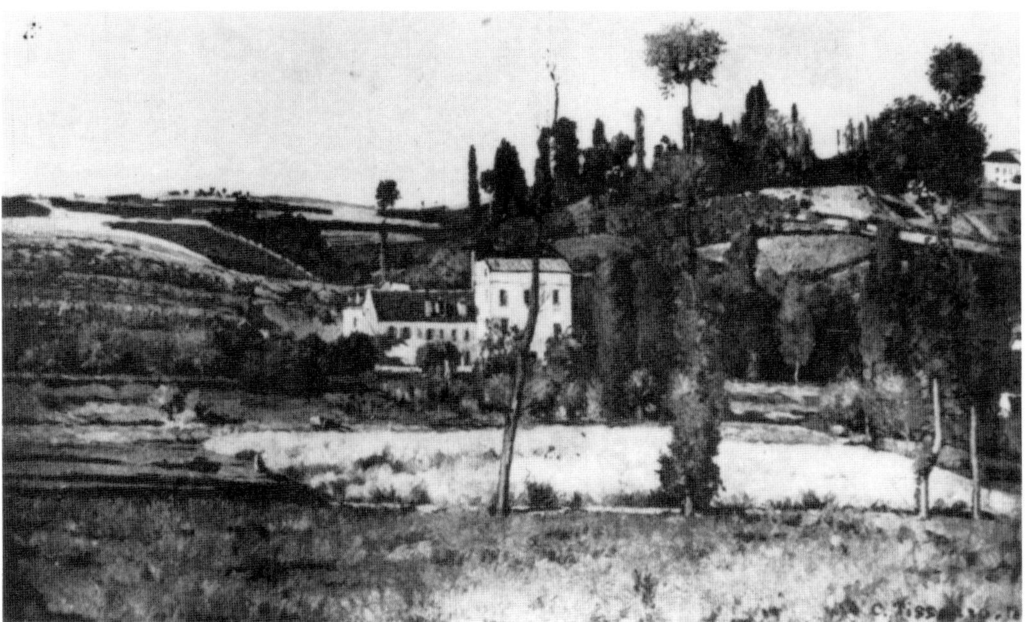

43. Camille Pissarro, *Le Moulin des Pâtis, près Pontoise* (P&V 62), 1868, oil on canvas, 90 × 150cm., private collection.

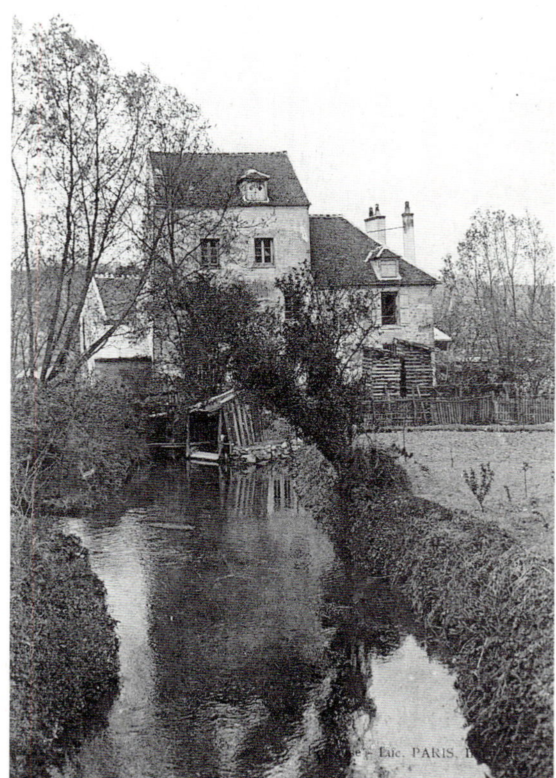

44. Moulin de la Couleuvre, early 20th century, postcard, Archives départementales du Val d'Oise.

45. Jules Lebas, *Le Moulin de la Couleuvre*, late 19th century, watercolor, private collection.

detached himself from and defunctionalized this traditional motif; but, by placing it at the center of the composition, he has also accepted it. This kind of ambivalence – both acceptance and rejection – is characteristic of Pissarro's painting throughout his career.

In 1883, a full fifteen years after *Le Moulin des Pâtis, près Pontoise* and during Pissarro's last year in Pontoise, the mill motif recurs in three more paintings: *Paysage à Osny, la vanne près du moulin* (pl. 47); *Lavoir et moulin d'Osny* (pl. 49); and *Le Ruisseau à Osny* (pl. 48), the latter two being most probably views of the moulin de la Couleuvre. This can be ascertained from looking at contemporary postcards or drawings of the mill (pls. 44 and 45) or from comparing the picture with Cézanne's painting, *Le Moulin de la Couleuvre, Pontoise* (pl. 46), executed in 1881. Both *Paysage à Osny* and *Lavoir et moulin d'Osny* are further illustrations of Pissarro's ambivalence in tackling a subject matter that carried Romantic connotations that were not to his taste. In *Paysage à Osny*, Pissarro rejected emphatically the mill motif, so that the mill is almost entirely out of the picture area – but not quite: a fraction of the shed attached to the mill can be seen on the right edge of the canvas. The picture ironically is a depiction of the lock (*vanne*) which is absolutely central to the functioning of the mill and yet which is here discreetly integrated into the landscape. In *Lavoir et moulin d'Osny*, as in *Paysage à Osny*, Pissarro has displaced the mill from a central position to the edge of the canvas, so that only part of the main building is visible. This is perhaps the most acute expression of Pissarro's ambivalence toward depicting mills: the mill is half accepted (within the frame) and half rejected (outside the frame).

The only painting of Pontoise in which Pissarro fully integrated a mill in a landscape is *Le Ruisseau à Osny*, although, here again, the edge of the canvas deprives the mill of its usual functional attributes – with the exception of the lock, which can be seen in the middleground. It is the stream of the title that is the focus of attention in this picture.

During the years 1872 and 1873, when Pissarro was including the grain fields and haystacks near Ennery in several paintings, he altogether avoided the mills that ground the grain. This general neglect is notable not only because of the prominent part played by mills in the Pontoisian landscape and the local eco-

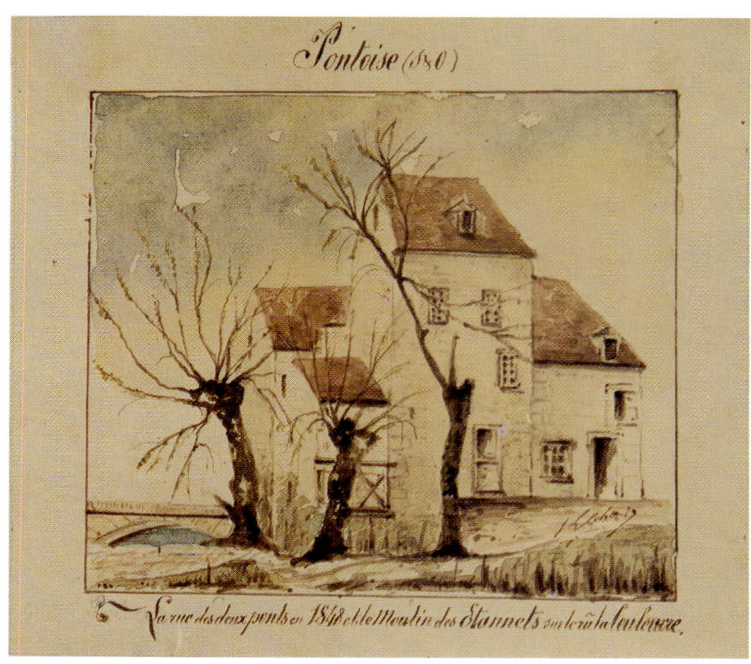

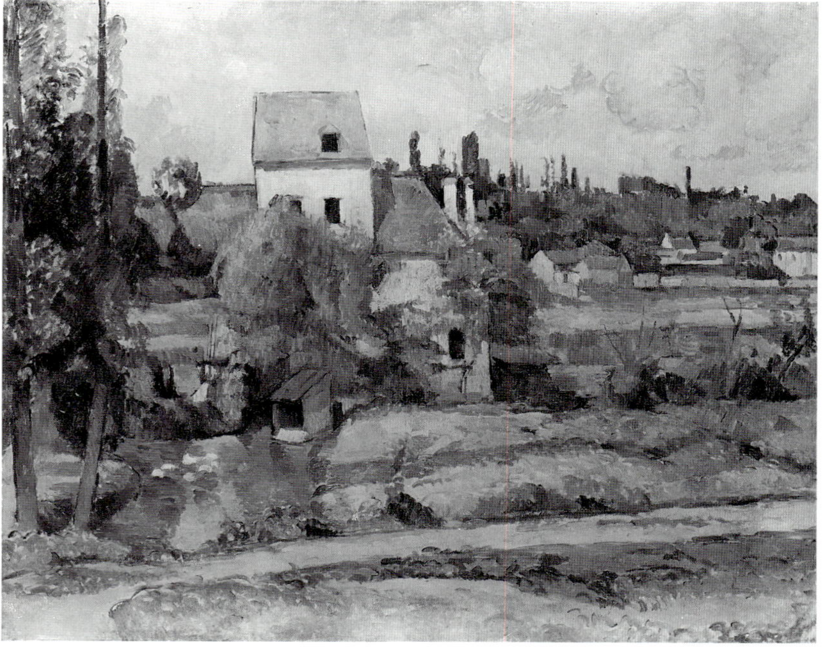

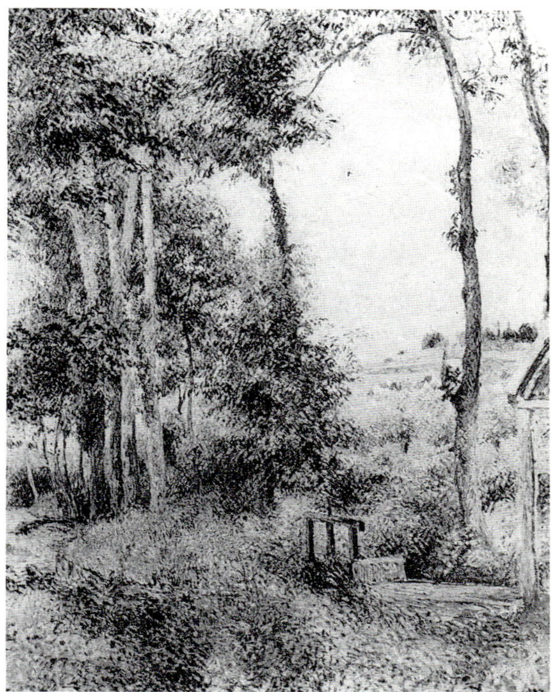

47. Camille Pissarro, *Paysage à Osny, la vanne près du moulin* (P&V 592), 1883, oil on canvas, 93 × 73cm., whereabouts unknown.

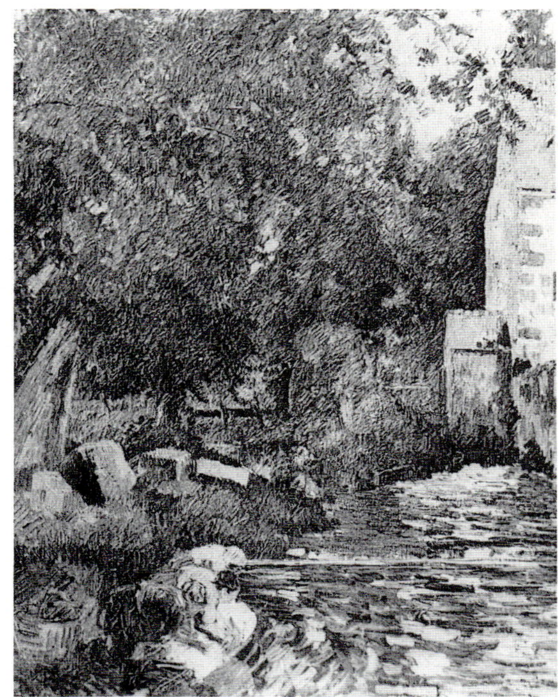

49. Camille Pissarro, *Lavoir et moulin d'Osny* (P&V 595), 1883, oil on canvas, 65 × 54cm., whereabouts unknown.

48 (above right). Camille Pissarro, *Le Ruisseau à Osny* (P&V 588), 1883, oil on canvas, 65 × 54 cm., private collection, Venezuela.

46 (left). Paul Cézanne, *Le Moulin de la Couleuvre, Pontoise*, 1881, oil on canvas, 73.5 × 91.5 cm., Nationalgalerie, Berlin.

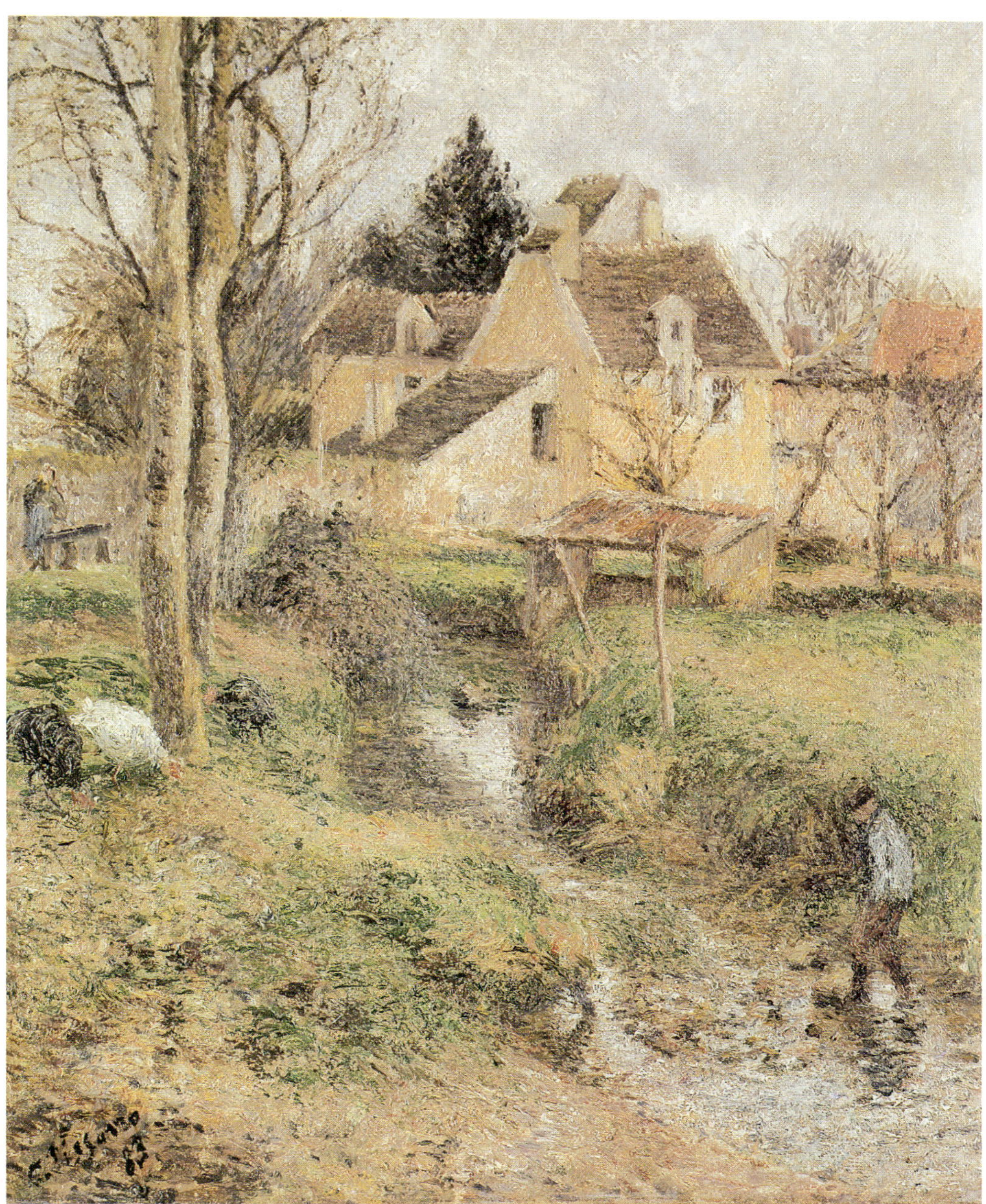

nomy, but because of their significance as motifs within the landscape tradition that, in other ways, Pissarro accepted.

A similar omission is that of the numerous quarries and quarriers of Pontoise. The route d'Ennery in the area of the Fond Saint-Antoine and the small canyons of Le Chou between L'Hermitage and Chaponval contained many quarries.[25] Although they do not play as important a role in the history of landscape painting as mills, quarries were common landscape motifs for nineteenth-century land- scape painters. Daubigny, Corot, Aligny, and many other artists depicted quar- ries, and piles of building material are significant features of town scenes.[26] Pontoise, with its position along a hilly plateau, was a regional center for quarry- ing throughout the eighteenth and nineteenth centuries. Much of the stone for the rebuilding of Paris came from the larger quarry regions south of the city, but the quarries of Pontoise did provide building material for local construction in the Région Pontoisienne and the northern suburbs of Paris.

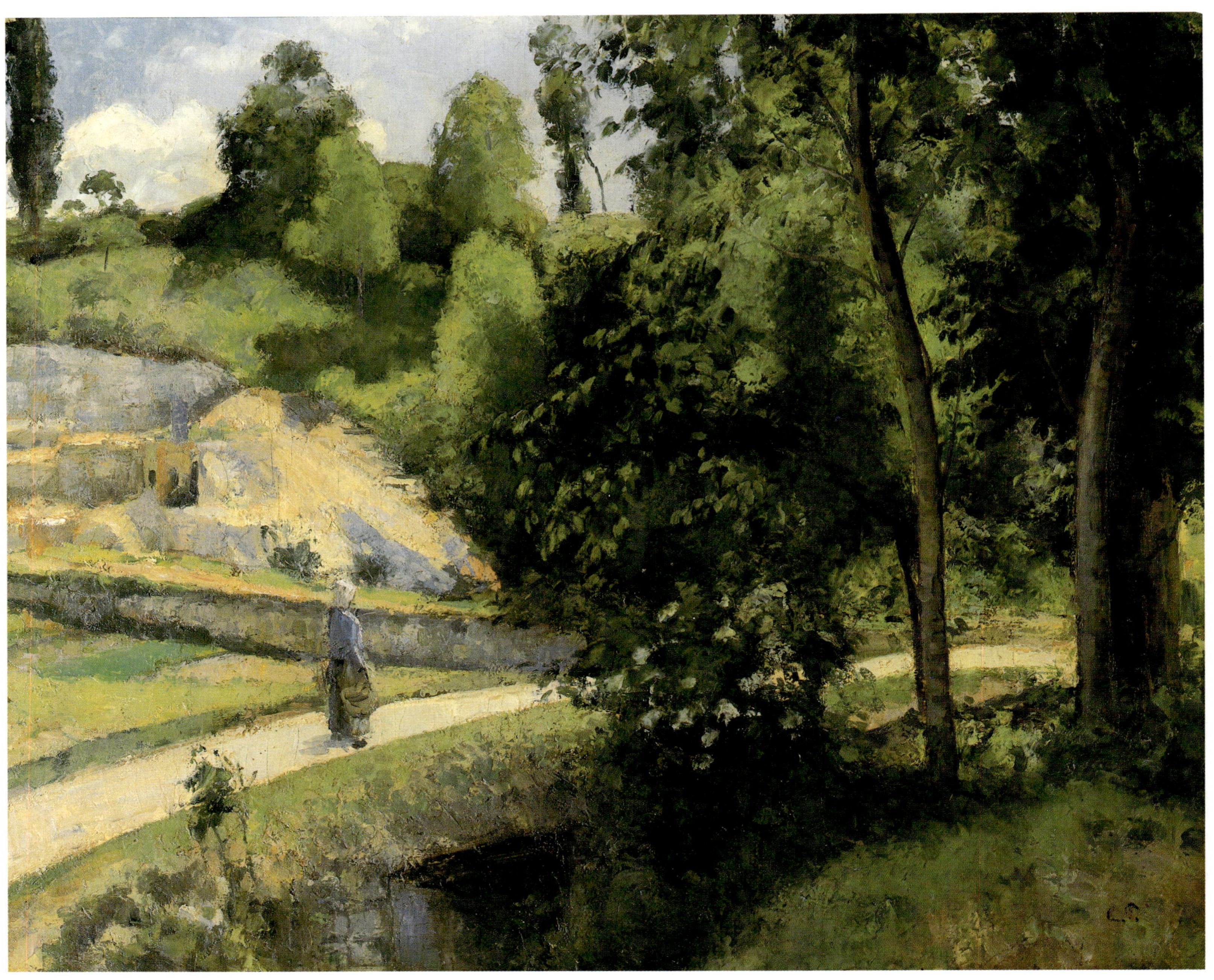

50. Camille Pissarro, *La Carrière, Pontoise* (P&V 251), *c.*1875, oil on canvas, 58 × 72.5cm., Rudolf Staechelin'sche Familienstiftung, Basel.

As in the case of the mills, the motif of the quarry is not totally absent from Pissarro's landscape paintings. The Courbetesque landscape, *Carrière, Pontoise* of *c.*1875 (pl. 50), together with two more paintings, *La Carrière à L'Hermitage, Pontoise*, 1878 (P&V 438) and *Les Carrières du Chou, Pontoise*, 1882 (pl. 51), all contain quarries. As with the *Moulin des Pâtis* and the other views of mills, Pissarro accepted the motif, but without its major defining features. Paintings of quarries were traditionally celebrations of human labor, of the will of man over matter, but Pissarro has avoided this approach in these three pictures. The figures are women, unconnected with the active labors of stone-cutting, and the quarries themselves are alluded to in the titles but not emphasized in the paintings. Human labor is absent, and the quarry is simply an element in the landscape.

* * *

What is clear from all these omissions is that Pissarro avoided the functional and the social aspects of the environment. Active labor and landscapes with prominent figures are almost totally absent from the iconography of Pissarro's Pontoise. The actuality of Pontoise was no more important for Pissarro than was *Pontoise touristique* or *Pontoise historique*. The painter's distance from much of the reality of the town is nowhere more evident than in his persistent avoidance of Pontoise itself. Returning to the dotted landscape map (fig. 1), it is evident to the viewer that the largest omission in Pissarro's Pontoisian landscape is Pontoise. He entered the town pictorially only twice, in 1872 to paint the *Fête de Septembre* (pl. 36) and in 1878 to paint the *Parc aux Charrettes* (pl. 38). The other dots cluster along the outskirts of Pontoise. Pissarro stood amongst the trees that line the

51. Camille Pissarro, *Les Carrières du Chou, Pontoise* (P&V 559), 1882, oil on canvas, 54 × 65cm., private collection.

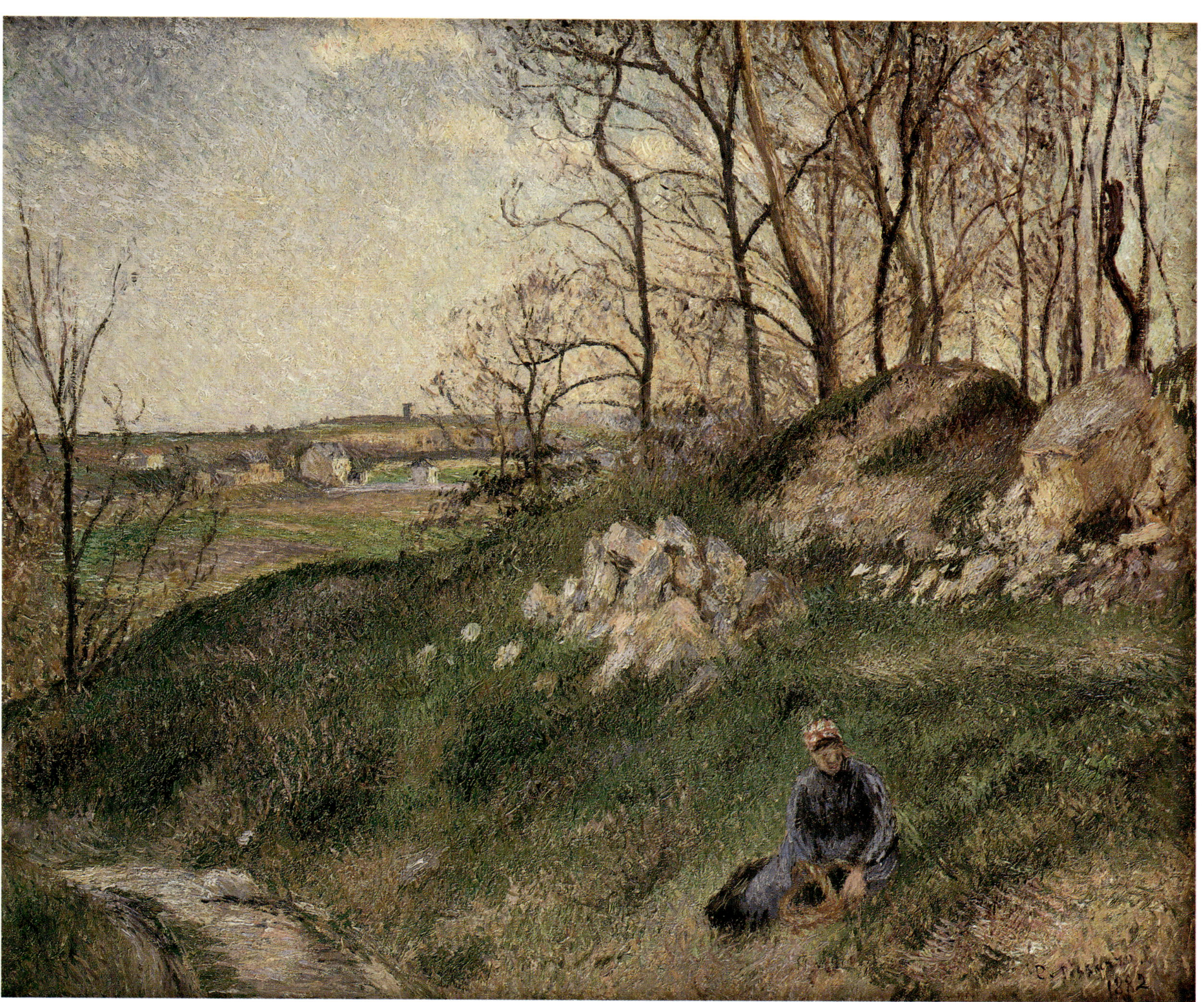

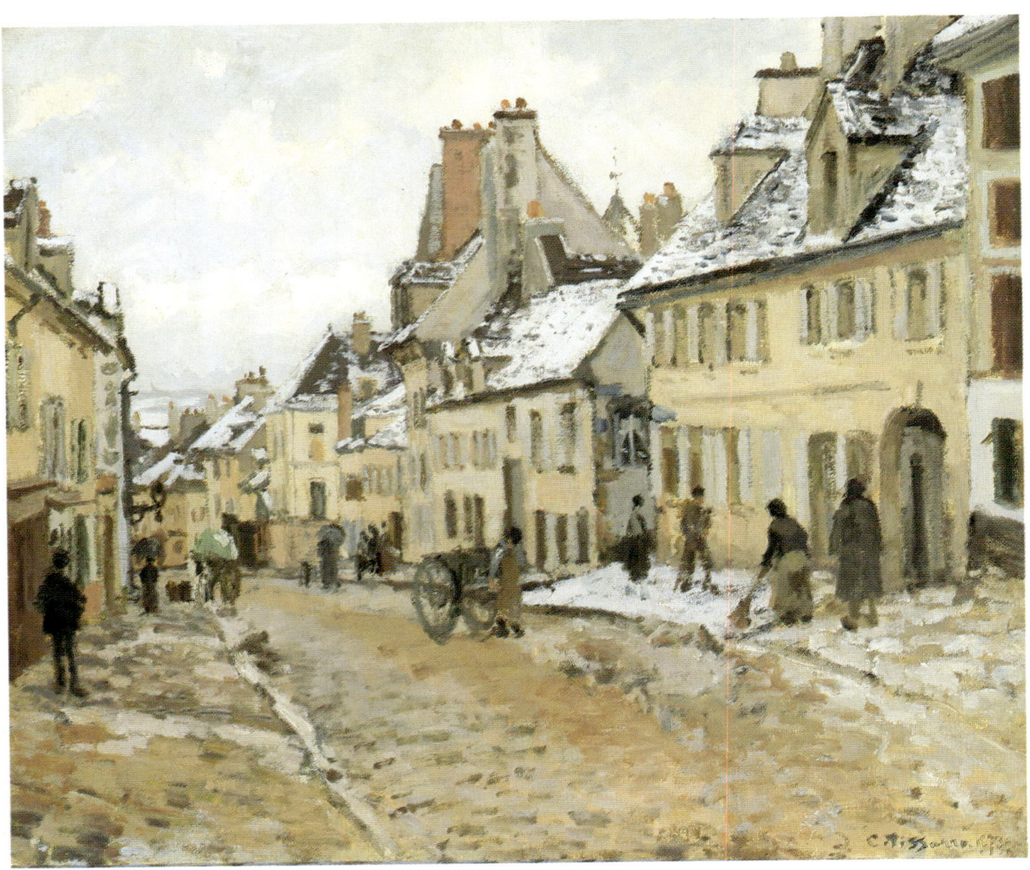

52. Camille Pissarro, *La Route de Gisors à Pontoise, effet de neige* (P&V 202), 1873, oil on canvas, 60 × 74cm., Bequest of John T. Spalding; courtesy, Museum of Fine Arts, Boston.

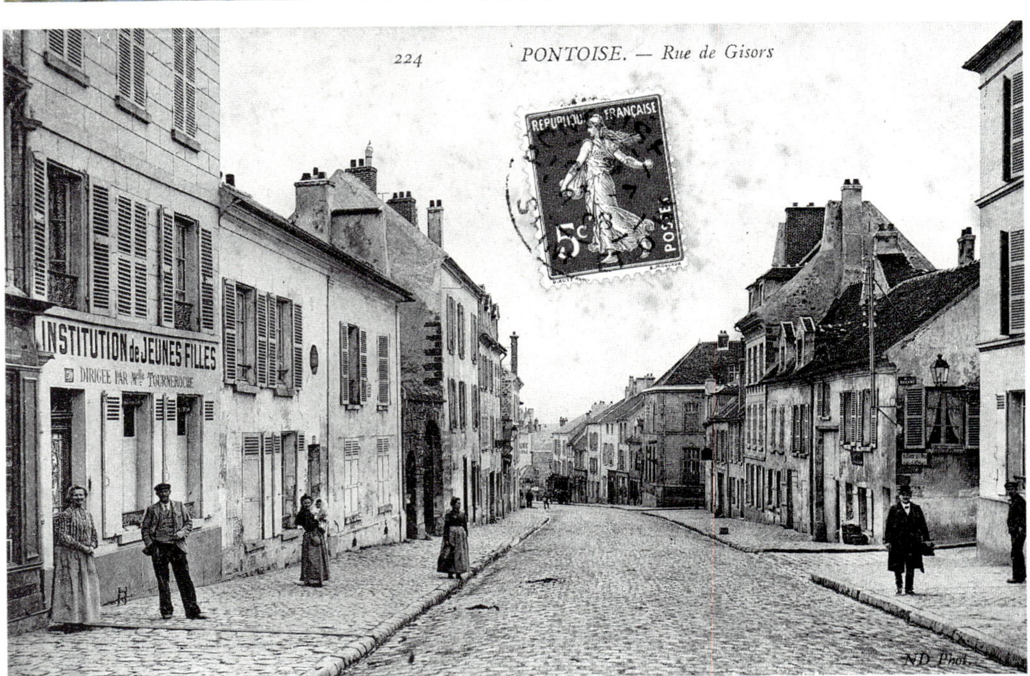

53. Route de Gisors, Pontoise, late 19th century, postcard, collection of M. Jean Hecquet, Paris.

avenue des Fossés; he hid in the foliage to paint the *Jardin public* in 1873 and 1874; he looked in from the outskirts of the route de Gisors in 1874 to paint his most illusionistically "urban" view of Pontoise, the *Route de Gisors* (pl. 52). Pissarro was a hoverer on the edge of activity, much like his more intensely isolated pupil-colleague Cézanne. He placed his easel on the various *routes* and on the *sentes* connecting those *routes*. He looked *at* Pontoise rather than *into* it. Pissarro's subject was Pontoise in general, not Pontoise in particular.

This observation is true for nearly all of Pissarro's pictorializations of Pontoise until the large market scenes of the 1880s, many of which were assembled in Osny and Eragny or in his studio in L'Hermitage from drawings done in the studio and slight sketches probably done in the markets themselves. Indeed, Pissarro's understanding of the market as the *raison d'être* of his secular Pontoise seems to have come rather late in his pictorial analysis of the site. His delayed acceptance of these active figure scenes stems most likely from his mid-century inability to consider urban subjects as landscape, as form in light. Pissarro accepted, probably throughout his life, the profound nineteenth-century dichotomy between city and country. As a landscape painter, he painted "nature," and, in spite of the broad, inclusive definition given to that word throughout the century, nature existed in opposition to concentrated urban civilization. The connection between the concepts "nature" and "space" is a key one in the theory of landscape painting, and it is not surprising that the urban views painted by landscape painters of the late nineteenth century are most often panoramic and inclusive views from above. Monet's important views of Paris from the Louvre are quintessential "city-scapes," or views of a city by a landscape painter. Neither Monet nor Pissarro could paint the concentrated, humanistic Paris described by Balzac, Zola and, in rarer moments, Flaubert, and painted by Manet and Degas, without compromising themselves as landscape painters. As any formal analysis of Pissarro's landscapes will quickly show, he was not a painter of space. His principal interest was solid form. Like the landscapes of Constable and Cézanne, the material presence of form is one of their primary characteristics. Yet, with his by now typical paradoxicalness, Pissarro seemed to share the landscape painter's fear of enclosed, claustrophobic spaces. The meddling of passers-by who ruined the painter's concentration or, to use Henriet's word, meditation, would have disturbed him greatly. Pissarro could conceive of a garden as nature, of a town in the landscape as nature, of a factory sited at the edge of a river as nature, of suburban sprawl as nature, all without penetrating the urban or semi-urban world of the town itself.

Pissarro's lack of attention to the small streets and picturesque corners of Pontoise is hardly surprising, especially when Richard's and Joanne's dislike of the interior of the town is recalled. Pissarro would never have been at home on a street that was "narrow and steep," no matter how picturesque.[27] In fact, all of his views of the town emphasize its large, public places. These public places and the larger streets leading into Pontoise gave Pissarro the opportunity to detach himself from his motif, to stand apart and at the edge. His fear of involvement, which had both personal and professional origins, was not compromised. The views of the parc aux Charrettes, the place aux Marchés, the Jardin public, the avenue des Fossés, the place du Tribunal, and the place du Vieux Cimetière are all planar alignments of concentrated urban form which stand apart from the viewer. Immersion is not Pissarro's aim.

What is perhaps most interesting about Pissarro's view of the town is its comparative modernity. As Pinckney and many subsequent historians of Paris during the Second Empire and the Third Republic have shown, the major aim of French urban planners throughout that period was to clear out the concentrated and claustrophobic sections of old cities and to replace them with airy boulevards, parks, and plazas. The difference between the Paris described by Balzac, Zola, and Eugène Sue and depicted by lithographers, and the Paris rebuilt by Haussmann and Napoleon III and depicted by the Impressionists could hardly be greater. In avoiding the "inner city" of Pontoise, Pissarro avoided more than urban reality: he was avoiding the traditional type of city that was at that time anathema to progressive intellectuals and planners. Like Monet, Renoir, and Manet, Pissarro preferred urban spaces to urban concentration.

The above list of the areas painted by Pissarro includes most of the public places of Pontoise. He was assiduous in his reporting of this aspect of the town. Most of these open areas encircled the town itself, forming a periphery of promenades, many of which were coincident with the ancient *fossés* or moats. Pissarro's careful inclusion of these public places in his pictorialization of Pontoise is further evidence of his interest in the general environment, the public and accessible world of Pontoise. Yet, we confront interesting exclusions in this list also. Pissarro never painted the large place du Petit-Martroy in the center of old Pontoise, except as a minimal setting in his later market scenes.[28] Nor did he paint the two small plazas in front of the town's major churches, although both of these plazas were represented in gouache by his friend, Piette. Perhaps his most notable omission was the rue Impériale, the most important new street in Pontoise. The rue Impériale was *the* Pontoisian street in the later nineteenth century. Most postcard views of the city show the place de la Gare and its continuation, the rue Impériale (pl. 17). Perhaps the Bonapartist associations of the street, combined with the fact that it centered axially on the church of Saint-Maclou, dissuaded Pissarro from painting it.[29] He avoided Pontoise's churches in other contexts, as has been shown, and, although politically he was a child of the Revolution, he was certainly not a Bonapartist.

Admissions

1 The agricultural landscape

Most contemporary critics who wrote about Pissarro's career considered him to be a painter of agricultural life, of a working landscape. Visual evidence for this contention is rich. Plots of well-tended land, carefully observed color and texture differences between fields of cabbage and grass, and figures who work in the fields are common elements of Pissarro's Pontoise. In fact, as many writers following Duret have observed, the agricultural aspect of Pissarro's iconography can be seen in contrast to the predominantly bourgeois and leisure character of the exactly contemporary landscape worlds of Monet, Sisley, and Renoir and connects Pissarro to the painters of peasant life of the middle of the nineteenth century. Yet, the agricultural character of Pissarro's Pontoise differs a good deal from the reality described in some detail in the last chapter.

The vast majority of the plots in Pissarro's Pontoise are small. He loved the *jardins suspendus*, described later in the century by Sagine, and the small *jardins potagers* in the region of Le Chou. The figures who work in his agricultural world work by hand with pre-modern, often out-moded, equipment. The plow sitting in the empty field of *Terres labourées* (pl. 54) is of a type that can be found in fourteenth- and fifteenth-century manuscript illuminations depicting French rural life. In fact, the plow had undergone a progressive modernization since the mid-eighteenth century, and iron plows with variable blades were a common feature on the land in the environs of Paris by the mid-nineteenth century.[30] What Pissarro accepted, pictorially, from the agricultural environment in which he lived was the small-scale garden agriculture, the kind considered by many historians and historical geographers to be the oldest and most basic.[31] Growing food stuffs for the family or for local sale on small, crowded plots of land resulted in a concentrated landscape, one that particularly appealed to Pissarro. His depictions of modern, large-field, partially mechanized agriculture are very rare; they are

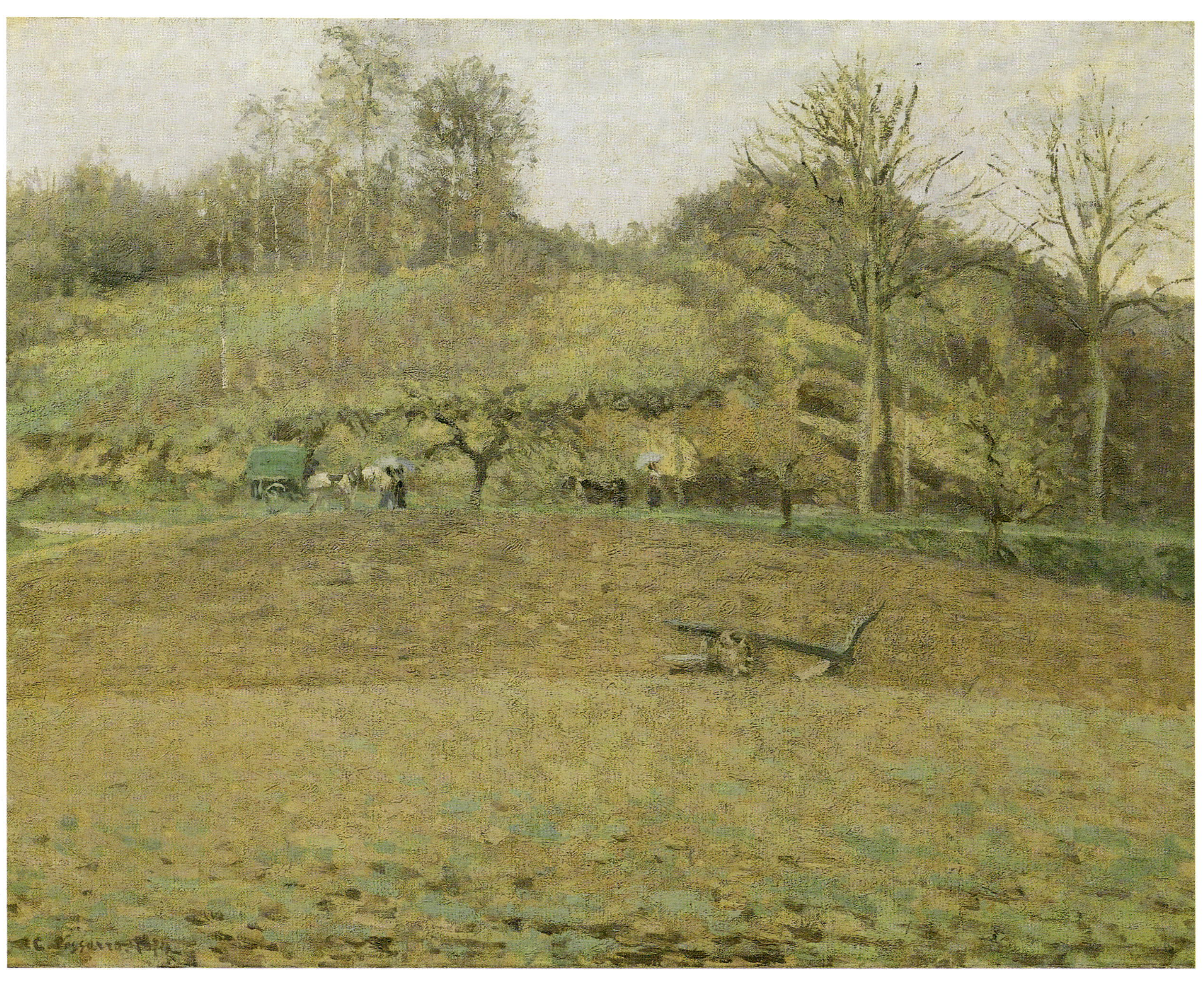

54. Camille Pissarro, *Terres labourées* (P&V 258), 1874, oil on canvas, 49 × 64cm., Pushkin State Museum of Fine Arts, Moscow.

confined, in fact, to a series of landscapes painted in 1872 and 1873, entitled the *Four Seasons* (pls. 132–35) and commissioned by Achille Arosa, and to another series of drawings related to the large gouache, *La Moisson*, exhibited at the Impressionist exhibition of 1882 (pl. 55).[32] These landscapes exist as exceptional images within Pissarro's work. Their spaciousness, the spread of the land across the almost panoramic format is very unusual for Pissarro, who preferred less insistently rectangular formats and greater complexity or formal interaction. The eye wanders lazily, almost without direction, across *L'Automne* (pl. 134), in contrast to the small, carefully interrelated movements of the eye from figures, to garden, to tree, to building, to garden again that characterize the viewing pattern for a typical garden landscape.[33]

If Pissarro avoided the crowded, claustrophobic world of the inner city with its narrow, steep streets, he was equally persistent in his avoidance of its opposite,

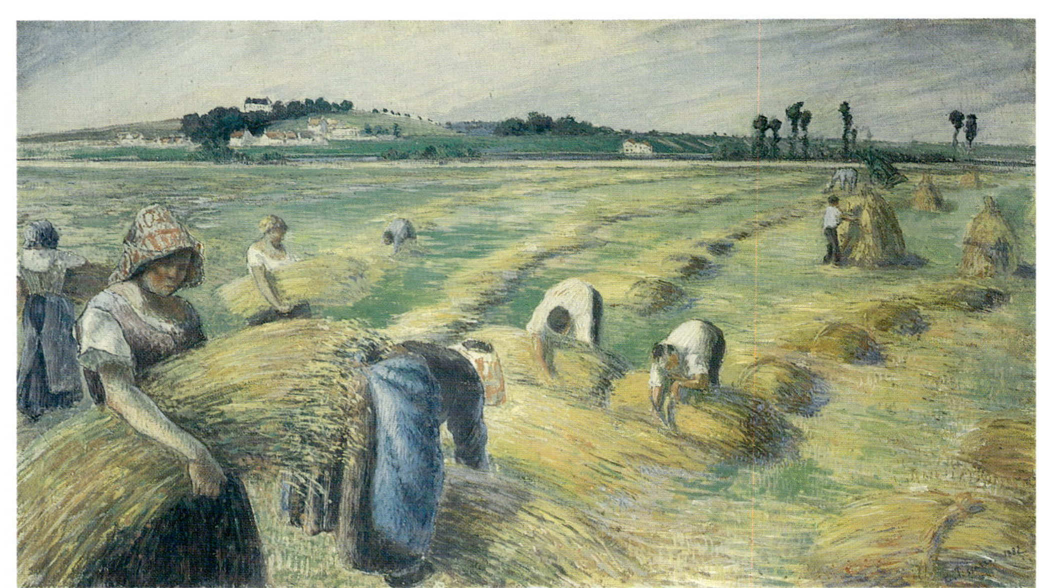

55. Camille Pissarro, *La Moisson* (P&V 1358), 1882, gouache on canvas, 70 × 126cm., The National Museum of Western Art, Tokyo.

the spacious field of the Vexin plain. His pictorial acceptance of garden agriculture shows a comparative rejection of the most cooperative or social of agricultures, grain cultivation, which was a common element both in the real landscape around Pontoise and in the peasant image as propagated by Millet, Lhermitte, and Breton. All those artists depict peasants working together in the fields at the time of the July harvest, sharing in the abundance of the earth. Such scenes of cooperative labor are non-existent in Pissarro's Pontoise, save in *La Moisson*, (pl. 55) which was painted rather late in Pissarro's Pontoise period. His Pontoisian "peasants" work alone or in pairs, often at separate tasks within the small-scale world of the garden. There is none of the mystical accord among men or between men and earth so crucial to the mid-century peasant image and to Pissarro's own arcadian peasant imagery of the 1880s and 1890s.

Another interesting facet of Pissarro's deemphasis of grain agriculture is that, although he allowed industrial images and motor-powered boats into his landscapes, he rejected agricultural progress as symbolized by mechanized farming, with the single exception of a picture painted in Montfoucault in 1876. He seems to have seen agriculture neither with the religious and moralizing eyes of the mid-century painters of peasant images nor with the progressive spirit of the Société d'agriculture et d'horticulture de Pontoise. He avoided both the cooperative and the mechanical aspects.

We confront, at this point, Pissarro's insistent and clearly intentional ambivalence toward his subject matter. Agriculture in Pissarro's Pontoise was neither real nor ideal. On the one hand, we gain a very imbalanced picture of Pontoisian agriculture in the 1870s, and on the other hand, we receive very little intellectual or moral elevation when confronted with an agricultural scene painted by Pissarro. His Pontoise would have suited neither Zola nor George Sand. In *Terres Labourées* (pl. 54), the image is clearly derived from Millet.[34] Yet gone for Pissarro is the sweeping simplicity of Millet's composition, the hymn to the temporary hope and eventual futility associated with seasonal labor both by Millet and later by Van Gogh. Pissarro's plow sits idly in a partially plowed field, while figures and carts move in monotonous quotidian rhythm in the background. He describes too many incidental forms for us. Our eye is distracted to the background. The plow, the icon of Millet's and Van Gogh's spacious landscapes, loses its significance.

Pissarro's admission of the agricultural life of Pontoise was, at best, a partial admission. He accepted only certain aspects and precisely those aspects least associated with previous peasant imagery. Without the grain harvest, the barnyard activity, and the grape harvest, the peasant imagery of Millet, Breton and Lhermitte would be impoverished. Pissarro, in fact, chose a relatively new aspect of agriculture to emphasize, the garden. Millet's only important image of a *jardin potager* is the large "narrative" landscape, *Printemps* (Musée d'Orsay), which was to have been part of group of four seasons on which the artist was occupied in his later years but did not complete. Again, Millet's concern for the unity of the landscape and with certain larger problems, such as the passage of time and the associated theme of renewal and redemption, are directly opposed to Pissarro's blander, more crowded, and finally more complicated images of gardens. Pissarro's agricultural views are never trapped in a significant moment. Rather, they are daily landscapes in which plots are spaded and weeded within the complex patterns of multi-harvest agriculture that characterize the *jardin potager*.[35]

2 *The river and the railroad: transportation and the extended landscape*

The river and the flower garden can be considered the archetypal subjects of advanced French landscape painting in the late 1860s and the 1870s.[36] To the twentieth-century mind, both of these subjects seem unproblematically genial, all but contentless; but their meanings in the 1870s were somewhat richer and more intricate. As any visitor to the Musée d'Orsay's vast holdings of mid-century landscape paintings can easily see, neither river scenes nor ornamental gardens are much in evidence. Corot, Chintreuil, Millet, Rousseau, Diaz, and most of the landscape painters who were the precursors of the Impressionists rarely painted large rivers, the watery routes that had ensured the economic and social unity of France for several centuries. Only small rivers and pools (*mares*) which interrupt the plains and forests of the landscape around Fontainebleau play a prominent part in the iconography of mid-century landscape painting. These pools, the most protected, private, intimate, and objective of nature's offerings of water, stand in opposition to the broad "avenues" filled with boats and lined with buildings that dominate the landscapes of Lépine, Sisley, Renoir, Pissarro, Monet, and Manet.

Yet, images of rivers abound in the various illustrated guides to the regions of France produced in the 1840s, '50s, and '60s. The topographical prints and drawings depicting the country from the seventeenth to the nineteenth centuries are veritable celebrations of its rivers.[37] As all these sources reveal, the image of the river is an ultimately nationalistic one. Rivers, like the "king's highways" of the seventeenth and eighteenth centuries, belong not to an individual, not even to a township, but to the nation. They are the thoroughfares that secure the continuing interdependence that in turn gives a modern nation the economic base for its unity.

Impressionist images of the river stem from these popular prints and from the paintings by Dutch artists of the burgeoning river and canal landscapes of the seventeenth century, especially those of Salomon van Ruysdael, Jan van Goyen, and their followers. Much, indeed most, Dutch landscape painting is a celebration of the then modern and expanding national system of canals and roadways, the avenues along which the interchange of an intensive capitalist economy occurred.[38] These two sources, prints and paintings, the former more immediate and accessible to the French painter of Pissarro's generation, are united in the pictures by Daubigny, who, with Jongkind, is the most important precursor of

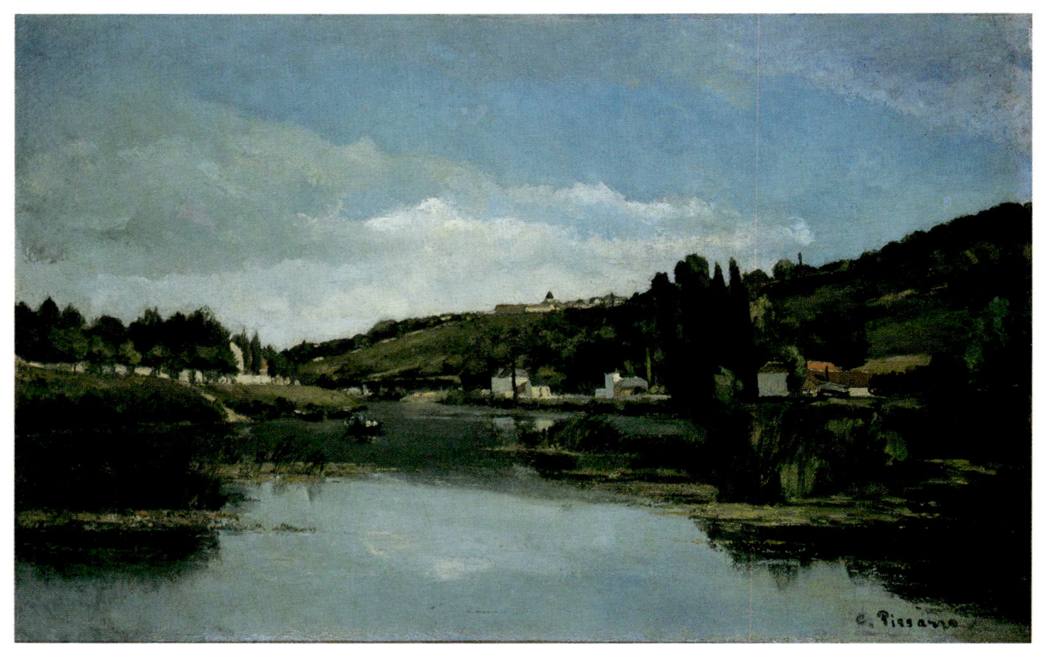

56. Camille Pissarro, *Bords de la Marne à Chennevières* (P&V 46), *c.*1864–65, 91.5 × 145.5cm., National Gallery of Scotland, Edinburgh.

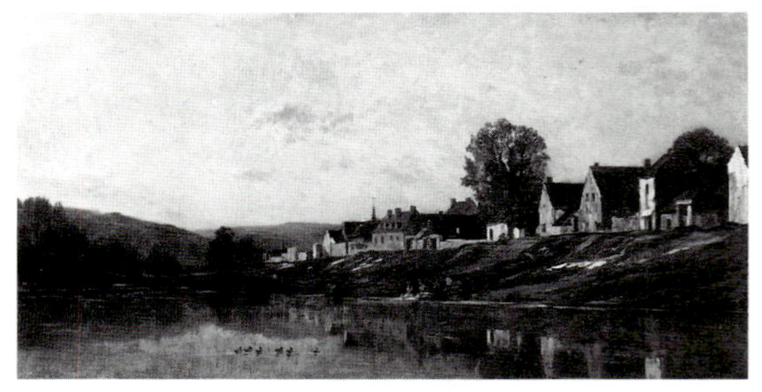

57. Charles François Daubigny, *Les Laveuses au bord de la Seine à Bonnières*, 1860, oil on panel, 34.5 × 66cm., Sotheby's, London (22 November 1988, lot 34).

the Impressionists. Daubigny's dual career as a travel illustrator and a Salon landscape painter made it uniquely possible for him to bring the popular nationalistic icon, the river, to the walls of the Salon. Pictures like *Bateaux sur l'Oise* and *Les Péniches*, both painted in 1865, combine the imagery of his popular prints, made, for the most part, in the 1850s, and the controlled technique and detailed surface of Salon pictures. The pictures and prints of Daubigny stand behind many of the images of the Oise and the Seine painted by Pissarro.[39] Pissarro's drawings of boating and rivers dating from the early and mid-1860s as well as the large landscape, the *Bords de la Marne à Chennevières* (pl. 56), exhibited in the Salon of 1865, stem directly from pictures such as Daubigny's *Les Laveuses au bord de la Seine à Bonnières* of 1860 (pl. 57).

The barge port of Pontoise was, with its agriculture, the principal source of the town's prosperity. Sagine, in his monograph of 1899, attests to the importance and the modernity of Pontoise's river port:

> The traffic on this river [Oise] is considerable, forming a network of direct links between Belgium, the industrial and commerical center of the north, and Paris and the whole of France. Gradually, mechanical traction is superseding animal traction. Almost all barges today are towed by tugboats, the so-called "steam-wasps."[40]

As though confirming Sagine's statement, the various travel artists who depicted Pontoise saw it as a port more than as a Gothic marvel or a picturesque collection of architectural forms in the context of a larger landscape. The Oise – and not just the Oise, but the most intensely active portions of its banks at Pontoise – provided the principal motif for the majority of *vues de Pontoise* executed in the eighteenth and nineteenth centuries. Pontoise was, as its name indicates, a bridge over the Oise, the place to which generations of Pontoisians and Vexinians brought their products and from which those products were sent on to the nation.

It is perhaps easiest to throw into relief Pissarro's view of the Oise and rivers in general by comparing it not with Daubigny's, but with the exactly contemporary depictions of the Seine by Monet (pl. 58). Discussions of Impressionist subject matter in the many books on that movement use the paintings of Monet in the

1870s as the "key" to Impressionism in what is thought to be its purest, most advanced form.[41] Impressionism is conceived as an art obsessed with the leisure of the bourgeoisie and with the rapidity of the modern world, symbolized most often by the train.[42] Monet's Seine, whether at Bougival or Argenteuil, is a river of pleasure and leisure. Its shores are lined with pavilions and their promenading inhabitants. Its surface is covered with sailboats and swimmers. Its waters are crowned by the railroad bridges that provide transport for the leisure boaters and bourgeois *promeneurs*. The contrast with Pissarro's Oise could hardly be greater. Factories and farms crowd *its* shores. Rural workers walk along the towpaths that line its banks. Horse-drawn and motor-powered barges navigate its regularized waters. Proletarian figures fish for their livelihood, fetch water for their domestic needs (being too poor to have their own wells or plumbing), or wash their linen and clothing. Pissarro's Oise is the organizing route of a crowded landscape. Both agriculture and industry press their demand on its waters.

But the differences between Pissarro's Oise and Monet's Seine are not only iconographical: they are formal and compositional. Unlike both Daubigny and Monet, whose *botin* and *bateau* floated the waters they painted, Pissarro virtually never left the banks of the river. His pictures cling almost obsessively to the shore, recording the trees, the fields, the figures *along* the river without entering its waters. Material form and not the sky or the reflective ripples of the water itself fills the surface of Pissarro's river views. The viewer and, of course, the painter are virtually always obviously set on dry land, and the pictorial and psychological effect of this is of crucial importance to an understanding of Pissarro's Oise and his view of river life.[43] For him, the river was a part of a transportation network that went beyond the confines both of Pontoise and of his pictures representing that town. The difference between this view and the leisure-oriented view of the

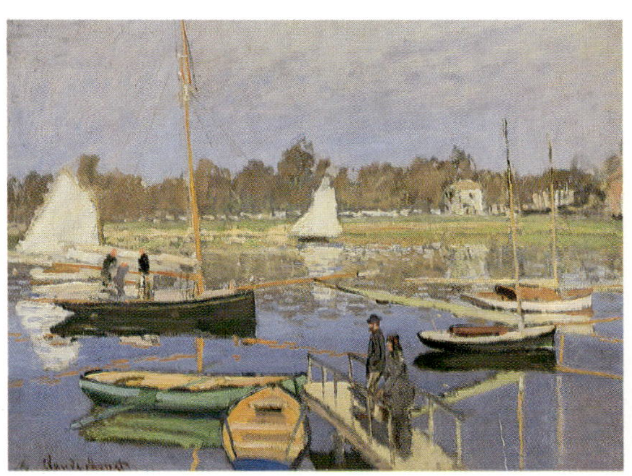

58. Claude Monet, *The Boat Basin at Argenteuil*, 1874, oil on canvas, 55 × 73cm., private collection, Dallas.

59. Camille Pissarro, *Péniches à Pontoise* (P&V 358), 1876, oil on canvas, 46 × 55cm., The Metropolitan Museum of Art; bequest of Mary Cushing Fosburgh, 1978 (1979.135.16).

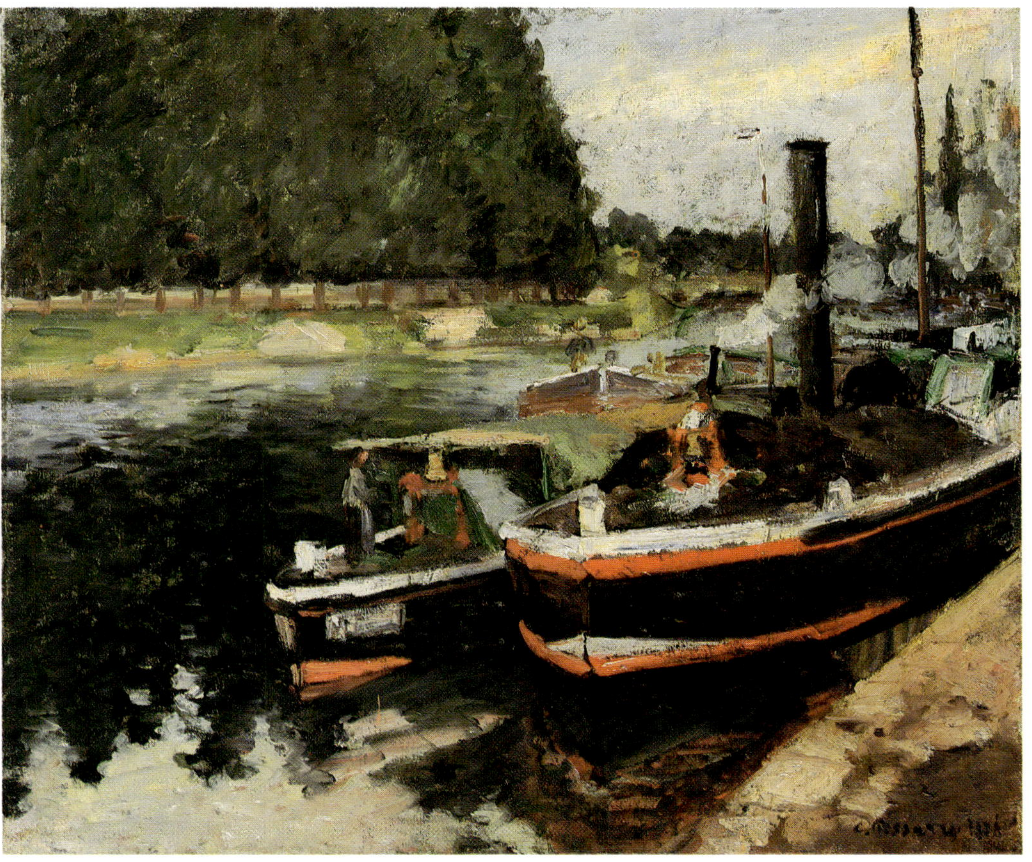

river that dominates Monet's depictions of the Seine at Argenteuil is very great indeed. Pissarro's Oise is observed as a world in motion from a static point of view. In countless paintings by Monet, on the other hand, the viewer is in motion, as are the boats that glide freely along the surface of the Seine. The purposeful and linear motion either parallel to the picture plane or penetrating its surface that is so characteristic of Pissarro's Oise views is in contrast to the freely sweeping and gliding movement of the sailboats in Monet's Seine. Among all Pissarro's river pictures of the 1860s and 1870s, despite his numerous depictions of *péniches* and rowboats, a sailboat appears in only one painting.[44]

But these iconographical and compositional contrasts between Pissarro's labor-oriented Oise and Monet's leisure-oriented Seine are not the only such contrasts that the modern viewer can make. Another iconographical contrast is perhaps more subtle, but equally important. It is possible to say that the railroad played the same role in Monet's landscape as the river played in Pissarro's. Railroad stations, both urban and suburban, are Monet's equivalents of Pissarro's towpaths and barge docks. It is the railroad bridge and not the river it so often crosses that is the principal motif of so many landscapes by Monet. It is the puffing train and not the river barges that knits together Monet's Rouen landscapes of 1872, as in *Le Convoi de chemin de fer* (pl. 79). Although Monet's attitude toward the technology represented by the steaming railroad train has not been analysed, it is certainly fair

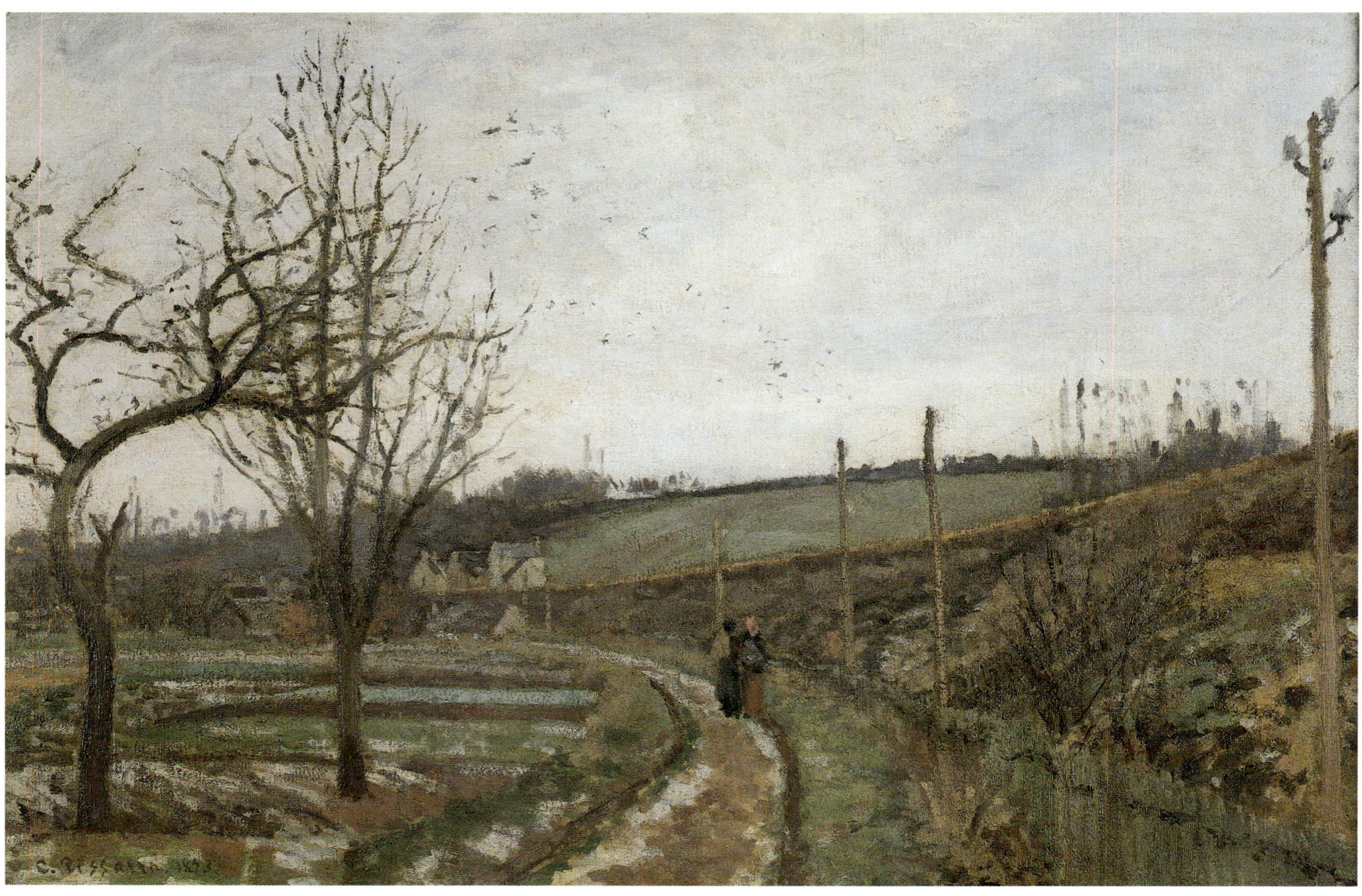

60. Camille Pissarro, *La Route au bord du chemin de fer, effet de neige* (P&V 205), 1873, oil on canvas, 62 × 81cm., National Museum of Western Art, Tokyo.

to say that he was much less qualified in his acceptance, either pictorial or social, of both industrialized technology and of rapid communication systems than was Pissarro. Indeed, Pissarro's acceptance of the river as the primary communication system within his landscape must be seen in the light of his comparative rejection of the railroad. Pissarro's pictorial references to the railroad are rare in an oeuvre in which industrial images are common. The most important of Pissarro's railroad images cluster in the year 1873, the same year in which he began his pictorial examination of the factory, which will be discussed at length in chapter 3. It is worthwhile to interrupt this discussion of Pissarro's river imagery with a brief mention of the railroad pictures because it seems clear that Pissarro's almost complete rejection of the railroad must be seen in the context not only of his industrial imagery, but of his acceptance of the river as a humanized and slow-paced mode of transportation which, if his pictures are evidence, he considered preferable to the train.

La Route au bord du chemin de fer, effet de neige (pl. 60), in many ways the most complex and meaningful of the group of railroad images painted in 1873, depicts neither the train nor the equally modern cast-iron railroad bridge that so fascinated Monet, but the steeply graded slopes leading up to the invisible tracks and the long string of telegraph poles that so often accompanied railroad tracks in the nineteenth century. Pissarro omitted the most exciting and *au courant* aspects of the railroad industry and concentrated instead on the permanent effect of that industry on the pre-modern environment of Les Pâtis. The composition is symmetrical, the one side devoted to nature, agriculture, and village life, and the other dominated by the railroad embankment and the telegraph poles. In the center is a rutted road with two tiny, almost tectonic peasant figures who stand at the nexus of the two worlds. Our eye follows the sweeping movement of the embankment back into the pictorial space, but is pulled again to the surface by the slower, centered figures and by the freely painted and graphic curves of the barren fruit trees on the far left of the composition. This extremely schematic, even intellectual landscape questions at a fundamental level the values of modern urban life and the rapid transportation and communication so vital to it. "Human scale," that most ambiguous concept so important to painters in the landscape tradition, is contrasted to "machine scale." The machine leaves an indelible mark on the landscape.

Rather than simply accepting or glorifying the railroad and its technology, Pissarro makes constant pictorial comparisons with the slower, hand-labor culture that the railroad age presumed to replace. In *Bords de l'Oise, printemps* (pl. 61), he places a puffing train in a broad, spacious landscape together with a barge on the Oise and a large cart moving along the route d'Auvers. The painter stands on the chemin d'Auvers and views this landscape of transportation systems through a linear screen of branches and trees. Again, the train is contrasted with older and slower modes of transportation and is viewed from a suspicious distance (compare also the train in the distance in *Environs de Sydenham Hill* [pl. 62], of 1871, and the same motif in the drawing *View from Upper Norwood* [pl. 76]). It is not the glorious machine puffing smoke that dominates so many images by Monet. Pissarro's only painted representation of the railroad bridge in Pontoise, *Le Pont du chemin de fer, Pontoise*, (pl. 63), places that bridge in the distance, where it has little, if any, forcefulness as a motif. This deemphasis of the railroad bridge can be seen in direct contradiction to its glorification by Monet in such pictures as his *Pont du chemin de fer, Argenteuil* (W 319).

Perhaps the most forceful landscape of the group and among the greatest French landscapes of the mid-1870s is *La Barrière du chemin de fer aux Pâtis près*

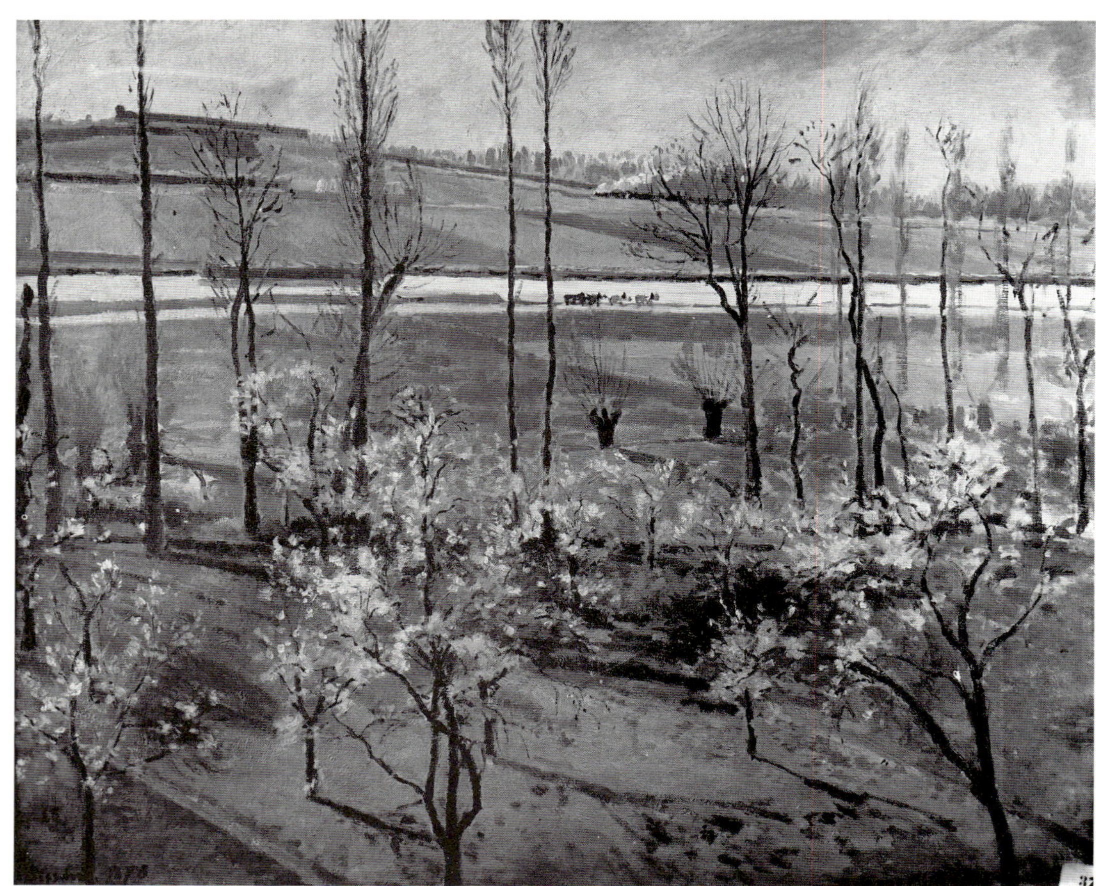

61. Camille Pissarro, *Bords de l'Oise, printemps*
(P&V 216), 1873, oil on canvas, 65 × 81cm.,
whereabouts unknown.

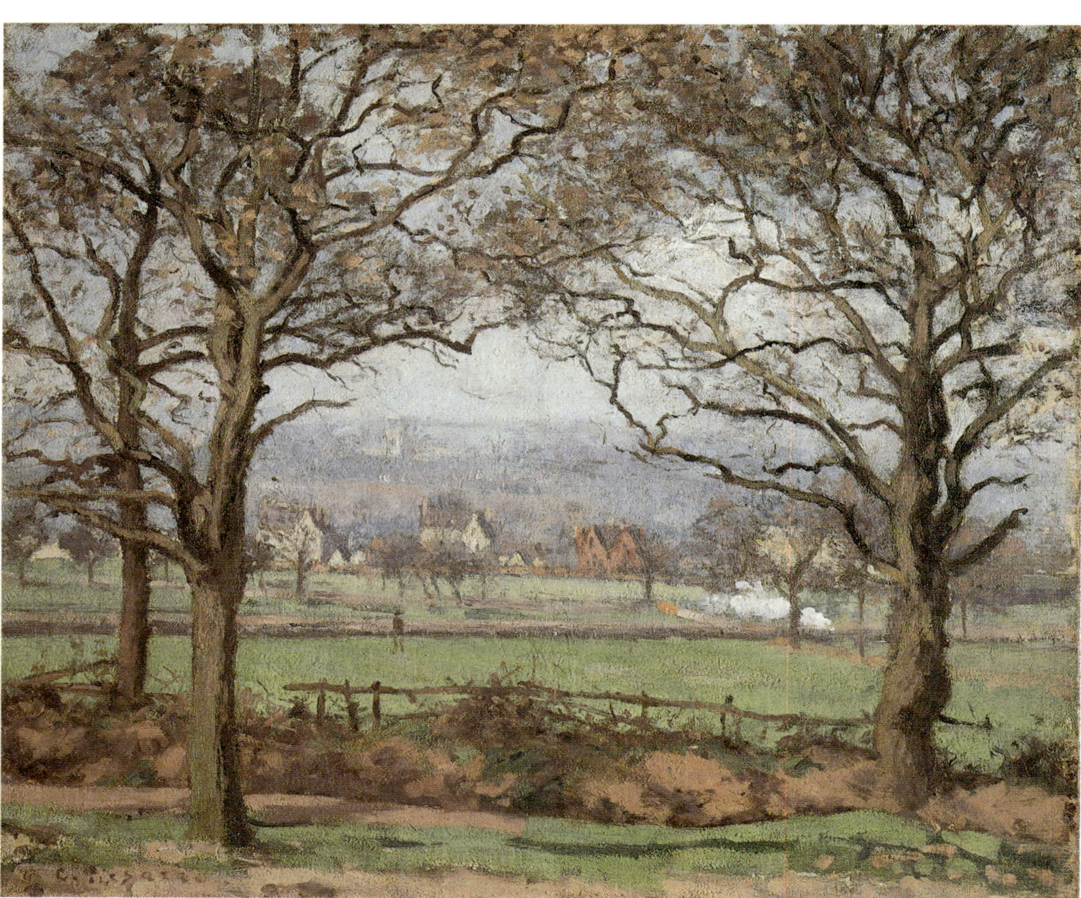

62. Camille Pissarro, *Environs de Sydenham
Hill (avec Lower Norwood au fond)* (P&V 115),
1871, oil on canvas, 43 × 53 cm., Kimbell Art
Museum, Fort Worth, Texas.

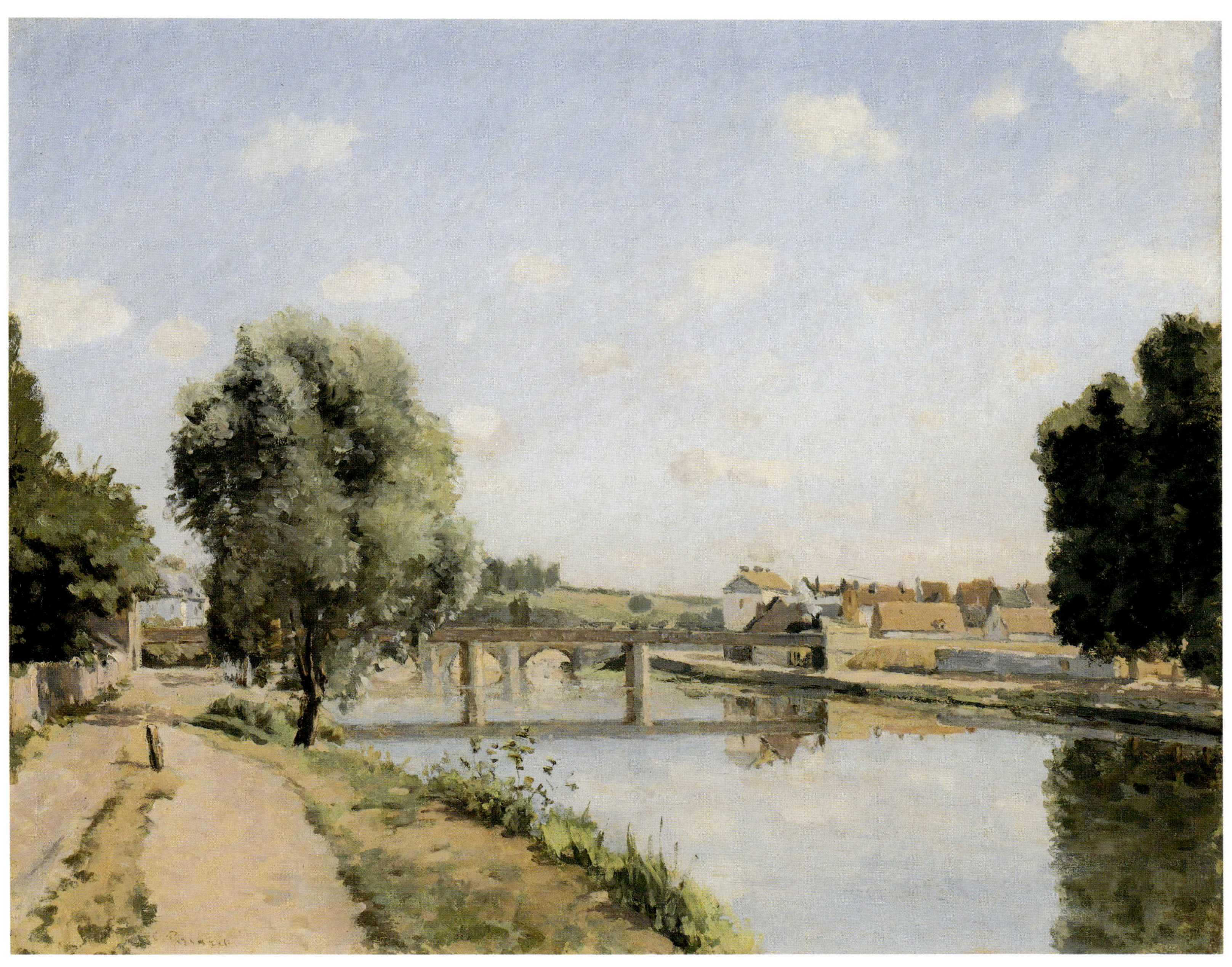

63. Camille Pissarro, *Le Pont du chemin de fer, Pontoise* (P&V 234), *c.*1873, oil on canvas, 50 × 65cm., Christie's, New York (16 May 1984).

64 (following pages). Detail of pl. 63.

Pontoise (pl. 65). In this picture, begun in 1873 and repainted in 1874, the railroad is represented not by a train but by a barrier that checks the ambulatory movement of the rural workers. The rigidly treated male and female figures are trapped in the insistent geometry of the barrier itself, which hinders both their progress and the viewer's plunge into a deeply gratifying pictorial space.[45] As all these examples indicate, Pissarro was suspicious of and possibly opposed to the railroad, and this suspicion, together with his relatively uncritical acceptance of the mechanical or motor-powered barges along both the Oise and the Seine, relates without doubt to the "canal versus railroad" struggle characteristic of the history of transportation in the late nineteenth century in England, the United States, and France.

What is particularly interesting about Pissarro's suspicious treatment of the railroad is that it is paralleled by Monet's rejection of the barge traffic that made the river into the viable system of transportation it remains today. If Pissarro

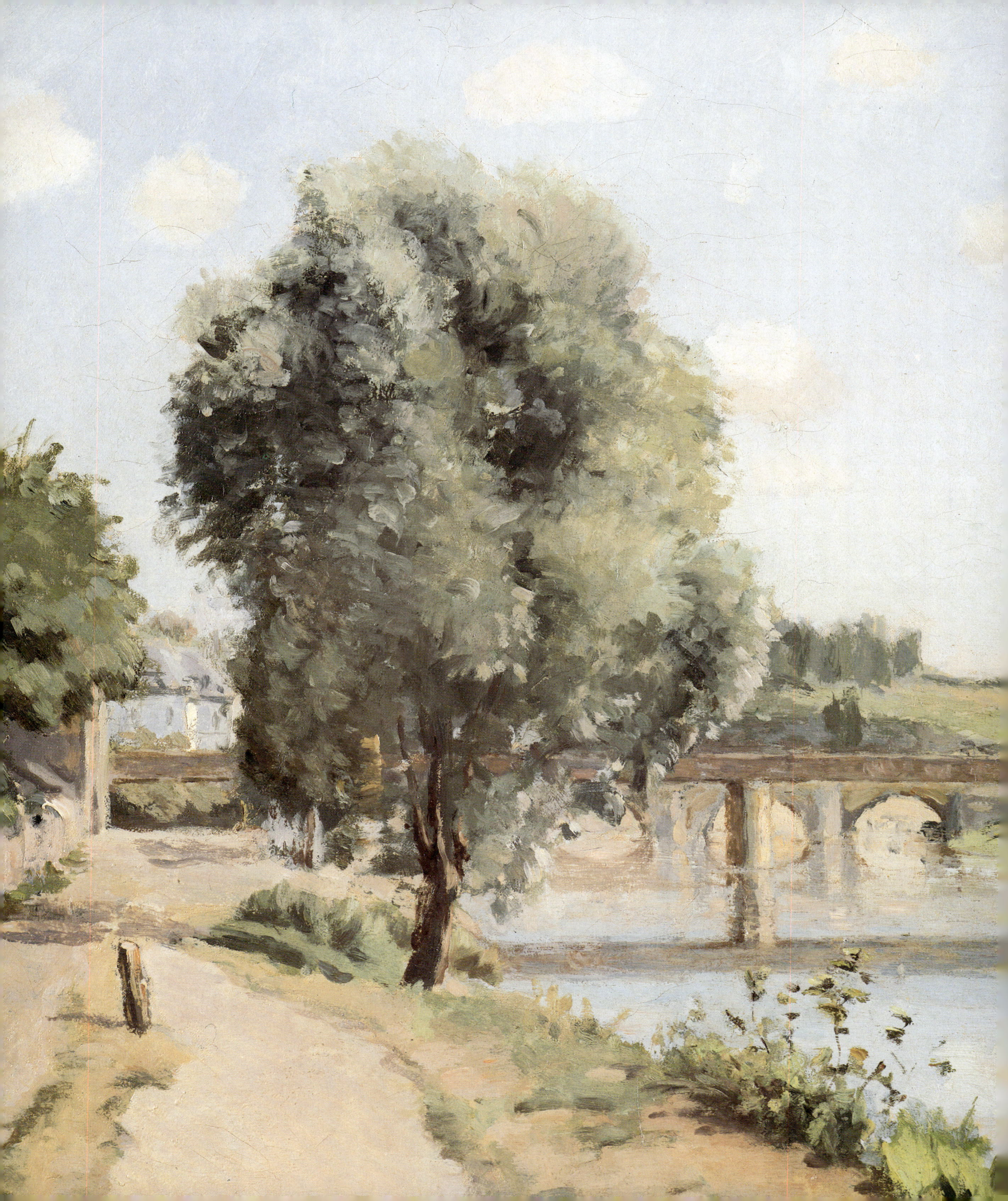

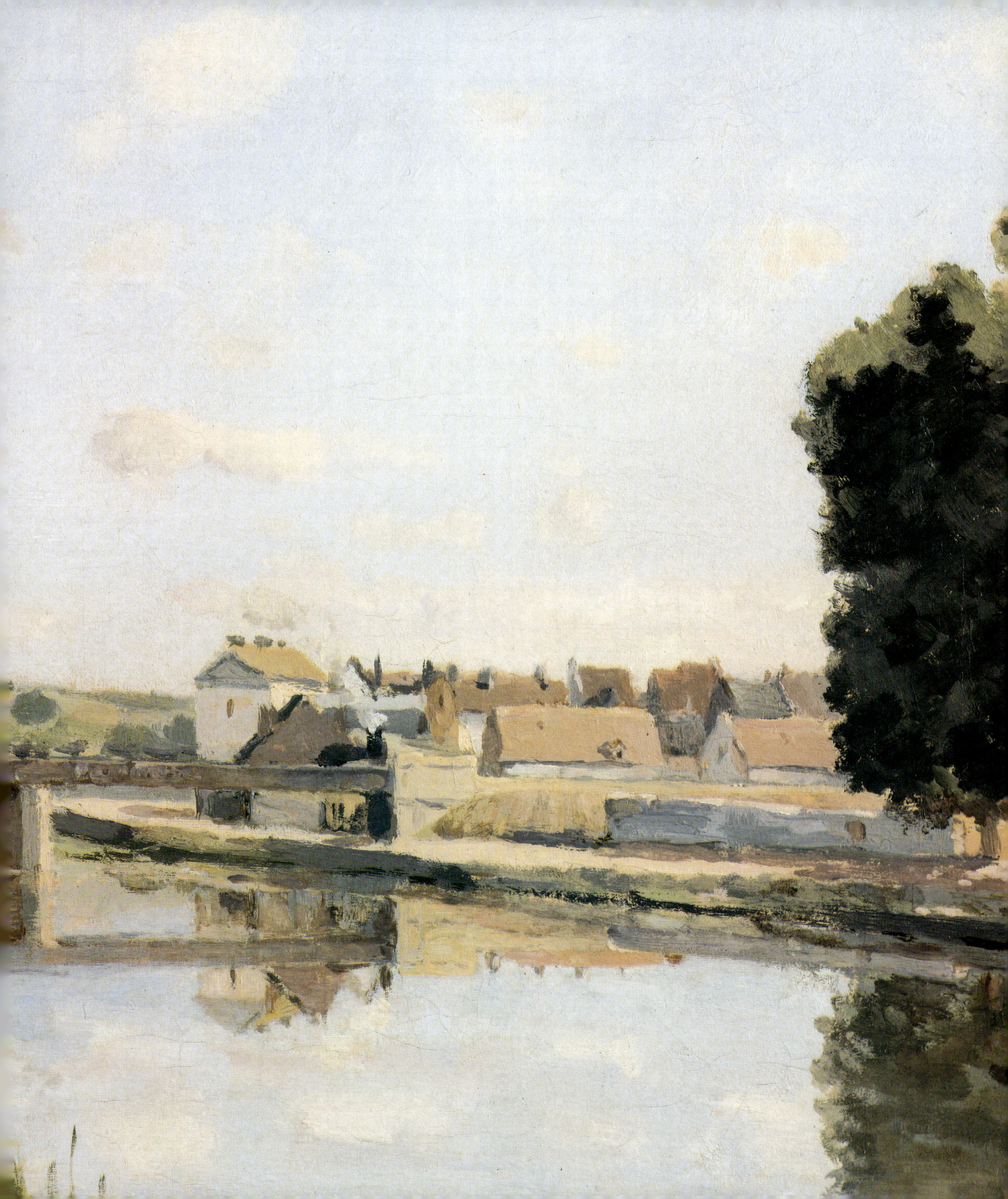

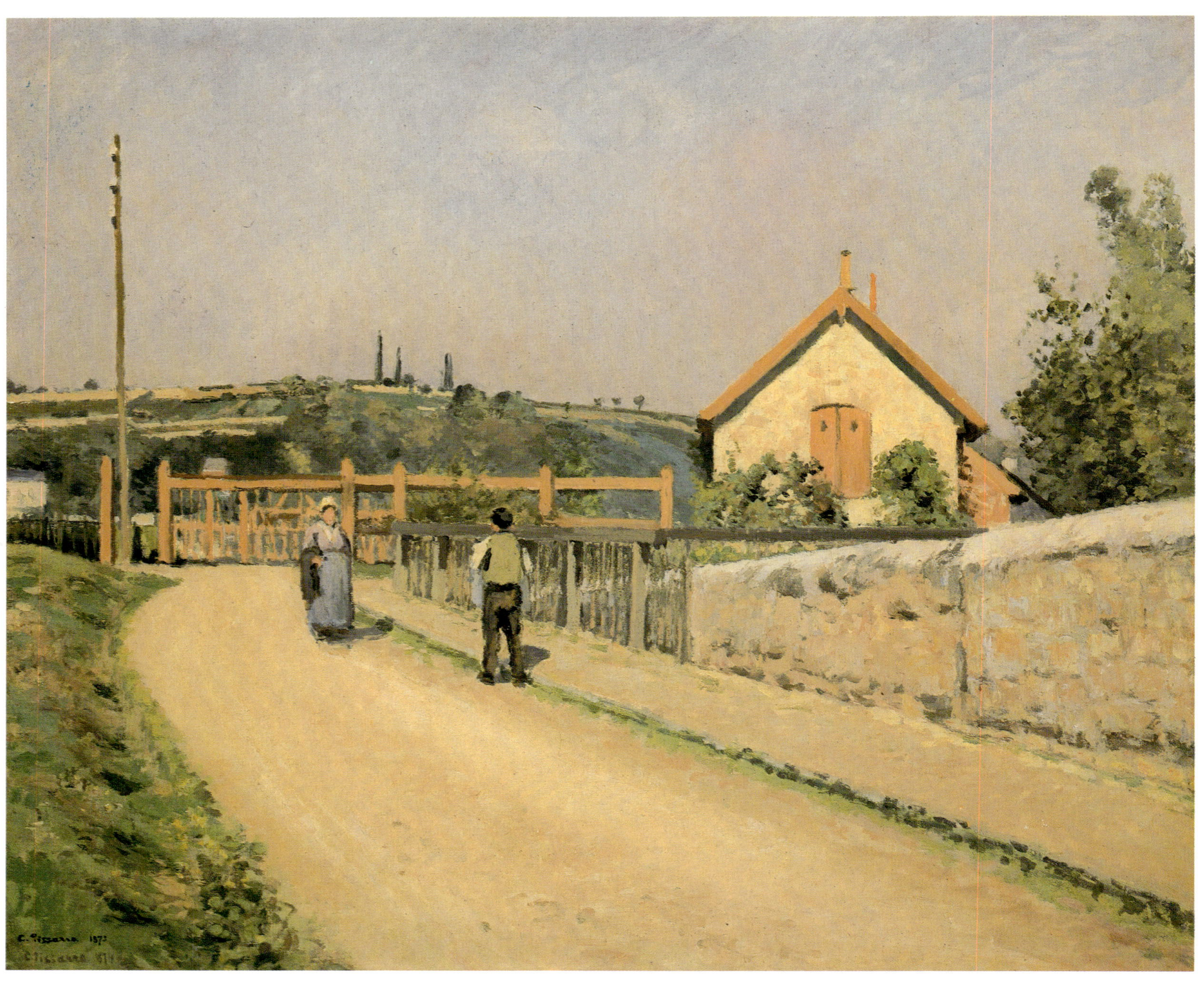

65. Camille Pissarro, *La Barrière du chemin de fer aux Pâtis, près Pontoise* (P&V 266), 1873–74, oil on canvas, 65 × 81cm., Phillips Family collection.

pictorially ignored the small sailboats and pleasure craft that must have occasionally wandered downriver from L'Isle-Adam or Auvers, Monet ignored the barges that regularly steamed or were pulled down the Seine toward the barge docks in Argenteuil or the large docks in Paris at Bercy. Although difficult to prove without further documentary evidence, it seems likely from pictorial evidence alone that Pissarro and Monet had decidedly different attitudes toward the railroad and modern technology. Pissarro always placed his trains in the midst of landscapes that contain rather than feature them. They are not the glorious motifs, rapid and exciting, that are such an evident feature of Monet's landscape. The marvelous train, exhaling voluminous smoke in Monet's *Le Chemin de fer dans la neige* (pl. 66) of 1875 is nowhere to be found in Pissarro's Pontoise. Monet's train speaks of the capital city, whose population inundated the town of Argenteuil at weekends and throughout the months of summer. Pissarro's land-

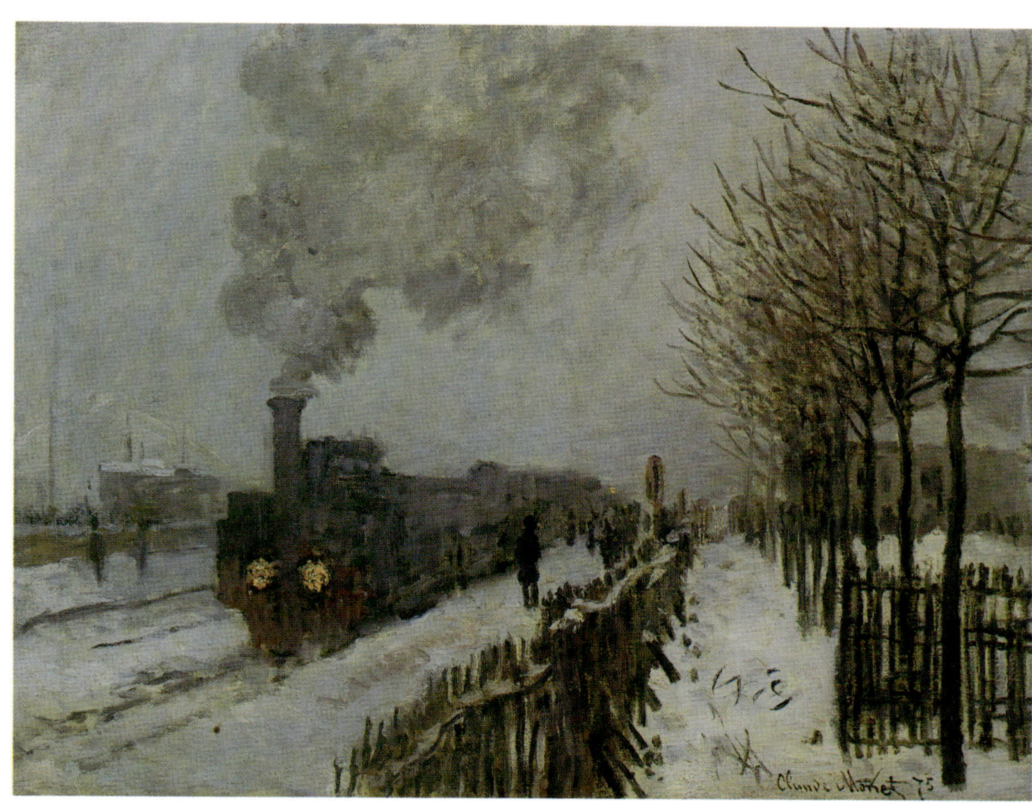

66. Claude Monet, *Le Chemin de fer dans la neige*, 1875, oil on canvas, 59 × 78cm., Musée Marmottan, Paris.

scape is seen from the local point of view. It is the stolid movement of the local "peasants" that Pissarro notes with such care, and not the momentary arrival of the train. Indeed, the very rapidity suggested by the image of a puffing train is all but antithetical to Pissarro's slower and more traditional landscape esthetic. His carefully observed world of forms, fitted neatly and laboriously into landscapes of almost puzzle-like complexity, is not conducive to the image of the train, a machine that bursts through the landscape with an energy unknown in Pissarro's rural world.[46]

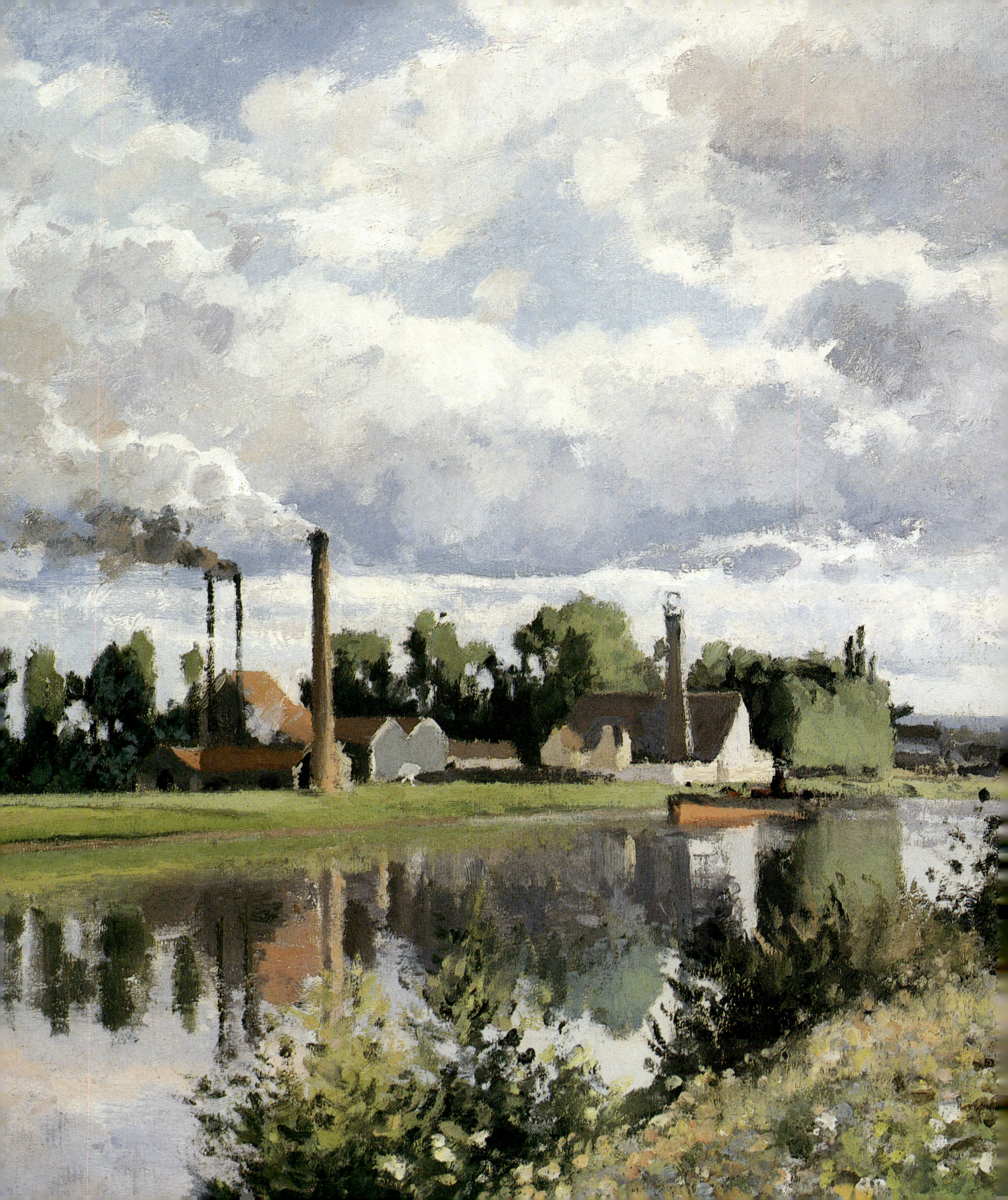

3 The Industrial Landscape: Pissarro and the Factory

Perhaps the closest approximation to iconography available to the historian of landscape painting centers around the concept of "motif." Although the word was used actively throughout the nineteenth century, it was never clearly defined. Many writers use it to signify a single object that is the central feature of a landscape painting. Others refer more generally to the framed view chosen by the painter as his "motif." The first of these definitions is objective and, therefore, iconic. The second has more to do with edges than objects or icons and presupposes an attitude toward the landscape that has little to do with Panofsky's methods. Obviously, the concept "motif" was confusing to the nineteenth-century landscape painter. Relating to the strength or even the dominance of a single form or group of clustered forms within the larger landscape, it shares close connections with the figure-versus-ground duality that plays a correspondingly important role in thinking about landscape. In the classical landscape tradition, a dominant or iconic form was avoided. Painters from Claude to Corot stressed the compositional interplay, either harmonious or contrastingly picturesque, among several forms rather than the strength of one single form, and the landscape painter's fascination with space and light is not conducive to pictorial concentration on a single objective motif. Nature, as most writers on landscape painting remind us, is not filled with significant form, but is a source of varied compositional ideas. Valenciennes's dislike of mountain landscape or French landscape, because of the dominance given in these settings to "nature" over "man," is related to his underlying concern for balance rather than dominance.[1] He wanted figures, vegetation, architecture, and geological forms to be unified within the landscape context, a context that is clearly anti-iconic.

Pissarro's general landscape esthetic relates quite clearly to the classical landscape tradition. He tended to avoid "motifs," as that word is objectively defined, to shy away from psychologically potent forms such as large figures, significant architecture, and even expressively gnarled trees, and to ground his landscape painting in the concepts of balance and pictorial unity. The major exception to this rule is, oddly enough, the factory that belonged in the 1870s to the firm of Chalon et Cie. and that dominated the Oise in the area of L'Hermitage where Pissarro lived. In 1873, Pissarro painted four important "factory-scapes" that represent the building, and another group of landscapes in 1876 centering on the enormous smokestack of the same factory. These works and the other less iconographically forceful images representing the many small factories near Pontoise form, without a doubt, the most sytematic investigation of the industrial image undertaken by any landscape painter of the Impressionist group. Occasional pictures by Monet, Sisley, Degas, and even Cézanne deal with the presence of industrial forms in the landscape, but do not show evidence of the concentrated probing of Pissarro's "series." These painters, particularly Monet, pay more attention to the mode of modern transportation, the train, than they do

67. Detail of pl. 75.

to the factory landscapes that were becoming as common around Paris as the tourist leisure towns favored by the artists.[2] Perhaps only Guillaumin with his various landscapes at Ivry and the industralized quai de Bercy in Paris approached the industrial landscape with a comparable directness (pl. 84).[3] Yet his paintings have their precedents in travel illustrations and are considerably less forceful than Pissarro's initial series of 1873. In fact, the industrial suburbs of Paris play a decidedly minor role in the iconography of landscape canvases painted in the *campagne de Paris* until the middle and late 1880s when they were taken up by painters of the Post-Impressionist group, particularly Signac, Luce, Seurat, and Van Gogh.

An intellectual historian would probably define two basic attitudes towards industry and industrial modernism in nineteenth-century France, attitudes that were equally strong but fundamentally opposing. The first was related to the positivist and progressive view of nature as the physical world including man and his works. This view cheerfully accepted industrialism and modernism. The second considered nature to be the absolute opposite of modern industrial civilization.

The simplest and most efficient example of the inclusive and positivist idea of nature which was current and perhaps dominant in popular French intellectual life is Gaston Tissandier's illustrated weekly magazine entitled *La Nature*.[4] The first issue appeared in 1873, the year in which Pissarro began his first significant pictorial examination of the factory, and it continued to publish throughout the rest of the nineteenth century. The subtitle of Tissandier's magazine is, in itself, revealing – "a periodical of the sciences and their application to the arts and to industry." In his introduction to the first issue, Tissandier made clear that he wanted all the diverse "specialities" of the sciences, the arts, and industry to be unified under the vaguely religious concept of nature. He, like Pissarro, Renoir, and so many artists and thinkers of the nineteenth and twentieth centuries, decried specialization and particularization, and his reason for founding and editing *La Nature* was to avoid this specialization by providing a magazine for everyone that covered everything. Industry, travel, and a kind of progressive idealism played a large part in Tissandier's optimistic journal.[5] An examination of the first year of *La Nature* tells us a great deal about the positivist and progressive idea of *la nature* in the France of the Impressionists. Illustrations include butterflies, factories, travel landscapes, railroad cars in plan and section, unborn fetuses, microscopic photographs, sections of leaves, and machines; and the first book reviewed by *La Nature* was Paul Poiré's short and influential *La France Industrielle*, first published by Hachette in 1873.[6]

This progressive or positivist view of nature had a good deal more importance in the European attitude toward landscape than has commonly been accepted. While it is indeed true that Salon landscape painting was "anti-progressive" or anti-industrial throughout the nineteenth century, the valuable tradition of tourist illustration and so-called popular landscape imagery paid considerable attention to factories within an industrial landscape world.[7] The importance given to industry in the landscape is best evidenced in Joanne's standard guide, *Les Environs de Paris*. This major source of information about the nineenth-century perception of landscape included several illustrated views showing smokestacks, steam boats, and trains. To Joanne and his readers, the environs of Paris were a modern landscape quite unlike the contemporary landscape portrayed by the Barbizon School and exhibited in the Salon and other prominent galleries. A similar fascination with the industrial component of real landscapes can be found in photographs of the middle and late years of the century, including the important images taken in the 1850s and 1860s by Adolphe Braun in his photographic surveys of France. For the student interested in the appearance of industry in the French landscape, there is no dearth of engravings, lithographs, and photographs at his disposal in the massive industrial sections in the Cabinet des Estampes of the Bibliothèque Nationale. The artists and photographers who turned their attention to industry were supported by the industrial economy; they were what we today call "commercial artists." The railroads, which, as Joanne made evident in his survey of their extent in France, controlled many other "industrial" elements of the French economy, provided the economic impetus that made travel art possible. It is no accident that railroads, factories, and the houses of their owners play an important role in the landscape iconography of Joanne and his illustrators.

The popular view of nature advanced by men like Joanne and Tissandier was the opposite of that represented by the landscape painters of the early and middle nineteenth century. The conception of nature as a place of escape from civilization—an idea as old as civilization itself—was as influential throughout the century as the opposing view. The industrial revolution had made a greater impact on the lives of men and their physical environment in a shorter time than any comparable revolution in the history of mankind, with the result that, as even a cursory examination will reveal, anti-urban and anti-positivist ideas about nature became general currency among many French artists and intellectuals. Writers as diverse in aim and in their relationship to modern society as George Sand and Jules Michelet glorified the peasant in their mid-century search for the truly good and meaningful life.[8] The difficulties of modern life were seen by the neo-Catholic Victor de Laprade and the atheist Emile Michel as the reason for the contemporary attempt to return to nature, for the rise in regionalism, and for the creation of the tourist who went in search of nature.[9]

Michelet's *La Mer* and *La Montagne* are great prose hymns to solitary escapes from civilization into a nature that is seen as an antidote to the confused and crowded life of the cities.[10] Elisée Reclus, the anarchist geographer admired by Pissarro, concurred with this view in an early and important article, "Du Sentiment de la nature dans les Sociétés Modernes," published in the *Revue des deux mondes* in 1866. Reclus considered mountain trips and nature excursions to be essential for the maintenance of mental and moral health in modern society.[11] Perhaps the clearest statement of this idea of nature as escape from modern life is found in Emile Michel's early essay, "Du Paysage et du sentiment de la nature a notre epoque," published in 1876.[12] Michel, who became an important historian of landscape painting in his later years and who painted landscapes in a rather tepid Barbizon School manner, decried the rapid change of the modern world and the dehumanizing effect of modern cities, recommending occasional excursions into nature as intermittent cures for the disease of modernism. Nature was equated by these writers with moral well-being; civilization, with waste, corruptness, and depravity.

Pissarro seems to have been intellectually interested in both attitudes. His training with the great mid-century landscape painters exposed him to the pre-modern and moralistic definition of nature as something rich and enduring from which the painter could derive inexhaustible inspiration. Yet his own paintings show evidence of a prolonged and fascinating relationship with the image of the factory, an image he both accepted and denied. It is perfectly clear that a painter's inclusion or exclusion of this image in the middle of the nineteenth century tells us a great deal about his attitudes toward nature. No important landscape painter of the mid-century painted a factory. Daubigny accepted industrial images in his popular prints, but never in his paintings, which depict pre-modern and rural settings. As numerous contemporary writers pointed out, the nature portrayed by these artists was the expression of a simpler world, a more "true," and therefore better world than the modern world of the city.

Pissarro's attitude toward the industrial revolution that had begun to transform France by the middle of the century and that was expanding rapidly in the Third Republic was anything but straightforward and is revealed in a stray phrase or an occasional sentence in his later correspondence. In a letter of 25 July 1883 to his son, he opposed art to industry in a manner characteristic of artists and intellectuals of his generation. Specialization, he tells Lucien, is the death of art and, by contrast, the very explanation of industry.[13] In another letter of July 1883, he complained that if the current economic slump did not let up, artists would be forced to work in factories.[14] Both these brief references to industry are essentially negative without being clear negations. In both, industry is contrasted with the arts and is, thereby, conceived as an element of culture that does not include the arts. Industry is specialized. The arts are generalizers and unifiers. Pissarro's example of the flexibility, the lack of specialization in the arts, is an interesting one: "Everything is worth drawing, everything! When you can capture the general character of a tree, then you can capture the human figure." For the Pissarro who wrote this passage, the goal of the artist was the comprehension of "form," not of forms. The typology and classification of forms, so crucial for the scientist and the industrial engineer, was not so important to the landscape painter.

It is clear that the images of the factory and the machine, the archetypal images of the industrial revolution and, hence, of the modern world, played a key role in the contemporary debate over the nature of man and what might be called the nature of nature. Michelet admitted factory workers to the cast of thousands in his book *Le Peuple* (1846), but found his ultimate solace during his exile writing *L'Insecte, L'Oiseau, La Mer,* and *La Montagne,* and had, in fact, based his study of the French people on the most "natural" of men, the peasant. Indeed, the basic thesis of *Le Peuple* is that the industrial revolution created class tensions absent from traditional society. Most nineteenth-century intellectuals were ambivalent in their response to the realities of industrial life. The realist Castagnary was among the earliest advocates of urban art, but he condemned a landscape by Jeanron for its inclusion of a telegraph pole: "What is there in common between this thread of brass, this industrial, useful product, and landscape, the refinement and the expression of the beautiful in nature?"[15]

Almost in opposition to Castagnary, Pissarro accepted the modern industrial elements of the landscape before most other landscape painters. Indeed, his paintings of Pontoise include the very telegraph poles that Castagnary condemned in 1857 (pl. 60), as well as factories, steam boats, and, at least to a very limited extent, trains. Yet, his treatment of the factory, which began in the 1860s and continued until his death, is far from consistent in the view of industry that it conveys. Pissarro's images of industry represent, finally, a painterly struggle to comprehend and to unify different aspects of modernity by a painter who never fully accepted it.

Studies of modern imagery in French nineteenth-century painting have made considerable progress in the last generation, especially with Hanson's work on Manet and Nochlin's or Weisberg's various publications on the so-called Realist painters.[16] These studies have stressed more often than not the acceptance of modern imagery by modern painters and have given scholarly credence to the famous phrase of Daumier, "one must move with the times" ("il faut être de son temps"). Yet, any analysis of the real character of many writers' and artists' "acceptance" of such imagery reveals their profound ambivalence to the modernity that we have often been taught to say they glorified. Bart's and Hemmings's discussions of Flaubert's modernism, Ruff's questioning analysis of Baudelaire's most problematic modernism, and Clark's remarkable work on the Impressionists suggest that their "acceptance" of modernity was anything but a straightforward one.[17] Many lecturers and writers are fond of pointing out factory chimneys and puffing trains as evidence of the progressive modernism of painters like Manet, Monet, and Degas, without considering that the inclusion of these unquestionably "modern" forms within a pictorial context does not imply agreement with or enthusiasm for the modern industrial world. Trains are compared pictorially by Degas to horses and carriages, by Pissarro to walking peasants, by Monet to the rivers they were superseding. The difficult juncture between modernism and pre-modernism is, in many ways, a obsessive theme of French painters of the Realist and Impressionist generation; in fact, the writings of "realists" like Zola and many of his disciplines show evidence of a contempt for several aspects of the modern world, a contempt that must be remembered when interpreting those smokestacks and trains.[18]

This chapter focuses on one painter's pictorial investigation of one factory. Although letters and other documents that unambiguously record Pissarro's attitudes to industry are lacking, the paintings are well known enough and the reality of the factory itself can be understood enough to make sophisticated analysis possible.

La Petite Fabrique

Pissarro had been attracted to, even fascinated by the image of the factory quite early in his career. A small canvas, undoubtedly painted between 1863 and 1865 and entitled *La Petite Fabrique* (pl. 68), depicts a factory in a village or suburban context. The building itself is typical of the small shed-like *fabriques* used for small-scale manufacture that were found in the environs of Paris throughout the early and mid-nineteenth century, before the massive industrialization later in the century and the construction of large factories or *usines*. This contrast between pre-modern *fabrique* and modern *usine* is very important in understanding Pissarro's painting of industrial architecture throughout the 1870s. Although there was some ambiguity in the use of the two words *fabrique* and *usine* in the nineteenth century, it is generally true that a *fabrique* was a smaller and often non-mechanized factory like those that had existed in Pontoise since the "industrialization" of the late Middle Ages. A *usine* was most often a large, mechanized factory. The *usine* is characteristic of the industrial revolution as we understand that term in the twentieth century.

Pissarro's *Petite Fabrique* would not have surprised the mid-nineteenth-century viewer familiar with the areas around Charenton, Saint-Denis, Bercy, or Creil which already contained numerous factories. Although Pissarro's style in this picture is broad and forceful, his subject matter is neither particularly modern nor defiant. The hour is either just after sunset or dawn. The factory is set into objective relief by the light cast from the sun; it is, in fact, the only apparently real object in the picture. The houses and hills are flattened and deobjectified. They act as a background screen for the space-displacing factory. The figures are undifferentiated and there only to indicate scale; their human presence, as is typical for Pissarro's figures of the 1860s, is minimal.[19] Yet, the factory, for all its pictorial

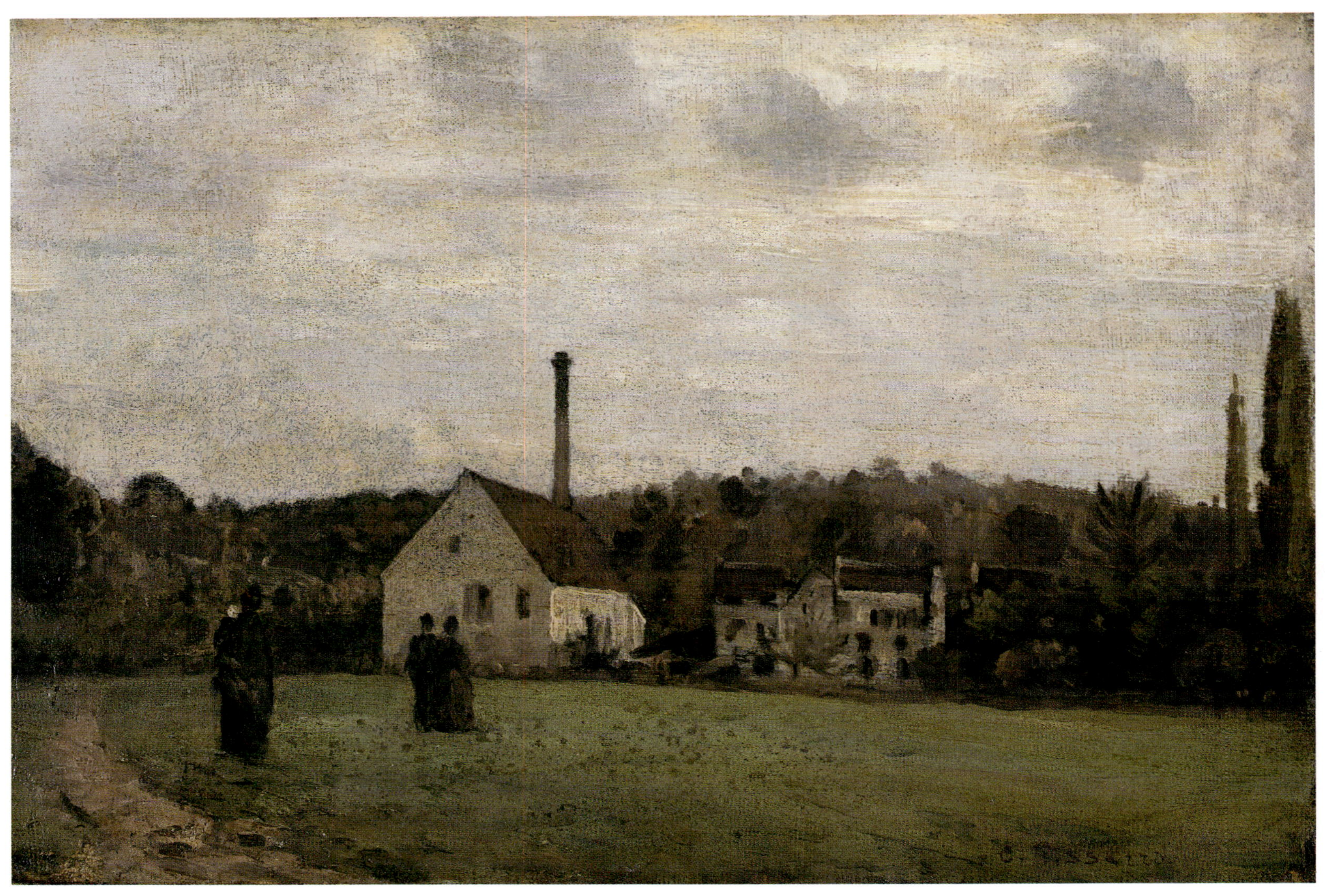

68. Camille Pissarro, *La Petite Fabrique* (P&V 66), *c*.1863–65, oil on canvas, 26.5 × 40cm., Musée de Strasbourg.

reality, has no smoke coming from the chimney and no sign of activity. It is inert, tectonic, and silent. If *La Petite Fabrique* is any indication, Pissarro's industry was not very industrious.[20]

What is particularly interesting about this small canvas is that it treats the factory so emphatically as a motif. With the exception of *La Tour du télégraphe à Montmartre* of 1863 (P&V 24), *La Petite Fabrique* is Pissarro's only surviving landscape of the 1860s with a centered motif. Both these pictures are attempts at pictorializing forms associated with modernity, and they are unique in Pissarro's work of that decade. All his other paintings of the 1860s are predominantly rural and contain several pictorial elements in interaction. By centering his attention on the factory and on the famous telegraph tower in Montmartre, Pissarro seems to have been addressing the potency of the motif *per se* as much as the abstract idea of pictorial composition.

One possible explanation for the presence of industrial motifs in Pissarro's early landscapes relates, perhaps surprisingly, to the kinds of motifs traditionally suggested to young landscape painters for inclusion in their works from the seventeenth to the end of the nineteenth centuries. *Moulin*, *fabrique*, and *usine* are words that recur frequently in books on landscape paintings, both historical studies and handbooks, written in the nineteenth century. Valenciennes, Le Carpentier, and Deperthes considered the *fabriques d'Italie* to be appropriate subjects for study, and small industry is a featured motif of a great many landscapes in the seventeenth-century Dutch tradition so admired by mid- and late nineteenth-century landscape painters. Although none of the sources discusses the precise meaning of these industrial buildings in their painted landscape contexts, the reasons for the interest in this type of structure are not difficult to guess. Factories and mills show man both triumphing over and in harmony with nature. These buildings, situated from the Middle Ages up to the nineteenth century on the river sites preferred by landscape painters, are physical evidence of the genial domination of man over his environment. They refer overtly to human industry and human intelligence. Nature is shown to be working for man. In fact, industrial architecture is one of the major types of architecture dominating the western landscape tradition: factories, ruins, churches, inns, country houses; or, in iconological terms, human industry, history, religion, travel, wealth.

Early Pontoise Factory-scapes and the Chalon et Cie. Group

When Pissarro reached Pontoise in 1866, he wasted little time before painting and drawing factories. Pontoise was one of the first painter's sites of the nineteenth century with any industry at all. A beautiful and well-known pencil drawing in the Wildenstein collection depicts the small distillery on the Viosne with its squat, square-sided smokestack, the river shed and taller smokestack of the Usine de

69. Camille Pissarro, *View of Pontoise*, 1867, pencil on paper, 28 × 45cm., Wildenstein & Co., New York.

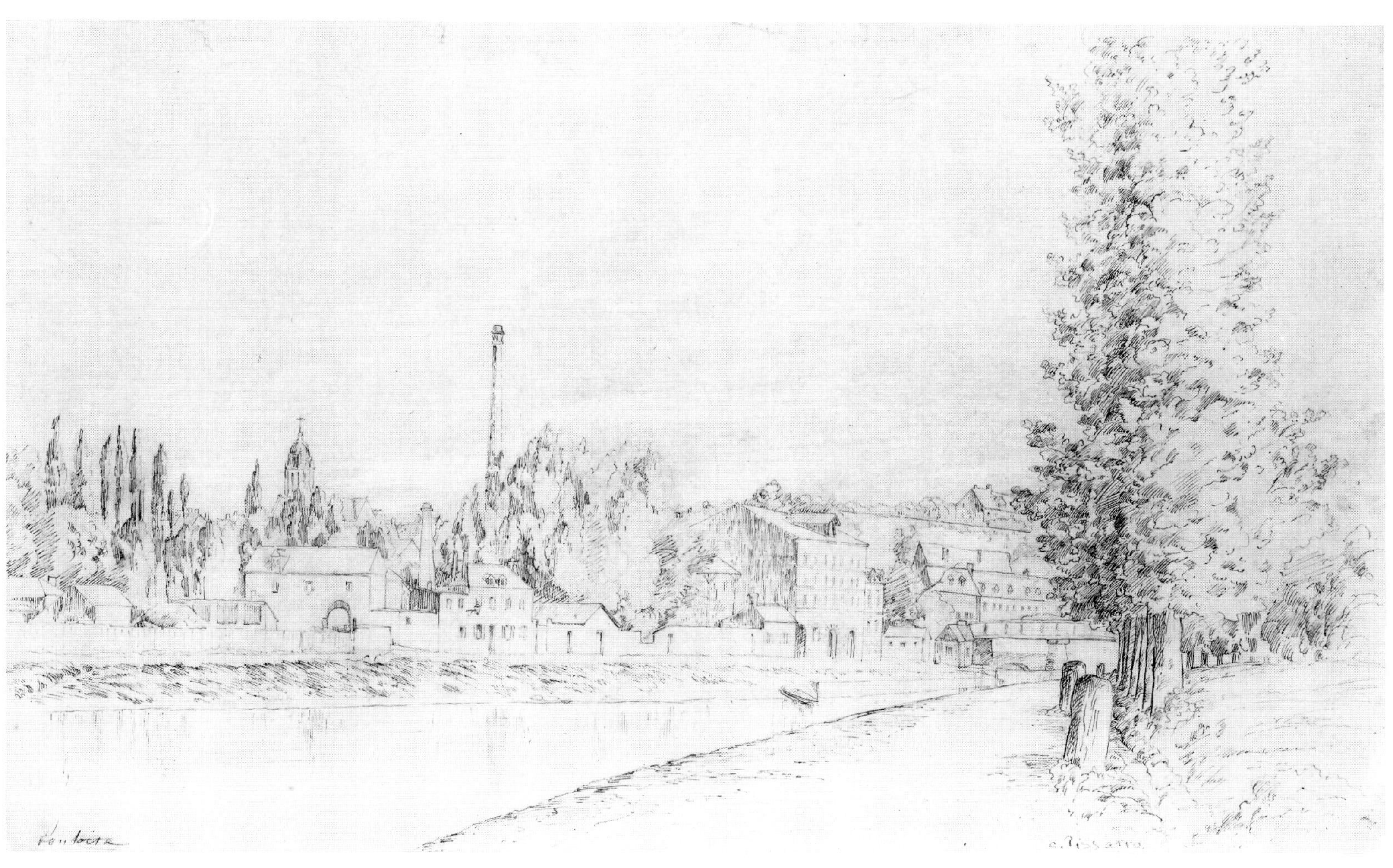

Gaz (which dates the drawing, in all probability to 1867 or 1868 because the Usine de Gaz was formally inaugurated in October of 1867), and the cast-iron railroad bridge built in 1864 and destroyed by the Prussians in 1870 (pl. 69).[21] Local industry, public industry, and public transportation take their place in this very modern landscape. Yet, Pissarro keeps this evidence of modest industry in check. The smokestack of the Usine de Gaz does tower over the crown of Saint-Maclou, but both are "out-verticalled" by the row of receding poplar trees on the right. In this starkly organized drawing, the man-made elements are subdued and underplayed. Unlike many of Pissarro's Pontoisian works, this drawing has surprising topographical accuracy. All the forms in the drawing were in fact there when Pissarro made it; but their iconic importance is subsumed by their simultaneous participation in the pictorial composition, which is strictly geometric and imparts to the drawing its cool, metaphysical quality. Neither the movement of the figures nor the passage of the clouds adds the dimension of time to these ordered volumes.[22]

Pissarro's evident concern in this drawing was compositional structure. The *idea* of the forms is not important. The factory has little importance *as* a factory. Rather it assumes its place in a landscape that contains rather than features it. The concept "composition" had an extraordinary importance in various literary and artistic movements of nineteenth-century France, an importance that goes beyond the classical or ideal landscape tradition. Baudelaire, whose discovery and translation of Edgar Allan Poe's important essay on composition marked one of the milestones in his own intellectual development; Flaubert, whose interest in ordered composition is clear from his letters and from Bart's essays on him; Manet, whose search through the history of western art for compositional ordering principles is well known; and Degas, whose interest in pictorial composition can best be called an obsession – all these men were concerned with the elusive interplay between the form as a thing in itself and the form as an element in a composition.[23] Pissarro's drawing, with its insistent ordering and its evidence of the artist's deliberate choice of forms that respond to the rectilinear format of the pictorial surface, fits well into this artistic tradition that stresses the artist's control over appearances.

The two factories that acted as the motifs in Pissarro's most important factoryscapes of the 1870s were constructed in the year immediately following the Commune and, sited in Saint-Ouen-L'Aumône, were additions to the Pontoisian landscape when Pissarro returned from Louveciennes in 1872. The paint factory of M. Arneuil was probably relatively small in that year. Cadastral records indicate that it acquired more sheds and a new smokestack later in the 1870s.[24] Chalon et Cie., then Chalon et Brenot, consisted only of the Italianate *fabrique* (pl. 70), which is the dominant motif of Pissarro's *L'Oise aux environs de Pontoise* (pl. 75). This latter building is typical of small-factory architecture in France during the late eighteenth and the nineteenth centuries. Its architecture was conservative, connecting it to the tradition of the Italianate *fabrique* familiar to students of Claude, Both, Poelenburg, Dughet, Valenciennes, and the travel artists of the eighteenth and nineteenth centuries. But the prosperity of the firm and the decisive policies of M. Chalon changed all that. During 1872 and early 1873, he began the hasty construction of a vast new *usine*, probably completed in the early months of 1873. This new building was both massive and brutal by comparison both with its forerunner and with the casual collection of sheds comprising the *fabrique* of M. Arneuil. The new factory gave the Oise an industrial character for the first time in the history of Pontoise. Its largest smokestack soared over every form in the environment, and its industrial image can be contrasted with its his-

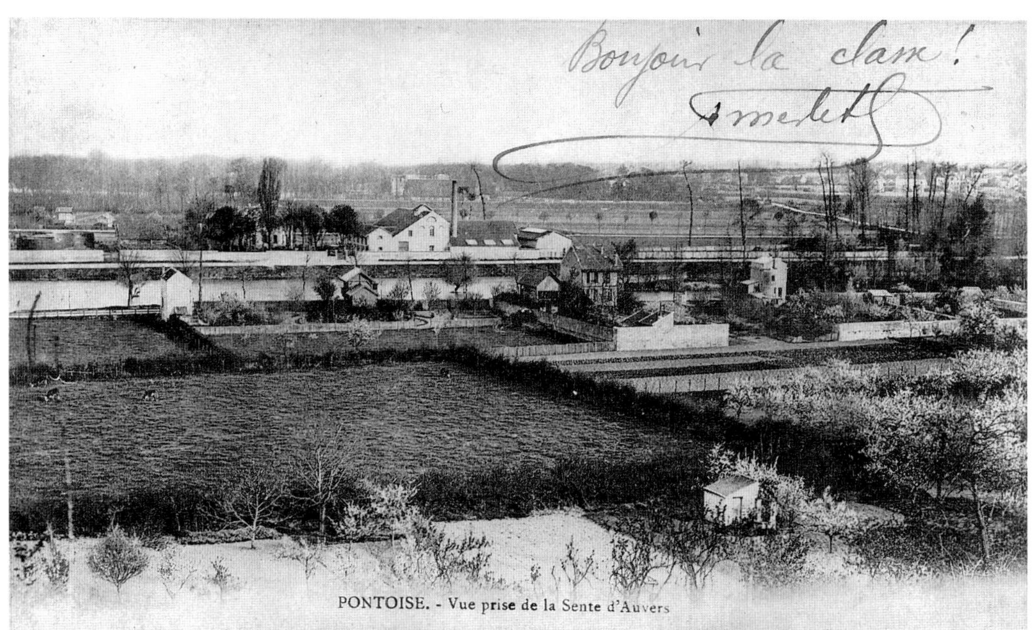

70. View of Pontoise from the Sente d'Auvers, late 19th century, postcard, collection of M. Jean Hecquet, Paris.

torical precursors, the *moulins* and the *fabriques*. These latter structures were small and numerous rather than massive and solitary. They were ranged not along the Oise, but along the smaller Viosne, where they merged into the picturesque, semi-rural landscape of Les Pâtis. M. Chalon built large, simple and, to the anti-modern eye, arrogant buildings on the alluvial plains to the northeast of Saint-Ouen. They related not to the town of Pontoise, but to the Oise itself. They existed almost entirely in terms of the developing barge traffic made possible by the vast canal network to which the Oise was connected. In Pontoise, only M. Chalon took full advantage of this key location, and his new factory, built to functional demands with no "applied" style, little finesse, and in great haste, was the subject for Pissarro's first and most important group of factory paintings.

The factory of Chalon et Cie. was a particularly potent form for Pissarro. It dominated the flat plains near Le Chou and stood directly across the Oise from the L'Hermitage quarter where the painter lived. He must have seen it practically every day as it rose up from the large field purchased by M. Chalon in 1872. Perhaps the separation created by the Oise between the painter and the building intensified its power as a pictorial motifs. The *usine* existed apart from Pissarro, in a environment of its own, canted slightly from the planar edge of the river bank which had been straightened and strengthened for the docking of *péniches*. It was the only potent or paintable form that Saint-Ouen had to offer, and all but a handful of Pissarro's paintings done in this area include the factory. For the Pissarro of the 1870s, Pontoise was hills, fields, hamlets, and towns, while Saint-Ouen was industry. Its position on the Parisian side of the Oise gave it an apt and peculiar connection with the kind of Parisian expansionism and modernism against which the town of Pontoise had fought since its founding in the early Middle Ages.

In 1873, Pissarro painted four canvases of the then new *usine* (pls. 71, 72, 74, and 75; see also pl. 73). These pictures share a centralized concentration and iconic simplicity that contrasts somewhat with Pissarro's contemporary pictures of spacious landscapes filled with many small-scale forms whose identity is subsumed in the general character of the landscape composition itself.[25] The strong-

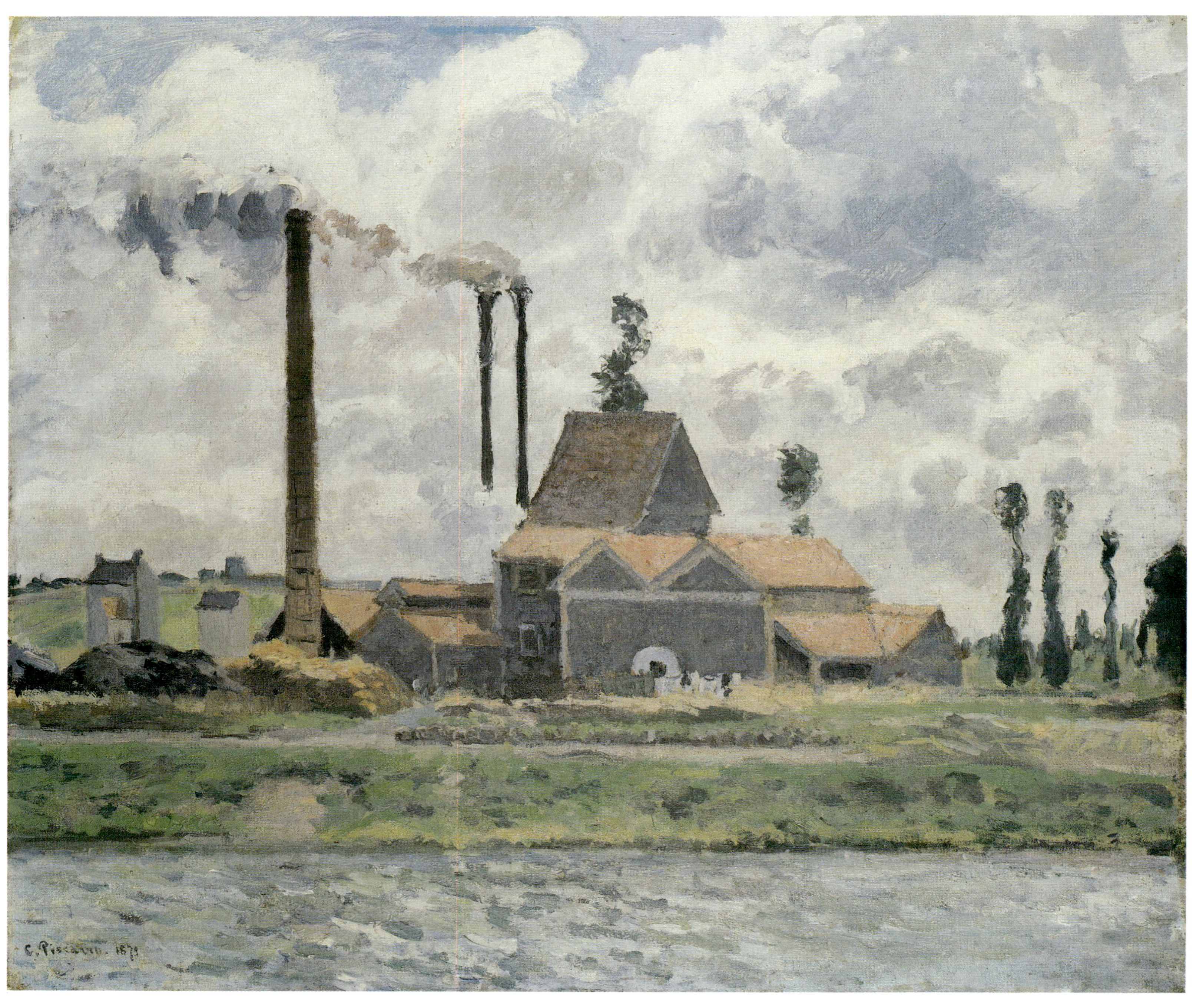

71. Camille Pissarro, *Usine près de Pontoise* (P&V 215), 1873, oil on canvas, 48 × 56cm., Museum of Fine Arts, Springfield, Massachusetts.

est and most iconic of the four, *Usine près de Pontoise* (pl. 71), is important enough to analyze in some detail. In it, the factory is awkward and complex. The roof of the central shed is exaggerated in its inclination and looms powerfully amidst the parallel sheds that covered the bulk of the floorspace. The structure is made illusionistically larger by Pissarro's inclusion of two tiny vertical dwellings at the left of the factory. According to the cadastral records for Saint-Ouen–l'Aumône and to Pissarro's other pictures of the area, these two buildings simply never existed. They are, perhaps, reversions to or memories of the dwellings that gave a populated context to Pissarro's earlier depiction of a factory, *La Petite Fabrique* of the early 1860s. Their extreme verticality relates them to the small houses then being built on very small plots by developers and real-estate speculators through-

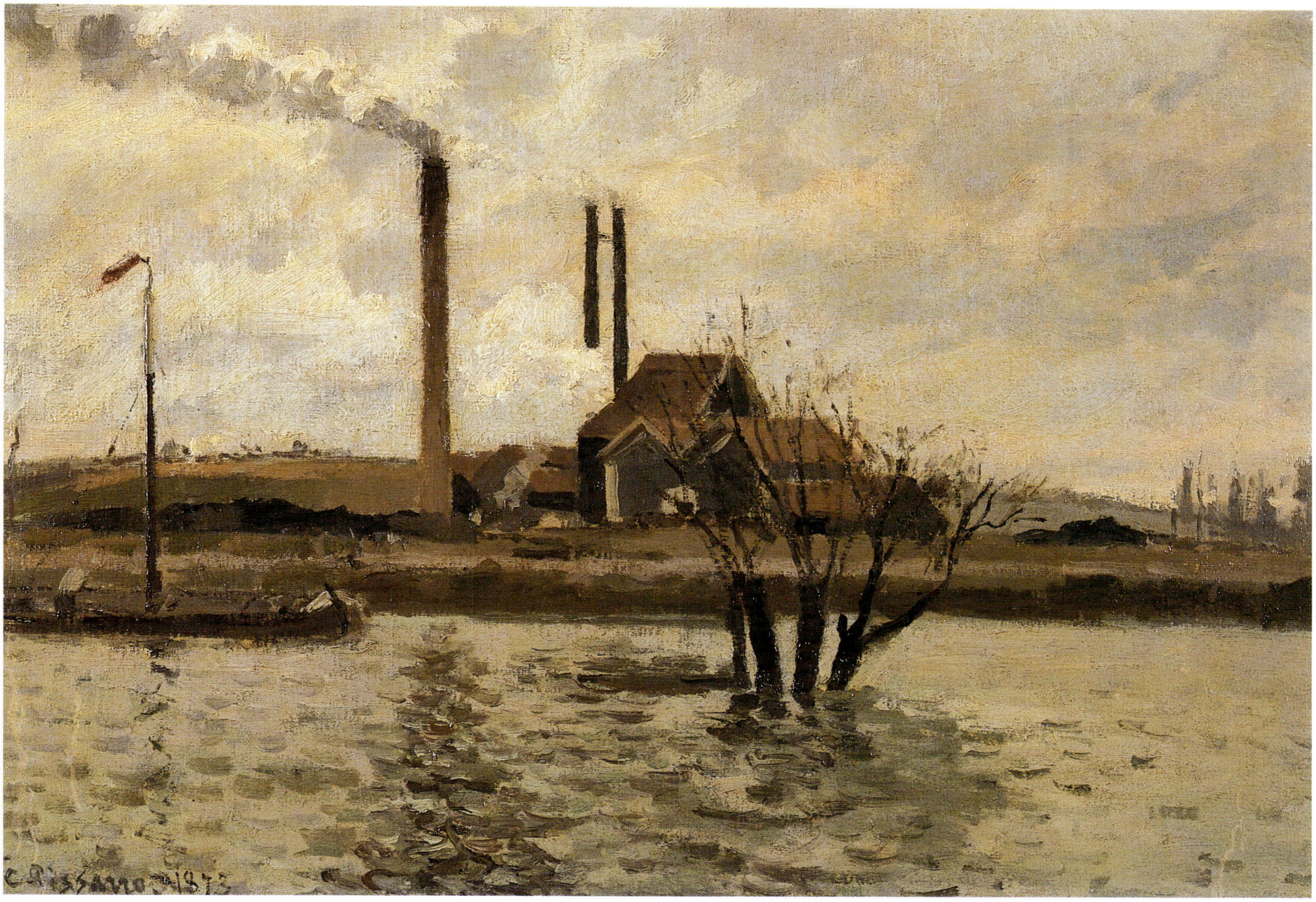

72. Camille Pissarro, *La Crue de l'Oise, Pontoise* (P&V 214), 1873, oil on canvas, 39 × 47cm., from the collection of the Earl of Jersey.

73. Camille Pissarro, *La Crue de l'Oise, Pontoise*, 1873, watercolor over pencil on paper, 17 × 25cm., collection of Mrs Paul Mellon, Upperville, Virginia.

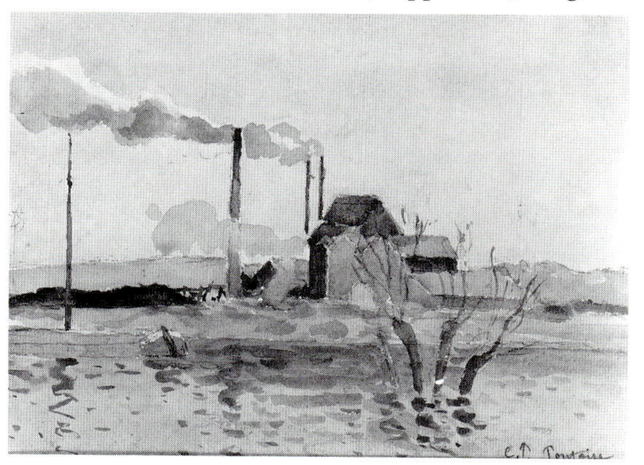

out the environs of Paris. Although these two dwellings do not form a dominant part of the composition, their imaginative introduction into the landscape gives them a greater importance in an interpretation of the picture than actual houses might have had. Their "strength" in the landscape is negligible, and they may have been introduced for that very reason. They suggest that the scale of this new factory, unlike any previously portrayed by the painter, is beyond what we might call "human scale," an abstract idea of great importance in the history and theory of landscape painting. The smallness of the houses, forms with which we readily identify, induces the viewer to push the foreground of the landscape back and gives the factory a greater illusionistic dominance as motif.

A significant oddity about this factory-scape within the context of Pissarro's oeuvre is its total lack of a populated and compositionally important foreground. Like Sisley, Pissarro was a painter of foreground and middle ground. He had a distrust of spaciousness, and his landscape paintings are most often comfortably confined works. Of the four pictures depicting the factory of Chalon et Cie., *Usine près de Pontoise* (pl. 71) and *L'Oise aux environs de Pontoise* (pl. 75), together with *La Crue de l'Oise, Pontoise*, a preparatory watercolor of 1873 (pl. 73), are all but unique in Pissarro's surviving paintings of the 1860s and 1870s for their lack

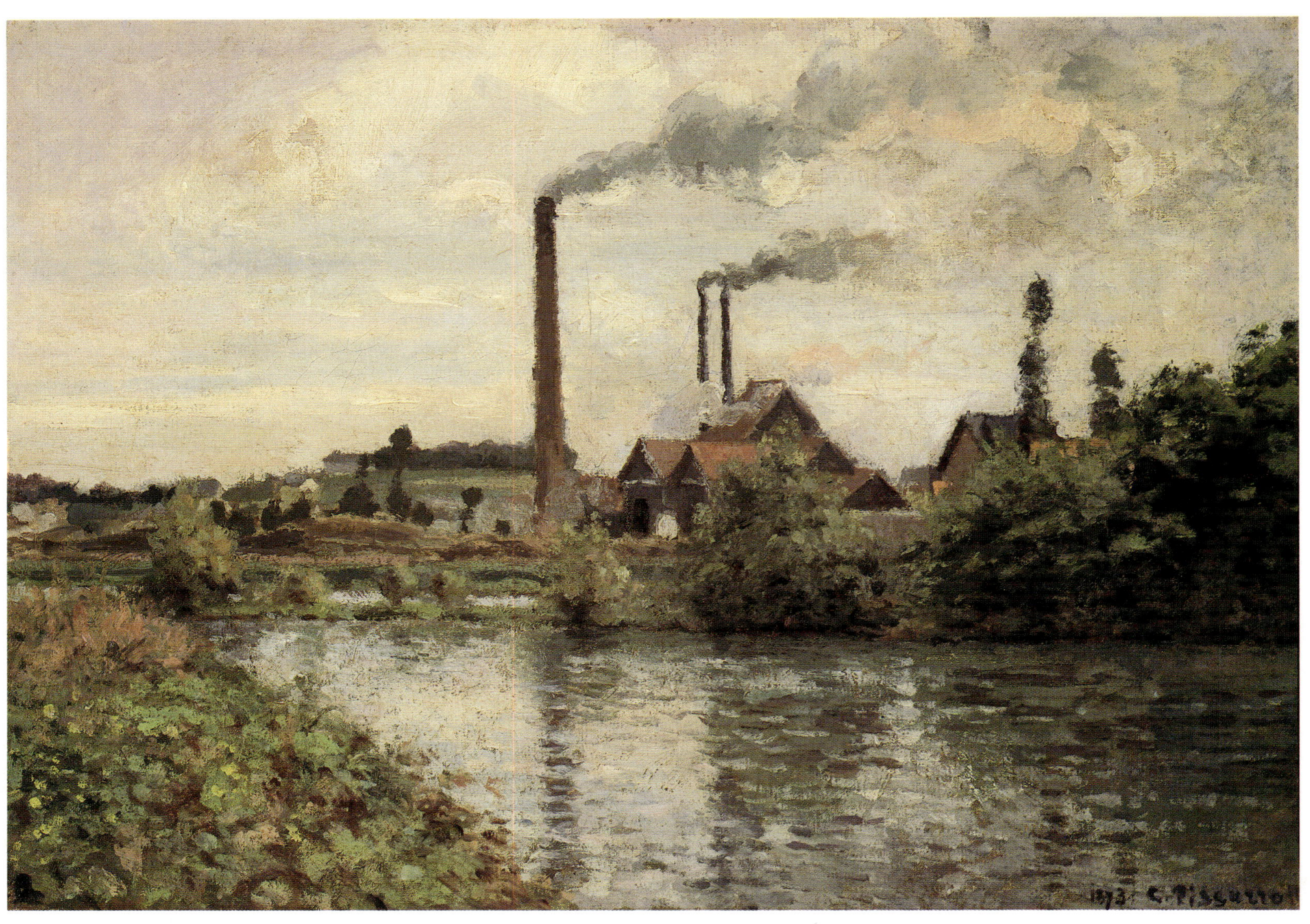

74. Camille Pissarro, *L'Usine à Pontoise* (P&V 217), 1873, oil on canvas, 45 × 54.5cm., Bronfman Foundation, Montreal.

of a humanized foreground. Pissarro's omission of the space occupied by the viewer and, therefore, of any acknowledgment of the viewer's existence must be considered a willful decision within the context of an oeuvre in which proximate forms predominate.

When *Usine près de Pontoise* is examined in detail, what appears to be a straightforward depiction of a single factory in fact involves many manipulations of actual appearance. The towering central shed, which Pissarro evidently wanted to enlarge for comparison with the two small houses already discussed, is illusionistically *lowered* by the canny placement of a poplar tree behind it. The compositional function of the tree is clear. It picks up the descending line of the smoke and the three smokestacks on the left and connects this line with the corresponding descending pattern of the poplar trees on the right. This descending smokeline aligns three forms: the smokestack at the front, the pair of smokestacks abutting the shed, and the tree in the back of the factory. Three different planes are compressed into one by forcing the elements of each into an abstract surface pattern. This kind of tension between flatness and objectivity, which enlivens so many pictures in the modern tradition, is used expressively and subtly by Pissarro. The picture represents an object trapped in planes. The factory gains importance and

84

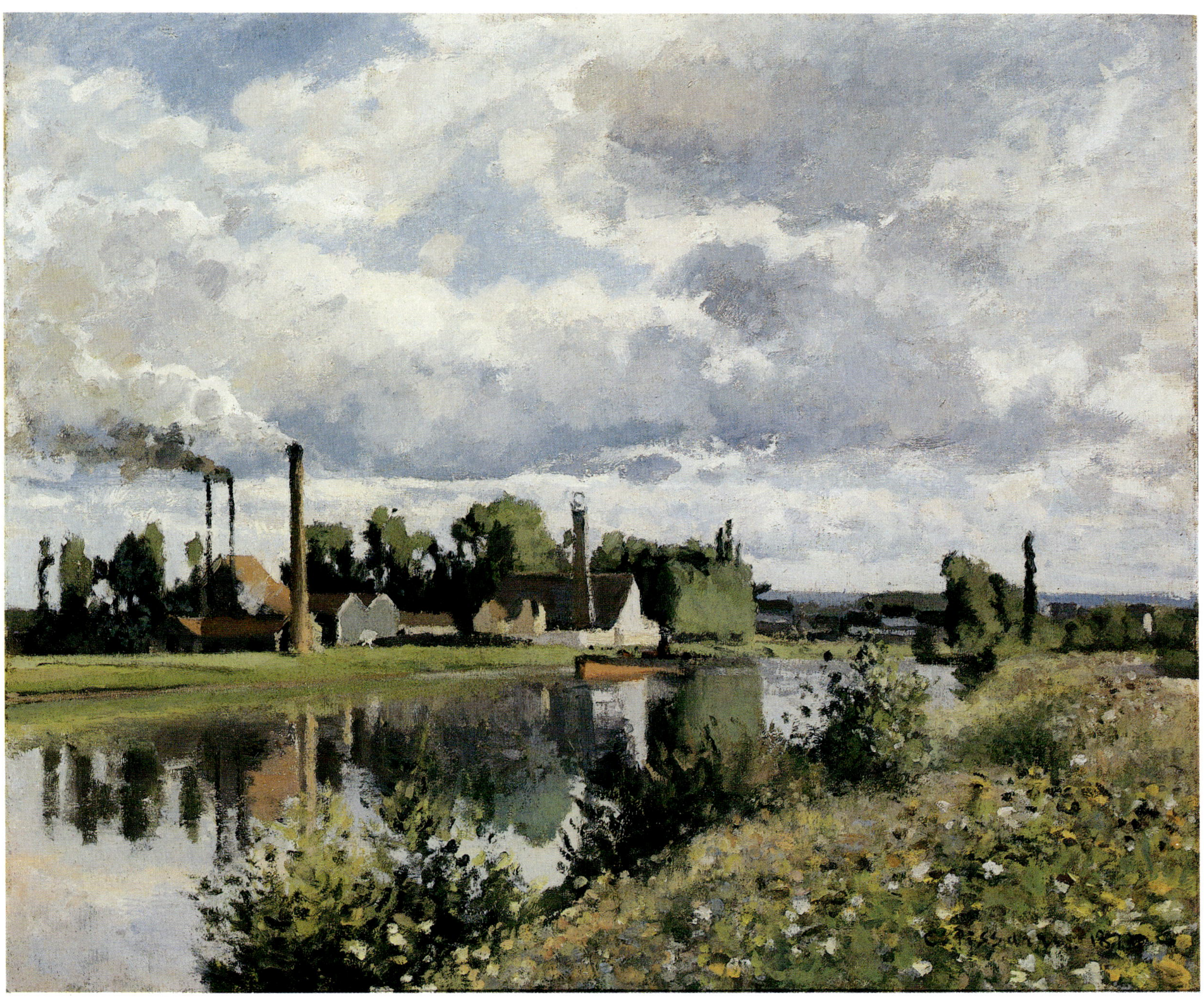

75. Camille Pissarro, *L'Oise aux environs de Pontoise* (P&V 218), 1873, oil on canvas, 45 × 55cm., Sterling and Francine Clark Art Institute, Williamstown, Massachusetts.

iconic singularity by the reduction of the pictorial space around it. It dominates its minimal setting; it demands interpretation.

The almost uncomfortable iconic power of the factory in *Usine près de Pontoise* can be seen more sharply by comparison with a drawing of an industrial landscape executed in 1870–71 and inscribed "Upper Norwood" (pl. 76). *Usine près de Pontoise* presents an ugly suburban factory in a frank, even crude manner. The factories along the Thames in *Upper Norwood* are small, rather intimate forms which nestle together at the foot of a hillside "adorned" by a pair of cows. Not even Pissarro's choice of winter for the season of this early sketch can dampen the good spirits, the harmony, and the unity of the landscape. A train puffs neatly across the middle ground. The long, leisurely line of factory smoke is parallel to the line of the foreground hillside, and the composition is unified into a central

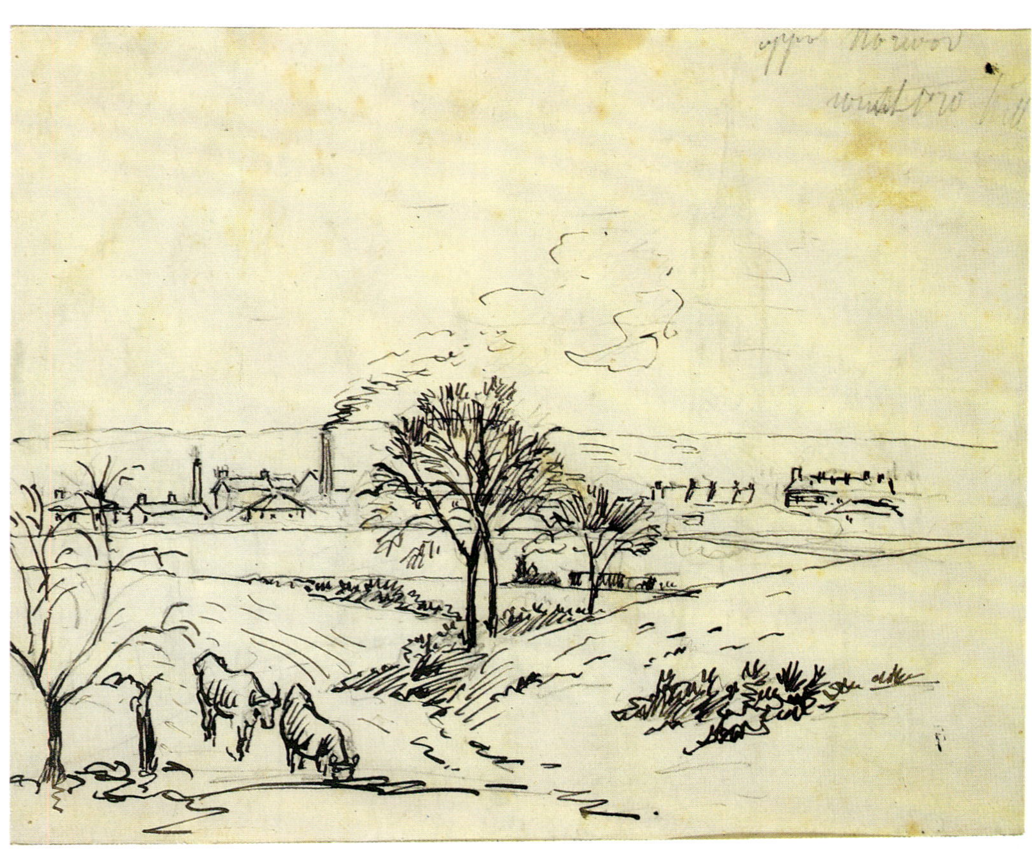

76. Camille Pissarro, *View from Upper Norwood*, n.d., pen and brown ink over pencil on paper, 16 × 20cm., Ashmolean Museum, Oxford.

lozenge anchored by the tree. Space, light, movement, and freedom characterize this small drawing.[26] Its meaning, if one can speak of a landscape having a precise meaning, revolves around the unity of city and country in the new world of the "agro-industrial village," the ideal of many mid- and late nineteenth-century intellectuals and social theorists.

The concept of the agro-industrial village, in many ways a conservative one, seems to have been derived from the dispersed and mill-related industry of the late eighteenth and early nineteenth centuries that was dependent on water power. The *fabriques* associated with this industry formed both the historical precedent in memory and fact for the romanticized concepts of Owen, Proud'hon, and other proponents of agro-industrial life, and the source for images of the factory in the nineteenth century.[27] Yet, by the Second Empire, newer factories were dependent on the rivers not for power, but for transport and sewage convenience, and with the improvement and extension of the railroad for non-passenger use, their dependence on barges and river traffic decreased as well. The *usine* of M. Chalon represents a transition point between early nineteenth-century water-powered industry like that of England and the river valleys of New England, and the factories in the industrial areas of modern cities, using portable fuel and producing portable products.

Usine près de Pontoise presents both the nineteenth- and the twentieth-century viewer with many of the critical problems inherent in what we call "realism." The picture's forthright structure gives the single dominating motif, the factory, a force it lacks in reality. Although today M. Chalon's *usine* has been enlarged and remodeled beyond recognition and has changed ownership several times, it is still ordinary, insignificant, and even rather small when compared with this much smaller painted image of it. The factories of Pontoise are, in fact, dominated by their setting. They stand in their own space, at the edge of a plain which was, in

86

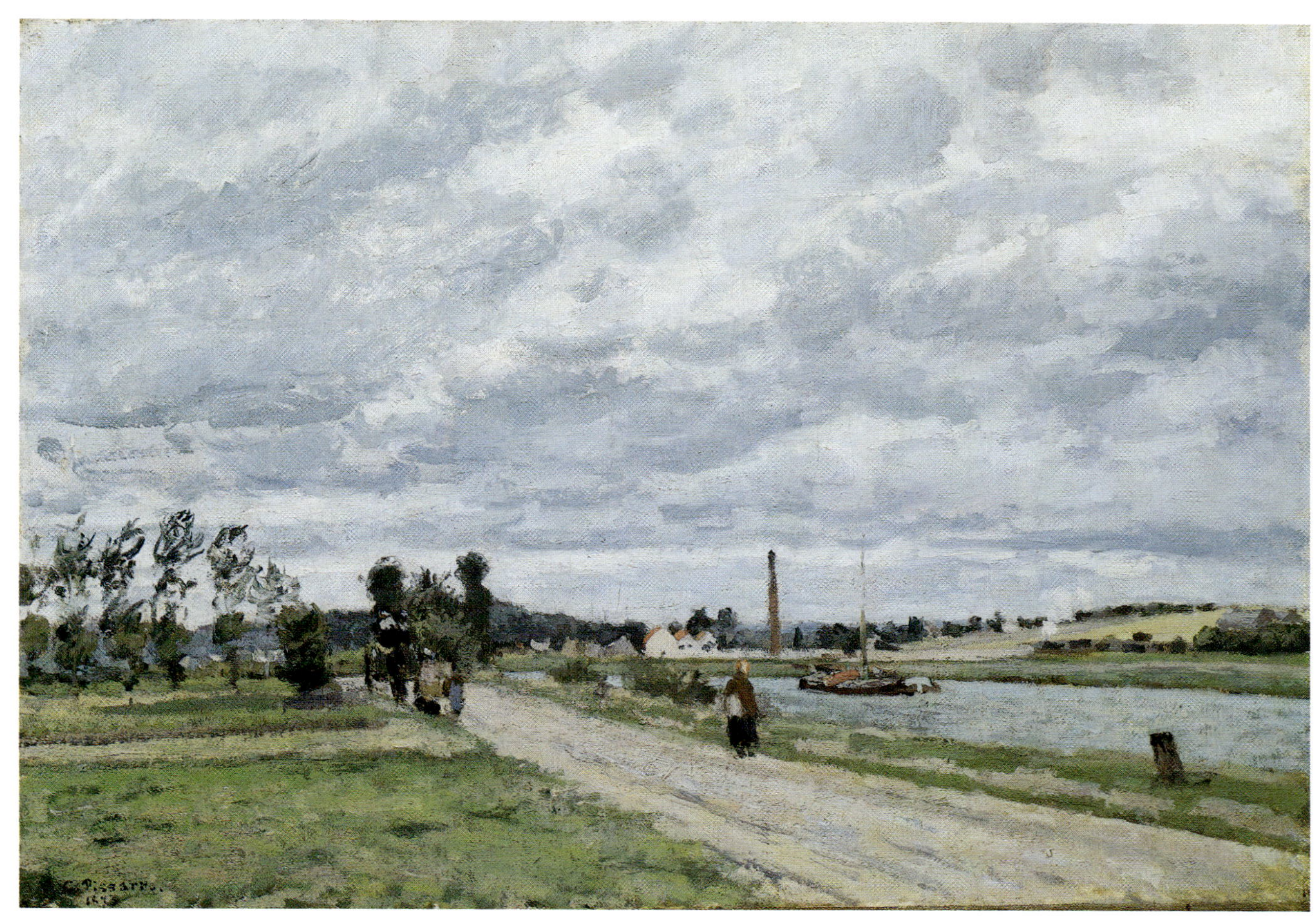

77. Camille Pissarro,
Bords de l'Oise, Pontoise
(P&V 222), 1873, oil on
canvas, 38 × 58cm.,
Indianapolis Museum
of Art; James E.
Roberts Fund.

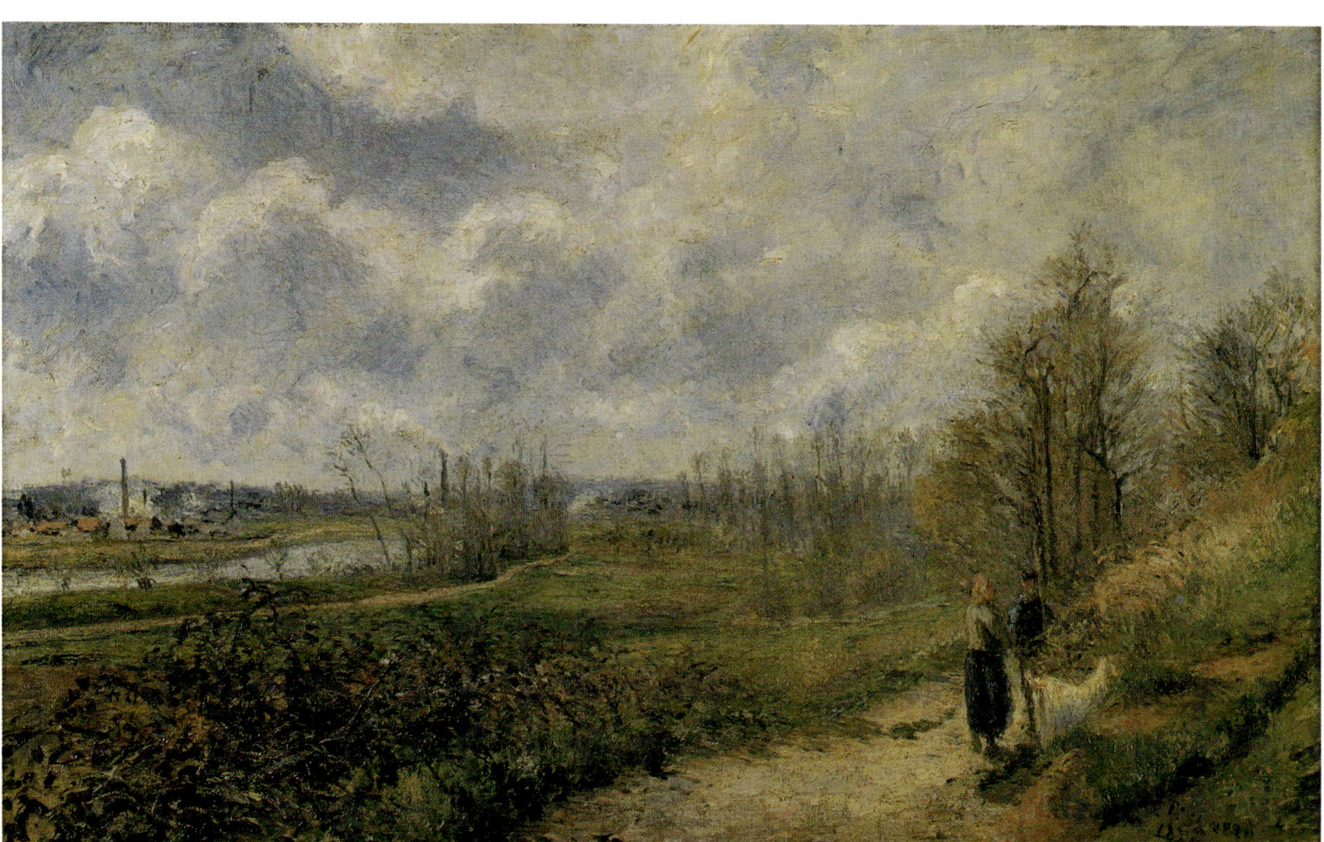

78. Camille Pissarro,
*La Sente du Chou,
Pontoise* (P&V 452),
1878, oil on canvas, 57
× 92cm., Musée de la
Chartreuse, Douai.

Pissarro's period, much more rural and spacious than it is today. Perhaps the best indications of the real importance of the factories in the Pontoisian landscape are Pissarro's rather more panoramic compositions such as *Bord de l'Oise, Pontoise* (pl. 77) of 1873, or, still better, *La Sente du Chou, Pontoise* (pl. 78), painted in 1878. The factories in these pictures are simply architectural elements in the natural landscape. Their existence is marginal and their meaning is subsumed in the general "mood" of the landscape. The four factory-scapes of 1873, with the possible exception of the relatively bucolic and often reproduced *L'Oise aux environs de Pontoise* (pl. 75), are both powerful and meaningful.

An analysis of the contemporary factory-scapes by Monet is instructive in this context. One can contrast, for example, Pissarro's 1873 *Usine près de Pontoise*, a relatively bleak and detached work in terms of the rest of his oeuvre, with Monet's *Le Convoi de chemin de fer* (pl. 79), painted in Rouen in 1872. Although Monet saw Rouen much as he did Argenteuil—as a glittering source of river landscapes in which pleasure boats play the largest role—he did make several important attempts to paint the industrial areas of the city. The most notably industrial of these views, *Le Convoi de chemin de fer*, is a detached and rapid image. The factories laminate the hillsides behind the rapidly moving trains, and the puffs of smoke push in rhythmic diagonals across the surface. As is often the case with Monet, the composition is conceived broadly, with several strong lines that unite the disparate and short brush-strokes. The subject matter of this picture is motion and steam rather than factories in the landscape.

In *Les Déchargeurs de charbon* (pl. 80) of 1875, Monet attempts to deal with industry in the landscape perhaps even more forthrightly than Pissarro's attempts in the Chalon et Cie. factory group. In spite of an elevated viewpoint and elegant diagonals that reflect Monet's interest in Japanese art, his landscape is an urban genre scene with dramatically receding pictorial space, moving and individuated human figures, and purposeful human activity. It is an empathetic view of an unpleasant activity, a view that can be considered social criticism only insofar as the labor of the workers is difficult and, to reuse Seitz's word, "dehumanized" in comparison with the work of the painter or the presumably bourgeois viewer of the picture.[28] The contrast with Pissarro could not be more extreme. None of the pictures of Chalon et Cie. has human figures, and, although two of them set the viewer on the river bank, they retain a distance between subject and viewer, provided by the river and the horizontal "wall" of the opposite bank. The lack of human presence in the landscape is as rare in Pissarro as the lack of a foreground. The fact that the views are depopulated renders them inert and dehumanized in comparison with other pictures by Pissarro, with Monet's *Déchargeurs de charbon*, and with virtually every other "industrial" painting of the period. Monet's picture reveals a view of modern industrial life that skirts between the picturesque in its variety and the sublime in its spaciousness and grandeur. Pissarro's view is much cooler, subtler, more detached, and, like its maker, more evasive. The meaning of Chalon et Cie., as it is depicted by Pissarro, is not so much to be found in what he admits to his pictures, but in what he omits.

The lack of empathy and pictorial enthusiasm for the motif is best understood by contrast with popular images of factories reproduced in the early 1870s. Although factories in the landscape had long been visible in magazine and guide-book illustrations, it is not until the 1860s and 1870s that magazine illustrators began to move inside the factories, to examine their functions in great detail. Both *Le Magazine pittoresque* and *L'Univers illustré* published many engravings of factories, and *La Nature* covered the industrial aspects of *la nature* at the expense of what one might think to be more "natural" topics. These illustrations stress over

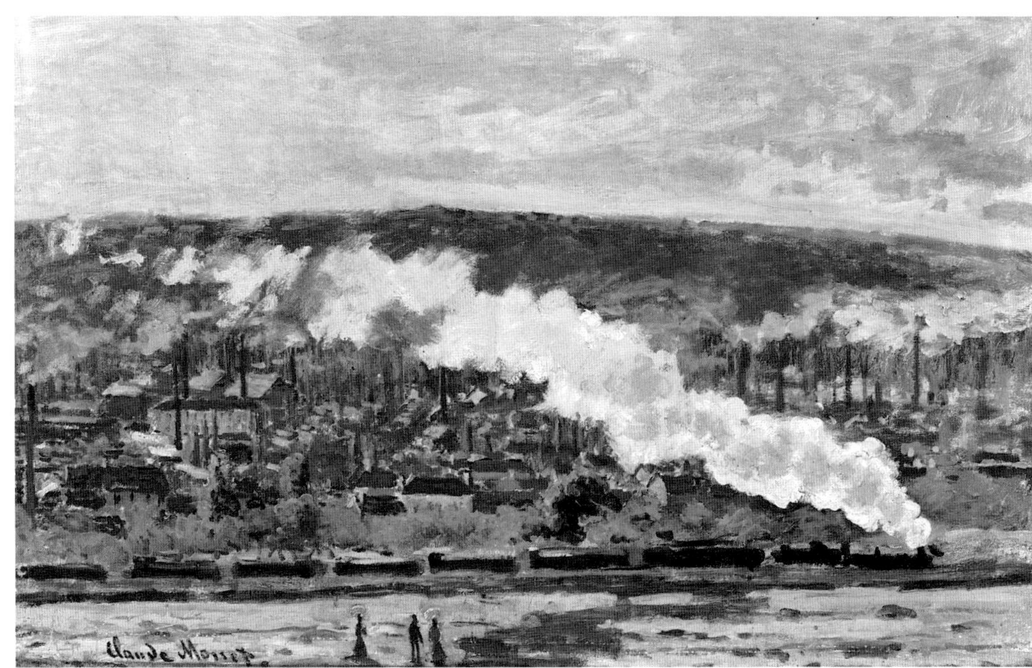

79. Claude Monet, *Le Convoi de chemin de fer*, 1872, oil on canvas, 48 × 76cm., private collection, U.S.A.

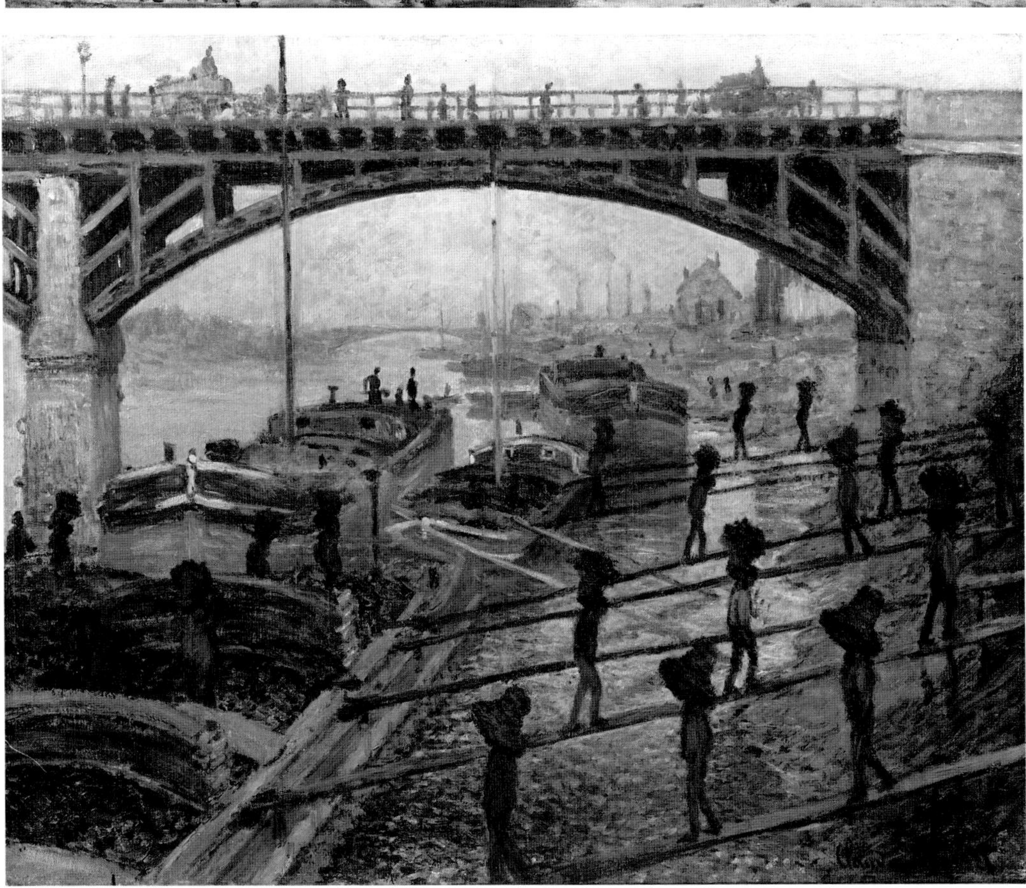

80. Claude Monet, *Les Déchargeurs de charbon*, 1875, oil on canvas, 55 × 66cm., private collection, France.

and over again the marvels of modern industry, its amazing inventiveness, its quick results. If change in the arts and the resulting concept of the "avant-garde" was reviled by most popular thinkers in France, they failed to display the same sort of timidity toward matters industrial. Most of the industrial views in magazines were not exteriors, as were the traditional tourist illustrations and the vast majority of paintings of industry, but interiors (pls. 81–83).[29] Rooms filled with

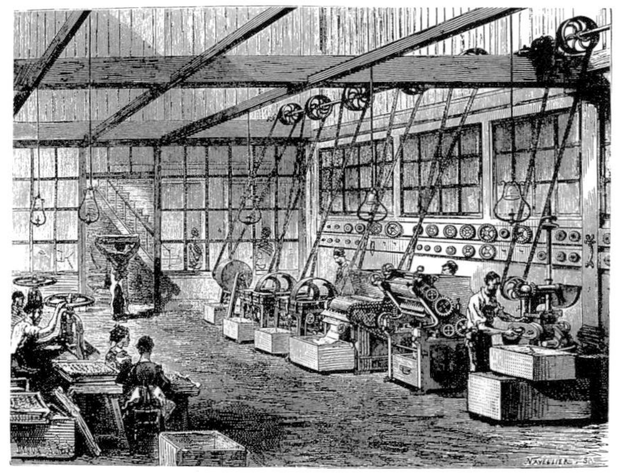

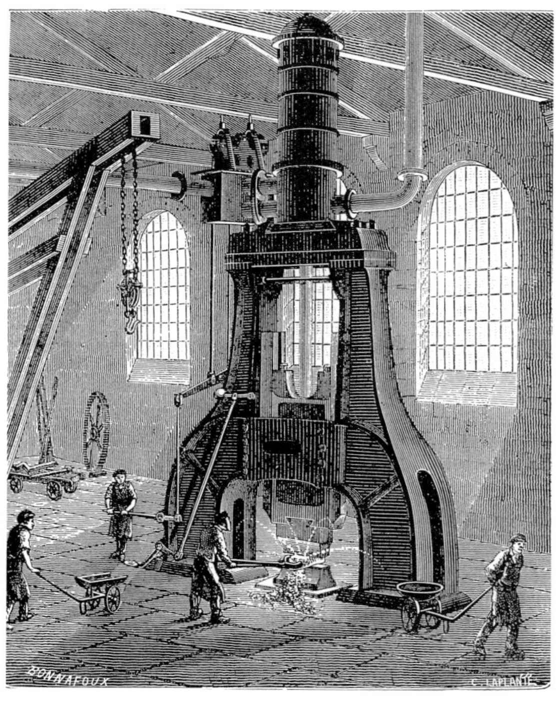

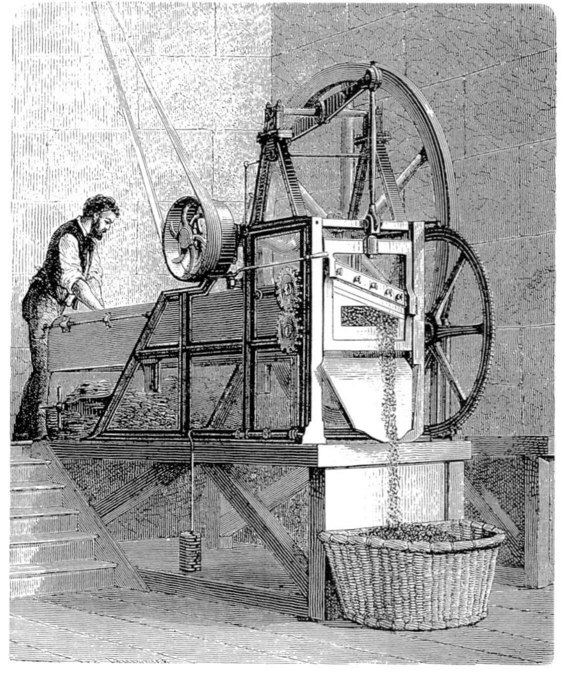

men making *baguettes* in front of long rows of ovens (surely not an image that the contemporary Parisian would admire), women sitting at endless lines of sewing machines, and men stuffing coal into flaming doors were not uncommon and did not shock and offend their contemporary audience in the way they do now.[30] But the real marvels of modern industry, the focus of industrial illustrations, were the machines, and the bigger they were, the more smoke and flames they produced, the fewer men visible, the better. These images show enormous cast-iron monsters that fill the picture space and are often accompanied by detailed descriptions of the function and capacity of the particular machine being illustrated. They fulfilled two purposes: education and advertisement. They made it possible for the contemporary general-reading public to know a great deal more about industrial processes than we do today.

In comparison with images of this kind, Pissarro's adoption of a distant, undetailed exterior view can be read as yet another omission. He gives us no indication of just what the factory is or, more fittingly, what it does. The process of industry did not concern the painter. The public had already entered the factories, involving itself in the marvelous inner workings of industrial processes and machines. Pissarro stood across the river and viewed the massive building as a detached observer.

Landscape painting is a quintessentially public art, an art that never invades, never reveals what is private, domestic, or even corporate. The landscape painter "looks over" forms, considering them in relation to each other and insofar as they exist in space and impinge on a pictorial surface. His aim is to unify and to organize forms rather than to analyze individuals or institutions. It is as a landscape painter that Pissarro confronted the new factory across the Oise from L'Hermitage in 1873. He emphasized his pictorial and personal detachment from the factory as much as he concentrated his pictorial efforts upon it. But it is the confrontation between Pissarro and the factory that is more significant for a history of landscape imagery. Pissarro never again painted a group of pictures of the same building in the same year. Until the Parisian panoramas of the 1890s, these paintings are Pissarro's most important, indeed his only important examinations of an architectural motif. Yet it is clear that Chalon et Cie. was not interesting to Pissarro for its architectural distinction, but simply as a factory, and hence as an objective encroachment of industry on the Pontoisian landscape. The four pictures, each different in size, composition, and landscape treatment, represent what may be the first sustained pictorial examination of modern industry in the history of art. It is quite possible, even probable, that Pissarro painted the factory several times in an effort to come to terms with industrial architecture using the traditional language of landscape. He wanted to place industry in his landscape. His earlier attempts, with the possible exception of *La Petite Fabrique*, had been timid and inconclusive. He preferred the semi-rural environment of L'Hermitage and Les Pâtis as the source of subjects for his synthetic landscape masterpieces of the 1860s, and his industrial landscapes painted in Bougival and Marly-le-Roi are rare. Although he lived near the latter towns, he chose to stay along the route de Versailles rather than to trudge down the steep hill for a day of industrial landscape painting along the Seine. It was only when industry entered so forcibly into his home environment in 1873 that he was provoked into this pictorial investigation of the modern factory.

The formal variety in the 1873 factory pictures indicates that they are not color studies or studies of an object captured at different times, as are so many of Monet's pictures representing an identical motif. Indeed, they seem to be painterly attempts to understand a form in a variety of formats. Although he was

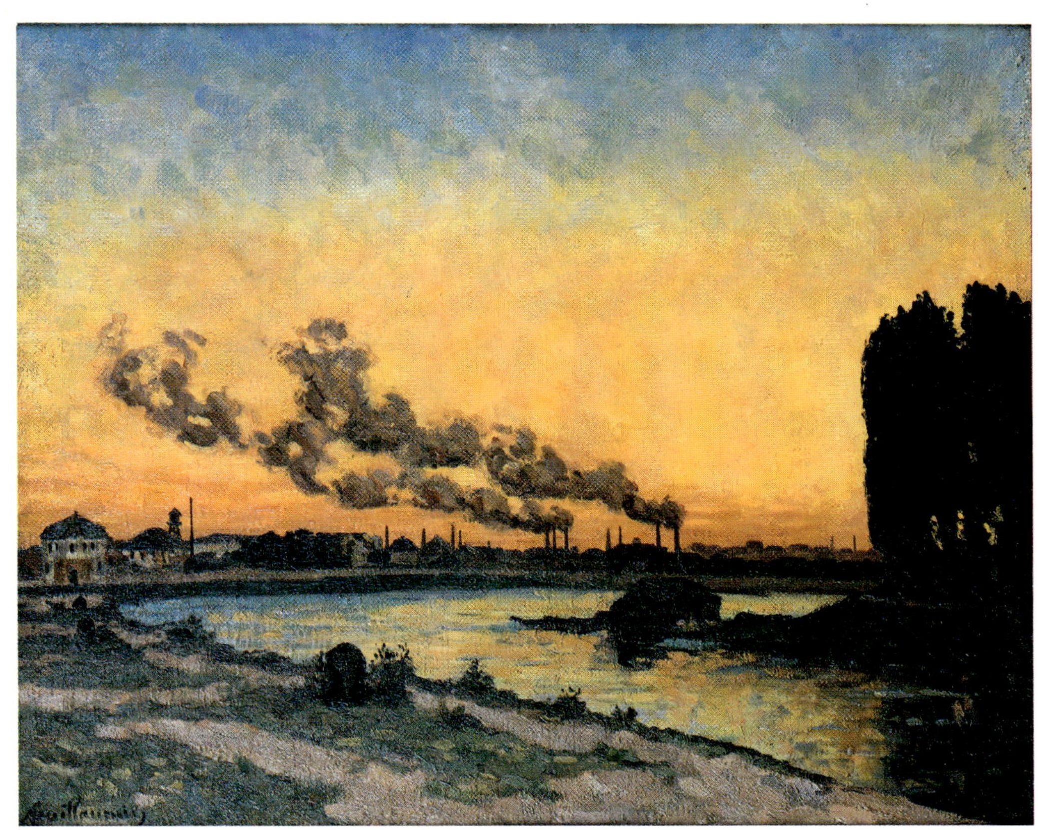

84. Armand Guillaumin, *Soleil couchant à Ivry*, *c*.1869, oil on canvas, 65 × 81cm., Musée d'Orsay, Paris.

81 (facing page top). *Intérieur d'une fabrique de savon de toilette*, from *La Nature*, Paris, 1874, vol. 2, p. 45.

82 (facing page center). *Marteau-pilon*, from Paul Poiré, *La France Industrielle*, Paris, 1880 (3rd edn.), p. 106.

83 (facing page bottom). *Machine à hacher le tabac*, from Paul Poiré, *La France Industrielle*, Paris, 1880 (3rd edn.), p. 283.

certainly not an intellectual, Pissarro was an intellectual painter. He analyzed forms and the relationships between forms in a detailed, almost grammatical fashion. His choice of a radically bounded landscape as *his* landscape gave him authority over a restricted range of form, from which, using existing and invented conventions, he created new landscape worlds. Yet, unlike many painters of his and later generations, he did not have a purely abstract approach to form. For Pissarro, the factory of Chalon et Cie. was a good deal more than a large form. These paintings suggest that he was interested in the idea of the factory as well as its form. For a realist painter of the 1870s, and especially for a painter of Pissarro's complex sensibilities, the two poles, form and idea (or content), were crucially interrelated.

The first indication of what would be Pissarro's ultimate artistic rejection of the new large-scale industry that the factory of M. Chalon clearly symbolized is *L'Oise aux environs de Pontoise* (pl. 75), the most attractive landscape of the 1873 group. In it, the factory re-enters the landscape. The river on which it is sited is a wide, leisurely diagonal leading into the picture, rather than a visual blockade. The viewer is given a reassuringly solid river bank from which to contemplate the picturesque, formally active group of factories. The older, more traditional *féculerie* is included in the landscape, although it is excluded from the other three pictures. The centrality and the whiteness of the factory are notable; the building anchors the landscape. The picture is, if anything, totally and refreshingly unproblematic. The factory is at home in the landscape, an element in a composed view rather than an icon to be analyzed and understood. The picture can be compared with the more comfortably traditional factory-scapes painted by Pissarro's good friend Guillaumin in the period 1869–73, most notably the *Soleil couchant à Ivry* (pl. 84), which was exhibited in the first Impressionist exhibition. Both Guillaumin and Pissarro viewed factories from a distance in the landscape. Their spectacular skies, a sunset for Guillaumin and icy blue clouds for Pissarro, dominate the landscapes. Nature holds her own against industry.

In the context of this study, the interest of *L'Oise aux environs de Pontoise* lies not in its relationship to the history of art but in its relationship to reality. Pissarro's alterations of the scale of recognizable forms have already been referred to, using as an example his diminution of the tower of Saint-Maclou in *Le Parc aux Charrettes* (pl. 38) of 1878. Many nineteenth-century critics discussed the process of enlargement of form in the making of a landscape painting.[31] Perhaps the most notable example is Philip Hamerton in his no-nonsense book entitled simply *Landscape*, published in 1885. Hamerton decried the heightening of mountains, the elongation of waterfalls, and other scalar exaggerations which he thought "Romantic" and opposed to the aim of landscape painting, which was, for him, the accurate depiction of significant natural scenery.[32] Yet neither Hamerton nor other critics mention the corresponding process of miniaturization or shrinkage that plays a large role in landscape painting, particularly for Pissarro. Forms of special interest are shrunk by Pissarro so that they become landscape elements rather than the motifs of the landscape.

There are several formal and psychological factors that contribute to the concept of "motif." The most obvious is scale. The motif must be large and conspicuous. It must overpower the background and dominate the space of the landscape. It must occupy the center of the picture, or at least court the center. It must be psychologically important. A tree is generally less potent than a human figure or a building. A church is more potent than a shop or a house. The centralization and the exaggerated scale of the apple tree in the famous *Potager et arbres en fleurs, printemps, Pontoise* of 1877 (pl. 159) are notable. Yet the question must be asked: is the tree the motif or is it a structural armature? The plethora of landscape objects that impinge on the formal existence of the tree impinge equally on its psychological importance, its "motifness." Clearly the tree is the motif of this landscape in a very partial sense. There is no reduction in the "motifness" of the factory in three of the four factory-scapes under discussion. The buildings in *Usine près de Pontoise* (pl. 71), *La Crue de l'Oise, Pontoise* (pl. 72), and *L'Usine à Pontoise* (pl. 74) are motifs. However, those in *L'Oise aux environs de Pontoise* are less motifs than objects. Pissarro, in his choice of a distant, three-quarter view and his inclusion of the *féculerie* has painted a complex arrangement of smaller industrial forms rather than a factory. He has both decentralized and diminished the factory relative to the environment. The factory is also diminished in the sense that Pissarro has made scalar alterations to the buildings relative both to each other and to their actual size. Cadastral maps of Saint-Ouen and Pontoise, as well as nineteenth-century postcards of L'Hermitage and of the site itself show that the new factory has been considerably reduced, more than halved in size, by Pissarro, and that it has been moved closer to the *féculerie* than it in fact was. The smokestack of the factory has been shrunk and the smokestack of the *féculerie* enlarged. The whole has been arranged so that the new factory appears to be behind the old one, rather than next to and almost in front of it along the river bank, thus further diminishing its importance. Pissarro has strengthened the older, smaller, and less prominent building and weakened the larger and more dominant one. To achieve a unity in his landscape, which demanded that the power of his motif be undercut and to a certain extent denied, Pissarro has altered the physical reality of his view markedly.

Clearly, the factory of M. Chalon both fascinated and, more importantly, disturbed Pissarro. His four pictures of it are attempts at comprehending modern industry by analyzing "the factory" as a form in itself and in the environment. His willful alteration of reality to suit pictorial conditions in the most attractive and conservative of the four paintings is evidence of a partial rejection of the factory, a rejection in which reality gives way to the conventions of landscape painting. Yet, an examination of Pissarro's later views of factories on the Oise will show an even stronger rejection.

The 1876 Group of Factory-scapes in Pontoise

The majority of Pissarro's later pictures of the factories along the Oise are large-scale river views in which the building plays a structural role as a distant object in the landscape. The tiny front shed of the complicated factory belonging to M. Arneuil is treated several times in isolation (P&V 219, 243, 250, 398, and two small pencil sketches of 1876–77 in the Ashmolean Museum, Oxford, B&L 99A and 100B). In all these pictures, Pissarro introduced only a very small part of a much larger establishment. The tiny shed with the tiny chimney has no importance in itself nor has it any potency in the landscape. It becomes a miniaturized symbol of industry along the banks of the Oise. The larger part of M. Arneuil's factory is allowed into only three landscape paintings. *Bords de l'Oise, Pontoise* (pl. 77) of 1873 depicts the factory as a rather stronger background element, but introduces a spatially and psychologically interesting foreground barge and a figure to counter the image of the building itself. The whole factory complex is depicted in only one picture, the panorama of Le Chou painted in 1878, *La Sente du Chou, Pontoise* (pl. 78), but here it is a mere element in a sweeping, spacious landscape.

After a hiatus of two years, devoted to the study of rural imagery, Pissarro began painting industrial scenes again in 1876. This year was an important one for Pissarro. He was shuttling between Montfoucault in Brittany and Pontoise, between a peasant and a modern landscape. He was active in the second Impressionist exhibition in April, opening himself again to the influence of the rest of the Impressionist group, especially Monet. He returned to Montfoucault after the exhibition to paint his most sustained series of harvest landscapes, including the oddly modern study of the threshing machine (P&V 367, collection of Lord Moyne) which he was to re-use nearly twenty years later in the *Travaux des Champs* (cf. B&L 376–78), the series of woodcuts from his own drawings on which he collaborated with his son, Lucien.

Pissarro returned to modern subjects in 1876, but his industrial landscapes of this year avoid any close connection with the industry they depict. Their evasiveness, their reticence can be seen most clearly in a group of five paintings that act, in many ways, as a response to the 1873 group. Their subject is the same factory on which Pissarro had focused in 1873, but this later group might be called "anti-motif" landscapes, and their oddness can be demonstrated by comparison with the earlier pictures.[33] Like the group of 1873, these five paintings are repeated images, re-exploring the same territory. Since none of the pictures in either the 1873 or the 1876 group was commissioned, they would appear to have been the result of Pissarro's doubts about modern industrial imagery.

The "easier" of the five landscapes are *Après la pluie, quai à Pontoise* (pl. 85) and *Le Quai du Pothuis à Pontoise (Hermitage)* (pl. 86). Although they are painted on canvases of the same size, the two pictures are not quite identical in composition. They were painted (or at least conceived) from the very long quai du Pothuis in Pontoise, looking upriver, across the Ile du Pothuis, toward the factory of Chalon

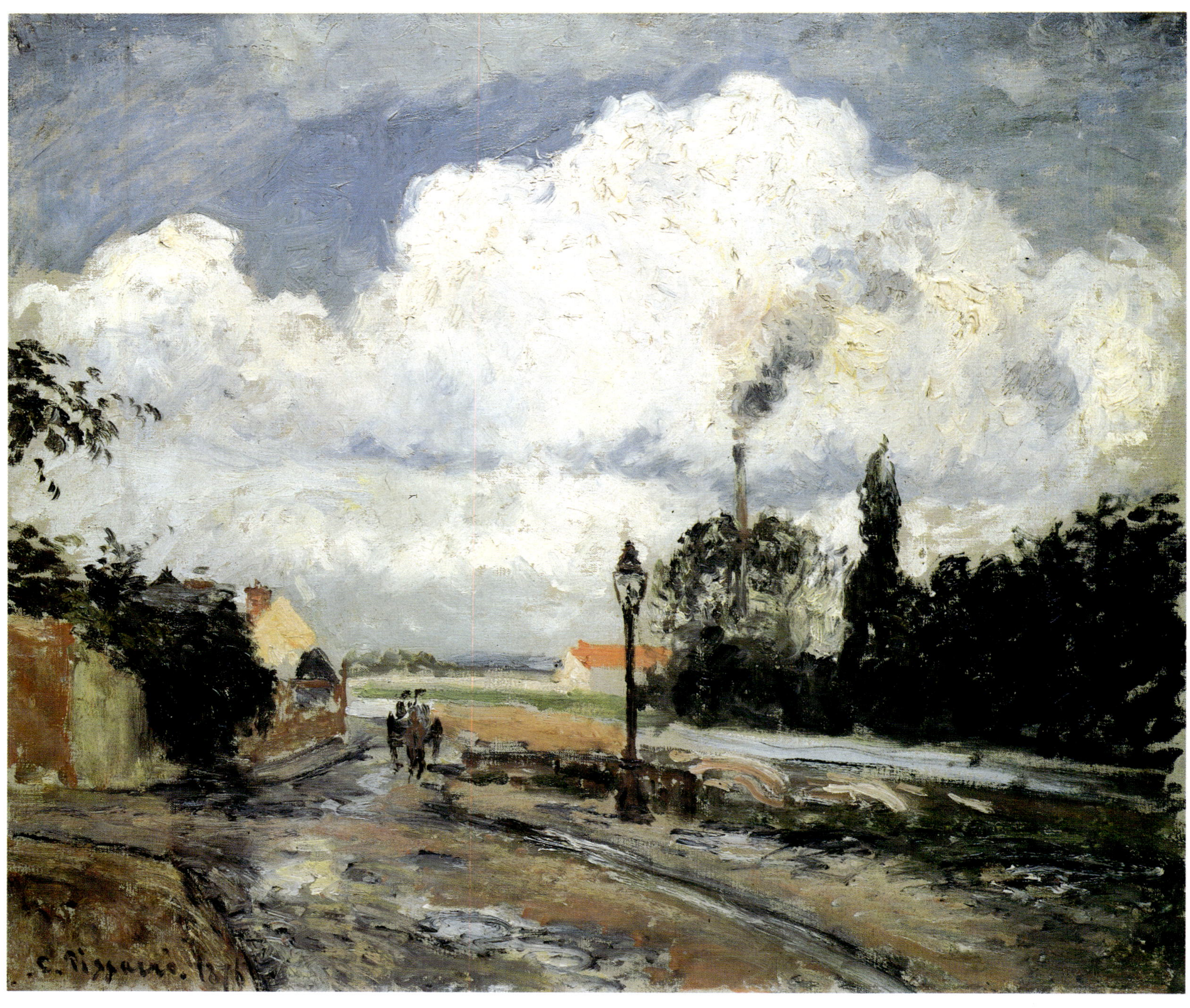

85. Camille Pissarro, *Après la pluie, quai à Pontoise* (P&V 355), 1876, oil on canvas, 46 × 55 cm., Whitworth Art Gallery, University of Manchester.

et Cie. In both pictures, the smokestack of the factory is an important vertical and background element. Yet, in contrast to the pictures of 1873, Pissarro placed himself in such a position that the prominent foliage of the Ile du Pothuis actually screens the factory buildings from view. As in other landscapes with factories painted in the same year and later, his emphasis is on the landscape rather than on the factory. In *Le Quai du Pothuis à Pontoise (Hermitage)*, the prominently centered barge and the complex forms of the domestic architecture on the quai du Pothuis impinge strongly on the pictorial importance of the smoldering smokestack. *Après la pluie*, which might be considered one of Pissarro's only witty landscapes, directs the viewer's attention to the centered lamppost, an element of progress that was certainly more visually innocuous than the smokestack with which it engages in a dialogue of verticals. These two pictures stand in direct formal and

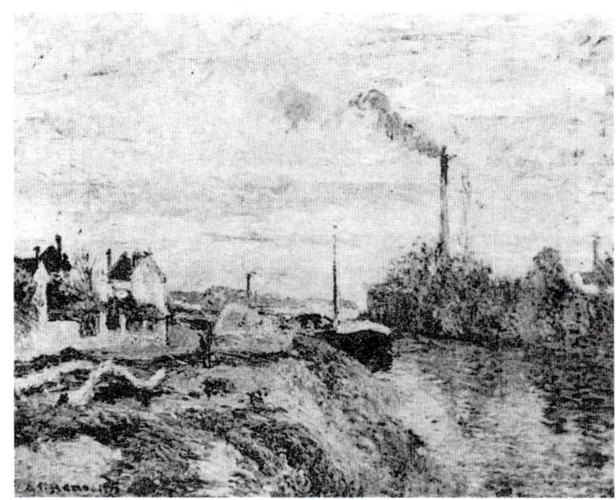

86. Camille Pissarro, *Le Quai du Pothuis à Pontoise (Hermitage)* (P&V 356), 1876, oil on canvas, 46 × 55.5cm., Sotheby's, New York (17 May 1990, lot 2).

87 (below left). Camille Pissarro, *L'Oise à Pontoise, temps gris* (P&V 353), 1876, oil on canvas, 53.5 × 64cm., Museum Boymans-van Beuningen, Rotterdam.

88 (below right). Camille Pissarro, *Bords de l'Oise, Saint-Ouen-l'Aumône* (P&V 354), 1876, oil on canvas, 55 × 65cm., whereabouts unknown.

iconological opposition to the series of 1873 (excluding, of course, *L'Oise aux environs de Pontoise*, pl. 75). In the earlier pictures, the foreground gives way to the middle ground. In the later pair, the space of the viewer is comfortable, ample, and clearly defined. In the background, the smokestack broods, a significant form overcome by almost trivial landscape details. The pictures represent in this way a contextual rejection of a once-powerful object. The factory is designified by its setting.

The remaining three paintings in the 1876 group are identically composed landscapes of the *féculerie* of M. Chalon (pls. 87 and 88). In painting them, Pissarro chose a spot on the towpath from which he had painted several earlier views of Pontoise itself. This time he looked upriver toward the two factories, old and new. (The viewpoint for this "trio" is almost directly across the river from the viewpoint of the pair just discussed.) As in the first two paintings of this group, Pissarro virtually centered his composition on the building, which is neatly framed by a strong lateral wall and by the foliage of the Ile du Pothuis. Only the smokestack is allowed "in" to Pissarro's group of three. He has hidden the large *usine* behind the *féculerie* which is, in itself, a bland, almost pre-modern industrial image not unlike that of *La Petite Fabrique* of 1863–65 or the *fabriques d'Italie* of the neo-classical landscape painter. All these pictures "crowd out" the same building that so confidently anchors the compositions of 1873. The 1876 group of three accepts the port, the small factory and the recently installed gaslight fixture, but not the *usine* with its canted roofs and brutal volumes. Unlike the 1873 group, all five of the 1876 landscapes are populated by variously occupied staffage figures, and the viewer is invited into the space of the landscape defined by diagonals.

Yet the meaning of the group of three within the later series is not easy to grasp. The paintings appear to contain a paradox. Pissarro has virtually omitted one factory and admitted, even emphasized another. The factories were owned by the same man. They were both involved in the distillation of local argicultural products and were, therefore, beneficial to the local economy in the same way, and both factories had been predominantly featured in Pissarro's pictures of the early 1870s.

The simplest explanation—that Pissarro thought the large factory ugly and

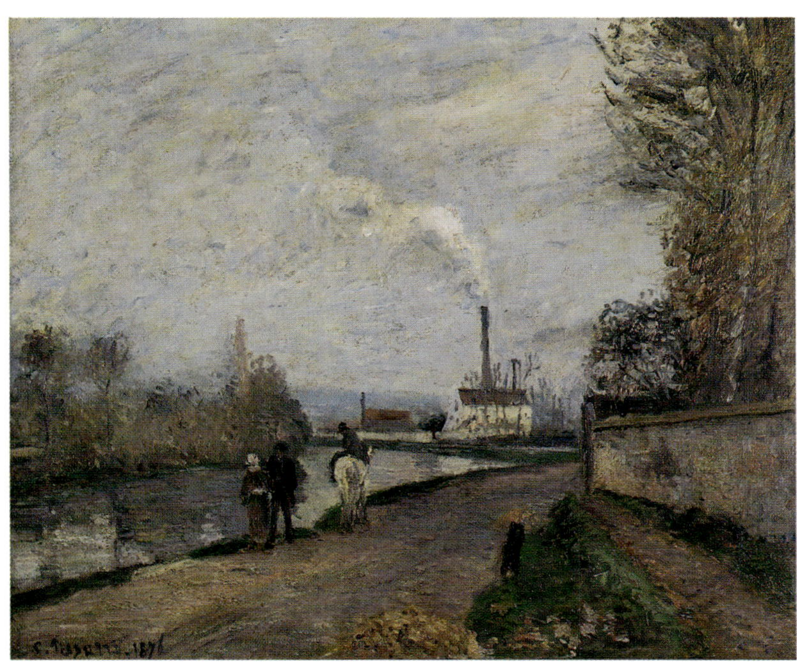

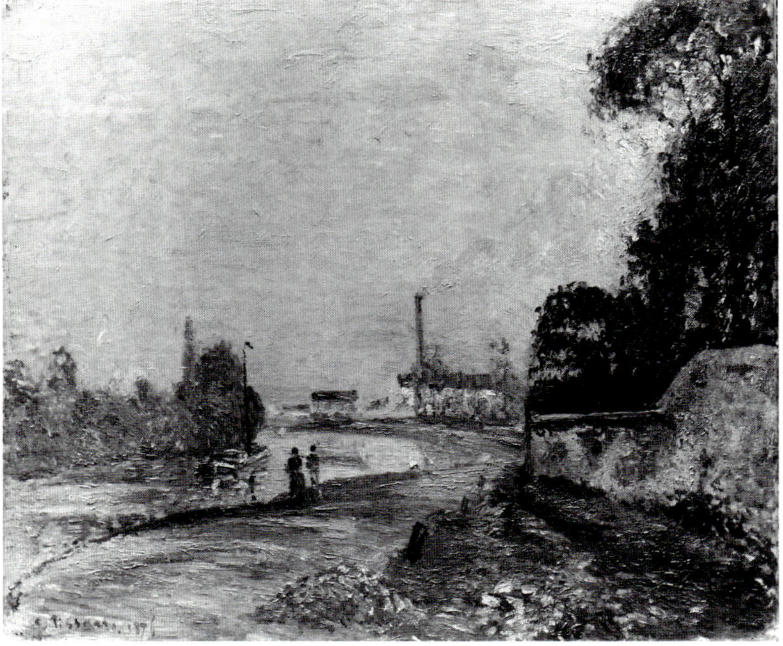

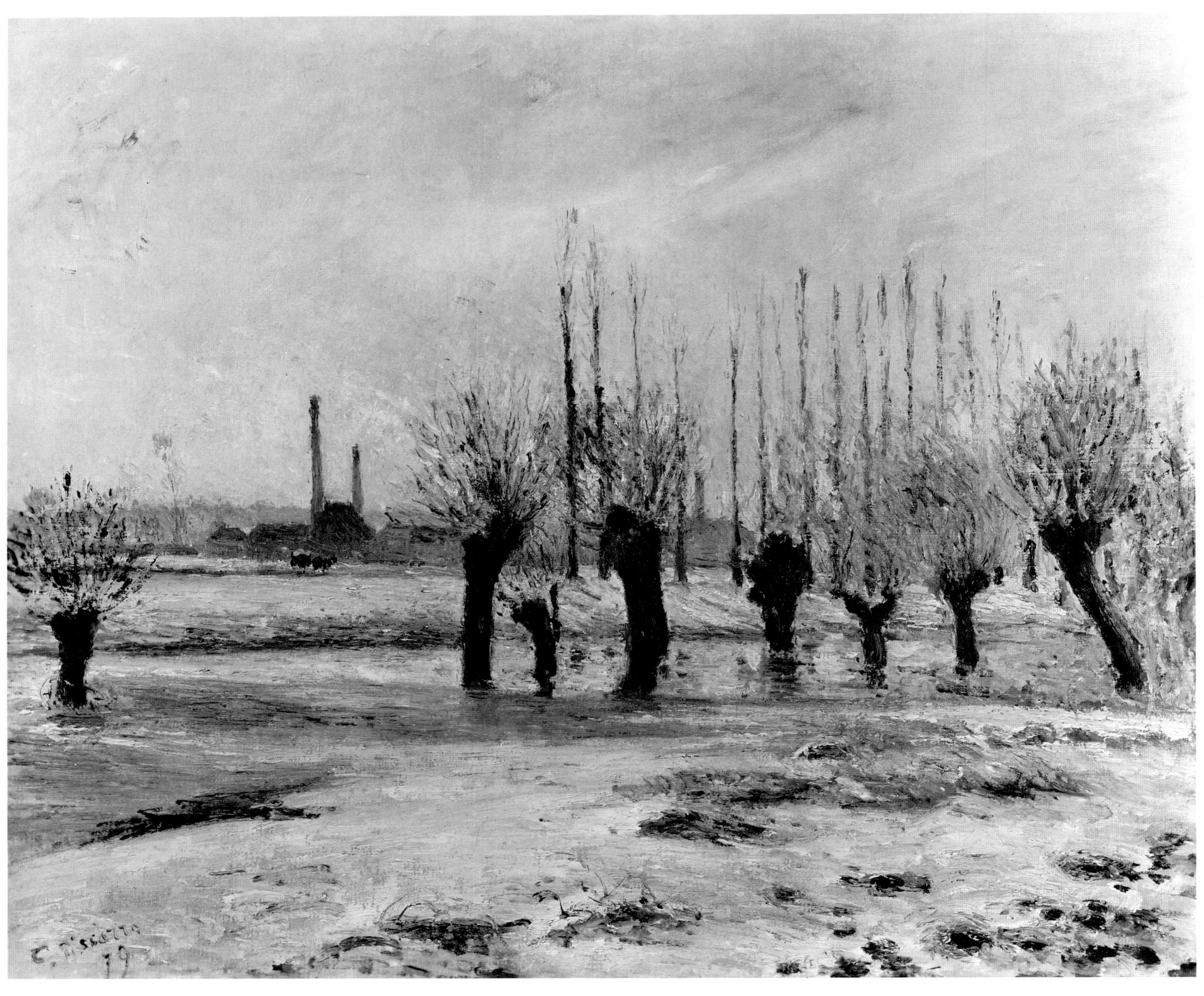

89. Camille Pissarro, *Effet de neige près Pontoise* (P&V 477), 1879, oil on canvas, 52 × 63.5cm., private collection, Switzerland.

therefore inappropriate to his pictorial aims—is not tenable, and perhaps the clearest way to explain his contextual rejection of the *usine* as well as the admission of the *féculerie* centers around the concept of motif. In painting this group of pictures, Pissarro composed a central motif landscape not unlike the three more distant views of the factory that he had painted in 1873. It would have been easy for him to compose a variety of landscapes from either side of the river that included only the traditional white *féculerie* built in 1871. He chose, however, to "banish" the larger factory from the illusionistic confines of his own landscape in a more important and provoking way. The three 1876 paintings do not represent a landscape in which the blighting feature existed just a bit to the right or to the left and therefore out of the painter's framed view; it was, as I have said, roughly in the center. If the landscape painter is a sort of minor god, as he was often considered to be in the nineteenth century, his creation must be in keeping with his tastes and inclinations. Pissarro, acting as a god, rejected the *usine* of M. Chalon from his difficult and evasive agro-industrial paradise.

Perhaps, in the final analysis, the word "rejected" is a little too emphatic, for, like all of Pissarro's omissions, this one was in some ways temporary. He did paint the whole factory complex once again in 1879. The picture, *Effet de neige près Pontoise* (pl. 89), is among the most masterful compositions painted by Pissarro in the 1870s. The roughly applied paint in the foreground gives the snow a massiveness and solidity, recalling the earlier winter landscapes of Courbet. The parallel rows of trees, one stunted and clipped for faggots and the other towering into the sky, define a landscape of screens slipping laterally through the frozen spaces of a winter day. The sky is cloudy and tinged with green and blue-green. The *usine* is a tiny background form, its smokestack made insignificant by the poplar trees, its mass overcome by the bulbous trunks of the foreground trees.

Living in a century in which industrial progress was considered vital to the drama of nation-building and of social elevation, Pissarro was suspicious of major industry. He was able to accept, even to glorify the smaller factories of the Oise, which he painted many times within the contexts of large and sympathetic landscapes. His artistic suspicion was reserved for the new *usine* of M. Chalon, but, as I have said, did not apply to the company itself. His argument can be interpreted as one concerned with scale. The small factories, rooted in village life, the modern outgrowth of the *petites fabriques*, so important in the landscape tradition, belonged to the rustic landscape. They and peasant markets and bourgeois houses find their place in his paintings. Indeed, if one can speak in economic terms, his landscape world is a world of petty capitalism. But he apparently rejected the emerging and soon-to-be-dominant large-scale industry, symbolized for him by M. Chalon's *usine*, a rejection that, in all probability, reflected Pissarro's attitude to modern industrial capitalism.

Pissarro's images of factories painted in the 1860s hover between two kinds of naturalism. They accept the inclusive world of the modern positivist by their very choice of subject, but they are certainly not the energetic and optimistic images found in travel books and magazines. Pissarro's selection of small industrial factories in predominantly rural contexts connects him to the classical landscape tradition more than to either the progressive modernism of his generation or the Romantic ruralism that dominated his profession. Like most landscape painters, Pissarro preferred the interaction of form to the forms themselves. The small-scale and physically complex world of the provincial town fascinated him. But the dominating, large-scale forms that characterized modern industrial architecture, and the domestic architecture of the socially ambitious bourgeoisie who controlled it, were antithetical to Pissarro's tastes, both pictorial and social.

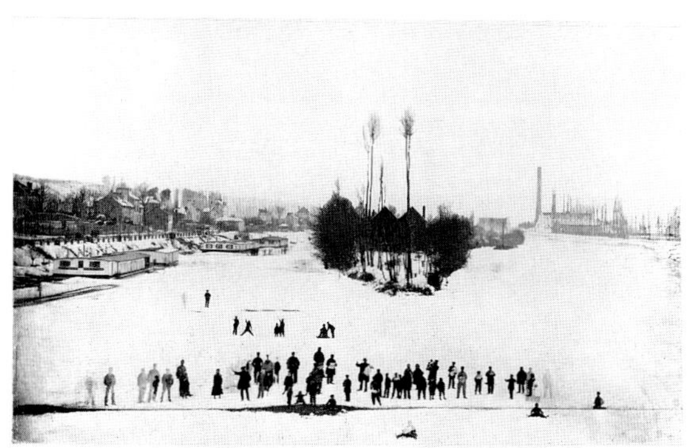

90. Pontoise, late 19th century, postcard, collection of M. Jean Hecquet, Paris.

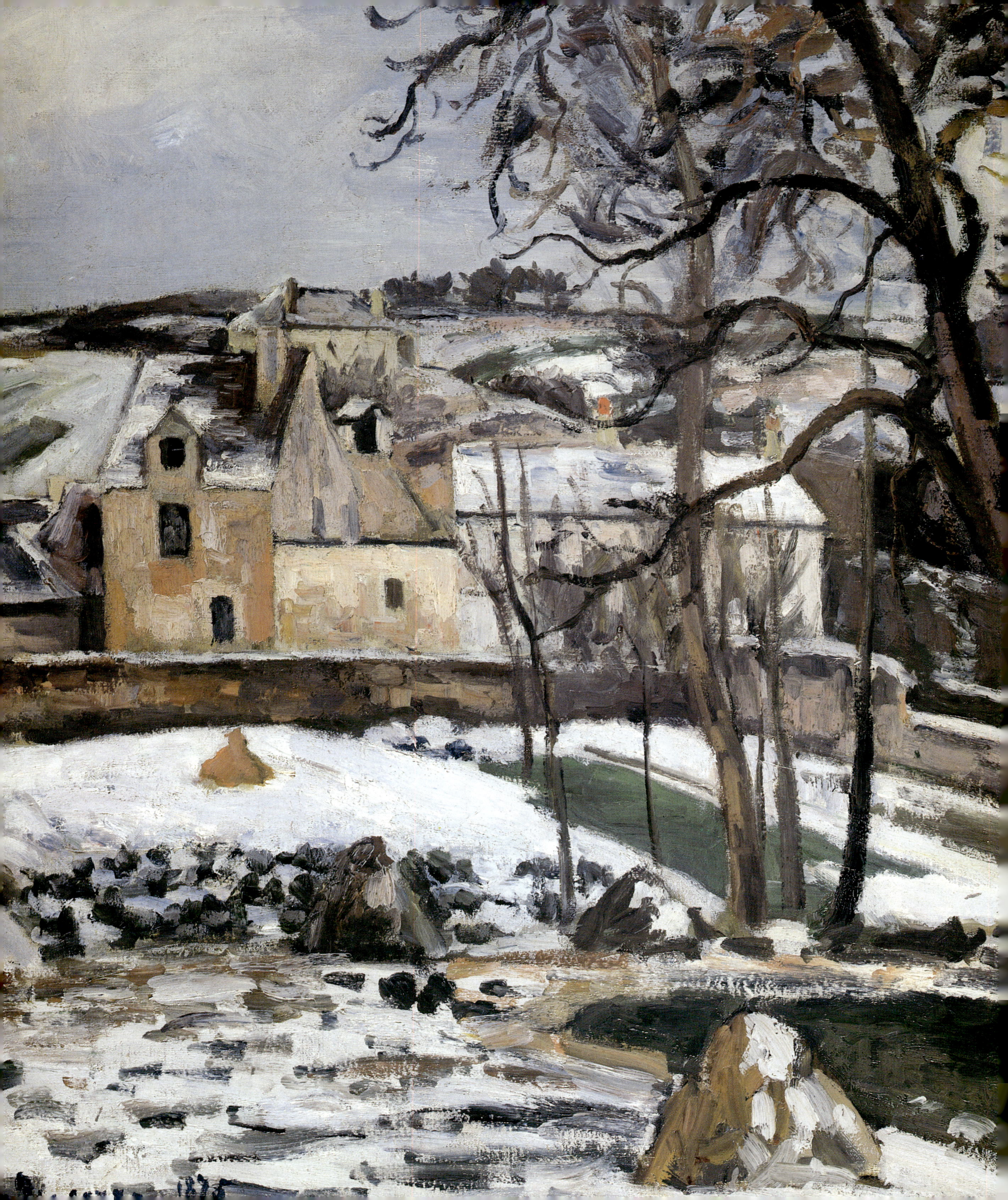

4 L'Hermitage: Home and the Landscape

The great majority of landscape paintings are travel images. They record the wanderings of modern western man across the surface of the earth. Their celebration is of roads, inns, cities, and vistas. They are alive to the possibility of movement and, by consequence, of escape from the pressures of urban life. The figures who inhabit the world of the landscape painter are wayfarers and travelers, free, for the most part, from worldly care and ambition. They stroll, rest, talk, draw, hunt, and amuse themselves, but they rarely work. The rooted, the domesticated landscape was, for all practical purposes, absent from the landscape production of the sixteenth, seventeenth, and eighteenth centuries. Residential architecture, at least of the ordinary varieties, is viewed through the eye of the passer-by, whose vision encompasses mills, inns, entire towns, glittering palaces, large country houses, and châteaux. This celebration of movement continued, of course, in the nineteenth century. Travel became more convenient, less expensive, and more widespread. The search for real paradises, lost cities, secluded natural environments, and intoxicating views that had characterized the work of painters as diverse as Frans Post, Jan Both, and Allart van Everdingen, was equally to be found in European landscape painting of·the nineteenth century. North American, English, French, and German artists traversed the surface of the earth recording the amazing landscapes they found. Valenciennes took the civilized world as his subject; Turner traveled throughout Europe; Corot wandered in Italy and France; Daubigny glided along the rivers of France in his *botin*. Even the Impressionist *promeneur*, walking slowly throughout the accessible paradise of the environs of Paris, must be seen as a continuation rather than a repudiation of this tradition. In many ways, the figures in fluttering dresses and walking suits painted by Monet, Sisley, and Renoir have their ancestry in the be-hatted and black-coated bourgeois travelers who populated the landscape worlds of the seventeenth century Dutch painters, and the railroad trains celebrated by artists from Turner to Monet are the modern progeny of the litters, carts, and carriages that are such evident features of seventeenth- and eighteenth-century landscape painting.

This travel tradition with its lateral spread out from the urban centers, across the earth, was countered in the nineteenth century by an equally strong pull back, a yearning for stability and for roots. *Nature, nation, naissance, natale*—these French words, used so often in nineteenth-century writings on landscape and modern civilization, have a basic etymological unity, a common ground in the concept of birth and origins. Personal roots provided the imaginative center for the work of many nineteenth-century French landscape painters. Enticed from their local milieux by ambition and accomplishment, they found themselves in what seemed and, no doubt was, a disinterested, sparkling, and unbridled Paris. Painters such as Courbet, Millet, and Cézanne grounded much of their imagery in the psychologically important world of the *pays natal*. The "nature" in their paintings reflected personal origins and familial ties. It was, somewhat paradoxically, but essentially, a nature of re-escape, of origins abandoned and resought. Courbet fled

91. Detail of pl. 113.

"

to Ornans and rooted his radical art of the 1850s in the region of his birth and in the portrayal of his own family. His *sauvage* manner was, like Cézanne's half a generation later, in opposition to the *politesse* of the capital which had provoked both the defiance and the brilliance of the young and proudly untrained provincial. Monet's persistent wanderings throughout the north of France in the 1870s were countered by his devotion, both pictorial and personal, to his young wife, Camille, and to the life of the garden and the house they shared.[1] And Pissarro's landscape of the 1870s is among the most physically constricted in the history of art, rarely extending more than 500 meters from his doorstep.

Yet the idea of the familial and the familiar landscape world is beset with complications. In general, the personal landscapes of the great nineteenth-century painters were of two types. The first was geographical – the pictorial home of the landscape painter was the area around his actual home. The second was iconographical – the landscape of the painter was a domestic one filled with images of homes, of daily life, of continuity. Courbet's and, to a great extent, Cézanne's pictorial homes were of the former type. They are familiar landscapes that were found within the area of the *pays natal*. Courbet's Ornans landscapes are rarely domestic. They are, more often, natural worlds that lack significant architectural and human presence. The landscapes of Constable, Millet, and Pissarro, however, are more iconographically domestic.[2] They are habitual worlds: domestic architecture predominates; the acts of daily life, in their oddly refreshing repetitiveness, are being carried out by the staffage figures. They are restricted worlds, free from the novelty and the sense of the unexpected that are so evident in the travel landscape tradition.

An explanation for Pissarro's fixation with a domestic landscape can be found in his own life. His childhood as the son of a success-conscious businessman was difficult, multilingual, and rootless. His home in St. Thomas, Virgin Islands, lacked a wholeness and stability to which he could turn for psychological and esthetic solace. He was raised in a French-speaking family in a predominantly Spanish- and English-speaking colony belonging to Denmark. His schooling was in Passy, now part of Paris, thousands of miles from his parental home. His later escape to Venezuela was made in the company of a young Danish painter. Compared with the lives of Chintreuil, Courbet, Millet, Monet, and Cézanne, Pissarro's childhood and young adulthood were much more problematic. His home environment had neither cultural nor linguistic unity. His family life as a child was incomplete and brief.

As if in response to this rootless, even homeless existence, Pissarro's landscapes form a succession of personalized worlds, of homes. Only the cities of Rouen, Le Havre, Dieppe, and Paris, which he began to paint intensively after 1883, are exceptions and are presented in esthetic opposition to the rural worlds dominated by his family and home. His trips were few, and his letters suggest that he disliked travel – that he disliked, that is, to be away from home.[3] His early visits to Paris were comparatively rare, solitary, and short, made for business reasons. He did not turn to that city as an important source of pictorial motifs until the 1890s. In fact, the majority of the paintings done in his Paris studio on the rue des Trois Frères in the late 1870s are interior family portraits, and his later Paris views were not painted from public places but from his hotel room. Like Constable's, Pissarro's environment was only alive to him if it was a personalized one. His journeys were not escapes, as were Monet's and Courbet's, but visits to friends or members of his family. His many paintings of England are the result of his sojourn there with his family in the early 1870s and of his later visits to his son Lucien. His choice of Montfoucault as an artistic base was motivated by the desire

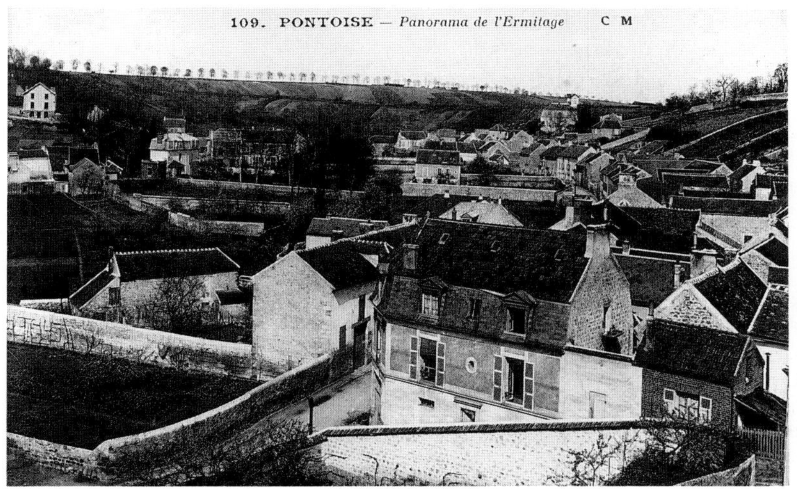

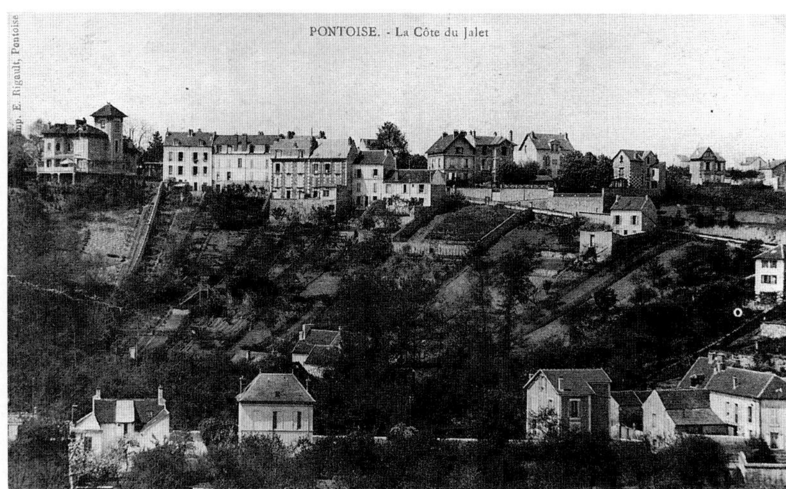

92. Panorama of L'Hermitage, Pontoise, late 19th century, postcard, collection of M. Jean Hecquet, Paris.

93. The Côte du Jallais, Pontoise, late 19th century, postcard, collection of M. Jean Hecquet, Paris.

to visit the home of his friend Piette where he might counter the rejection and financial disappointment of the first Impressionist exhibition by grounding his art in a real rural milieu. His paintings of the traditional artist's town, Moret, near Fontainebleau, did not mark a return to a famous mid-century site, but. were rather the result of a visit to his son Georges; and his depictions of the Norman coast near Dieppe were prompted by the invitation of his friend Octave Mirbeau who had a country house on the coast. Unlike Monet and Renoir, Pissarro did not make trips in search of motifs. He painted the world around him, the comforting and domestic world of personal connections. Unlike Monet and Renoir, Pissarro professed a complete indifference to the colorful and exotic attraction of the Mediterranean coast. He even turned down Cézanne's invitation to come to stay with his family in Aix-en-Provence.

It seems clear that Pissarro considered L'Hermitage rather than Pontoise itself to be his home. With the exception of the very brief period of 1872 when the family resided in the house at 16 rue Malebranche near the Jardin public, all the Pissarro addresses in Pontoise were in L'Hermitage. There is little pictorial and no documentary evidence of Pissarro's interest in the other semi-rural areas surrounding the town of Pontoise. L'Hermitage was the only part of Pontoise on which he lavished his attentions, and his pictorialization of it is, without doubt, the most concentrated examination of a small place in the history of landscape painting. Never have so many paintings sprung from so small a landscape.

Pissarro's L'Hermitage is more remarkable for its iconographical than its geographical domesticity. It was not only physically small, but, when compared with the sites of other landscape painters, it was also unusually densely populated (pl. 92). There were few empty spaces and no uninterrupted expanses. Homes filled the valleys and crept up the hillsides (pl. 93). It would have been all but impossible to find a framed landscape within it that had neither figures nor houses, and Pissarro never did. An escape from the populated landscape of the town or the city was not possible in L'Hermitage; it was a crowded landscape in which the solitary human presence that played such an important part in Romantic landscape tradition was overtaken by the social context. The cool woods and stormy seas of Courbet, the sublime mountains of Turner, Michelet, Reclus, and Cézanne, the anti-human quality of Monet's rocks at Belle-Isle and his cliffs at Etretat – these landscapes of escape in which nature is seen in opposition to the world of man are antithetical to Pissarro's L'Hermitage. In Pissarro's landscape, people lived together, united against the emptiness of nature.

For all its physical isolation within its own bounded landscape, L'Hermitage was and had always been an appendage to Pontoise itself. It is probable that the formation of the hamlet was a late eighteenth-century phenomenon, coinciding with the rural improvement that occurred throughout the Vexin area at the end of the *ancien régime*.[4] A quick look at any of the eighteenth-century maps of Pontoise reveals a single row of buildings along the unnamed Côte des Grouettes and several winding roads and paths (pl. 7). The L'Hermitage that Pissarro knew consisted of these buildings and paths, as well as the very straight Second Empire street, rue de L'Hermitage. This latter road, on which at least two of the Pissarro family houses were located, was new in almost every way and contrasted markedly with the older and renamed rue du Fond de L'Hermitage on which the family lived between 1866 and 1868. The old L'Hermitage had been the dwelling place of market gardeners and small farmers as well as the growers for the Pontoise wine market, which retained its importance until the mid-nineteenth century. Their houses stood between the rich loam gardens of the valley and the steeper, drier, and sunnier vineyards on the Côte des Grouettes. The houses huddled together. Their barnyards were constricted. There were no ornamental flower gardens and no front yards. They abutted the street, conserving all the available land in the valley and along the restricted hillsides for cultivation. While the rue du Fond de L'Hermitage clung to the edge of the hillside, the new rue de L'Hermitage cut through much of the central garden lands with a ruthless linearity. Unlike the older street, it was lined shortly after its construction in the early 1860s with new commercial establishments and larger *maisons bourgeoises*. These houses stood back from the street in the middle of ornamental gardens that usurped the same garden land that the peasant houses had tried so hard to conserve. The houses themselves and the gardens that surrounded them were hidden from the prying eyes of the passers-by by large stone walls and protective gates. These walled rectangles contrasted clearly with the usually communal patchwork of plots in the larger garden area that ran along the rue du Fond de L'Hermitage.

As is obvious from this description, the L'Hermitage of Pissarro's day presented two aspects: peasant hamlet and suburb. These two worlds existed in tight and moderately successful juxtaposition. Each way of life was represented by a street. The rue de L'Hermitage had cafés, a shop, and gas street lamps by 1867 or 1868.[5] The rue du Fond de L'Hermitage had none of these amenities. Each of the streets maintained its own landscape, its own character, and stood on its own side of the valley. Pissarro's home environment embodied the very social tensions between old and new, rural and urban, peasant (or semi-peasant) and bourgeois that were such a marked characteristic of his age. Although it was a domestic and, at least to some extent, a rural landscape, L'Hermitage was also a modern and modernizing landscape.

It is in the period of the late 1860s and early 1870s, when L'Hermitage was being transformed from agrarian hamlet into modern suburb, that Pissarro became fascinated with images of a modernizing rural landscape. His acceptance of both the traditional and the modern aspects of such an environment is notable, and is reflected in his choice of obviously dualistic sites for his landscape paintings. The mistitled *Paysage à Pontoise* (P&V 309, Musée d'Orsay), of 1869–70 (actually painted at Louveciennes, and previously misdated to 1875) is a clear case in point.[6] The subject is intensely traditional, a farm in the landscape. The long rectangular format is reminiscent of Daubigny. A screen of trees on the left is clearly Corotesque, as is the pretty figure of a young peasant girl watching her goats while dangling her feet in a stream. Yet in contrast to these bucolic images,

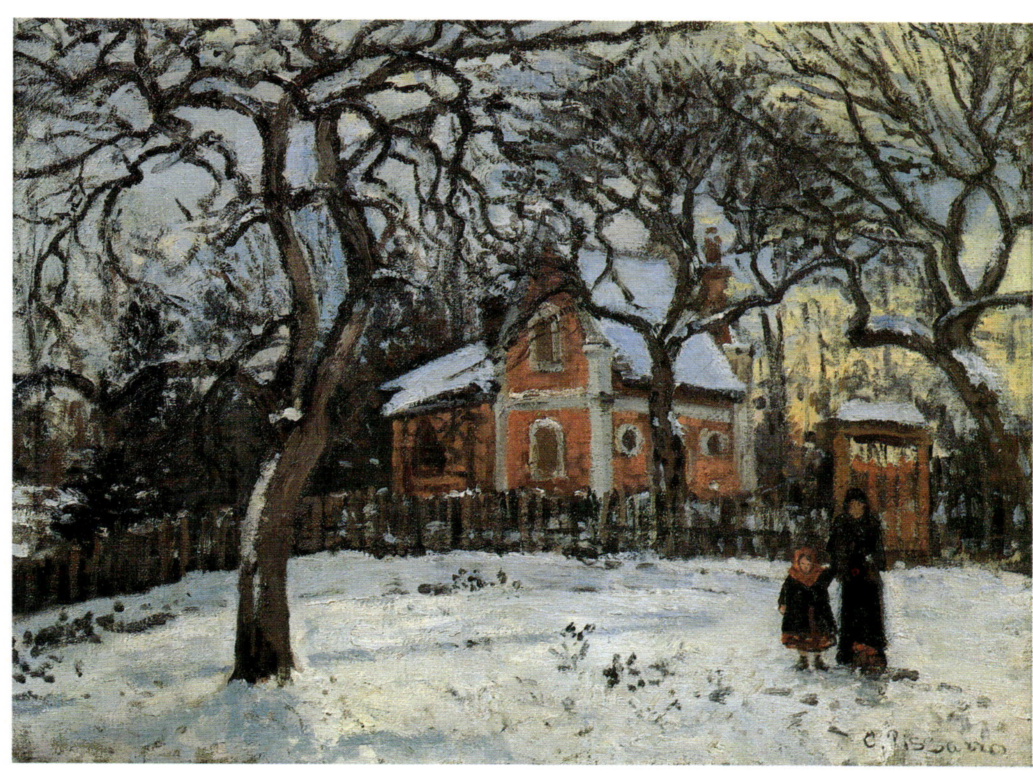

94. Camille Pissarro, *Châtaigniers à Louveciennes*
(P&V 146), *c*.1872, oil on canvas, 40 × 54cm.,
Musée d'Orsay, Paris.

the landscape is marred by a large construction site in the middle ground, and the
field is gouged with the fresh ruts of wagon wheels.

New bourgeois country houses also became a feature of the Pissarro landscape
in the Louveciennes pictures of the early 1870s and demonstrate Pissarro's acute
awareness of urban encroachment upon the countryside. *Le Châlet, la maison rose*
(P&V 82, Musée d'Orsay) depicts a brilliant-red house in the center of a cultivated
landscape. *Châtaigniers à Louveciennes* (pl. 94), also datable to the period 1871–72,
is a portrayal of Pissarro's favorite group of chestnut trees in Louveciennes with
the backdrop of another red house and two rather "posed" bourgeois figures. The
brilliantly composed *Village de Voisins* (P&V 139, Musée d'Orsay) of 1872 sports
another bourgeois house, several gates to more extensive properties, and a face-
less but well-dressed female stroller. Pissarro's pictures of Louveciennes vacillate
clearly between the bourgeois landscape of the route de Versailles and the peasant
landscape of the older road parallel to it, both of which were visible from his front
yard. Pissarro recorded the changes in this very socially fragile landscape more
fully than any landscape painter of his generation.[7]

The implications of these remarks is that Pissarro was a painter who understood his environment, who was open to both its aspects, traditional and modern.
Yet, this is only partially true. Any careful look at Pissarro's actual life in L'Hermitage coupled with a close examination of his pictures of it reveals that he was
more distant from his own home environment than virtually any nineteenth-
century landscape painter. Pissarro's interest in L'Hermitage was more often
formally than iconologically motivated. Pissarro did not treat L'Hermitage as the
environment it was, depicting its changes of mood and its enormous physical
complexity. L'Hermitage *in toto* was never a pictorial motif. In fact, his pictorialization of it is closely related to the more restricted concept, *coin*. Rather than
painting L'Hermitage, Pissarro painted certains "coins de L'Hermitage" which,
for many reasons that evade the historian's grasp, he found picturable.

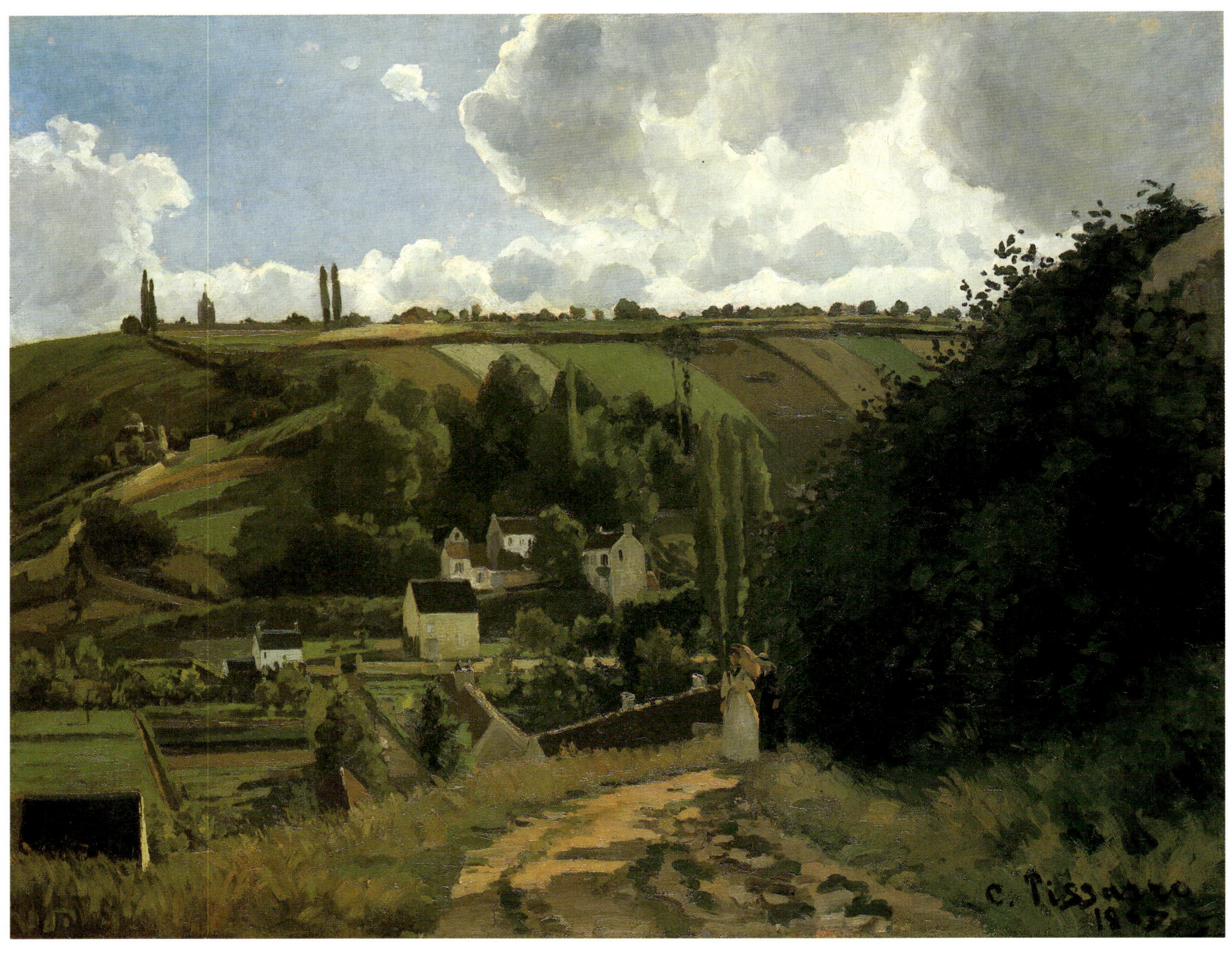

95. Camille Pissarro, *La Côte du Jallais, Pontoise* (P&V 55), 1867, oil on canvas, 87 × 115cm., Metropolitan Museum of Art, New York; bequest of William Church Osborn.

Coin, which means literally "corner," is a fundamentally elusive and informal landscape term which was used widely throughout the middle and late nineteenth century.[8] *Coin* lacks the importance or even the singularity of "motif." It is less positively forceful, more arbitrary. Many painters sought out picturesque *coins* of well-known sites to avoid the obvious and previously depicted motifs favored by conventional landscape painters. This attitude toward the landscape pervades Pissarro's oeuvre, with the arguable exception of the late urban pictures painted in Rouen and Paris. He preferred the little-known, the informal aspects of landscape. His reasons for this preference were, I think, twofold. First, he desired originality and wanted to avoid close competition with other landscape painters. In a letter to Lucien of 21 August 1885, he hints at his attitudes toward forceful or established motifs: "You mentioned a study on which you have begun to work, of *Les Graves*, a motif that Guillemet, the Daubignys (father and son) as well as many others have painted. But alas, how it has been interpreted! I doubt whether you will be able to do much work; tranquility and reflection coupled with a

104

passion for one's subject are necessary for good work."[9] This is suggestive and a little vague. Pissarro indicates his desire to paint original or fresh motifs rather than reinterpreting the motifs of others, yet his use of the word "passion" in this connection is surprising to the careful student of his work. If there is one major element lacking in Pissarro's esthetics, it is passion. His attitudes to his own motifs, as revealed in either his letters or his pictures, do not show much evidence of passion. He failed to repeat motifs enough to suggest passion by infatuation and, when he did include a powerful motif, he persistently used pictorial devices designed to deny its power.

In fact, the lack of passion in Pissarro's landscapes underlies another reason for his preference for *coins* more than motifs. The *coin* lacks strong meaning: it is an odd, framed portion of an environment and is, by definition, part of a larger whole. The painter, in choosing a *coin*, is not constrained so clearly as he is when he depicts a recognizable motif. His painting need not be as faithful or as accurate in its rendition of the subject. The *coin* landscape is contrastable not only with the motif landscape but with the *vue* landscape so often considered to be the predominant Impressionist landscape mode. The *vue* is not a formal or focused landscape, but a lateral extension of land, that is, *land-scape*. Its visual inclusivity is opposed to the intrinsic exclusivity of *coin* landscapes. Among all of Pissarro's depictions of L'Hermitage, there is not one general view of the quarter. His *Côte du Jallais, Pontoise* (pl. 95) and *Vue de L'Hermitage, Côte du Jallais, Pontoise* (pl. 96) are rather limited attempts at a panoramic sweep or view. They are too insistently ordered, too rigidly concerned with matters compositional, with the interlocking of the parts of the landscape, to pay much attention to spatial extension. Other landscapes from the surrounding *côtes* looking down into L'Hermitage are screened, particularized, and often highly distorted depictions of the quarter. Depicting the whole environment of L'Hermitage never interested Pissarro; he did not stand back and project his painterly gaze over it as he did over the plains of Vexin, over the Oise river, or over the Champs de Saint-Martin in the early 1870s. He did not, in short, observe L'Hermitage as Adolphe Joanne advised in

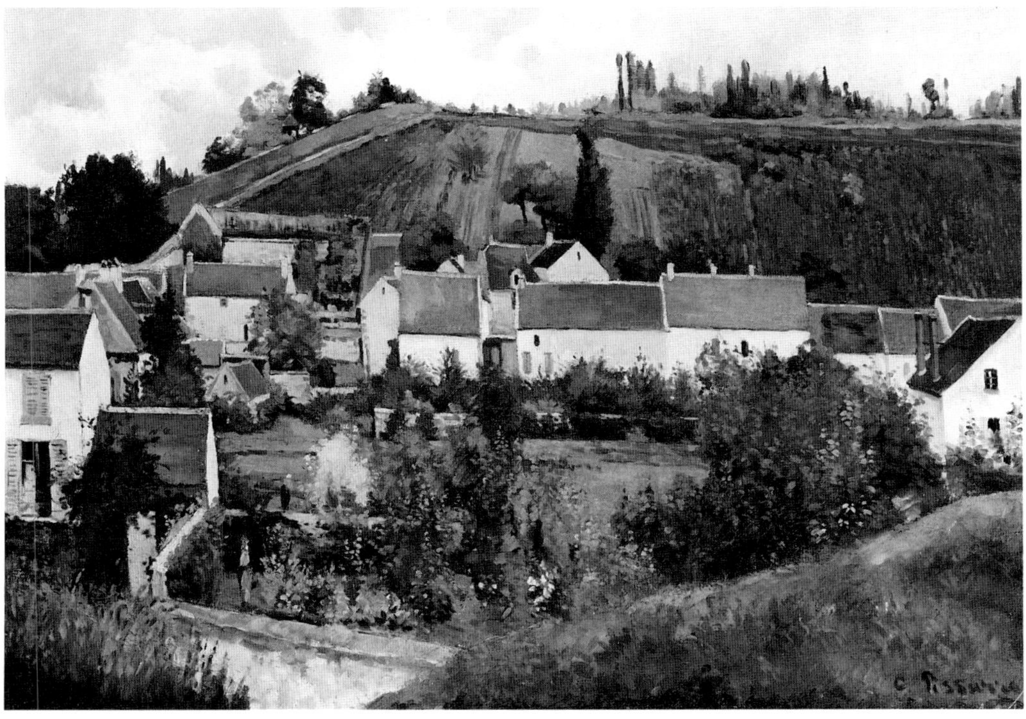

96. Camille Pissarro, *Vue de L'Hermitage, Côte du Jallais, Pontoise* (P&V 57) *c.*1867–68, oil on canvas, 70 × 100cm., private collection.

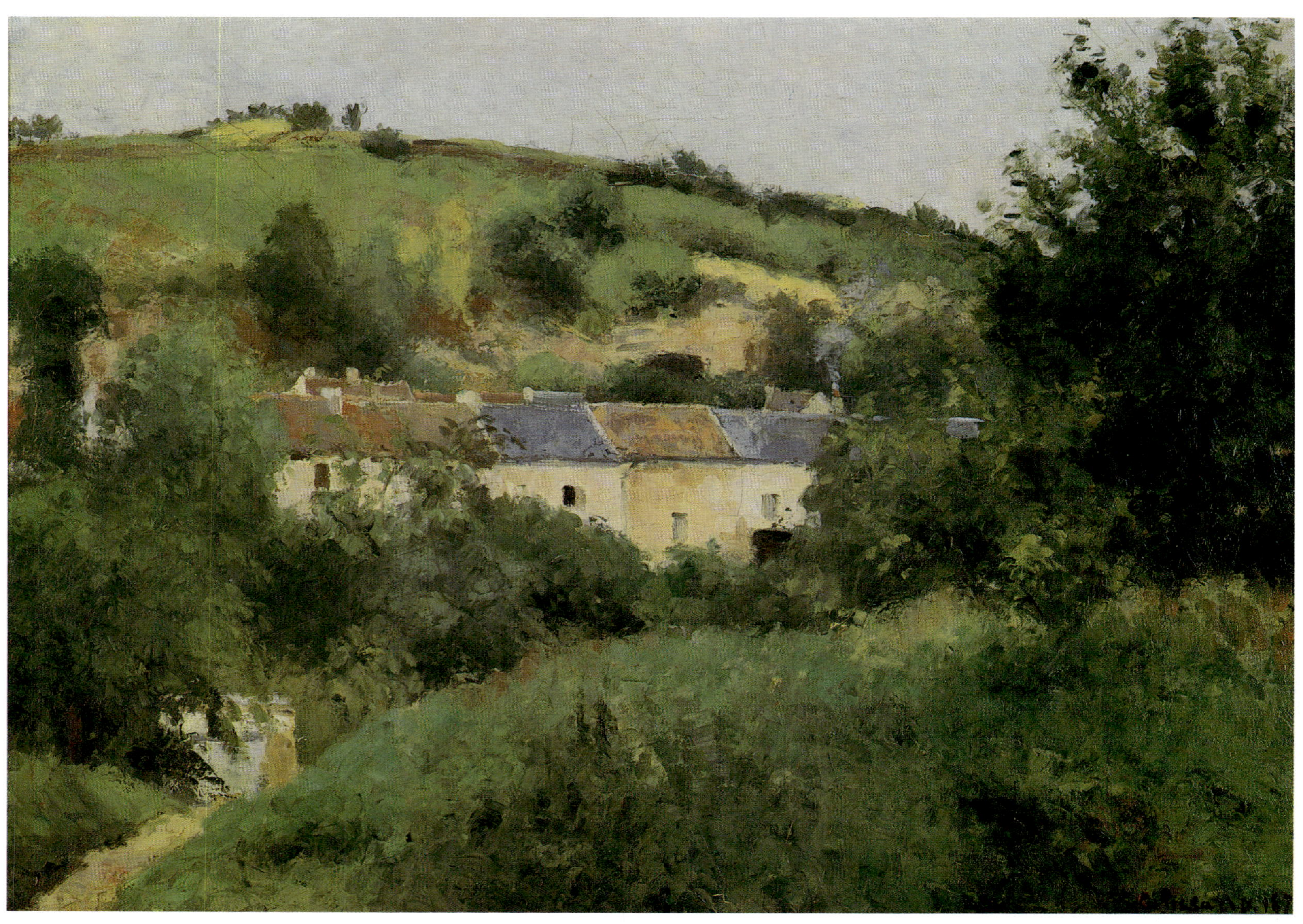

97. Camille Pissarro, *Le Sentier du village* (P&V 310),
1875, oil on canvas, 39 × 55.5cm., Rudolf Staechelin'sche Familienstiftung, Basel.

his guidebook. Joanne recommended the hamlet not for its architecture, its small
river, or its fields, but for the variety of views obtainable from its various steep
hillsides. This recommendation was endorsed by the many contemporary postcard views of L'Hermitage, but, after his first Pontoise period of 1866–68, Pissarro avoided those *vues* with singular persistence.[10]

The rue du Fond de L'Hermitage was densely populated, complex, and intensely
traditional. Its appearance was little different from that of one of the streets in
the ancient and nearby village of Ennery. Its houses were smaller versions of the
famous courtyarded farms for which the Région Parisienne is famous. Small
yards, tiny walled and terraced gardens, and concentrations of gabled shed-like
structures gave the street a picturesqueness lacking in the newer, wider, and more
convenient rue de L'Hermitage. Yet Pissarro painted the rue de L'Hermitage at
least seven times and never painted the rue du Fond de L'Hermitage except from a
distant vantage point. (Two canvases depicting the same scene in the autumn and
winter [P&V 209 and 238] probably represent the group of eighteenth-century
houses in which the artist lived in these years; they are certainly as close in spirit
to the rue du Fond de L'Hermitage as Pissarro ever came.) Pissarro's deemphasis
of this street is strange, particularly since its rural architecture is virtually identical

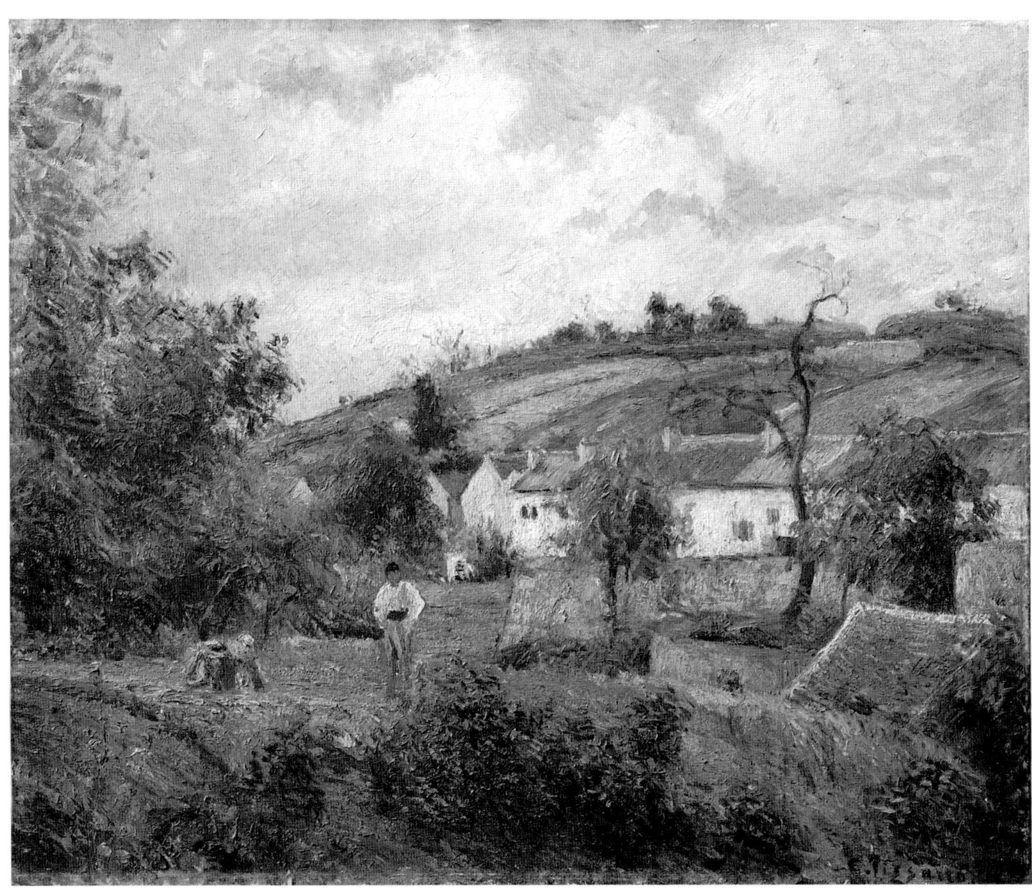

98. Camille Pissarro, *L'Hermitage, Pontoise* (P&V 447), 1878, oil on canvas, 55 × 65.5cm., Öffentliche Kunstammlung Basel, Kunstmuseum.

both to that he portrayed in the early 1860s and to that of the streets of Le Valhermeil and Chaponval which interested him in 1873 and 1880. Again, we confront an omission in Pissarro's apprehension of the landscape, and one of considerable proportions.

In many ways, the rue du Fond de L'Hermitage *was* L'Hermitage. Its inhabitants had been rural laborers and small landowners since the eighteenth century and continued to work the gardens and plots in the region in spite of the industrial encroachments and the resulting labor drain of the late nineteenth century. The population of L'Hermitage was concentrated along this street. The oldest families and the most established of its inhabitants lived there. Its yards, domestic interiors, and gardens would have provided ample pictorial matter for Millet or Lhermitte, but they were virtually ignored by Pissarro. The most baffling thing about this omission is that it seems to have been reserved for L'Hermitage itself. Pissarro *did* paint barnyards, peasant interiors, harvest scenes, and other aspects of peasant life in several key periods during the 1870s, but he simply did not paint them in L'Hermitage. Montfoucault provided the source for the majority of these depictions of pre-modern rural life. Pissarro avoided the traditional and the rural *only* in his own home landscape.

Pissarro rarely discussed his surroundings in his correspondence, and, as is often the case with this most complicated of painters, the explanation for this odd and deliberate omission must be sought in the pictures themselves.[11] *Le Sentier du Village* (pl. 97) of 1875 portrays the houses of the rue du Fond de L'Hermitage from a viewpoint on the pathway that leads from the rue de L'Hermitage to the rue Victor-Hugo on the Côte Saint-Denis. He created an imaginary scene in which the foreground slope of the hill rises slightly so that it screens the newer

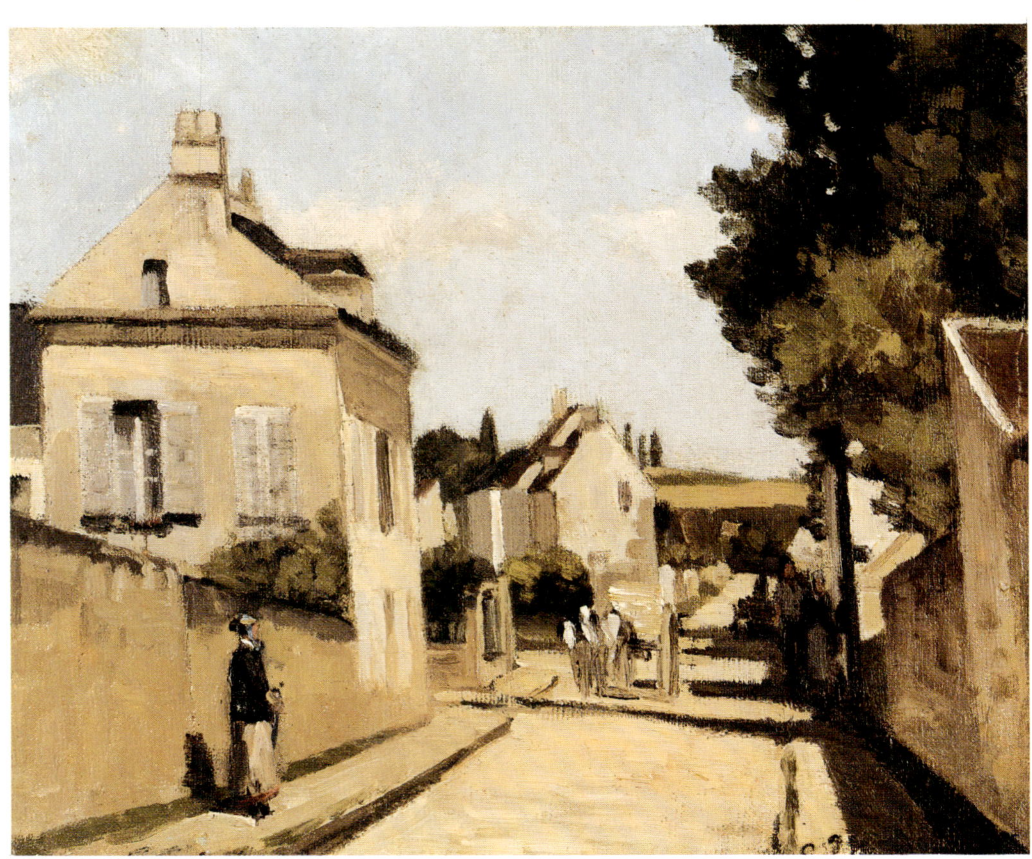

99: Camille Pissarro, *Rue de L'Ermitage, c.*1866–68, oil on canvas, 32 × 40cm., private collection.

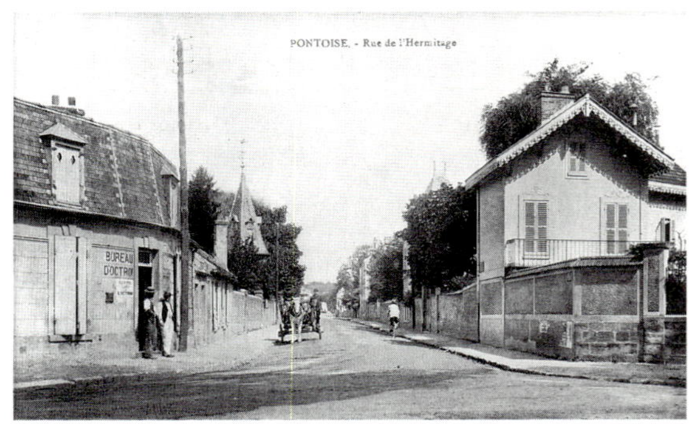

100. Rue de L'Hermitage, Pontoise, late 19th century, postcard, collection of M. Jean Hecquet, Paris.

buildings on the rue de L'Hermitage (which it, in fact, does not do) and then added the clustered foliage that screens the ends of the rue du Fond de L'Hermitage and forces it to become a long central band around which the palette-knife vegetation circulates. What interested Pissarro about the rue du Fond de L'Hermitage was not its peasant-genre aspect or its existence as a "scenic fact," to borrow a phrase from Champa, but its structural linearity. The structural aspect of the street plays a major role in the landscape composition. *L'Hermitage, Pontoise* (pl. 98) of 1878 and *L'Hermitage à Pontoise, effet de neige* (P&V 341) of 1876 treat the rue de Fond de L'Hermitage similarly as a structural band that organizes the pictorial surface.

Locus and Genius Loci

Geoffrey Hartman, in his series of essays on Wordsworth, discusses what Wordsworth calls "spots" in nature that have a peculiar emanative power for the poet and to which he directs his art.[12] The notion is a particularly fruitful one, I think, for analysis of landscape imagery. The poet or painter who is "spot-fixated" attaches his attention to a precise place which has for him a *genius loci*, a spirit of place. Pissarro's locative precision, the exactness of many of his landscape titles, suggests that he too was susceptible to a *genius loci*, that he was esthetically swayed by the power of particular "spots" or places in nature.

For the painter of the *genius loci*, subjectively significant spots (historians of landscape would probably use the word motif) are of supreme importance. A mountain, a waterfall, a ruin, a lake, a pond, or a deserted building – all these motifs are emblematic. Pissarro's L'Hermitage possessed none of these spots,

108

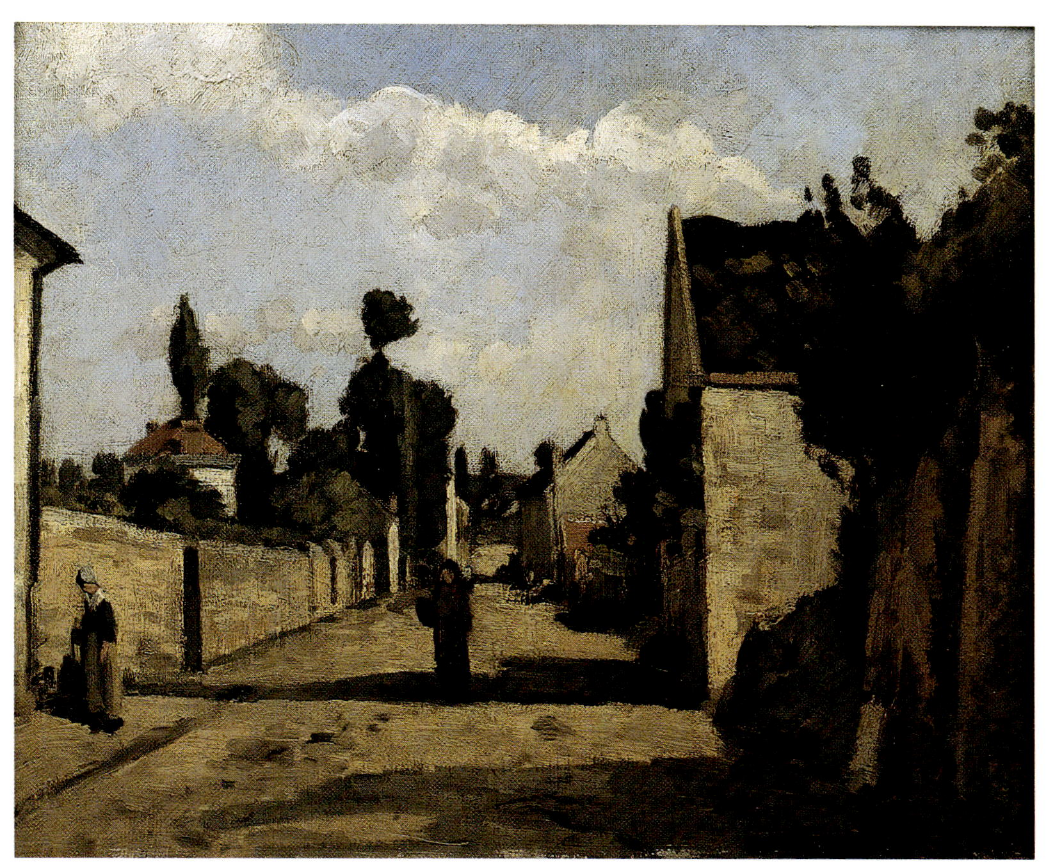

101. Camille Pissarro, *Rue de L'Ermitage, c.*1866–68, oil on canvas 38 × 46.5cm., collection of the Tel Aviv Museum of Art; bequest of Lilli Schocken, Jerusalem–New York, 1959.

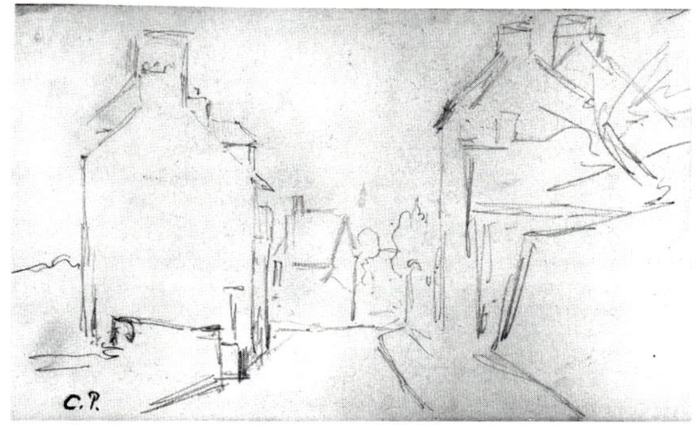

102. Camille Pissarro, *Rue de L'Ermitage, c.*1866–68, pencil on paper, 11 × 18.5cm., Sotheby's, London (8 Apr. 1976).

none of these subjectively important motifs from which the meaning of the landscape emanates. This is particularly evident when one views at length not only Pissarro's omission of potent or associative landscape elements, but also his treatment of three major landscape areas on which he concentrated a great deal of his attention in L'Hermitage: the rue de L'Hermitage, Les Mathurins, and the Côte de Maubuisson.

Pissarro's seven surviving landscape paintings of the rue de L'Hermitage vary in date, palette, format, size, and, of course, style.[13] The two earliest versions, neither of which are included in the catalogue raisonné, were undoubtedly painted in 1866–67, during Pissarro's first years in L'Hermitage (pls. 99 and 101). They depict the then new rue de L'Hermitage rather than the rue du Fond de L'Hermitage on which the Pissarro family was at that time living. Both seem to derive from schematic pencil sketches (pl. 102) and are structured views of the tight, constrained, even geometrical architecture that characterized the low-budget rural construction of the Second Empire. These two pictures represent the street with a detached blandness, one focusing on the north end and the other, on the south. Both were painted from almost exactly the same spot. This representation of the street as two separate streets characterizes all five later representations of the rue de L'Hermitage (pls. 103, 104, 105, 106, and 107). Pissarro, it seems, took pains to disguise the sameness and, thereby, the single identity of the street. The seven images in no way constitute a series. Rather, they vary the character of the street as much as possible and the possibility of variety is further increased by Pissarro's altering the season, the format, the facture, and the palette. One street, a scant two blocks in length, becomes seven totally different paintings. The motif *qua* motif is denied by Pissarro. His fascination is not with the precise meaning or even with the subjective power of the rue de L'Hermitage, but with the pos-

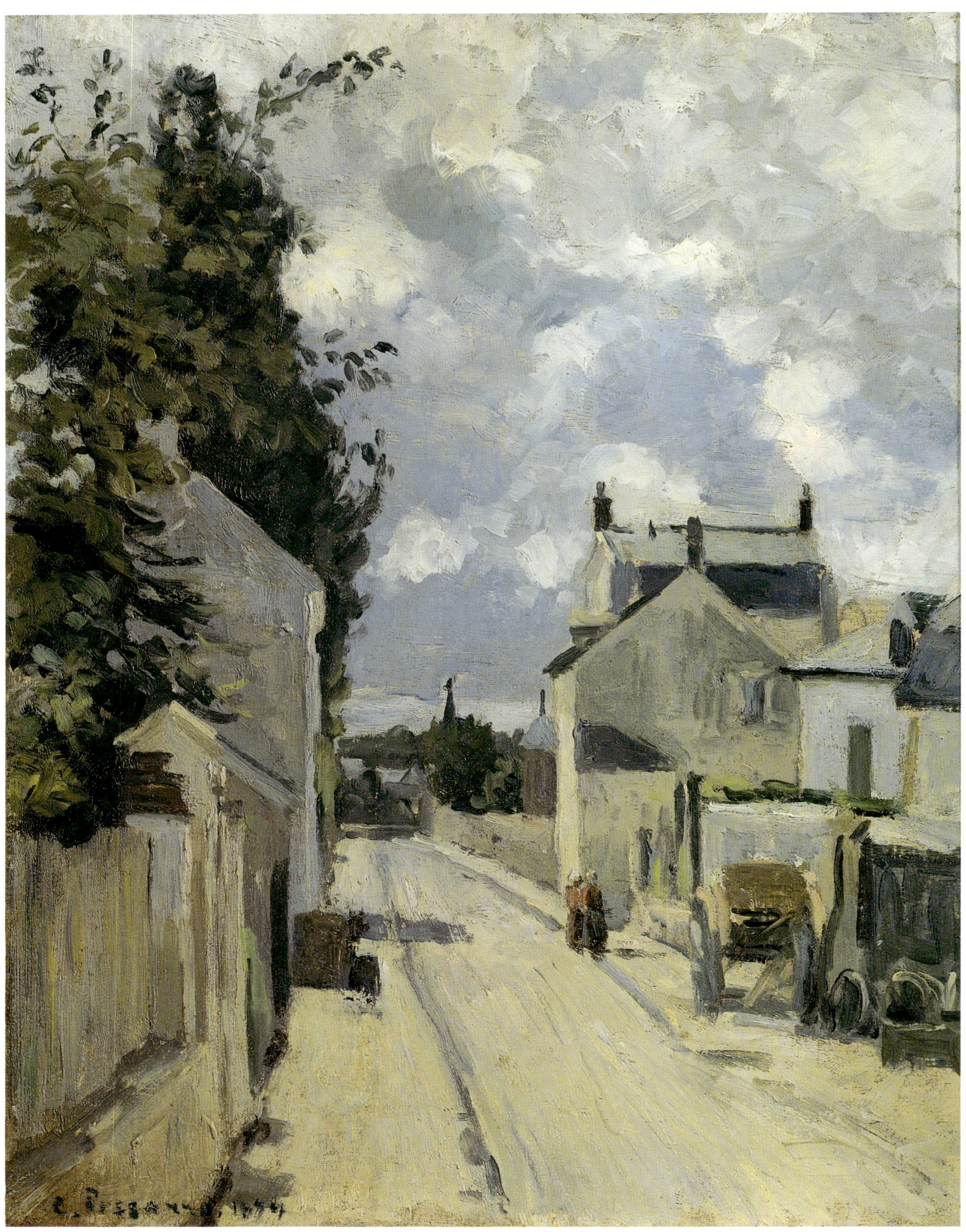

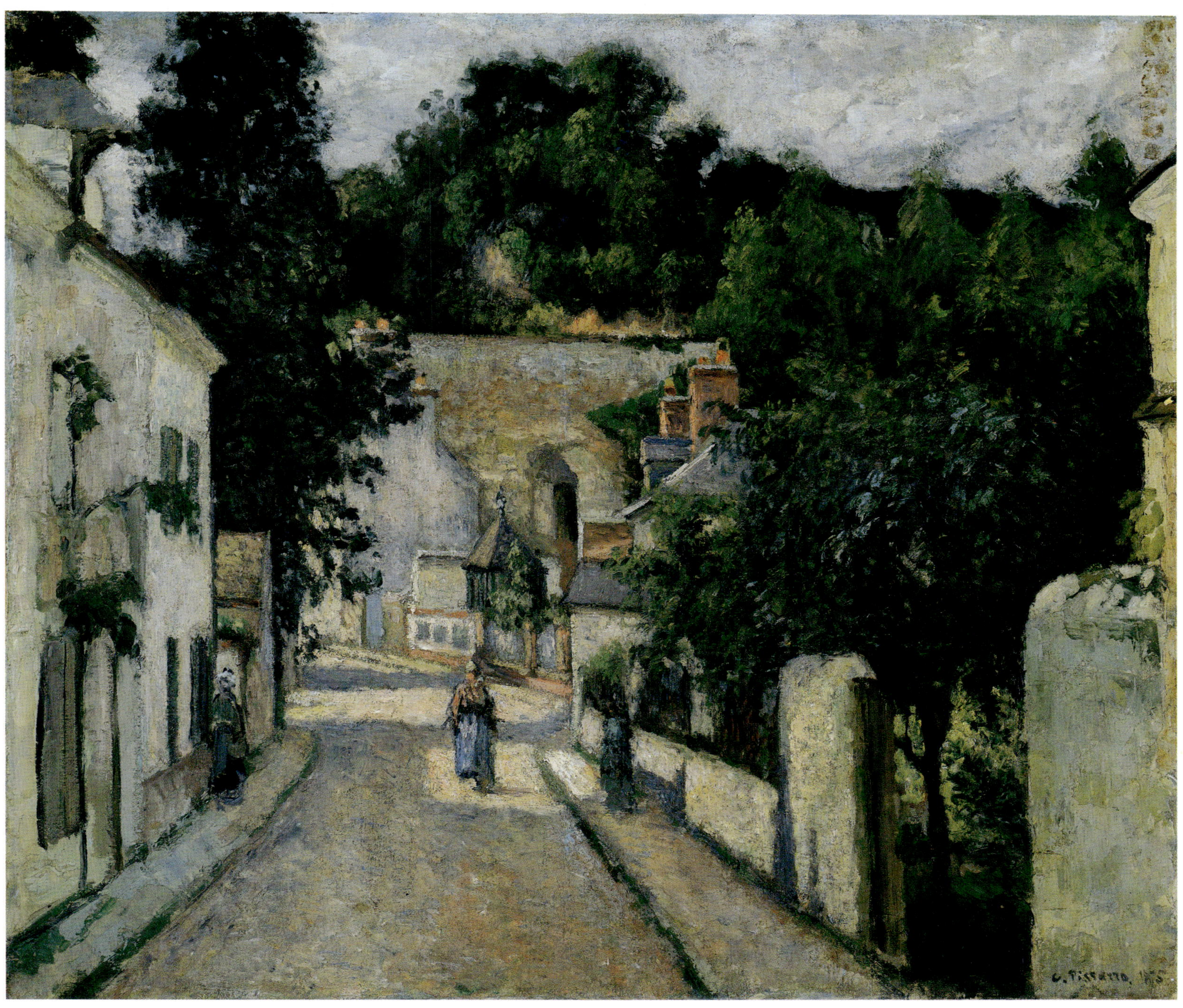

104. Camille Pissarro, *Rue de L'Hermitage à Pontoise* (P&V 305), 1875, oil on canvas, 58 × 69cm., National Gallery of Canada, Ottawa.

103. Camille Pissarro, *Rue de L'Hermitage, Pontoise* (P&V 264), oil on canvas, 41 × 32cm., collection of Arthur. E. Imperatore.

sibility of making a variety of pictures *from* the rue de L'Hermitage. We see, quite clearly, in fact, that the rue de L'Hermitage was not a Wordsworthian or Romantic "spot" for Pissarro. It did not emanate a *genius loci*. Not only was it too bland subjectively to have power as a motif—Pissarro chose, as always, an intrinsically uninteresting subject—but, in addition, he chose to vary it so conscientiously that even its identity as the rue de L'Hermitage is undermined. Ludovic-Rodo and Lucien Pissarro were able to identify it as the rue de L'Hermitage only once in their catalogue titling.

One can make the same observations even more strongly about Pissarro's various pictures painted near and of the Château des Mathurins. Pissarro was assiduous in his reporting of this small region just slightly beyond the bounded

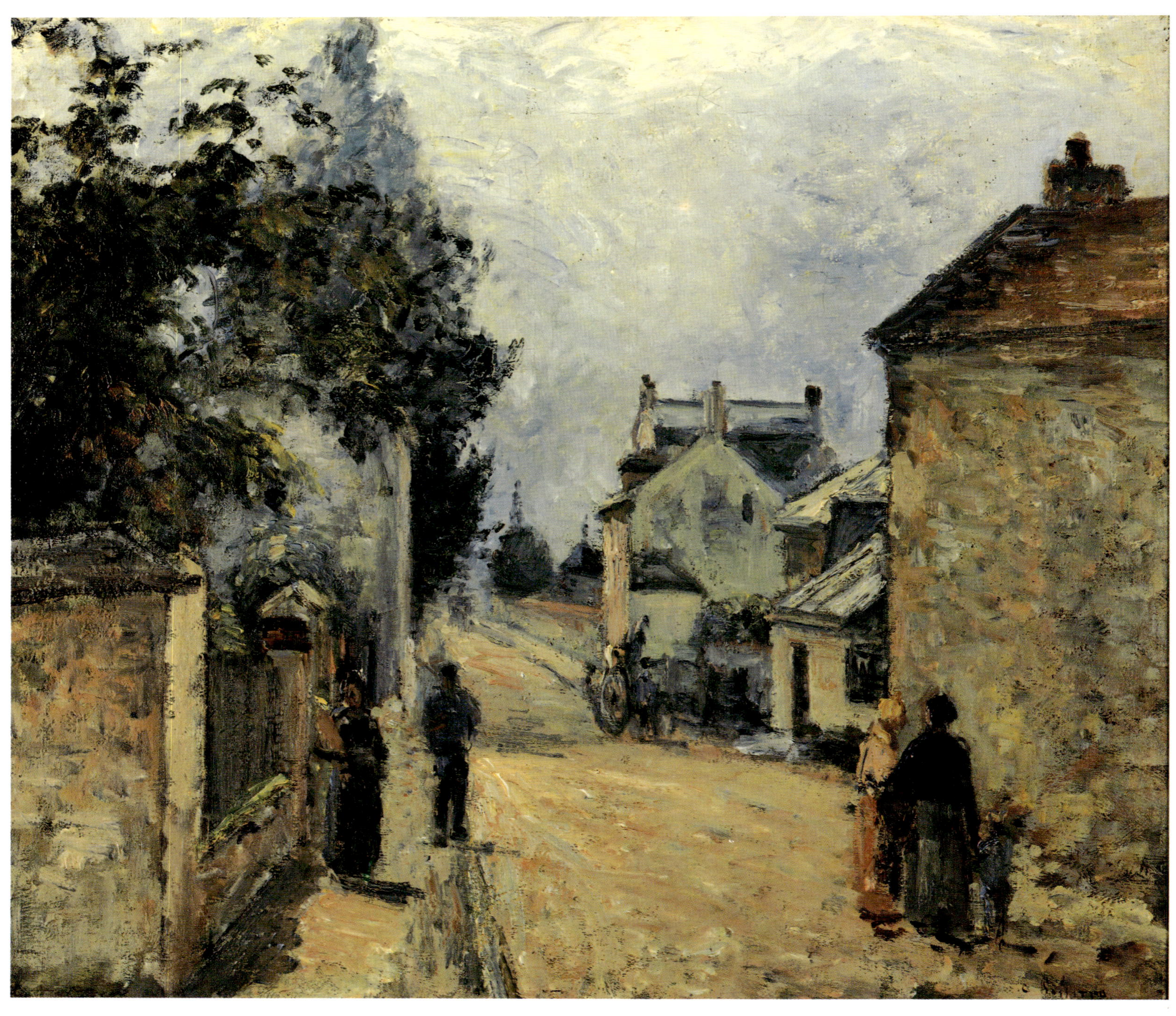

105. Camille Pissarro, *Une rue à L'Hermitage* (P&V 391), *c*.1877, oil on canvas, 46 × 56cm., Rudolf Staechelin'sche Familienstiftung, Basel.

area of L'Hermitage proper. He seems to have felt freer here than in the populated heart of L'Hermitage between the rue de L'Hermitage and the rue du Fond de L'Hermitage. In painting the various (and varied) pictures along the Route d'Ennery, his physical movements were minimal. The area from which he painted could be reached in five minutes from any of his various houses in L'Hermitage (except the last one, from which it would have required a slightly longer walk of eight or ten minutes).

Like the seven pictures of the rue de l'Hermitage, the three exterior views of the Château des Mathurins are as different as possible from one another. *Pontoise, Les Mathurins (ancien couvent)* (pl. 108) and *Route de Saint-Antoine à l'Hermitage, Pontoise* (pl. 109) were painted from a similar position slightly above the route

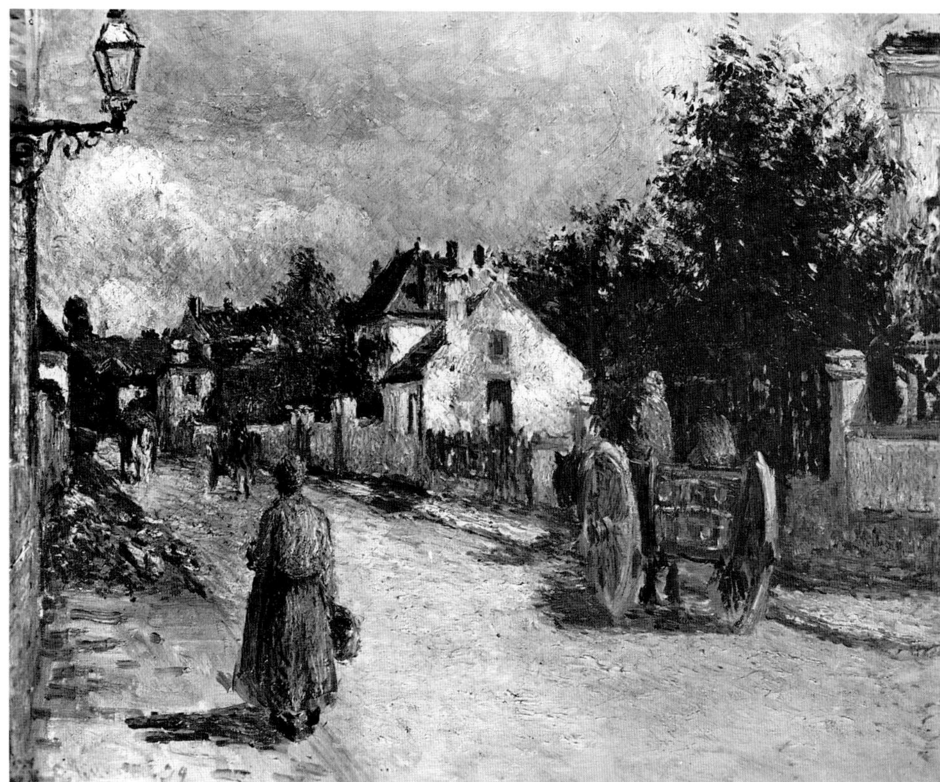
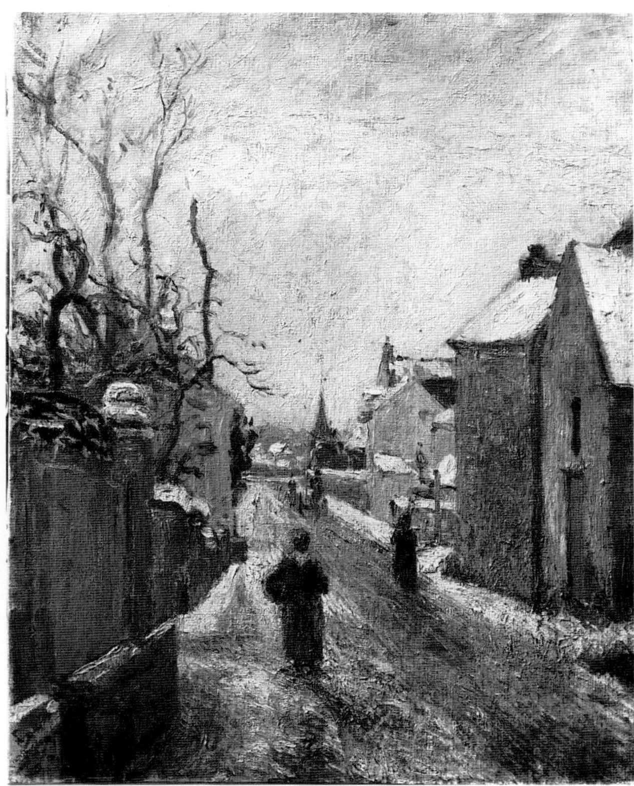

106. Camille Pissarro, *Route à Pontoise*, 1879, oil on canvas, 38 × 46cm., private collection, U.S.A.

107. Camille Pissarro, *Rue à L'Hermitage, Pontoise, effet de neige* (P&V 479), 1879, oil on canvas, 46 × 38cm., whereabouts unknown.

d'Ennery or the route de Saint-Antoine (which is a continuation of the rue de l'Hermitage). Yet, they were painted in different seasons; the later picture (pl. 109) makes extensive use of a palette knife and large brushes; and the composition of the earlier is more insistently grid-like and balanced than the later, more active, diagonal-based composition. It is evident from even this brief description that Pissarro has made deliberate alterations. He has very consciously returned to a motif, but not without waiting and not without remembering, perhaps even consulting, his last version of it. His esthetic is determined by a desire for variety. Again, the power of the motif is only a small part of the meaning of the picture. Pissarro himself evidently thought more about season and style than subject. Indeed, the last of the three pictures, *Les Mathurins, Pontoise* (P&V 397), carries this desire for variety through stylistic alteration even further. The format, the composition, the terrain, the season, the facture – indeed, almost everything – is altered. As we have seen so often with Pissarro, the context overwhelms the content.

These three pictures are not the only ones painted by Pissarro in the area. What he did in painting the rather constricted landscape near the Château des Mathurins was, quite simply, to turn around in the center of the small pseudo-valley and to paint various compositions of the road and the surrounding hillsides. There is, as a result, no motif. The painter stood in the landscape and, with the minimum of physical movement, created eight paintings. Three of these, already discussed, represent the château itself (pls. 108 and 109, and P&V 397); the five others are *Effet de neige à l'Hermitage* (P&V 307), *Chemin montant, environs de Pontoise* (pl. 111), *Route du Fond de L'Hermitage, Pontoise* (pl. 110), *La Route d'Ennery* (P&V 402), and *La Route d'Ennery à L'Hermitage, Pontoise* (pl. 112). Again, the variation of mood, season, format and palette is evident, but that variety is amplified by a corresponding variety of framed "sections" taken from the larger landscape. The concept of *coin* enters the discussion again: the landscape as a whole did not

108. Camille Pissarro, *Pontoise, Les Mathurins (ancien couvent)* (P&V 212), 1873, oil on canvas, 59 × 73cm., whereabouts unknown (lost in World War I).

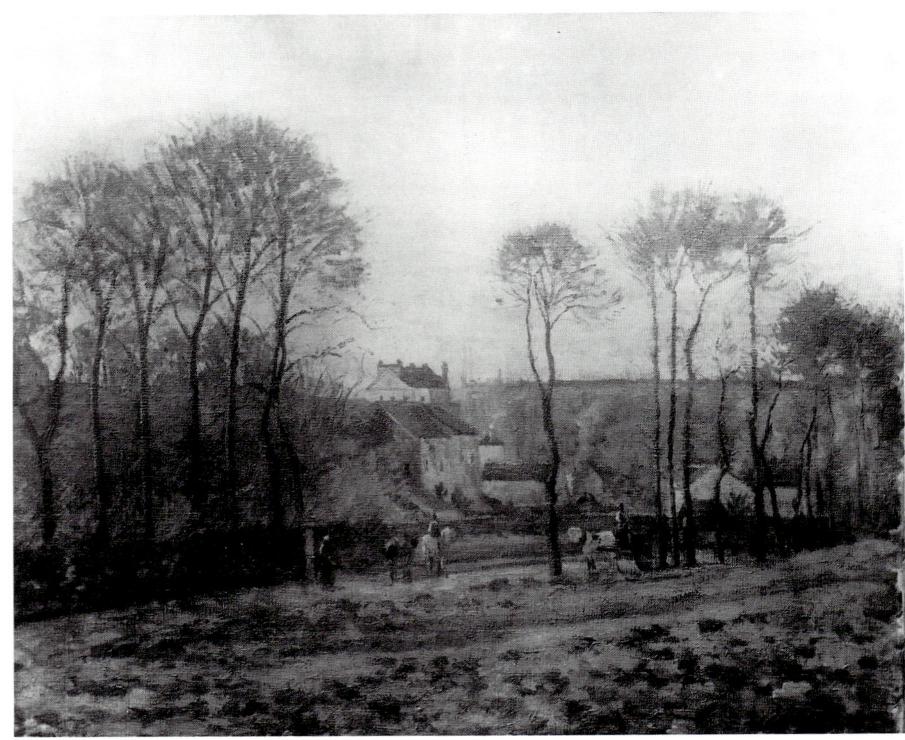

109. Camille Pissarro, *Route de Saint-Antoine à L'Hermitage, Pontoise* (P&V 304), 1875, oil on canvas, 52 × 81cm., private collection, on loan to the Kunstmuseum, Basel.

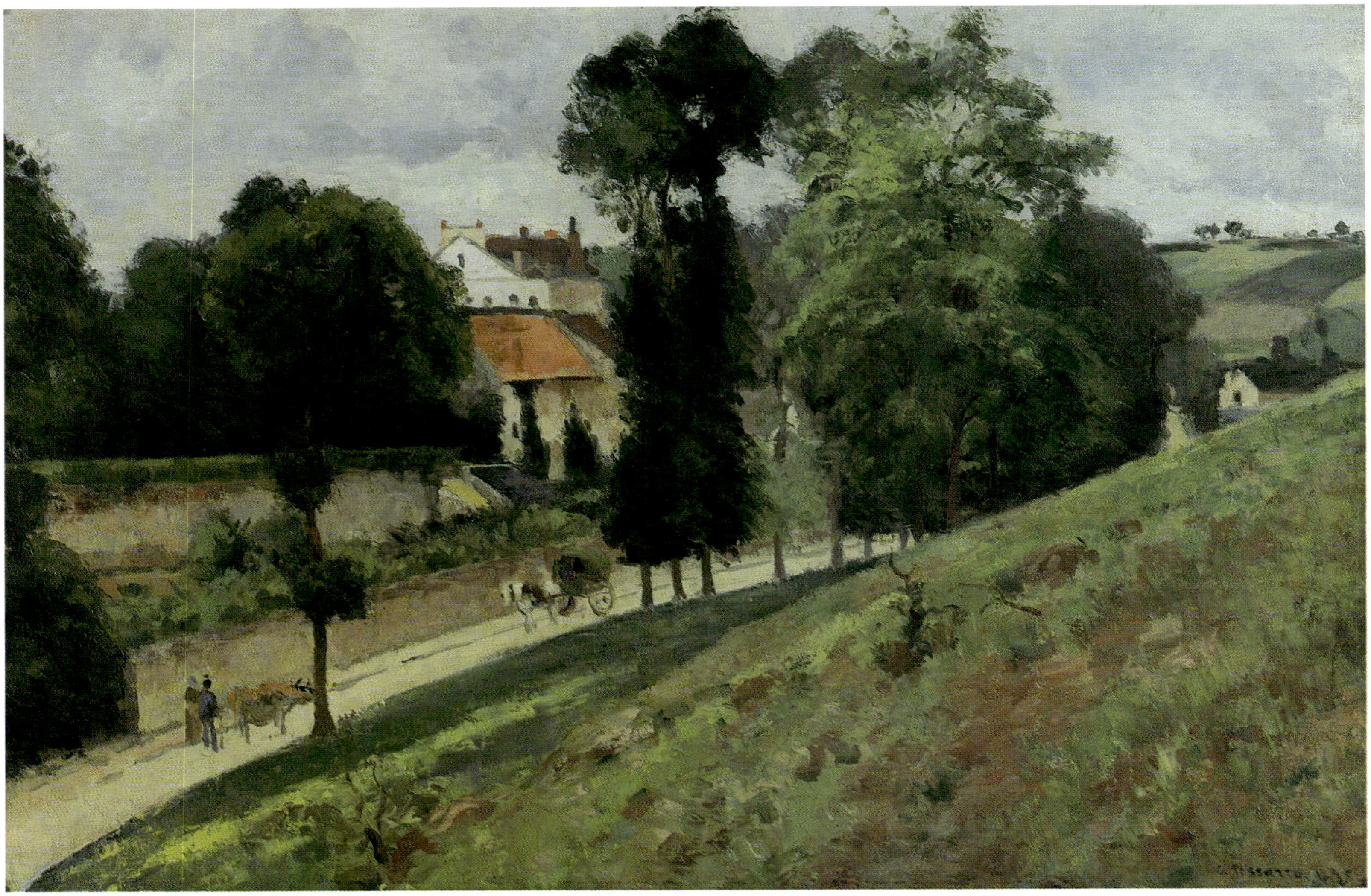

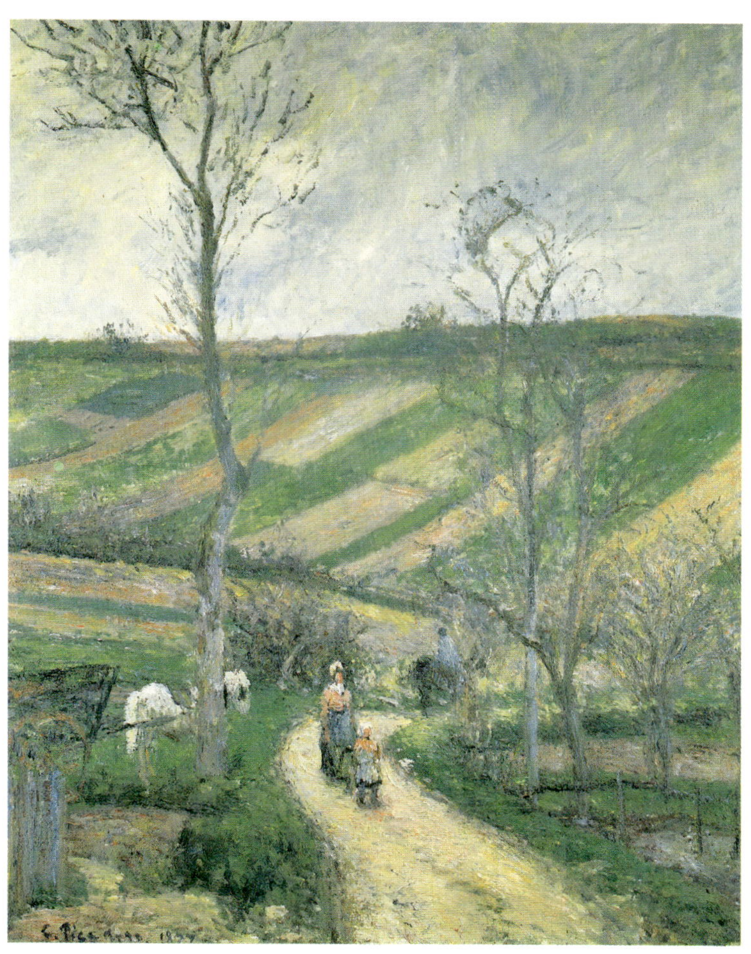

110. Camille Pissarro, *Route du Fond de L'Hermitage, Pontoise* (P&V 385), 1877, oil on canvas, 65 × 55cm., private collection.

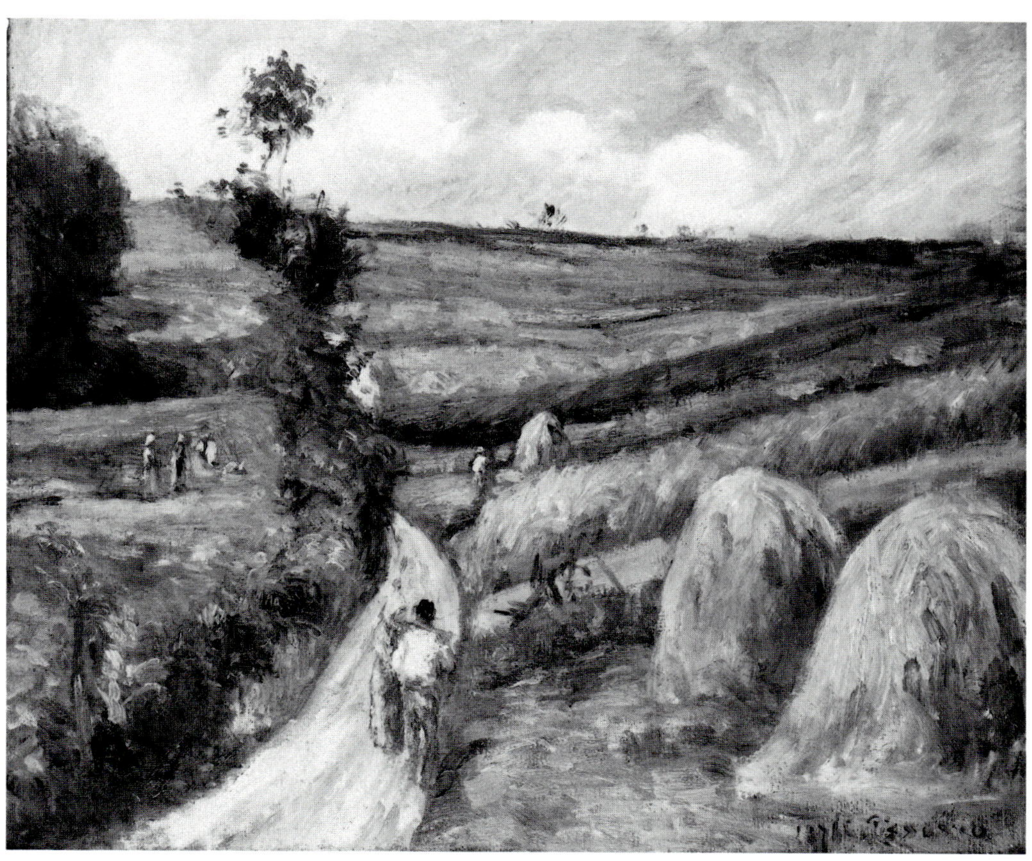

111. Camille Pissarro, *Chemin montant, environs de Pontoise* (P&V 351), 1876, oil on canvas, 46 × 55cm., Sotheby's, London (24 Apr. 1963, lot 8).

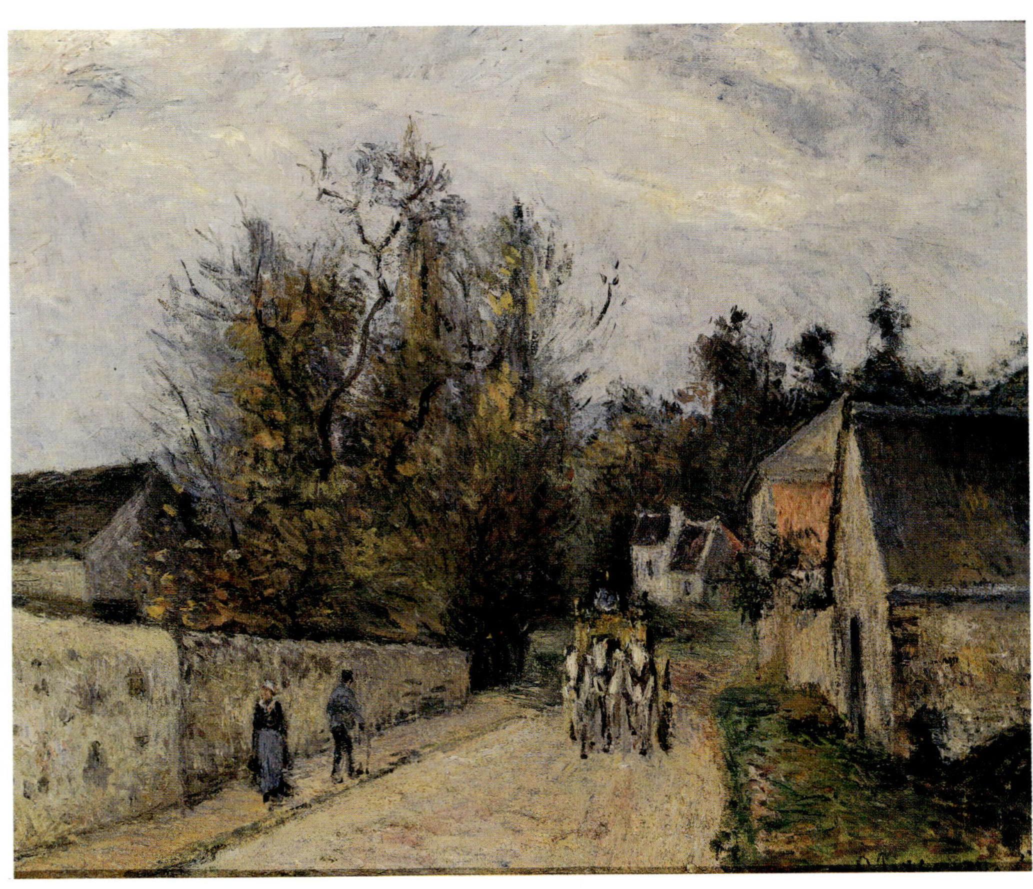

112. Camille Pissarro, *La Route d'Ennery à L'Hermitage, Pontoise* (P&V 411), 1877, oil on canvas, 46 × 55cm., Musée d'Orsay, Paris.

interest Pissarro; rather, he divided a homogenous landscape into *coins*, thus creating the effect of greater diversity than the actual scene would have afforded when perceived with a single sweep of the eye.

The same generalizations – of turning slightly to adopt differently framed views, of altering formats and styles, of making many compositions from one restricted area – apply as well to Pissarro's depictions of the misnamed Côte de Maubuisson, which he painted a great many times. His tendency was not to adapt format and motif to each other, to create Henriet's almost mystical accord between the subject and style, but rather to use style, motif, and format as independent variables, each of which can be altered to produce a diversity of landscape paintings. Pissarro's landscape esthetic comes very close to the analytical. With the exception of the three virtually identical views of the small factory of M. Chalon (pls. 87 and 88), the only repetitions of a motif in L'Hermitage or Pontoise itself contain enormous seasonal variation. *Un Coin de L'Hermitage, Pontoise* (P&V 262, Oskar Reinhart Sammlung, Winterthur) was painted in the summer of 1874 and remade as *L'Hermitage à Pontoise, effet de neige* (P&V 341, Galerie Schmit, 1977) in the winter of 1876. *Côteau de L'Hermitage, Pontoise* (P&V 209, Durand-Ruel collection) was "winterized" to become *Effet de neige à L'Hermitage, Pontoise* (P&V 238). Season, like motif and style, were all part of the language of landscape, to be used to provide a variety of paintings from a tiny landscape.

One confronts, at this point, the remarkable abstractness and detachment of Pissarro's landscape vision. Instead of treating his home environment as a source of domestic scenes, he used it as a small, accessible, and variable source of *coins* which could be painted in as many ways as possible. Pissarro did not search for motifs in the manner described by Henriet. Rather he painted almost in the way

116

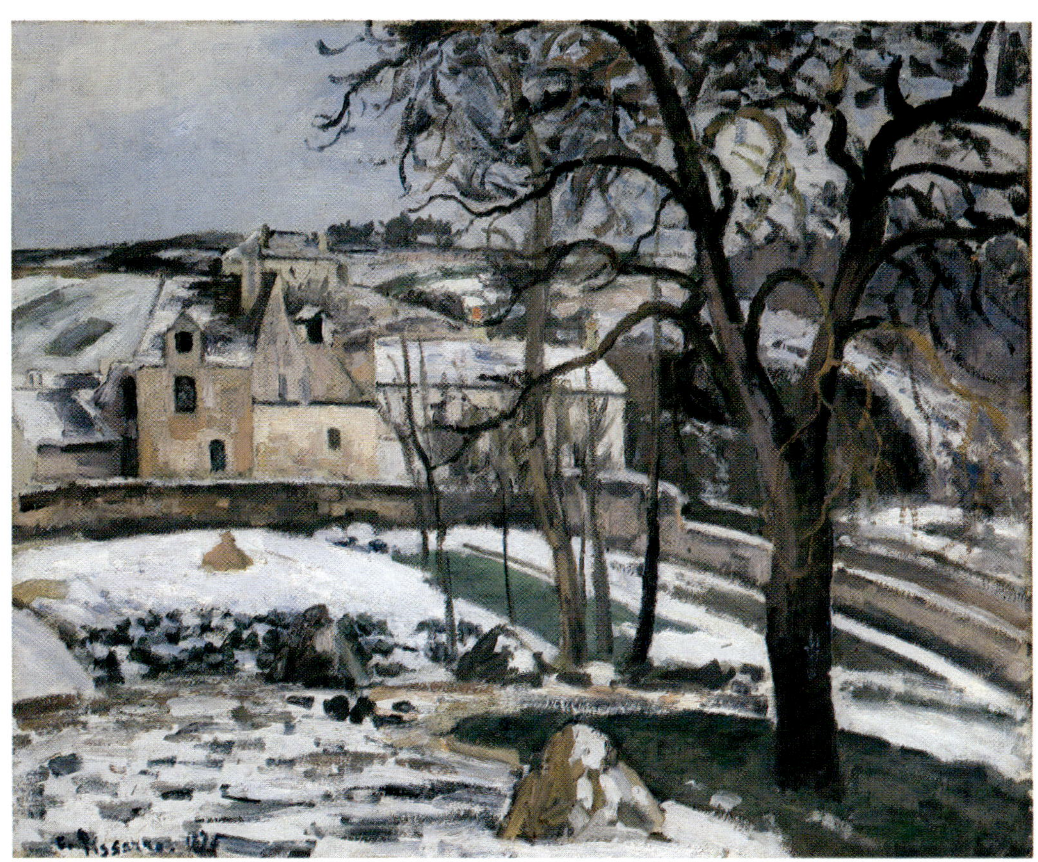

113. Camille Pissarro, *Effet de neige à L'Hermitage, Pontoise* (P&V 297), 1875, oil on canvas, 54 × 65cm., Sotheby's, London (4 Apr. 1989, lot 9).

that Le Carpentier hinted at in his *Essai sur le paysage* of 1817. For Le Carpentier – and for Pissarro – the precise landscape is almost unimportant to the landscape painter. The painter can, according to Le Carpentier, paint a great landscape painting in any landscape.[14] Here we see the key to Pissarro's peculiar landscape vision in the Pontoise period, one which is, perhaps, surprising to students of this most family-conscious painter. Pissarro's home environment was important to him because it was varied and accessible rather than because of an abstract *genius loci* or of any psychological attachment to it as home. Pissarro's vision of L'Hermitage was, if anything, a structural vision, one more concerned with balance and a deliberate blandness than with any forcefully associationist concepts of landscape.

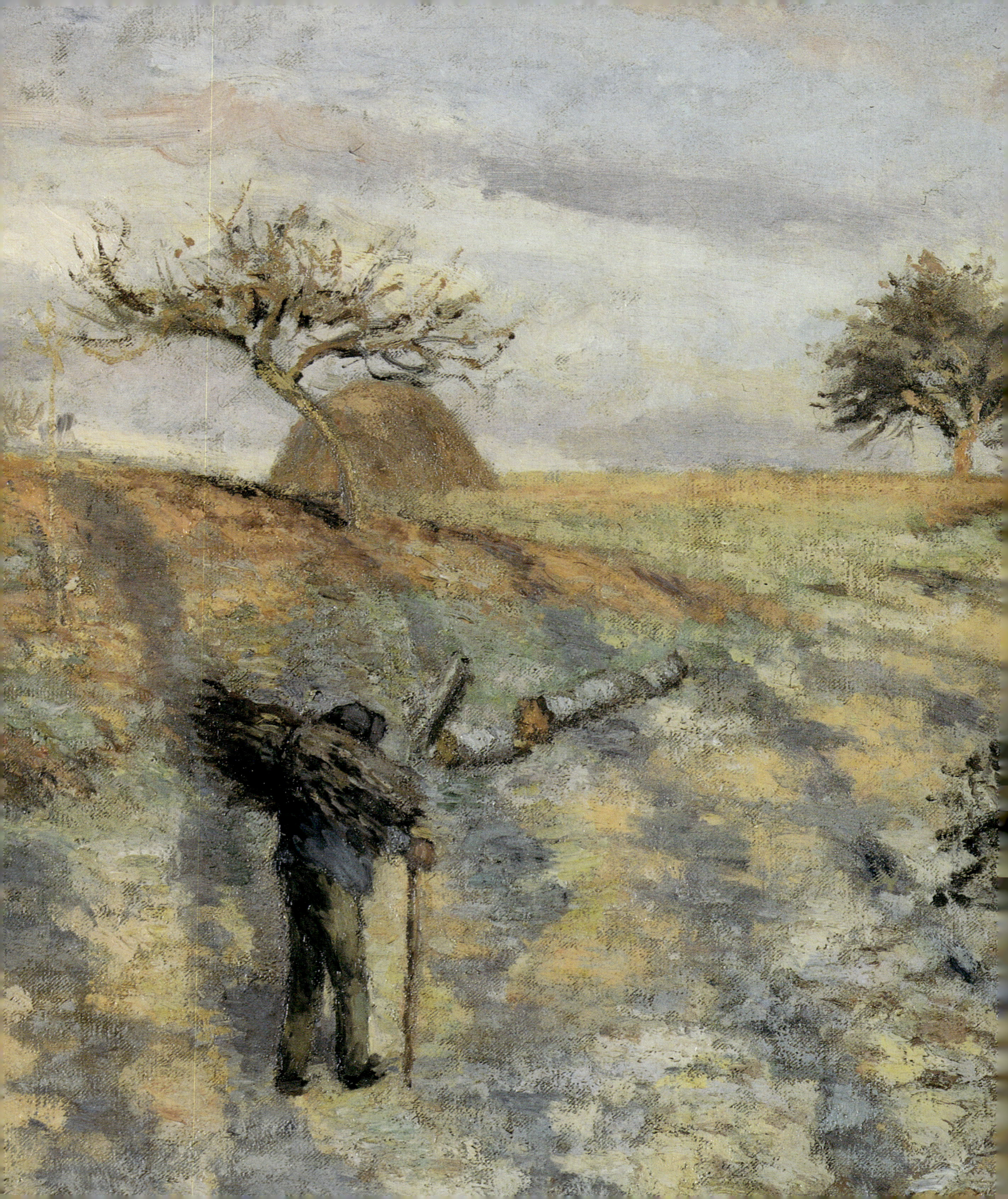

5 *The Figure in the Landscape: Pissarro and the Society of Pontoise*

One of the principal definitions of landscape painting is an art in which the background dominates the figures. The implications of this are clear – the business of the landscape painter is "background" and not figures. The dichotomy, while a rather pleasing and critically easy one, does not apply so straightforwardly to the actual history of landscape painting. In spite of the fact that there were notable "pure" landscape painters (Claude, Ruysdael, Van Goyen, Valenciennes, Rousseau, Michel, and Daubigny), many of the greatest and most famous landscape painters from the sixteenth to the nineteenth centuries were figure painters as well. Indeed, most of the great nineteenth-century landscape painters fit into the latter category. Corot, Courbet, Monet, Pissarro, Cézanne, Seurat, and Gauguin made important contributions to figure painting, and Poussin, who in the nineteenth century was considered the greatest French landscape painter, stands firmly as a model for this kind of twofold career.

Throughout the history of the genre, landscape painters have been dissatisfied with the expressive confines of their craft, with its lack of monumental humanism. The strength of the "ideal-figure-in-the-landscape" tradition, best exemplified by "bather" landscapes, can be seen throughout the nineteenth century as a desire to transcend "pure" landscape or, perhaps more accurately, to unify landscape painting and figure painting. Yet there is a notable and important lack of empathy, of humanized depth, in the world of the landscape painter. The large "figure-in-the-landscape" pictures of Monet, Pissarro, Cézanne, and Gauguin have a detached blandness. Monet is clothes-conscious. Pissarro is pose-conscious. Cézanne is form-conscious. Gauguin is color-conscious. Their figural scenes, while they often possess at least a hint of genre veracity, lack the believability and psychological connectiveness that is so important in genre paintings. The figures exist predominantly as figures. They are problems for the landscape painter, whose major concern is with a "correct" and harmonious relationship among the figures or between the figures and the background rather than with the creation of psychologically potent forms, which is the principle concern of the genre painter.

Much of this detachment stems from the essential ambivalence toward the human figure that is at the root of landscape painting. The figure in the landscape is, to corrupt Riegl's phrase, an insignificant form among forms. The landscape painter's world, with its pervasive unity and balance, must be in keeping with the landscape painter's desire to homogenize reality by minimizing the importance of empathetic forms. For Frédéric Henriet, the human figure is like a center of attraction that absorbs surrounding details to its own advantage, and, as such, has to be underplayed by the landscape painter, who must establish between his figures and his landscape an exact equation of dependence and submission.[1] Throughout the landscape tradition, the figure is deemphasized by the landscape painter, the force of its humanity curtailed. The painter's most obvious weapon is

114. Detail of pl. 115.

scale. Human beings in landscape paintings are most often tiny staffage figures whose placement is of greater importance than their pose, costume, or expression.[2] Deperthes, whose discussion of the human figure is a very short section in a long book on landscape painting, gives his highest praise to the perfectly placed figure and implies that the human figure plays only a generalized role as the psychological connector between the viewer and the landscape, allowing the former a mediated entrance to the latter.[3] Yet, in spite of the undeniable importance of this role, Deperthes refuses to allow the figure to partake fully in the meaning of the landscape. Figures heighten rather than define that meaning. Their existence, while important, is clearly of a secondary nature. The relative insignificance of the figure for the landscape painter can be seen most clearly in Le Carpentier's important treatise on landscape painting published in 1817. In his discussion of "la grammaire du paysage," Le Carpentier mentions the four seasons, the four times of day, all types of trees, rocks, mountains, waterfalls, water, and sky, without a single reference to the human figure.[4]

Clearly, the landscape figure plays a variety of roles, depending on the sensibility of either the artist or the age, but, whatever those roles, they are always secondary. Certain painters in the landscape tradition have avoided the problems of the figure altogether. Ruysdael, Koninck, and Everdingen often painted landscapes that are all but unpeopled, and, in the mid-nineteenth century, painters as diverse in esthetic temperament as Rousseau and Chintreuil painted natural worlds totally devoid of human presence. For Le Carpentier, the landscape painter was born in "silence and solitude . . . far away from the traffic of the world," and Henriet's landscape painter studied alone in the fields, far from the persistently nagging presence of his fellow men.[5] Even Deperthes, whose thinking along these lines was rooted in classical mythology, recommended replacing the academic study of the human figure with the study of the tree.[6] It is probably not accidental that Pissarro made exactly the same remark more than half a century later.[7] For Deperthes and Pissarro, the painter could simply learn the recipes for correct figure drawing, but he must devote his life to the structural apprehension of nature by experimental representation of selected natural forms or scenes.

Landscape painters, since the origins of their profession in the sixteenth century, have been closely associated with the urban world, and the nineteenth-century landscape painter was no exception.[8] The Parisian art market absorbed the vast majority of landscape paintings in this century, followed by the increasingly important regional capitals of Rouen, Lyon, and Marseilles. Landscape painters made "inroads" into the country from these urban centers, and, although an increasing number of painters lived *in situ*, they made frequent trips in and out of cities to sell their "wares" and to engage in professional discourse. With their profession firmly rooted in the city and in the values of urban capitalism, the painters themselves were problematic figures in the landscape. Their society was most often a society of other landscape painters, men who were neither bourgeois nor peasant, who lived fully in neither the city nor the country.[9] Most landscape painters, from the time of Valenciennes and his numerous students through the so-called generation of 1830 to the Impressionists and even the Cubists, painted in groups, alienated from the rural society they often depicted. Perhaps the fullest account of the life of a landscape painter to survive from the period of the Impressionists is Frédéric Henriet's *Le Paysagiste aux champs*, which was published first in 1866 and appeared in a revised, extended edition in 1876. The book records the small, but complicated society of landscape painters who formed colonies of roving, even rootless men. "By forming such groups, in those artistic resorts,

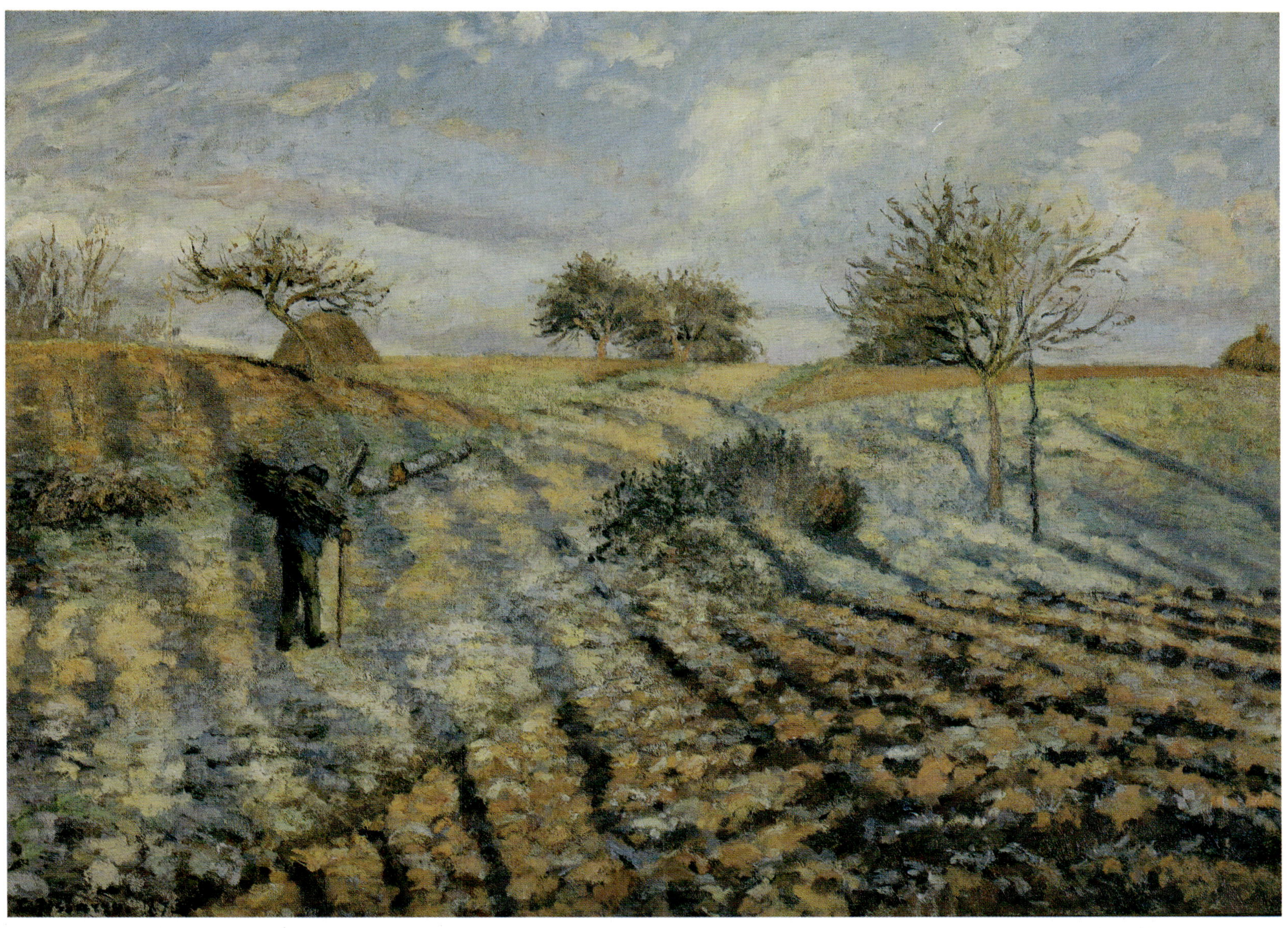

115. Camille Pissarro, *Gelée blanche, ancienne route d'Ennery, Pontoise* (P&V 203), 1873, oil on canvas, 65 × 93cm., Musée d'Orsay, Paris.

landscape painters league together against boredom. They transfer their studio life, habits, and language and the confusion of the boulevards into the open field." The landscape painter is, for Henriet, "an essentially intermittent being."[10] He lives inbetween rather than "in." He is detached from the urban society of the bourgeoisie, whom he most often despises, and from the rural society of the peasant and the provincialite, whom he pities. "He is," as Henriet succinctly put it, "a social parasite."[11]

Henriet's ideas illuminate more fully than any other nineteenth-century writing the peculiar social situation of the landscape painter. Although many studies of the "modern artist" stress the alienation of the avant-garde artist from his host society, little if any mention has been made of what might be called the double alienation of the avant-garde landscape painter during the same period.[12] Indeed, Henriet's landscape painter is a sort of suspended being, who sees rather than experiences life. He has an inexact, even abstract place in society. His "inbetweenness" or social ambivalence is very clearly related to the formal ambivalence that he displays toward the human figures who populate his world. He is, in many ways, a man who is all but totally detached from the world as it is conventionally or socially understood.

Of all the late nineteenth-century landscape painters, Pissarro would be one of the last to be accused of this kind of detachment. Unlike Cézanne, who all but totally eliminated genre figures from his landscape world, Pissarro populated his scenes with real figures going about their daily lives. Unlike Monet's figures, who are, for the most part, transient trespassers from the cities who walk along rivers or through country fields, Pissarro's figures belong, or seem to belong, to their surroundings, connected and unproblematic. Of the pictures painted in Pontoise, very few are lacking in important human presence and, in those that are, the absence of figures is important in an interpretation of the landscape.[13] The nature painted by Pissarro has none of the "silence and solitude" considered necessary by Le Carpentier and the mid-century landscape painters who followed him. Most of Pissarro's paintings have a sizable population of figures, nearly as many as there are in seventeenth-century landscapes. They speak of Claude, Van Goyen, Hobbema, and, of course, Poussin.

In keeping with the classical landscape tradition in which he worked, Pissarro was primarily concerned with the placement of his figures in the larger context of the landscape painting more than with what has already been called their genre veracity. Their forms are often blockily defined, their gestures stiff and awkward, but their placement is always secure and premeditated. Almost any example will do. The peasant figure carrying faggots on his back in the important landscape of 1873, *Gelée blanche* (pls. 114 and 115), is balanced by a pair of leafless fruit trees that respond to his shape and location, thereby locking him into the landscape by association and alignment with natural form. The figure is as much a part of the landscape as the trees. They are equally natural, equally indigenous. In other landscapes, figures stand or walk on the roads and paths that lead in and out of Pontoise, giving shape to the space, acting as structural verticals, and frustrating the viewer's natural inclination to move rapidly inward. The two women strolling on the path that leads into *La Côte du Jallais, Pontoise* (pls. 95 and 116) stand at the very point on the road at which it disappears from our sight. By occupying that position, they emphasize the separation between the world of the body and the world of the eye, a separation that Pissarro makes subtly and often in his landscapes of the 1860s and 1870s.[14] They stand at the nexus of those worlds, facing the viewer. They block his inward motion, keeping him forward, in from of the landscape, which is the true and truly inaccessible subject of the picture.

These latter examples, and there are, of course, many more, are evidence of Pissarro's positive and, in a way, intellectual use of figures. As much as Valenciennes, Michallon, Deperthes, and Corot, Pissarro analyzed the demands of the landscape composition before placing his figures. Very few of Pissarro's landscape figures of the 1870s share the seeming casualness that is evident in those of Monet, Sisley, and Renoir. Pissarro was not and could not have been the painter of the infamous black flecks (*lichettes noires*) of Louis Leroy's Monet. In fact, Leroy, in his review of the first Impressionist exhibition, chided Pissarro for the crudity of the subject as much as for the crudity of the execution in *Gelée Blanche*, provokingly and appropriately invoking the name of Michallon in the same sentence.[15] Pissarro was a landscape painter in the ideal landscape tradition, and few aspects of his art support this thesis more tellingly than do his figures. The scalar deemphasis combined with the carefully considered compositional placement would have been admired by Vernet, Valenciennes, or Michallon. In many ways, Pissarro's Pontoise is an awkwardly modern Arcadia. His landscape world is often more classical, as that word has been applied to landscape, than Cézanne's unpeopled, if geometricized landscapes or than Seurat's landscapes with their persistently stylized, constrained figures.

116. Detail of pl. 95.

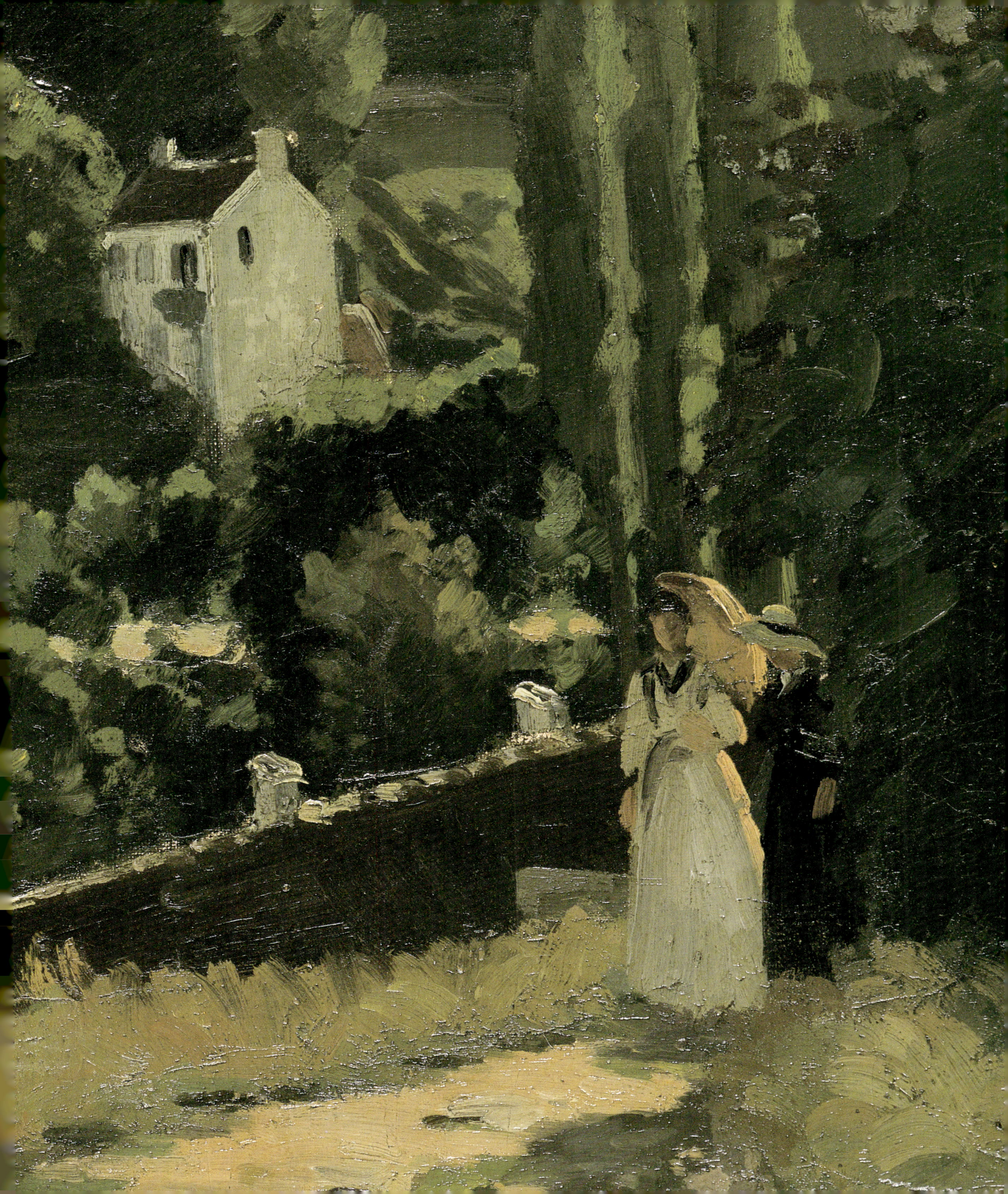

Although it has long been treated as a peasant hamlet by writers about Impressionism, the society of Pissarro's Pontoise is, reflecting the actual social make-up of the town, a divided one. The humbler "peasant" figures, be-aproned and besmocked, are countered by a large number of figures who can only be called bourgeois. These latter figures are most often *promeneurs* or purchasers, and they distinguish themselves from the large figural population of peasants by their costume. They are "dressed up" and form part of the fashion-conscious, modern population of Pontoise.

Class contrast between traditional and modern populations is rare in French painting of the nineteenth century. Monet, Sisley, Manet, and Renoir were little interested in the peasantry. Lhermitte, Breton, and Millet ignored the bourgeoisie, both provincial and Parisian. Bourgeois figures are notably absent from the production of the Barbizon School and its many later offshoots. Perhaps only Jules Bastion-Lepage was able to accept both worlds: the peasant, associated with his own humble origins, and the bourgeois, associated with the urban aspirations to which he succumbed at an early age.

Yet, in spite of the lack of a balanced and comprehensive representation of different social groups in nineteenth-century French art, class contrasts are common in the landscape tradition of the seventeenth and, perhaps surprisingly, the eighteenth centuries. What is probably Claude's earliest important picture, *Mill on a River* (pl. 117) of 1631, makes a clear distinction between the northern bourgeoisie, here a sketching party dressed in actively silhouetted black, and the native population of impoverished figures dressed in colorful rags and rejected garments. Claude's picture presents a case of contrasts: wealth and poverty, leisure and labor, art and life. Bourgeois and *bombaccianti* simultaneously populate the landscapes of the Italianate painters who played such an important role in landscape painting of the seventeenth century. It is interesting to contrast these works with those by Dutch landscape and genre painters of the seventeenth century. Class contrasts were welcomed in their depictions of Italy, where the peasantry was a colorful curiosity to be described by the traveler. In paintings of Holland itself, however, the worlds of the country and the city, of agriculture and commerce, are more strictly divided. Pictures that include both classes are comparatively rare in Holland in the seventeenth century, as they were in France in the nineteenth century.

Yet the landscapes of Vernet and Hubert Robert painted in France in the middle and late eighteenth century bring the Italianate class contrasts into France itself. Robert's pair of pictures depicting the destruction or "liberation" of the gardens at Versailles after the revolution (Gulbenkian Museum, Lisbon) are intentional delineations of class differences, more biting and less ambiguous than pictures in the Dutch or French Italianate tradition mentioned above. But this inclusion of diverse classes within a single pictorial format is not connected solely with the radical social and political upheavals at the end of the eighteenth century. Vernet's series of landscape paintings devoted to the description of the major building projects of eighteenth-century France – roads, harbors, and bridges – make a clear delineation between social classes. There are both workers and watchers, proletariat and bourgeois, in Vernet's French landscapes.

Pissarro's Pontoise, with its peasants and its far-from-prosperous bourgeoisie, is not exactly comparable to any of the examples above. Vernet and the Italianate tradition stand not in the foreground but in the background of our minds when we view a landscape by Pissarro painted in Pontoise. There is no clear relationship

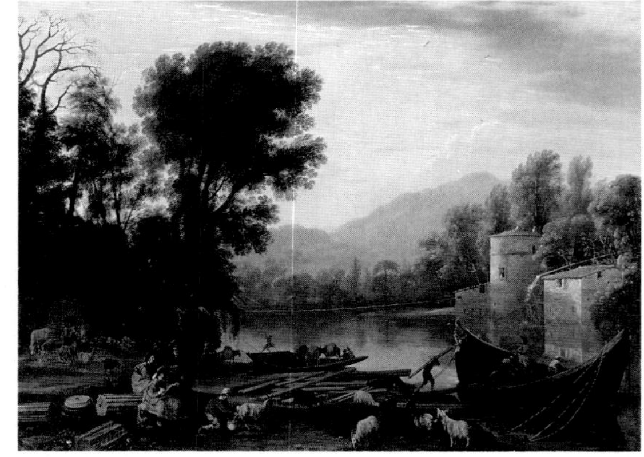

117. Claude Lorrain, *Mill on a river*, 1631, oil on canvas, 61.5 × 84.5cm., Seth K. Sweetser Fund; courtesy, Museum of Fine Arts, Boston.

118. Detail of pl. 38.

124

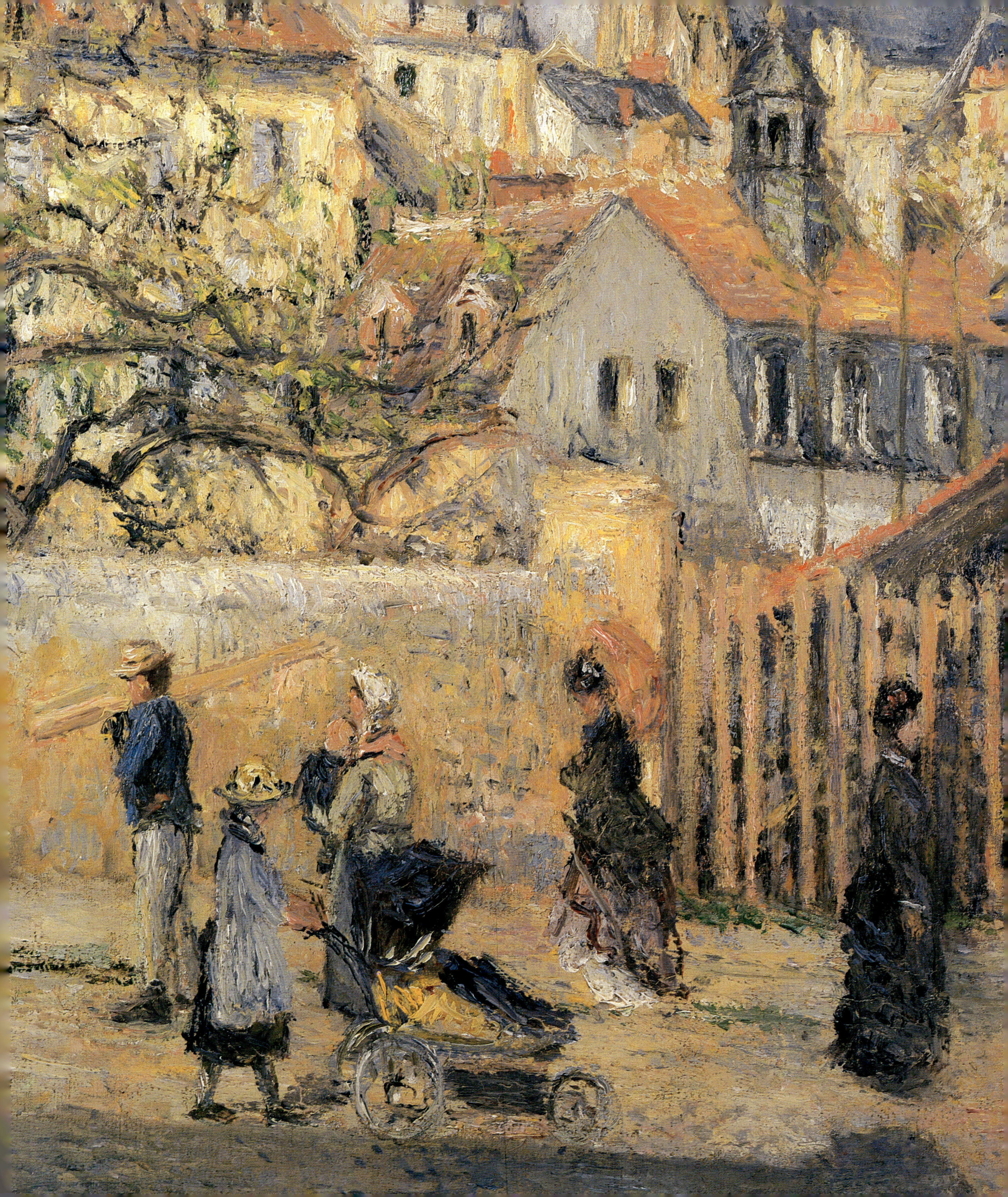

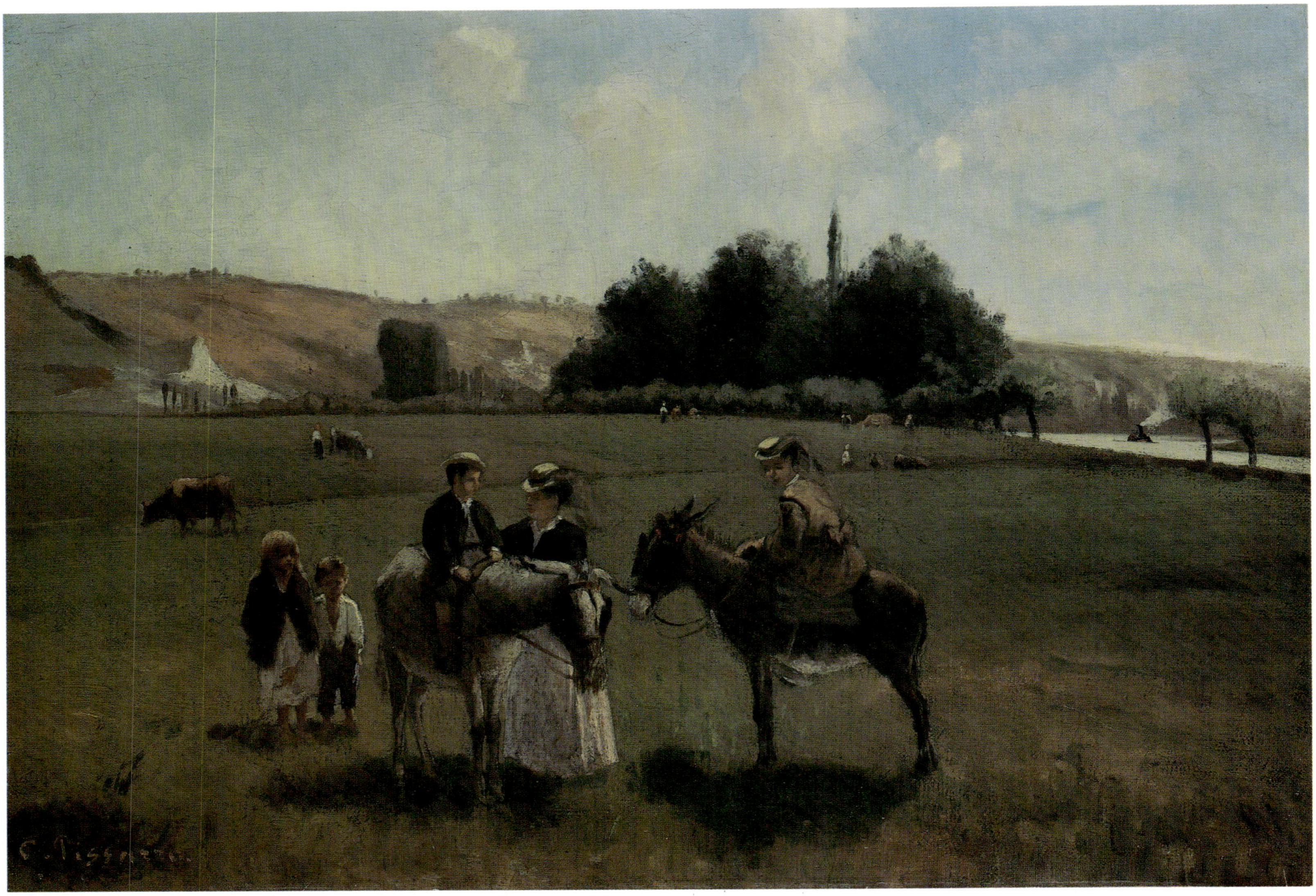

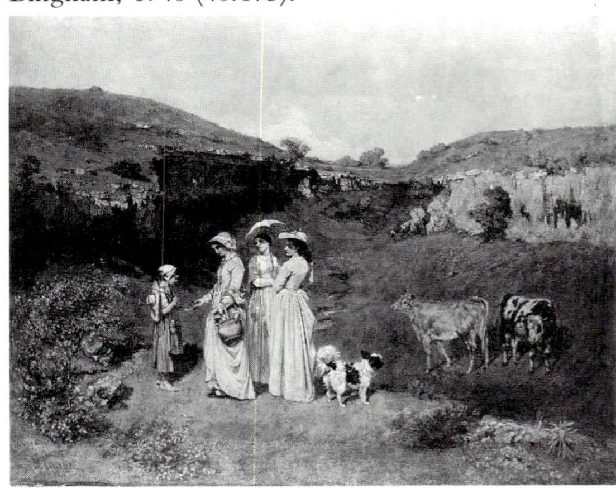

119. Camille Pissarro, *La Promenade à âne à La Roche-Guyon* (P&V 45) *c.*1865, oil on canvas, 35 × 52cm., Mr. Tim Rice, London.

120. Gustave Courbet, *Les Demoiselles de village*, 1851, oil on canvas, 195 × 261cm., The Metropolitan Museum of Art; Gift of Harry Payne Bingham, 1940 (40.175).

between those who are ordered and those who order in Pissarro's less socially sophisticated landscapes. His figures are essentially unrelated to each other. There are few paintings in which bourgeois figures and peasant figures are simultaneously present. Bourgeois figures virtually never talk to or stand with peasants or workers, even in the rare market scenes, like *La Charcutière* of 1883 (P&V 615, Tate Gallery, London). The *promeneurs* in *La Côte du Jallais* (pl. 116) or in *Promenade au bord de l'eau, Pontoise* (P&V 404, whereabouts unknown) are bourgeois in a peasant landscape with no peasant figures. The peasant figures in many of Pissarro's landscapes move along the roads or work in the fields with no supervision from the bourgeoisie. The two classes, for the most part, exist in isolation. Even the figures who walk together in the restricted and laterally defined foreground of *Parc aux Charrettes, Pontoise* (pl. 118) are barely aware of each other's presence. The worker and the bourgeois have no hierarchical relationship to one another as they do in the paintings of Vernet, Both, or Claude.

There is, however, some evidence that Pissarro was fascinated by social tension, by the problematic relationship between the modernizing or progressive class, the bourgeoisie, and the traditional class, the peasantry. The most obvious instance of this tension manifested in pictorial terms is the often reproduced *Promenade à âne à la Roche-Guyon* (pl. 119). Painted in the middle 1860s, this small

126

picture derives its composition and, to a certain extent, its imagery from Courbet's large and more famous *Les Demoiselles de village* (pl. 120) exhibited at the Salon of 1852. Both Pissarro's and Courbet's pictures examine rural class issues. In both, wealthy figures are seen in the same landscape context as poor figures. Although Courbet's picture is socially ambiguous (the three girls, the painter's sisters as the Three Graces, are giving alms to a peasant girl who is tending the cattle), Pissarro's smaller picture is defiant and seemingly obvious in its social message. A bourgeois woman is out with her two children, who are both seated on donkeys in a sunny field near the Seine, which Pissarro depicted many times in the late 1850s and early 1860s. Standing next to this well-dressed group are two children of the lower classes, dressed like *bombaccianti* in ill-fitting hand-me-downs, staring all too plaintively at the scene of plenty. Pissarro has not spared us the irony of contrasts. His aim is social, if not subtle. His pictorial emphasis is on the "haves," but his sympathy is clearly with the "have-nots." When compared with contemporary figure paintings such as Manet's *Déjeuner sur l'herbe* (Musée

121. Camille Pissarro, *La Route de Rouen, les hauteurs de l'Hautil, Pontoise* (P&V 151), 1872, oil on canvas, 42 × 55cm., private collection, Dallas.

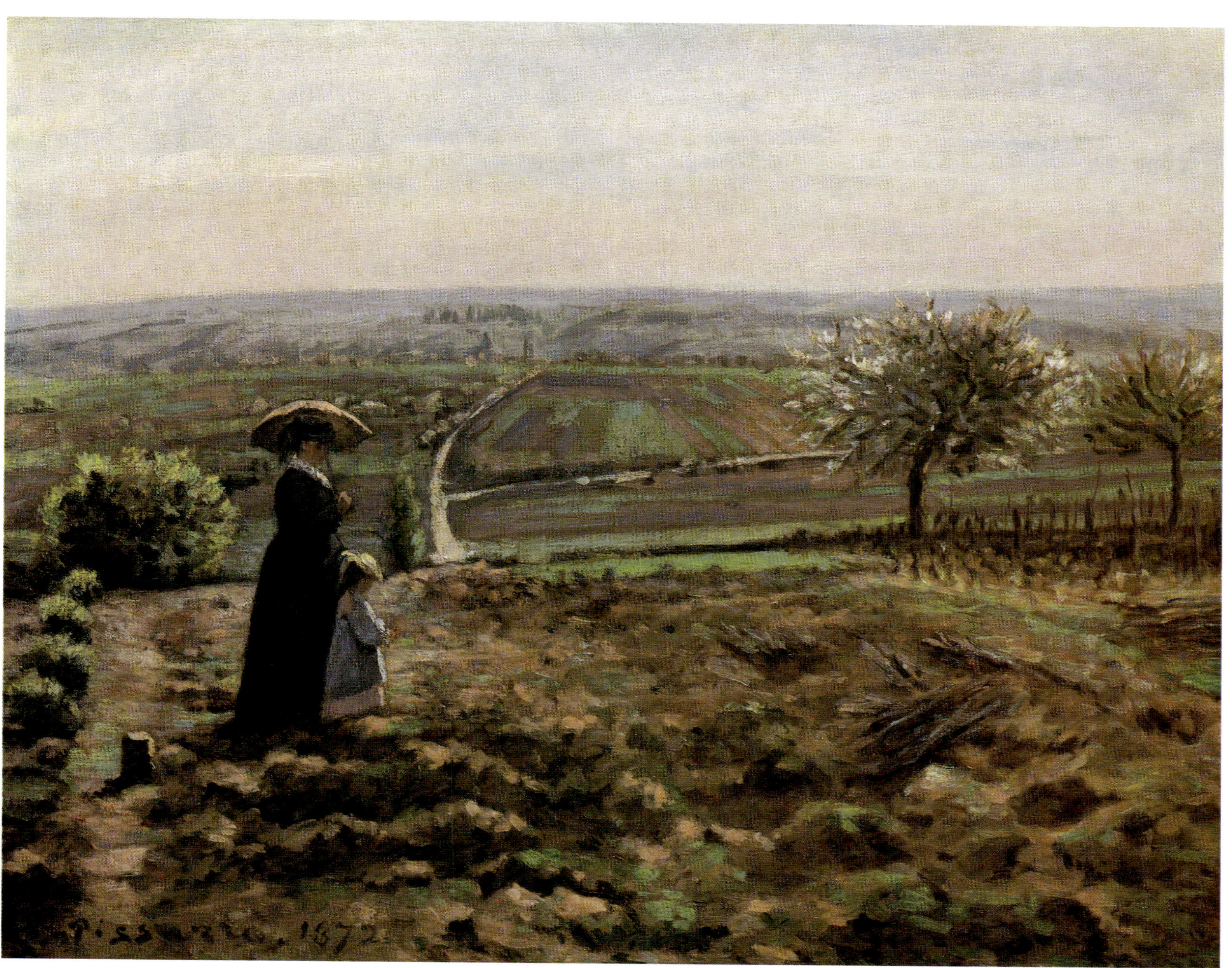

d'Orsay), Monet's *Women in the garden* (Musée d'Orsay), or Renoir's urban landscapes of the late 1860s, Pissarro's small picture is pregnant with social implications. No landscape painter of the 1860s was as sensitive to social tensions as Pissarro. His only depiction of La Grenouillère near Bougival (P&V 174) puts this almost archetypal pleasure spot into juxtaposition with a small factory, and his single concentrated study of a bourgeois *promeneur, La Route de Rouen, les hauteurs de l'Hautil, Pontoise* (pl. 121) shows a well-dressed woman and her daughter (Mme. Pissarro and Jeanne) walking in the dirty ruts of a plowed field.

These examples attest to the social questioning in Pissarro's pictures of the 1860s and early 1870s. *La Promenade à âne à la Roche-Guyon*, in spite of the apparent superficiality of its social message, is a complex picture, involving itself at several levels with the problem of the human figure in the landscape. This small canvas was almost Pissarro's first and only attempt until 1874 to paint a figure painting or, at least, to allow the human figure as such to dominate the landscape into which it is set.[16] The broad plains near La Roche-Guyon are very much a background in this picture. Pissarro, the landscape painter, is showing an interest in that conflict between the figure and the landscape, an ancient pictorial conflict that is complicated for him by the additional level of meaning of the class conflict. To whom we ask, does the landscape belong? The classically balanced landscape has been doubly questioned by the young Pissarro with the help of Courbet. The figures usurp the power of the landscape, and the social tension, which is to play such an important role in Pissarro's thinking about the modern France he depicted, undercuts the merely "figurative" role of the mother, her children, and the watchers. The tensions of the painting are double tensions that Pissarro rarely confronted quite so strongly. Even the benign bond between a mother and her young children is put into a larger social context. The horsed and the unhorsed—that ancient class distinction in aristocratic art since the Roman Empire—is used anew by Pissarro. For the Pissarro of *La Promenade à âne*, even the seemingly innocent play of children is part of the larger social and economic system of the Second Empire.

This painting stands behind Pissarro's landscape production of the 1860s and 1870s in much the same way as *La Petite Fabrique* of 1863–65 underlies his later paintings of industrial France. For Pissarro, the role of the bourgeois figure in the landscape was a problematic one. He was never able to accept the bourgeois landscape as fully, even joyfully, as Monet or Renoir. His treatment of the bourgeois figure as a problem with both social and pictorial consequences has its basis in the nineteenth-century landscape tradition, as is made clear by Henriet's discussion of the social ambiguity of the landscape painter himself and his related concept of the human figure as a "center of attraction." This latter idea led many, indeed most landscape painters of the nineteenth century, to populate their landscapes with what were or seemed to be indigenous figures, figures in complete accord with the nature in which they stood. Bourgeois figures, dressed in the elegant clothes of the fashionable drawing-room or the carriage, belonged in gardens, but not on country walks—until, of course, the rise in popularity of the rural promenade by the end of the Second Empire. Impressionist painters from Monet to Caillebotte viewed nature with the eyes of the urban *promeneurs*. Pissarro, rooted more firmly in the landscape tradition, was suspicious of their presence in any landscape.

It is possible, however, to exaggerate the importance of *La Promenade à âne à la Roche-Guyon*, to let it act as the "explanation" of later, more ambiguous images. In a career characterized by a notable dedication to radical politics, Pissarro, perhaps paradoxically, never again painted a picture with such obvious social intention.[17] The bourgeois figures in Pissarro's large, almost Cartesian series of

122. Detail of pl. 41.

128

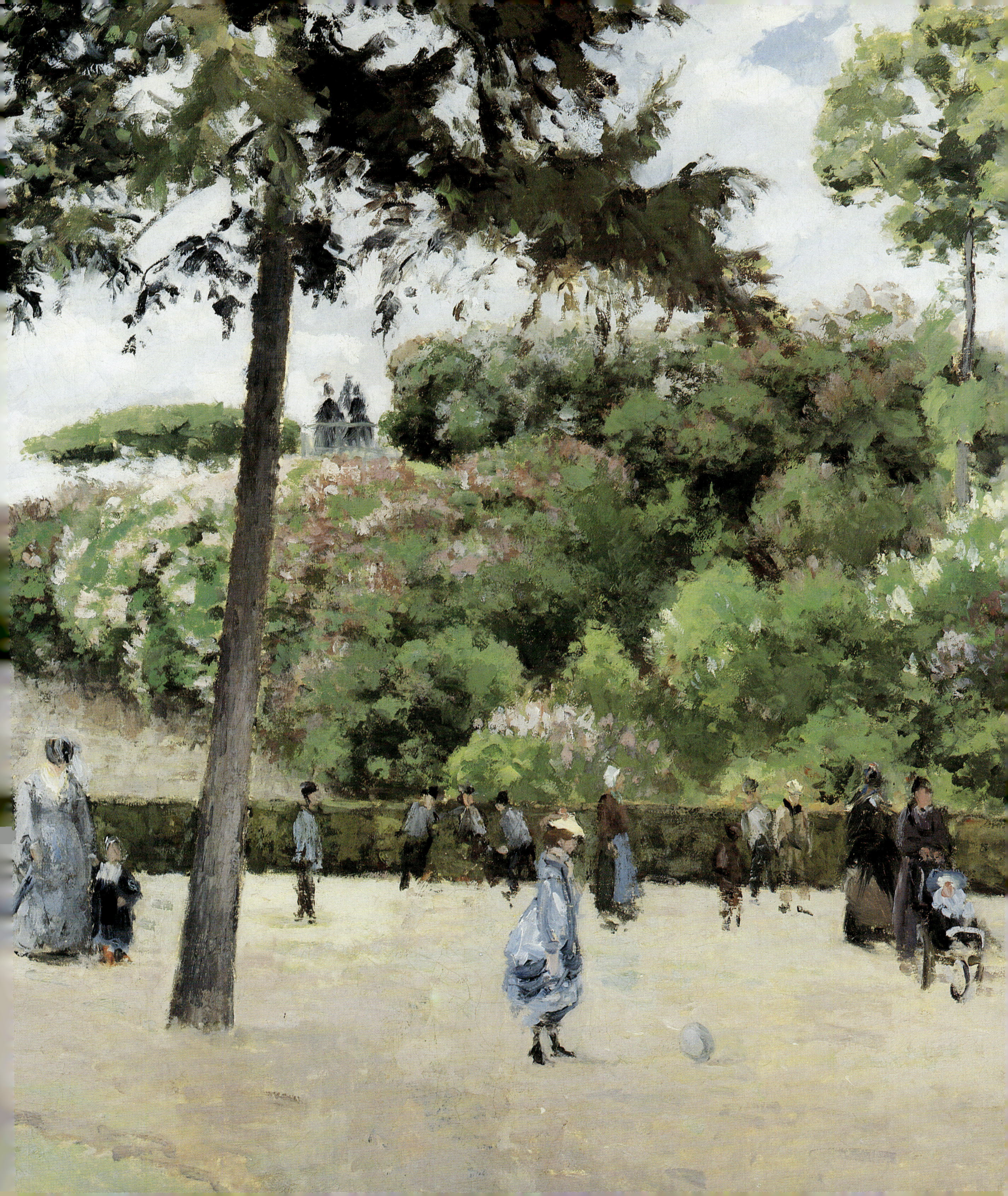

Pontoise landscapes painted in 1872–73 play ordinary roles. They very rarely disrupt the continuity of the landscape or townscape into which they are set. The reason for their "belonging" relates to Pissarro's use of them not as symbols for the bourgeoisie, not as figures whose identity is their class, but as themselves indigenous figures. There are virtually never bourgeois figures where there ought *not* to be bourgeois figures. They are seen, most often, against the appropriate background of the town itself. They stroll, gossip, and stand idly along the road in *Le Tribunal de Pontoise, Place Saint-Jean* (P&V 211, Peter Salm Collection, New York) of 1873. Children play together while their mothers chat and watch in the pictorially fascinating *Le Jardin de la Ville, Pontoise* (pl. 122). The figures are absolutely "at home" in their town setting. They belong as much as the rural workers belong in the market, on the road, or in the field.

We confront again a case of Pissarro's ambivalence and fundamental indecision. In a handful of pictures, the bourgeois figure is depicted as an intruder or outsider in the country setting, while he is at home in other, less problematic pictures. Pissarro's depictions of the bourgeoisie are the most forceful, at least socially, when they approach figure painting, when the figure becomes the "center of attraction" that Henriet wanted so desperately to avoid. However, the landscape figures, which they generally are, are recessive, and their meaning is severely constrained. One is reminded, in this latter context, of the advice given by John Thomas Smith to the young Constable: "Do not set about inventing figures for a landscape taken from nature," Smith warned, "for you cannot remain an hour in any spot, no matter how solitary, without the appearance of some living thing that will in all probability accord better with the scene and time of day than will an invention of your own."[18] We must remember, in considering this advice in terms of Pissarro's work, that Pontoise was a landscape rich in bourgeois figures. They strolled up the rue de L'Hermitage and down the many quays along the Oise. They amused themselves in the parks and town squares. Their presence was manifest in this small, modernizing town with its ancient bourgeois roots.

Pissarro's landscape figures derive fundamentally from the real landscape. In spite of his dislike of crowded or urban scenes, he retained an interest in all aspects of the environment. As we have seen, his landscapes, unlike those of Renoir, Sisley, and Monet, include both the bourgeois and the peasant, both the modern and the traditional. They show a modernizing and a divided Pontoise not altogether unlike the real Pontoise. Monet's Argenteuil is a considerably more unbalanced portrait of a rather similar town. The bourgeois presence was, of course, more notable in Argenteuil, with its larger river and greater ease of access to the capital. Yet, as a glance at many postcards readily demonstrates, the local agriculturalists and workers, both men and women, outnumbered the fashionable bourgeoisie that populate the predominantly modern worlds of Renoir, Monet, and Caillebotte. Perhaps the most important conclusion that one can draw in this context about landscape paintings of Pissarro is that they reflect social distinctions but, with one or two notable exceptions, do not stress class tension. Henriet, Corot, Boudin, and Jongkind stand behind Pissarro more than did Courbet.

Pissarro and the Rural Workers of Pontoise

Rural workers are, of course, much less problematic than bourgeois figures to the landscape painter. They belong, quite simply, in nature. They are at home in the fields from which they sustain their living, on the paths along which they move in habitual rhythms, and in the hamlets in which they and their families have lived for centuries. As rural workers, the great majority of Pissarro's figures partake of the broad, generic meanings of rootedness and continuity, meanings that characterize much of the peasant imagery in nineteenth-century France.

Most of the rural workers who inhabit Pissarro's landscape are tiny staffage figures. They had, in many ways, as great a psychological distance from the nineteenth-century viewer as the *bombaccianti* had from the seventeenth-century viewer. They recede into landscapes, defining the scale of a roadway, conforming to the planar architecture of their pictorial homes, crouching into pictorial niches created by bending branches and the curved silhouettes of hillsides. They are figures of the middle ground, never tiny dots or flecks as were Monet's urban street figures of the 1870s or Pissarro's own later street figures. Even those few who stand boldly in the foreground plane, as does the *vachère* in the small summer landscape, *Paysage à Chaponval* (pls. 167 and 169) or the potato gatherer in the *Récolte des pommes, Pontoise* (pl. 170) are tiny and oddly distant figures. They seem to be middle-ground figures who are accidentally inhabiting the foreground. They stand in the tectonic splendor of another world.

With the single exception of Robert Herbert's famous essay on the peasant image in French art, Pissarro's detachment from the peasant figures who populate his pictures has never been adequately studied.[19] All nineteenth-century writers from Duret to Lecomte assume Pissarro's intimate knowledge of the peasantry, his complete immersion in his rural milieu. Their phrases have that kind of lilting moralism so common in contemporary descriptions of rural landscapes and their painters. Lecomte described Pissarro in 1890 as "profoundly knowledgeable of the quintessential intimate details of rural life ['la vie agreste'], familiar with the exact appearances of things and people in the countryside."[20] Arsène Alexandre called Pissarro a workman and historian of the fields ("historien des champs").[21] This attitude has survived to the present day. John Rewald states the case bluntly: "Rather than glorifying the rugged existence of the peasants, he placed them without any pose in their habitual surroundings, thus becoming an objective chronicler of one of the many facets of contemporary life."[22]

In fact, Pissarro's attitude toward the peasantry seems to have been a complex affair, involving as much detachment as familiarity, as much digust as admiration. His pictures of *la vie agreste* suggest very little of the "quintessential intimate detail" and the "exact appearances" so ringingly intoned by Lecomte, and his letters are virtually empty of references to peasants. His only notable statement about the peasantry occurs in a rather late letter dated 21 April 1892 to the novelist-critic Octave Mirbeau. The letter had been quoted only once in the Pissarro literature until its recent publication in the collected correspondence and had not previously been given adequate attention. Pissarro had just read a second-hand booklet by the Russian nobleman and anarchist, Peter Kropotkin, which he sent at the end of April to Lucien in London. Kropotkin, he writes, "believes that one should live the life of a peasant in order to understand them properly. It seems to me that one has to be excited by one's subject in order to render it properly; but is it necessary to be a peasant? . . . Let us first of all be artists and then we shall have the ability to feel everything, even a landscape, without having to be a peasant."[23] The passage is a curious one in a number of ways, but mostly because it stands, amidst thousands of lines of surviving prose, as Pissarro's only sustained remark about the peasantry, his principal human subject. It is fascinating for another reason, too. Pissarro avoided substantive discussion of any sort in his letters, and this is among a mere handful of questioning passages in his entire existing correspondence. What is particularly revealing is that Pissarro should choose this aspect of Kropotkin to discuss. Kropotkin's books of the period before 1892 were, if anything, broadly utopian and concerned with his anarchic proposal for the participation of the entire human population in mechanized, modern agriculture. Pissarro seems to have been rankled by a minor, inessential idea or phrase in Kropotkin, which he has remembered out of any proper context in a letter to the young Mirbeau.[24]

What the passage makes clear is that Pissarro lived as a bourgeois among peasants or rural workers. He was, by choice, an "other" in the context of the hamlet or village. He countered or attempted to counter an idea that was common in middle or late nineteenth-century France among Romantic intellectuals like George Sand and her followers that the peasant, with his "naïve" and "real" vision could perceive nature better than city dwellers, and that the landscape painter or rural novelist should approach the life style of the peasant in order to be able to perceive rural nature adequately.[25] Pissarro, like the other Impressionist painters, repudiated this idea. He lived with a fairly large and definitely bourgeois establishment in various hamlets and villages. He did not attempt to emulate Millet who, in turn, emulated the peasant in his choice of dwellings, in his persistent efforts at gardening, and in his dress. Even the elderly Corot, who painted such "civilized" landscapes, was often compared to a peasant in his appearance and consciously chose to simplify his desires and appearance in keeping with the life style of the country. Any reading of the major biographies of French landscape painters of the nineteenth century will reveal that the peasant was an important part of the painter's alter-ego. The peasant's simplicity, his lack of pretense, and his 'naïveté," the most important qualities for the nineteenth-century landscape painter, were eagerly cultivated by the city dwellers who form the largest part of the population of landscape painters. Pissarro, in arguing against Kropotkin, was denying his need for a connection with the peasantry. He understood the landscape *without* living like a peasant, which, looking at Millet, Pissarro felt was a dangerous existential choice: from an artistic point of view, it resulted, according to him, in a shallow and odiously sentimental rendering of the peasants' lives; from a political and social point of view, it was sheer hypocrisy.

Although it is doubtful that Pissarro concurred with many, indeed any of Kropotkin's ideas in the 1860s and 1870s, his glorification of market gardening in the Région Parisienne must be seen in markedly different terms than the peasant image of Millet, Breton, Sand, Balzac, or even Zola. These painters and writers focused their pictorial and descriptive attention on what we might call "true" or "real" peasants who lived far from the city of Paris, far from the varieties of modernism that emanated from that capital throughout the eighteenth and nineteenth centuries.

As the separate discussion of Pontoise has already established, the peasantry, as we understand it today and as it was most often defined in the nineteenth century, was all but dead in the Pontoise of the latter decades of that century. The rural worker was part of an increasingly modernized, partially mechanized cash-crop and hired-labor system of agriculture. As such, the "peasantness" of Pissarro's Pontoise is largely mythical. His landscapes appear to be rather than are peasant landscapes. The rural workers who walk down the roads and till the fields of his landscapes ran machines, rotated crops, and participated in a sophisticated marketing system that served the city of Paris as much as it did Pontoise itself. The agriculture of Pontoise, like that of Argenteuil, consisted of the modern market gardens that were so much admired later in the century by Kropotkin. These are the rural workers who were to act as the basis for his new anarchist state.[26]

While it is true that Pissarro celebrated a modernizing, if small-scale agriculture in his paintings of Pontoise and L'Hermitage, he was not a very detailed or even trustworthy chronicler of the life and work of these latterday "peasants." Indeed, perhaps the only painter who seriously studied the world of agriculture in the then modern France was Léon Lhermitte.[27] The difference between Lhermitte and Pissarro, arguably the two major painters of *la vie agreste* active in the last third of the century, is the difference between a figure painter and a landscape painter; between a man concerned with a partially (and necessarily) idealized recording of the real peasant life amidst which he lived, and a painter of rural landscapes in the Région Parisienne. It is to Lhermitte that we look for moving, accurate, and humanized depictions of the dying peasant class in the north of France. His Salon entry of 1882, *Le Pays des moissonneurs*, shows a homeless and exhausted Norman family sitting in the courtyard of a large wheat farm while the husband and father collects his pay from the *paysan riche* who owns the farm. Lhermitte, although stylistically conservative, even *retardataire* to the modern eye, was a far more knowledgeable and empathetic painter of the rural world than was Pissarro. Indeed, the title "historien des champs" applied almost perfectly to Lhermitte and hardly at all to Pissarro.

Except for the three rather lengthy stays of 1874, 1875, and 1876 in Montfoucault with his friend Piette, Pissarro probably never viewed rural life at close hand. His pictures of Osny and Ennery, the two wheat-growing villages of the Vexin plateau closest to Pontoise, are somewhat timid views of main streets, mills, and other public scenes. They show no evidence of intercourse with the native population. They are anything but "intimate." Pissarro's pictures of the rural workers in and around his own landscape at L'Hermitage are landscape paintings with figures. The figures, like most landscape figures, populate rather than define the landscape. The landscape triumphs over the figures.

Yet, when compared with the landscape figures of the other major Impressionists, Pissarro's staffage figures have greater variety and seemingly a greater "truth." A simple glance through the landscapes of Monet painted in the 1870s reveals a surprisingly narrow range of human activity. The vast majority of Monet's figures stand or walk in simple erect poses. They very rarely *do* anything. The same generalizations can be made about the landscape figures of Sisley and Renoir. Pissarro's figures tend gardens, chat by the side of a roadway, push wheelbarrows, wait for trains to pass, fish in the Oise, and carry faggots on their backs. The list, while a rudimentary one, is easily contrastable with the lists that one could compile for the landscape figures of Monet, Sisley, and Renoir in the same decades and very comparable with a list of the activities of the landscape figures in Corot's French landscapes. Using the large collection of paintings by Corot now in the Musée d'Orsay as a sample, such a list would include washing clothes, tending cattle, walking along paths, boating in the river, feeding the family pig, resting in the fields, and riding horseback. The connection with Pissarro is evident. The younger painter's landscape esthetic was essentially determined by Corot, the most important landscape painter in France during the middle of the nineteenth century. Pissarro's figures play a minor role in the landscape, as they had for Corot. Yet they lend a certain specificity and reality to that landscape by virtue of their various activities. Unlike Monet and Sisley, Pissarro was concerned with the purpose as well as the placement of his figures.

In contrast to the staffage figures, Pissarro's large figural studies of peasants, most of which were painted in the period 1879–83, show peasant figures who are generally doing nothing against a background of almost undifferentiated green with a very high horizon line. All the pictorial, psychological, and historical problems with which Lhermitte involved himself in his studies and Salon pictures – the portrayal of real figures performing real activities in their own environment – are tactfully avoided by Pissarro.[28] His full-scale peasant figures are almost exclusively pretty girls or young women. They are the kind of peasants whom travel writers had been accustomed to admire since the eighteenth century in their detached, often sexist accounts of their unavoidable coach rides through rural Europe on the way to Paris, London, and Rome.[29]

In the figure paintings of 1879–83, Pissarro enlarged the figures so that they are no longer staffage figures. He allows them instead to dominate their surroundings. He contorts their limbs in active, even distracting poses; he averts their gazes so as to deny psychological interaction with the viewer; he distorts the conventional relationship between the ground plane and the figure as Degas was doing at the same time, tilting the ground plane forward and pushing it around the figure so that the viewer seems, most often, to be looking down on the peasant. In fact, many of the peasant paintings of 1882 are of rural women wearing simple costumes lying or sprawled on the ground (pl. 123). The figures relate to the resting peasant type that one finds easily in the paintings of Courbet, Corot, and even Bastien-Lepage. But, when comparing Pissarro's *Le Repos, paysanne couchée dans l'herbe, Pontoise* (pl. 124) to Courbet's *Harvest* (Petit Palais, Paris) or Bastien-Lepage's *Rest after the Harvest* (Musée d'Orsay) of 1882, Pissarro's peasant girl loses much of her real connection with the resting peasant type. Her work is only loosely defined, indicated by the rake lying at her side. Unlike Bastien-Lepage and Courbet, Pissarro gives us no confirmation of the task the girl has been working at. The more one explores images of this type – and Pissarro painted an important series of female peasants in 1882–83 – the more evident are their manifold distances from reality, the problematic, unrealistic, almost anti-genre stance that they take vis-à-vis both the peasant image in past art and the viewer.

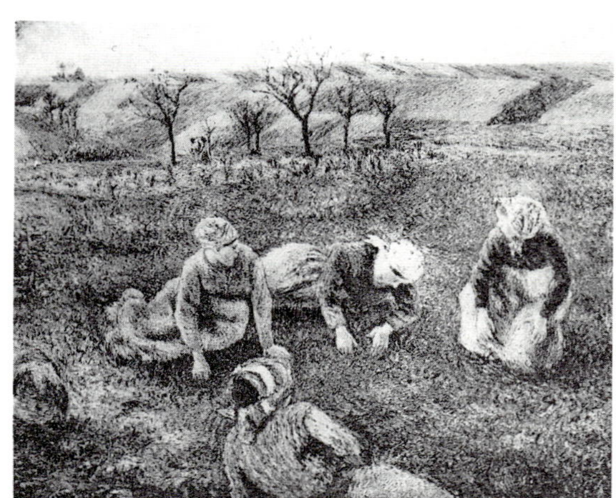

123. Camille Pissarro, *Les Sarcleuses, Pontoise* (P&V 563), 1882, oil on canvas, 63 × 77cm., whereabouts unknown.

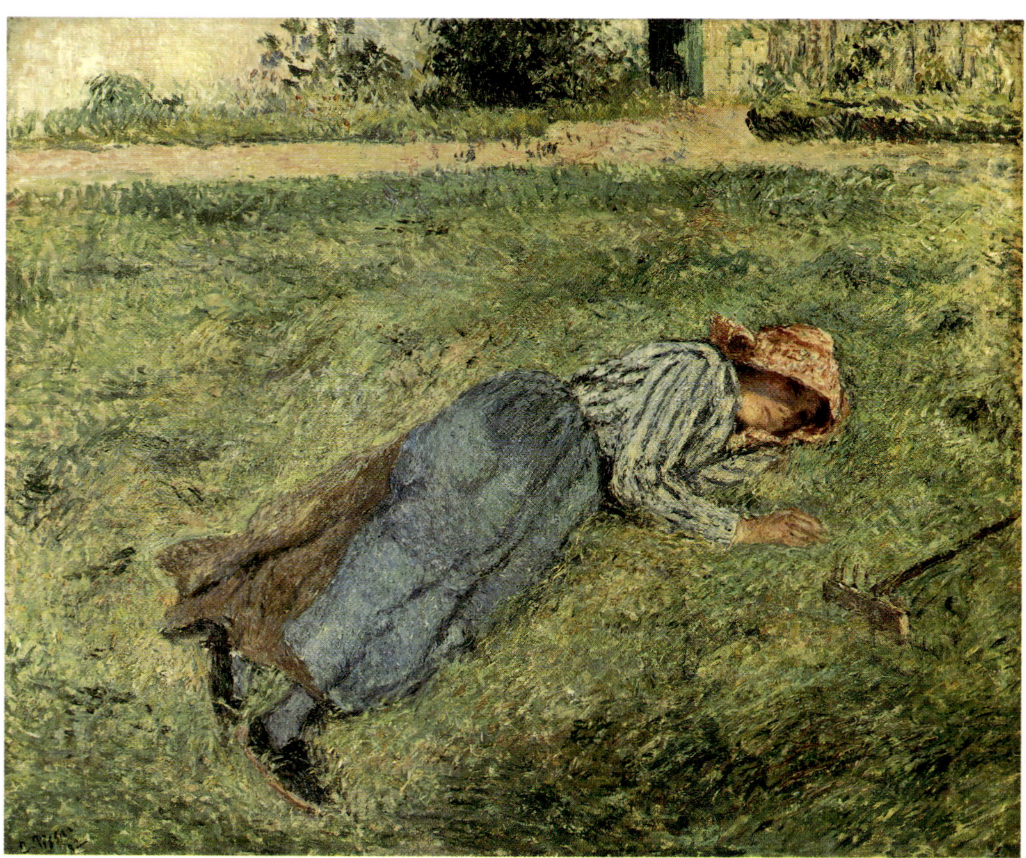

124. Camille Pissarro, *Le Repos, paysanne couchée dans l'herbe, Pontoise* (P&V 565), 1882, oil on canvas, 63 × 78cm., Kunsthalle, Bremen.

Pissarro's large figures are servant girls and hired models arranged calculatedly against grassy backgrounds.[30] In fact, the backgrounds are so simple, so uncluttered with accessory forms, that the oddness, the distortion of their poses is emphasized. The viewer reads the peasant women of the early 1880s as *posed* figures. What fascinated Pissarro was not the relationship between figure and ground, but, quite simply, the figure. He was not primarily interested in their social status or lack thereof, but in their bodies. They are figures as much as they are peasants, and they must be interpreted as attempts or experiments in figure painting made by a landscape painter, rather than as genre scenes. They are, as such, abstract and unreal. Comparing these figures to the peasant women of Millet, Breton, Bastien-Lepage, Lhermitte, or even Bouguereau activates our sense of their strangeness and places them art historically as the logical precursors of the contorted Breton peasants painted by Gauguin and Bernard in the latter 1880s.

The Frontal Figure and the Landscape Tradition

The great majority of figures in the landscape tradition are absorbed either in their own lives or their own thoughts. Shepherds and shepherdesses dangle their feet in the water. Resting travelers gaze wistfully at the view. Gypsies talk or sing in small groups. Acquaintances gossip a bit before going their respective ways. Workers load ships while merchants supervise the scene. These occupied and preoccupied figures dominate nineteenth-century landscape painting as well. Yet Pissarro, who was seldom a purely inventive painter, borrowed from a type of landscape figure, one who is neither occupied in a task nor preoccupied with his own thoughts. This is, simply, the frontal figure. Although only a handful of these figures exist in Pissarro's landscape, they are special enough to be examined with some care. They tell us, in many ways, more about the peculiar social tensions between the landscape painter and the inhabited landscape he paints than any other figures in landscape painting.

These figures stand in stiff, frontal poses with their arms hanging loose at their sides, and they face the viewer with an affected directness. They first appear in Pissarro's pictures of the late 1860s and can be related, in a distant way, to Manet's staring women of the early and middle years of that decade. The disconcerting effect of the staring Victorine in *Déjeuner sur l'herbe* or *Olympia* is an often referred to aspect of Manet's many-sided and undeniable avant-gardism. Pissarro's smaller, less obvious figures have never been noticed by students of landscape painting, but they play a decisive role in any proper elucidation of his own very difficult and evasive esthetics.

Several examples of the frontal figures can be mentioned, but it is perhaps best to treat one example in detail. *Vue de Pontoise, quai du Pothuis* (pl. 126) is a startlingly bold, planar, and geometric townscape. Although almost encrusted with architectural form, the painting is populated by only two figures, a very small population for a townscape painted in the nineteenth century. The figures, a bourgeois couple standing in the left foreground, have a crucial formal role in the picture, interrupting the only space-suggesting diagonal of the picture, blocking a recessive arch of the bridge, and providing a strong vertical in an area of the picture devoted to small-scale horizontal forms. Clearly, Pissarro needed figures at precisely this place in the landscape. They are in no way random or fortuitous wanderers, and they certainly do not appear to be. They stand still, but are not engaged in conversation and show no close relationship either to each other or to

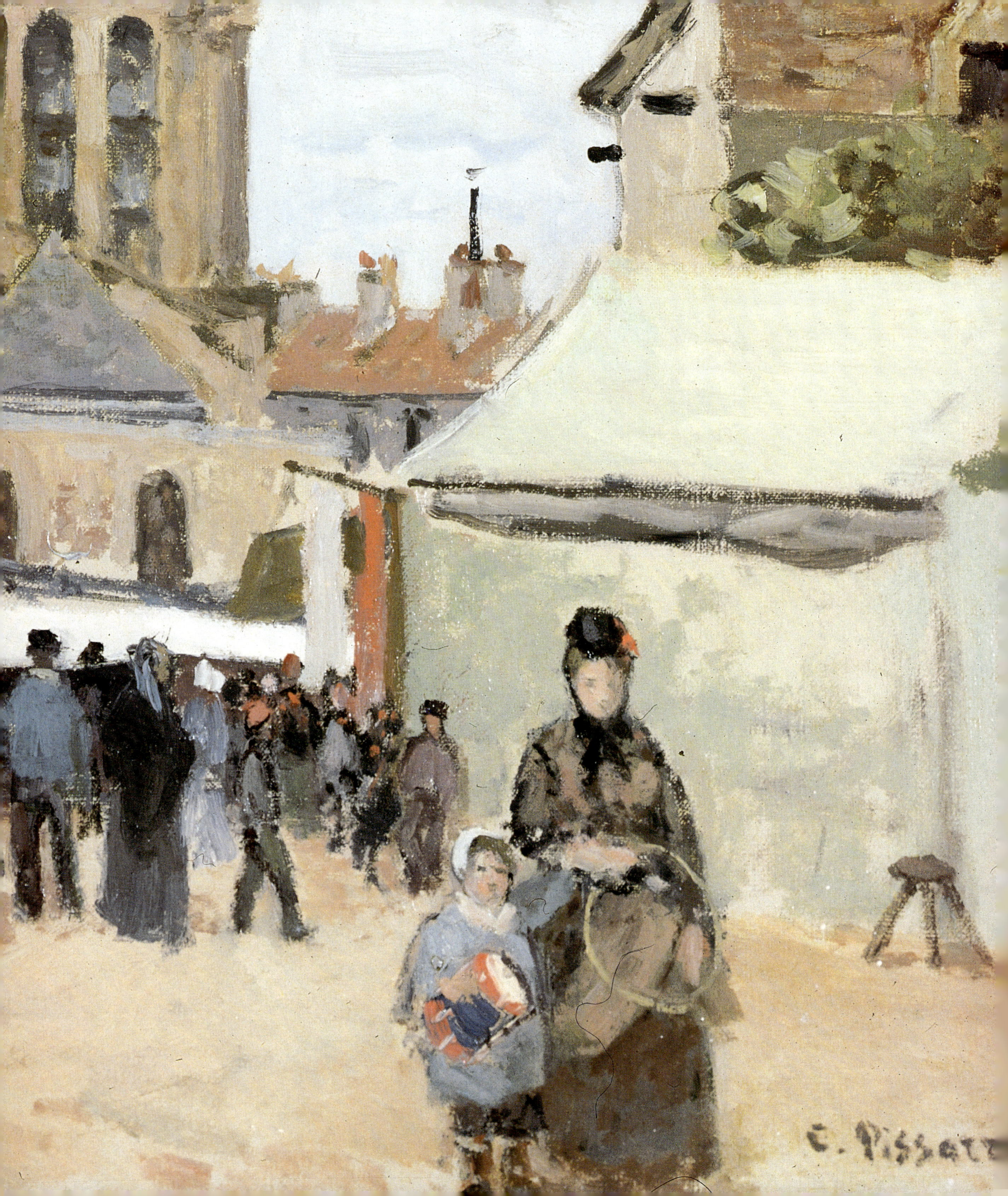
C. Pissarro

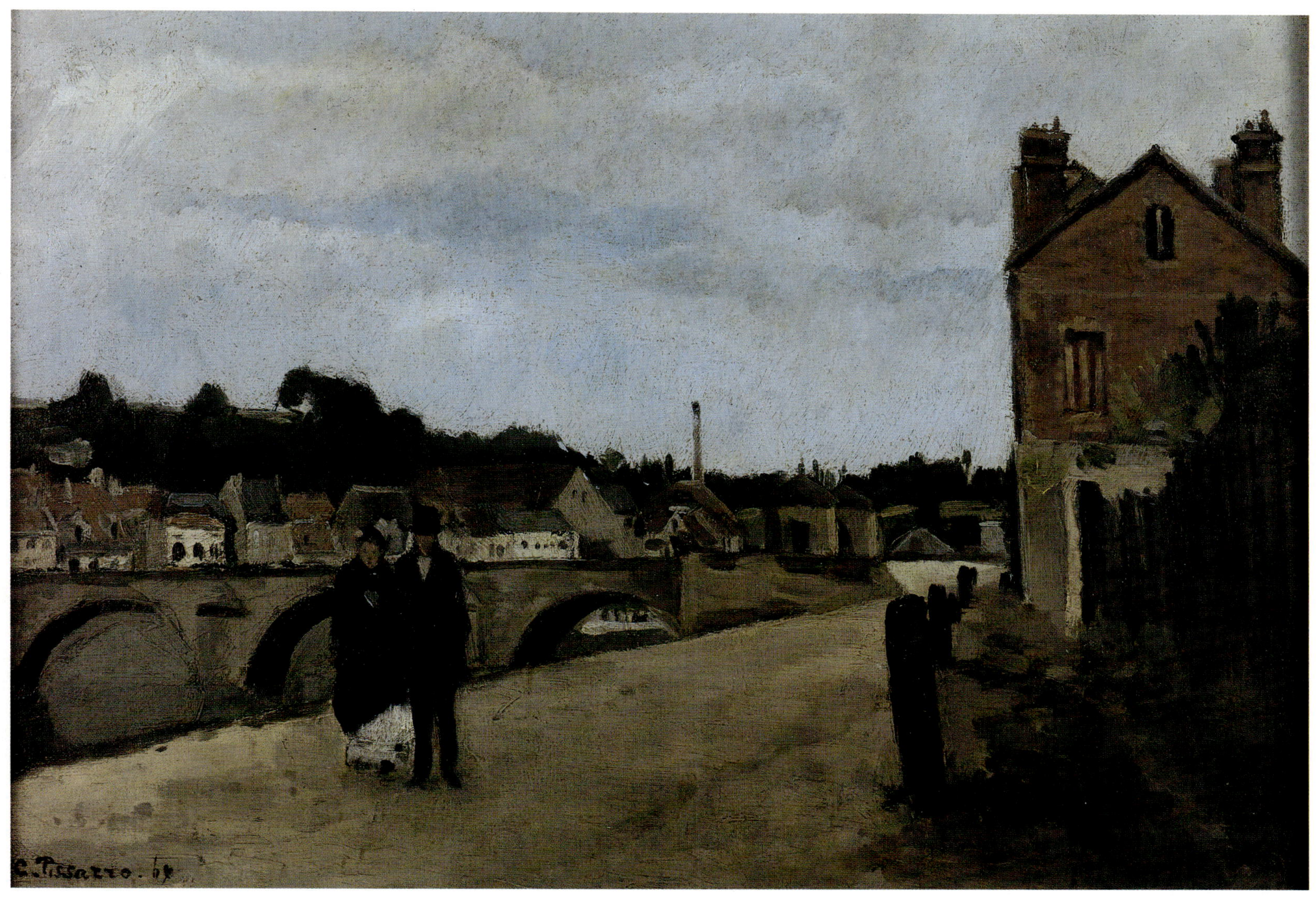

126. Camille Pissarro, *Vue de Pontoise, quai du Pothuis*, 1867, oil on canvas, 31 × 45.5cm., collection of the Tel Aviv Museum of Art; bequest of Lilli Schocken, Jerusalem-New York, 1959.

125. Detail of pl. 36.

the landscape in which they are very obviously set. They are out-of-place figures paradoxically fixed in place. Even their color is artificial, and intentionally so. They wear precisely the black and white that was in the process of being banished from Pissarro's palette and that, in the context of the picture, is clearly separable from the natural colors of the buildings, the trees, and the sky.[31]

Yet these matters of placement and color are not their primary oddities, which are, rather, their pose and their frontality. Why are they frontal? The answer lies, I think, in their role vis-à-vis the pictorial space. They, like the two frontally posed *promeneurs* in *La Côte du Jallais* (pl. 116), keep the viewer *out* of the picture much more forcefully than a casually posed, occupied figure would. If Pissarro had replaced them with a pair of peasant women chatting to a dock worker, a typical arrangement in many simpler landscapes of the nineteenth century, the careful, almost puzzle-like planarity of his composition would have been destroyed. The viewer would simply read around such a little genre group. The frontal couple allows nothing of the sort. They not only reinforce the flatness and planarity of the picture, they exaggerate it. They continually "square us off." We are always in front of them, no matter where our eye wanders along the surface of the picture. They make it all but impossible for us to imagine ourselves into the limited pictorial space that Pissarro does provide.

The *promeneurs* in *La Côte du Jallais* are not only frontal figures, but a frontal bourgeois couple. The sober appropriateness of their clothing and its suggestion of discreetness and respectability make them more formidable figures than a pair of gawking peasants in town for the day would have been; and it is true that most of Pissarro's frontal figures are bourgeois figures dressed up for a walk.[32] The woman and her daughter standing beneath the arched web of tree limbs in *Châtaigniers à Louveciennes* (pl. 127) are clear examples, but there are many others as well. Bourgeois figures in frontal poses were perhaps slightly ridiculous to Pissarro. They do not belong in the landscape as do Corot's washer-women and nymphs,[33] Millet's peasants, Monet's women in the garden, or Gauguin's South Sea islanders. They look forward to Seurat's hieratic, geometrized figures which play pictorial and social rather than psychological roles. But their forthright stares render them more disturbing than Seurat's predominantly profile figures who engage in social intercourse within the planarized stringencies of his landscape world. Seurat's figures are no less occupied with their own lives for all the geometric limitations on their movements. Pissarro's figures engage *us* and not each other. They, like Manet's prostitutes, charge the pictorial surface with a tension grounded in social and psychological doubt.

Like most landscape painters of his own or of the previous generation, Pissarro disliked the bourgeoisie, finding them pretentious, vulgar, and stupid.[34] This opinion, although related in many cases to radical politics, was held by those who aspired to be aristocrats as well as by socialists and anarchists. Pissarro's proforma dislike of the bourgeoisie undoubtedly has a bearing upon the "stick" figures that inhabit his landscape world. His bourgeois frontal figures wear their clothes like wooden dummies. However, Pissarro was not consistent in this matter and painted frontal peasants as well. I turn, for my single example, to his greatest painting of 1877, *Côtes Saint-Denis à Pontoise* (pl. 154). In this large yet oddly constrained picture, a peasant woman and her child stare at us from behind the naked branches of winter (pl. 128). They are not awkward and defiant figures, as are the bourgeois couples discussed above. Rather, they recede into the vegetation and stare out from the protected confines of another world. The landscape, even without the figures, is among the most complex and pessimistic pictures in Pissarro's oeuvre. Its layered surface is as thick and rutted as the muddy road that runs off the picture on the left. The branches and limbs of the trees form screens upon screens, cutting and interrupting forms in what is almost a frenzy of linear energy. Yet the pathos and melancholy of the picture is most forcefully communicated by the peasants. Their presence is not assertive, but, when we find them, as we inevitably do, they haunt us, forcing us back into ourselves, making us uncomfortably aware of our own presence in the landscape.

The frontal figures confront us with the problem of "being" in the landscape, a problem of continuous importance to the landscape painter. The *Vue de Pontoise, quai du Pothuis* and *Côtes Saint-Denis à Pontoise* are, in most ways, uncomparable images. They are stylistically dissimilar, technically different, and chronologically separated by a decade at a time in the history of art characterized by extremely rapid change in almost every aspect of pictorial creation. Yet, for the iconographer of landscape images and the student of "social" landscapes, they have a startlingly similar message. In the earlier image, the geometric order and the almost obsessive tidiness of man's world, the town, is confronted with notable directness. Its inhabitants are forceful, even shameless in their respectability. In the later image, the disturbing complexity of pre-modern rural nature is confronted, and its inhabitants are "natives," timid watchers, who lurk in the vegetation, waiting. How compelling this picture must have been when it made its

127. Detail of pl. 94.

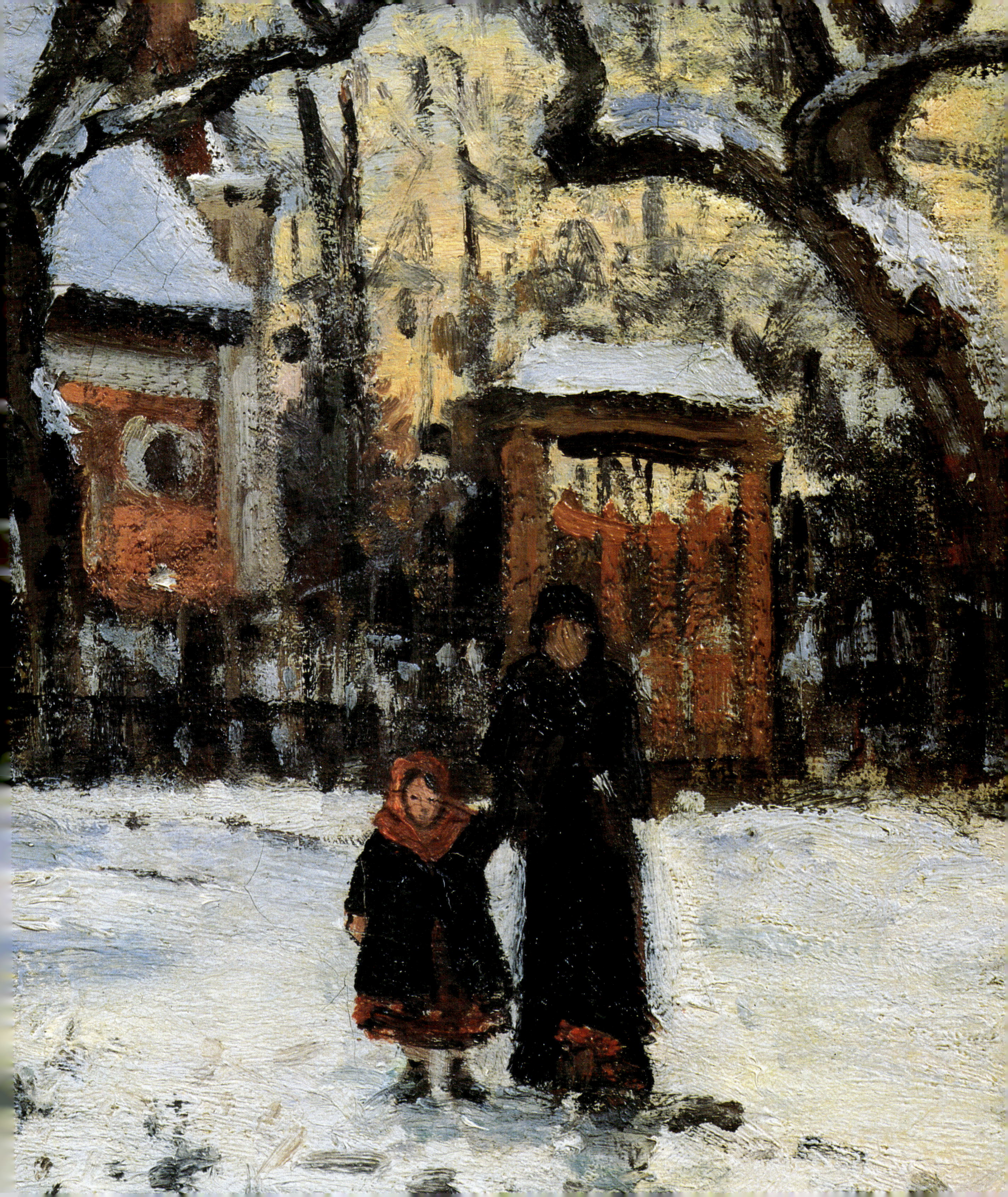

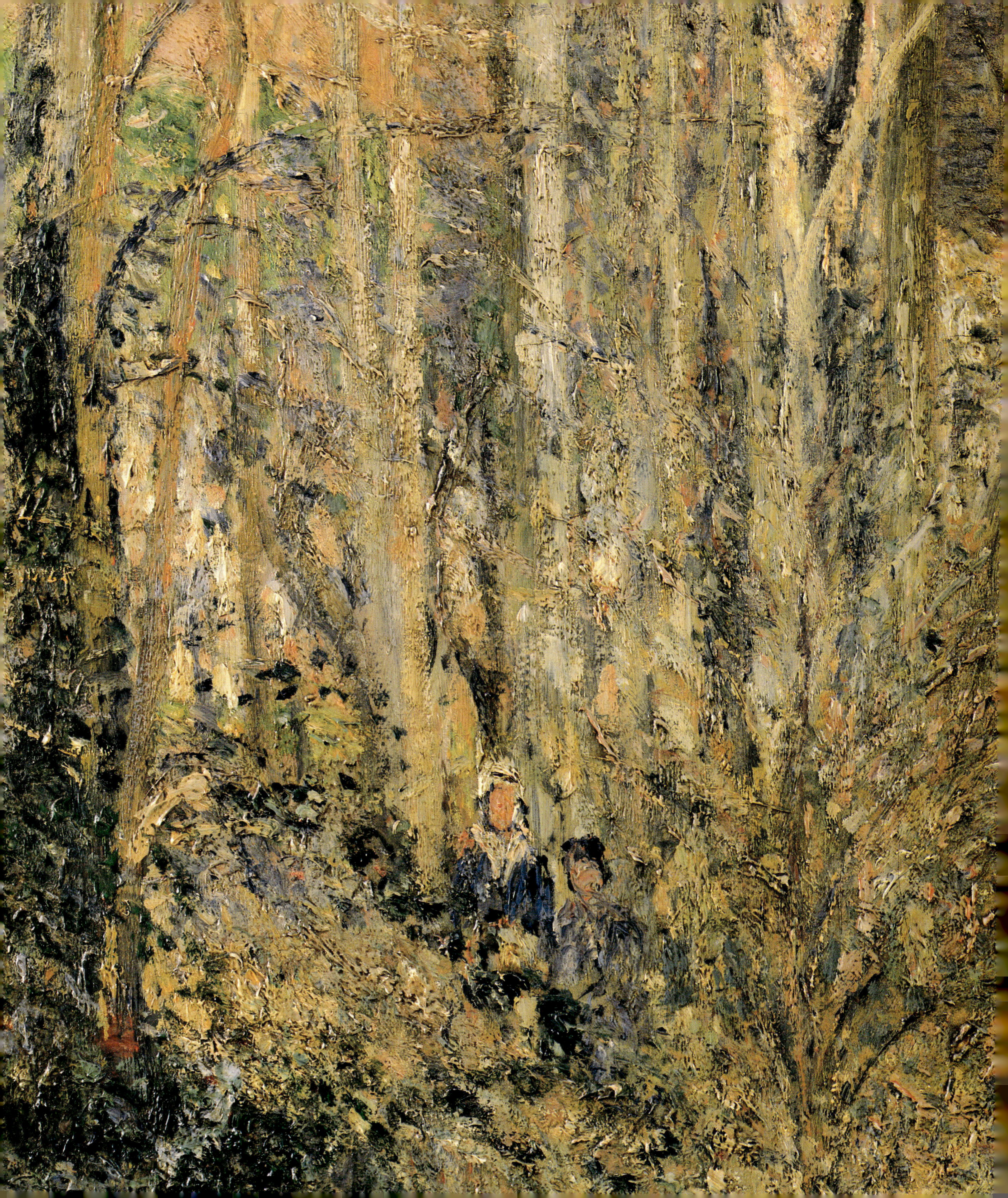

first appearance at the third Impressionist exhibition of 1877. It hung probably alone on a small wall, in the same room with Renoir's greatest figure painting of the 1870s, the *Moulin de la Galette* (Musée d'Orsay). Scarcely could two more opposite paintings be imagined – Renoir's, with its delightful acceptance of the urban bourgeoise at their leisure in Paris, and Pissarro's, with its layered ambiguities, its suspicion, its ultimate acceptance of a state of alienation.

The frontal figures, although they represent a minority of Pissarro's landscape figures, address themselves to Henriet's concept of the landscape painter as "an intermittent being" quite clearly. With all their posed presence, they remind us continually that we are the viewer and that the painter, arranging at will, has altered nature to meet certain pictorial, personal, and esthetic aims. Pissarro's nature, intimate as it might appear to be, is in fact a detached and sometimes defiant nature, which stands apart from us as it stood apart from him.

128. Detail of pl. 154.

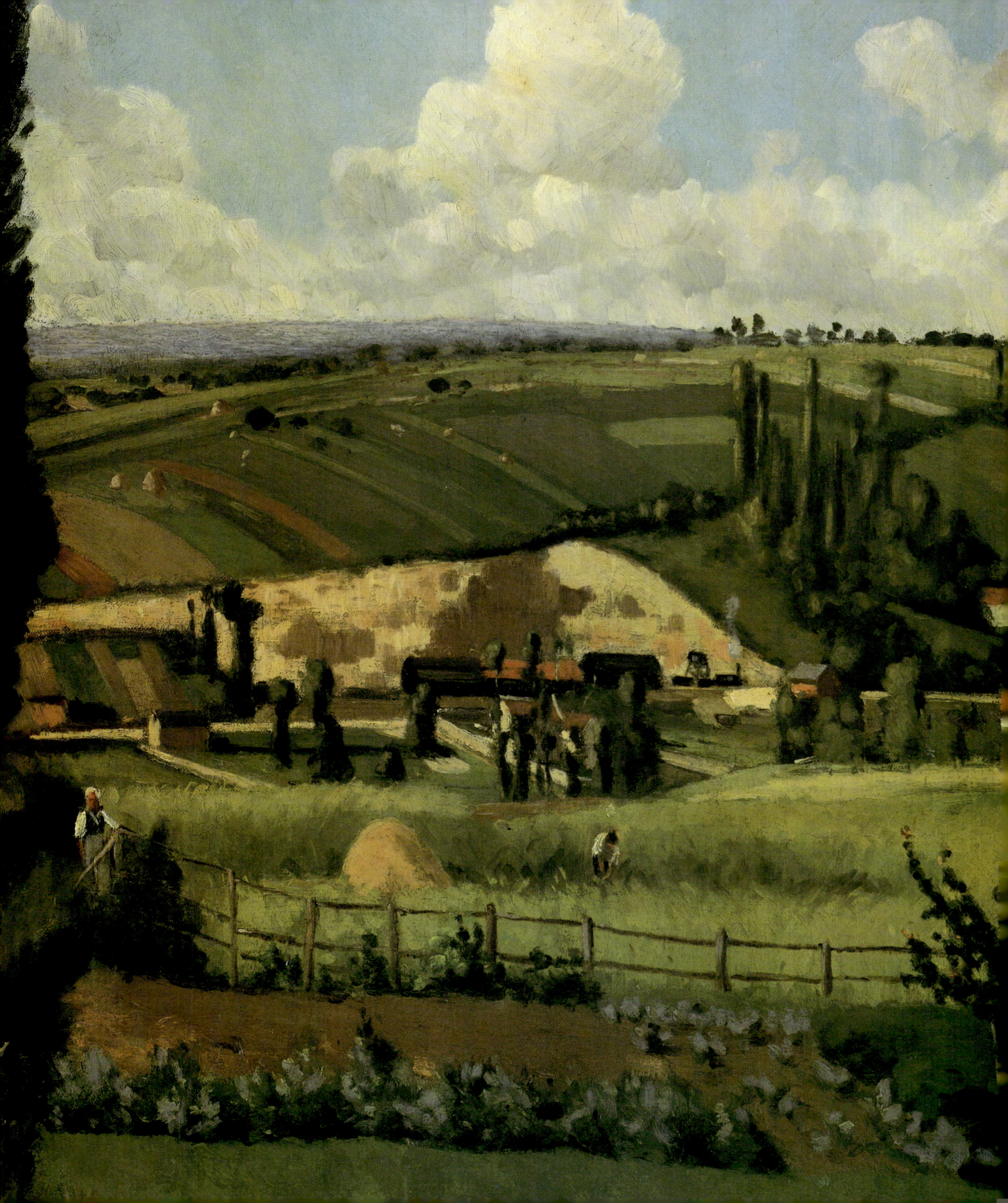

6 Progressions and Regressions

It is well known that Pissarro played a major role in the movement called Impressionism. This role is particularly evident in his correspondence, which reveals a constant attention to matters artistic. He wrote literally thousands of letters, many of which are lost today.[1] The extant letters show how he soothed or attempted to soothe temperamental squabbles among his fellow artists. From his Pontoisian vantage point, he kept the fledgling organization of artists together and created at least some form of what we today call solidarity among a disparate group of men and women. In keeping with this overwhelming body of documentary evidence, students of Impressionism, most notably John Rewald, have stressed Pissarro's crucial role in what might be called the sociology of the movement.[2] His even-tempered character has been extolled in paragraph after paragraph of prose. His "heroic" attempts at battling both personal poverty and internal dissension among his friends have been written about at length. What is lacking, however, is a clear understanding of his own artistic development within the movement that he maintained so carefully that he has often been called its father.

An intensive study of Pissarro's development in the Pontoisian period reveals a process of considerable complexity. There are at least four totally distinct sub-periods which interrupt what many writers have considered to be the continuity of that most Impressionist decade. These sub-periods do not combine to form a unified style. The word fitful can best be used to characterize his career at this time. There is little that is linear or progressive about it.

Many writers have discussed Pissarro's career as a slow and perhaps rather dull, even relentless, evolution through the predominant styles of late nineteenth-century painting. His early work has always been linked with mid-century landscape painting, the 1870s, with Impressionism, the 1880s, with Neo-Impressionism, and the 1890s, with a synthetic Impressionism involving a brighter palette, more contrived compositions, and a wider range of subject matter.[3] The logically progressive character of Pissarro's art has been a feature of Pissarro criticism since the 1890s. Georges Lecomte referred in 1892 to "the different phases of the logical evolution of his talent," to "a slow rise toward a more integral art," and later, in describing his character, to "the progressive and normal development of his personality."[4] Arsène Alexandre made similar remarks in 1896, discussing Pissarro's career as a steady evolution, free from the nervousness that characterized both modern painting and modern life.[5] Even Holl, in his underrated study, *Après l'Impressionnisme*, written in 1910, structured Pissarro's career as "an important and reasoned rise."[6]

Ostensibly, the elements of stability in Pissarro's career were great. While undeniably poor, he did not suffer the intense poverty experienced by Monet in the late 1870s. His letters to Murer, Gachet, and Duret lack the dramatized pathos and abjectness of Monet's letters written just prior to the death of his wife in 1879.[7] Pissarro lived in a reasonably stable environment within the supportive context of a large immediate family and, more importantly from the financial point of view, of a large and wealthy extended family.[8] His paintings were rarely heaped with the scorn leveled against those of Monet, Cézanne, and Renoir, nor did he suffer the neglect experienced by Lépine, Guillaumin, Béliard, and the many lesser Impressionists. He lived in the same small hamlet, L'Hermitage, near Pontoise, for most of this decade.

Yet any close study of Pissarro's life in the 1870s undermines the rather benign, "unified" image of the painter from Pontoise. His career in that small town was interrupted by important periods in Louveciennes, suburban London, Montfoucault in Mayenne, Brittany, and, of course, Paris. His letters to Dr. Gachet reveal a preoccupation with the health of his family undoubtedly related to the frail condition and early death of his daughter, Jeanne. His domestic arrangements in L'Hermitage were not as settled as might appear: surviving correspondence indicates that the family had at least three addresses there between 1873 and 1883, and references in letters suggest that there may have been more.[9] The motivations for the moves were probably twofold: the size of the growing family, and the rising or falling of the family finances. However, what is of interest in this context is not the reasons for the moves, but the fact of the moves. The family was unstable within a stable environment. Their funds and their friends came from outside.

Two general attitudes towards Pissarro's career persist in the historical and critical commentaries on Impressionism written in the twentieth century. The first is that Pissarro was the oldest and, therefore, the most conservative of the Impressionists. This point of view stresses his lengthy apprenticeships with Corot, Courbet, and Chintreuil and contrasts his apparent lack of boldness with the "inventiveness" of Monet and even Renoir.[10] The second emphasizes Pissarro's susceptibility to outside influences and treats his career as a series of responses to the inventions of other painters. Material to support this latter contention is largely confined to Pissarro's adoption of Seurat's and Signac's "divisionist" technique in the latter 1880s.[11] The present chapter will propose an alternative structure best called "progressions and regressions," a structure combining both these essentially correct evaluations of Pissarro's position in the history of modern art, but lacking their pejorative connotations.

The words "progression" and "regression" have been chosen for very specific reasons. Historians and social scientists who have focused their attention on modern or post-industrial history have been rightly obsessed with modern man's desire for change and his simultaneous need for continuity. The many studies of the process of modernization in both European and Third World countries have stressed the traumas and psychic scars experienced by its victims.[12] Like most men of his own highly mobile generation, Pissarro at once desired "improvement" and yearned for stability. His imagery skitters between industry and agriculture. He claimed in a letter to his son, Lucien, that the disease of modern times was change, all the while fighting for "improvements" in both art and society that would necessitate change.[13] His almost obsessive attachment to Impressionism is evidence enough of his desire to make what Harold Rosenberg has called a tradition of the new. Like the so-called futurists after him, Pissarro made "modern" pictures of pre-modern subjects or, as the discussion of his struggle with the image of the factory has shown, rather unmodern pictures of decidedly modern subjects. His entire career is characterized by a vacillation between the modern and the pre-modern. Like so many other "modernist" painters, he grappled both with the traditions of the history of art and with the immediate and variable stimuli of modern life, even in its relatively provincial, Pontoisian manifestations.[14]

Perhaps the most interesting aspect of Pissarro's complicated development in the Pontoisian period is the degree to which the visual stimulus that the landscape afforded him was much less important for the formation of his esthetic than were outside pressures and influences, whether verbal or visual. It was not Pontoise, but Théodore Duret, Claude Monet, Gustave Courbet, and Edgar Degas who, both separately and in combination, gave Pissarro the impetus for the often extreme stylistic and iconographic changes that characterize his art in the years 1867–83. Following the advice or example of these men, he altered his perception of the natural environment markedly. The raw visual impression so often considered to have been of paramount importance to the "Impressionist" painter was less important for Pissarro than ideas about art and the various ways of making it.

The phases of the Pontoisian period can be characterized in two ways: first, by analyzing the paintings themselves in the kind of detail to which art historians are accustomed and, second, by graphing the frequency of motif types and mapping the points from which Pissarro painted landscapes in any given year. These latter methods, more in keeping with the statistical approach of many sociologists and social historians, are in some ways more useful to the art historian than the conventional practice of stylistic and iconographical analysis because they set unified periods of time into clear relief. They abstract the analysis from the level of intimate and fundamentally descriptive connoisseurship to the general typological cataloguing of many works of art. There are, however, advantages to the more traditional method. General arguments can be concretized in a descriptive analysis of a single work of art. For that reason, several works will be discussed in some detail within each of the sections devoted to a sub-period of Pissarro's Pontoisian career.

1866–1868   Structural Realism: The First Pontoise Period

Pissarro arrived in Pontoise in October 1866, established a residence on the rue du Fond de L'Hermitage, and remained there until January 1869, when the family moved to Louveciennes. Seventeen paintings of Pontoise, fourteen of which are included in the Pissarro-Venturi catalogue and three of which have come to light since its completion, survive in published form. They have a distinct uniformity of style and represent a logical outgrowth of the constructivist landscape mode that Pissarro had developed by the mid-1860s following the example of Corot's early landscapes.[15] The pictures share a similarity of palette, tending toward greens, some greys, and earth tones. The bright accent colors that Pissarro had used in the early and middle 1860s are no longer evident.[16] Certain pictures, such as the *Vue du Pontoise, quai du Pothuis* (P&V 60, Kunsthalle, Mannheim), *Paysage aux Pâtis, Pontoise* (pl. 130), and *Vue de Pontoise, quai du Pothuis* (pl. 126) are almost monochromatic and show an evident Corotesque concern for the study of value rather than hue. The surfaces of all three canvases are divided into large rectilinear areas of paint possessing a density and literalness that recall the oil studies painted by Corot in the 1820s and 1830s. The pictures are orderly arrangements of painted marks and are evidence of Pissarro's interest in rigid pictorial structure and, by extension, in the artist's willful control over nature. As such, they evoke the Aristotelian view of nature as something to be ordered and improved by man, so important in the French landscape tradition with its roots in Poussin.

Paysage aux Pâtis, Pontoise will serve well as an emblem of Pissarro's obsessive ordering, his monochromatic palette, and the literalness of his paint handling during the first Pontoise period. The "banding" of nature into insistent parallels,

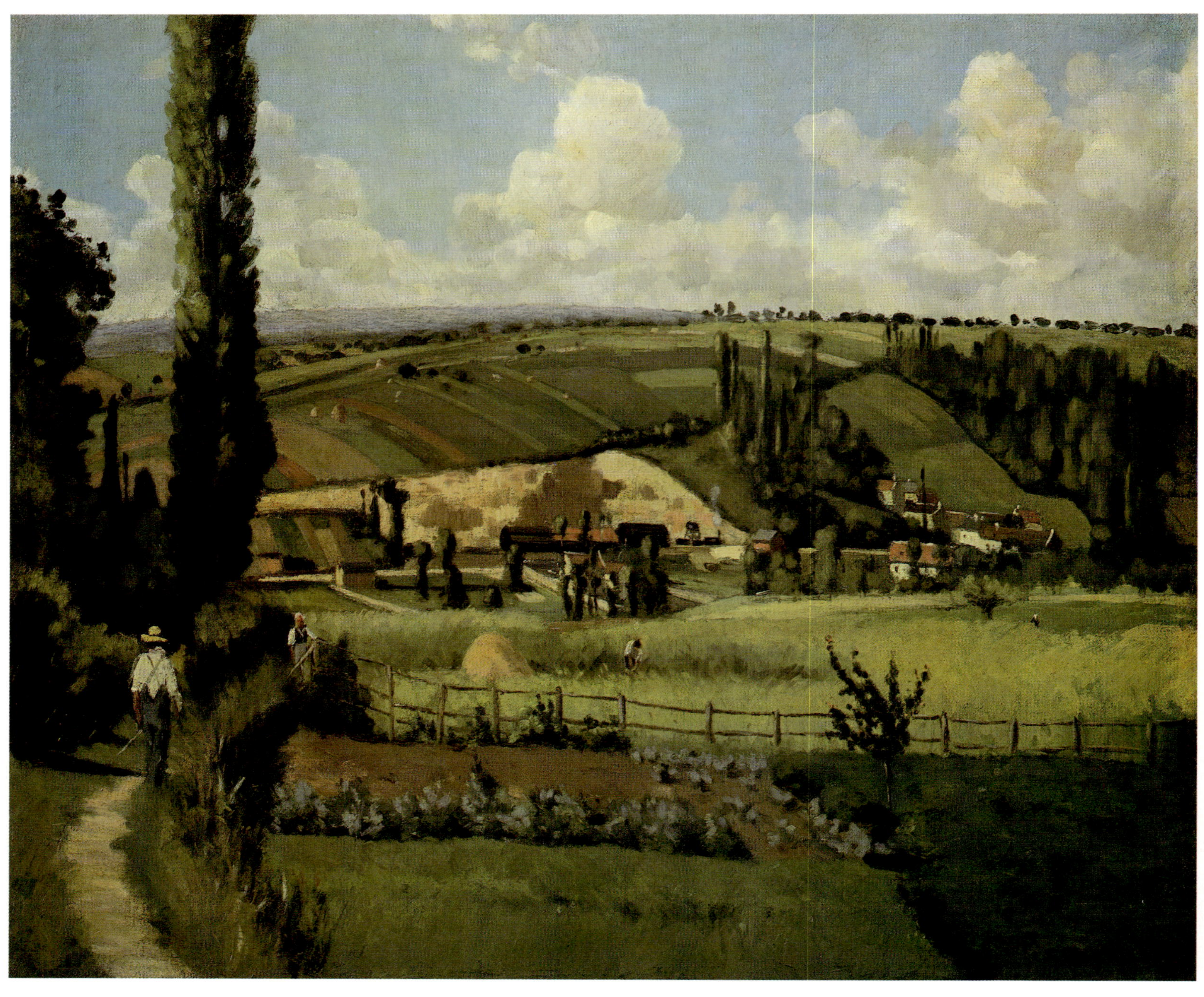

130. Camille Pissaro, *Paysage aux Pâtis, Pontoise* (P&V 61), 1868, oil on canvas, 81 × 100cm., private collection.

which Champa relates to Daubigny and sees as a characteristic of Pissarro's pictorial structure in the 1860s, is especially evident in this picture.[17] Because of the painter's viewpoint, just above the descent of a rather steep hill, the landscape lacks a middle ground and emphasizes an almost strident foreground with a clearly structured repoussoir poplar tree and three scale-giving figures. There is no visible connection between the foreground and the background, which is a carefully defined arrangement of separately applied patches of paint, each representing a tree, a roof, a field, or a quarry. Pictorial penetration is possible only along the slightly curved foreground path, uncomfortably attached to the left edge of the picture. The figures and the poplar tree block this penetration by the viewer as much as they encourage it. The viewer must read along or across the landscape. All Pissarro's pictorial devices dichotomize the tactile (foreground) and the visual (background) realms of experience and reinforce the viewer's detachment from nature. The location from which Pissarro painted this landscape is not difficult to determine, in spite of the fact that twentieth-century construction has totally altered the agricultural character of the landscape. The picture was painted from the hillside near the village of Cernay overlooking the Viosne Valley with its hamlet, Les Pâtis. Yet it is clear that topographical accuracy was not Pissarro's concern. The floor of the Viosne valley with its distinctive mills, old farms, quarries, and small forests, all of which would have fascinated a topographical tourist illustrator, play a minor role in Pissarro's landscape. The rich human and architectural character of the site is eschewed.

In painting *Paysage aux Pâtis, Pontoise*, Pissarro gave himself over most fervently to the fields with their controlled green patches. For an agricultural landscape, this picture is unusually green. The color was most often reserved for *sous-bois* or park landscapes in the nineteenth century, and yellows, browns, and golds, the colors of earth and ripened grain, predominate in paintings of field agriculture. Grain fields were most often depicted during the harvest season and not, as in here, in late spring or early summer. The green of the landscape is probably rooted in the vegetative landscapes of Chintreuil, whom Pissarro met at Corot's studio in the 1860s, and recalls the often quoted advice that Corot gave to Pissarro during the same period: "Study values—We do not see the same way. Where you see green, I see grey and beige. But this is no reason why you should not work on your values, for there lies the root of everything."[18]

Interpretation of *Paysage aux Pâtis, Pontoise* is not an easy task. The tiny hay-

131. Camille Pissarro, *L'Hermitage à Pontoise* (P&V 56), 1867, oil on canvas, 90 × 150cm., Wallraf-Richartz-Museum, Cologne.

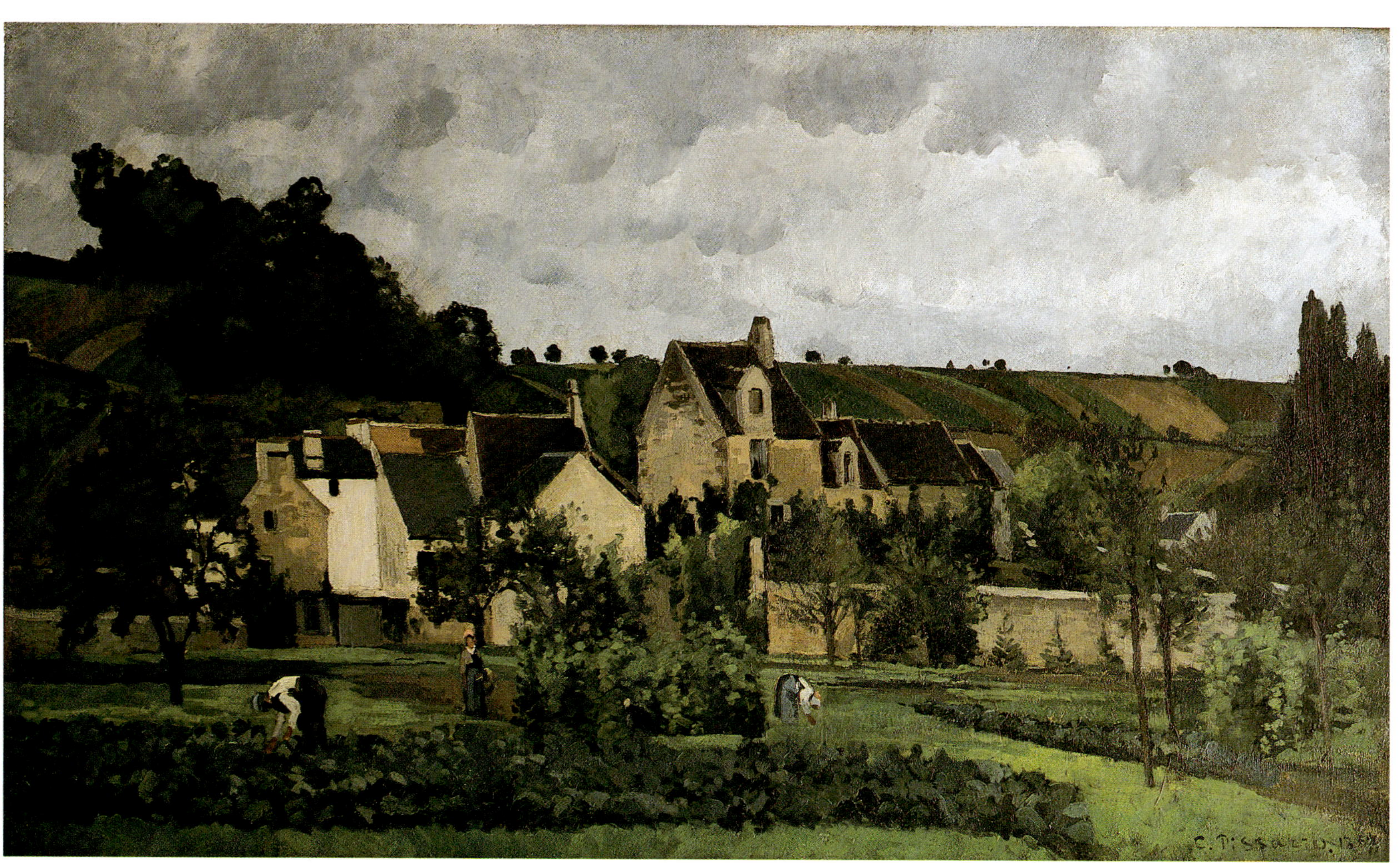

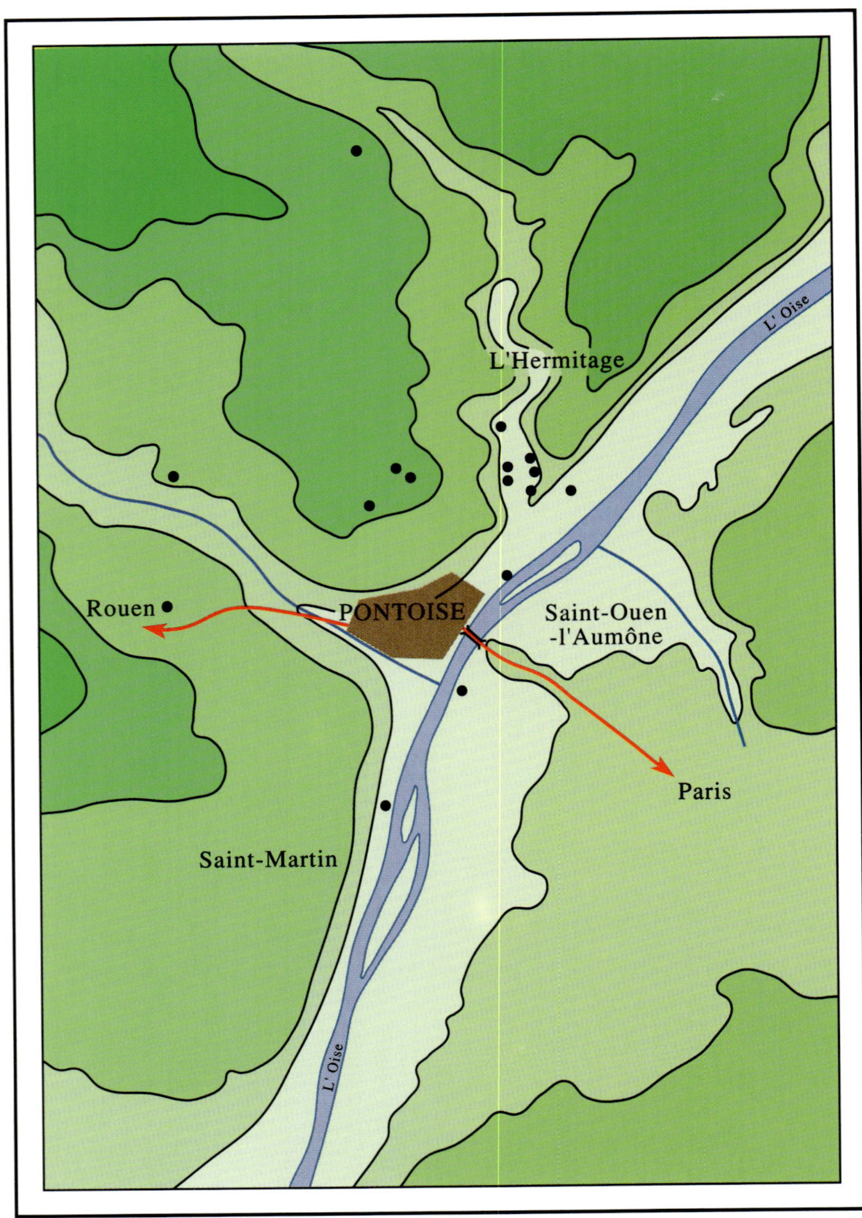

Fig. 2. Map of Pontoise as portrayed by Pissarro, 1866–68.

stack and its associated rural workers are neither clear enough nor dominant enough to suggest a link with the then well-established tradition of harvest genre painting. The buildings are neither detailed nor central enough to be considered a motif. The repoussoir tree is so intently vertical and so cropped as to be virtually meaningless as an image. Pissarro's concern with the spatial and pictorial tensions in landscape, with the differentiation between foreground and background, is characteristic of his paintings in the first Pontoise period.

Although most of Pissarro's large exhibition landscapes of this period depict motifs in L'Hermitage, other landscapes that survive are more representative of the whole of Pontoise (fig. 2).[19] *Paysage aux Pâtis* and *Le Moulin du Pâtis* (pl. 43) record the Viosne valley. The two semi-industrial river landscapes of 1868, *Vue de Pontoise, quai du Pothuis* (pl. 126) and *Vue de Pontoise, quai du Pothuis* (P&V 60), confront the urbanity of Pontoise as forcefully as the landscapes of L'Hermitage confront its agrarian hamlets. *L'Entrée de Pontoise, route de Gisors* (P&V 63, Kunsthistorisches Museum, Vienna) and the small orchard scenes painted near the so-called "maison du Père Gallien" focus on the plateau region near the remains

148

of the sixteenth-century fortification called "la Citadelle." The mistitled *Les Jardins de L'Hermitage, Pontoise* (P&V 52, Narodni Galeri, Prague) is the first recorded Pissarro landscape of the area called Le Chou where Berthe Morisot had painted in 1863. Two oil sketches and a pencil drawing which undoubtedly date from this period depict the then new rue de L'Hermitage with its walled *maisons bourgeoises* and incipient commercial establishments (pls. 99, 101, and 102).[20]

What is interesting to a student of Pissarro's attitudes toward reality is that the paintings of the first Pontoise period act as a kind of precursory summary of Pissarro's paintings of Pontoise made during the 1870s and 1880s. The home-centeredness that is such a remarkable feature of Pissarro's Pontoise is evidenced both in the concentration of the pictures in the area of L'Hermitage and in his choice of this more familial and accessible site for the larger exhibition landscapes painted both *plein-air* and in the studio. Pissarro's attempts at recording the entire environs of Pontoise, pursuing both range and depth, are also notable (fig. 2). The two urban river landscapes are provincial versions of the kind of city-scapes that Monet and Renoir painted during the same year in Paris.[21]

As far as the environs of Pontoise are concerned, Pissarro made pictorial use of two areas, Les Pâtis and L'Hermitage. He did not venture past Le Chou toward the villages of Le Valhermeil and Chaponval which were to provide him with rural motifs for several isolated canvases in 1872 and 1873 and were to fascinate him in the early 1880s. Nor did he make any pictorial exploration of Saint-Ouen-l'Aumône, the site of the vast majority of his later industrial views. It is certainly possible that, in choosing Les Pâtis and L'Hermitage, Pissarro, then a relative newcomer to Pontoise, was following the advice of Adolphe Joanne, who re-commended exactly those two regions for rural promenades in his guidebook of 1856, still the standard guide to the environs of Paris in the latter 1860s.[22]

What is evident from this brief discussion of the geographical range of Pissarro's landscape sites and the resulting range of his imagery is that the latter was as complicated an amalgam of imageries as his style was an amalgam of predominant mid-century styles. In painting the *quai* landscapes and the route de Gisors, Pissarro adopted the subject matter of travel illustrators rather than that of landscape painters. The illustrations in Joanne's guide or even in the almost exactly contemporary guide to Paris and its environs produced for the Exposition Universelle of 1867, are comparable in their placement of structured figures in city-scapes and along waters. In depicting L'Hermitage as a peasant landscape, Pissarro derived his stimulus not from the site itself, but from the tradition of rural imagery exemplified by the paintings of Corot, Millet, and even Daubigny. In placing bourgeois figures on the route de Gisors and along the chemin des Mathurins, Pissarro aligned himself not only with the tourist-guide illustrators, but with the painters of the modernist-realist tradition formally inaugurated by Manet in 1863. The list could extend further in any exhaustive analysis of Pissarro's stylistic development in the latter 1860s, but there is little doubt that Pissarro was what one might call a synthetist landscape painter in the first Pontoise period, although a synthetist of a different type than the well-known painters of that name a generation later. No landscape painter of his generation had as complete a response to "reality," and the very richness of his pictorial apprehension of the landscape is evidence of a desire fully to comprehend various "realities" within "reality."

It is interesting, in this context, to observe that Pissarro was responding, perhaps consciously, to many of the criticisms of landscape that had become frequent in the 1850s and 1860s. Writers from Baudelaire to Castagnary complained of the excess of the commonplace in landscape, of the lack of distance between real and pictorial worlds. Pissarro responded, not by abandoning the real world, but by restructuring it and thereby taking it from the realm of sensation to that of formulation or construction.

1868–1872   Three Interludes in Three Years

Pissarro left his house on the rue du Fond de L'Hermitage in 1868 for a larger, more recently constructed house on the route de Versailles above the village of Louveciennes. Although his reasons for the move are not recorded in any document, it was most probably made so that he might work in consort with Monet, Sisley, and Renoir, all of whom were living and working in the relatively small suburban landscape that stretched from Bougival down the Seine to the village of Marly-le-Roi.[23] The move is, in itself, a telling one. Pissarro deserted his own landscape for one crowded with significant younger painters. It is clear that he was looking ahead, away from the amalgamated style and imagery of the first Pontoise period to the more suburban imagery of the region around Louveciennes and the more loosely brushed style of the younger Monet. The change in Pissarro's style during that period has been noticed by all major critics of his career and has been forcefully isolated by Lionello Venturi in a section of his stylistic analysis of Pissarro's development in the catalogue raisonné. Venturi called the phase "la formation du goût impressionniste." Neither Venturi nor subsequent scholars had, until recently, given proper attention to the importance of Monet for both Pissarro's style and his imagery in this period during the latter 1860s.[24] Pissarro's style changed suddenly and dramatically. His pictures became more complex, more concerned with subtle observations of vegetation, water movement, and small-scale rhythms of light. His facture became more variable and he admitted the ephemeral and the gestural into an art from which they had been all but totally absent. The small, wrist-gesture strokes that are so important for the esthetic of Impressionism, as they had been for the esthetic of both Daubigny and Jongkind, are introduced into a pattern of brushstrokes that had been insistently rectilinear and, therefore, parallel to the picture plane.

Between his move to Louveciennes in 1868 and his removal to Pontoise in 1872, Pissarro was subject to a wide variety of influences. His exposure to the work of Monet has already been mentioned, and Rewald has published remarkably similar winter landscapes painted by Monet and Pissarro on the route de Versailles in Louveciennes during the winter of 1869–70.[25] The seven-month period in England in 1870–71 provided Pissarro not only with access to the landscape paintings of Turner and Constable, but also to the contents of the National Gallery and what was then the South Kensington Museum (now the Victoria and Albert Museum).[26] Christopher Lloyd, in an important article in the *Burlington Magazine*, has pointed to several possible instances in Pissarro's paintings where he appears to have borrowed sources from works seen during his visits to the London museums.[27] Pissarro's move back to the house on the route de Versailles, Louveciennes, in 1871, allowed him to apply the lessons learned in England to the landscape most associated with Monet and the French avant-garde painters around him. He refined a style that had resulted from intimate exposure to the landscape painting of the generation of 1830, to the young painters around Monet, to the Dutch landscape tradition, and to the great English landscape painters of the late eighteenth and early nineteenth centuries. The history of landscape painting lay behind Pissarro when he made his decision to return to Pontoise in February of 1872.

It is probable that, when the history of Impressionism is rewritten in another hundred years, Pissarro's paintings of 1872 and 1873 will be considered his masterpieces, as great, in their way, as Corot's work from his first trips to Italy or as Monet's landscapes from the late 1860s. Pissarro's style in the classic Pontoise period derived from the combined example of Monet and Turner, grafted to his by then familiar version of Corot's style. The small-scale patches of the facture undoubtedly come from Monet. The palette, whose earth tones were enlivened by various purples, yellows, pinks, and pale oranges, relates to the late landscape palette of Turner, whose work stands behind so many of the watercolors and paintings of the London period. Yet both these influences are subsumed by the overwhelmingly Corotesque quality of Pissarro's art. His composition, his intimacy of observation, his love of small-scale value gradations observed in complicated arrangements of form, and his insistently geometrical compositions owe their most profound debt to Corot, the greatest French landscape painter of the nineteenth century.[28] Paintings like the delicate *La Maison rouge* of 1873 (P&V 221, Portland Museum of Art) are structured by value gradation within the

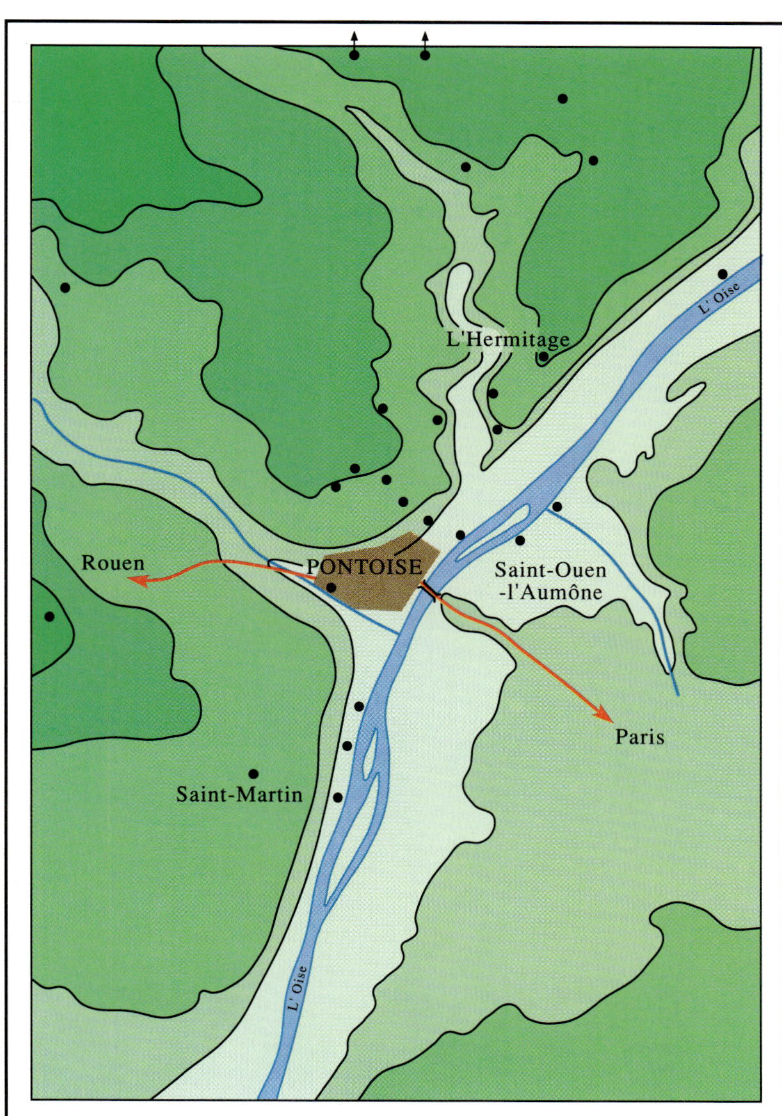

Fig. 3. Map of Pontoise as portrayed by Pissarro, 1872.

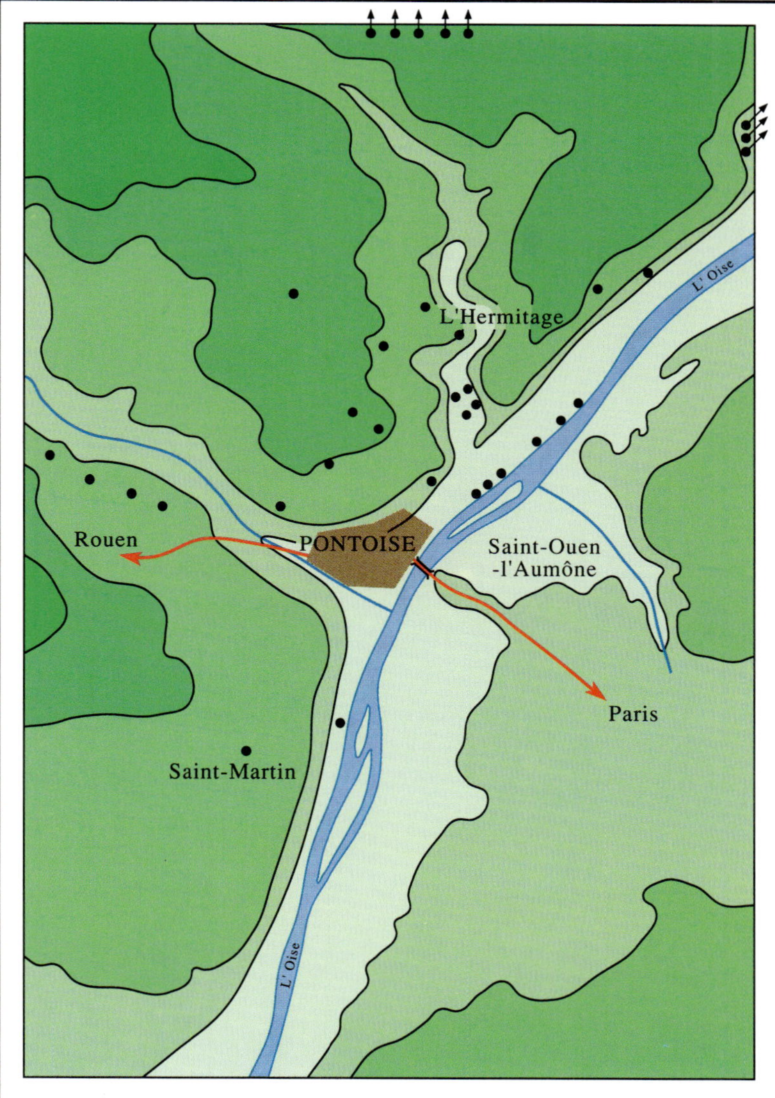

Fig. 4. Map of Pontoise as portrayed by Pissarro, 1873.

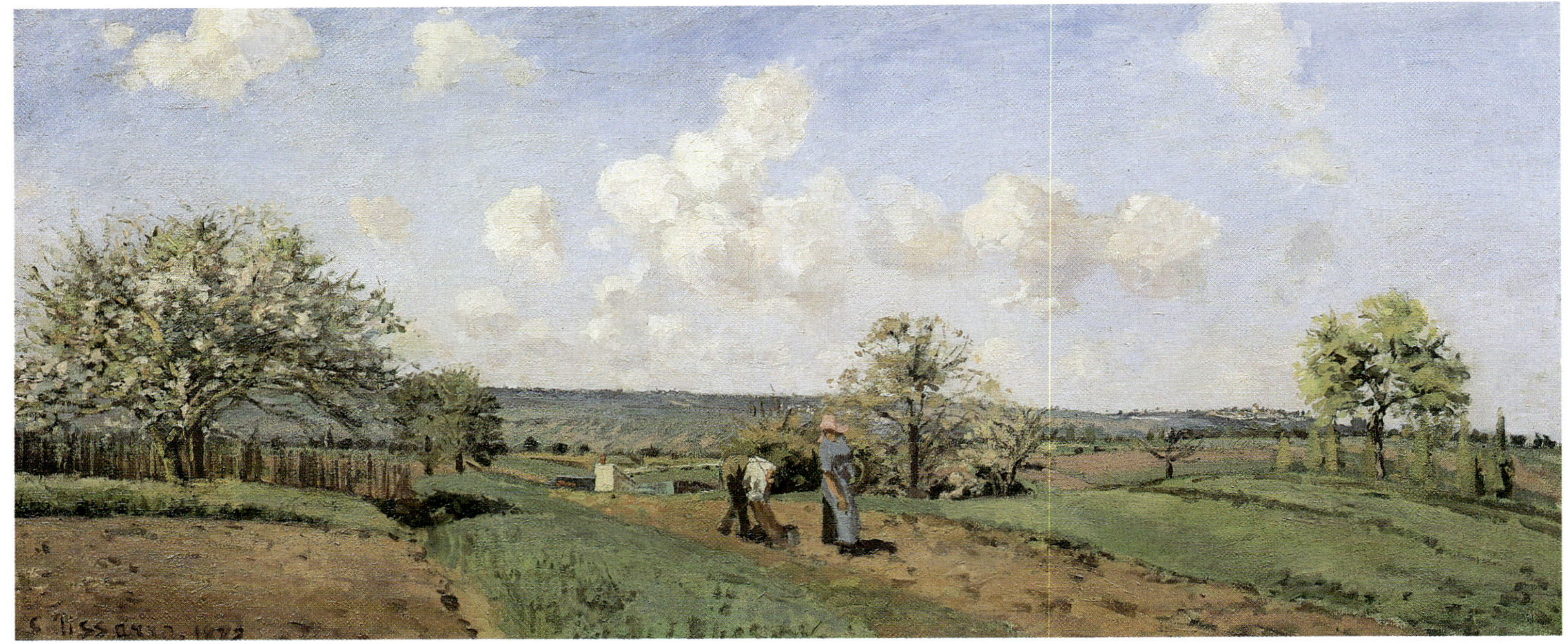

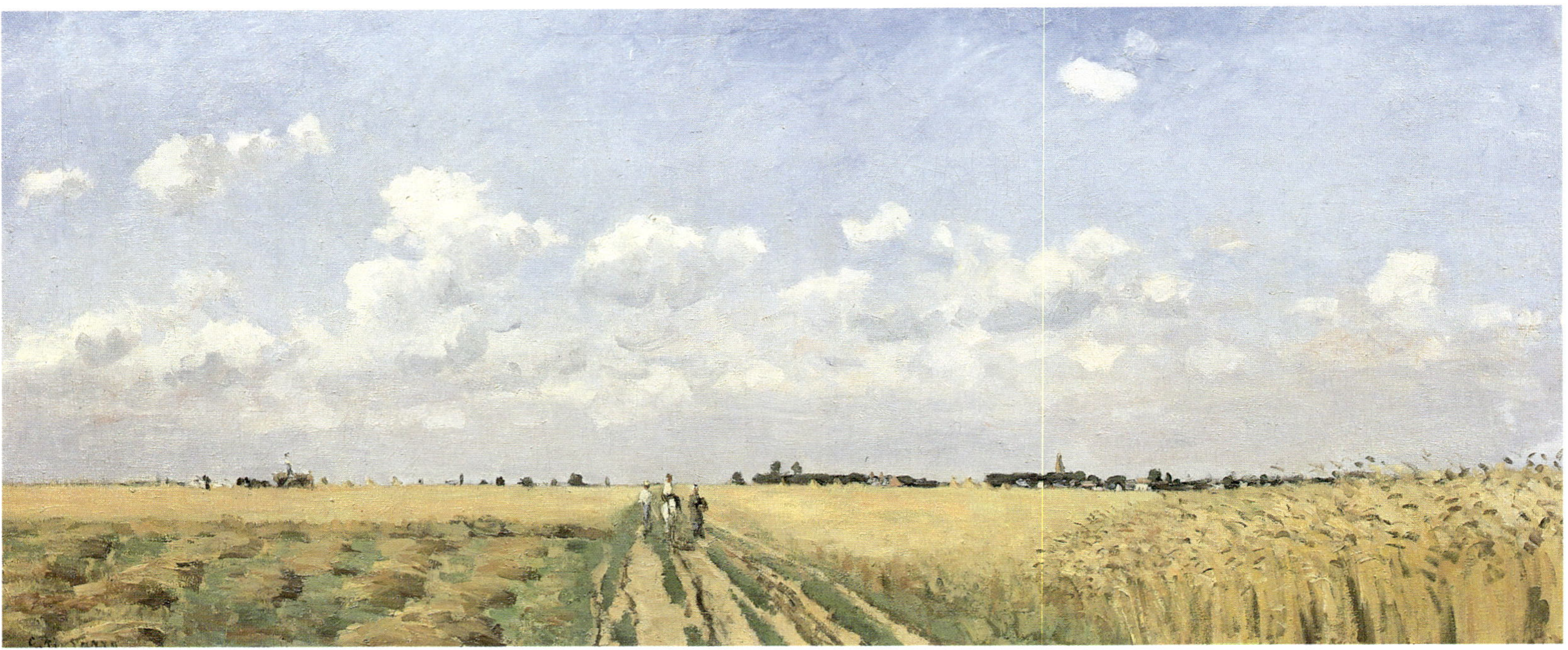

132 (top). Camille Pissarro, *Le Printemps* (P&V 183), 1872, oil on canvas, 55 × 130cm., private collection, Madrid.

133. Camille Pissarro, *L'Eté* (P&V 184), *c.*1872, oil on canvas, 55 × 120cm., private collection, Madrid.

several simple hues included in the palette. Corot of the Roman landscape sketches comes most forcefully to mind in this context.

"Classic" is a difficult word and is often misused in writings about art and architecture. Yet the desire to attain what some have called a "classic moment" has been a feature of both art and art criticism since the Renaissance, and the concept applies very well to Pissarro at this point in his career. Pissarro's landscapes in the classic Pontoise period are distant, balanced worlds in which man and his architecture dominate nature, whose rhythms are controllable and essentially benign. Pissarro's view of agriculture in this period continues to veer away from the predominantly "genre" character of agricultural imagery in French painting of the previous generation. The laboring figures who inhabit the foreground plane of so many landscapes of the first Pontoise period become tinier

152

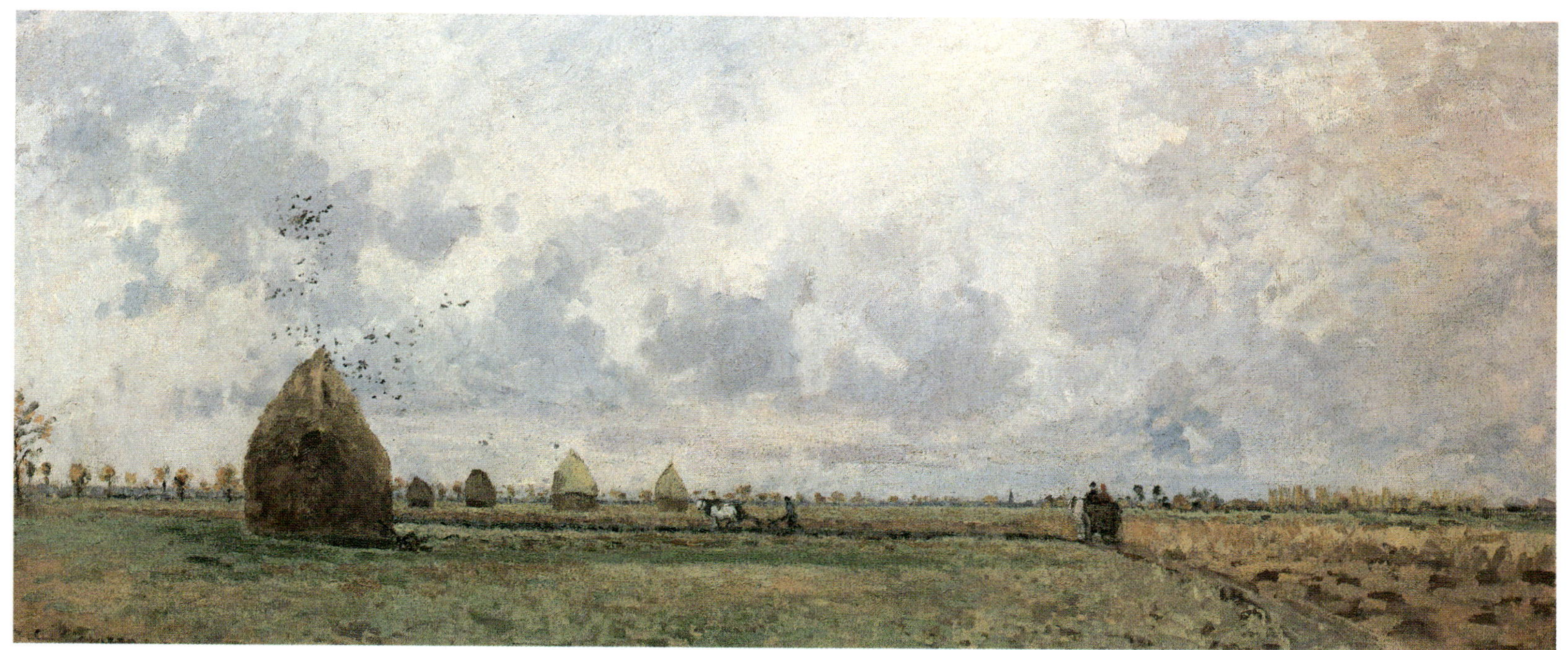

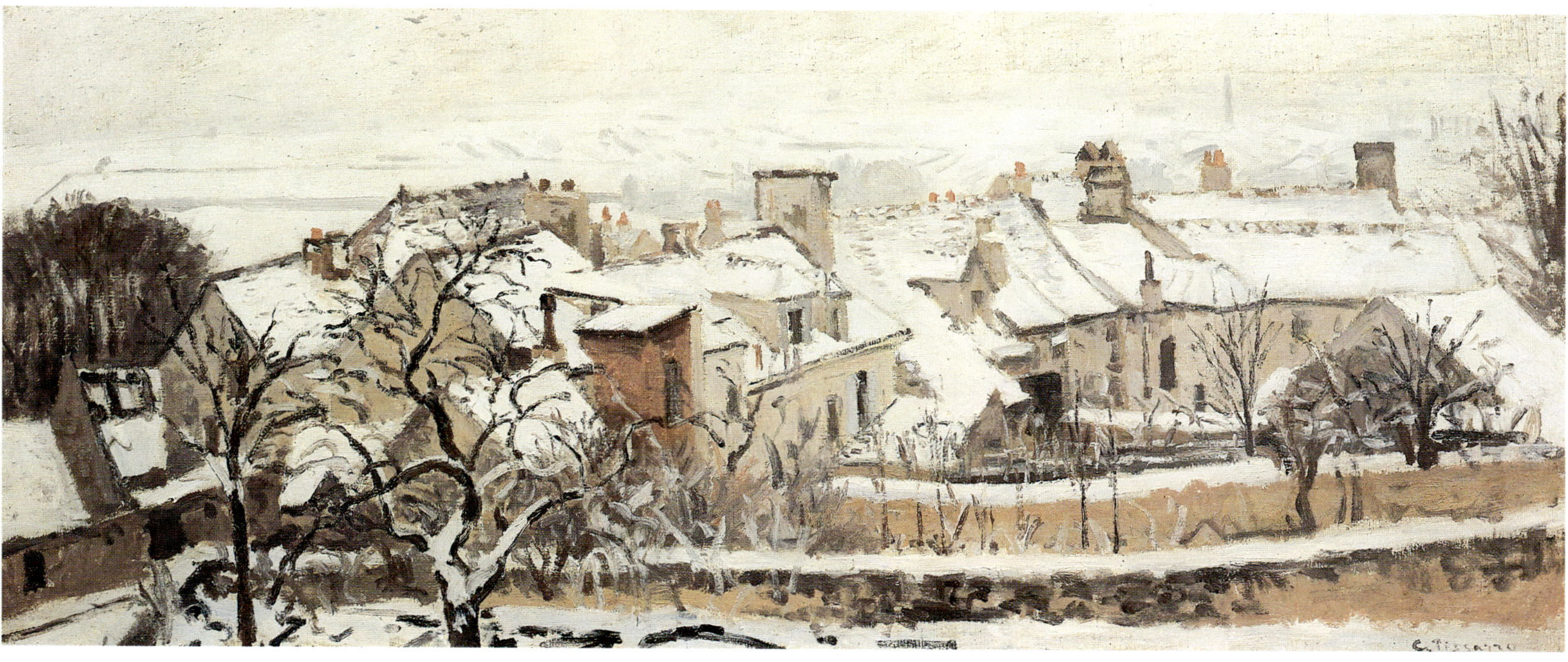

134 (top). Camille Pissarro, *L'Automne* (P&V 185), *c*.1872, oil on canvas, 55 × 130cm., private collection, Madrid.

135. Camille Pissarro, *L'Hiver* (P&V 186) *c*.1872, oil on canvas, 55 × 130cm., private collection, Madrid.

and more recessive in the classic Pontoise period. The earthy, consciously crude presence of the peasant which is so important a component of mid-century peasant imagery gives way to the landscape, with its sweeping horizons and cloud-dotted skies. The pictorial style of the classic Pontoise period is characterized by small-scale patches of paint, reduced versions of the planar rectangles of the first Pontoise period. These orderly marks are relieved by the short, wrist-gesture strokes so often associated with depicting movement, and, therefore, with Impressionism. The style of the classic Pontoise period shows a balance between construction and sensation that Pissarro never again achieved.

The classic Pontoise period is epitomized by *Les Quatres Saisons* (pls. 132–35), painted in 1872 and 1873. With the exception of *L'Hiver*, the pictures in this series describe an expanding world. Both *L'Eté* and *L'Automne* represent the Vexin

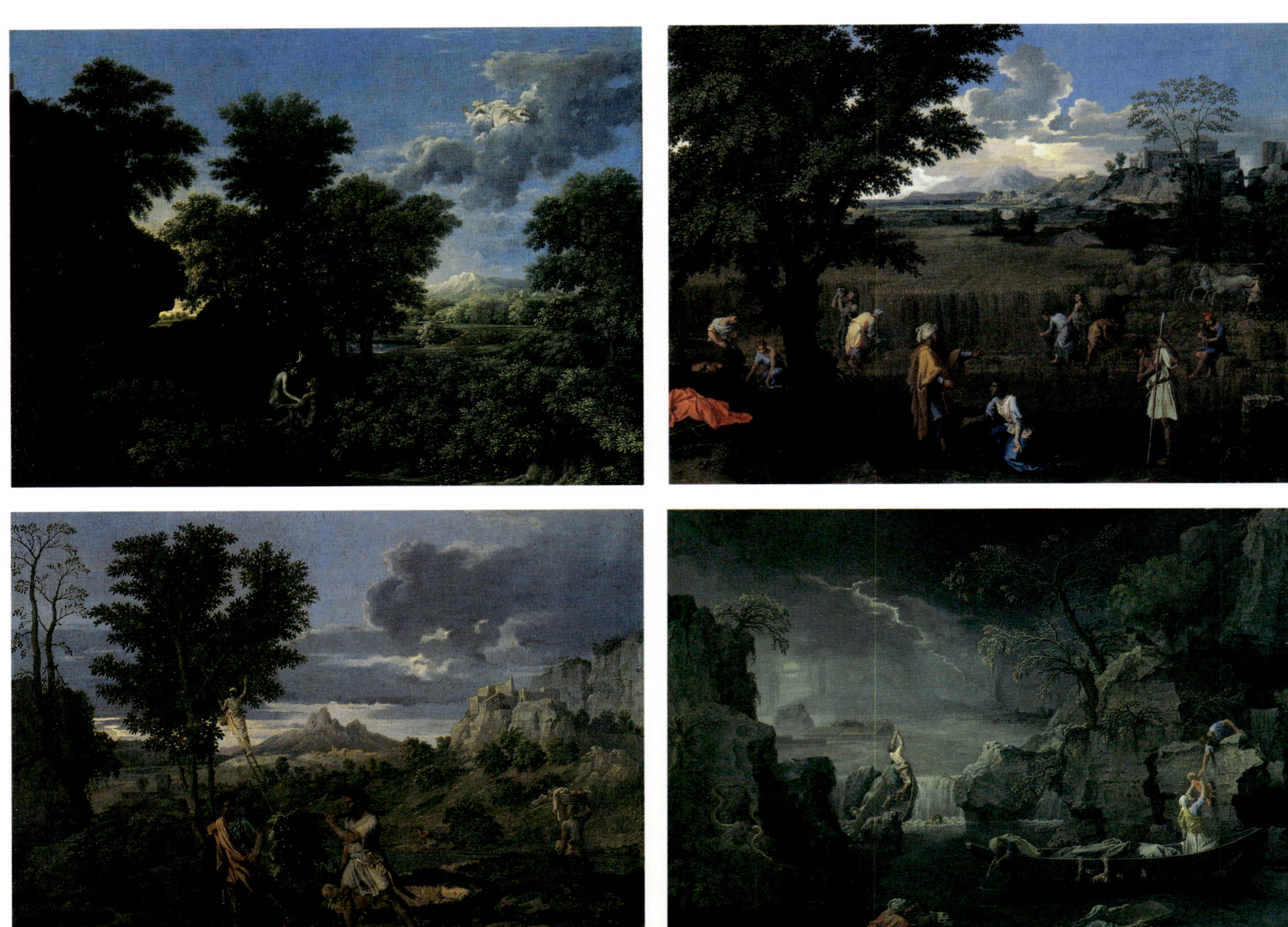

136–39. Nicolas Poussin, *Les Quatres Saisons*, 1660–64, oil on canvas, each 118 × 160cm., Musée du Louvre, Paris.

plateau, the landscape of limitless horizons that was to act as the motif for Van Gogh's last landscape paintings. Man, within this horizontal world, is a tiny, almost insignificant creature, overcome by the plenty of "*la terre.*" The iconographical origins of the pictures rest ultimately in the series of landscapes depicting the four seasons painted by Poussin in the latter 1660s and acquired by Louis XIV from Cardinal Richelieu's collection (pls. 136–39). Poussin's series stands at the root of the seasonal preoccupations that characterize nineteenth-century French landscape painting from Valenciennes to Monet. Landscape painters, according to virtually every writer of the nineteenth century, are responsible for describing the great seasonal rhythms of nature, her cosmic and non-material qualities, as much as they are responsible for describing her forms. The four seasons and their analogue, the four times of day, made nature more ideated and less literal than simple visual reality.

Pissarro's *Quatre Saisons* represent a spacially extended and, of course, classicized view of nature *in toto*. The four seasons, a strictly metrical division of the calendar associated with certain major agricultural rhythms by arcadian theorists, have their roots in classical antiquity and in the neo-classical writings and paintings of the Renaissance and various later "neo-classicisms," whether of the seventeenth, eighteenth, or nineteenth centuries. Most regional European temporal divisions were based on the astrological system of the months rather than the grander classical *quatro-partite* system. Pissarro was aligning himself with the tradition of Poussin by the very act of painting this series, an alignment very much in accord with his orderly esthetic in the early 1870s. It is Pissarro the neo-classicist who emerges so strongly in *Les Quatre Saisons.*

Without too great a digression from the historical outline of this chapter, Pissarro's *Quatre Saisons* can be profitably compared with those of Poussin and with the almost contemporary series of four seasons by Millet. It is interesting to note that, in spite of the prominence given to matters seasonal in the many books on landscape painting in the nineteenth century, there are very few *summae* or series groupings of all the seasons in one pictorial format.[29] Of all the major French landscape painters, only Poussin and Millet had painted such a series. Pissarro would definitely have known Poussin's series, but he was probably unfamiliar with Millet's, which was left unfinished at the painter's death and later dispersed. For Poussin, the cycle of nature was anything but regenerative. By combining the classical idea of seasonality with Old Testament subjects, Poussin endowed the seasons with an inevitability that all but denies the "cycle" itself and suggests the ultimate reality of the fall of man.[30] Millet, although he lacks the biblical references, paints a version of the four seasons that shares much of Poussin's grim determinism. For Millet, it is the relentlessness of the cycle itself, the impossibility of redemption of the earth, that takes the place of Poussin's latent religious iconography.[31] Although these summary accounts of the content of two very complex cycles are inadequate, they do point up the contrast with Pissarro's "modern" view of the same subject.

Like Millet and Poussin, Pissarro viewed the four seasons as an agricultural allegory. He represented, more or less, the same activities in the same seasons. But there the similarity ends. Pissarro's *Quatre Saisons* are optimistic and iconographically simple. By using the panoramic format favored by Daubigny and used by many mid-century artists, Pissarro has freed himself from much of the iconography of the seasons. There are no potent forms, no allegorical subjects, and, by diminishing the forms, he has distanced the viewer from his landscape, which can be read with a grand detachment. The eye reads quickly and dramatically in and along the surface of the ever-productive earth because he has avoided any powerful foreground forms. Even winter, a landscape of almost savage severity for Poussin and Millet, is, for Pissarro, a huddle of warm houses, gathered at the base of a protective hillside against the inclement weather. *Les Quatre Saisons* suggest that redemption on earth is possible, and, not only on earth, but in France and in Pontoise. Although Pissarro echoed the classical landscape tradition in painting a seasonal series, his own view of the four seasons cannot be read as a conservative or derivative image. *Les Quatre Saisons* are as much characterized by their departure from the artistic and literary tradition associated with the seasonal cycle as are the paintings of Manet by their departure from the High Renaissance and Baroque models that stand so emphatically behind them.

Les Quatre Saisons can be read in almost every way as a *summa.* They take their place within two of the most productive years in Pissarro's career. The images can be taken as proof—as much a proof as the painter's own testimony or the words of friends and subsequent historians—of his faith in France after the debacle of the Franco-Prussian War. They can be justifiably seen as the single most important manifestation of Pissarro's interests during the classic Pontoisian period.

140 (following pages). Detail of pl. 134.

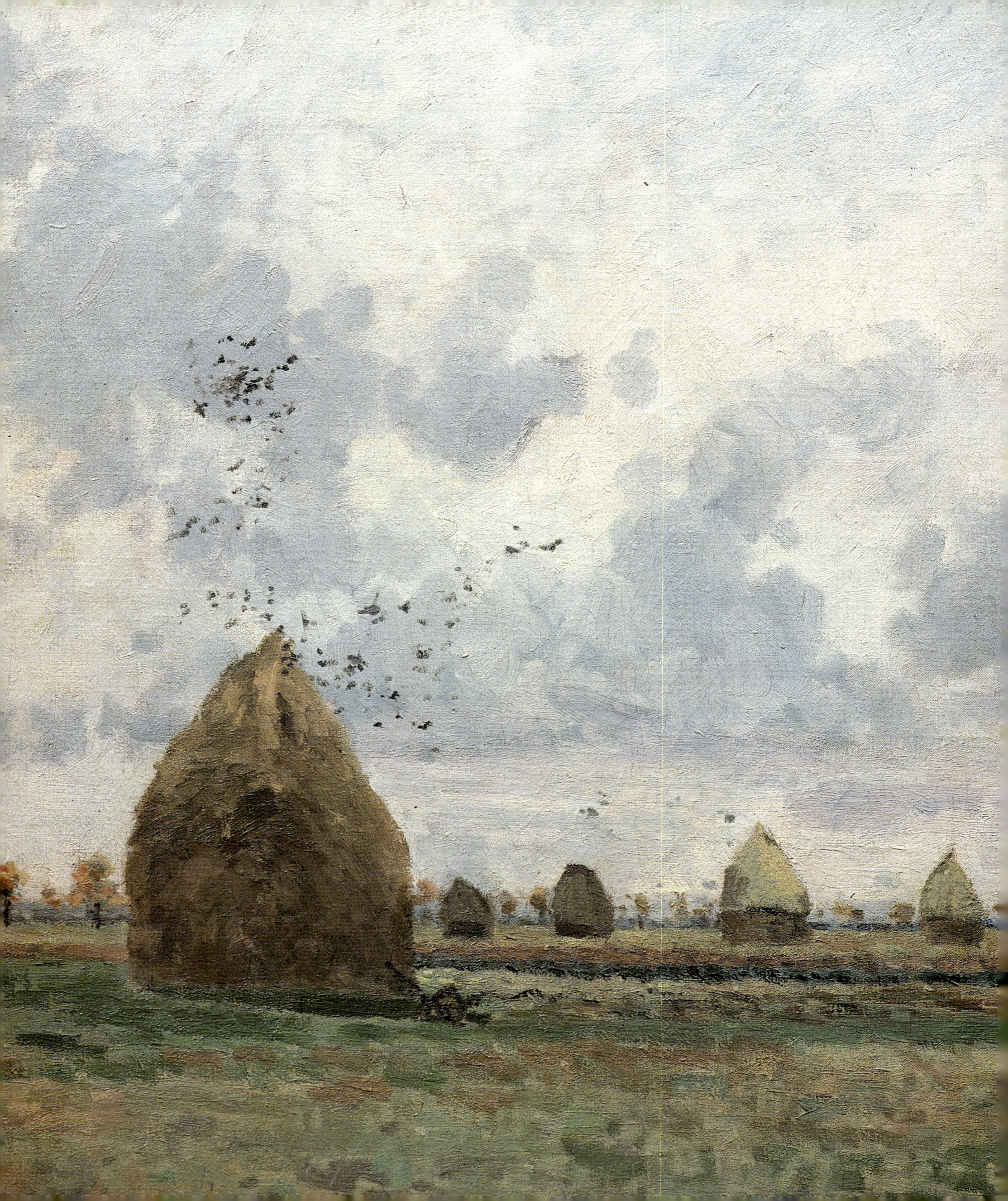

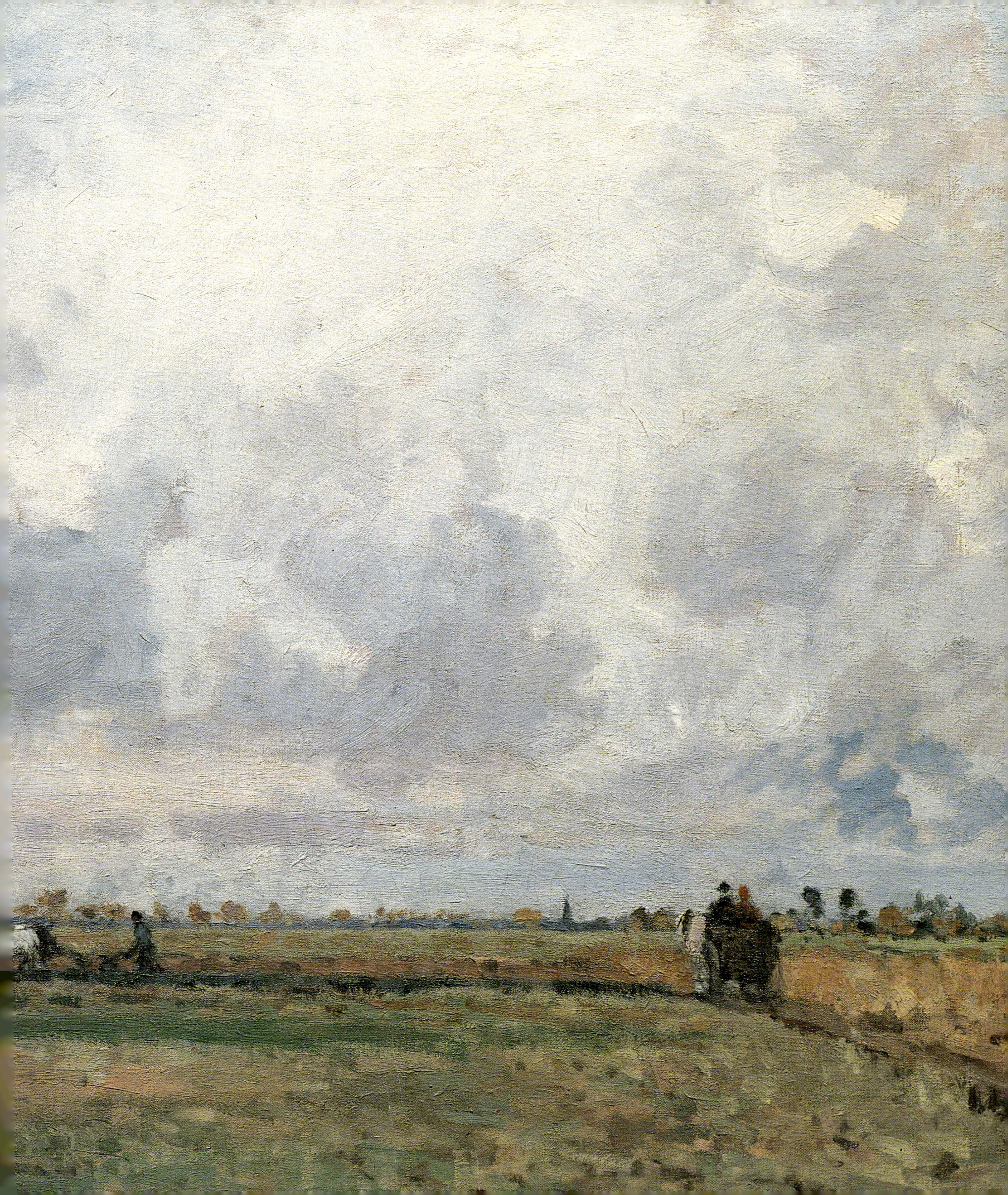

Pissarro took Pontoise by storm, at least pictorially, when he returned there from London in February of 1872. Site maps of that year and the next reveal an unparalleled range (figs. 3 and 4). There is no "home in the landscape," as discussed in chapter 4. In fact, the sheer variety of motifs was more important to Pissarro in these years than at any other time in his career. Images of the intensely rural thatched cottages near Auvers (P&V 228, 229); of the wheat harvests and haystacks near the Vexin town of Ennery (pls. 133, 134, and P&V 223, 225, and 233); of the concentrated *jardins potagers* of L'Hermitage (P&V 164, 165, 209, 226, 227, 238); of the small plowed fields laminating the hillsides that bordered the route Saint-Antoine (pl. 60, and P&V 220); of the Oise and its towpaths (pls. 63, 77, 141, and 142, and P&V 159, 160, 161, 219, 222, 234); of the factories belonging to Chalon et Cie. and to M. Arneuil (pls. 71, 72, 74, 75) — all these iconographically diverse images date from the classic Pontoise period. Iconologically, the images range from the traditionally rural to the absolutely modern, from agriculture to industry. Images of water are considerably more important than they had been in the rather earth-bound first Pontoise period, reflecting, of course, an esthetic impetus from Daubigny, Monet, and, to a lesser extent, Sisley, whose contemporary river landscapes are often so startlingly similar to those painted by Pissarro in the classic Pontoise period. Pissarro was experiencing a professional optimism he would not feel again until the 1890s. He was alive to the landscape, allowing its multiple realities to affect him more fully than ever before.

What is perhaps most telling about this period of Pissarro's career in Pontoise is that he seemed to consider himself to be the visual historian of the town. Indeed,

141. Camille Pissarro, *Bords de l'eau à Pontoise* (P&V 158), 1872, oil on canvas, 55 × 91cm., collection of Lucille Ellis Simon.

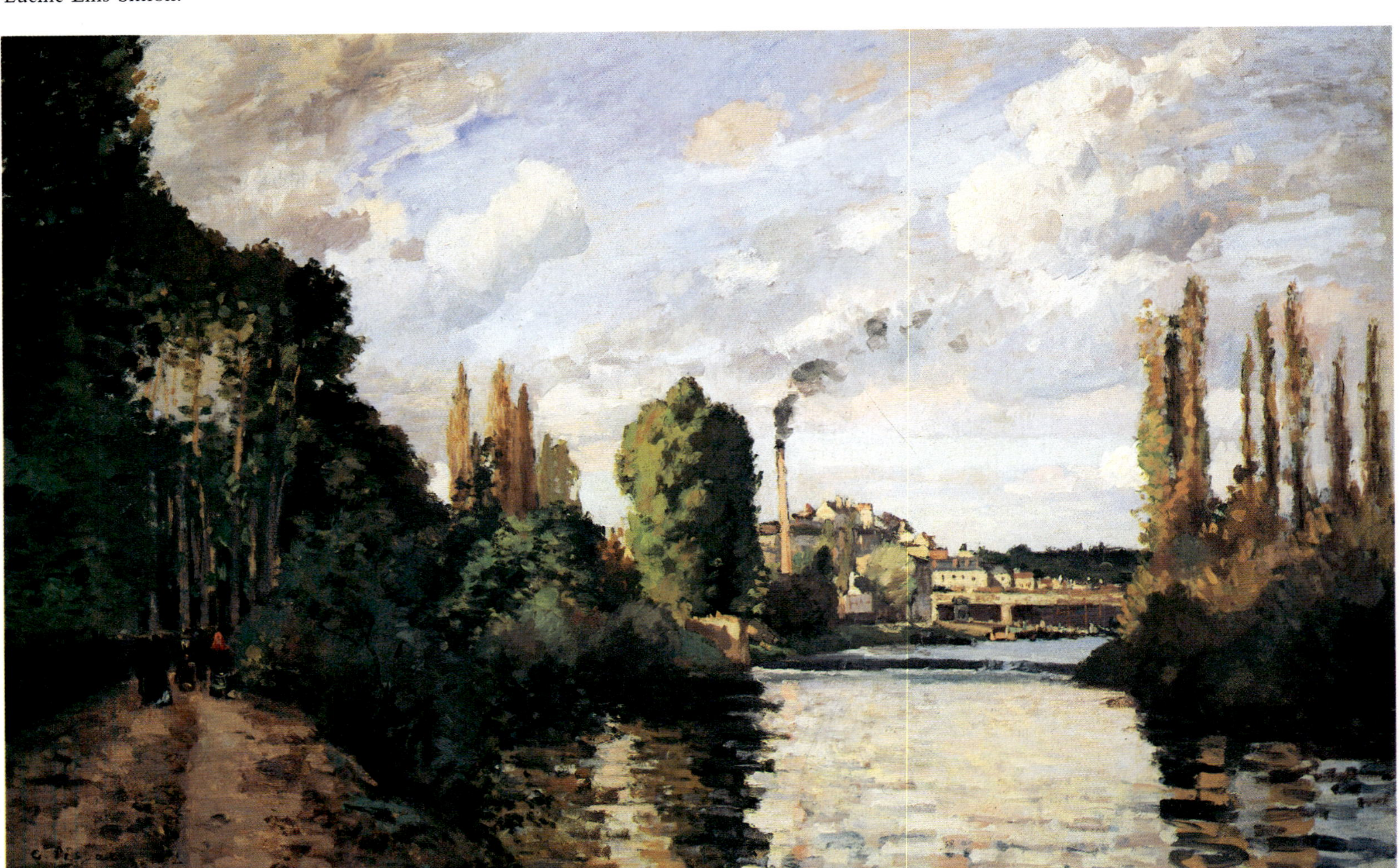

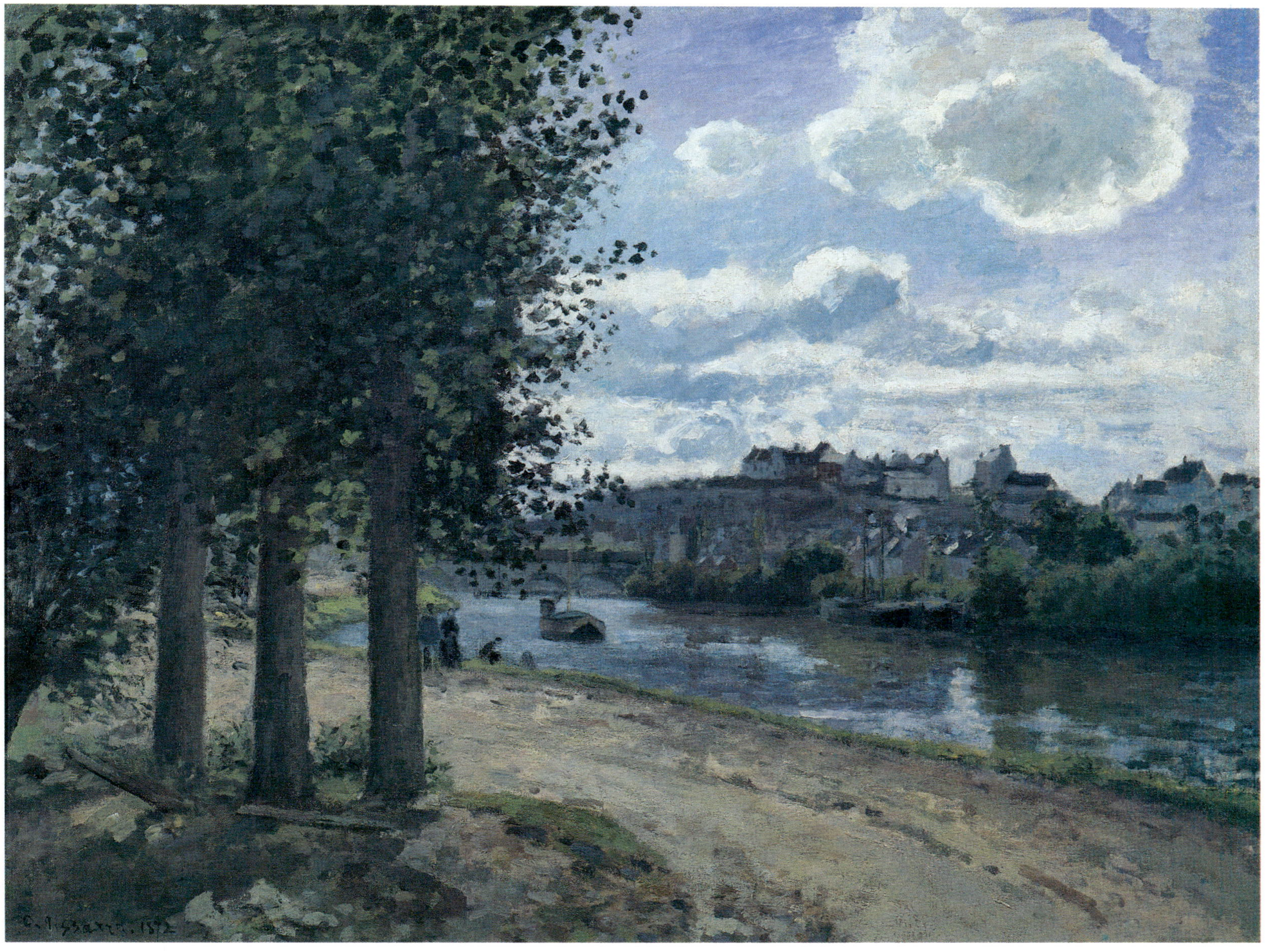

142. Camille Pissarro, *Pontoise, bords de l'Oise* (P&V 182), 1872, oil on canvas, 54 × 73cm., courtesy of the Lefevre Gallery, London.

the term "historien des champs," applied to Pissarro by the art critics of the 1890s, can be altered in the classic Pontoise period to "historien de Pontoise." The connection between Pissarro's painted images of L'Hermitage and Les Pâtis and the guidebook recommendations of Joanne has already been noted. There are, however, more telling connections to be made in the classic Pontoise period, connections that lend credence to the assertion that Pissarro was the visual historian of the town during those short years. All guidebook entries that describe Pontoise include discussion of the two major events of the year, the Foire Saint-Martin, held in November, and the earlier and smaller Fête de Septembre. The Foire Saint-Martin, which continues to be celebrated in modern Pontoise, has its origins in the late Middle Ages and is among one of the oldest communal fairs in the environs of Paris. Several popular illustrators had published views of it, and Gustave Doré, who contributed several items to the *iconographie de Pontoise*, illustrated the event twice.[32] Pissarro painted both these important local events in 1872, along with his views of the traditional rural life, the life of the ports, the roads in and out of the town, the various suburbs, and the town's fledgling industry. In addition, he began his almost methodical depiction of the urban spaces of Pontoise, many of which had been either created or improved during the Second Empire. He was, as is evident from this simple list, assiduous in his attention to every part of the environment and to the civic events that marked the year in Pontoise. A student of the site itself would learn more from the paintings executed in the two years of the classic Pontoise period than from all Pissarro's other paintings of the town combined.

In returning from Louveciennes and its restricted imagery to Pontoise, Pissarro had returned to his own landscape, rejecting implicitly the kind of landscape world endorsed by Monet and Renoir for the more bracing "realities" of his own. His style, although technically unchanged since Louveciennes and Upper Norwood days, broadened somewhat. His palette became lighter and brighter, although he continued to show a Corotesque obsession with value structure rather than hue. His execution became more confident and unproblematic without losing its fundamentally geometric quality. What Pissarro did in his paintings of this period was to revel in the sheer variety of the site. The style itself is relatively simple to describe. The facture consists of uniformly small patches of paint which overlap subtly to achieve a unified, but variegated surface. There is none of the complex layering, the optical interpenetrations of form and color that are ostensibly Impressionist. For Pissarro of the classic Pontoise period, architecture clearly predominated over nature and was used to order, humanize, and schematize his pictorial world. Its function is at once formal and iconological. What is most notable, almost unique about the pictures of this period is their spaciousness. As a rule, Pissarro avoided the depths of the landscape. He was, to borrow Champa's useful terminology, a painter who organized rather than composed nature.[33] His interest in parallelism was all but antithetical to an interest in space. Yet there are many pictures of an unrivaled spaciousness in these two years, years that mark, in many ways, the apex of Pissarro's career as a landscape painter.

The iconographical and the geographical range of Pissarro's Pontoise during the classic Pontoise period separates his esthetic from the contemporary esthetics of Monet, Renoir, and Sisley, whose response to the landscape was much less various and much more repetitive in iconography. With the important exception of the factory, which has been discussed separately, Pissarro virtually never painted the same subject twice during this period. He seems to have made a decision to be an objective recorder of the various realities of Pontoise, and he employed a style that is characterized by a schematic simplicity and a pictorial detachment. Pissarro did not search for established or picturesque subjects in the manner described by so many writers on landscape in the middle part of the nineteenth century. Rather, he developed a mode of vision that he applied quite consistently to the various realities around him. In 1896, Gustave Geffroy called Pissarro's pictures of Pontoise a "series"; if any group of paintings justifies that title, it is the views of Pontoise that belong to the classic Pontoise period.[34]

1874–1875   *The New Ruralism: Pontoise and Montfoucault*

The open, receptive vision of the classic Pontoise period gave way in the middle of the 1870s to a phase of intensive experimentation with peasant life and rural imagery. The family moved from their small house on the rue Malebranche near the Jardin public first to another small, rather dark, and inconvenient house on the

143. Detail of pl. 144.

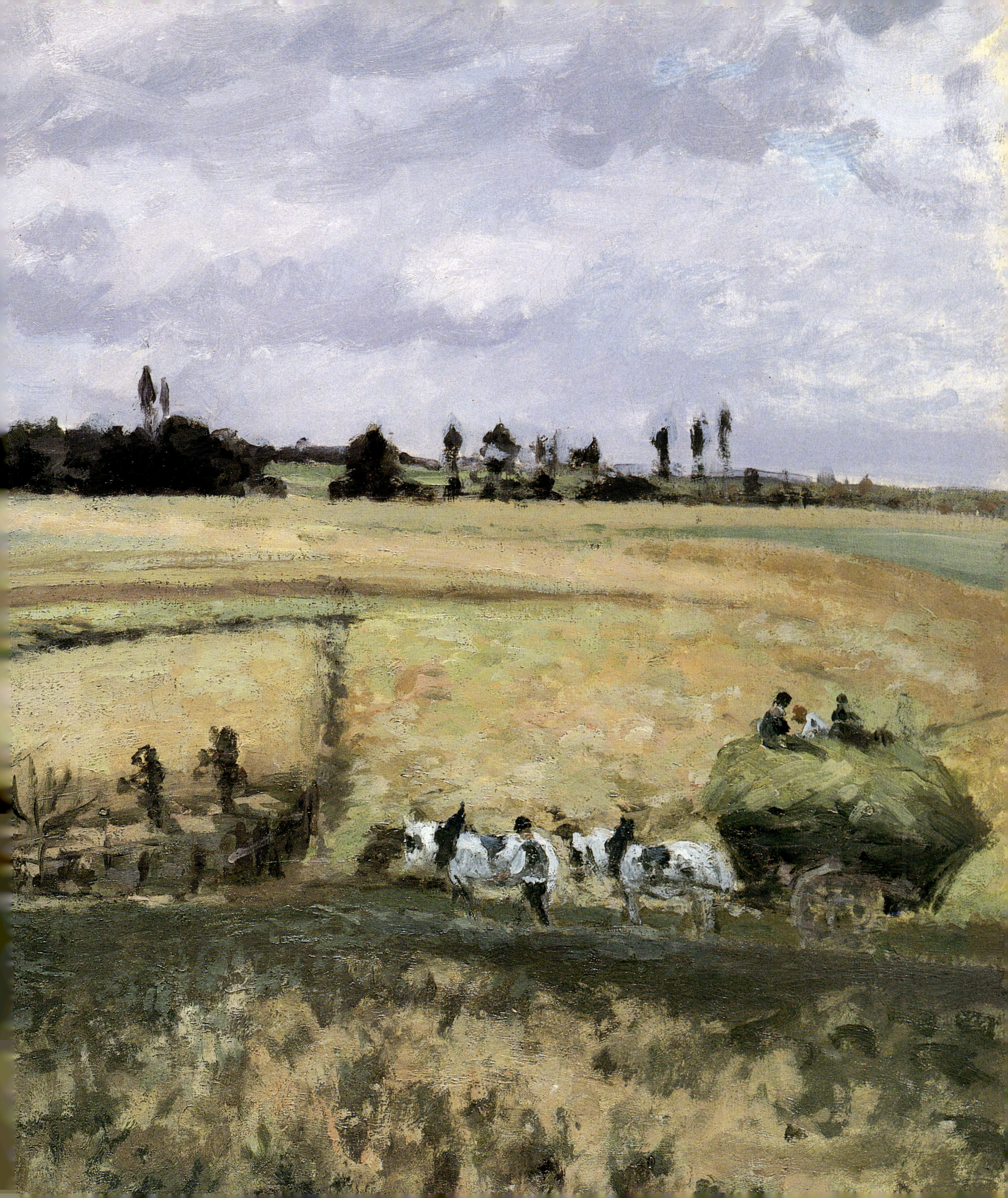

quai du Pothuis, and finally to a larger, lighter, and drier house at 26, rue de L'Hermitage in October 1873.[35] By the late spring of 1874, Pissarro had altered his palette, his facture, his iconography, and his attitude toward pictorial space to form a new style almost directly at odds with that of the classic Pontoise period. The period between 1874 and early 1876 can be called one of regression, whose character and causes will be studied below. Pissarro's pictorial attention in the years 1874, 1875, and 1876 was not lavished exclusively on Pontoise, but rather was divided between Pontoise and the farms near Montfoucault, where his closest friend, Ludovic Piette, owned property. Montfoucault presented a completely new kind of landscape for Pissarro. The area around this, the capital town of Mayenne, maintained an agriculture that was totally different from the village agriculture of the Parisian *campagne*. Small, isolated farms surrounded by their own enclosed fields, hedgerows, and ponds gave the region a landscape structure much like that of southern England. Pissarro himself called Mayenne "the true countryside" ("la vraie campagne") in a letter to Duret written just before his departure to Montfoucault in October 1874, a countryside that he contrasted, by implication, to the modernized countryside with its rural workers in Louveciennes and Pontoise.[36] Although Pissarro had visited Montfoucault with Piette several times in the 1860s, his three lengthy trips of 1874, 1875, and 1876 produced many more images and represent a concerted attempt at portraying and, therefore, understanding a kind of landscape that was, in many ways, foreign to his tastes and inclinations.

The change in Pissarro's attitude toward the landscape can be seen clearly in *Terres labourées* of 1874 (pl. 54), painted in Pontoise prior to Pissarro's departure for Montfoucault. Whereas the landscapes in *Les Quatre Saisons* (pls. 132–35), allow the viewer to be immersed in the unproblematic horizontal expanse of fields, this small landscape is marked by a constraint of format. The season is fall or early winter, a season that predominates in the paintings of this "new-ruralism" period. The earth is not the green of the first Pontoise period, but golden and brown. Yet optimistic images related to harvest and the richness of the earth are lacking. The plow, resting idle in the middle of a half-plowed field, is an allusion to Millet's *L'Hiver aux Corbeaux* (Kunsthistorisches Museum, Vienna), which Pissarro, like Van Gogh after him, probably knew from the engraving by Delaunay.[37] The horizontal banding of the composition, which was a notable feature of the landscapes from the first Pontoise period, is now blatant and uninterrupted. Comparison with a similarly composed landscape of 1872, *Paysage à Pontoise* (pl. 144) indicates Pissarro's greater interest in traditional ruralism in the mid-1870s and his resolute denial of any real pictorial space. The earlier landscape contains both a freely painted group of repoussoir trees, which acts as a compositional anchor, and an entrance path leading directly to the distant road. The harvest wagon in the middle distance alludes to the earth's bounty. The earthy, brown-gold tonality of *Terres labourées* is in opposition to the varied and lighter palette of the earlier painting. Pissarro virtually omitted the sky from the later landscape, a formal and, of course, iconological change that characterizes many landscapes of the Montfoucault period. The expanse of sky and space that lent a definite optimism to the paintings of the classic Pontoise period has disappeared from those of the years 1874 and 1875.

The paintings of 1874 show ample evidence of a change in both style and iconography. Pissarro's facture became more dense and his brushstrokes broader. His palette darkened considerably and consisted predominantly of earth tones and greens. His attention turned from distantly viewed landscapes to the concentrated space of the barnyard, populated with figures and defined by complex arrange-

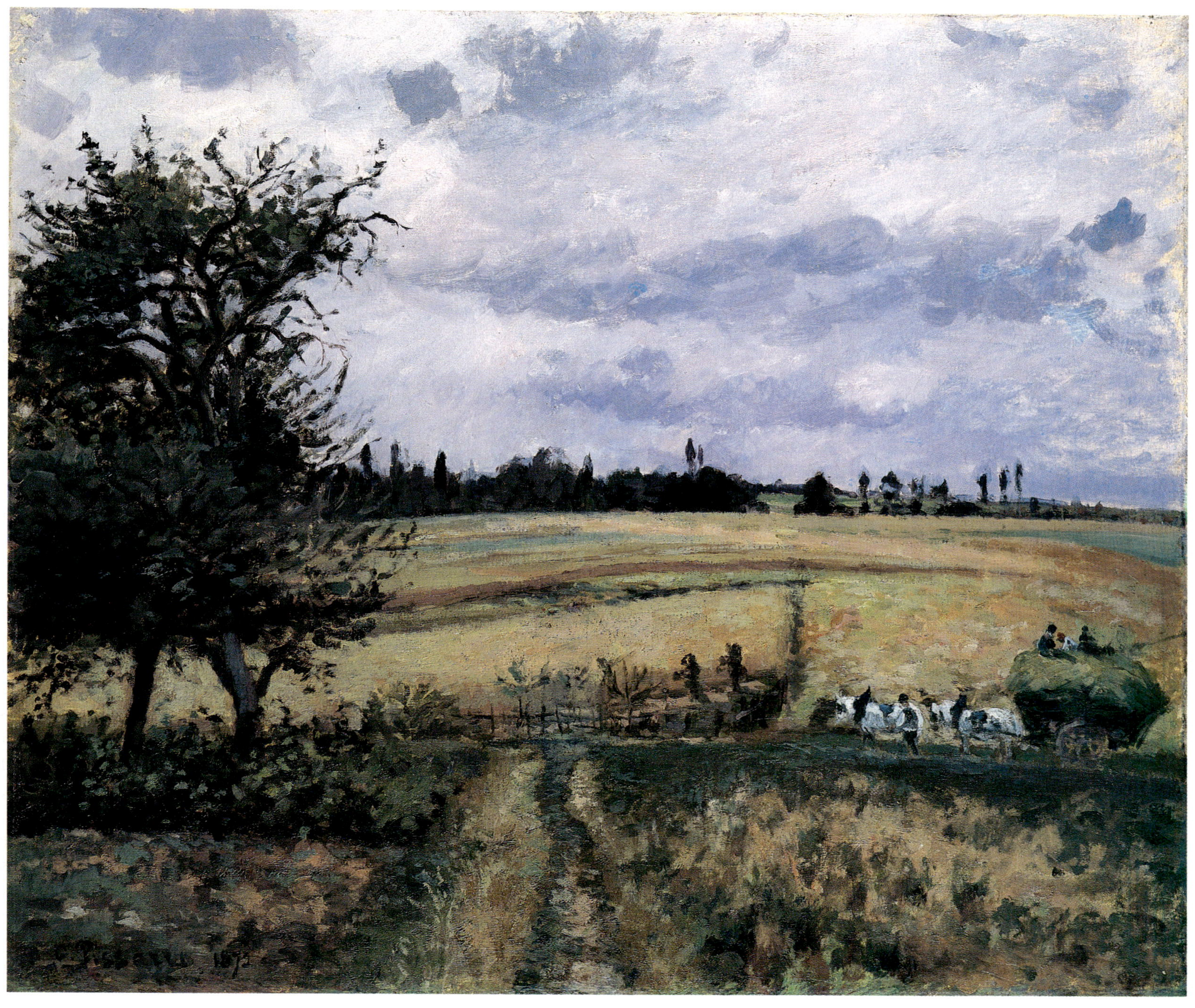

144. Camille Pissarro, *Paysage à Pontoise* (P&V 163), 1872, oil on canvas, 46 × 55cm., Ashmolean Museum, Oxford.

ments of form.[38] The importance of Courbet in Pissarro's stylistic amalgam increased again to the point of overwhelming the aspects of Monet that remained in the modern style of the early 1870s. Millet, who had never been an important artist for Pissarro, gained prominence for him for the first time in 1874. The sheer physical reality of form – its weight, mass, and proximity – became Pissarro's overriding concern in the Montfoucault period, and that reality was expressed by the material presence of paint itself. Pissarro built up paint on the surface to suggest "real" mass and to give literalness to illusionistic objects. For the Pissarro who repainted the *Barrière du chemin de fer* in 1874 (pl. 65), paint did not describe light, as it did so often for Monet; it was not linear and calligraphic as it was in Sisley's paintings of the mid-1870s; nor was it an indicator of movement, rustling and windswept, as in so many Renoir landscapes of the 1870s. Pissarro layed paint

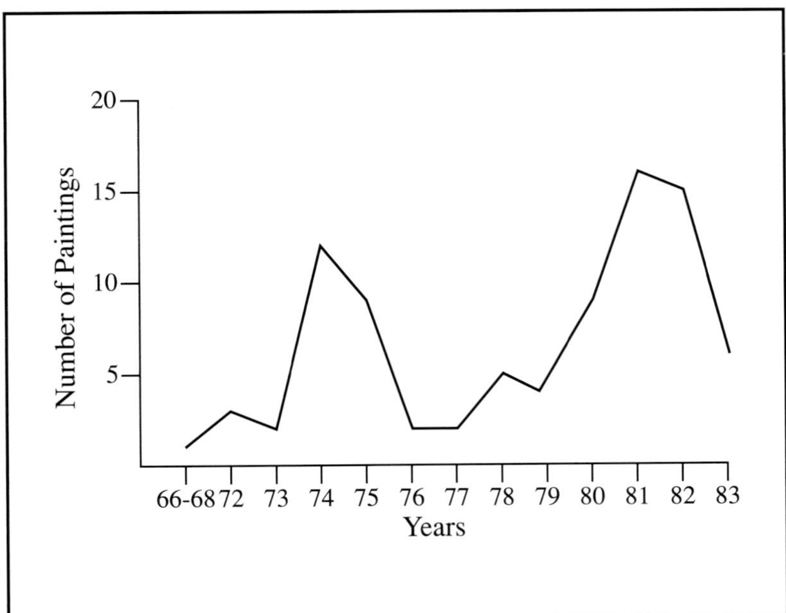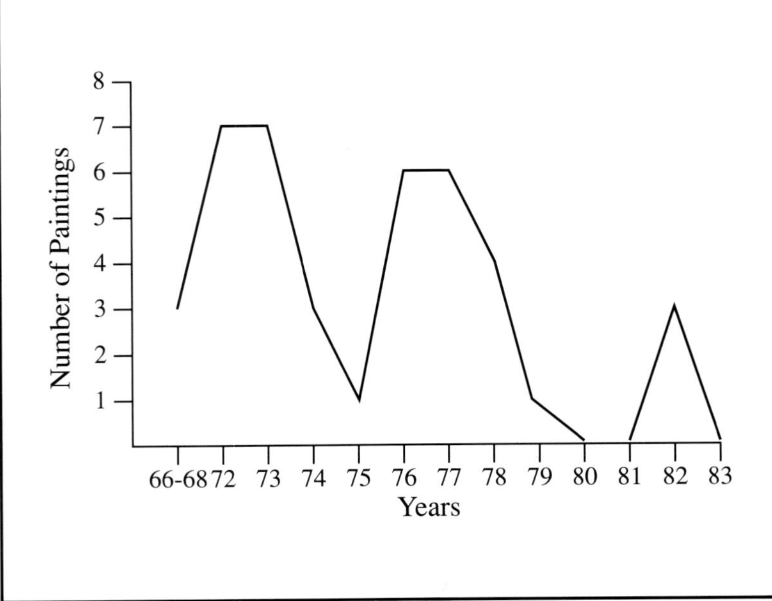

Fig. 5. Graph showing the number of figure pictures (including portraits) by year.

Fig. 6. Graph showing the number of river landscapes by year.

on the surface to suggest mass and weight in a manner matched in the period only by Cézanne.[39]

What is interesting in this context is that Pissarro's move to Montfoucault was not the cause of his new ruralism and his investigation of subjects and techniques rooted in the art of the Barbizon School and Courbet. The origins of this change lay not in a place, but in a series of attitudes. Pissarro, it must be remembered, did not leave for Montfoucault until the fall of 1874, after the closing of the first Impressionist exhibition in Paris. Graphs charting Pissarro's use of motif types year by year (figs. 5 and 6) and the maps of the areas around Pontoise painted by Pissarro (figs. 7 and 8) show dramatic changes in the year 1874, changes made prior to the move to Montfoucault. The painter restricted the geographical and iconographical scope of his activities markedly in that year. Not only does ruralism characterize the imagery of the Montfoucault pictures, but it applies to Pissarro's views of Pontoise as well. The "modern," urban character of Pontoise as it is revealed in the classic Pontoise period gives way to a traditional and pre-modern view of the same environment. The site maps of the years 1874 and 1875 look remarkably like those of the first Pontoise period. There is a distinct preference for L'Hermitage landscapes, a return to the bounded landscape that had provided the material for Pissarro's most successful landscapes of the 1860s, the pictures admired by Zola and Duret. Indeed, one view of the rue de L'Hermitage (pl. 103) is almost a remaking of the two views of that street painted in 1866–67 (pls. 99 and 101).[40]

Théodore Duret is the key figure in relation to this change in Pissarro's style. The critic was the first conscientious historian of Impressionism and the father of Impressionist studies. His early recognition of the Impressionists was more forceful and active than that of its other apologists, Castagnary, Zola, and Burty. Both Castagnary and, later, Zola had written about and understood Pissarro's paintings of the 1860s. Zola's discussion of the raw power of Pissarro's naturalism serves as a bracing counter to the weaker, arcadian Pissarro created by the critics of the 1890s. But neither Castagnary nor Zola had encouraged Pissarro personally. Duret wrote to Pissarro throughout the early 1870s and purchased paintings from him.[41] His letters to Pissarro of 1873 contain the germ of his ideas on Impressionism and were the first significant attempts at differentiating the esthetic

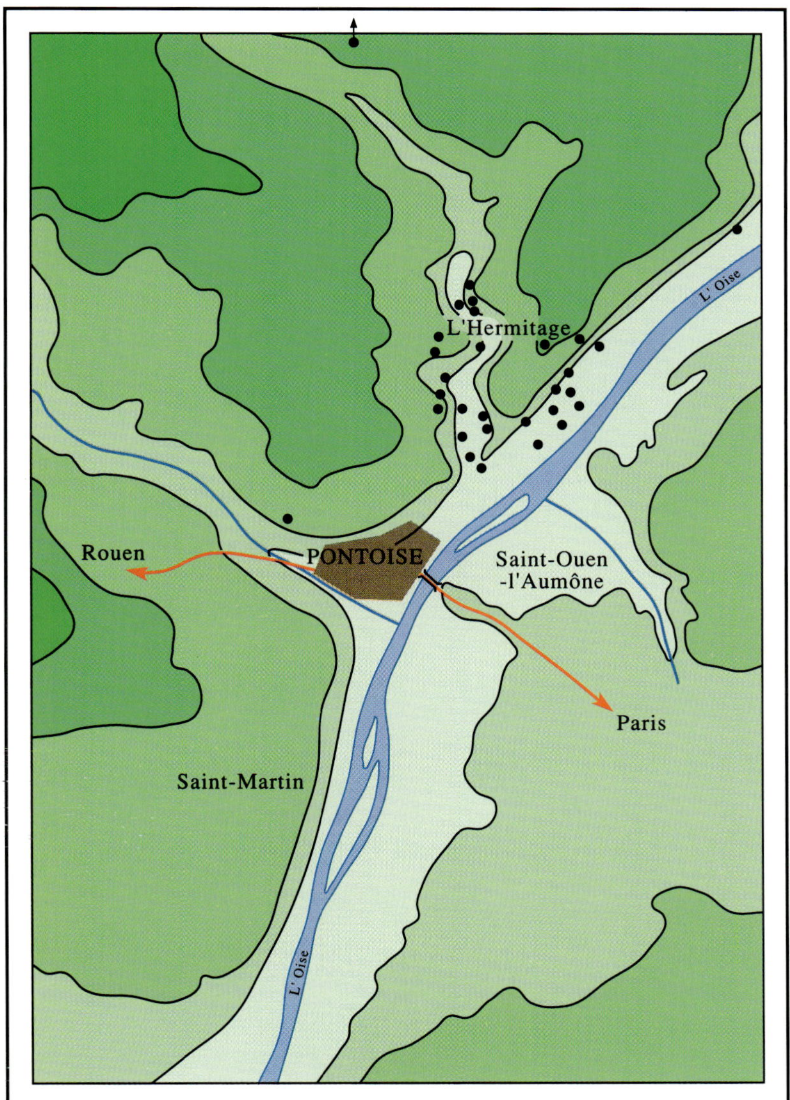

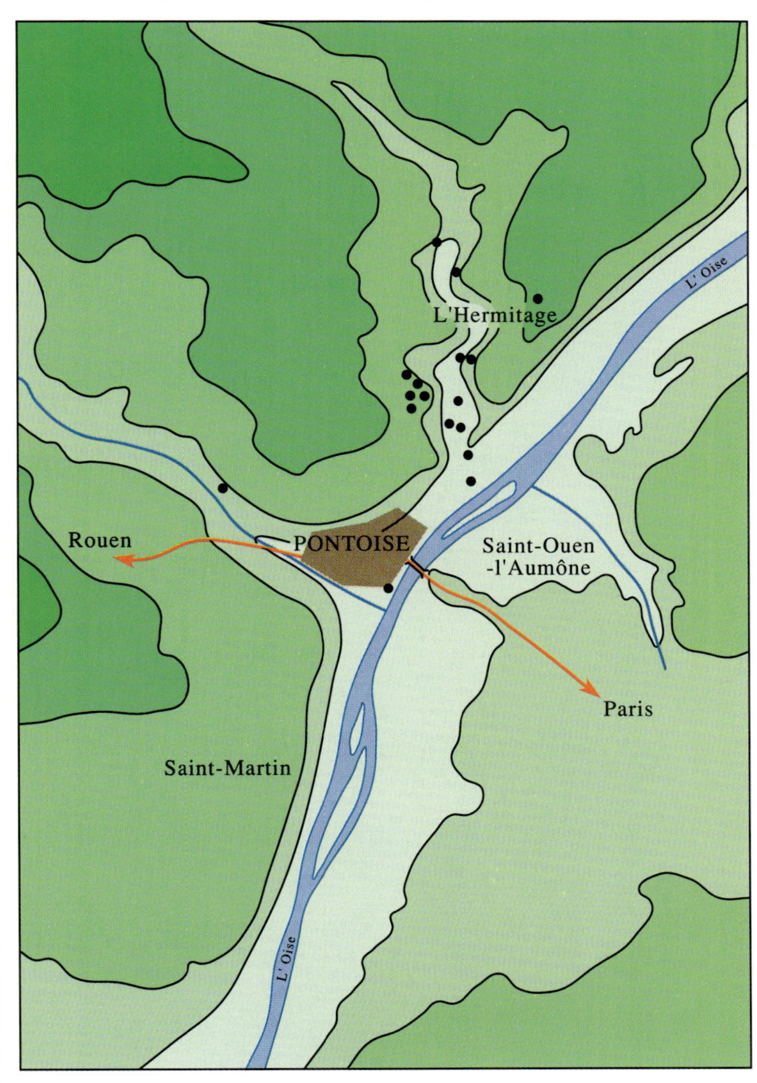

Fig. 7. Map of Pontoise as portrayed by Pissarro, 1874.

Fig. 8. Map of Pontoise as portrayed by Pissarro, 1875.

personalities of the three painters he considered the most important Impressionists: Monet, Pissarro, and Sisley. Duret's concern for Pissarro's well-being can hardly be exaggerated, and the painter wrote back intimate but respectful letters to the critic. A particularly important letter written by Duret on 6 December 1873 is worthy of some quotation:

> I persist in thinking that nature, with its rustic fields and its animals is that which corresponds best to your talent. You do not have the decorative feeling of Sisley, nor the fantastic eye of Monet, but you do have what they don't, an intimate and profound feeling for nature, and a power in your brush that makes a good painting by you something with an absolute presence. If I have any advice to give you, I would tell you not to think of either Monet or Sisley, don't preoccupy yourself with what they do; go your own way; in your path of rustic nature, you'll go into a new path, both as far and as high as any master.[42]

Pissarro responded to Duret with these words:

> Thank you for your advice, you should know that I have thought about what you've told me for a long time. What has kept me for a long time from painting after nature, is simply the difficulty of finding available models, not only in

order to paint but also in order to do proper studies of the subject. However, I will soon try to do it again; this will be very difficult because you should not think that these paintings can always be done from nature, that is to say, outside. It will be very difficult.[43]

Three figure paintings of peasant genre dating from the spring and summer of 1874 are clear attempts at wrestling with "la nature vivante" and "la vie agreste" and are undoubtedly direct pictorial responses to the advice of Duret. Duret succeeded in turning Pissarro away from Monet's style back to a kind of acceptable, even "academic" imagery of rural nature that was, in most ways, antithetical to the bourgeois leisure world in which the other major Impressionist painters operated. *La Femme gardant une vache* (P&V 263, private collection, Japan), *La Récolte des pommes de terre* (pl. 146), and *La Gardeuse de vache* (P&V 296, whereabouts unknown) are all composed figure paintings of traditional peasant motifs sited in Le Chou. *La Récolte des pommes de terre* looks astonishing to a student of Pissarro's landscapes of the classic Pontoise period and fits more comfortably with the arcadian peasant images of the 1880s and 1890s, when Pissarro returned to the composition in various media.[44] Without the direct evidence of the Duret-Pissarro correspondence in December 1873, one would be inclined to reject the date of 1874 for this picture.

Unlike most paintings by Pissarro completed in Pontoise, *La Récolte des pommes de terre* is not topographically precise. Pissarro chose as his landscape motif two houses in Le Chou which were also painted by Cézanne (pl. 145) and Aguiar (Musée d'Orsay). In the painting, the hill is radically planarized and heightened, forming a backdrop for the figures. Henriet's and Daubigny's interest in "savoir voir" is here replaced at Duret's insistence by a constructivist interest closer to "savoir faire" or "savoir construire." The figures are clearly constructed rather than observed, and several drawings for them survive.[45] When compared with Pissarro's *vues*, markets, public gardens, fair scenes, and industrial river landscapes of the preceding two years, almost everything about this painting is uncharacteristic. At once awkward and academic, *La Récolte des pommes de terre* was completed in the same year in which Monet, Manet, and Renoir were painting their genial garden and river landscapes in nearby Argenteuil, and in which Sisley explored the outer reaches of the Seine with his characteristic delicacy of vision. Before the first Impressionist exhibition had sunk from the minds of the Parisians, Pissarro was retrenching, making his initial preparations for the ideal peasant-figure compositions that obsessed him in later years. Although none of the figures relates precisely to a prototype in Millet, the subject of the potato harvest is clearly Milletesque (see *La Récolte des pommes de terre*, Walters Art Gallery, Baltimore, and *L'Angelus*, Louvre), and it is, of course, no accident that Millet's name was mentioned by Duret in connection with Pissarro's earlier in the same letter quoted above.[46]

What is particularly interesting to the student of modern art about *La Récolte des pommes de terre* is not its Milletesque imagery or its clearly constructed, one might even say "anti-*plein-air*" quality, but its color. In this painting and many others from the period of the new ruralism, Pissarro seems to have realized both the expressive and the structural importance of hue. Gone, at least comparatively, is the Corotesque concern for small-scale shifts in value that order the landscape. Instead, the color of *La Récolte des pommes de terre* is liberally applied in thickly painted areas and shows evidence of Pissarro's interest in color structure. The brilliant yellow blouse of the crouching peasant woman in the center is shaded with saturated purple, the orange of her apron with blue (pl. 147). Adjacent areas

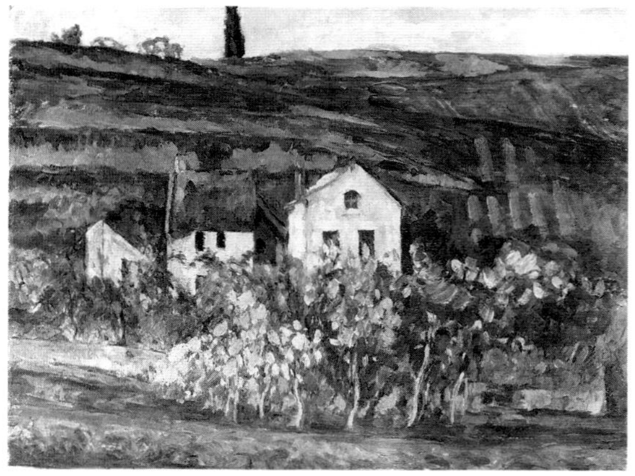

145. Paul Cézanne, *Auvers, small houses*, 1874–75, oil on canvas, 40.5 × 54.5cm., courtesy of the Fogg Art Museum, Cambridge, Mass.; bequest of Annie Swan Coburn.

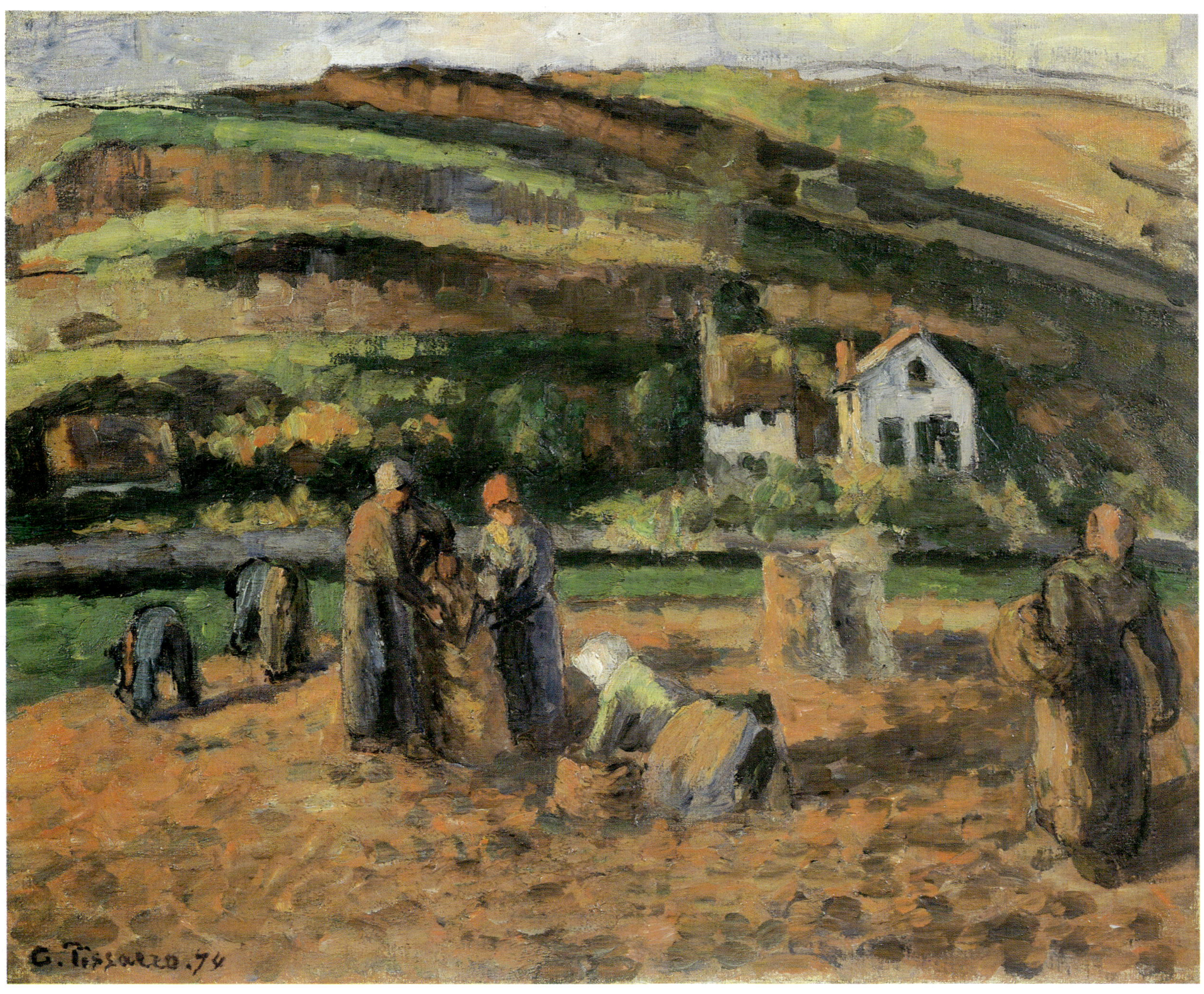

146. Camille Pissarro, *La Récolte des pommes de terre* (P&V 295), 1874, oil on canvas, 33 × 41cm., Mr. and Mrs. Sacerdotti, London.

of almost strict color opposites can be found throughout the painting, which has a resulting optical brilliance that the works of the classic Pontoise period lack. In spite of what are in many ways the regressive characteristics of *La Récolte des pommes de terre*, both its color and its contrived and constructed composition look forward to the anti-Impressionist esthetics of the 1880s and 1890s. Pissarro's ruralism was very evidently a new ruralism, not a simple application of mid-century imagery and style.

In keeping with his new interest in constructivist peasant imagery, Pissarro's attitude to industry and other modern subjects was transformed in 1874. Industrial images are rarer in the Montfoucault period than they had been in the classic Pontoise period, and the three paintings of 1874 that include a factory can all be read as repudiations of the industrial or modern world. *Bords de l'Oise à Pontoise* (P&V 250, whereabouts unknown) denies formal potency to the factory of M.

Arneuil by treating it as a background feature, interrupted by the insistent presence of the foreground vegetation. In the small vertical landscape of 1874, *Bords de l'Oise* (P&V 245, Fogg Art Museum, Cambridge, Mass), the factory is again screened from view and attention is focused on the pre-modern, manual labor of a male peasant. *Effet de matin, environs de Pontoise* (P&V 243, whereabouts unknown) emphasizes the bleak and thickly painted expanse of a ploughed field on a winter day. It is clear that, in 1874, Pissarro retreated artistically from the modern town of Pontoise, returning to the smaller landscapes of L'Hermitage in order to focus more effectively on pre-modern agricultural images. The comparative failure of the first Impressionist exhibition in this year, a failure predicted by Duret, seems to have resulted in Pissarro's abandoning his comprehensive treatment of Pontoise. He had already painted all the public places in the town with the single exception of the parc aux Charettes. He had painted all his images of the Vexin plateau. He had taken the picturesque stroll down the Oise to Saint-Martin for the last time.

The magnitude of the change experienced by Pissarro in 1874 is difficult to overemphasize, and it is clear that the ultimate source of his new ruralism was Duret. The critic realized with an exaggerated clarity the difference between the two major Impressionist landscape painters, Monet and Pissarro, and encouraged them to develop what he defined as their own specialities rather than to work as members of the revolutionary "cadre" to which he is known to have been opposed. Duret's role within the stylistic and iconographic history of Impressionism was vital. He diversified, or, at least, encouraged the diversity of the movement from the outset. He pushed Pissarro away from the site-based, total landscape, from his role as "historien de Pontoise" toward the role he would occupy, at least intermittently, for the rest of his life—"historien des champs."

In 1875, Pissarro painted a group of landscapes structured very broadly with the palette knife, canvases that provide further and even more conclusive evidence for the creative and intentional conservatism of both his style and his iconography in the mid-1870s. This group of pictures, long recognized by Pissarro scholars and treated in some detail by John Rewald, is of crucial importance in a critical discussion of Pissarro's technique. The palette knife was used as a "signature" tool by Gustave Courbet, its most famous proponent, but has never received widespread critical attention in discussions of Impressionist technique, probably because its use in the nineteenth century was almost exclusively limited to that artist.[47] The simplest characteristic of this technique is a ruggedness of surface that achieves a certain brutality in several experiments made by Pissarro in the mid-1860s, for example, *Nature morte* (P&V 50, Toledo Museum of Art, Toledo, Ohio) of 1867. Yet, in the hands of a master—Courbet in the 1860s and Pissarro in 1875—it is a technique of great range and suppleness. Courbet used it most successfully in the *sous-bois* of the 1860s, such as *La Remise de Chevreuils* of 1866 (Musée d'Orsay), to suggest both the flickering of foliage and the visual impenetrability of the dense forests in the region of the Loue that he preferred. The thick, flat areas of color interpenetrate and layer to suggest advancing form rather than receding space.

Of the four major palette-knife landscapes painted by Pissarro in Pontoise, *Le Petit pont* (pl. 28), *La Carrière, Pontoise* (pl. 50), *Le Sentier du Village* (pl. 97), and *Le Chemin montant L'Hermitage, Pontoise* (P&V 308), any one will form a useful subject for analysis. *La Carrière, Pontoise* (pl. 50) has always been dated 1874, but must be placed with the other palette-knife paintings, all of which are dated 1875.[48] The landscape abounds in "conservative" features. The repoussoir is

147. Detail of pl. 146.

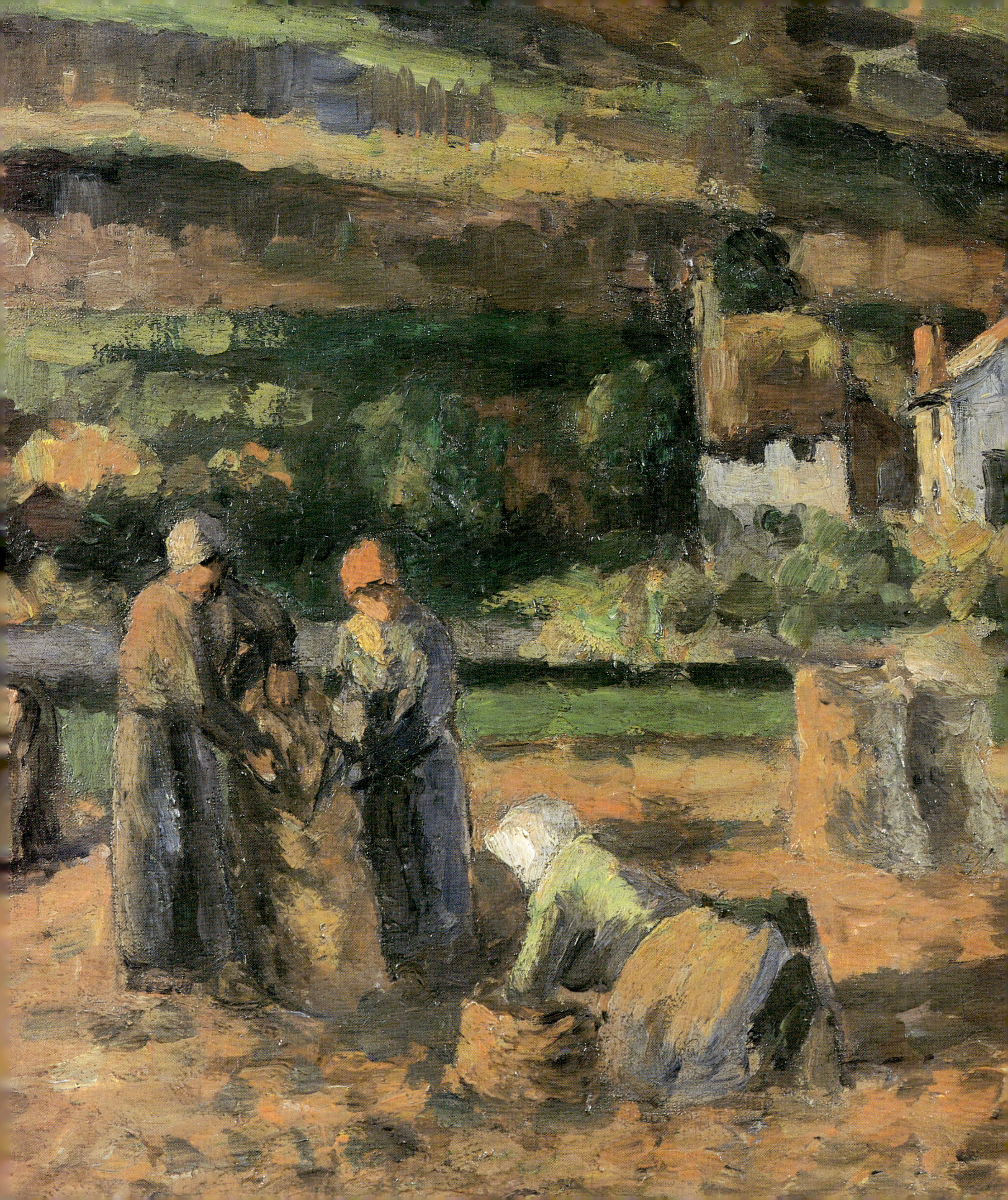

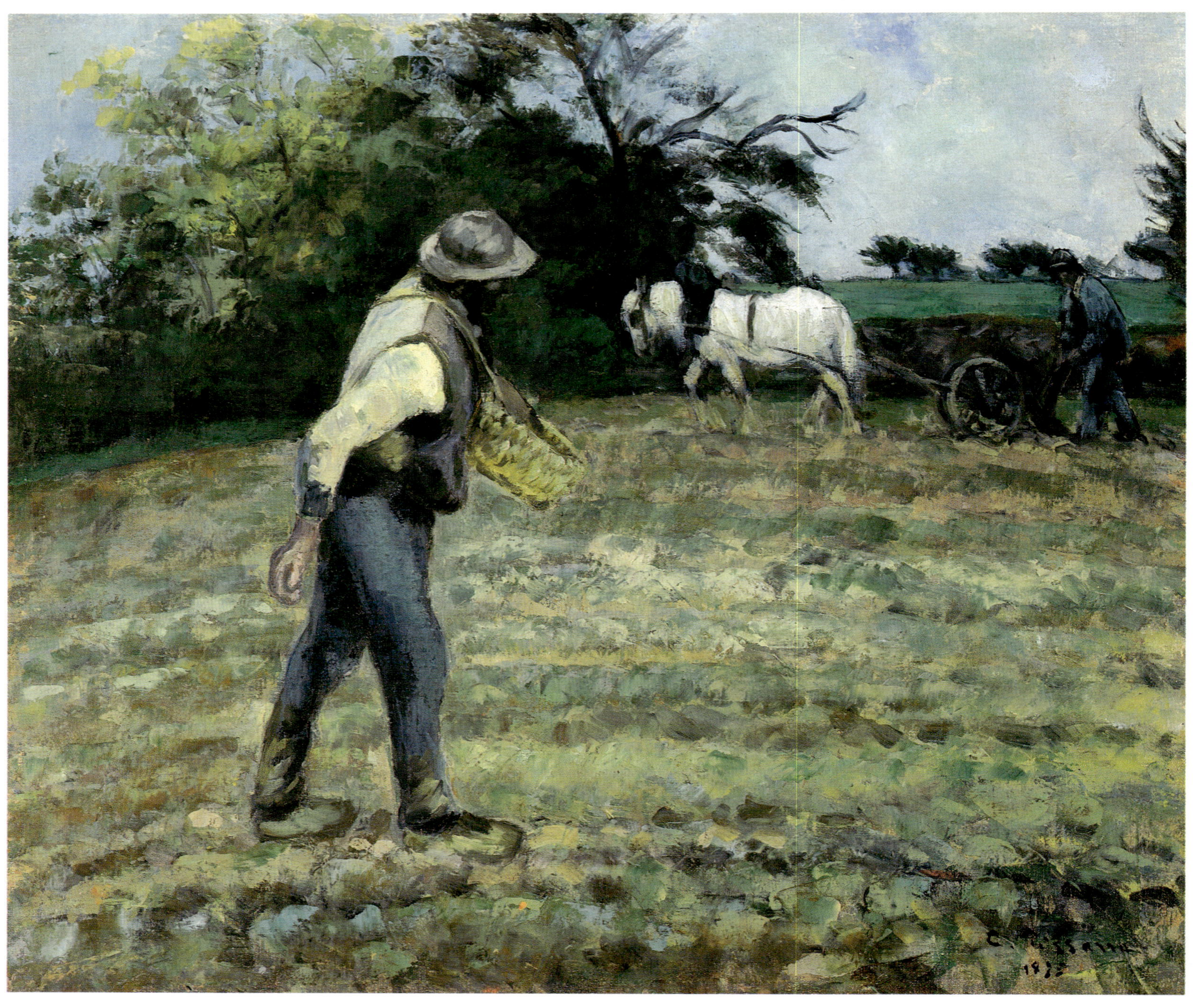

148. Camille Pissarro, *Le Semeur, Montfoucault (semeur et laboureur)* (P&V 331), oil on canvas, 1875, 46 × 55cm., private collection, Dallas.

retardataire in palette, treatment, and structure, relating closely to a vertical *sous-bois* painted by Pissarro in the mid–1860s (P&V 54, whereabouts unknown) and a drawing of the same period in the Ashmolean Museum, Oxford (B&L 57). The quarry motif, although deemphasized by Pissarro in keeping with his practice of designification already discussed, is also mid-century in origin and rare in Impressionist iconography. The painting, like so many painted by Pissarro in the 1860s, is a stylistic amalgam of Courbet, Corot, and Chintreuil. Daubigny, so important as a precedent for Pissarro's river landscapes of the classic Pontoise period, is of no importance for him in the Montfoucault period. *La Carrière, Pontoise* is an image for which precedents abound. It looks backwards; its strength lies in its creative eclecticism.

The same can be said for the superb 1875 figure painting, *Le Semeur, Mont-*

170

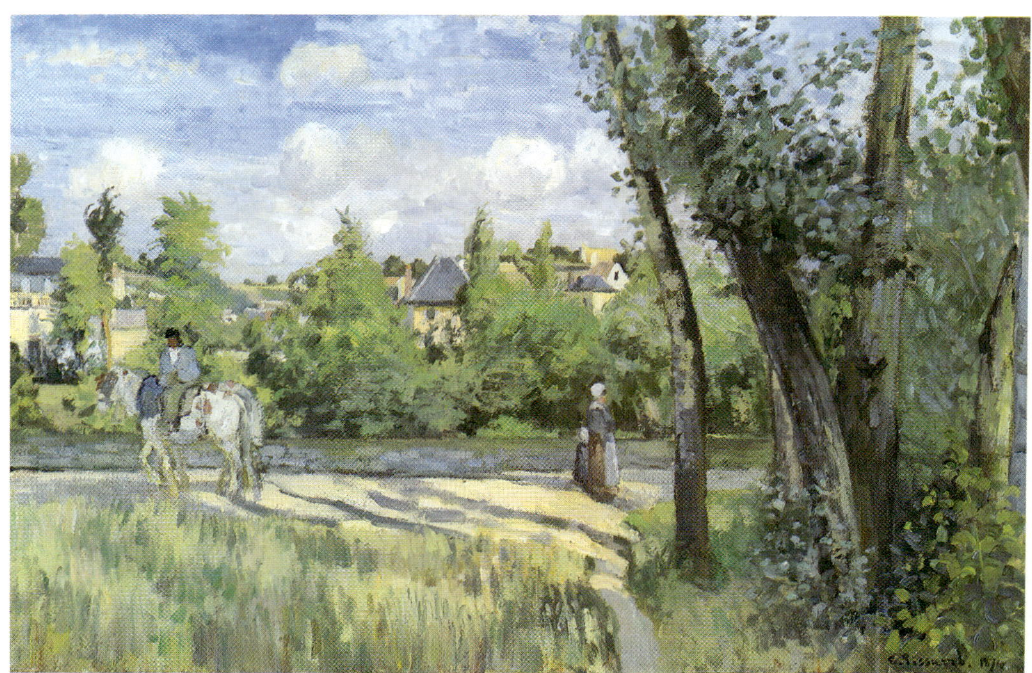

149. Camille Pissarro, *Paysage, plein soleil, Pontoise* (P&V 255), 1874, oil on canvas, 52.5 × 81.5cm., Julia Cheney Edwards Collection; courtesy, Museum of Fine Arts, Boston.

150. Jean-François Millet, *The Sower, c.*1865, pastel, 47 × 37.5cm., Sterling and Francine Clark Art Institute, Williamstown, Mass.

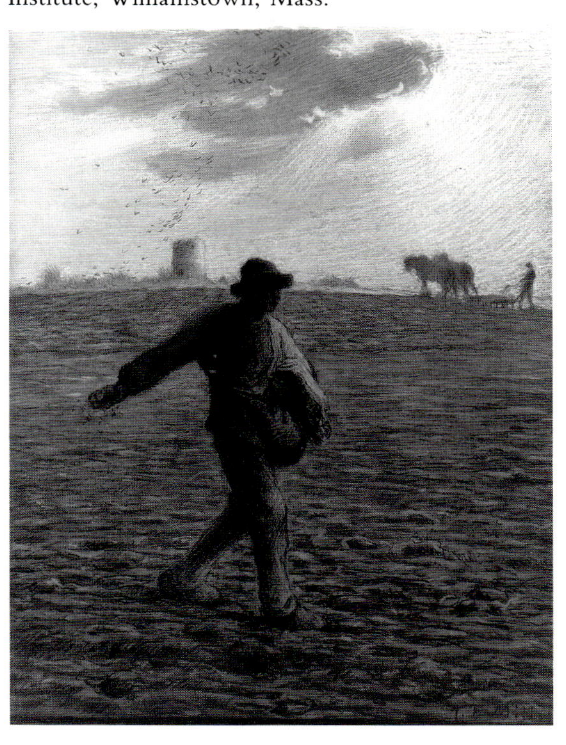

foucault (pl. 148). Yet, in this case, Pissarro includes Millet even more forcibly than Courbet as a source. The figure is derived directly from Millet's famous sower, but not from the earliest canvases of 1848, but the later, more decorative versions (pl. 150). With a figure clearly indebted to Millet and a furrowed field with obvious relationships to Courbet, this difficult small picture is anything but "Impressionist." One cannot imagine Pissarro "finding" this figure in nature, working from a series of sessions *en plein air*, and finishing the canvas with the kind of directness popularly associated with the movement. Here, we have a work of art built on the shoulders of other artists, powerful, but powerfully indirect. How the young Cézanne must have learned from this example—and how much must he have taught his teacher.

The period of new ruralism is among the most difficult in Pissarro's career to evaluate. The best paintings stand at the nexus of the new and the old, relating much more forcefully to precedent than the exactly contemporary paintings of Monet or Sisley. Pissarro is in many ways more comparable to Manet and Degas in his relation to the history of art than he is to the other landscape painters with whom he is most often grouped. Paintings like *La Récolte des pommes de terre* and *Paysanne poussant une brouette* (pl. 151) have extraordinary power, a power that comes from their forthright grafting of the new technique of color-opposite construction onto an imagery securely rooted in nineteenth-century French art. The maps and graphs illustrated in this book help perhaps more than the analysis of any one painting to demonstrate the changes in Pissarro's esthetics during this difficult period between the first and the second Impressionist exhibitions. It is, in fact, misleading to characterize Pissarro's esthetic in this period by the example of *La Récolte des pommes de terre*. Its brilliant color, while a feature of some paintings of 1874–75, is absent from many other "green" landscapes, such as *Paysage, plein soleil, Pontoise* (pl. 149), in which value construction is as significant as hue is in *La Récolte des pommes de terre*. The relatively monochromatic palettes and the use of bright color accents rather than paired color-opposites connect the palette-knife canvases forcefully to the art of the mid-century, from which Pissarro, more than any other Impressionist painter, drew his inspiration.[49]

171

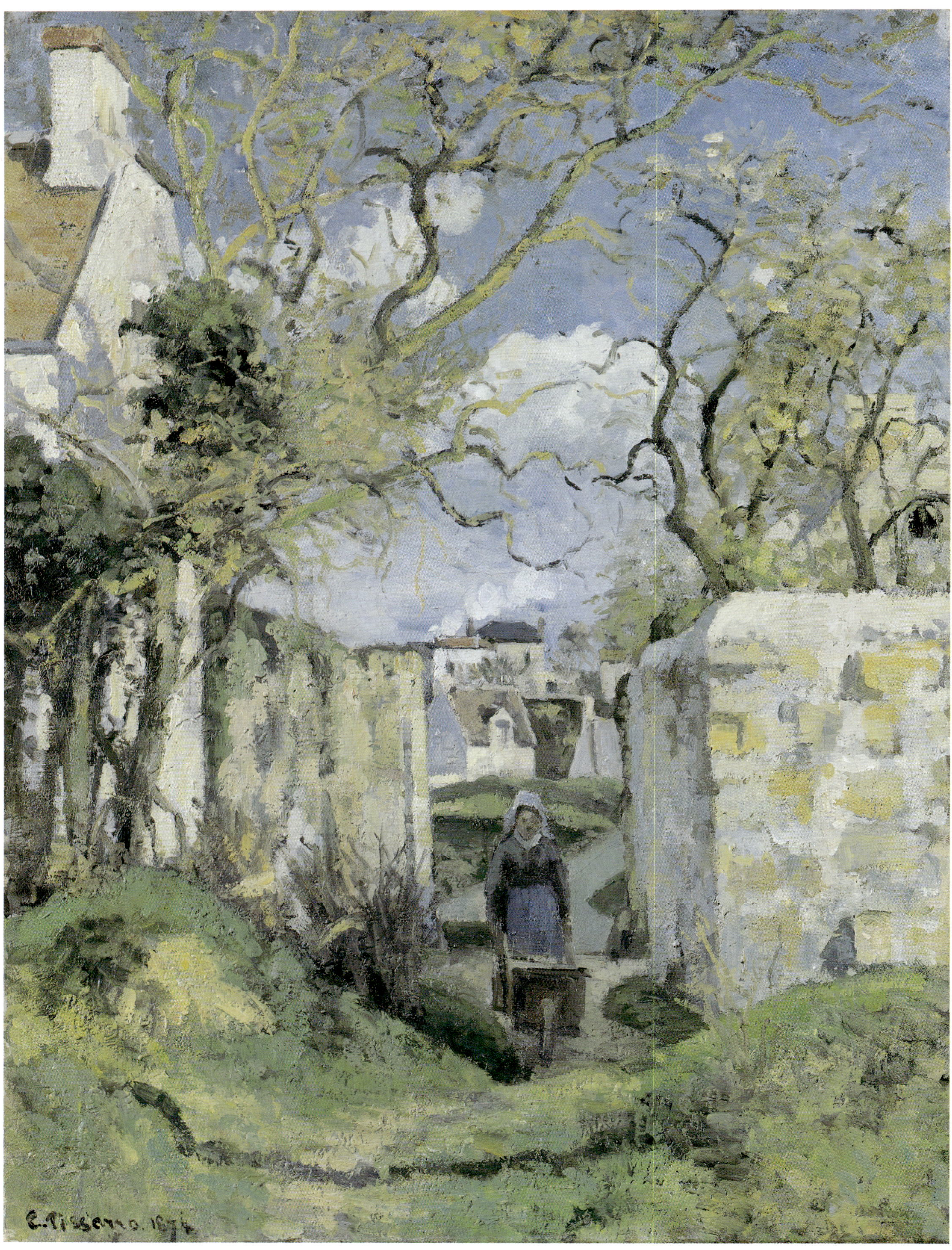

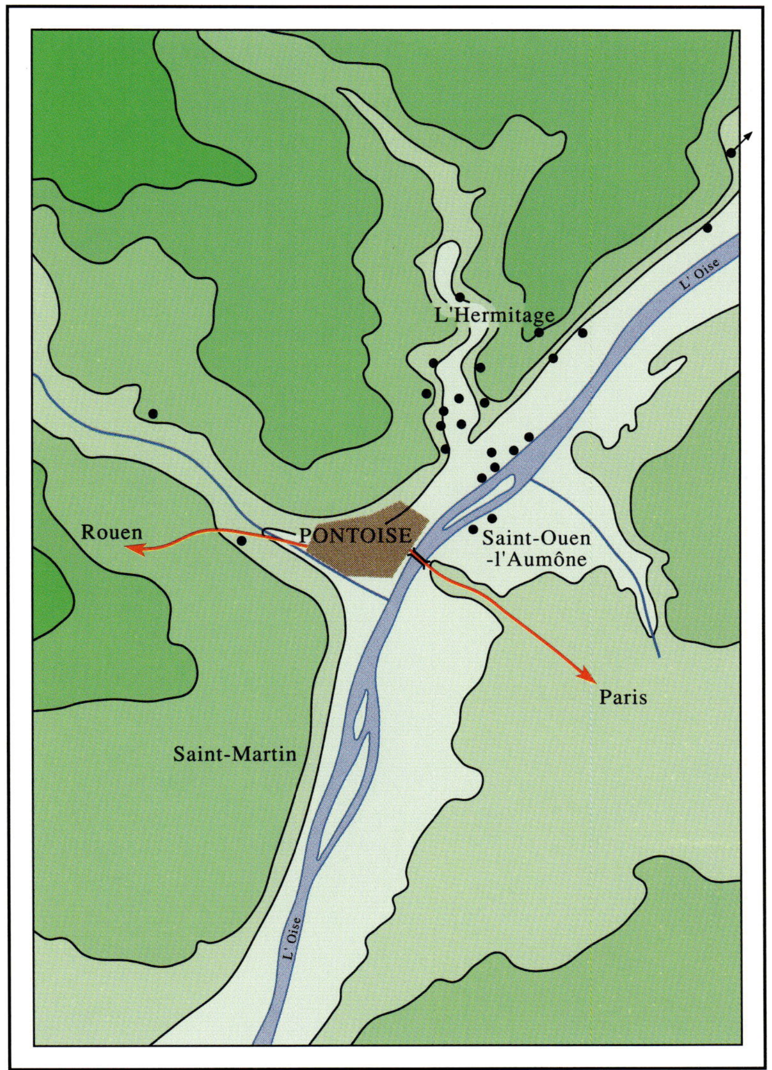

Fig. 9. Map of Pontoise as portrayed by Pissarro, 1876.

151. Camille Pissarro, *Paysanne poussant une brouette, Maison Roudest, Pontoise* (P&V 244), 1874, oil on canvas, 65 × 51cm., Nationalmuseum, Stockholm.

1876   A Confusion of Realms

Both iconological and formal analyses indicate that 1876, Pissarro's last year spent shuttling between Pontoise and Montfoucault, was a confused and variable year for the painter. It saw a partial, but important return to the modernist subject matter, of the early 1870s (figs. 5, 6, and 9) and an experimentation with a complex, multi-layered, and, for the first time, truly "Impressionist" facture. The second Impressionist exhibition held in April of that year exposed Pissarro to the recent paintings of Monet, with whom Pissarro had not corresponded since January 1874, nor seen since the first Impressionist exhibition in April of that same year. The exhibition reintroduced Pissarro to Paris and to the avant-garde urban art from which Duret had tried, with some success, to avert him.

Pissarro's depictions of the Pontoise landscape in 1876 range in their subject matter from scenes of traditional agricultural labor to the rather grand, leisure-garden scene painted at Les Mathurins, *Le Jardin des Mathurins, Pontoise*. He painted his first detailed study of the *guêpes à vapeur* on the Oise and returned to industrial imagery.[50] Yet, in spite of this new variety of motif types and this readmission of industrial imagery, Pissarro's range of landscape sites in Pontoise remained narrow and essentially unchanged from the constricted patterns of the

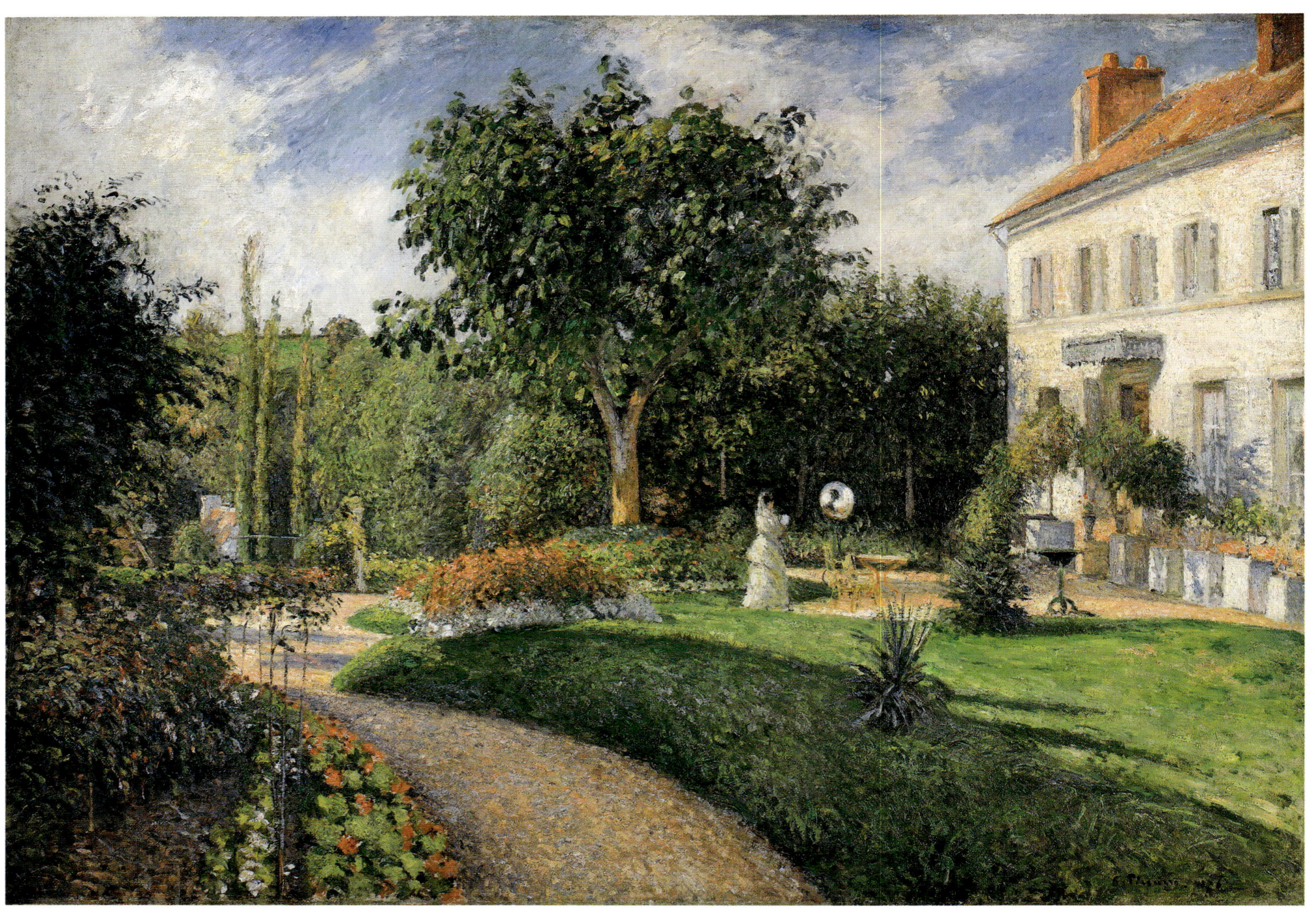

152. Camille Pissarro, *Le Jardin des Mathurins, Pontoise* (P&V 349), 1876, oil on canvas, 113 × 165cm., Nelson-Atkins Museum of Art, Kansas City, Missouri (Nelson Fund).

previous two years. The physical geography of Pissarro's Pontoise was the same in 1876 as it had been in 1875, but his perception of the landscape included many more recently built structures and frankly identical forms. The river and its "modern" life increased considerably in iconological importance in 1876. Yet the change was apparent not only in Pissarro's treatment of Pontoise: even his perception of the landscape at Montfoucault altered. Canvases such as *La Fenaison à Montfoucault* (P&V 363, Sotheby's, New York, 10 May 1988) and *La Moisson à Montfoucault* (P&V 364, Musée d'Orsay) have a spaciousness and geniality that recall *Les Quatre Saisons*. As a direct result of his trips to Paris and his re-exposure to the other Impressionists, Pissarro's work in 1876 sets the isolationist ruralism of the Montfoucault period into relief. His retreat from the suburban imagery of the Impressionists was not resolved enough to withstand the pressures from Paris, pressures that he would feel for the rest of his life.

The year 1876 produced few masterpieces. The pictures are wide-ranging, difficult, and, of course, variable. Their evasiveness, their lack of a unifying style, betray a painter uncertain of his artistic direction. Indeed, the stylistic vacillations of 1876 contort the surface of many pictures. The industrial images reveal in many ways a suspiciousness of the industrial world they depict. They exaggerate

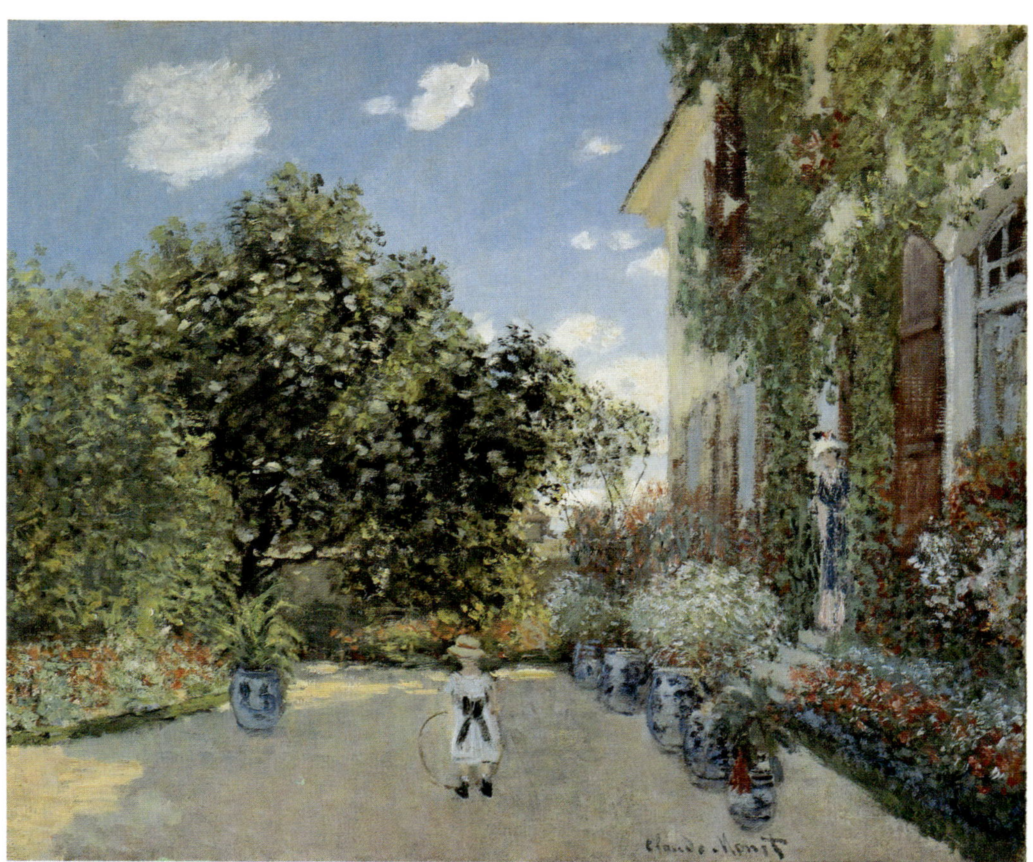

153. Claude Monet, *La Maison de l'artiste à Argenteuil*, 1873, oil on canvas, 60 × 73 cm., Art Institute of Chicago; Mr. and Mrs. Martin A. Ryerson Collection, 1933.1153.

the incidental foreground forms and lack any concentration on a motif. The rural images include modern, mechanized threshers (P&V 367, collection Lord Moyne, and P&V 368, collection of the Hon. James Smith) as well as pre-modern, barnyard tools.[51] Both agricultural and industrial images are treated with equal ambivalence.

Even Pissarro's technique shows the dichotomous quality observed in his iconography in that most fitful year. Certain landscapes are complex renderings of many forms with tiny, intertwining brushstrokes very unlike the heavily painted landscapes of the Montfoucault period and the carefully tended landscapes of the classic Pontoise period (see particularly P&V 343, Mazeul de Arta, Bucharest, and P&V 370, Rudolf Staechelin'she Familienstiftung, Basel). As such, they relate clearly to the landscapes of Monet exhibited in the second Impressionist exhibition. Others are characterized by a large, broadly brushed facture which traps forms into planes and stems logically from the palette-knife pictures of 1874–75 (P&V 337, whereabouts unknown; P&V 339, Sotheby's, New York, 14 May 1985, lot 20; and P&V 341, Galerie Schmidt, Paris, summer 1977). Still others show a mixed facture, a combination of small touches and larger areas of evenly applied color, as, for example, *L'Oise à Pontoise, temps gris* (pl. 87).

The second Impressionist exhibition clearly had profound effects on Pissarro. His large garden landscape, *Le Jardin des Mathurins, Pontoise* (pl. 152), was conceived in response to Monet's enormous *Déjeuner* (Musée d'Orsay), although its massing and composition are closer to *La Maison de l'artiste à Argenteuil* (pl. 153), which was not in the exhibition. Pissarro's river landscapes are echoes in an industrial key of Monet's river landscapes painted in Argenteuil. Yet Pissarro's landscapes could never be confused with those of Monet, and it is evident that the older artist was attempting to improve on his model rather than simply borrowing from it. The large garden picture is conceived as a series of clearly defined masses that assume their places in an almost volumetric landscape. The brushstrokes, while small, are constrained within the forms they describe, lacking the independent gestural quality so important for Monet. Again, Pissarro's use of color in *Les Jardin des Mathurins, Pontoise* recalls *La Récolte des pommes de terre* in its frequent juxtaposition of areas of color opposites within a generally green landscape.

1877–1878 Impressionist Years

No member of the Impressionist circle was more crucial to the survival of the movement than was Pissarro. However, in pictorial terms he was rather late in his adoption of many of the major stylistic and iconographical aspects of the Impressionist style as it has come to be understood by twentieth-century critics. The preoccupation with movement and reflection that characterized the paintings of Monet, Sisley, and Renoir was not a feature of Pissarro's esthetic until 1877. Yet the paintings of 1877 and 1878 are assiduous in their use of Impressionist imagery, including river scenes and bourgeois figures. The palette-knife constructions of the Montfoucault period were replaced in 1877 by almost diaphanous, windswept trees and wavy waters, evoked with many short, wrist-gesture strokes like those that Monet and Sisley had been using intermittently since the late 1860s. The heaviness of both the imagery and the style of the Montfoucault period, undercut in that most problematic of years, 1876, gave way in 1877 to a freely brushed style and a more decidedly modern imagery.

It is tempting to say that Pissarro returned to Pontoise in 1877, that he concerned himself once more with the site itself after the conscious ruralism of the mid-1870s; and the statement is partially true. He painted "reversions" of several canvases of the classic Pontoise period which manifest a desire to reconnect himself with the Pissarro of that period. *Terre labourée en hiver, avec un homme portant un fagot* (P&V 381, formerly collection of Sam Salz) is a remaking of *Gelée blanche, ancienne route d'Ennery, Pontoise* (pl. 115). *Bords de l'Oise, Pontoise* (P&V 403, Williams College Museum of Art, Williamstown) is clearly a new version of *Au bord de la rivière, Pontoise* (P&V 160, Musée de Saint Gallen, Switzerland). Distant views with many small forms that are all but absent in the paintings of the Montfoucault period reappear in what must be called the Impressionist years (pl. 78, and P&V 409, Kroller-Müller Museum, Otterlo, and P&V 412, Dr. Nathan, Zurich). Yet, in spite of these attempts at returning to the Pontoise of the classic period, the paintings of 1877–78 lack the range of subjects and the interest with the site as a whole that are characteristic of that earlier period. The site maps (figs. 10 and 11) prove that Pissarro remained rooted, for the most part, in L'Hermitage and the immediately adjacent hillsides and river areas. Although many of his landscapes became spacious again during those years, the painter moved very little in the real landscape to paint them.

Pissarro painted two kinds of landscapes in 1877–78: thickly painted, almost scumbled landscapes with predominantly rural subjects (*Côtes Saint-Denis à Pontoise*, pl. 154 and *Le Verger, Côtes Saint-Denis à Pontoise*, pl. 155); and freely painted landscapes representing subjects in motion (*Bords de l'Oise à Pontoise*, pl. 156 and *Un Coin du jardin à L'Hermitage*, P&V 396, Musée d'Orsay). The latter type of images, which in many ways dominates the period, is related to a series of very small paintings to which one must turn for a proper understanding of Pissarro's problematic Impressionism. In fact, Pissarro began, in 1877, to paint

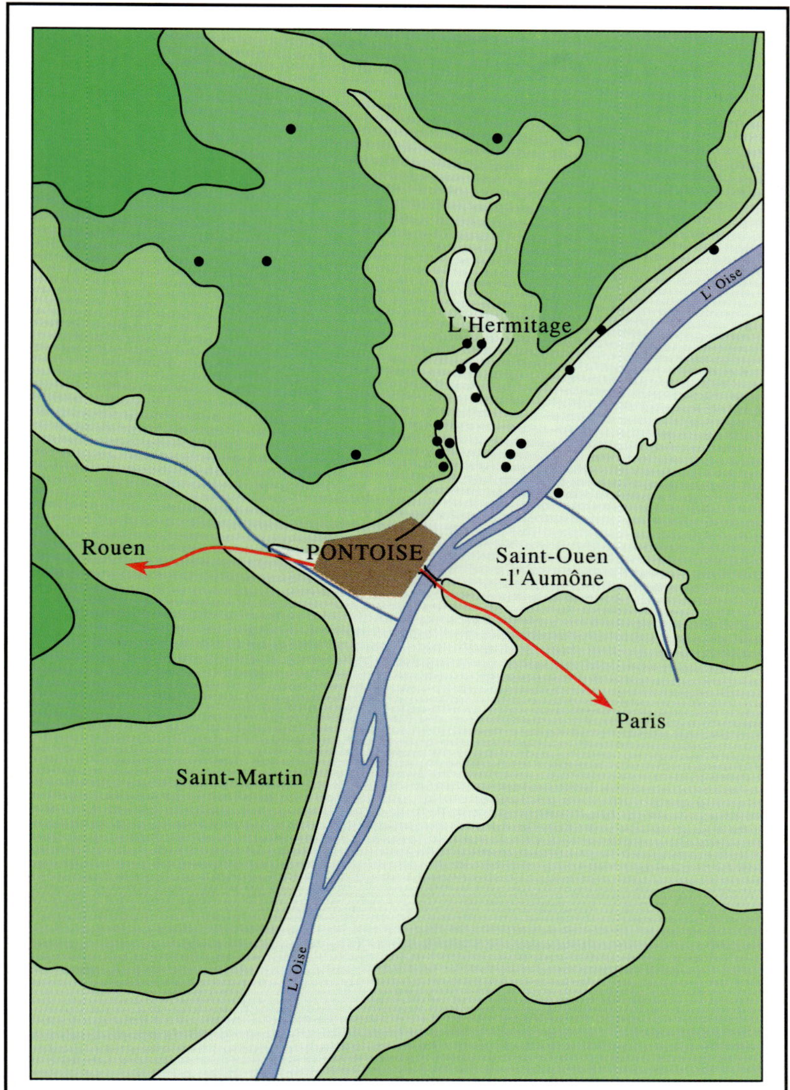

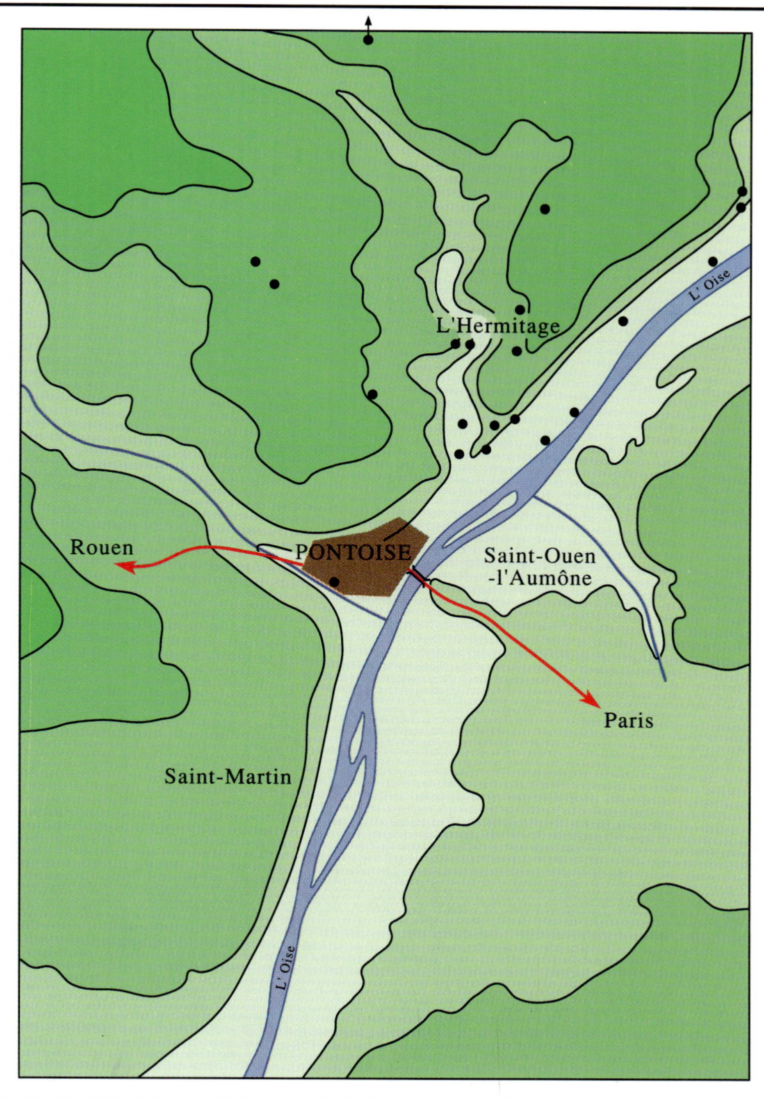

Fig. 10. Map of Pontoise as portrayed by Pissarro, 1877.

Fig. 11. Map of Pontoise as portrayed by Pissarro, 1878.

tiny *esquisses* which he used as a chromatic and compositional basis for larger, finished paintings. This technique, which has long been considered anathema to the Impressionist landscape painter, relates the pictorial process of Pissarro in the late 1870s to that of Seurat, who made elaborate series of small studies in preparation for large canvases in the 1880s.[52] These small sketches act as an historical bridge between the academic *esquisse-étude-tableau* progression, frequently violated by the academicians themselves, and the anti-Impressionist landscape program of the various Neo-Impressionist painters.

Pissarro's small *esquisses*, all of which were executed on *carton* like the Seurat studies for the *Bathers at Asnières* (National Gallery, London), can be divided into two types: those directly related to larger canvases (pls. 156 and 157) and others that might be called independent. Pissarro seems to have considered these tiny preparatory studies to have been independent works of art. Most of them are signed, but an unusually high percentage are undated.[53] There are, in fact, no dated pairs, so that connection between the *esquisses* and the related paintings has not been noted in the literature. Their very existence seems inconsistent with the idea of Impressionism. Yet what is odd and revealing is that the pictures that come from the sketches are the most fleeting, simple, and freely conceived of Pissarro's career. *Bords de l'Oise à Pontoise* (pl. 156) is as different from *Côtes Saint-*

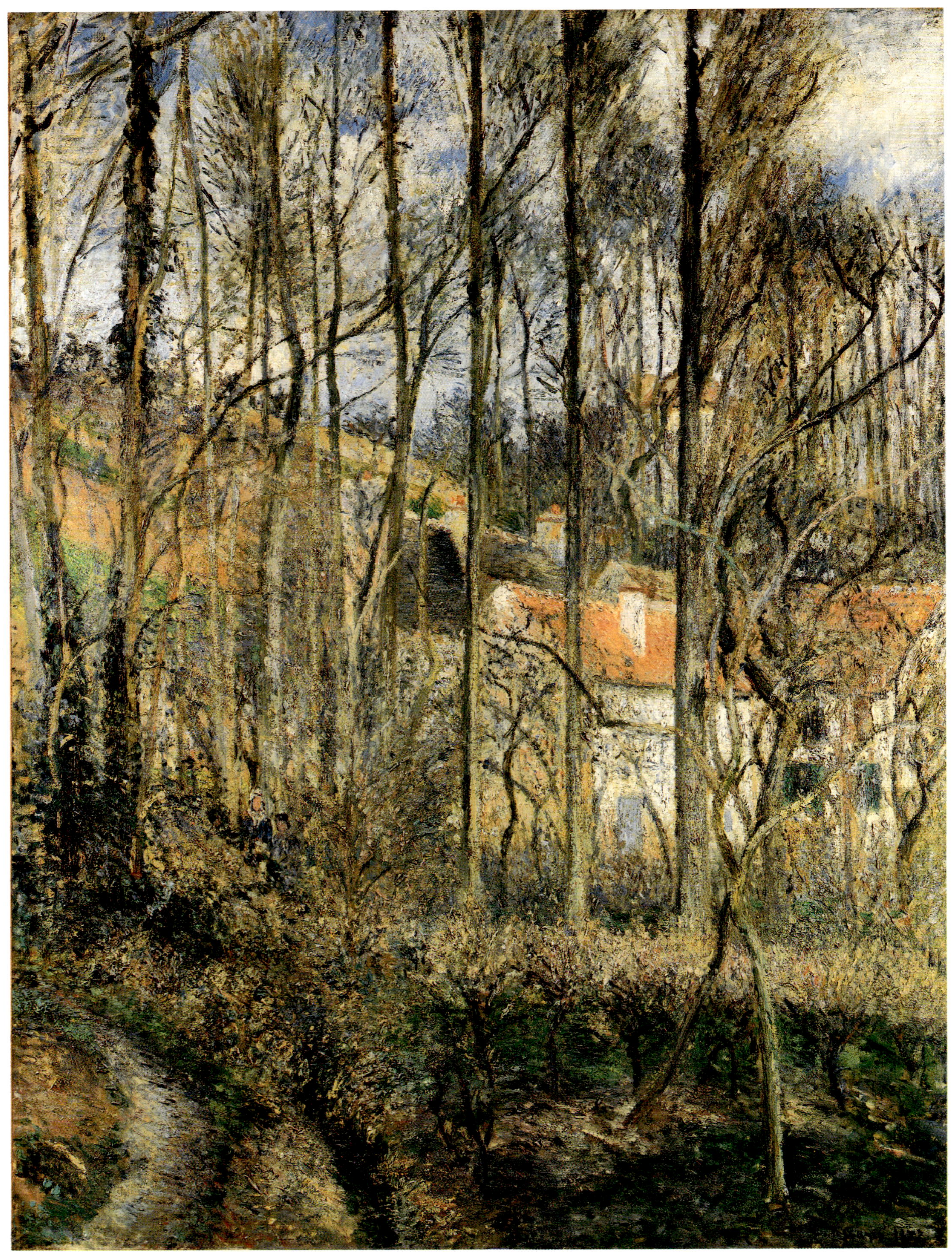

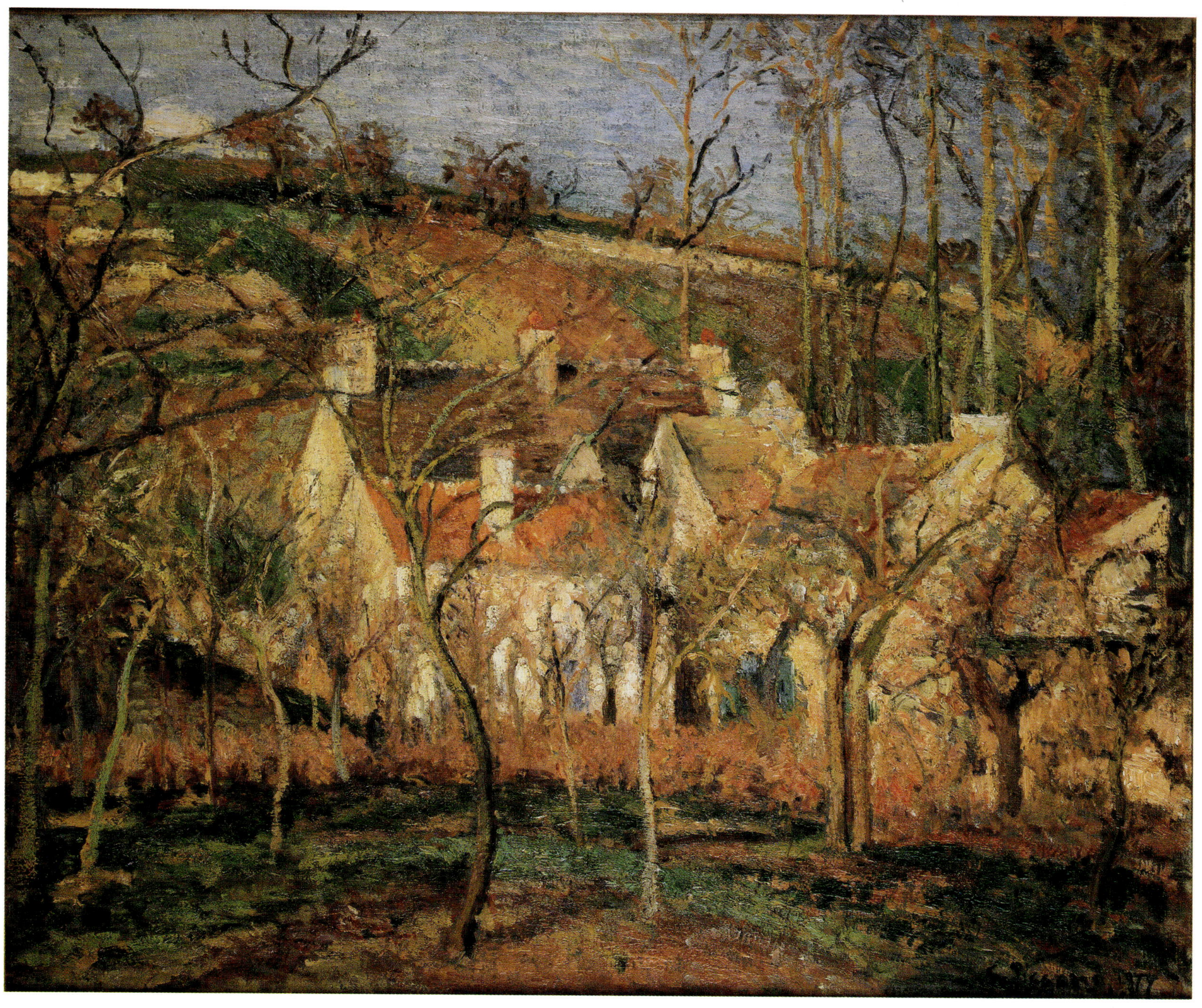

155. Camille Pissarro, *Le Verger, Côtes Saint-Denis à Pontoise* (P&V 384), 1877, oil on canvas, 54.5 × 65.5cm., Musée d'Orsay, Paris.

154. Camille Pissarro, *Côtes Saint-Denis à Pontoise* (P&V 380), 1877, oil on canvas, 115 × 87.5cm., courtesy of the Trustees of the National Gallery, London.

Denis à Pontoise (pl. 154) of the same year as a Monet is from a Cézanne. *Bords de l'Oise à Pontoise* is freely conceived; its "motif" is motion. The wind whips the foliage; the water rushes by. The brushstrokes that describe all this motion are applied with a notable freedom and apparent spontaneity. *Côtes Saint-Denis à Pontoise*, on the other hand, is massively complex, melancholic, screened, and stable. Its subject is centered, solid, and traditional within the iconographic context of European landscape painting since the seventeenth century. *Côtes Saint-Denis à Pontoise* can be read as an extension of the imagery of the Montfoucault period, taking into account the advances in Impressionist style made during the same year by Monet in his series of the Gare Saint-Lazare, five of which were exhibited at the third Impressionist exhibition in April 1877. By contrast, the landscapes for which small studies survive, although spontaneous in

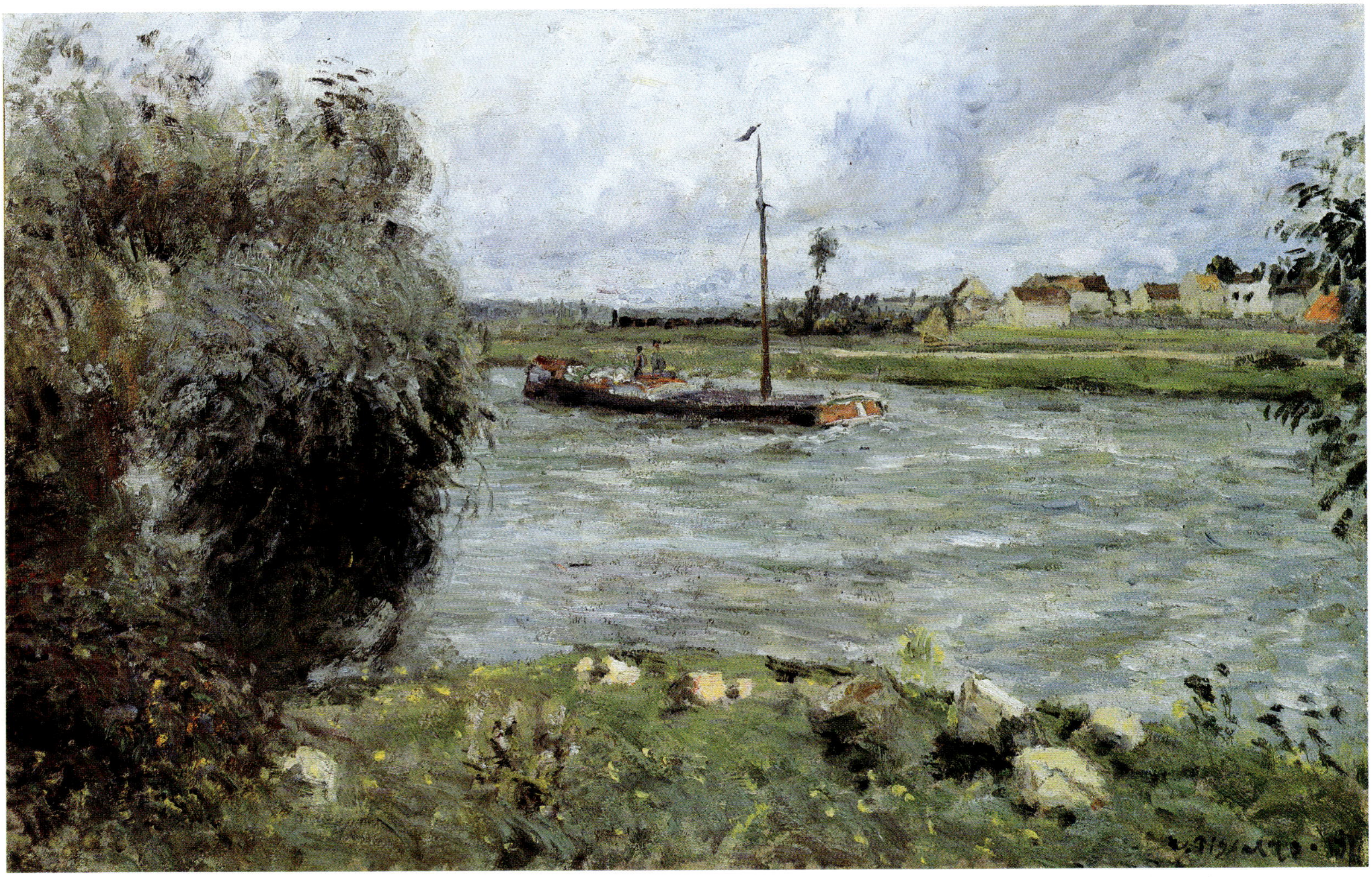

156. Camille Pissaro, *Bords de l'Oise à Pontoise* (P&V 399), 1877, oil on canvas, 52 × 81cm., private collection

157. Camille Pissaro, *Bords de l'Oise, environs de Pontoise* (P&V 401), *c*.1877, oil on cardboard, 11 × 14cm., destroyed in World War II.

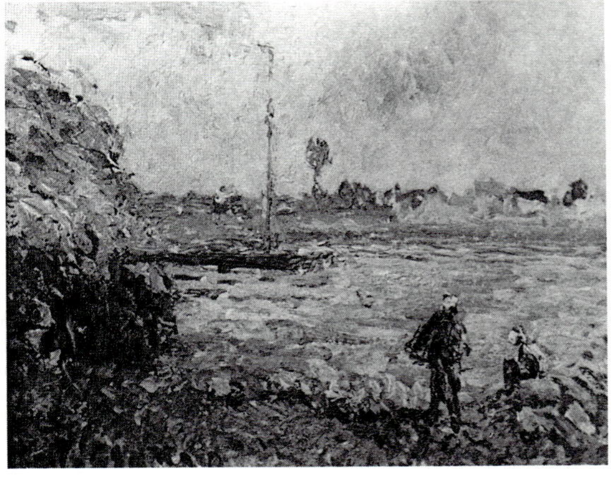

appearance, were clearly contrived images for Pissarro, images for which studies were necessary.

Why did Pissarro paint these *esquisse-tableau* pairs? Why did he paint "Impressionist" *esquisses* for "Impressionist" paintings? As Champa has shown in his persuasive analysis of Pissarro's sketch for *The Towpath* (Glasgow Art Gallery and Museum), painted in 1864, Pissarro used the sketch as a mode of blocking and arranging the composition in a highly traditional manner.[54] Yet, as early as 1864, Pissarro failed to refine his manner of execution for the larger canvas. He simply enlarged the sketch, facture and all, as if he were putting a colored slide into a slide projector. The size is, therefore, the key difference, indeed the only major difference, between the *esquisse* and the finished picture.

It is clear that the *esquisse* provided Pissarro with a miniature means of achieving the unified effect before the laborious production of a large painting. Read in the same manner employed by Champa, the sketches become tiny studies of "spontaneity" for medium-sized pictures of "spontaneity." They are, in many ways, attempts rather than studies, which is why the word *esquisse* has been used rather than the word *étude*, preferred by Pissarro himself and his son, Ludovic-Rodo.[55] Indeed, their existence as attempts rather than totally independent pictures can be seen most easily in comparison with several earlier pictures by Monet representing the same motif. *Le Bassin d'Argenteuil* (Rhode Island School of Design Museum, Providence), the *Bridge at Argenteuil* (Mellon Collection, Upperville,

180

Virginia), and *Le Pont d'Argenteuil* (Musée d'Orsay) are all versions of the same subject in the same season using the same structural and compositional devices. The language is crucial in this context. The pictures by Monet, which are nearly identical in size, are versions of a composition, not attempts or trials. They are independent and different works of art, not quite a series in the pure sense of that term, but rather variations on a motif. By contrast, Pissarro's choice of a tiny format for his sketches lessens their relative importance and indicates, beyond a doubt, that they are studies or trials. It is likely that similar studies of this kind have been lost or discarded, given that other canvases of 1877 and 1878 are related in style and motif to the pictures for which sketches on *carton* do exist.

As in the example of *The Towpath* mentioned above, Pissarro used a sketch technique in both the *esquisses* and the larger canvases painted in the Impressionist period.[56] In fact, if exhibited separately, the large pictures would be considered remarkably fresh and vigorous "impressions" by the standards of Pissarro's own career. His most free and exuberant pictures of the Impressionist decade were not based on direct perception and *plein-air* involvement with the motif, but on a process of pictorial transformation of "reality," involving the intermediate step of an *esquisse*.[57] This is not to say that Pissarro painted the larger versions of these pairs entirely in the studio. They were quite probably finished or even worked a great deal out of doors, in keeping with the warm-weather pleasantness of their motifs. Yet, the very existence of the sketches tempers any interpretation of the spontaneity of the pictures and raises and question of the nature of Pissarro's Impressionism and, by consequence, of Impressionism itself.

There is little doubt that Pissarro considered Monet to be the greatest landscape painter of the late nineteenth century. In spite of their differences in social background, life style, politics, and temperament, and aside from minor lapses of judgment, Pissarro was among the most sympathetic judges of Monet's career. His own removal to Louveciennes after the isolated first Pontoise period has been interpreted in this chapter as a turn toward the developing avant-garde of Monet and away from the premeditated and stylistically eclectic paintings of that period. Pissarro's career of the 1870s can be read as a vacillation between Monet and the painters of the generation of 1830, between the anti-intellectual, modern, and brilliantly "optical" painting of the younger man and the anti-urban, moralistic, and constructivist painting of the Barbizon School. Pissarro's approach to the style of Monet in the early 1870s has been described above, as has his rejection of both the iconography and the style of the younger artist during the Montfoucault period.

Pissarro's paintings of 1876, 1877, and 1878 can be interpreted as a return to Monet. The older painter had not assimilated technical and compositional input from the younger since the period 1869–70. Monet had made key changes in his facture and his subject matter during the early and middle 1870s, and Pissarro, frustrated by his attempts at creating a new, unsentimental ruralism, broadened his art in 1876. The three Impressionist exhibitions of 1876, 1877, and 1878 gave Pissarro a greater exposure to the recent painting of Monet than he had ever experienced, an exposure that was possible without close personal contact. In fact, the friendship between Pissarro and Monet, never a great one, began to wane as the 1870s continued. Their correspondence, now published in large part in Wildenstein's biography and catalogue raisonné of Monet's paintings, shows a cluster of letters in the early 1870s, before the first Impressionist exhibition. The next letter, which came after a pause of several years, was a formal condolence from the Pissarro family on the death of Camille Monet in 1879. Monet replied with equal formality.[58]

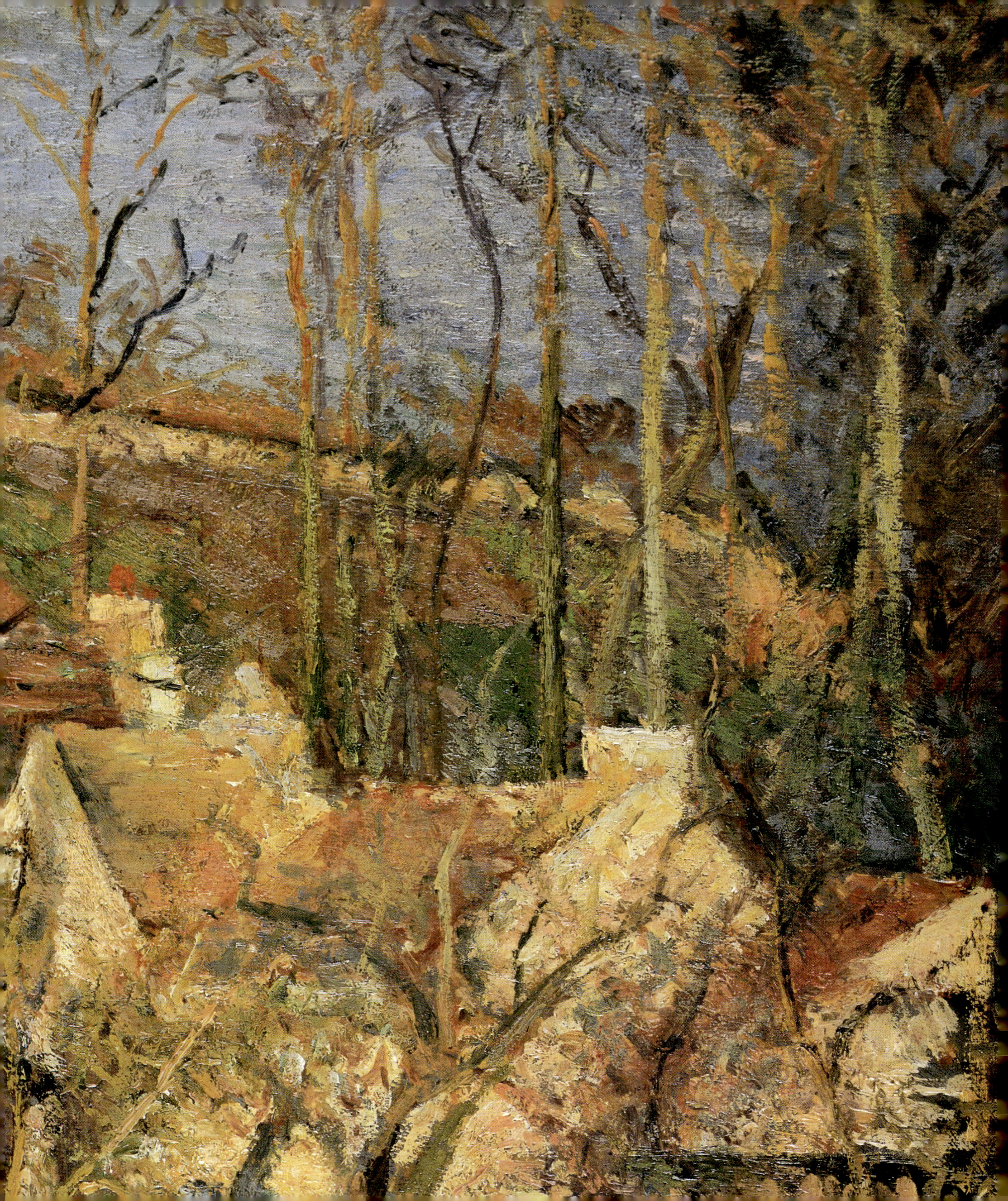

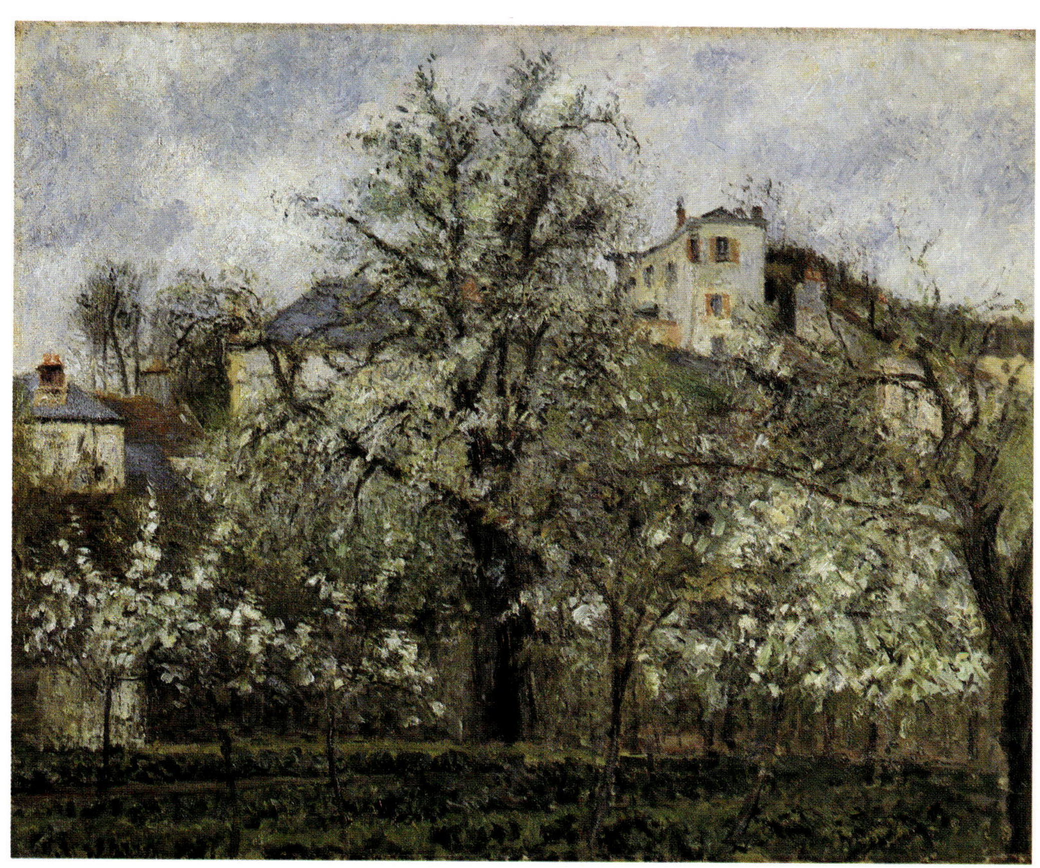

159. Camille Pissarro, *Potager et arbres en fleurs, printemps, Pontoise* (P&V 387), 1877, oil on canvas, 65 × 81cm., Musée d'Orsay, Paris.

Pissarro's adoption of the *esquisse* mode of pictorial conception must be seen as what psycho-analysts would term an approach-avoidance to the example of Monet. Pissarro's greatest paintings of 1877, to take one year as an example, are not the "Impressionist" pictures discussed above, but pictures in the synthetic rural tradition. *Côtes Saint-Denis à Pontoise* and *Le Verger, Côtes Saint-Denis à Pontoise*, with their intensely traditional subjects and their surfaces reminiscent as much of Rousseau and Diaz as of Monet, are Pissarro's masterpieces of this period. It is clear when confronted with these pictures that Pissarro was more at home in the stable environment of the rural landscape. Earth, not water, was what truly fascinated him. The familiar motifs of L'Hermitage allowed him to experiment more fully with problems of technique and color; indeed, the thickness of the paint on canvases such as *Le Verger, Côtes Saint-Denis à Pontoise* suggests that he painted layer upon layer rather than attained a certain compositional level in miniature before beginning the full-scale picture (pl. 158). John House's recent work on Monet's methods suggests that Monet himself used this technique of adding to the composition in discrete layers, covering the *esquisse* and thereby creating the finished picture.[59] Both Pissarro's use of the Impressionist sketch and Monet's probable layering process indicate that Impressionist working methods were far more intellectual and premeditated than the textbooks would have us believe.

Coloristically, Pissarro made few changes or advances in the Impressionist years. He continued to paint two kinds of pictures, as he had since 1874. One is characterized by the obvious juxtaposition of warm and cool colors and by a mutual heightening of the palette using color-opposites. Perhaps the most important picture of this type painted in the Impressionist years is the justly famous *Le Verger, Côtes Saint-Denis à Pontoise* (pls. 155 and 158) first shown in

158. Detail of pl. 155.

the Impressionist exhibition of 1877. Its surface is covered with brilliant areas of pure color that interact in a variety of ways to produce an optical tension rare in Impressionist painting of the 1870s. There is a wider range of hue than of value in this canvas, and the palette is highly saturated. The contrast with pictures like *Potager et arbres en fleurs, printemps, Pontoise* (pl. 159) or *Chemin sous bois, en été* (P&V 416, Musée d'Orsay) could hardly be greater. The latter pictures are as much characterized by their relatively monochromatic palette and their value modulations as the former is by its polychromatic palette and its concern with hue. Pissarro adjusted his approach to his subject during these years. There is quite simply no such thing as a specific Pissarro palette during the 1870s. He worked with different palettes even during the same year.

1879–1883 Forms of Departure: The Last Pontoise Period

In 1879, Pissarro began the most extensive period of pictorial experimentation in his career, a period that lasted well into the 1880s and resulted in his inconclusive acceptance of Neo-Impressionism in 1885. Pissarro's interests during the years 1879–83 were so varied that complete discussion of them will not be attempted here. Rather, this section will outline, as concisely as possible, the nature of those interests and, more importantly, will suggest that Pissarro paid less attention to Pontoise as a site during this period of intense esthetic experimentation than at any other time of his stay there. He reworked in the studio earlier compositions painted from nature. He was particularly interested in rigid pictorial structure of a kind he had never used before. He began a long program of figure painting in which the landscape of Pontoise is all but non-existent.[60] His working methods became even more complex than they had been in the Impressionist period. More preparatory drawings were executed. Sketchbooks were increasingly used for direct transcription of vision. Prints became an important part of his oeuvre for the first time. Gouaches and watercolors increased in size and number. All of these varied interests suggest a fundamental questioning of the kind of painting normally associated with Impressionism, the *plein-air* sketch, and a more complicated, highly mediated relationship with "reality" than a simply optical one. For Pissarro in the last Pontoise period, the simple equation between seeing and representing advocated by Henriet in *Le Paysagiste aux champs* was both undesirable and impossible.

Dans le potager à Pontoise, paysanne bêchant (pl. 161) will serve as an emblem of this fascinating phase in Pissarro's career. The painting itself is formidable in its complexity. There are many pictorial issues involved in its making; its surface and its composition are both worthy of sustained investigation.

The surface of *Dans le potager à Pontoise, paysanne bêchant* is covered with uniformly small, even minute touches of paint (pl. 163). There are no large, uncomplicated forms treated with the planar simplicity that characterizes Pissarro's pictures of the periods 1866–68 or 1874–75. The surface is nervous, but it is also substantial. There is little about it that is fleeting or ephemeral. It is clear from the sheer multiplicity and the insistent minuteness of the strokes that the surface took a long time to create. The picture records, in detail, the labors of the artist. The material presence of the paint, which had fascinated Pissarro so intently in the first Pontoise and the Montfoucault periods, is very evident here. The surface is painterly, without a doubt, yet how unlike the fluid, painterly surfaces associated with that word. Like the constructive brushstrokes of Cézanne, each small touch of paint registers a separate act.

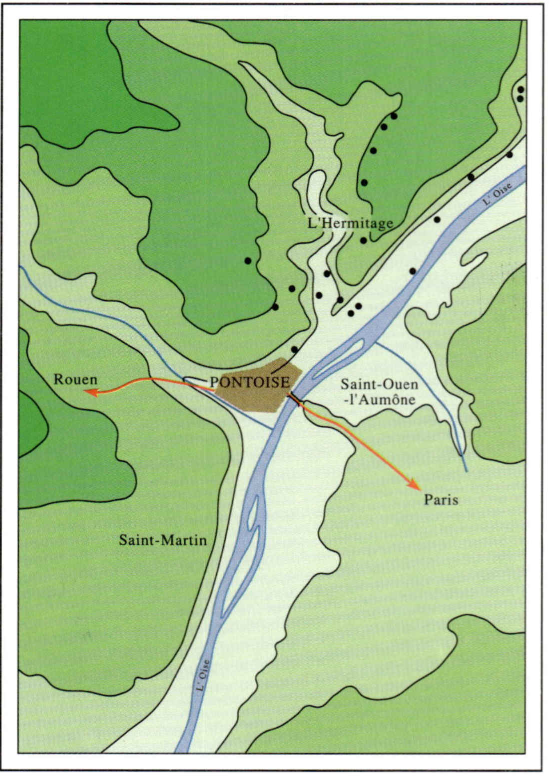

Fig. 12. Map of Pontoise as portrayed by Pissarro, 1879.

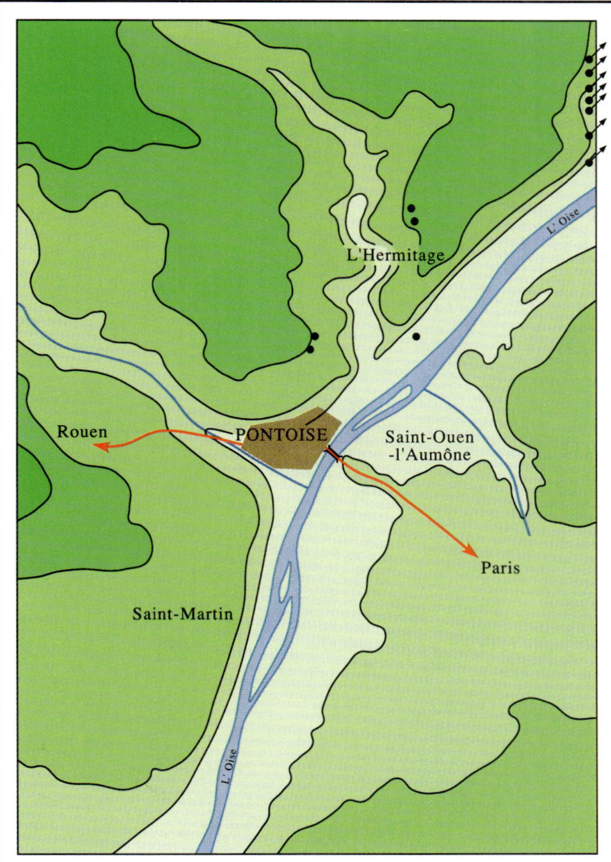

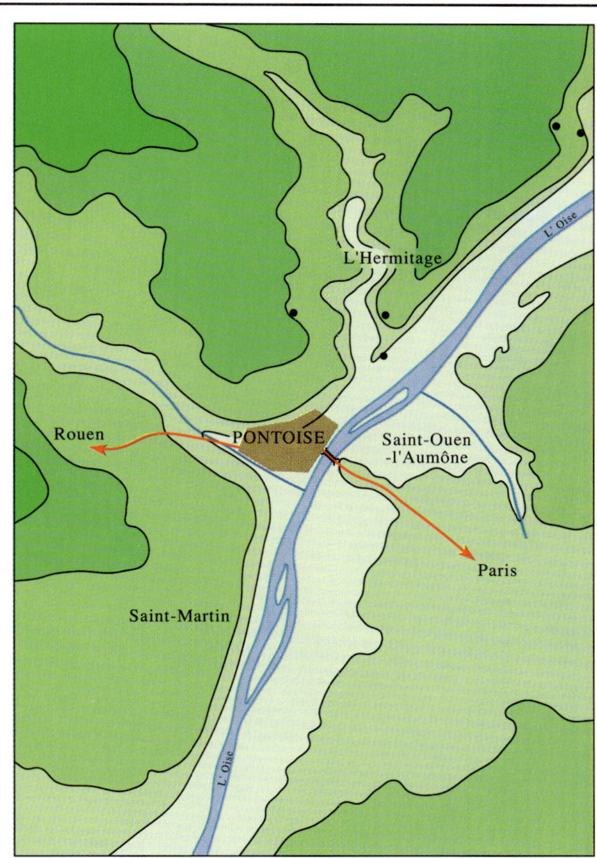

Fig. 13. Map of Pontoise as portrayed by Pissarro, 1880.

Fig. 14. Map of Pontoise as portrayed by Pissarro, 1881.

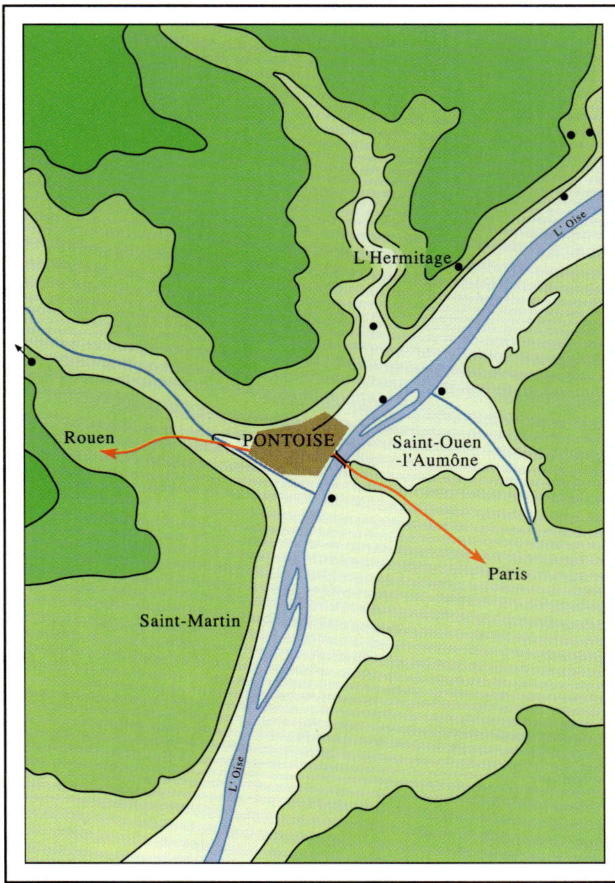

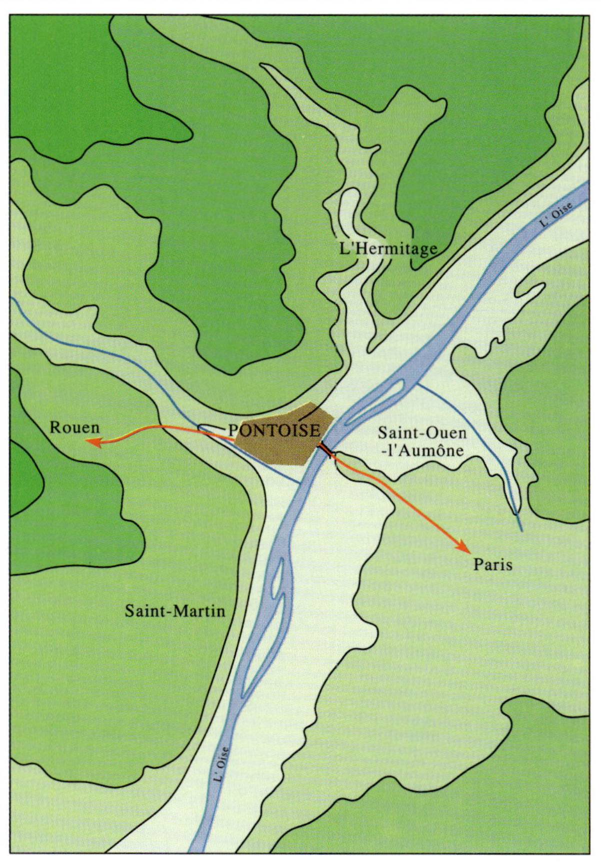

Fig. 15. Map of Pontoise as portrayed by Pissarro, 1882.

Fig. 16. Map of Pontoise as portrayed by Pissarro, 1883.

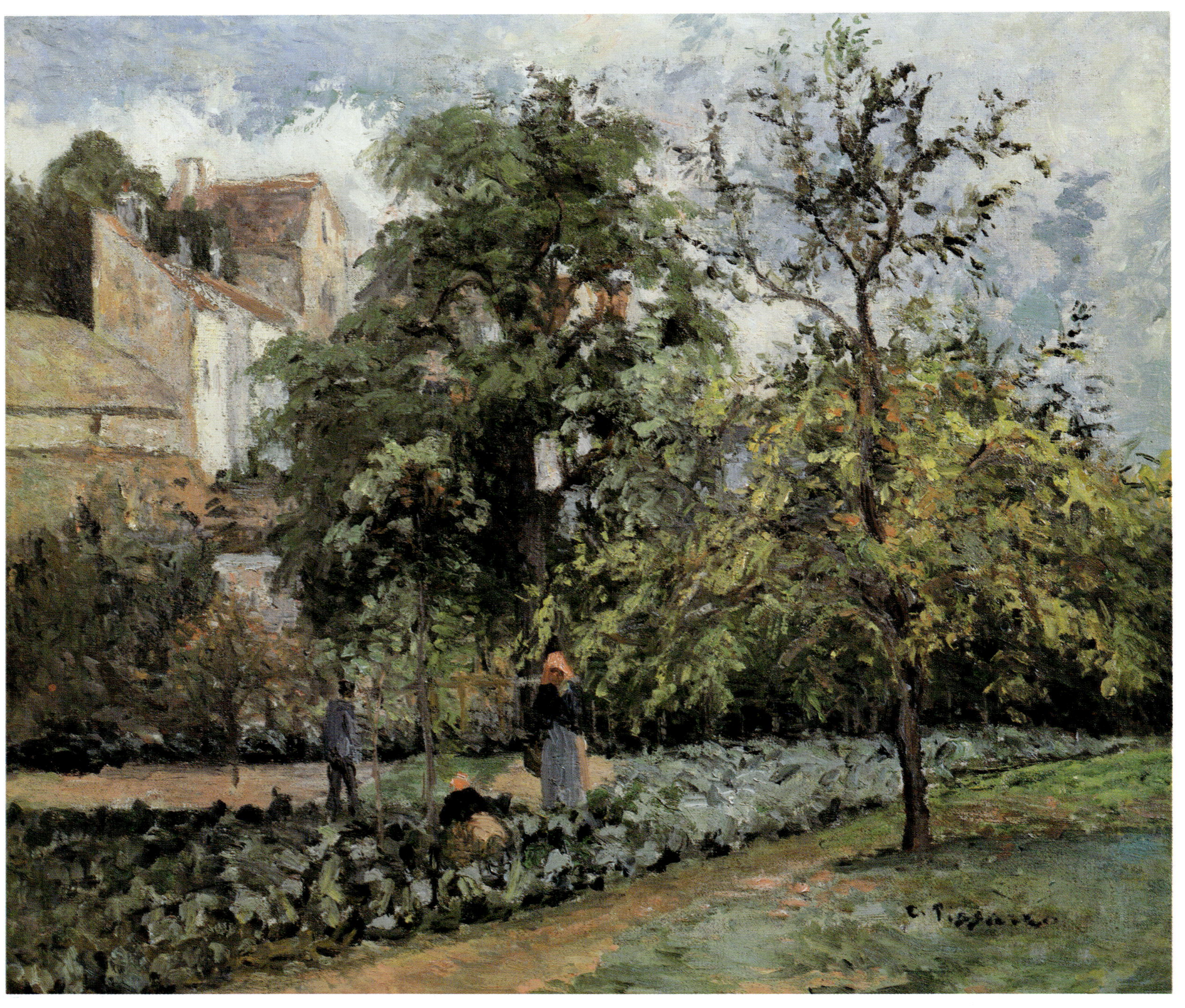

160. Camille Pissarro, *Le Verger à Maubuisson, Pontoise* (P&V 345), 1876, oil on canvas, 38 × 46cm., private collection.

In this picture Pissarro was essentially combining the characteristics of the many different types of facture with which he had been working in the 1870s: the literalness of the paint handling in the palette-knife constructions of 1875; the orderliness and repetitiveness of the facture in pictures of the first Pontoise period; the short strokes created by the gesture of a wrist which are rooted in the "Impressionist" facture of Monet – all these are combined in a "constructive" stroke that Pissarro developed at the same time as Cézanne's more geometric version of the same name.

There is nothing of the sketch in *Dans le potager à Pontoise, paysanne bêchant*. All the evidence forces our interpretation of the surface and its relation to the act of painting to a point where adjectives like "careful," "controlled," "detailed," and

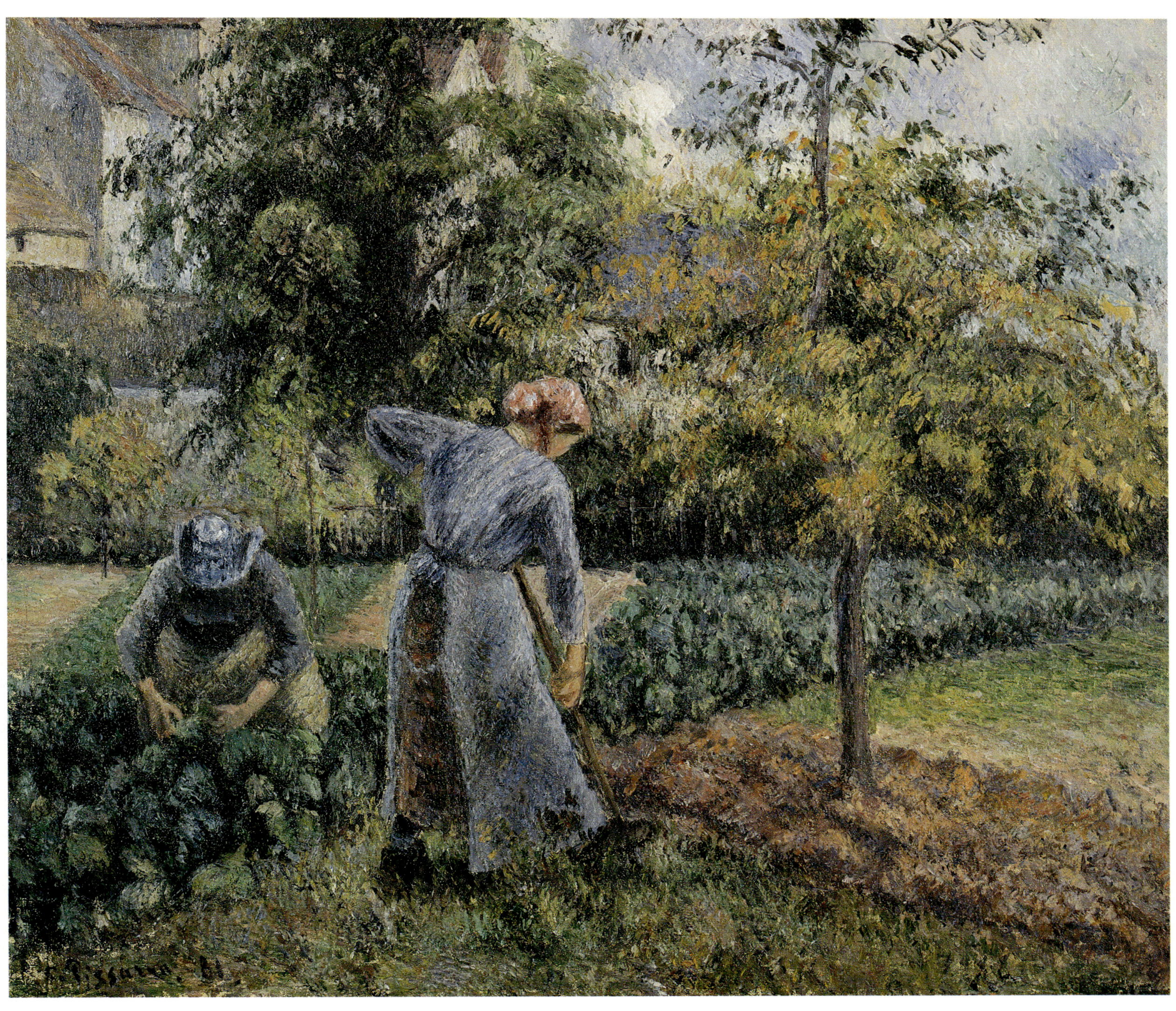

161. Camille Pissarro, *Dans le potager à Pontoise, paysanne bêchant* (P&V 534), 1881, oil on canvas, 46 × 55cm., Nieson Shak collection, Scotchplanes.

162 (following page). Detail of pl. 160.

even "ordered" ring truer than the ubiquitous "sketchy." Examined in detail, the tiny strokes play a variety of pictorial roles. Some cling insistently to the forms they define, folding around the bodies of the figures, defining the countable heads of cabbage, and giving substance to the trunk of the tree. As such they are "materializers" of form. Other strokes, of a remarkably similar character, are marshaled into parallel skeins of paint that add spatial and directional variety to a rather flat composition. They have, in these areas, a decorative rather than a strictly constructive significance. Still others play loosely across the surface disguised as leaves or spots of light. With the important exception of these latter examples, all the strokes in the picture are regular and ordered. They build forms and define planes.

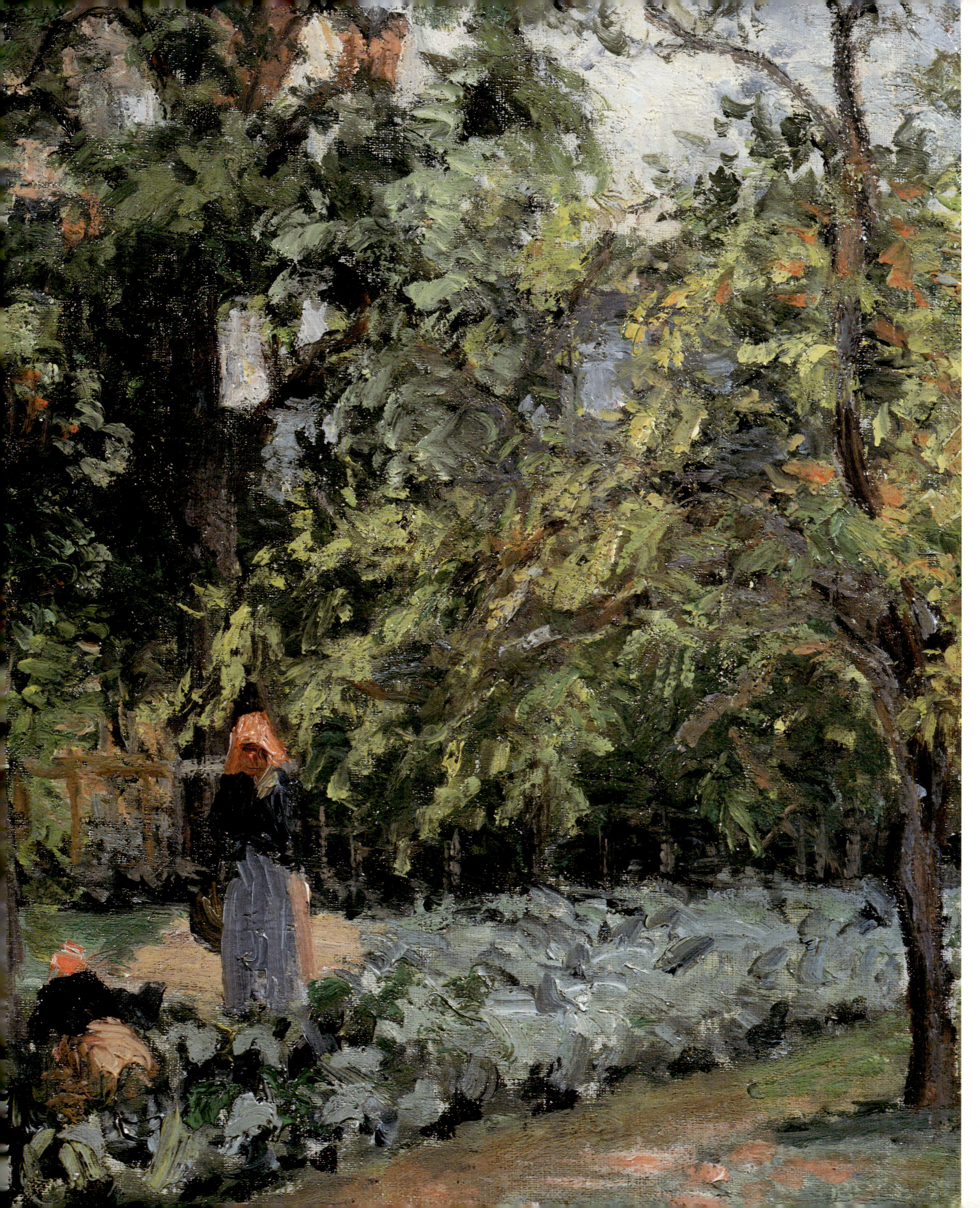

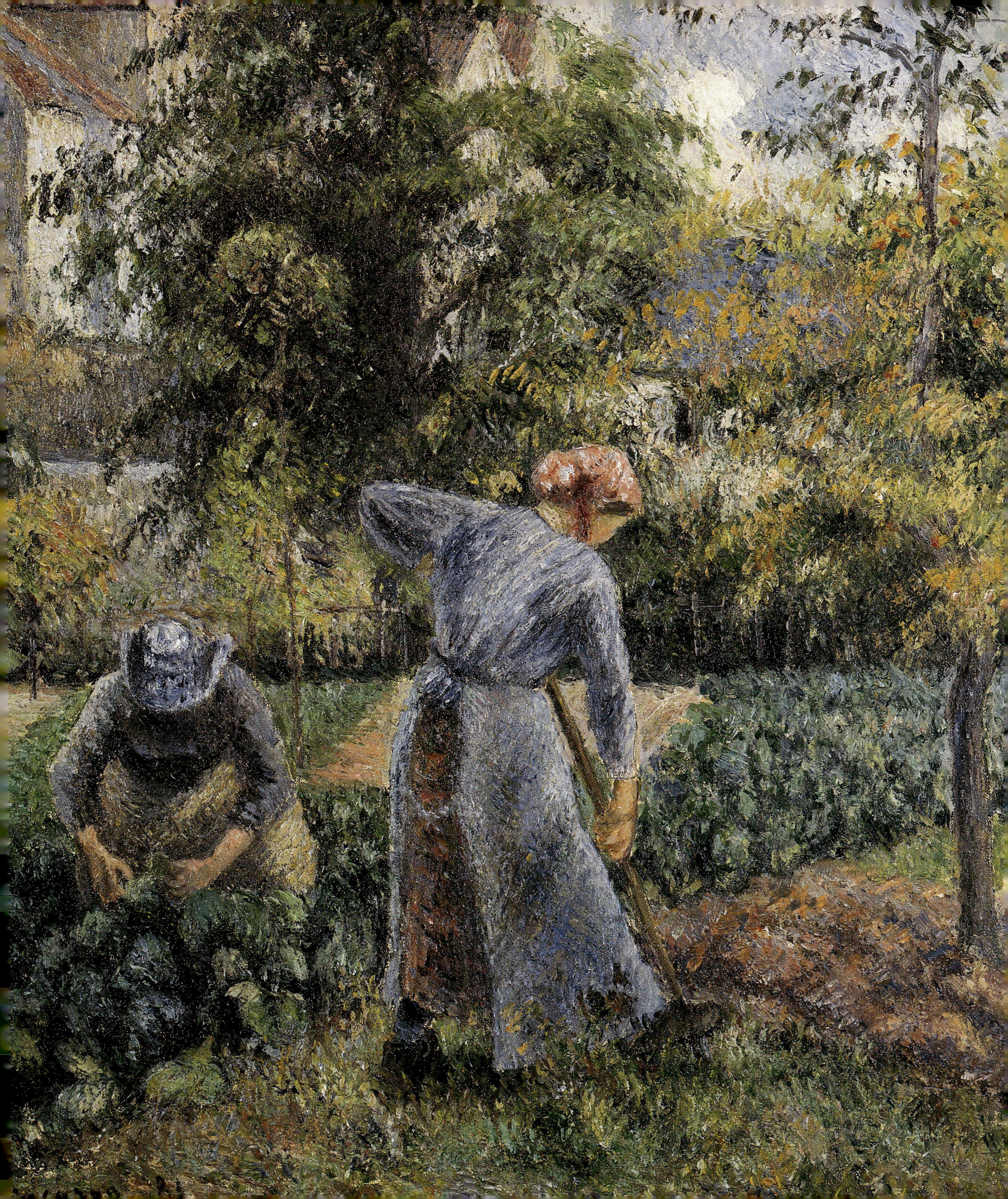

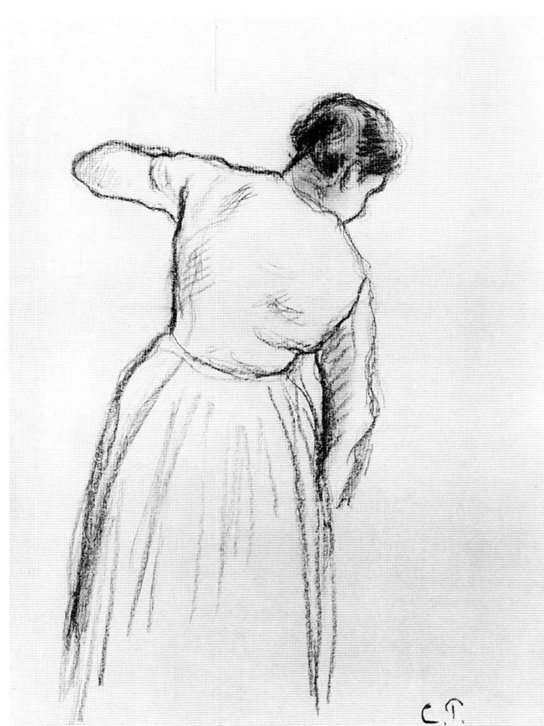

164. Camille Pissarro, *Paysanne bêchant, c.*1880s, charcoal on paper, private collection.

163 (previous page). Detail of pl. 161.

This chapter has recorded in its general outlines Pissarro's ambivalence to the painting of Monet and has discussed the way in which this ambivalence manifested itself throughout the 1870s. The "dialectic" of Pissarro's development is concentrated in *Dans le potager à Pontoise, paysanne bêchant.* The fluttering leaves, the white flecks of light on the kerchief of the peasant woman, and the windy movement of the clouds along the blue sky are all ephemeral. They have their origins in the Impressionist pictures painted by Pissarro in the years 1877–78. In these passages, light and motion, which obsessed landscape painters from Deperthes to Monet, are trapped by Pissarro's dancing brush, yet, trapped only in these passages. The remainder of the picture does not allow such lack of control, such surrender to the momentary. Pissarro takes the tiny Impressionist strokes, pulls them together, refuses, for the most part, to allow them to move freely across the surface. The design of the picture is always paramount. The painter's gestures are determined in advance both by the compositional schema, which will be discussed shortly, and by the essentially constructivist attitude toward the stroke of paint. Objects are built up partly illusionistically and partly literally with pieces of color applied, overlapped, and repeated. The surface of *Dans le potager à Pontoise, paysanne bêchant* eschews the unwieldy variety of strokes that had characterized his oils in the years 1876–78. Disorder and the ephemeral are allowed only a small portion of the surface of this picture and are forced to play a part in the ordered landscape. Both the apparent and the substantial aspects of nature are reconciled in this landscape. An analysis of the facture taken on its own reveals Pissarro's desire to do "both and" rather than "either or"; to transcend the dichotomy that had plagued his career.

Dans le potager à Pontoise, paysanne bêchant is, in all probability, the most insistently ordered landscape of Pissarro's oeuvre and, in addition, was probably the most ordered landscape to have been painted by a major French landscape painter for at least a generation. In examining its carefully balanced composition, the viewer thinks backward to Poussin and to the classical tradition that he initiated, or, alternatively, forward to the rigidly geometric landscapes of Seurat, Signac, and even several of the Symbolist painters of the 1890s. This landscape represents an antithetical response to the Impressionism of sensation.

A simple description of the composition will further clarify the anti-Impressionist stance of *Dans le potager.* It is, like several other pictures of the period 1879–81, for example, *Paysage à Chaponval* (pl. 167), rigidly divided into thirds by the large figure and the tree. The horizon is implacably horizontal, allowing no irregularity to the surface of the earth itself. These divisions of the picture surface refer to the pictorial format itself and are countered by an important diagonal substructure which provides a canted, "other" order to the landscape. Unlike any of the other landscapes by Pissarro discussed above, the key to this composition is the figure. The entire landscape represents an attempt to unite landscape and figure more fully than Pissarro had ever done previously. The back of the woman is shadowed with a thin vertical band that is, in turn, connected both to the vertical form of the section of her skirt exposed by the apron and to the distant vertical of a large tree growing on the hillside that separates Le Chou from L'Hermitage. The figure is, therefore, verticalized and chained into the natural order. Yet, she is not merely a standing figure. Her primary meaning lies in her activity, and it is precisely this activity that relates to the diagonal substructure of the composition. Her elbow, the line of her skirt, and her hoe are all parallel and strictly perpendicular to the diagonal edge of the cabbage field. The technique is not unique to Pissarro: many landscape painters of the classical tradition have made similar use of a vertical and a canted ordering principle. Poussin is, of course, the most prominent example. The famous landscape with St. John at Patmos, now in the Art Institute of Chicago, keys the canted tree into the pictorial order by making it strictly perpendicular to the slope of the distant mountain that it intersects on the surface of the picture. For the Pissarro of *Dans le potager à Pontoise, paysanne bêchant*, both orders of the landscape, the vertical and the diagonal, respond to the figure. She and her activity are literally locked into the composition.

The origins of this picture are not unlike those of several other landscapes of the early 1880s. It is, simply, a structured remaking of an earlier, looser composition from the Impressionist period, *Le Verger à Maubuisson, Pontoise* (pl. 160). Pissarro had chosen this latter picture for inclusion in the fourth Impressionist exhibition of 1879 and, after seeing the picture in the context of the exhibition, attempted a literal remaking, a structured "critique" of his earlier manner. The earlier picture becomes, in this manner, an *esquisse* for the later. The changes Pissarro made in both the composition and the facture were all made in the service of order. The human figure became more dominant, usurping power from the landscape and creating a tension between figure and ground lacking in Pissarro's esthetic of the Impressionist period. The more or less casually balanced order of the earlier canvas is tightened into an *a priori* ordering system. The loose, almost buttery facture of the earlier picture (pl. 162) is replaced with a regularized facture. Impressionism is read by Pissarro as a progressive phase in the history of art "vers un art plus intégral."

It is clear from this example that Pissarro was deeply concerned in the last Pontoise period with the creation of a single viable style that would transcend the partial Impressionism of the preceding period. The fourth Impressionist exhibition prompted him not only to remake *Le Verger à Maubuisson, Pontoise*, but to use other exhibited pictures as the basis for new "synthetic" landscapes. *La Côte des Grouettes, Pontoise, temps gris* (P&V 314, collection of M. Lefèvre Foinet, Paris), was chosen for the exhibition of 1879 and "remade" after that exhibition to become *Paysannes dans les champs, Pontoise* (P&V 515, Sotheby's, New York, 14 November 1984, lot 15). Again, Pissarro chose one of his most Impressionist pictures, enlarged the figures, and ordered the facture to produce a masterpiece in no way related to the casual, *plein-air* esthetic of the earlier picture.

If Monet was the most important artist for Pissarro in the decade of the 1870s, he was replaced in the last Pontoise period by Degas. Degas encouraged Pissarro's active experimentation with drawing and print making. His abortive group project to publish a journal of prints, *Le Jour et la Nuit*, gave Pissarro the opportunity to work with the complexities of intaglio print making, and freed him from his single-minded attention to oil painting. As has already been implied, Pissarro became an *artist* rather than a *painter* in the last Pontoise period. The work on his drawings and prints carried out by this author and Christopher Lloyd revealed a surprising increase both in the number of drawings, gouaches, and prints during the period, and in the range of subjects and styles encouraged by this new interest in media.[61] The impetus for this surely comes from Degas. Pissarro had been exposed to drawings, pastels, and gouaches by that master in all the Impressionist exhibitions; indeed, Degas was notable for contributing preparatory studies and drawings to the first Impressionist exhibition, and his concern with the potential for exhibiting all stages of the art-making process is in distinct contrast to the Impressionist preoccupation with the oil painting itself. Pissarro's admiration for Degas was practically boundless. In a letter of 1883, he described Degas unreservedly as "without doubt, the greatest artist of our age."[62] It seems probable that the fascination with different media that characterizes the mature art of Degas

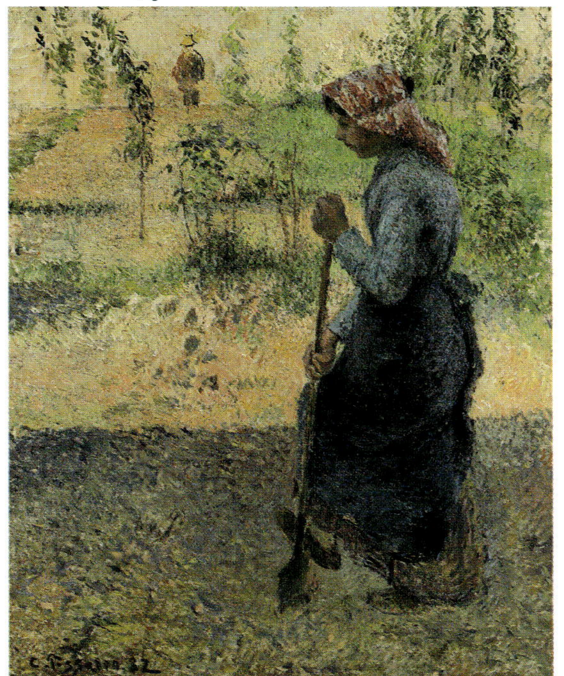

165. Camille Pissarro, *Etude de paysanne en plein air (paysanne bêchant)* (P&V 577), 1882, oil on canvas, 65 × 54cm., private collection.

was communicated to Pissarro and transformed by the older artist to suit the rural imagery of the last Pontoise period.

Several important generalizations can be made about Pissarro's imagery in these years. The most obvious and probably the most important is that architecture definitively lost its central role in his construction of the picture, a role particularly noticeable in the pictures of the first Pontoise period, the classic Pontoise period, and during the first year of the Monfoucault period. The pictorial importance of architecture and, by association, of tectonic forms is related to the "balanced" landscapes of the classical landscape tradition, in which nature, architecture, and weather define each other without the dominance of one or the other. Nature varies and soothes the landscape. Architecture structures, rationalizes, and, of course, "humanizes" it. Weather enlightens and temporalizes it. The classical balance between these three elements, the creation of a harmonized, if bland, pictorial world, was seriously undermined by Pissarro, first in the Montfoucault period, then in the Impressionist period, and more radically in the last Pontoise period. With few exceptions, trees and vegetation dominate the pictures. Screened landscapes, which form a very minor subtype in Pissarro's paintings of the late 1860s and early 1870s, predominate during the late 1870s and early 1880s. *Bords de l'Oise, Pontoise* (P&V 250), for example, is clearly the pictorial prototype for *Bords de l'Oise près Pontoise, temps gris* (P&V 434, Musée d'Orsay). In the second picture, the same vegetation is allowed to curve in great swooping rhythms and interrupt the factory structure in a manner similar to the rhythms of the trees in the heavily screened landscapes of the same period, such as *Paysage sous bois a l'Hermitage* (P&V 444, Nelson-Atkins Museum, Kansas City), and the related print (D 16), and the enormous *Le Fond de L'Hermitage* (pl. 166). The esthetic roots of these works lie in the *sous-bois* of the Barbizon School, in the silvery screens of the late Corot, and in the foliated late landscapes of Courbet. Pissarro, during the last Pontoise period, observed civilization from nature. The trees form a complex and partial pictorial barrier between the viewer and the humanized world with which he most clearly identifies.

The examples cited in the last paragraph set the highly structured pictorial world of *Dans le potager à Pontoise, paysanne bêchant* into relief. Pissarro's work of the last Pontoise period is as much characterized by dichotomies as it was in the previous decade. Although his style and his imagery are almost constant throughout the period, his compositions are various and all but contradictory. A single example will clarify the nature of these dichotomies. The famous and often reproduced *Paysage à Chaponval* (pl. 167) is, with *Dans le potager à Pontoise, paysanne bêchant*, among the most structured landscapes in Pissarro's oeuvre. Again, the structure applied to the picture is one of surface proportion and linear organization. The landscape is divided laterally into thirds. The *vachère* is positioned in a small "picture within a picture" which is proportional to the picture itself. She stands, in addition, on a ground plane that defines a perfect square with the shimmering but observable edge of the repoussoir tree on the left (pl. 169). As structural devices, these can be contrasted with the tectonic "imagery" of the classic Pontoise period. In the earlier period, Pissarro used architecture to define the pictorial structure by arranging it in certain positions that relate to the pictorial format and that define and reinforce the edge of the canvas itself. For the Pissarro of the period 1866–74, architecture represented the structure of the landscape and was, therefore, a structural "imagery" easily found in village nature. He grounded the structure of the picture in the actual structure of man-made reality. This is quite different from the general and extrinsic structure of many landscapes in the early 1880s. The structure of *Paysage à Chaponval* has nothing to do with archi-

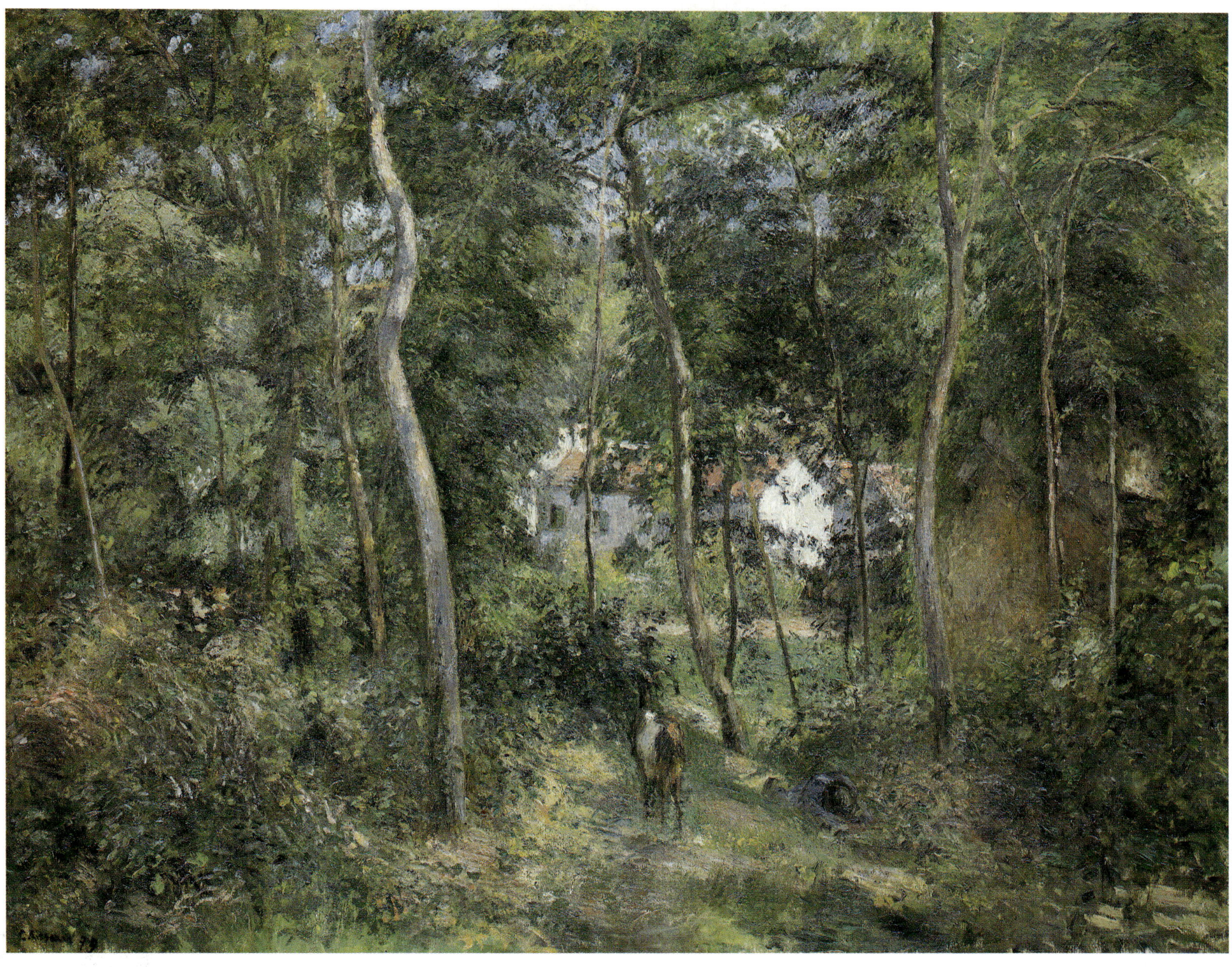

166. Camille Pissarro, *Le Fond de L'Hermitage* (P&V 489), 1879, oil on canvas, 126 × 162cm., Cleveland Museum of Art; Gift of the Hanna Fund, 51.356.

tecture. Architecture is an element in a landscape structured by the artist's willful division of the pictorial surface into geometric areas.

Paysage à Chaponval can be contrasted in almost every way with landscapes like *Chaumières au Valhermeil* (pl. 168), exhibited at the Impressionist exhibition of 1881. The softened, curvilinear forms of the thatched cottages, the free arcs of the road, and the wandering linear pattern of the branches predominate in this brilliantly anti-ordered landscape. The starkness of pictorial order in *Paysage à Chaponval* stands in sharp contrast to the richness and apparent randomness of the Valhermeil landscape, in which the forms within the landscape seem to obey their own expressionist dictates. Yet the two pictures are painted with the same facture, have nearly identical and equally traditional motifs, and are both correctly dated 1880 by the artist himself. Again, the vacillation, the dichotomy that runs throughout Pissarro's career comes into sharp focus. This time, Monet and suburban realism are not pitted against Duret and traditional ruralism. Nor is the dichotomy of a technical nature: heavily painted, objective nature is not opposed

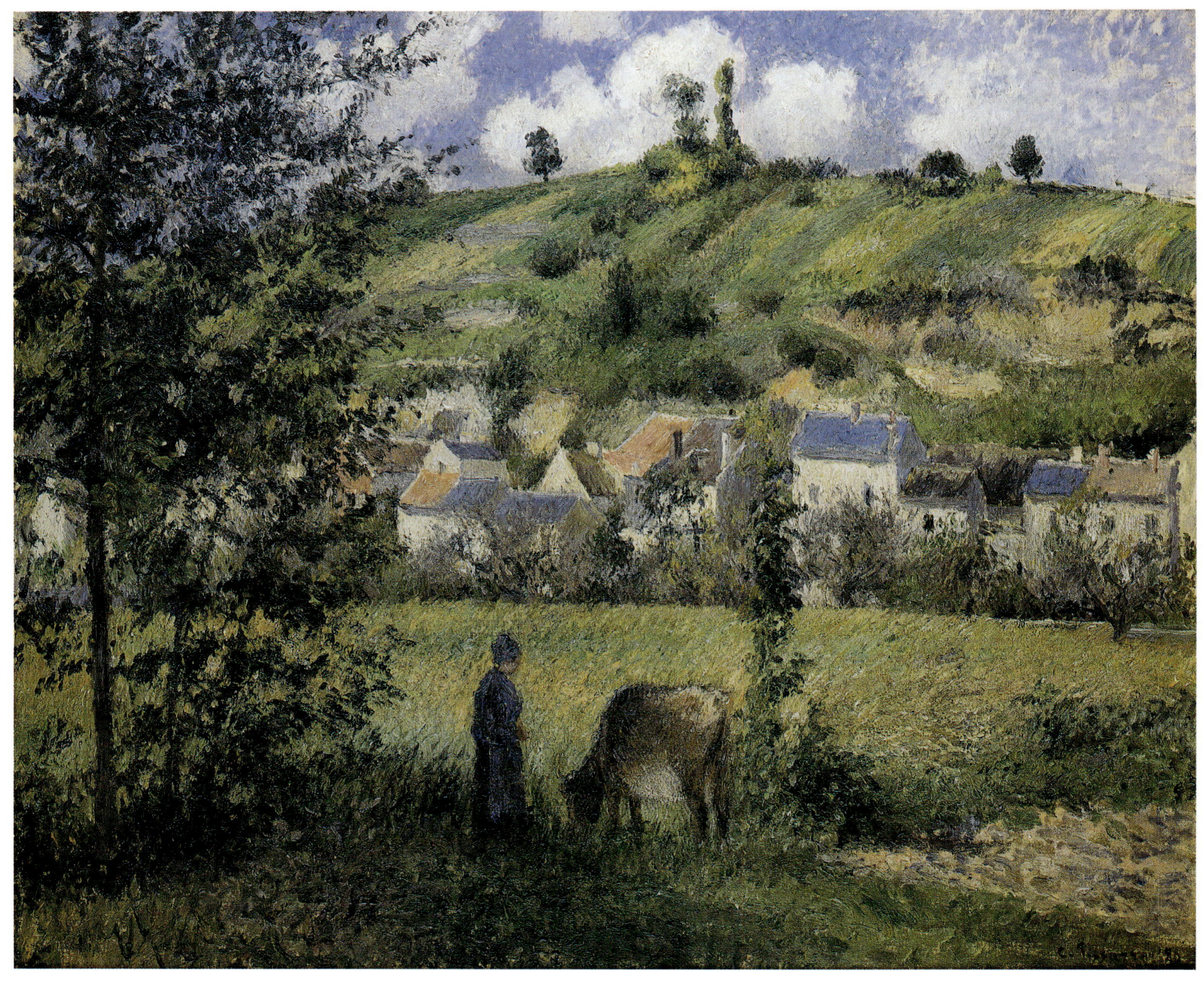

167. Camille Pissarro, *Paysage à Chaponval* (P&V 509), 1880, oil on canvas, 54 × 65cm., Musée d'Orsay, Paris.

to lightly brushed, transient, and random nature. Pissarro, in painting these two pictures of two virtually identical villages, using the same facture, in the same year, was confronting the issue of structure itself. *Paysage a Chaponval* and *Chaumières au Valhermeil* could almost be exhibited as a pair with the titles, "The Nature of Structure" and "The Nature of Appearance." Pissarro has distilled the two opposing views of nature that run throughout the history of western culture: the Aristotelian view (nature, without the mind, is chaotic and must be structured to be understood) and the pre-Socratic (or Heraclitean) view (nature is constant change and disorder, presenting man with no possibility of structured apprehension). The issue involved in these two pictures is enormous and resounds throughout the centuries. Pissarro, in addressing himself to it so directly, was again asking the question of the nature of pictorial order and pictorial unity and the relation of that order or that unity to "real" nature.

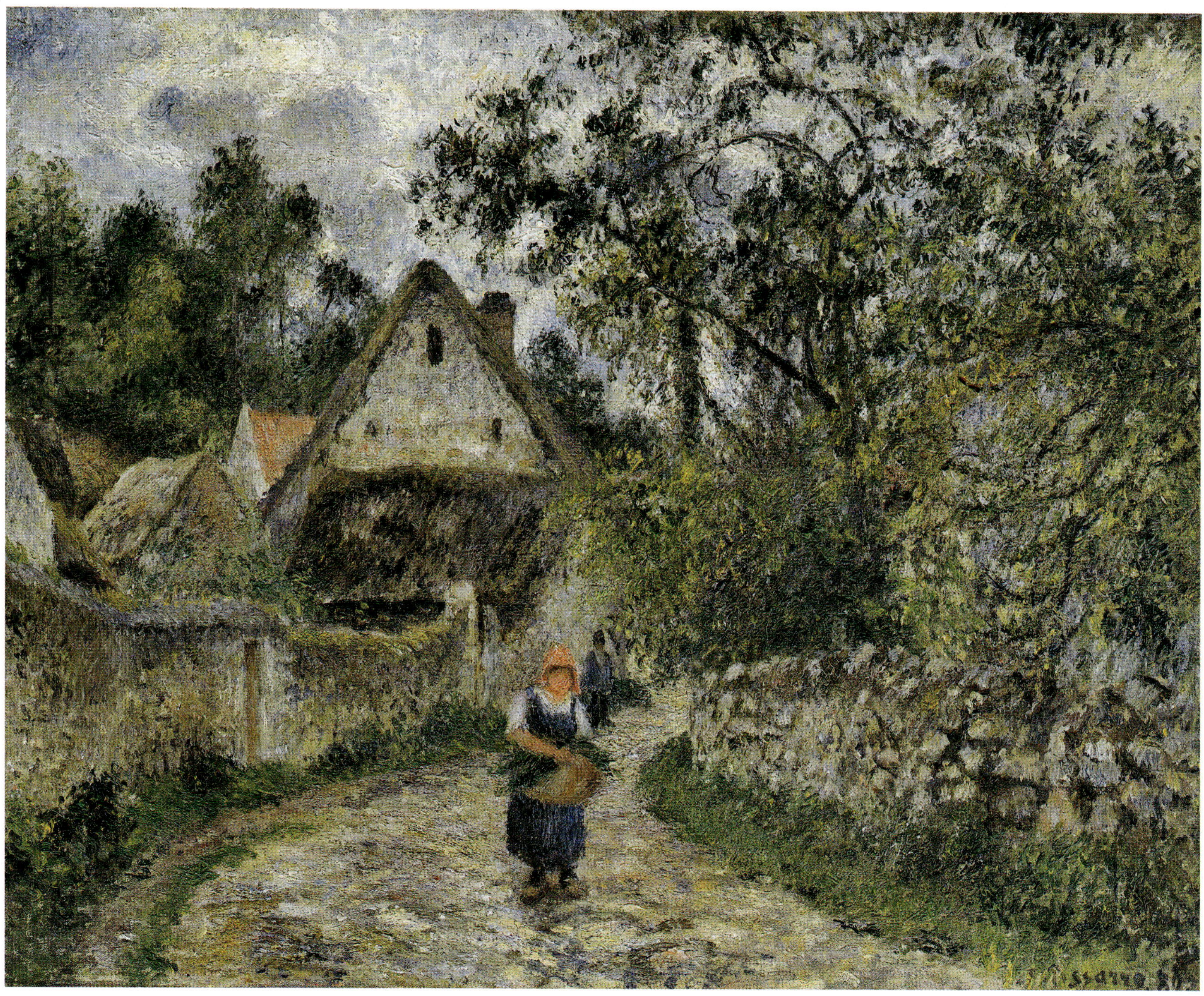

168. Camille Pissarro, *Chaumières au Valhermeil (avec figure)* (P&V 511), 1880, oil on canvas, 59 × 73cm., collection of G. Draikis.

The existence of these two pictures in the same year is a clear indication that Pissarro's response to the landscape had become increasingly abstract. Although the names of the hamlets, Le Valhermeil and Chaponval (the two sites he preferred to all others in the last Pontoise period) are almost always communicated to the viewer in the titles of pictures, the pictures themselves are clearly less interesting topographically than those of the classic Pontoise period. Pissarro's landscape motifs become so repetitive in the last Pontoise period as to deny iconological significance to the sites themselves. Not only were the hamlets of Le Valhermeil and Chaponval physically separate from Pontoise, thus indicating a "departure" from the Pontoisian landscape painted so faithfully in all other Pontoise periods, but the character of these small villages was such that they would have appeared typical and even dull to any Parisian viewer of landscape in the early years of the 1880s. How they are like the landscapes painted around

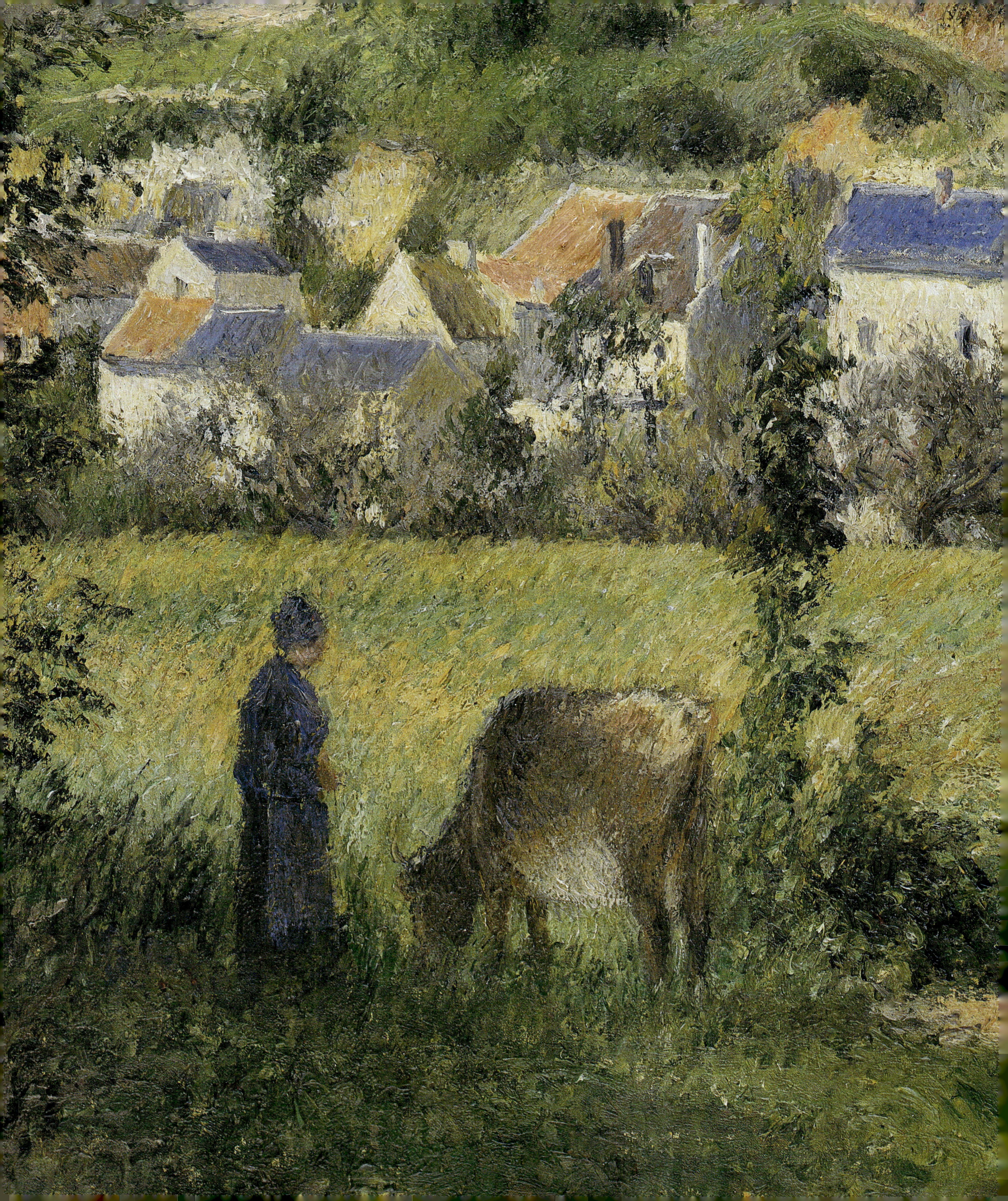

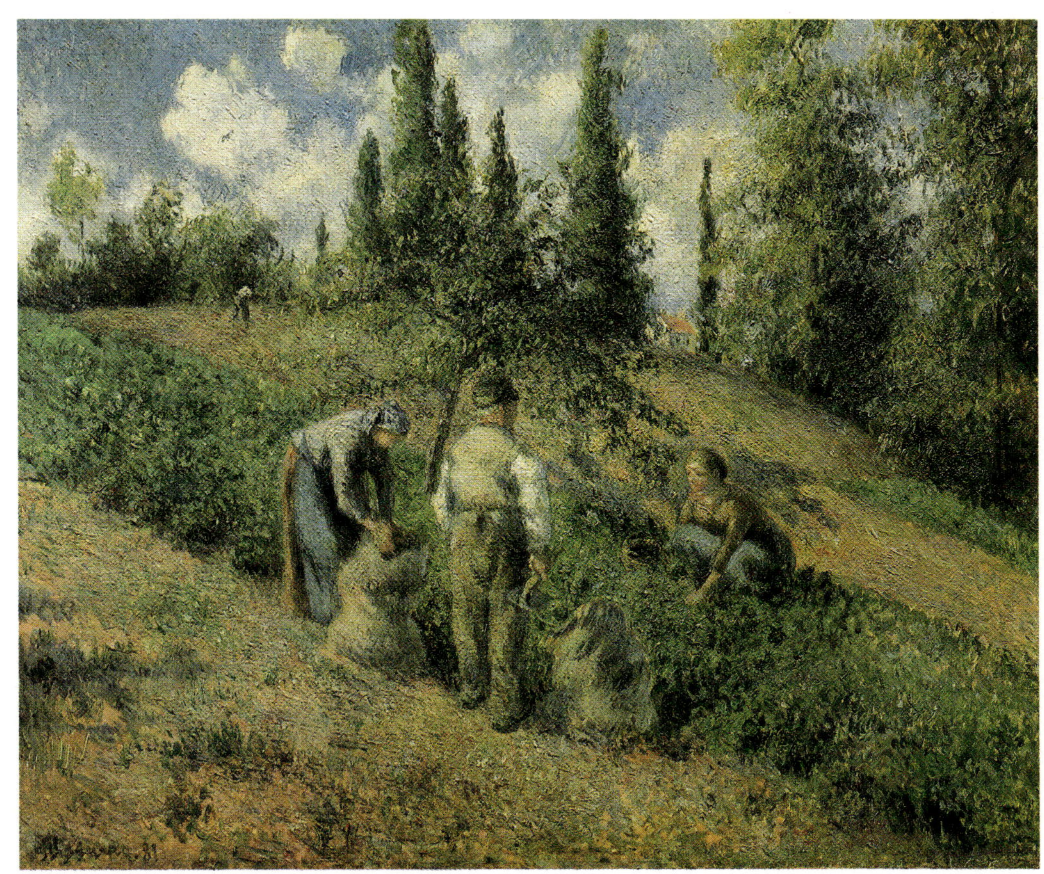

170. Camille Pissarro, *Récolte des pommes, Pontoise*
(P&V 516), *c.*1880, oil on canvas, 46 × 56cm.,
Metropolitan Museum of Art; Robert Lehman Col-
lection, 1975 (1975.1.197).

169. Detail of pl. 167.

Barbizon, Fontainebleau, Cernay-la-Ville, and many other sites mentioned by
Henriet in his books of the 1860s and 1870s. Even the small-scale industrial
elements allowed to creep into Pissarro's landscape during the first year of the last
Pontoise period are seen from the vantage point of a rural field or a footpath too
small for carts or wagons. Pissarro began in this period to address himself to the
larger esthetic questions involved in the nature of landscape painting and became
less interested in imagery.

During the years 1881, 1882, and 1883, Pissarro delved into the formal realm of
figure painting *per se*. His landscape production, which had dominated his art
since his early years in Venezuela, dwindled significantly. The vacillation of 1880
between tectonic structure and natural curvilinearity was subordinated to the new
dichotomy between landscape painting and figure painting.

The figure painting of Pissarro is beyond the scope of both this chapter and this
book and demands separate attention. It is crucial, however, to stress the increased importance of the figure in its own right for Pissarro in the early years of
the 1880s. His tendency toward "monumental" figure painting, hinted at in the
discussion of *Dans le potager à Pontoise, paysanne bêchant*, is paralleled in the work
of Renoir, who began enlarging and "classicizing" his figures in the late 1870s and
made his famous trip to Italy in the winter of 1881–82. On the other hand, it is
exactly opposed to the lack of figures in Cézanne's landscapes and in Monet's
landscapes after the death of his wife, Camille, in 1879. Renoir, Pissarro, and even
Degas moved away from Monet and from landscapes with motifs that directly
confront the viewer. Pissarro's technical experimentation and his prolonged study
of artificial pictorial structure and of the human figure must be seen as part of a
general reaction against landscape painting by the advanced painters of the 1870s
who contributed so significantly to its independent history.

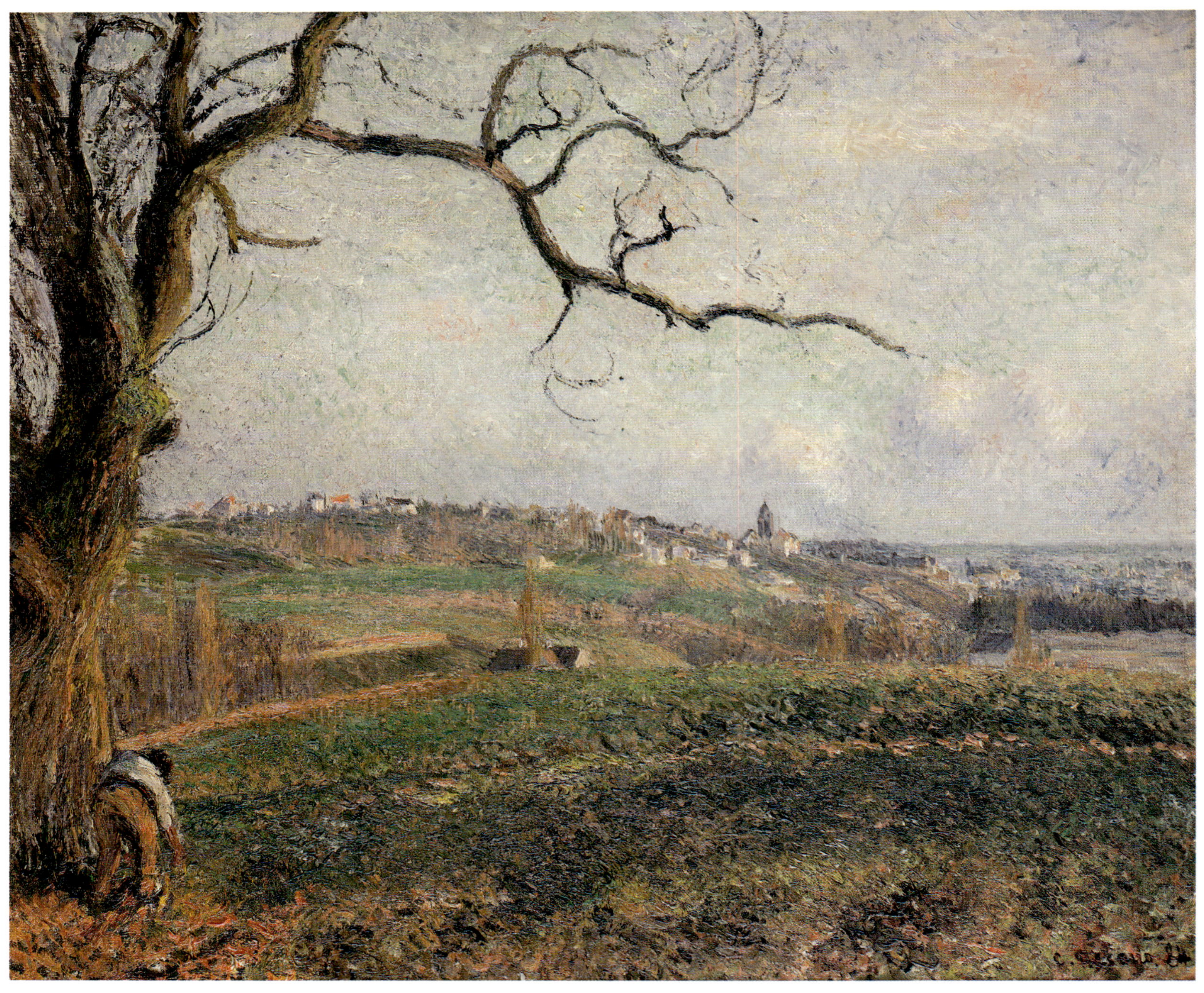

171. Camille Pissarro, *Vue de Pontoise* (P&V 628), 1884, oil on canvas, 59 × 73cm., private collection.

As the examples in this brief survey have indicated, Pissarro began the last Pontoise period with a questioning of the nature of the art-making process and a consequent interest in media. He followed this interest with an investigation of the pictorial structure of "reality." This phase gave way to a struggle that runs throughout the history of landscape painting between landscape painting and figure painting. All these phases are unified by a single pictorial style, a single facture. They evidence a profound distance from the "reality" of Pontoise; they represent "forms of departure."

The last Pontoise period ended with a brilliant and real departure, although a temporary one, for the capital city of Normandy, Rouen. The excitement of this trip for Pissarro cannot be overstressed. It allowed a period of reflection and concentration, far from the family and the problems of the Impressionist movement itself which were plaguing him in 1883. His pictures painted both in and after Rouen have a freedom of execution, an involvement in several levels of landscape reality, and a lack of studied artfulness that is everywhere at odds with the pictures of the last Pontoise period. Pissarro had, it seems, exhausted a landscape once again, and it was necessary for him to move on to another. His move to the village of Osny, a village in the grain-producing area of the Vexin plateau only eight kilometers from Pontoise, coincided with his visit to Rouen and his decision to leave the Pontoisian landscape once and for all. The search for a new landscape was a protracted one, suggesting once again that the quality of the landscape site was very important for Pissarro. His last years in the Pontoise region were punctuated with a series of exploratory trips that finally led to the definitive move to Eragny--sur-Epte, where the painter remained until his death in 1903. Eragny, like the village of Osny and the hamlets of Le Valhermeil and Chaponval, was a traditional rural area with little of the modernized farming and none of the industrial imagery so evident around Pontoise itself. In accepting a traditional rural landscape as his own landscape, Pissarro paid homage to the early advice of Duret, advice so important in the history of Pissarro's ruralism. Yet Pissarro played this traditional rural landscape against the urbanity and the modernism of both Paris and Rouen throughout the rest of his life. Gustave Geffroy, in his review of the Pissarro exhibition of 1898 in Paris at Durand-Ruel, quite correctly divided Pissarro's mature career into two parts, rural and urban. He spoke in his characteristically fervent style of the "appearances of country life" ("apparitions de la vie de campagne") as opposed to "the spectacles of city life" ("les spectacles de l'existence des villes"). His words are, of course, modern. The countryside, in its purified, almost Virgilian simplicity, is an "apparition." The city, as it was to be for Léger, its most forceful apologist in the twentieth century, is a "spectacle." As Geffroy makes clear, Pissarro's pictorial world thrived on the very dichotomy with which he struggled so forcefully in the Pontoisian period. The vacillations between Monet and the mid-century, between suburb and city, between wrist gesture and controlled areas of paint, between order and "chaos," all were accepted by the painter in his mature styles. The indecisions plaguing his work during the Pontoise period did not disappear when he left that town in 1883, but they became much less apparent and much less urgent than they had been in the difficult decade of the 1870s.

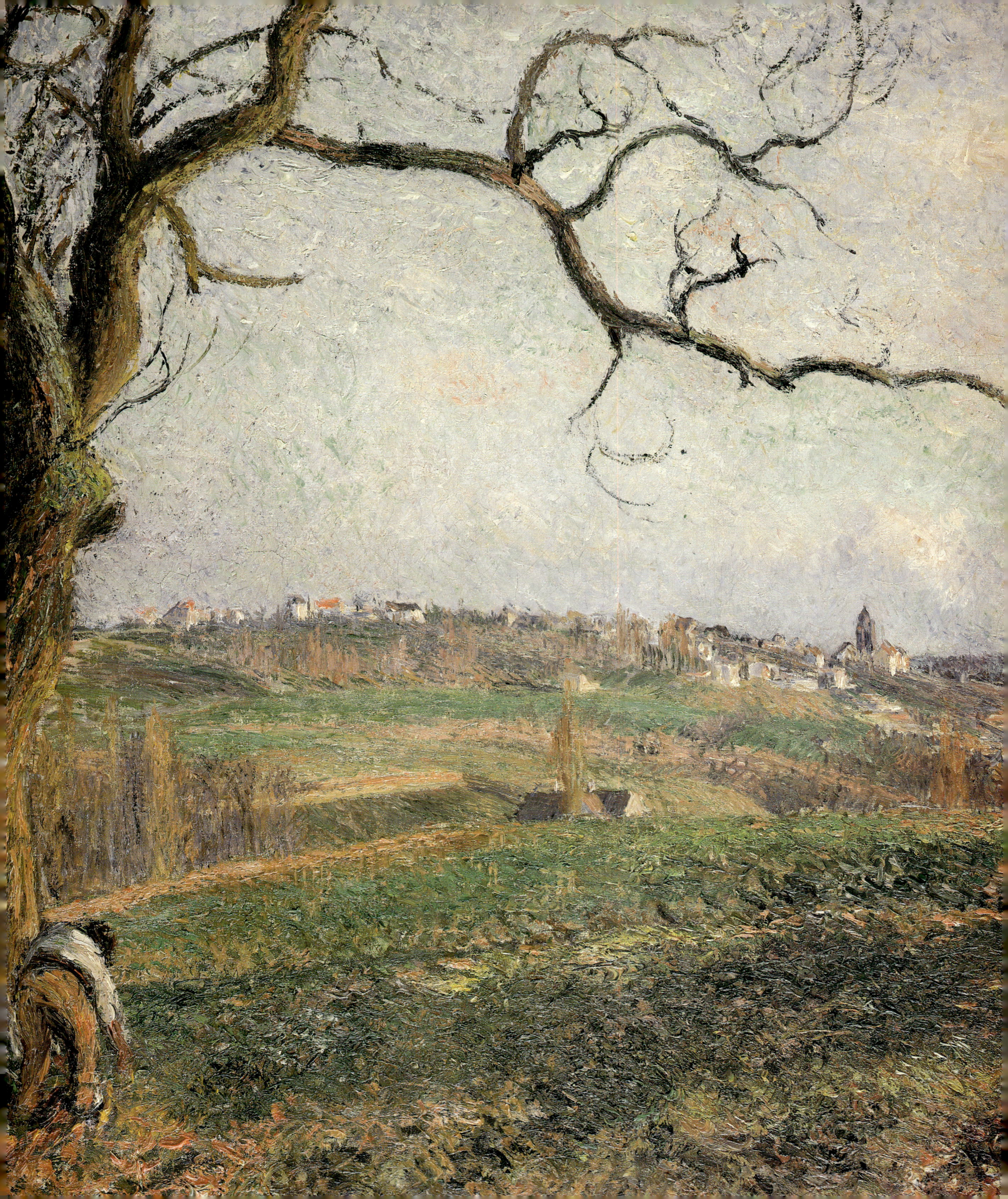

Conclusion

The basic problem for the student of Pissarro and Pontoise is one of discontinuity. In many ways, the painter and the place had very little to do with each other, in spite of more than a decade of intense interaction. Pissarro virtually ignored both the visible history and the bustling economy of Pontoise in his many representations of the town. There is, in fact, little about his pictures to suggest that he was very well informed about Pontoise. However, the idea that Pissarro was detached from Pontoise is in direct contradiction to the conventional view of him. Thousands of words have been written about his love for nature and his profound knowledge of this or that place, but the words are curiously hollow and repetitive. Neither Duret nor Lecomte can convince us that Pissarro either knew or cared very much about the realities of peasant life or the lives of the industrial proletariat in any one of the various places he inhabited and painted. Indeed, the words of these critics, whether in letters, books, or critical articles, have a suspicious sameness about them. Duret and Lecomte *wanted* Pissarro to have understood a great deal more than he himself did. Their ideas have more to do with a vague cultural yearning for origins, for an Arcadia, for an escape from what were seen as the pressures inherent in modern life, than they have to do with Pissarro. Yet Lecomte hit the very center of Pissarro's concerns in writing not about his subject matter, nor directly about his style, but about his working methods. His words, repeated in several contexts, bear quotation once again:

> Certainly Camille Pissarro painted thousands of studies and hundreds of canvases after nature. But, from an early stage in his career as a painter, passionately involved in research, most of his paintings were executed in the studio, with much deliberation, after studies made directly in front of the motif, in absolute keeping with the original emotion. . . . Camille Pissarro abandons himself freely to his sensation, which he would never give up for any theory or any system. But he also constructs, he selects, he arranges.[1]

These sentences were written in the early 1920s and were based on Lecomte's writings of the 1890s which were, in turn, based on long conversations with the painter himself. Superficially, they are connected with the distinctly anti-Impressionist or anti-*plein-air* esthetics current in France during the last decade of the nineteenth century. As this study has shown, however, they can be applied with little trouble to the decade of the 1870s, which has always been considered the most natural and the most "naïve" of Pissarro's career. The last sentence of the quotation above, with its rhetorical repetition of the subject, gets at the heart of Pissarro's problematic esthetics. It is clear that he tried to abandon himself to the reality of Pontoise and that his most faithful efforts to do so were made in what has been called the classic Pontoise period. Yet the remainder of his career in that town had progressively less to do with Pontoise and more to do with various concepts of construction and order. He made more attempts to be a figure painter than he did to understand the "peasantry" he was painting. His "vegetative" esthetics of the latter 1870s and early 1880s have more to do with the

172. Detail of pl. 171.

theory of landscape and with concepts of "natural order" than they have to do with the landscape in which he painted.

While it is true that Pissarro's paintings of Pontoise tell us a great deal more about the environment of that town than the paintings of Monet tell us about the areas around Argenteuil or Vétheuil, their central concern is not with actual appearances but with structure. Pissarro sought the nature of nature, if such an awkward phrase is permissible, and not nature itself.[2] His paintings, with their insistent planarity and their refusal, with very few exceptions, to be either sensuous or spacious, stubbornly resist our attempts to explain them. They are neither real nor ideal and illustrate what Henriet revealingly called "the respective limits of the ideal and the real."[3] Yet, pictorial structure and color aside, it would be a mistake to deny totally Pissarro's interest in Pontoise itself. Although the depth of his "realist" vision decreased as the 1870s continued, his pictures record so many parts of the environment in so many different seasons and moods that one can hardly claim that Pissarro's detachment from Pontoise was complete. Rather, one must consider the "reality" of the site as one of the several components of Pissarro's almost analytic landscape esthetic. The site, the season, the time of day, color, value, facture, and composition were all interdependent variables which could be altered at the will of the painter. Pontoise as a site was important for Pissarro, but it was only relatively important—one element in what might be called his grammar of landscape.

It is, in the final analysis, landscape itself that interested Pissarro. He was, like Valenciennes, Le Carpentier, Deperthes, Corot, and so many other writers and painters of the nineteenth century, concerned with the structure of appearance and the creation of a balanced and holistic world, lacking the confusion and the tension of real experience. As Lecomte, with his characteristic appreciation of Pissarro's structural vision, put it in 1922, "Pissarro was long concerned with blending together solid constructions with the richest strokes of color and with retaining synthetically the large and powerful shapes of nature."[4]

The Camille Pissarro that this book reveals was among the most stubbornly complicated artists of the late nineteenth century. His career lacks the unified and progressive character found in those of many of his contemporaries—Cézanne, Monet, Seurat, and Degas. Perhaps only Manet, a painter who was never very important for Pissarro, was as complicated and elusive an artist. Pissarro's drawings, paintings, and prints are often more "difficult" to interpret than those of other, better-known artists of his age. It is, of course, the "difficulty" of Pissarro that attracts modern viewers to him, not his apparent naïveté, his honesty, or his goodness—all of which are the qualities that have been extolled for three generations of Pissarro criticism and scholarship. It is this "difficulty" that has become increasingly clear with each new volume of his correspondence that has been published, and further made clear with the publication of the *Catalogue of drawings by Camille Pissarro in the Ashmolean, Oxford* in 1980, the same year in which the first major monographic exhibition devoted to Pissarro, since 1930, was held.[5] The drawings reveal his true stature and show him not as an artist of supreme technical facility like Degas, but as one whose relationship with reality was among the most mediated in the history of realist art.

Perhaps the most perplexing historical question that one must ask at the end of this analysis of the relationship between an environment and a series of landscape paintings is what the analysis has told us about the nature of Impressionism. A large question of this sort hinges on the smaller, but equally crucial question of whether Pissarro really was an Impressionist at all. Writings about Impressionism, voluminous as they are, have a surprising sameness. We are taught that

Impressionists sought immediate and fugitive effects of nature, that they glorified the landscape sketch and altered the European artistic concept of "finish," and that they were concerned with a brilliantly colored world, dominated by primary hues and lacking the lugubrious darkness of earlier European art. This analysis of Pissarro's Pontoise has shown that he was anything but an artist of the immediate and fugitive effects of nature, that his landscapes are often extremely "finished," and that, while he was frequently ahead of his time in his interest in the pictorial properties of hue, his interest in value modulation continued throughout the 1870s. It becomes increasingly clear to students of Impressionism and Impressionist criticism that, when modern critics talk about the general characteristics of the movement, they are really talking about the general characteristics of Monet's art. This view has certain critical advantages in that a clarity and consistency of approach is possible when we allow one artist to speak for the much more complex movement of which he was only one part. Yet, such a view is certainly both inaccurate and unfair to the other important artists. Pissarro, to most scholars of Impressionism, was a *retardataire* artist, lacking the boldness and the imagination of Monet. His interest in peasant and rural imagery shows that he was not as "modern" as Monet or Renoir, both of whom celebrated the life of the urban or suburban bourgeoisie. His carefully constructed landscapes look stilted if one thinks that Impressionism should be gestural, rapid, and ephemeral.

It is possible to turn the tables and to create a definition of Impressionism with Pissarro at the center. This definition would view the period as a struggle between the traditional values of the landscape esthetics and the realities of modern life and landscape. In such a view, Monet's art would seem narrow in its acceptance only of the bourgeois world. Monet's style, to follow this logic, would lack the experimental quality and the struggling attempts to unite past and present, sensation and construction, so evident in Pissarro's style throughout the 1870s.

Both critical methods are, of course, wrong. Neither Monet nor Pissarro, nor Sisley nor Degas are quintessential Impressionists. The movement was composed of all these major talents, and our attempts at dealing with it must come to terms with the diversity of trends encompassed by the many Impressionist painters. The task is not as easy one. Detailed studies of the imagery, the drawings, the working methods, and the lives of the painters are still needed. Clearly, the collective history of the movement so brilliantly assembled by John Rewald is not a complete history.[6] There were more discords, diversities, and disagreements than even Rewald records. Certain historiographical advances have been made. The trend of treating Impressionism as a unified movement, fighting the rigid standards of the Academy, has declined in recent years.[7] Studies of contemporary criticism have shown that the Impressionists were not so perniciously reviled as we have been taught, and studies of their finances have taught us and will continue to teach us that they were not starving artists at the mercy of a corrupt system. The sociology of the movement is now well understood owing to recent revisionist history. The art-historical information on the Impressionist movement has greatly increased in the past decade, particularly when compared with the literature on Impressionism produced in previous decades; indeed, whether it be the brilliant pictorial history of the Blundens or the attempt at comparing postcards to paintings, as Rewald has done, or whether it be the studies of Sam Hunter or Phoebe Pool, which, although lacking the sociological sophistication of the above, offered the same treatment of pictorial concerns, overall the same clichés of Impressionism were being perpetuated.[8]

Champa has taken part in re-evaluating the significance of this multi-faceted and extraordinarily complex movement with his careful pictorial history of

Impressionism in the 1860s.[9] Wildenstein contributed considerably to a more thorough understanding of the movement with his four-volume catalogue of Monet's paintings.[10] Varnedoe and Lee have made valuable contributions in the study of Caillebotte;[11] Christopher Gray has given adequate treatment to Guillaumin;[12] and many scholars have made great strides toward a clear understanding of Degas.[13] Since then, of course, and in contrast to the 1970s, the 1980s seem to have witnessed an explosion of literature on Impressionism. Yet, one cannot fail to remark that there is still no essay evaluating Monet's industrial imagery, only one clear attempt at understanding the working methods of the Impressionists,[14] and no discussion of Impressionist color that compares in scope with the work done on the color of Seurat, Van Gogh, or even Cézanne. The list could continue almost indefinitely, and it indicates the degree to which the 1870s and the early 1880s suffer from a particular paradox: although visually more exposed to a wider public than any other period of art, this is still among the least studied periods in the historiography of French painting. We know a good deal more about Realism in the 1850s and 1860s and about what has come to be called Post-Impressionism in the late 1880s and 1890s than we know about Impressionism itself.

This study of Pissarro and Pontoise has revealed several important things: that Pissarro did not have a naïve and merely "optical" relationship with his environment; that he tended to avoid powerful and previously depicted motifs in his search for a seemingly objective view of his environment; that his understanding of the environment in which he lived was perhaps not so great as one may have thought; that his acceptance of modernism and industrial imagery was not unqualified; that he had complicated working processes not altogether unlike those of his precursors, the Barbizon School; that his styles changed frequently and suddenly in short periods of time, and his search for a new art was a complicated, halting affair; that his place within the history of art, particularly the history of French art, has been underplayed in attempts to emphasize Impressionism as a purely "modern" movement. This list, confused and diverse as it may appear, is evidence of the fact that we have made many mistakes and/or omissions in our treatment of both Pissarro and Impressionism, and that much work remains to be done before more conclusive assessments can be made.

It is perhaps best to end this investigation of Pissarro in Pontoise by emphasizing his position as a bridge between the great French painters of the mid-nineteenth-century and the great French painters of the end of the century. It was Pissarro, not Monet, Sisley, Renoir, or even Manet, who was the teacher of Gauguin, Cézanne, and, quite possibly, Seurat. *La Récolte des pommes de terre* (pl. 146), that odd and awkward picture completed in 1874 on the advice of Duret, looks back to Millet and forward to Cézanne, Seurat, and Gauguin. These monumental figures in a landscape, even a landscape so small, emanate a power that continues through the rest of the nineteenth century in French art. The volumetric and rhythmic treatment of the figures and the setting anticipate Cézanne, as does the structural juxtaposition of warm and cool colors. The frank use of color opposites and the rigidity of the composition stand behind Seurat's important compositions of the early 1880s. The Pissarro who sought advice from Corot when he arrived in France in 1855 and the Pissarro who struggled to combine the concern for structure with Monet's cult of "sensation" in his paintings of the 1870s is anything but a *retardataire* painter who pales in comparison with Monet. Pissarro's place in the history of nineteenth-century French art is more secure and more important than that of Monet, who, like so many great artists, stands more forcefully out of his own time than he does in it.

Notes

Introduction

1. Jules Castagnary, "Salon de 1866, Le Nain–Jaune," *La Liberté*, May 1866, pp. 3–4. Castagnary's essay on landscape is among the two or three most thoughtful contributions to the theory of landscape written in the 1860s. His discussion of the "immense retour vers la nature et la verité" is, in the final analysis, a despairing one, written between the generations of great French landscape painters of the nineteenth century. He considered the genre of secondary importance to the history of art and thought that the mental faculties necessary for understanding a landscape were of a rather low or ordinary kind. He finally rejected landscape as being too literal, too concerned with banal representation of banal nature.
2. Louis Brès, "Le Paysage provençal et son influence au point de vue littéraire et artistique," Académie de Marseilles, Marseilles, 1883.
3. See particularly André Gouirand, *Les Peintres provençaux*, Paris, 1901. The literature on Provence and on the local characteristics of its culture needs to be reviewed by students of Cézanne, whose own regionalist sympathies are of enormous importance in a proper understanding of his career.
4. Frédéric Henriet, Champfleury, and A. de la Fizelière, *La Vie et l'oeuvre de Chintreuil*, Paris, 1874, pp. 78–84.
5. This generalized idea is basic to French landscape theory and was advanced early in the century by Valenciennes. In fact, Valenciennes thought that coloring, modeling, and perspective were to be found in nature rather than applied to it, and he based his entire esthetic on drawing and painting from nature. See P.-H. de Valenciennes, *Eléments de perspective practique à l'usage des artistes, suivis de réflexions et conseils à un élève sur la peinture, et particulièrement sur le genre du paysage*, Paris, 1800, pp. 398–407.
6. Sisley's moving and rather pathetic attempts to gain some form of fame are recorded by O. Reuterswärd in "Sisley's 'Cathedrals'–a study of the 'Church at Moret',' *Gazette des Beaux-Arts*, March 1952.
7. Frédéric Henriet, *Le Paysagiste aux champs*, Paris, 1876, chapter 2, "Les Colonies des Artistes." This section of the book is the only one written in the 1870s. The rest of the material is drawn from Henriet's writings, published and unpublished, of the 1860s.

Henriet's book, chatty and thoughtless as it first appears to be, is the essential document for the student of landscape painting in France during the late nineteenth century. It is a mine of information and, more particularly, the expression of a series of attitudes held by many, perhaps most landscape painters of the generation of the Impressionists. Henriet neither admired nor knew the Impressionists very well, but his book tells a great deal that makes it easier to understand the essential qualities of their art.

8. Many late nineteenth-century writers mention the sheer number of landscape painters and the tiresome profusion of landscape images in the Salons. It is always important to remember in studies of French landscape painting of this period that the genre was considered to be, and probably was, overpopulated. Henriet stressed the cliquishness of landscape painters and was definite about the fact that many of them lived in the country for economic as well as esthetic reasons. The landscape in which most painters operated had almost as many painters as peasants. One recalls here Degas's disparaging and cynical remark about those landscape painters "cluttering" the countryside and his wish to see the gendarmes shoot them all down (Etienne Moreau-Nélaton, "Deux heures avec Degas," *L'Amour de l'art*, July 1931, p. 267).
9. The most brilliant and provocative discussion of this landscape in print is Marc Bloch's long essay, "L'Ile-de-France (le pays autour de Paris)," *Revue de Synthése historique*, vols. 25 and 26, Paris, 1912 and 1913. Bloch points out the lack of real historical significance of the Ile-de-France. It is a psychological rather than a geographical region. He refuses, therefore, to limit or define its borders precisely, saying that it is the area that surrounds Paris, an area defined more by a city than by the precise character of its own terrain.
10. Most of these places are mentioned in all the biographical studies, most of which stem from Adolphe Tabarant, *Pissarro*, Paris, 1924. Others, like Chailly and Nanterre, are recorded on drawings in Pissarro's hand. For examples of drawings executed in Montmorency, see B&L 49A, 49B, 49C, 50, 51; in La Roche-Guyon, B&L 52, 53; in Chailly, B&L 60; in Nanterre, B&L 61.
11. Champa's analysis of the early style of Pissarro can be found in the chapter devoted to that artist in his *Studies in Early Impressionism*, New Haven and London, 1973, pp. 67–73.

Rewald's discussion of Pissarro's sources is more concerned with personal interaction with the painters rather than with acute stylistic analysis of specific pictorial traits derived from them. See his short biographical treatment of the artist in *C. Pissarro*, New York, 1963. Cogniat's treatment of Pissarro's career is brief, but very well balanced (*Pissarro*, Paris, 1974). For the mention of Chintreuil and Desbrosses, see Charles Kunstler, *Pissarro: villes et campagnes*, Lausanne and Paris, 1967, p. 14, and see Cogniat, *op. cit.*, p. 30. Rewald refers to Pissarro's meeting Chintreuil while working "in the country around Paris," in his *History of Impressionism* (4th revised edn.), New York, 1973, p. 50.

12. There are several sources for items in the *iconographie de Pontoise*. The topographical albums in the Cabinet des Estampes, Bibliothèque Nationale form the largest grouping (*Topographie de la France, Val-d'Oise*). There are several drawings representing Pontoise in the Destailleurs Collection also in the Bibliothèque Nationale. The collections of the Société historique et archéologique de Pontoise et du Vexin français are also comparatively rich, as are the Archives de Val-d'Oise, Pontoise. The largest group of nineteenth-century photographic images of Pontoise is in the collection of M. Jean Hecquet, a former Pontoisian now living in Paris.
13. The best treatment of pictorial activity in the Pontoisian region can be found in Rudolphe Walters's short article "Les Impressionistes dans le Vexin français," *Bulletin du sociéte historique et archéologique du Vexin français*, 1973. Walters mentions both Morisot and Rousseau without giving precise pictorial references. There is also material related to pictorial activity in the Pontoisian region in *Les Peintres des Bords de l'Oise*, Musée de Pontoise, 1974. There is no mention of Morisot in this latter source, and the small *esquisses* by Rousseau that were chosen for the exhibition lack any precise reference to their site and might as easily have been painted around Barbizon as around Pontoise.
14. Both *L'Oise à Pontoise* (P&V 174, collection of The Earl of Jersey) and *Le Lavoir à Pontoise* (P&V 175, Musée d' Orsay) represent the Seine near Bougival. Landscape photographs by a wealthy landscape photographer of the 1870s in Louveciennes and postcards of the same region make site identification possible. The buildings on the river in P&V 175 are, in fact, some of the outbuildings called La

Grenouillère. *Barrage sur la Seine à Bougival* (P&V 125, Parke-Bernet, 26 and 27 April 1972, illustrated in color) was, in fact, painted near the Château de Saint-Martin in Pontoise looking across river to the small buildings in Saint-Ouen-l'Aumône. The correspondence between Lucien and Ludovic-Rodo Pissarro in the early and mid-1930s contains many discussions of the precise site of a painting by their father. Some of the decisions they made have proved to be incorrect. (The correspondence is unpublished and has been destroyed. Partial transcripts were made by Mr. Bensusan Butt, who has kindly made them available to the author.)

15. Throughout the nineteenth century, L'Hermitage was spelled L'Ermitage. Pissarro, however, spells it both ways, and modern usage is to have the "H." In keeping with the latter and for the sake of consistency, the spelling "L'Hermitage" is used in this book.

16. The escape from the Paris art capital to the *pays natal* which was so important for Cézanne and Courbet have been adequately discussed in the literature relating to those two artists. T.J. Clark in *Images of the people*, London, 1973 (see chapter, "Courbet in Ornans and Besançon 1849–50," and particularly pp. 98 ff.) and other sources have emphasized the importance of the Loue Valley for Courbet, although their treatment of the paintings most often stresses the large figural compositions submitted to the Salon in the 1850s and deemphasizes the more numerous and equally important landscapes and animal compositions in which Courbet specialized during the 1860s and 1870s. Cézanne's affected "provincialism" has always been noted in the Cézanne literature, and it is possible to differentiate easily between the "greened" landscapes that he painted in the Ile-de-France and those more coloristically balanced and complex landscapes painted in Provence.

17. Although it is difficult to discuss Pissarro's landscape titles with a great deal of authority, the listings for the Impressionist exhibitions and for the early Salons to which Pissarro contributed are dominated by titles with precise locations. This preoccupation with place led the painter's son, Ludovic-Rodo, to create titles with place names for the untitled portion of the artist's oeuvre. Although a precise numerical study has not been done, general study suggests that locative titles were much rarer in landscape paintings of the middle of the nineteenth century, which tend to be titled by times of day (crépuscule, soleil couchant, soleil levant) or generic names that have no locative precision (coup de vent, ruines, mare de campagne, etc.). The titles of the Impressionists and their contemporaries have a good deal more information about the exact site or motif. The fact that they are painted "en face du motif" is admitted rather than denied, in keeping with their *plein-air* esthetics.

18. Henriet, *Le Paysagiste*, pp. 131–35. This section of Henriet's book is, unfortunately, one of the weakest. His ideas are extremely significant, but his flippancy of tone and the shortness of the chapter make it impossible for him to discuss them adequately.

19. Frédéric Henriet, *Les Campagnes d'un paysagiste*, Paris, 1891, p. 69. Henriet's passage is an interesting one because, in it, he rejects the "savoir faire" esthetic by telling the painter that he paints the totality of nature and not objects. If one knows how to paint skies, trees, rocks, walls, etc., one knows nothing in Henriet's view: "Il faut chaque jour que l'on est devant la nature s'imaginer que l'on peint pour la première fois."

20. It is revealing and significant to remember, in this context, that Henriet especially disliked what he termed "l'artiste voyageur" because he merely observed and never understood nature. Henriet and most landscape theorists of the nineteenth century recommended patient study of a single landscape rather than constant travel to intoxicating sites. See Henriet, *Le Paysagiste*, pp. 153–56.

21. See particularly, Reidemeister's orgy of photographic comparisons in *Auf den Spuren der Maler der Ile de France*, Berlin, 1963; Rewald, *C. Pissarro*; and William C. Seitz, *Monet*, New York, 1960. The technique of juxtaposing modern photographs and photographs of nineteenth-century landscape paintings is not, however, limited to these three scholars. Earl Loran has also made extended use of the method in *Cézanne's Composition*, Berkeley and Los Angeles, 1963, and one finds frequent comparisons in the best illustrated monographs and catalogues on Van Gogh and Monet (for example, the recent exhibition catalogue *Van Gogh à Paris*, Musée d'Orsay, February-May 1988, where juxtapositions of Van Gogh's paintings and postcard views of the sites depicted can be found).

22. Discussions of the peculiar "distortions" made by landscape painters has received some treatment in the literature on Cézanne, particularly Loran, *op. cit.*, and H.L. Sherman, *Cézanne and Visual Form*, Columbus, Ohio, 1952. One of the most interesting nineteenth-century discussions of this subject can be found in P.G. Hamerton, *Landscape*, London, 1885.

23. Marie-Louise Vincent, *George Sand et le Berry*, Paris 1919; Geoffrey Hartman, *Wordsworth's Poetry*, 1787–1814, New Haven, 1964.

24. See particularly Graham Reynolds, *Constable: The Natural Painter*, London, 1965; the catalogue for the monographic exhibition at the Tate Gallery, *Constable: Paintings, Watercolours and Drawings* by Leslie Parris, Ian Fleming-Williams, and Conal Shields, London, 1976, and the work on which most Constable studies are based, C.R. Leslie, *Memoirs of the Life of John Constable, R.A.*, London, 1843. Constable and Pissarro shared a comparable fixation on landscapes in which they lived and with which they seem to have had powerful connections. However, any prolonged comparison between their respective attitudes towards place becomes a study in contrasts. Martin Reid's attempts at discussing the "geography" of Pissarro's landscapes painted in suburban London can be found in "Camille Pissarro: three paintings of London. What do they represent?" *Burlington Magazine*, vol. 119, April 1977, pp. 253–61, and "The Pissarro family in the Norwood area of London, 1870–71, where did they live?" in *Studies on Camille Pissarro*, London, 1986, pp. 5ff. For a comparison between Pissarro and Constable, see Christopher Lloyd, *Camille Pissarro*, Geneva, 1981, p. 51. Pissarro's attitude toward possible influences from Constable and the English School carried a certain ambiguity. In a letter to the English critic Wynford Dewhurst in November 1902, Pissarro wrote: "In 1870 I found myself in London with Monet and we met Daubigny and Bonvin. Monet and I were very enthusiastic over London landscapes.... We also visited the museums. The watercolours and paintings of Turner and Constable . . . certainly had an influence on us . . . they shared more in our aim with regard to plein-air, light and fugitive effects." Yet, on reading Dewhurst's book on Impressionism, Pissarro wrote to the author in 1903: 'I do not think, as you say, that the Impressionists are concerned with the English School, for many reasons too long to develop here. It is true that Turner and Constable have been useful to us, as all paintings of great talent have, but the base of our art is evidently of French tradition" (Lloyd, *op. cit.*, p. 26).

25. Janine Bailly-Herzberg, ed., *Correspondance de Camille Pissarro*, vol. 1 (1865–85), Paris, 1980; vol. 2 (1886–90), Paris, 1986; vol. 3 (1891–94), Paris, 1988; vol. 4 (1895–98), Paris, 1989. The final volume (1899–1903) is due to be published shortly.

26. *Mon cher Pissarro*, Paris, 1985 (with commentary by Janine Bailly-Herzberg).

27. There are several editions of the letters to Lucien, of which the first published in French was *Camille Pissarro, lettres à son fils Lucien*, ed. John Rewald, Paris, 1950. However, this edition is by no means a complete one. The original letters are in the Ashmolean Museum, Oxford and the complete correspondence from Pissarro to his son Lucien is included in Bailly-Herzberg, *op. cit.* Anne Thorold is planning to publish a new edition of the letters from Lucien to his father in 1991.

1   Pontoise: The Landscape Itself

1. See particularly Léon Thomas, *Bibliographie de la ville et du canton de Pontoise*, Pontoise, 1883 and Henri Lemoine, *Manuel de bibliographie générale du département de Seine-et-Oise*, Paris, 1945. There is also a useful short bibliography of essential sources in Jean

Gressier, Jean-Marcel Champion, Alain Demurger, Jacques Dupaquier, Gilles Gaucher, Jean Hecquet, and Jean Lecuir, *Pontoise: 2000 ans d'histoire*, Pontoise, 1973. Marc Bloch discusses regional bibliography in the Ile-de-France in "L'Ile-de-France (le pays autour de Paris)," *Revue de Synthèse historique*, vols. 25 and 26, Paris, 1912 and 1913.

2. The society began an intensive publishing venture in 1879. See the *Mémoires de la Société historique et archéologique de Pontoise, du Val d'Oise, et du Vexin*, which continues publication to this day.

3. Paul Joanne, *Dictionnaire géographique et administratif de la France*, Paris, 1899, vol. 5, pp. 3613–14.

4. E. Sagine, "Ville de Pontoise," 1899, unpaginated manuscript, Archives Nationales, Versailles.

5. *Description générale et particulière de la France: voyage pittoresque de la France*, vol. 4: *Paris et ses environs*, n.d. The section on Pontoise is very short, but plate 24 is an elaborate view of the town featuring the old bridge, Saint-Pierre, the ruins of the Château, and some port activity in the foreground.

6. M. l'Abbé Trou, *Recherches historiques, archéologiques, et biographiques sur la ville de Pontoise*, Pontoise, 1841. For Trou's brilliant section on the revolutionary destruction, see pp. 326–29. Trou's book is one of a large number of local histories written in the 1830s and 1840s by local priests, savants, and aristocrats. Most of these books were the basic source material for the first generation of popular guidebook writers. All of the prominent entries on Pontoise of the Second Empire are essentially based on Trou's often erroneous account of the history of that town. For a good bibliography of early urban and town histories of the type written by Trou, see Philippe Dollinger, Philippe Wolff, and Simone Guenée, *Bibliographie d'histoire des villes de France* Paris, 1967.

7. Bloch, *op. cit.* p. 135.

8. Trou, *op. cit.*, p. 2.

9. J.-B. Richard, and E.-M. St. Hilaire, *Guide du voyageur aux environs de Paris dans un rayon de 60 kilomètres* (3rd edn.), Paris, 1840, pp. 345–46. The text of the first edition, published in 1826, is virtually identical.

10. Adolphe Joanne, *Les Environs de Paris* (2nd edn.), Paris, 1872, pp. 265–69. The text in the editions of 1856 and 1872 is almost the same and is based largely on Trou. In fact, Joanne refers to several buildings mentioned by Trou that never seem to have been in Pontoise at all.

11. *Ibid.*, p. 266.

12. Louis Barron, *Les Environs de Paris*, Paris, 1886, p. 565.

13. Trou, *op. cit.*, p. 357, refers to two "grandes et belles usines."

14. Adolphe Joanne, *op. cit.*, p. 268.

15. The most readily available summary account of agriculture in the area around Pontoise can be found in Danielle Allezard et Lucienne Lamy, *L'Agriculture du Vexin français*, Paris, 1970.

16. An excellent summary of the history of canals in the north of France can be found in Raymond Lazzarotti, *L'Industrie et les complexes industriels dans la vallée l'Oise*, Paris, 1968, pp. 25–37.

17. For the clearest discussion of the urbanization of Pontoise and the improvement of the docks in the nineteenth century, see Charles Gantois, "Les anciennes fortifications de Pontoise, leur disparitions, l'urbanisme à Pontoise au XIXème siècle," *Mémoires de la société historique et archéologique de Pontoise et du Vexin français*, vol. 50, Pontoise, 1943, pp. 166–87.

18. *Guide pittoresque du voyageur en France: Département de Seine-et-Oise*, Paris, 1834, p. 6, where the streets are described as "étroites et très escarpées."

19. Adolphe Joanne, *op. cit.*, p. 20.

20. For an illustration and discussion of the opening of the rue Impériale, see *L'Illustration, journal universel*, 16 October 1869.

21. *Description générale et particulière de la France*, p. 524.

22. *Almanach historique de Pontoise et du IIème arrondissement de Seine-et-Oise*, Pontoise, 1803, p. 29.

23. H. Moser, *Annuaire administratif, statistique, agricole, industriel, et commerciel de Seine-et-Oise*, Versailles, 1865, pp. 539–40.

24. *Statistique de la France; industrie: résultats généraux de l'enquête effectuée dans les années 1861–1865*, Nancy, 1873, pp. 666–69.

25. The information in this paragraph is derived exclusively from the well-kept cadastral records of Saint-Ouen-l'Aumône. None of the statistics has been published.

26. Sagine, *op. cit.*

27. For an excellent study of the markets of Vexin, including those of Pontoise, see Eugène Bougeatre's *La Vie rurale dans le Mantois et le Vexin au XIXème siècle*, Meudon, 1971, pp. 154–57. Bougeatre's book is filled with fascinating details derived for the most part from reliable local statistics. His picture of the peasant and market economy can be profitably contrasted with Pissarro's rather thin pictorial version of the same subject.

28. An excellent discussion of the railroad and other modes of public transportation can be found in Bougeatre, *op. cit.*, pp. 145–46.

29. Moser, *op. cit.*, p. 539.

30. It is relevant to recall that "peasant" and "paysan" have different connotations in English and French. "Paysan" derives from "pays" (land or country) and is almost devoid of the disparaging connotation its equivalent has in English. The French term indicates simply the origin of the subject: a man from the land or the country. In the nineteenth century eighty per cent of the French population lived off the land and were thus "paysans."

31. Jacques Dupaquier, *La Situation de l'agriculture dans le Vexin français (fin du XVIIIème siècle et début du XIXème siècle) d'après les enquêtes agricoles*, Paris, 1964. See also Georges Lefebvre, *Etudes sur la Révolution Française*, Paris, 1936, pp. 279–367.

32. Perhaps the most succinct and relevant description of this rather complex form of "peasant" life can be found in Henri Baudrillart, *Les Populations agricoles de la France, Normandie et Bretagne, passé et présent*, Paris 1885, especially pp. 140–147. Much of Baudrillart's rather impressionistic treatment of his subject is corroborated with considerable statistical material by Eugen Weber in *Peasants into Frenchmen: The Modernization of Rural France, 1870–1914*, Stanford, 1976.

33. Olwen Hufton, *The Poor of Eighteenth-Century France, 1750–1789*, Oxford, 1974, especially pp. 15–17, 48–51, 69–107.

34. Perhaps the most stimulating, if occasionally overly general discussion of the peasantry in European history can be found in Emmanuel Le Roy Ladurie's collection of essays, *Le Territoire de l'historien*, Paris, 1973, in the chapter, "La Civilisation rurale."

35. Such information is readily apparent after consulting the listing of property rentals and wages in the Archives Communales de Pontoise. A general study that corroborates much of the information and gives many parallels is Michel Philipponeau's excellent book, *La Vie rurale de la banlieue parisienne: étude de géographie humaine*, Paris, 1956. Allezard and Lamy, *op. cit.*, also discuss the "cross-patterning" and confusion in the various economic realms.

36. General and specific discussions of modernization in the French countryside in the eighteenth and nineteenth centuries are too numerous to mention. A recent study, however, outweighs all its predecessors in the amount of material used to support the conclusions: Weber, *op. cit.*

37. All the above information is derived from Sagine, *op. cit.*

38. The modernization of agriculture in the late nineteenth century is one of the most difficult subjects related to the progressive history of France in that period. Most of the international expositions, magazines, articles in the press, and "how-to" books written from the Second Empire to the end of the century stress the mechanical progress and change which was beginning to characterize French agricultural life. On the other hand, students of rural life from Baudrillart to Weber have stressed the time lags involved in the actual acceptance of mechanized tools. The literature for Pontoise is almost ambivalent on this point. Perhaps the monograph on Osny, written in 1899 by Signot, is the most reliable and informative source available to us. Signot's monograph is much more expert than Sagine's contemporary monograph on Pontoise, and both were written in preparation for a series of communal monographs to be exhibited at the International Exposition of 1900 in Paris. All these monographs are now housed in the Archives Nationales in Ver-

sailles, but xeroxed copies of relevant monographs are in all departmental archives.

39. Henri Le Charpentier, *Calendrier historique de Pontoise: éphémérides quotidiennes de l'histoire de cette ville*, Pontoise, 1882. The book is fascinating and useful not only for its factual information, which is literally listed in calendrical form, but also because it is an ancestor of the "daily" or ordinary history which has been the major contribution of French historians to the historiography of the twentieth century.

40. Both newspapers are accessible in the Bibliothèque Nationale branch in Versailles.

41. Adolphe Joanne, *op cit.*, pp. 268–69.

2 Pissarro's Pontoise: Omissions and Admissions

1. Most of these observations are based on the author's own visits to the sites painted, with the aid of the various catalogues raisonnés, postcards, and other visual tools.

2. See particularly the essay by Champfleury in Frédéric Henriet, Champfleury, and A. de la Fizelière, *La Vie et l'oeuvre de Chintreuil*, Paris, 1874, p. xvii. Hamerton also makes note of Chintreuil's powers of endurance in the landscape (*Landscape*, London, 1885, p. 18).

3. See especially Frédéric Henriet, *Les Campagnes d'un paysagiste*, Paris, 1891, pp. 35–38 ("il nous faut aller chercher le motif," he writes in a letter to Harpignies). Thoré's discussion of his rural walks in the company of Rousseau are in the introduction to his "Salon" of 1844.

4. Examples are too numerous to mention, the most prominent include *Bonjour M. Courbet*, exhibited in the Salon of 1855 (Musée Fabre, Montpellier), Cézanne's pencil drawing of Pissarro (Cabinet des Dessins, Louvre), and Gauguin's two versions of *Bonjour M. Gauguin*, 1889 (Narodni Gallery, Prague and Armand Hammer Collection, Los Angeles).

5. Hartman's discussion of Wordsworth's "spot syndrome," *Wordsworth's Poetry, 1787–1814*, New Haven, 1964, pp. 84–87, is relevant to an analysis of nineteenth-century landscape painting, much of which reveals an obsessive interest in certain "spots" in nature or in time.

6. For a discussion of the seigneurial property before and after the sale of lands in the *vente des biens*, see Georges Lefebvre, *Etudes sur la Révolution Française*, Paris, 1936, pp. 279–367. References to the specific properties in Pontoise are too numerous to note. The reader could consult virtually any history of the town written since Trou's account of 1841 as well as any of the major guidebooks included in the Select Bibliography. The French obsession with the large country house or château has never been adequately stressed in discussion of French landscape perception. The French château was as important an element in the landscape for Frenchmen as the more thoroughly studied English country house

was for Englishmen. There is no clear discussion of the country house in the iconography of landscape painting, but it played an important part in the seventeenth century as well as in the eighteenth and nineteenth centuries.

7. The châteaux of Pontoise are mentioned in virtually every guidebook that includes the city. A good modern source is *Pontoise et ses environs*, edited by *L'Echo Pontoisien*, Pontoise, 1931.

8. The most ready proof of these assertions can be found by working through the topographical volumes for France in the Cabinet des Estampes, Bibliothèque Nationale, or the huge Destailleurs Collection of topographical drawings (also Bibliothèque Nationale) assembled by the architect who designed many of the country buildings for the Rothschilds in England and France, including Waddesdon Manor.

9. See Daniel Wildenstein, *Claude Monet: biographie et catalogue raisonné*, Lausanne and Paris, 1974; entries for W 422 and W 433.

10. Pissarro's political radicalism is so well known that prolonged discussion of it is no longer necessary. Benedict Nicolson's article of 1946, "The Anarchism of Camille Pissarro," *The Arts*, [London], no. 11, is still the best source, although it somewhat overemphasizes its points and makes Pissarro a more rabid *politico* than he in fact was. Pissarro's remarks about the bourgeoisie can be found at many points throughout his correspondence, and they are almost always disparaging. For two rather ordinary examples, see Camille Pissarro, *Lettres à son fils Lucien*, ed. John Rewald, Paris, 1950, pp. 72, 73, 77, and 265. A more recent and better-documented analysis of Pissarro's "emotional rather than intellectual" anarchism, will be found in Ralph E. Shikes and Paula Hays Harper, *Pissarro: his life and work*, New York and London, 1980, pp. 226–41. Shikes and Harper present the reader with a much more varied, balanced, and complete understanding of Pissarro's anarchism by including excerpts of some of Pissarro's favorite readings by authors such as Jean Grave, P.-J. Proud'hon and Kropotkin. See also Christopher Lloyd, *Camille Pissarro*, Geneva, 1981, pp. 135–42, which interprets Pissarro's anarchism in the context of the social and geographical oppositions: wealth/poverty, city life/rural life. See also Ralph E. Shikes, "Pissarro's political philosophy and his art" in *Studies on Camille Pissarro*, London, 1986, pp. 35–54.

11. For the connections between the painting and the parc de Marcouville, see Leopold Reidemeister, *Auf den Spuren der Maler der Ile de France*, Berlin, 1963.

12. See Jean Gressier, *et al.*, *Pontoise: 2000 ans d'histoire*, Pontoise, 1973, p. 153.

13. The books by Desraimes that Pissarro would have known contain both opinions that he might have held and other, almost directly

contrary opinions. She was an agglomerative intellect in the nineteenth-century mode, not altogether unlike Mme. Blavatsky, who attempted to combine all knowledge in one theory and succeeded only in confusing everything. See especially, *L'Ancien devant le nouveau*, Paris, 1869, and *France et progrès*, Paris, 1873. Although it is very tempting to connect stray sentences from Desraimes's writings with the paintings of Pissarro, such connections would be unfair both to Pissarro and to Desraimes.

14. See *Archives de Camille Pissarro*, Hôtel Drouot, Paris, 21 November 1975, no. 138. (The name Desraimes is misspelled.)

15. For a more complete discussion of Pissarro and Monet, see pp. 62 ff.

16. For a general discussion of this phenomenon, see Emmanuel Le Roy Ladurie, *Le Territoire de l'historien*, Paris, 1973, p. 161. Both Sagine in his monograph on Pontoise of 1899, and Signot, in his monograph on Osny of the same year, make similar statements (both, unpaginated manuscripts, Archives Nationales, Versailles). A good modern discussion of rural architecture in Vexin can be found in Eugène Bougeatre, *La Vie rurale dans le Mantois et le Vexin au XIXème siècle*, Meudon, 1971, pp. 32–38. All these discussions, plus Eugen Weber's more recent summation in *Peasants into Frenchmen: the Modernization of Rural France, 1870–1914*, Stanford, 1976, suggest that the kind of rural architecture that had been the stock and trade of peasant genre painting in the mid-nineteenth century was rapidly disappearing from the real French rural scene in the latter part of the century.

17. The most complete recent discussion of the peasant as "sauvage" is in Weber, *op. cit.*, pp. 3–22. It must be mentioned, however, that this view of the peasantry, although common in the France of the middle and late nineteenth century, was not the only one. Both nationalistic and pantheistic views of the peasantry were equally important and form key components of the peasant image.

18. For a detailed analysis of the religious situation in nineteenth-century France, see the important article by Y.-M. Hilaire, "La pratique religieuse en France de 1815 à 1878" in *L'Information historique*, pp. 57–69 (quoted in Jean-Marie Mayeur, *Les Débuts de la Troisième République, 1871–1898*, Paris, 1973, p. 136) and see the graphs organized by Fernand Boulard, *Archives de sociologie des religions*, January–June 1971, p. 80.

19. Adolphe Tabarant, *Pissarro*, Paris, 1924; Charles Kunstler, *Pissarro: villes et campagnes*, Lausanne and Paris, 1967, p. 10. Further treatment of Pissarro's religious background with extensive use of unpublished family archival material is included in Shikes and Harper, *op. cit.*

20. In a letter from Frédéric Pissarro to his son Camille dated 7 October 1859, and published in Shikes and Harper, *op. cit.*, p. 51, the father invites his son to celebrate the yearly Jewish

family celebration: "Your mother asks me to write to invite you to come for dinner with us today, because this is the evening when we celebrate Kipur and on this solemn occasion the whole family should be together." Camille probably accepted his father's invitation, but as Shikes and Harper rightly insist: "The explanations Frédéric felt impelled to give indicated how far away the son had drifted."

Pissarro's wife's parents were traditional Roman Catholic farmers who kept vines in Burgundy. Pissarro met Julie when she was a maid in his mother's house in Paris in 1860. Julie remained Pissarro's common-law wife for ten years before they married in a non-religious wedding. Pissarro's mother never approved of her son's liasion nor of his marriage with Julie. Pissarro all his life kept well away from churches and synagogues, which he saw as breeding grounds of the most perverse hypocrisy, and he brought up his children on the same principles, thereby establishing a family tradition of atheism or free-thinking.

21. Pissarro's depiction of the Jardin public is fascinating for other reasons. Most guide-book writers who mention Pontoise praise the extraordinary views from the Jardin public, which is sited at the top of a hill overlooking the plains of Montmorency. After the construction of the Eiffel Tower (1887–1889), Pontoisians could see it clearly from the Jardin (*Pontoise et ses environs*, ed. *L'Echo Pontoisien*, p. 38). Pissarro's view of the garden emphasizes not the most important part of the garden, the view, but the rather uneventful plaza in front of the view. His inclusion of the tip of the tower of Notre-Dame de Pontoise puts the oddity of his landscape into relief.

22. It is, perhaps, a slight exaggeration to say that the Foire Saint-Martin was a secular festival. Its religious origins were well known in the nineteenth century, mostly because of Abbé Trou's history of the town which stressed the religious institutions so heavily. By the nineteenth century, it had become a very rowdy and lively fête which retained very few of its original religious overtones, (see Weber, *op. cit.* and Bougeatre, *op. cit.*, pp. 152–43). The two illustrations of the Foire Saint-Martin by Gustave Doré were published in 1852 (see *Topographie de la France, Val-d'Oise*, Cabinet des Estampes, Bibliothèque Nationale). For further discussion of the Foire Saint-Martin and Pissarro's several versions of it, see p. 159.

23. The map is clearly reproduced in Sagine, *op. cit.*

24. In George Sand's *La Mare au Diable*, the mill owner was a cut above other peasants and was actively engaged in cheating them. Peasant lore contains many stories related to the mill owner and to trips to the mill (see particularly Marie-Louise Vincent, *George Sand et le Berry*, Paris, 1919. Land surveys

in France in the seventeenth, eighteenth, and nineteenth centuries record a great many mills. Unfortunately, an iconography of landscape painting has not yet been written, at least, not one that discusses the important architectural motifs of landscape paintings and their probable meanings.

25. Although it is much better in its treatment of the region south of Paris, the best article on the quarries and quarriers of the Région Parisienne is Henri Raulin, "Les Carriers et les tailleurs de grès de la région Parisienne," *Arts et traditions populaires*, vol. 9, no. 3, July and September 1961. The industry, which provided stones for the large rebuilding and repaving projects in Paris during the Second Empire, became increasingly important in the nineteenth century. Although it employed a great many peasants who fled the overpopulated countryside, the majority of workers were foreign by the turn of the century. The quarries of Pontoise are mentioned by Sagine, *op. cit.*, and in most of the statistical accounts of the Pontoisian economy published in the nineteenth century. Their economic importance was almost as great as that of the grain mills which Pissarro also avoided in his work.

26. The quarries near Fontainebleau are the subjects of many drawings and paintings of the 1820s and 1830s. Pissarro himself owned a Corot drawing of a quarry with large, cut stones and several tiny figures. (The drawing is presently in the collection of the Ashmolean Museum, Oxford.) Corot also juxtaposed the facade of Chartres cathedral with a large pile of cut stones in *La Cathédrale de Chartres* (Musée d'Orsay).

27. See pp. 155 ff.

28. It is interesting to note that the only prominent view of that picturesque plaza painted in the period of Pissarro's stay in Pontoise is by his friend, Ludovic Piette. This large water-color of 1877, the year of Piette's death, now in the Musée de Pontoise, seizes the motif forcefully on a market day and is filled with hundreds of busy human figures and many genre details. It can be contrasted in almost every way with Pissarro's only picture of a market painted in the 1870s, *Fête de Septembre, Pontoise* (pl. 36). Piette's view, with its swooping, spacious curve and its detailed depiction of the architectural ambiance, is very different for the planar, awkward world of the market that Pissarro painted five years before.

29. Only a slight pencil drawing (B&L 158) records this view which Pissarro saw many times after emerging from the train. This drawing, done on the blue lined paper he used in 1883 to jot down landscape and city-scape notes during his trips to find a new house for the family, was clearly made as he came out of the station of his return home to Pontoise, possibly for the last time.

30. The bibliography related to the modernization of the plow in France is so vast that it

would daunt any reader. Perhaps the most complete history and discussion of the plow in print can be found in E.-O. Lami, *Dictionnaire encyclopédique et biographique de l'industrie et des arts industriels*, 7 vols., Paris, 1881. The entry, pp. 684–850, was written by the greatest expert on the plow in France during the late nineteenth century, J.-A. Grandvoinnet, who had written the very important *Traité de mécanique agricole* in 1854, and had published a serious and widely read journal of progressive agriculture, *Le Génie rural*, between 1858 and 1875.

31. See, for example, Daniel Faucher, *La Vie rurale vue par un géographe*, Toulouse, 1962. pp, 96–98, 181–83. Faucher's book is among the most sensitive and intelligent books on agriculture written in the twentieth century in French. It is not, strictly speaking, historical. Rather, in writing about agriculture for city dwellers, Faucher is more phenomenological in his approach. For further discussion of Faucher's book in relation to Pissarro, see note 35 below.

32. See P&V 183–86, 225, and 233, and several drawings in the Ashmolean Museum, Oxford.

33. See pl. 22 and P&V 226, 227, 231, 242, 262, 444, and 447.

34. See p. 162.

35. It is interesting to note in this context that most writers on rural cultivation in the nineteenth and twentieth centuries divide it into agriculture and horticulture, the cultivation, respectively, of field and garden. Although respectable treatises on the art of gardening had appeared in France as early as the sixteenth century, interest in gardening waned in the nineteenth century in spite of the profitability of the profession. Indeed, the modernization of cultivation led to a distinct shift of attention away from garden agriculture and work by hand to field agriculture and work by machine or groups of men working, in a way, as a machine. Perhaps the most popular and simple agricultural handbook was T.-H. Barrau, *Simples Notions sur l'agriculture*, Paris, 1868 and 1883 (the years Pissarro arrived in and left Pontoise). Barrau devoted the most of his attention to large-scale agriculture and implied in several sections that gardening and small-scale agriculture was a lower-class activity. He was, no doubt, correct, but his relative designification of horticulture was normal for writers on agricultural matters and places Pissarro's celebration of this daily activity into clearer perspective. Pissarro's horticultural landscape was, in this way, anti-progressive. For a good discussion of this subject, see Daniel Faucher, *Le Paysan et la machine*, Paris, 1954.

36. An iconography of Impressionism has not yet been written. The generalizations made by Arnold Hauser in *The Social History of Art* are very provocative, but do not apply especially well to the imagery of artists like Sisley and Pissarro. Most of the generalizations

made in the following pages are my own and derived, quite simply, from the recent catalogues raisonnés, which have made the iconographer's task so much easier.

37. This generalization cannot be supported in any single note. The reader is referred to the illustrations of the town of Pontoise which, almost without exception, focus on the river and the port life of the town from the seventeenth to the end of the nineteenth centuries. The reader is also encouraged to look at the "popular" or illustrative prints of Daubigny published by Delteil and the illustrations to Louis Barron, *Les Environs de Paris*, Paris, 1886, which are dominated by river scenes with the associated imagery of the train and the factory, so important for the Impressionists.

38. See Wolfgang Stechow, *Dutch Landscape Painting of the 17th Century*, London, 1966.

39. Daubigny's importance for Pissarro should not be over-stressed. Champa's discussion of Daubigny and Pissarro in *Studies in Early Impressionism*, New Haven and London, 1973, p. 75, makes use of a rare Daubigny with no water. Daubigny is in many ways probably closer to Monet than he is to Pissarro. The leisure aspects of the river and the painter's use of a boat are both emphasized by Monet and Daubigny; Pissarro's preference for remaining on dry land is in contrast both to Monet and to Daubigny.

40. Sagine, *op. cit.*

41. Arnold Hauser, *The Social History of Art*, New York, n.d. (Vintage Books), pp. 166–225.

42. It is interesting to note that the only element of industry present in Monet's suburban landscapes is the train. Few factories mar the edges of the Seine in his landscapes.

43. For a discussion of one of the prominent landscapes in which the viewer is *not* obviously on land, see pp. 83–84.

44. This is *Bords de Rivière*, of 1871 (P&V 124, formerly in Degas's collection and exhibited at Nortman & Brod, London, June 1985, illustrated in the catalogue). The site is between Marly-le-Roi and Bougival along the Seine.

45. The relationship between the figures and the very rigid, tectonic structure of the barrier interested Pissarro to such an extent that he made a lithograph of the center portion of the composition in 1874. This composition has been mistitled both by Delteil (D 130) and, more recently, by Melot as *Une Rue à patures à Pontoise*.

46. Indeed, Pissarro's only composition that makes a feature of a railroad train completed in the Pontoisian period is *Le Pont de chemin de fer a Pontoise* (D 37), an etching of which only two proofs of two states survive. This etching has always been dated 1883, the year of Pissarro's departure from Pontoise, and the date is plausible considering Pissarro's sudden burst of pictorial nostalgia in that year. He drew the place de la Gare and the rue Thiers for the first and last time (B&L 158B), and made two last views of Pontoise from the hillside of Osny (P&V 587 and 628). The railroad image remained exceptional in Pissarro's oeuvre, and the fact that so few impressions of D 37 survive and that those that do are very faint and unlike others of the early 1880s suggest that Pissarro rejected the composition.

3 The Industrial Landscape: Pissarro and the Factory

1. P.-H. de Valenciennes, *Eléments de perspective pratique à l'usage des artistes*, Paris, 1800, pp. 620–22.

2. For a general discussion and several good charts concerning industrialization in France in the late nineteenth century, see *Atlas historique de la France contemporaine: 1800–1965*, Paris, 1966, pp. 87f. Raymond Lazzarotti in *L'Industrie et les complexes industriels dans la vallée de l'Oise*, Paris, 1968, discusses in some detail the industrial growth in the area of France in which Pontoise is located. He pays special attention to the major industrial developments of Creil, Compiègne, Chauny, and Saint-Quentin in the second half of the nineteenth century.

3. See Christopher Gray's excellent monograph, *Armand Guillaumin*, Chester, Conn., 1972.

4. Tissandier's journal, *La Nature*, was among the most popular magazines of the late nineteenth century. Degas was familiar with it (see Theodore Reff, *Degas, The Artist's Mind*, Metropolitan Museum of Art, New York, 1976).

5. Tissandier also played an important role in the history of photography. He published the first manual for the practical photographer in French, *La Photographie* (Paris, 1840), which appeared in English in 1842.

6. For a provocative discussion of the beginnings of the positivist concept of nature see Jean Ehrard, *L'Idée de nature en France à l'aube des lumières*, Paris, 1970, pp. 385–416.

7. With the exception of the work of Twyman and Adhémar on landscape lithographs in Britain and France in the early and mid-nineteenth century, there is little serious work on the very large tradition of popular landscape. The illustrations in guidebooks, done by unstudied artists such as Nicolas Chapuy and Hubert Clerget, form a cohesive grouping that begs examination. No serious student of landscape and perception in France during the nineteenth century can afford to ignore the so-called "popular" tradition. The best sources are, quite simply, the illustrated guidebooks produced in France from the eighteenth to the early twentieth centuries; the drawings for these illustrations, collected *en masse* by Destailleurs and presented in bound form to the Cabinet des Estampes, Bibliothèque Nationale; and the prints and drawings in local archives and the *archives départementales*.

8. See *The Sand-Flaubert Correspondences*, translated by A.C. McKenzie, New York, 1921. In a letter written from Nohant in August 1867, Sand discusses the peasantry of the north coast of France: "In order to go on with my novel, I must see the countryside near the channel that all the world has not talked about, and where there are real natives at home, peasants, fisherfolk, a real village in the corner of the rocks.... You told me that the population of the coast was the best in the country and that there are real dyed-in-the-wool, simple-hearted men there. It would be good to see their faces, their clothes, the houses, and their horizons." Although it is perfectly clear that Sand was not anti-progressive, she spent a good deal of her intellectual and moral energy on the countryside with its pre-modern inhabitants and very little time in the modern city, the property of Balzac. For Michelet, see *Le Peuple*, Paris, 1846.

9. For Michel's writings, see note 12, below. Laprade is perhaps the most prolific and, in many ways, the most difficult of French nineteenth-century writers concerned with the idea of nature and its relationship to other aspects of modern reality. His three most important books are *Le sentiment de la nature avant le christianisme*, Paris, 1866; *Le sentiment de la nature chez les modernes*, Paris, 1868; and *Histoire du sentiment de la nature*, Paris, 1882. In all these books, especially the latter two, he is obsessed with the relationship between nature and industry, on one hand, and nature and religion, on the other. He defines three kinds of "rapport" with nature in his last and most complex book: the material rapport, associated with industry; the intellectual rapport, relating to science; and the moral rapport, perceivable only through art. His categorizations indicate that he considered any interpenetration between industry and nature conceptually impossible, because the latter predates the former and is, therefore, original. An intellectual history of the idea of nature in the late nineteenth century is absolutely essential before more complete generalizations about the nature of landscape painting of the period can be made.

10. Jules Michelet wrote a good deal of "nature" prose during his exile in the Second Empire and throughout his later years. His writings, emotional as they may seem to the modern reader, were an important early influence on the anarchist geographer, Elisée Reclus (see note 11, below). See Jules Michelet, *La Mer*, Paris, 1861, for a discussion of bathing resorts on the north coast of France that exactly parallels Boudin's early interest in the subject and predates the interest of Monet and the other Impressionists in the beach. The book ends with a glorious section entitled "Vita nuova des nations," in which bathing in the sea is put forward as a means of improving

the moral and mental health of modern man. *La Montagne* was published in 1868 and is essential to any understanding of mountain landscape in the nineteenth century.

11. Elisée Reclus, "Du Sentiment de la nature dans les sociétés modernes," *Revue des Deux Mondes*, 15 May 1866, pp. 352–81. This important article is filled with valuable insights for the student of landscape perception in modern times. Reclus talks about the extraordinary fascination which the "view from above" has for most men (p. 353). He writes a brief history of mountain climbing which is very useful for the beginner. He views the city from the mountain top and compares the vast urban migrations to the barbarian invasions of Rome! Clearly, industrial modernism, the cause of the population movements he so decried, was never admired by this fiercely individualistic geographer.

12. Emile Michel, "Du Paysage et du sentiment de la nature à notre époque," lecture delivered to the Académie de Stanislas, 11 May 1876. In spite of the relative obscurity of its source, this long lecture is one of the three or four indispensable documents to the student of landscape painting and landscape perception in modern times. Michel relates the modern love of the out-of-doors to the crowding of the cities, the nervousness of modern time, and the alienation of the modern individual from his family and his native roots. He decries industry in the city and in the countryside: "Vous savez, messieurs, ce qu'était autrefois la ferme; un amas de bâtiments groupés dans un décousu le plus pittoresque autour d'une grande cour pleine d'animation; aujourd'hui, la ferme est aussi une usine. L'homme y est reduit au rang de serviteur docile des machines" (pp. 14–15).

13. "Tout est bon à dessiner, tout! Quand on sait voir le caractère générale d'un arbre, on voit la figure. Il ne faut pas etre specialiste, c'est la mort de l'art et, par contre, de tout ce que l'on ferait pour l'industrie" (Janine Bailly-Herzberg, ed., *Correspondance de Camille Pissarro*, Paris, 1980, vol. 1, p. 223).

14. *Ibid*.

15. See Joseph C. Sloane, *French Painting between the past and the present: artists, critics, and traditions from 1858 to 1870*, Princeton, 1951 and 1973, p. 100.

16. Anne Coffin Hanson, *Manet and the Modern Tradition*, New Haven and London, 1977 and 1979. Nochlin's views on the subject are set forth in many publications, but summarized in *Realism*, Baltimore, 1971. See also G.P. Weisberg. *The Realist Tradition: French Painting and Drawing, 1830–1900*, Cleveland, 1980.

17. See B.F. Bart, *Flaubert*, New York, 1966; F.W.J. Hemmings, *Culture and Society in France, 1848–1878*, New York, 1971, pp. 113–18; Marcel Ruff, *Baudelaire*, New York, 1966; T.J. Clark, *The Painting of Modern Life, Paris in the Art of Manet and his Followers*, New York, 1985.

18. Zola, the French writer who accepted modernism most fully in his series of novels beginning with *Thérèse Raquin* in 1867, made a convincing fictional case for the decadence of modern society. The industrial worker and the urban proletariat were anything but pleasing characters in Zola's world. For a general discussion of the fear of decadence, which paralleled the so-called "progress of realism" in French literary and artistic culture, see A.E. Carter, *The Idea of Decadence in French Literature*, Toronto, 1958.

19. For a more complete discussion of the frontal, "stick" figures of this type, see chapter 5.

20. Pissarro's distant and planar view of the factory can be contrasted to both earlier and contemporary views of industrial sites. Bonhomme visited a large industrial section of Indret (Loire-Atlantique) in the years immediately following the revolution of 1848 and painted extremely animated, specific, and exciting interior and exterior views showing a large population of workers actively engaged in their various tasks. A good source of industrial views in reproductive form is *La Première Révolution industrielle. La documentation photographique*, 5–296 and 5–297, Paris, 1969 (for the Bonhomme, see plates 13–14).

21. For the exact dates of these constructions, see Henri Le Charpentier, *Calendrier historique de Pontoise: éphémérides quotidiennes de l'histoire de cette ville*, Pontoise, 1882, pp. 83, 95. The finished oil version of this drawing (not in P&V) has been recently discovered and is in the Timkin Gallery, San Diego.

22. The lack of temporal concern separates Pissarro somewhat from French Neo-Classical painters of the nineteenth century. Although Pissarro's esthetic of the late 1860s is decidedly geometric and classically ordered, he does not share their concern for the time of day and the season of the year. This lack of emphasis on the temporal aspects of the scene forces the viewer's attention on the forms themselves and their surface interaction, rather than on the refreshing movement of the wind or the passage of cumulus clouds.

23. For Baudelaire, Poe's essay had an importance beyond its obvious qualities (see Ruff, *op. cit.*). Even Gertrude Stein discovered the significance of abstract composition in the work of Cézanne, which she bought with her brother at Vollard's gallery in 1902. The concept of composition has an enormous and recurring importance in the theory of art throughout the eighteenth and nineteenth centuries and was not an "abstract" development of Cézanne who passed the idea along, through his example, to the Cubists, for whom it became an obsession. See Bart, *op. cit.*; any basic monograph of Manet; and Reff, *op. cit.*

24. All the specific information related to the factories in Saint-Ouen-l'Aumône used in this chapter derives from the property records and the "Plan cadastral parcellaire de la commune de St. Ouen-l'Aumône." The in-formation on the construction of the various wings and additions to the factories can be found in *Propriété non bâtie*, vol. 1. The factories belonging to M. Arneuil are first listed in 1873 and were added to in 1876. Chalon et Brenot started construction in 1872, finished in 1873, added in 1876, 1877, and 1878. The records are rather confusingly listed, and it is possible that entries do not correspond exactly to the date of construction.

25. While generally true, this remark is somewhat qualified because Pissarro was more decidedly motif-conscious in the years 1872–73 than at any other time in his Pontoisian career. For a full discussion of this period and its particular esthetic see chapter 6.

26. The drawing was used as the basis for a fan composition, *Paysage à Upper Norwood*, which is not in P&V, but is included in Mark Gerstein's dissertation, "Impressionist Fan Compositions," Harvard University.

27. The concept of an agro-industrial economy that served local rather than national or corporate needs is very basic to the anarchist philosophy which Pissarro was to adopt so forcefully in the 1880s and 1890s. The bibliography of the idea is vast and beyond the scope of this study. A good summary of the concepts held by Owen and many other social theorists of the nineteenth century can be found in Peter Kropotkin, *The Conquest of Bread*, London, 1906 (first published in Paris under the title *La Conquête du Pain* in 1892), especially pp. 252–60: "Agriculture can only prosper in proximity to factories. And no sooner does a factory appear than the infinite variety of other factories *must* spring up around, so that, mutually supporting one another by their inventions, they increase their productivity" (p. 260).

28. William C. Seitz, *Monet*, New York, 1960, p. 94. Seitz incorrectly dates the picture 1872. Wildenstein dates it 1875 on the basis of a sale of that year (see Daniel Wildenstein, *Claude Monet: biographie et catalogue raisonné*, Lausanne and Paris, 1974, p. 270.

29. Even exterior views of factories published in the popular press in the 1870s were more exciting and animated than Pissarro's cool and confusing *Usine près de Pontoise*. See the dark satanic mill illustrated in *L'Univers Illustré*, vol 13, 1870, p. 69, with an accompanying article by the industrial correspondent, Henry Muller, on consumption and creation – the economic system with an industrial basis on which twentieth-century economic systems are based. All the illustrations for the Muller article depict smoky marvels with working human figures and purposeful activity.

30. Again, the volumes labeled "l'industrie" in the Cabinet des Estampes, Bibliothèque Nationale, are filled with relevant examples. Most of my descriptions have been chosen from random notes on illustrations of industry from the 1860s and 1870s.

31. Linda Nochlin, ed., *Sources and Documents in*

the History of Art: Impressionism and Post-Impressionism, 1874–1904, Englewood Cliffs, 1966.

32. P.G. Hamerton, *Landscape*, London, 1885, pp. 110–14.

33. It is possible that Pissarro turned his attention to the factories again in 1876 because they themselves were enlarging in that year (see note 24, above).

4 L'Hermitage: Home and the Landscape

1. The author is presently working on a study of Monet's private imagery. This will focus on the dialectic of private-public, garden-river which plays such an important part in any proper interpretation of Monet's imagery.

2. Constable is, in many ways, the painter in the history of art who is the most significantly rooted in a domesticated environment. Graham Reynolds, in his excellent *Catalogue of the Constable Collection at the Victoria and Albert Museum* (London, 1960), asserts that Constable never traveled expressly for subjects and that his landscape was dominated by personal associations. He quotes C.R. Leslie, without source, who believed that "the subjects of his works form a history of affections" (p. 17). Constable was capable of forming attachments to new localities to which he might be attracted by bonds of personal "interest" (p. 19).

3. See, for example, the letter to Lucien dated 6 June 1898, Janine Bailly-Herzberg, ed., *Correspondance de Camille Pissarro*, Paris, 1989, vol. 4, p. 487.

4. In fact, the cadastral records of Pontoise indicate that at least two thirds of the buildings in L'Hermitage were constructed in the nineteenth century.

5. Information about the construction of the rue de L'Hermitage is relatively scanty. It is never mentioned in published histories of Pontoisian urbanism, such as Gantois's important study of 1933 (see chapter 1, note 17). This is most probably because the information in the cadastral records is curiously incomplete. Most of the lists of house sales and leases suggest that the building of the street took place in the early 1860s when so much other physical improvement was taking place in Pontoise. All the new houses that lined it were constructed in the first two years of Pissarro's stay in L'Hermitage.

6. For other canvases depicting the same motif, see P&V 83 (dated 1870), 126 (dated 1871), and 190 (misdated in P&V as "vers 1872" and mistitled, *Le Degel, Pontoise*). The two dated examples prove that the motif was in Louveciennes. The style of P&V 309 is also much more in keeping with the paintings of 1869–70. The construction site is present in P&V 190 as well.

7. There are no bourgeois houses in the landscapes painted or drawn by Pissarro in the period between 1855 and 1868. It seems reasonable to assert that he was a painter of the peasant environment in the mid-century tradition until the bourgeois landscape encroached upon his own home landscape.

8. The term was made famous, of course, by Zola, whose well-known definition of art is "un coin de la création vu par un temperament."

9. "Tu me parles d'une étude que tu as commencée, les *Graves*, motif que Guillemet, Daubigny père et fils, et *tutti quanti* ont fait. C'est très beau, mais hélas, quels interprètes! Je me doute bien que tu ne peux travailler beaucoup. Il faut le calme, la réflexion et en meme temps la passion de son sujet pour faire quelque chose de bien" (Bailly-Herzberg, *op. cit.*, vol. 1, p. 341).

10. It is interesting to compare Pissarro's attitude toward his home environment with the exactly contemporary urban art of Manet and Degas. Both the latter artists were also concerned with the "slice" of visual reality. Their compositions are selective, often crowded with figures or forms, definitely not comprehensive. They can be contrasted with the total views or views from above which had dominated urban imagery for several centuries.

11. The fact that Pissarro avoided discussion of the various landscapes in which he painted is, in itself, fascinating. The letters of Chintreuil, Henriet, and many late nineteenth-century landscape painters are filled with references to the landscapes in which they painted. Pissarro is extraordinary for the lack of descriptive attention he paid to his surroundings in his correspondence. His landscape sensibility did not extend to the verbal realm, in spite of the fact that he discussed matters related to art obsessively in what is perhaps the most voluminous correspondence written by any late nineteenth-century painter.

12. Geoffrey Hartman, *Wordsworth's Poetry, 1787–1814*, New Haven, 1964, pp. 84–89.

13. Apart from the two unpublished paintings mentioned in the text and illustrated in pls. 99 and 101, the remaining five are *Rue de l'Hermitage, Pontoise*, (pl. 103); *Rue à l'Hermitage à Pontoise* (pl. 104); *Une rue à l'Hermitage* (pl. 105); *Rue à l'Hermitage, Pontoise, effet de neige*, (P&V 479, ex-collection Meirowsky, Berlin); and *Rue de l'hermitage, Pontoise* (not in P&V, published in John Rewald, *C. Pissarro*, New York, 1960. p. 115.

14. C.-J.-F. Le Carpentier. *Essai sur le paysage*, Paris, 1817, pp. 45–50.

5 The Figure in the Landscape: Pissarro and the Society of Pontoise

1. Frédéric Henriet, *Le Paysagiste aux champs*, Paris, 1876, pp. 117–19.

2. The "smallness" of figures was stressed even in the earliest writings about landscape. Edward Norgate in *Miniatura: or the Art of Limning*, written *c.* 1650, made the following remark: "Now for figure and passengers in your landscape, let them lessen and lose both in size and color as they are neare or farre off" (Martin Hardie ed., Oxford, 1919, p. 53).

3. J.-B. Deperthes, *Théories du paysage*, Paris, 1818, pp. 151–52.

4. C.-J.-F. Le Carpentier, *Essai sur le paysage*, Paris, 1817.

5. *Ibid.*, p. 25; Frédéric Henriet, *Les Campagnes d'un paysagiste*, Paris, 1891, pp. 35–36.

6. Deperthes, *op. cit.*, pp. 68–69.

7. See p. 76.

8. Even Norgate, in his treatise of 1650, finds the landscape painter in the city. The painter, in Norgate's telling of the story, creates a landscape painting from the verbal description of a landscape that a gentleman has just visited. The distance between the painter and site is absolutely central to Norgate's idea of a landscape painter. He does not imitate nature, but recreates it (*op. cit.*, p. 45).

9. Henriet, as usual, summed up this peculiar position better than anyone else: "Passant tour à tour de l'ardent milieu parisien au calme des champs, des discussions fécondes de l'hiver aux paisables travaux de l'été, sa vie est une perpetuelle antithese." ("Shuttling back and forth from the hectic Paris milieu to the peaceful life of the fields, from the fruitful discussions of the winter to the quiet work of the summer, the artist's life is a constant contradiction"; *op. cit.*, p. 105.)

10. *Ibid.*, pp. 101f.

11. *Ibid.*, p. 230.

12. Critics from Thompson to Rewald have stressed the modern artist's alienation from both real and artistic society; historians of modern culture have discussed the alienation of the modern urban individual. The word is all but overburdened with significance. Perhaps Renato Poggioli's *The Nature of the Avant Garde* is the most succinct text dealing with alienation and the modern artist. On the same subject, see also the illuminating article by Fred Orton and Griselda Pollock, "Avant-gardes and Partisans reviewed," *Art History*, vol. 4, no. 3, September 1981, pp. 305ff.

13. See pp. 83–84.

14. See pp. 65–67.

15. *Centenaire de l'Impressionnisme*, Grand Palais, Paris, 1974, pp. 259–60.

16. Two notable exceptions are *La Bonne* (P&V 53, Chrysler Museum) of *c.* 1867, the first full-size figure painting in Pissarro's oeuvre; and the monumental *La Route de Versailles à Louveciennes* (P&V 96, Bührle collection, Zurich) of 1870, in which Madame Pissarro, dressed as a bourgeoise (in a long black dress) converses with a maid across a fence that may symbolize the unbridgeable class barrier.

17. Pissarro's most forcefully social or political art is restricted to drawings, usually made for

private use, and to the one great project, *Turpitudes sociales*, completed in 1890, but never published during Pissarro's lifetime.

18. C.R. Leslie, *Memoirs of the Life of John Constable, R.A.* (2nd edn.), 1945, p. 6. Constable's connection with French landscape painting of the mid-nineteenth century needs to be reviewed. Sensier translated Leslie's entire book, presumably for publication, in the early years of the 1850s. The manuscript is now in the Bibliothèque d'art et d'archéologie, Université de Paris. For Pissarro's attitude toward Constable, see Introduction, note 24.

19. Robert L. Herbert, "City and Country: the rural image in French painting from Millet to Gauguin," *Artforum*, February 1970, pp. 44–55.

20. "Possesseur profond des essences intimes de la vie agreste, familier avec des aspects exacts des choses et des êtres de campagne" (Georges Lecomte, "Camille Pissarro," *Les Hommes d'aujourd'hui*, vol. 8, no. 366, 1890, unpaginated). Lecomte stressed Pissarro's total familiarity with the rural milieu and the peasantry in all his writings about Pissarro. Longer sections can be found in his preface to *L'Exposition Camille Pissarro*, Durand-Ruel, Paris, 1892, pp. 11–18.

21. Arsène Alexandre, preface to *L'Exposition Camille Pissarro*, Durand-Ruel, Paris, 1896, p. 14: "Pissarro comme ouvrier et comme historien des champs" ("Pissarro as a workman and historian of the fields").

22. John Rewald, *C. Pissarro*, New York, 1963, p. 20.

23. "Croit qu'il faudrait vivre comme les paysans pour bien les comprendre. Il me semble qu'il faut être emballé par son sujet pour le bien rendre, mais est-il nécessaire d'être paysan? ... Soyons d'abord artiste et nous aurons la faculté de tout sentir, même un paysage, sans être paysan" (Janine Bailly-Herzberg, ed., *Correspondence de Camille Pissarro*, Paris, 1988, vol. 3, p. 217). This letter, now in the Cabinet des Dessins, Musée du Louvre, is substantially quoted by Georges Lecomte in *Camille Pissarro*, Paris, 1922, p. 95. The letter is among the longer and more despairing of Pissarro's letters. In it, he worries about his upcoming exhibition at Durand-Ruel and about his inability to be a successful artist. It records Pissarro as an "être intermittent", who fears Paris because he visits it so rarely, and who is unable and unwilling to *become* a peasant.

24. In another letter to Lucien, dated 2 May 1887, Pissarro takes an unusually vehement stance against Millet, after the publication of two of the artist's letters in *Le Figaro*. These letters revealed Millet's politically reactionary views and his opposition to the Commune, to Courbet's art, and to socialism. Pissarro commented in his letter on the tendency to identify Millet with the peasantry: "Judging Millet's painting *L'Homme à la Houe*, the socialists had counted Millet in their ranks and held him as one of theirs, thinking that an artist who had suffered so much, a greatly gifted peasant ["ce paysan de genie"] who had translated some of the most heartbreaking aspects of an old peasant's life, necessarily had to share their ideas. Not at all! The great artist himself raised the most indignant objections!" (Bailly-Herzberg, *op. cit.*, vol. 2, p. 157). This letter makes an interesting complement to the letter of 21 April 1892, quoted above.

25. The most succinct statement of this idea that I know is expressed in the preface to George Sand's *François le Champi*, Paris, 1852.

26. It is interesting to note that Pissarro all but ignored the most "modern" aspect of the rural economy of Pontoise, the market, until the last Pontoisian period. His figures generally walk along the road or work in generalized tending poses in the various gardens around the town. The aspect of exchange is underplayed by Pissarro in the vast majority of peasant pictures painted in Pontoise.

27. André Theuriet, *La Vie rustique, compositions et dessins de Léon Lhermitte*, Paris, 1888.

28. There are two exceptions: the painting done in 1875 representing a sower in the foreground and a plowman at work in the background, *Le Semeur, Montfoucault (semeur et laboureur)*, pl. 148, and the study for this painting, *Etude de paysan (semeur à Montfoucault*, P&V 331, ex-collection Bonin (see also *The Sower*, pen and ink, B&L 307, and the woodcut of the same subject in the Ashmolean Museum, Oxford); and *Le Père Melon sciant du bois, Pontoise* (P&V 499), painted in 1879 and owned by Gauguin (Christies, New York, 15 May 1985, lot 16). This last picture is one of two views of Père Melon; the other represents a resting figure (P&V 498). The composition is rather awkward and centered. Again, it is likely that Pissarro made a conscious decision to paint a scene of active labor, centered the figure, simplified the background considerably, and reduced the peripheral elements in the picture. When compared with Henriet's compositions, Pissarro is concerned with considerably simpler pictorial problems to which he addressed himself with a directness unknown to Lhermitte.

29. For this generalization, I am indebted to my wife who has done a great deal of reading in travel literature of the eighteenth, nineteenth and early twentieth centuries. For a parallel in the history of art, one need only read the letters of Gauguin written from Pont Aven, Martinique, or Tahiti. He was obsessed with female figures and sexuality. Pissarro's women, while chaste, clearly relate to this male-dominated travel tradition, another indication of Pissarro's distance from the "reality" around him.

30. Pissarro's only lengthy discussion of his figure paintings occurs in a letter of 22 July 1883 to Lucien: "J'ai peu travaillé dehors cette saison, le temps est peu favorable, et je suis poursuivi par l'idée de faire certains tableaux de figures qui me donnent bien du mal pour la conception. Je fais des espèces de petits cartons; quand j'ai bien ruminé la chose, je me mets à l'oeuvre. J'ai fait poser Nini pour les petites charcutières en plein vent [he refers to the picture in the Tate, P&V 615, for which there are so many pencil drawings and studies] .... Quant à mes grandes toiles, j'en ai deux que tu connais, que je rumine depuis deux ans" (Bailly-Herzberg, *op. cit.*, vol. 1, p. 232).

31. The problem of the inclusion of black in the painter's palette is a considerable one for the student of Impressionism. A great deal of the published literature contends that the color was removed from the palette of the Impressionists by the late 1860s in opposition to the academic method of "greyed" shadows. Lecomte, among Pissarro's biographers and apologists, repeated over and over, beginning with his essay in *Les Hommes d'aujourd'hui, op. cit.*, that Pissarro removed black from his palette by 1865. Pissarro himself surely read these articles and seems to have implicitly accepted and therefore perpetuated several errors of this kind made by Lecomte. He was, like the elder Sisley, anxious to be more "modern" than he in fact was. One can find black in his pictures throughout the 1870s and 1880s.

32. One can find similar frontal figures in pls. 36, 41, 65, 91, 95, 151, and 168, and P&V 60 (Kunsthalle, Mannheim), 138 (Musée d'Orsay, Paris), 139 (private collection), 220 (Durand-Ruel, Paris), 261 (Museo de Bellas Artes, Buenos Aires), 311 (Christie's, London, 30 March 1981, lot 33), 364 (Musée d'Orsay, Paris), 370 (Rudolf Staechelin'sche Familienstiftung, Basel), 438 (Sotheby's, New York, 6 May 1979, lot 208), and 465 (Janice Levin's collection, New York).

33. It is clear, however, that the only major source for these figures is Corot. See particularly *Vue de Tivoli*, 1843 (Robaut 451); *Saint-André-en-Morvan*, 1842 (Robaut 424); *Le Chemin de Sèvres* (Robaut 1464); and *Marcoussis*, 1865 (Robaut 1302).

34. See pp. 40–41.

6 Progressions and Regressions

1. A complete listing of published letters as well as the whereabouts of unpublished letters in public collections can be found in Janine Bailly-Herzberg, ed., *Correspondence de Camille Pissarro*, Paris, 1980, vol. 1, pp. 9–11. Unfortunately, Pissarro's correspondents during the 1860s and 1870s were not so conscientious about saving his letters as he was about saving theirs.

2. See particularly, John Rewald, *The History of Impressionism* (4th revised edn.) New York, 1973. A great many of the documents Rewald uses to construct his remarkably detailed account of the movement were, in fact, the

letters from dealers and artists to Pissarro that he saved throughout his life. The movement was dependent on Pissarro, both as an actor and as an archivist.

3. In fact, the division of late nineteenth-century French painting into decadal units has been so widespread that too few attempts have been made to see longer periods of continuity or, alternatively, shorter periods of more subtle stylistic transformations. The decades from the 1860s to the "fin de siècle" are as prominent as the "thirties," "forties," and "fifties" in the folk history of the United States in the twentieth century. Intensive study of individual artists is needed to counter this trend.

4. Georges Lecomte, preface to *L'Exposition Camille Pissarro*, Durand-Ruel, Paris, February 1892, p. 1.

5. Arsène Alexandre, preface to *L'Exposition Camille Pissarro*, Durand-Ruel, Paris, 1896.

6. J.C. Holl, *Après l'impressionnisme*, Paris, 1910, p. 58.

7. For the letters to Murer, Gachet, and Durer, see Bailly-Herzberg, *op. cit.*, vol. 1. Monet's letters of 1879 are published in most complete form in Daniel Wildenstein, *Claude Monet: biographie et catalogue raisonné*, Paris 1974, vol. 1, pp. 436–38.

8. The importance of Pissarro's extended family to the financial well-being of his immediate family has only recently been adequately analyzed in Ralph E. Shikes and Paula Hays Harper, *Pissarro: his life and work*, New York and London, 1980, pp. 52–53. Pissarro was given considerable support by his family throughout his early career. The exaggerated idea of the avant-garde artist rejected by a selfish bourgeois family and reviled by the public is not at all applicable to Pissarro. It was not until March 1872, when Pissarro was forty-two, and Durand-Ruel started to buy regularly from him, that he gained financial independence from his mother.

9. The addresses are 26, rue de L'Hermitage, 18 bis, rue de L'Hermitage, and 32, quai du Pothuis. They are listed in their probable sequence. Pissarro moved to the first house in October of 1873. He refers to it in a letter to Gachet of 11 October 1873 (Bailly-Herzberg, *op. cit.* vol. 1, p. 81) and in a letter to Duret written on 31 October 1873 (*ibid.*, p. 85). The address at 18 bis rue de L'Hermitage can be found at the bottom of a letter written to Murer on 13 October 1877 (*ibid.*, pp. 105–106). The most definitive treatment of Pissarro's addresses can be found in T. Meray's article, "Pissarro à Pontoise", *L'Echo de Cergy-Pontoise*, December, 1974. Unfortunately, Meray turns up more questions than he, or anyone, can answer.

10. This view is somewhat at odds with the prevailing idea expressed in the nineteenth century and today that the Impressionists were relatively untrained "anti-academic" artists. Georges Lecomte, in his writings about Pissarro, from the initial article, "Camille Pissarro," for *Les Hommes d'Aujourd'hui* (vol. 8, no. 366) in 1890 to the full-scale biography of 1922, stressed the importance of Pissarro's *lack* of training for the formation of his own authentic style. With a secure knowledge of Pissarro's long period of artistic apprenticeship under several important artists of the mid-nineteenth century, modern historians of his career have realized the essential inaccuracy of Lecomte's ideas. Major students of Pissarro's sources and training include Tabarant, Rewald, Cogniat, and Champa.

11. This rather uncomplimentary, although essentially correct, view is commonly found in general books on Impressionism or late nineteenth-century French art. Focillon, Meier-Graefe, Francastel, and many subsequent historians of the movement have considered Pissarro to be a good, safe, and uninventive artist.

12. The literature on modernization is vast. The best bibliographical guide to the literature is John Brode, *The Process of Modernization, an annotated bibliography of the socio-cultural aspects of development*, Cambridge, Mass., 1970. A ready source of summaries of the major theorists of modernization in the late nineteenth and early twentieth centuries is Lewis A. Coser, *Masters of Sociological Thought*, New York, 1971. See particularly the sections on Durkheim, Simmer, and Weber, pp. 129–263.

13. Bailly-Herzberg, *op. cit.*, vol. 2, p. 30 (3 March 1886): "La France est malade, mais de quoi? – voilà la question! Elle est malade de transformation, elle peut y passer, c'est certain, cela dépend des autres pays de l'Europe. S'ils sont eux aussi tant soit peu dans la même voie, on en verra du neuf. Evidemment, cela ne peut durer!" This letter and several other remarks in the correspondence indicate that the picture of the "political" and "radical" Pissarro first presented by Benedict Nicolson in "The Anarchism of Camille Pissarro," *The Arts*, [London], no. 11, [1946], presents only one side of Pissarro's complex nature. He desired stability and a "return" to a simple, ordered world. His radicalism pales in comparison with many social and political radicals of the twentieth century.

14. For a short and suggestive article on Pissarro's sources in the history of European art, see Christopher Lloyd, "Camille Pissarro and Hans Holbein the Younger," *Burlington Magazine*, vol. 117, November 1975, pp. 722–26. It is, however, difficult to use the word "source" with any precision in Pissarro studies. His transformations of a source are often so sweeping that it is perfectly possible to deny its existence as a source. He seems to have used the history of art very broadly and, perhaps, with an imperfect visual memory. For juxtapositions of some of Pissarro's works with various sources in European art, see also Christopher Lloyd, *Camille Pissarro*, Geneva, 1981, pp. 44, 50, 51, 98, 120, 128, where the author establishes evocative links with artists such as Raphael, Hobbema, Pieter de Hooch, Francesco Albani, etc.

15. The word "constructivist" is used in this way not in connection with the early twentieth-century artists of that name, but as Theodore Reff uses it in his analysis of the development of the "constructive stroke" in the painting of Cézanne. See note 39 below.

16. For a brief and highly critical discussion of Pissarro's use of these accent colors, see Kermit Champa, *Studies in Early Impressionism*, New Haven and London, 1973, pp. 70–71.

17. *Ibid.*, pp. 69, 71, and 73–79.

18. "Il faut étudier les valeurs. Nous ne voyons pas la même façon. Vous voyez vert et moi je vois gris et blonde. Mais ce n'est pas une raison pour que vous ne travailliez pas les valeurs, car cela est au fond du tout." This quotation seems to have come from Pissarro himself and was repeated several times in the early literature. One source is Alexandre, *loc. cit.*, p. 7.

19. Champa discusses the larger pictures, which were evidently painted for the Salon, more fully than any other commentator. He treats the views of L'Hermitage as a series in the manner of Monet's series views painted from the Louvre in 1866 and 1867. The idea is an interesting one and is at least partially valid. The major pictures represent the sides of the valley in which the hamlet was situated. They are, in this way, a more "complete" series than Monet's views from the Louvre, which face in only two directions. The site maps given in this book offer a visual recreation of the grouping. See Champa, *op. cit.*, pp. 73–79.

20. For further discussion, see pp. 108–9.

21. See particularly Renoir's *Le Pont des Arts* (Norton Simon Museum, Pasadena, California) and Monet's *The Quay of the Louvre* (Municipal Museum, The Hague).

22. Adolphe Joanne, *Les Environs de Paris*, Paris, 1856, pp. 268–69: "The banks of the river Oise offer pleasant walks. From the hillsides of L'Hermitage (in the northeast) beautiful views can be enjoyed. These hillsides (15 minutes walking distance from the town) owe their name to a hermitage that was established there in the fifteenth century by Jean Dupin. Alternatively, you can walk up the Viosne valley toward Osny. It is approximately a two-hour walk (there and back). Osny is a village with 467 inhabitants, pleasantly located in the Viosne valley, where several mills are powered by the river. From Osny, it is possible to return to Pontoise along the right bank of the Viosne."

As this brief excerpt from Joanne's text suggests, there is considerable work to be done on the frequent intersections between the views of a place offered by guidebooks and those offered by landscape painters. The fact that Impressionist nature is very much the nature experienced by the weekend traveler has been noticed many times in general studies of the movement, but the connection with the guidebooks that orchestrated and even determined the movements and the ideas of these leisure-loving landscape figures has never been clearly expressed. With few exceptions, like the one under discussion, Pissarro's does not seem to have perceived places in the same way as a guidebook tourist. A study of the connection would be much more profitable for Monet, Renoir. and Sisley.

23. There is considerable need for an analysis of the painting done in the environs of Bougival, Louveciennes, and Marly-le-Roi at the end of the 1860s and in the first years of the 1870s. Champa has begun the process in *Studies in Early Impressionism*, but his treatment is essentially ahistorical, and a greater understanding of Impression could result from more thorough investigation of existing source material relating these key sites, for example: the work on Louveciennes by Jacques and Monique Lay (*Louveciennes hier et aujourd'hui*, Louveciennes, 1975) and the excellent municipal archives in all three towns (for a keener apprehension of the social structure of the landscape); the contemporary guidebook literature, particularly the evocative essay by Victorien Sardou in the *Guide à Paris et aux environs de Paris* prepared for the Exposition Universelle of 1867; the extensive collection of photographs of Louveciennes taken in the period 1856–75, now in the collection of Mme. Guy Merle d'Aubigny in Paris (for an analysis of the differences between "real" and illusionistic landscapes).

24. For a discussion of the complex interrelationship between Monet and Pissarro during the early years of Impressionism, see the exhibition catalogue, *Pissarro*, London, Paris, and Boston, 30 October 1980–9 August 1981, pp. 16–17 and 79–81.

25. John Rewald, *C. Pissarro*, New York, 1963. The parallel, while interesting and convincing, is not quite as close as it could be. Another, unpublished version of the *Route de Versailles*, by Pissarro, from the George A. Lucas collection, Maryland Institute, on indefinite loan to the Walters Art Gallery, Baltimore, is much closer in both composition and viewpoint. See the London-Paris-Boston exhibition catalogue, *op. cit.*, p. 80.

26. The close connection between Turner and Pissarro has not been emphasized in recent literature, but was very important both for Pissarro and for his early apologist-critic, Georges Lecomte. Lecomte, anxious as he was to prove that Pissarro and not Seurat had discovered the optical properties of the simultaneous contrast of color and had applied them to pictures, traces Pissarro's interest in complimentaries to Turner (*op. cit.*). While Lecomte's notions are both exaggerated and incorrect, he was right in giving such importance to Turner. Pissarro's palette of the early 1870s was very much affected by the pastel palette of Turner's late watercolors and oils. Even the importance given to the watercolor

process increased for Pissarro in the same period due to the example of Turner.

27. Lloyd, *Camille Pissarro*.

28. Of modern historians of art, only the Germans, notably Meier-Graefe and Novotny, have given prominence to Corot in their evolutionary histories of modern art. Corot is, with Pissarro, the crucial link in a line of neo-classical painters that runs from Poussin to Seurat and plays what is arguably the dominant role in significant French painting of the seventeenth, eighteenth, and nineteenth centuries. Corot studies have lacked the probity and depth of analysis that has characterized the study of Impressionist and Post-Impressionist artists by American, British, and French art historians of the last generation.

29. For the best discussions of seasonality in French writings on nineteenth-century landscape, see P.-H. de Valenciennes, *Eléments de perspective pratique, à l'usage des artistes*, Paris, 1800, pp. 427–79; C.-J.-F. Le Carpentier, *Essai sur le paysage*, Paris, 1817, pp. 51–100; and J.-B. Deperthes, *Théories du paysage*, Paris, 1818, pp. 37, 69. Later in the century, the writings about landscape tend to underplay both seasonality and the analogous concept of the four times of the day in favor of discussions of idealization, the search for a motif, and the social life of the landscape painter. It is probably fair to say that most significant writing about landscape produced in the period between 1855 and 1890 deals with the social landscape, with the prevailing changes in culture that necessitated a "return" to nature. In spite of this relative lack of attention in the literature, the idea of seasonality was very important in landscape practice. For some discussion of Pissarro's use of the seasons as part of what Le Carpentier called "la grammaire du paysage," see chapter 4. Seasonality was of enormous importance for Monet also; in fact, it could be profitably argued that he used the seasons and the four times of the day as the major temporal divisions in his landscape titles and that his love of the transient aspects of nature has its theoretical roots in the writing of Deperthes.

30. The best discussions of Poussin's cycle are Anthony Blunt, *Nicolas Poussin*, New York, 1967, pp. 322–26, and Kurt Badt, *Die Kunst des Nicolas Poussin*, Cologne, 1968, pp. 556–68. Badt's discussion incorporates much of the earlier literature, paying particular attention to Friedländer.

31. Millet's *Four Seasons* were exhibited as a group in the large Millet retrospective in Paris and London, 1976 (for a complete discussion, see Robert L. Herbert, *Millet*, Paris, 1976, pp. 293–301). The canvases were exhibited in the Gavet sale in 1875 (an exhibition and sale that Pissarro probably attended, see note 45 below), but they were probably unknown to Pissarro in 1872–73.

32. See chapter 2, note 22 for reference to Doré's illustrations. There is another popular illus-

tration of the fair which dates from 1886, three years after the Pissarro family left Pontoise and its environs.

33. Champa, *op. cit.*, p. 75.

34. Gustave Geffroy "L'Art d'aujourd'hui: Camille Pissarro," *Le Journal*, 18 April 1896.

35. The house at 26 rue de L'Hermitage was described by Pissarro thus: "c'est pas gai, mais c'est propre, et il y a beaucoup de place" (*Lettres impressionnistes au Dr. Gachet et à Murer*, Paris, 1957, p. 29). It is tempting to say that Pissarro's new ruralism in the mid-1870s was prompted by the move itself, and there is no persuasive evidence to the contrary in the correspondence with Duret.

36. Bailly-Herzberg, *op. cit.*, vol. 1, p. 95. (20 October 1874).

37. Sheldon Cheney, *The Role of Vincent Van Gogh's Copies in the Development of his Art*, Garland Press, 1976, p. 276. See also, Herbert, *op. cit.*, p. 238.

38. It is the physical constriction of the landscape motifs chosen by Pissarro that separates his landscape esthetic of the mid-1870s from that of the 1860s. Champa's discussion of Pissarro's career in the earlier decade applies, in most ways, equally well to the new ruralism period.

39. Reff's article, "Cézanne's Constructive Stroke," *Art Quarterly*, Autumn 1963, is really the best and the only intelligent study of the relationship between Cézanne and Pissarro in the decade of the 1870s. It is, of course, a commonplace to say that Pissarro "tamed" and "ordered" Cézanne's voluptuous esthetic, but the precise mechanics of that ordering has been very little discussed. Since Reff's article, more interest overall has been expressed on the complex and multilayered relationship between Pissarro and Cézanne; the reader could, in particular, refer to the chapter, "Pissarro, Cézanne and the School of Pontoise" in Shikes and Harper, *op. cit.*, pp. 115–30; see also Lloyd, *Camille Pissarro*, pp. 62–72, for a telling juxtaposition of several of their works, and their shared interest in constructive strokes. The relationship between the two painters will receive investigation in an exhibition planned for Los Angeles, Dallas, and Paris in 1994.

40. Similarities between the two periods led both Ludovic-Rodo Pissarro and, subsequently, the Louvre to date *Paysage à Pontoise* (P&V 309, Musée d'Orsay) to 1875 rather than to the more accurate 1869–70. For further discussion of this misdating, see p. 102, above.

41. See note 7 above for the correspondence.

42. "Je persiste à penser que la nature agreste rustique avec animaux, est ce qui correspond le mieux à votre talent. Vous n'avez pas le sentiment décoratif de Sisley ni l'oeil fantastique de Monet, mais vous avez qu'ils n'ont pas, un sentiment intime et profond de la nature, et une puissance de pinceau qui fait qu'un beau tableau de vous quelque chose d'absolument assis. Si j'avais un conseil à vous donner, je vous dirais ne pensez ni à

Monet, ni à Sisley, ne vous préoccupez, pas de ce qu'ils font, allez de votre côté, dans votre voie de la nature rustique, vous irez dans une voie nouvelle, aussi loin et aussi haut qu'aucun maître" (Bailly-Herzberg, *op. cit.*, vol. 1, pp. 87–88).

43. "Merci à vos conseils, vous devez savoir qu'il y a longtemps que je pensais à ce que vous me dites. Ce qui m'a empêché longtemps de faire la nature vivante, c'est tout simplement la facilité d'avoir des modèles à mon disposition, non seulement pour faire le tableau mais pour étudier la chose sérieusement. Du reste, je ne tarderai pas à essayer encore d'en faire, ce sera fort difficile car vous devez vous douter que ces tableaux ne peuvent se faire toujour sur nature, c'est à dire, dehors. Ce sera bien difficile" (*ibid.*, vol. 1, pp. 87–88).

44. See P&V 859 (1893) and 1405 (1886).

45. Two sheets closely related to the painting are in the Fink Collection, Palm Beach, Florida.

46. The connection between Millet and Pissarro has been made in the Pissarro literature since Duret. Lecomte and Geffroy wrote at some length about it, but their remarks have more to do with the general similarity between the peasant genre of the two artists than with any specific connections between the paintings and drawings. Pissarro himself had a complicated and not altogether consistent idea of Millet. His letters of the 1880s and 1890s show a mixed respect and contempt for the earlier artist. whom he accuses, in the final analysis, of sentimentality. Pissarro could have been exposed to the work of Millet in the mid-1870s in a variety of ways. Popular prints of his compositions were very common by that period, and it is likely that Pissarro either possessed several or was familiar with them. The painter owned at the time of his death three etchings either by Millet (D 33) or by his brother, Jean-Baptiste Millet (D 32 and 34), but it is not known when he acquired these prints. The largest grouping of Millet's drawings, paintings, and pastels was assembled for the famous Gavet sale in 1875 (see Herbert, *op. cit.* p. 307). Given Pissarro's interest at this time in peasant genre and in compositions in which the figure dominated its setting, it is reasonable to assume that he attended the exhibition. However, many of the most notable of his peasant compositions and those most ressembling Millet prototypes were executed before the Gavet sale. A more detailed discussion can be found in B & L, pp. 17–18 for the period under scrutiny, and also pp. 39–40 and 43. In this context, it is safe to say that, while Millet was important to Pissarro as an artist who addressed himself to many of the same problems, Pissarro seems to have steered clear of Millet as a direct source for either his style or his compositions. His motifs often have their prototypes in Millet, but his handling of those motifs is decidedly different.

47. See Rewald, *C. Pissarro*, and Champa, *op. cit.*, pp. 74–75.

48. This earlier dating was initiated by Ludovic-Rodo Pissarro in the catalogue raisonné of 1939. There is, however, no documentary evidence supporting the separation of this painting from the others in which the palette knife was used in all or part of the process of execution. Rewald perpetuates the incorrect earlier dating in his monograph of 1963 (pp. 100–101).

49. It is difficult to argue with any consistency that Impressionism represents a shift in the history of art from chiaroscuro or value construction to hue construction. Although the increase in the availability of tube-packed and uniformly processed paints made it easier for the Impressionist painter to experiment with color than it had been for his Barbizon School precursor, the importance of value structure within the Impressionist formal vocabulary is difficult to exaggerate. Contrary to many written opinions, Impressionist paintings, especially those of the 1870s, look perfectly clearly structured in black and white photographs, and simple examination of them shows that they are much more monochromatic than critics have been willing to admit. The idea that Pissarro or Monet eliminated black from their palettes by the late 1860s, as Lecomte would have us believe, is nonsense when one stands in front of almost any painting by either man done in the 1870s. R.F. Brown's reconstruction of Pissarro's palette in 1870–75 fails to include the black which is very evident in the pictures themselves ("The color technique of Camille Pissarro," unpublished Ph.D. thesis, Harvard University, 1952). The idea that the interest in hue replaced interest in value is a very appealing one, but disregards both the precedent of painters like Turner and Delacroix and the actual practice of the Impressionists.

50. These two paintings, *Bords de l'Oise: environs de Pontoise*, (P&V 357) and *Péniches à Pontoise* (pl. 406), look back to a painting of the *péniches* on the Seine executed in 1872 under the direct influence of Monet, *La Seine a Port-Marly* (P&V 187). Again, the images constitute a return for Pissarro to modernist, Monet-oriented imagery.

51. Pissarro reused the compositions with the mechanical threshers in his last hymn to "la vie rurale," *Les Travaux des Champs*, a publication with a complex history for which Camille Pissarro designed compositions that were engraved on wood by his son, Lucien. The composition of the mechanical thresher was in fact posthumously published in Emile Moselly, *La Charrue d'érable*, Paris, 1912.

52. It is interesting in this context to note that Daniel Wildenstein has published a similar pairing of a tiny *esquisse* and a larger painting executed by Monet in 1874. The two images, W 319 (Musée d'Orsay) and W 320 (Musée Marmottan), are unique in Monet's published oeuvre. Wildenstein does not speculate on the reasons for this oddity within Monet's career. Other examples of a "sketchy" and a

"finished" composition published in the first volume of Wildenstein's catalogue raisonné are virtually identical in size, indicating that they were independent compositions, one of which was "worked up" for sale or exhibition. They make it perfectly clear that Monet worked "vertically" on his compositions, painting layer on layer, rather than blocking out a composition, finding tonalities in a small format, and applying those findings toward the creation of a larger, exhibition picture. A great deal of work still remains to be done on Impressionist working methods, but see Bernard Dunstan, *Painting Methods of the Impressionists*, New York, 1976, and Christopher Lloyd and Richard Thomson. *Impressionist drawings from British public and private collections*, The Arts Council of Great Britain, 1986 (an exhibition catalogue that specifically explored the role of drawing in Impressionism). A thorough evaluation of the complex importance of drawing within Pissarro's oeuvre is given in Richard R. Brettell and Christopher Lloyd, *Catalogue of the drawings by Camille Pissarro in the Ashmolean Museum*, Oxford, 1980.

53. This fact is, in itself, suggestive that Pissarro thought rather less of *esquisses* than he did of paintings. Unlike Sisley, Renoir, and Monet, Pissarro was an assiduous dater of his pictures. He was, in fact, obsessed with his own pictorial development as reflected by the history of his paintings. Unfortunately, he did not date his prints, gouaches, drawings, or watercolors with the same conscientiousness.

54. Champa, *op. cit.*, pp. 70–71. Unfortunately, Champa's analysis, while correct in large measure, does not seem to have been based on a direct examination of the paintings. The sketch for *The Towpath* is in the Fitzwilliam Museum, Cambridge.

55. It is interesting to note that Pissarro virtually never used the word *esquisse* in his surviving correspondence. Ludovic-Rodo Pissarro's use of *étude* in the catalogue raisonné to describe these small studies would have been applauded by his father. The word *esquisse*, with its implication of rapid movement of the hand and a consequent summary treatment of the subject, was perhaps too ephemeral for Pissarro, who was, as this book implies, obsessed with the ordering of appearance.

56. This lack of any real difference in the surface character of the *esquisses* and the larger paintings differentiates Pissarro's pairings from the sole example of such a pair in the work of Monet, mentioned in note 52 above. The execution of the larger picture is decidedly more complex and descriptive in the Monet pairing.

57. Among all early writers on Pissarro, Lecomte was the only one to understand fully the manifold distances between art and reality that Pissarro's art presupposes. In his article of 1890, "Camille Pissarro" for *Les Hommes d'aujourd'hui*, he claimed that "M. Pissarro fixe au pastel ou à l'aquarelle les effets

transitoires, puis, loin du site, se livre à un travail de synthèse philosophique . . . . Seuls, subsistent les caractères durables." The passage was reused with only slight changes in the introduction by Lecomte to *L'Exposition Camille Pissarro* (Durand-Ruel, Paris, February 1892, p. 9), as well as in Lecomte's review of the same exhibition in *Art et Critique*, 6 February, 1892, pp. 49–52. The passage shows the degree to which Pissarro was concerned *throughout* his career with the kind of "synthetic" or anti-scenic concept of landscape painting for which the Post-Impressionist period is so well known.

Although there are many overstatements and historical inaccuracies in the criticism of Lecomte and Mirbeau in the 1890s, it is likely that Pissarro himself read and approved their writings before they were published and considered them to have been a fair representation of his own evolution. The departures they make from fact are, therefore, revealing in themselves and deserve separate consideration.

58. Wildenstein. *op. cit.*, pp. 427–39.
59. Much of this information is derived from conversations with John House and observations of the canvases themselves. It is absolutely necessary that work on Impressionist technique be done from analysis of the works themselves rather than from the often inaccurate information provided by the early critics.
60. Like all historical generalizations, there are exceptions to those made in this chapter. Pissarro's interest in the human figure did become decidedly more important to him in 1879, especially with the large studies of "Père Melon" at work and at rest (P&V 498 and 499), but he began to re-examine the

human figure not in 1878, but in 1879. It is interesting to note that two of the figural genre compositions begun in 1878 (P&V 471 and 472) are "reversions" of a painted study of 1875 (P&V 332), which had clearly been made on the advice of Duret in the Montfoucault period. Again, the model of progressions and regressions, of periods that exist in an almost antithetical relationship to those that immediately precede and follow them, but that contain works that echo, often directly, a picture from two or three years earlier, is readily observable in Pissarro's career. The same generalizations cannot be made about the work of any other major painter in the 1870s.

61. See Brettell and Lloyd, *op. cit.*, pp. 126.
62. Bailly-Herzberg, *op. cit.*, vol. 1, p. 204. The letter was written on 9 May 1883 and sent before Pissarro moved to Eragny.

Conclusion

1. "Assurément, Camille Pissarro a peint des milliers d'études et des certaines de toiles d'après nature. Mais, de bonne heure dans sa carrière de peintre passionnément chercheur, la plupart de ses toiles les plus importantes sont composées à l'atelier, avec beaucoup de méditation, d'après les études faites directement en face du motif, dans toute la vérité de l'émotion ressentie . . . Camille Pissarro s'abandonne librement à sa sensation, qu'il ne sacrifie à aucune théorie et à aucun système. Mais il construit, il choisit, il ordonne" (Georges Lecomte, *Camille Pissarro*, Paris, 1922, p. 69).
2. The useful distinction established by Spinoza in his *Ethics* between *natura naturans* and *natura naturata* is enlightening in the present context. Pissarro, of all the Impressionists, was undoubtedly more concerned with *natura naturans* than with *natura naturata*, thus revealing more in common with such twentieth-century artists as Mondrian rather than with Matisse, for instance.
3. Frédéric Henriet, *Le Paysagiste aux champs*, Paris, 1876, p. 134.
4. Lecomte, *op. cit.*, p. 35.
5. See the exhibition catalogue, *Pissarro*, Hayward Gallery, London, 30 October 1980–11 January 1981; Grand Palais, Paris, 30 January–27 April 1981; Museum of Fine Arts, Boston, 19 May–9 August 1981.
6. John Rewald, *The History of Impressionism* (1st edn.) New York, 1946.
7. See the exhibition catalogue *Post-Impressionism*, Royal Academy of Arts, London, and National Gallery of Art, Washington, D.C., 1979–80.
8. M. and G. Blunden, *Impressionists and Impressionism*, Geneva, 1970 and 1980; and Phoebe Pool, *Impressionism*, London, 1967.
9. Kermit Champa, *Studies in Early Impressionism*, New Haven and London, 1973.
10. Daniel Wildenstein, *Claude Monet: biographie et catalogue raisonné*, 4 vols., Lausanne and Paris, 1974.
11. Kirk T. Varnedoe and Thomas P. Lee, *Caillebotte*, Houston, 1976–1977; and Christopher Gray, *Armand Guillaumin*, Chester, Conn., 1972.
12. Gray, *op. cit.*
13. Theodore Reff, *Degas, The Artist's Mind*, Metropolitan Museum of Art, New York, 1976.
14. John House, *Monet: Nature into Art*, New Haven and London, 1986.

Select Bibliography

The following bibliography is not intended to be exhaustive. It contains all major items cited in the references as well as other books that the author has either consulted frequently or has used as the basis for a concept.

Pissarro

The most intelligent and comprehensive bibliography devoted to Pissarro was compiled by Martha Ward for the 1980–81 exhibition held in London, Paris, and Boston (see *Pissarro, 1830–1903*, Boston, 1980, pp. 250–261). There are two earlier bibliographies of the Pissarro literature, both of which make a complete listing of the source material redundant in this context. Ludovic Rodo Pissarro and Lionello Venturi included an exhaustive bibliography, arranged chronologically, in *Camille Pissarro, son art–son oeuvre*, 2 vols. Paris, 1939. Their listing includes all newspaper articles, reviews of exhibitions, ephemera, and books about Pissarro published before their date of publication. Research for this book has included most of the material listed in this bibliography, but with emphasis on the nineteenth-century critical literature and the more important books, articles, and reviews from the twentieth century.

Modern sources for the study of Pissarro are included in the excellent annotated bibliography in John Rewald's revised and expanded edition of *The History of Impressionism*, New York, 1973. Although necessarily more selective than Pissarro and Venturi, Rewald includes all important books, exhibition catalogues, and articles. He omits most newspaper articles and references to recent editions of popular monographs on Pissarro. Although several publications post-date Rewald's bibliography, none contribute new material or new interpretations. One important omission in the Rewald bibliography is Barbara Shapiro's excellent exhibition catalogue, *Camille Pissarro: the Impressionist Printmaker*, Boston, 1973. Perhaps the best of the recent monographs on Pissarro is the late Raymond Cogniat's *Pissarro*, Paris, 1974.

Pissarro's complete correspondence is currently being published (Janine Bailly-Herzberg, ed., *Correspondance de Camille Pissarro*, Paris, 1980–89). The first four volumes (1865–1894) have appeared and the final one is forthcoming. John Rewald includes references to all the published correspondence of Pissarro in *The History of Impressionism*, p. 645. Since publication of this bibliography, the Pissarro family has sold their holdings of the letters written to the artist throughout his life. Although widely dispersed throughout the world at present, the most important letters are quoted either in whole or in part in *Archives de Camille Pissarro*, Hôtel Drouot, Paris, 21 November 1975. The letters from Monet to Pissarro have been recently published in Daniel Wildenstein's *Claude Monet: biographie et catalogue raisonné*, 4 vols., Lausanne and Paris, 1974.

In addition to the published correspondence. the author has consulted the following archival sources:

Pissarro Archives: Ashmolean Museum, Oxford   These contain the letters written by Lucien and Camille Pissarro between 1883 and 1903, the correspondence of Lucien himself, and the letters of other family members, including some letters from Madame Pissarro, Camille's wife.

Duret Archives: Cabinet des Dessins, Musée du Louvre, Paris   These includes the important correspondence between Camille Pissarro and the critic Théodore Duret.

Murer Archives: Bibliothèque d'Art et d'Archéologie: Université de Paris, Paris   These include the correspondence between Pissarro and Eugène Murer.

Landscape Painting

Adhémar, Jean, *Les Lithographies de paysage en France à l'époque romantique*, Paris, 1937.

Adhémar, Jean, *Les Joies de la nature au XVIIIème siècle*, Paris, 1971.

Allemand, Hector, *Causeries sur le paysage*, Lyons, 1877.

Bacler, Dalbe, *Menales pittoresques et historiques des paysagistes*, Paris, 1803.

Bart, Benjamin F., *Flaubert's Landscape Descriptions*, Ann Arbor, 1956.

Baudelaire, Charles, *Art in Paris: 1845–1862*, ed. and trans. Jonathan Mayne, London and New York, 1965.

Baudelaire, Charles, *The Painter of Modern Life*, ed. and trans. Jonathan Mayne, London and New York, 1965.

Boisseau, Henri, *Cours de paysage*, Paris and London, 1843.

Bouyer, Raymond, *Le Paysage dans l'art*, Paris, 1894.

Breton, Jules, *Oeuvres poetiques*, Paris, 1887.

Champa, Kermit, *Studies in Early Impressionism*, New Haven and London, 1973.

Charlot, Marcel, *Paysages et paysans*, Paris, 1898, illustrated by Lhermitte.

Couture, Thomas, *Paysage: entretiens d'atelier*, Paris, 1869.

Crepy, J.B., *Nouveau cayer de paysage*, Paris, 1781.

Deperthes, J.-B., *Théories du paysage*, Paris, 1818.

Deperthes, J.-B., *Histoire de l'art de paysage*, Paris, 1822.

Du Camp, Maxime, *Les Beaux Arts à l'exposition universelle et aux salons de 1861 à 1867*, Paris, 1868.

Fardwell, Frances Virginia, *Landscape in the works of Marcel Proust*, New York, 1948.

Fraipont, G., *L'art de peindre du paysage*, Paris, 1892.

Hamerton, P.G., *Landscape*, London, 1885.

Henriet, Frédéric, *L'Été du paysagiste*, Paris, 1866.

Henriet, Frédéric, *Le Paysagiste aux champs*, Paris, 1876 and Château Thierry, 1913.

Henriet, Frédéric, *Les Campagnes d'un paysagiste*, Paris, 1891.

Henriet, Frédéric, *Les Eaux-fortes de Lhermitte*, Paris, 1905.

Henriet, Frédéric, Champfleury and A. de la Fizelière, *La Vie et l'oeuvre de Chintreuil*, Paris, 1874.

Herbert, Robert L., *Neo-Impressionism*, New York, 1968.

Herbert, Robert L., "City and Country: the rural image in French painting from Millet to Gauguin," *Artforum*, February 1970, pp. 44–55.

Lanoé, G. and T. Brice, *Histoire de l'école française de paysage*, Paris, 1901.

Lanoé, G. and T. Brice, *Histoire de l'école française de paysage depuis Chintreuil jusqu' à 1900*, Paris, 1905.

Laprade, Victor de, *Le Sentiment de la nature avant le christianisme*, Paris, 1866.

Laprade, Victor de, *Le Sentiment de la nature chez les modernes*, Paris, 1868.

Laprade, Victor de, *Histoire du sentiment de la nature*, Paris, 1882.

Le Carpentier, C.-J.-F., *Essai sur le paysage*, Paris, 1817.

Lenoble, Robert, *Histoire de l'idée de nature*, Paris, 1969.

Leslie, C.R., *Memoirs of the Life of John Constable, R.A.*, London, 1843 and 1945.

Mandevare, N.-A.-M., *Principes raisonnés du paysage à l'usage des écoles des départements de l'empire français*, Paris, 1804.

Michel, Emile, "Du paysage et du sentiment de la nature à notre époque," Académie de Stanislas, Paris, 11 May 1876.

Michelet, Jules, *Le Peuple*, Paris, 1846.

Michelet, Jules, *La Mer*, Paris, 1861.

Michelet, Jules, *Le Montagne*, Paris, 1868.

Mornet, Daniel, *Le Sentiment de la nature en France de J.J. Rousseau à Bernadin St. Pierre*, Paris, 1907.

Nochlin, Linda, ed., *Sources and Documents in the History of Art: Impressionism and Post-Impressionism, 1874–1904*, Englewood Cliffs, 1966.

Nochlin, Linda, *Realism and Tradition in Art: 1848–1900*, Englewood Cliffs, 1966.

Nochlin, Linda, *Realism*, Baltimore, 1971.

Paulhan, Fr., *L'Esthétique du paysage*, Paris, 1913.

Poinat, Jean, *Les Maîtres du paysage en littérature*, Montbuisson, 1916.

Reclus, Elisée, "Du Sentiment de la nature dans les sociétés modernes," *Revue des Deux Mondes*, 15 May 1866, pp. 352–81.

Reidemeister, Leopold, *Auf den Spuren der Maler der Ile de France*, Berlin, 1963.

Reynolds, Graham, *Catalogue of the Constable Collection in the Victoria and Albert Museum*, London, 1960.

Rieu-Edelmann, *La Forêt de Fontainebleau dans l'estampe et la photographie d'après les collections topographiques du cabinet des estampes de la Bibliothèque Nationale*, Diplome de l'Ecole de Louvre, Paris, 2 October 1973.

Rilke, Rainer-Marie, *Le Paysage*, trans. Maurice Betz, Paris, 1942.

Sagne, J., *Le Sentiment de la nature dans l'oeuvre de Stendhal*, Zurich, 1932.

Sloane, Joseph C., *French Painting Between the Past and the Present: artists, critics, and traditions from 1848 to 1871*, Princeton, 1951 and 1973.

Thenot, *Cours complet de paysage*, Paris, 1834.

Thenot, *Les Règles du paysage*, Paris, 1841.

Thomson, D.C., *The Barbizon School*, London, 1891.

Thoré, Théophile, *Salons de W. Burger, 1861–1868*, Paris, 1870.

Twyman, Michael, *Lithography, 1800–1850*, London, 1970.

Valenciennes, P.-H. de, *Eléments de perspective pratique à l'usage des artistes, suivis de réflexions et conseils à un élève sur la peinture, et particulièrement sur le genre du paysage*, Paris, 1800.

Vander-Burch, H., *Essai sur la peinture de paysage à l'huile*, Paris, 1839.

Villeneuve, *Cours de paysage*, Paris, 1837 and 1841.

Pontoise and its Environs

Allezard, Danielle and Lucienne Lamy, *L'Agriculture du Vexin française*, Paris, 1970.

Almanach historique de Pontoise et du IIème arrondissement de Seine-et-Oise, Pontoise, 1803.

Annuaire de l'arrondissement de Pontoise, 1889: Administration, Commerce, Industrie, Pontoise, 1889.

Annuaire de Seine-et-Oise, 1872, Versailles, 1872.

Bougeatre, Eugène, *La Vie rurale dans le Mantois et le Vexin au XIXème siècle*, Meudon, 1971.

Brule, J.-C., *Trois Communes de la Basse Vallée de l'Oise: Cergy, Jouy-le-moutier, Vaureal, de la fin de l'ancien régime à 1850; Etudes de la Région Parisienne*, 15, 16, 17, and 18, Paris, 1967–1968.

Bulletin de la Société d'agriculture et d'horticulture de l'arrondissement de Pontoise, 1850–1881 in 6 volumes.

Castelnau, Fernande, *Val d'Oise: anecdotes d'hier et d'aujour'hui*, Paris, 1972.

Charlot, A., "Ennery," 17 September 1899, Archives Nationales, Versailles.

Depoin, J., *Histoire populaire de Pontoise*, Pontoise, 1889.

Description générale et particulière de la France: voyage pittoresque de la France, vol. 4: *Paris et ses environs*, n.d.

Dictionnaire des communes, hameaux, écarts, fermes, et châteaux isolés du département de Seine-et-Oise, Versailles, 1858.

Duclos, Georges, *Pontoise féodal et souterrain*, Pontoise, 1968.

Duvivier, A., "St. Ouen-L'Aumône," 24 September 1899, Archives Nationales, Versailles.

L'Echo Pontoisien, ed., *Pontoise et ses environs*, illustrated by H. Bourguignon, Pontoise, 1931.

Egion, A., *Essai sur le département de Seine-et-Oise*, Paris, 1839.

Gantois. Charles "Les anciennes fortifications de Pontoise: l'urbanisme pontoisien au debut du XIX siècle à nos jours," *Mémoires de la Société historique et archéologique de Pontoise et du Vexin français*, vol. 50, 1943, pp. 113–87.

Garner, Prefet, *Description géographique, physique, et politique du département de Seine-et-Oise*, Paris, 1806.

Gressier, Jean, et al., *Pontoise: 2000 ans d'histoire*, Pontoise, 1973.

Guide pittoresque du voyageur en France: Département de Seine-et-Oise, Paris, 1834.

Joanne, Adolphe, *Les Environs de Paris*, 1856 and 1872.

Lazzarotti, Raymond, *L'Industrie et les complexes industriels dans la vallée de l'Oise*, Paris, 1968.

Le Charpentier, Henri, *Calendrier historique de Pontoise: éphémérides quotidiennes de l'histoire de cette ville*, Pontoise, 1882.

Lemoine, Henri, *Le département de Seine-et-Oise de l'an VIII à 1871*, Versailles, 1943.

Mataigne, H., *Notes historiques et géographiques sur Auvers-Sur-Oise*, Pontoise, 1885.

Mataigne, H., *Auvers-sur-Oise, 1906–1924*, Pontoise, n.d.

Moser, H., *Annuaire administratif, statistique, agricole, industriel, et commercial de Seine-et-Oise*, Versailles, 1865.

Richard, J.-B. and E.-M. St. Hilaire, *Guide du voyageur aux environs de Paris dans un rayon de 60 kilometres*, Paris, 1826 and 1840.

Sagine, E., "Ville de Pontoise," 1899, Archives Nationales, Versailles.

Signot, "Osny," 24 September 1899, Archives Nationales, Versailles.

Thomas, Léon, *Bibliographie de la ville et du canton de Pontoise*, Pontoise, 1883.

Thomas, Léon, ed., *Chroniques retrospectives sur Pontoise*, Pontoise, 1883.

Trou, M. l'Abbé, *Recherches historiques, archéologiques, et bibliographiques sur la ville de Pontoise*, Pontoise, 1841.

The Peasantry

Arland, Marcel, ed., *Le Paysan Français à travers la littérature*, Paris, 1941.

Benoit, J., *Histoire des paysans et leurs conditions à travers les siècles*, 1854.

Bonnemère, E., *Histoire des paysans depuis le fin du moyen âge jusqu'à nos jours*, 2 vols., 1856.

Dareste, C. and La Chavanne, *Histoire des classes agricoles en France depuis St. Louis à Louis XVI*, 1854.

Donial, H., *Histoire des classes rurales en France et de leurs progrès dans l'égalité civile et le propriété*, 1857.

Dordan, E., *Le Paysan français d'après les romans de XIXe siècle*, Toulouse, 1923.

Faucher, Daniel, *Le Paysan et la machine*, Paris, 1954.

Leymarie, M.-A, *Histoire des paysans en France*, 1849.

Walter, Gerard, *Histoire des paysans de France*, Paris, 1963.

Related Readings

Atlas historique de la France contemporaine: 1800–1965, Paris, 1966.

Barrau, T.-H., *Simples Notions sur l'agriculture*, Paris, 1868 and 1883.

Barron, Louis, *Les Environs de Paris*, Paris, 1886, illustrated by Fraipont.

Baudrillart, Henri, *Les Populations agricoles de la France, Normandie et Bretagne, passé et présent*, Paris, 1885.

Bloch, Marc, "L'Ile-de-France (le pays autour de Paris)," *Revue de Synthèse historique*, vols. 25 and 26, Paris, 1912 and 1913.

Brès, Louis, "Le paysage provençal et son influence au point de vue littéraire et artistique," Académie de Marseilles, Marseilles, 1883.

Brode, John, *The Process of Modernization, an annotated bibliography of the socio-cultural aspects of development*, Cambridge, Mass., 1970.

Castagnary, Jules, "Salon de 1866," *La Liberté*, 5–13 May 1866.

Claval, Paul and Etienne Juillard, *Région and regionalization dans la géographie française*, Paris, 1967.

Demangeon, Albert, *La maison rurale en France*, Paris, 1937.

Du Camp, Maxime, *Les Chants modernes*, Paris, 1855.

Ehrard, Jean, *L'Idée de nature en France à l'aube des lumières*, Paris, 1970.

Exposition universelle internationale de 1878 à Paris: le matériel et les procédes des industries agricoles et forestières, Paris, 1880.

Faucher, Daniel, *La Vie rurale vue par un géographe*, Toulouse, 1962.

Festy, Octave, *L'Agriculture pendant la révolution française, l'utilisation des jachères, 1789–1795*, Paris, 1950.

Flory, Thiebaut, *Le Mouvement régionaliste français*, Paris, 1966.

Fohlen, Claude, *Le Travail au XIXe siècle*, Paris, 1972.

Gachon, Lucien, *La Vie rurale en France*, Paris, 1967.

Gallois, Lucien, *Régions naturelles et noms de pays: étude sur la Région Parisienne*, Paris, 1908.

Geikie, Sir Archibald, *Landscape in History and other Essays*. London, 1905.

Girardin, J., and A. du Breuil, *Traité elémentaire d'agriculture* (4th edn.), Paris, 1885.

Gouirand, André, *Les Peintres provençaux*, Paris, 1901.

Grandvoinnet, J.-A., *Traité de mécanique agricole*, Paris, 1854.

Grandvoinnet, J.-A., ed., *Le Génie rural*, Paris, 1858–75.

Gravier, J.-F. *Régions et Nation*, Paris, 1942.

Hartman, Geoffrey, *Wordsworth's Poetry, 1787–1814*, New Haven, 1964.

Hauser, Arnold. *The Social History of Art*, New York. n.d.

Hufton, Olwen, *The Poor of Eighteenth-Century France, 1750–1789*, Oxford, 1974.

Joanne, Adolphe, *Atlas historique et statistique des chemins de fer français*, Paris, 1859.

Joanne, Paul, *Dictionnaire géographique et administratif de la France*, Paris, 1899.

Kropotkin, Peter, *The Conquest of Bread*, London, 1906.

Lami, E.-O., *Dictionnaire encyclopédique et biographique de l'industrie et des arts industriels*, 7 vols., Paris, 1881.

Lay, Jacques and Monique, *Louveciennes: hier et aujourd'hui*, Louveciennes, 1974.

Lefebvre, Georges, *Etudes sur la Révolution Française*, Paris, 1936.

Lemoine, L., *Les Artisans et l'industrie*, Paris, 1883.

Le Roy Ladurie, Emmanuel, *Le Territoire de l'historien*, Paris, 1973.

Meline, J., *Le Retour à la terre*, Paris, 1905.

Menon, P.-L. and R. Lecotte, *Au Village de France, la vie traditionelle*, 2 vols., Paris, 1945 and 1956.

Michel, Emile, *La Forêt de Fontainebleau*, Paris, 1909.

Mikesall, Marvin W., "Landscape" in *International Encyclopedia of the Social Sciences*, vol. 8, pp. 575–80.

Noilhan, H., *Histoire de l'agriculture et l'ère industrielle*, Paris, 1965.

Philipon, Charles, *Paris et ses environs reproduits par le daguerréotype*, Paris, 1840.

Philipponneau, Michel, *La Vie rurale de la banlieue parisienne: étude de géographie humaine*, Paris, 1956.

Ponce, I., *La Culture pratique*, Paris, 1869.

Ponce, I., *Traité d'agriculture pratique et d'économie rurale*, Paris, n.d.

Proud'hon, P.-J., *Lettre à M. Blanqui sur la propriété*, Paris, 1841.

Raulin, Henri, "Les Carriers et les tailleurs de grès de la région Parisienne," *Arts et traditions populaires*, vol. 9, no. 3, July and September 1961.

Sauer, Carl Otto, *Land and Life*, Berkeley, 1925 and 1963.

Schlatter, R.B., *Private Property, the History of an Idea*, New York, 1951.

Sigaux, Gilbert, *Histoire de tourisme*, Geneva, 1965.

Statistique de la France; industrie: résultats généraux de l'enquête effectuée dans les années 1861–1865, Nancy, 1873.

Statistiques de la France, Année 1872, Paris, 1875.

Thiers, Adolphe, *De la propriété*, Paris, 1848.

Tissandier, Gaston, ed., *La Nature*, Paris, 1873–1917.

Tulippe, Omer, *L'Habitat rural en Seine-et-Oise*, Liège, 1934.

Vincent, Marie-Louise, *George Sand et le Berry*, 2 vols., Paris, 1919.

Weber, Eugen, *Peasants into Frenchmen: The Modernization of Rural France, 1870–1914*, Stanford, 1976.

Williams, Raymond, *The Country and the City*, New York, 1973.

Zeldin, Theodore, *France: 1848–1945, vol. 1: Ambition: Love and Politics*, London, 1973.

Photographic Credits and Acknowledgments

Photographic material has been supplied by the owners except in the cases listed below. The list contains also relevant credit and copyright lines.

1, 23, 29, 31, 39, 112, 115, 136, 137, 138, 139, 155, 159, 167: © Photo Réunion des Musées Nationaux; 3, 4, 102, 111, 113: Sotheby's, London; 7, 8, 9, 10, 11, 19, 25, 26: Archives départementales du Val d'Oise; 13: David Carritt Ltd, London; 21: A.E. Dolinski Photographic, San Gabriel, Calif.; 33, 51, 168: Christie's Colour Library, London; 36: Sotheby's, New York; 38, 161: Carmel Wilson; 41: Honolulu Academy of Arts; 42, 121, jacket: Tom Jenkins, Dallas; 46: Staatliche Museen, Berlin; 50, 97, 105, 109: © Colorphoto Hans Hinz Allschwil-Basel; 61, 80, 88, 107, 108: Archives Durand-Ruel, Paris; 62: Michael Bodycomb; 63: Christie's, New York; 65: Brian Merrett/Jennifer Harper; 66: © Photo Routhier; 79: Paul Tucker; 81, 82, 83: courtesy of the Trustees of the British Library, London; 96: Knoedler & Co., Inc., New York; 103: Steven Sloman © 1985. Courtesy of Christie's, New York; 110: Öffentliche Kunstsammlung Basel; 130: Malcolm Varon, N.Y.C. © 1982; 131: Rheinisches Bildarchiv, Cologne; 141: Los Angeles County Museum of Art; 151: Staatens Konstmuseer, Stockholm; 164: courtesy of Sam Salz.

The following have been extremely helpful in obtaining photographic material for this book, and the authors and publishers would like to extend their thanks:

Annamarie Andersen (Galerie Koller, Zurich); Irina Antonova (Pushkin State Museum of Fine Arts); Mme. Françoise Balignano (Musée de la Chartreuse, Douai); Dr. Dominick Bartmann (Berlin Museum); Dr. Per Bjurström (Staatens Konstmuseer, Stockholm); Susan Boyles (Indianapolis Museum of Art); Mr. Charles R. Bronfman; John E. Buchanan, Jr. (Dixon Gallery and Gardens, Memphis); Ms. M. Paige Carter (Museum of Fine Arts, Boston); many people at Christie's, especially the Hon. Charles Allsopp and James Roundell in London, and Michael Findlay, Frank Giraud, and Diana Kunkel in New York; Deanna Cross (Metropolitan Museum of Art, New York); Mrs. Codiuta Cruceanu (Muzeul de Arta al R.S. Romania, Bucharest); Ms. France Duhamel (National Gallery of Canada); Caroline Durand-Ruel Godfroy: Dr. George E. Ellis (Director, Honolulu Academy of Arts); Dr. Manfred Fath (Städtische Kunsthalle Mannheim); Mrs. Marianne Feilchenfeldt and Dr. Walther Feilchenfeldt; Sammie S. Friedman (Louis Stern Galleries, Los Angeles); Dr. Christian Gelhaar (Director, Kunstmuseum, Basel); Prof. W.H. Gousel (Museum Boymans-van Beuningen, Rotterdam); Heather Haskell Museum of Fine Arts, Boston); M. and Mme. Jean Hecquet; Robert Henning Jr. (Santa Barbara Museum of Art); Ernest Herman; the Earl of Jersey; the Lefevre Gallery, London, especially Desmond Corcoran and Martin Summers; Mr. George Levy (Blairman & Sons); Mrs. Ann Meers; Nicole Misrahi; Mrs. Ruth A. Mueller; Mr. and Mrs. Arthur Murray; Mary Ann McSweeny (Sterling and Francine Clark Art Institute); Mr. Tatsuji Ohmori (curator, Bridgestone Museum of Art, Tokyo); Mary Pfeifer (Los Angeles County Museum of Art); Ivan E. Phillips; Mr. Tim Rice; Laura Richens (Memphis Brooks Museum of Art); David Rockefeller; Conchita Romero (Caylus, Madrid); Anne Roquebert (Musée d'Orsay); Baron Edmond de Rothschild; Dr. S. Salzmann (Director, Kunsthalle, Bremen); Marc Scheps (Director, Tel Aviv Museum of Art); Manuel Schmit (Galerie Schmit, Paris); many people at Sotheby's, especially Majorie Delpech, Lucy Dew, and Michel Strauss in London, and Roberta Lux, Judy Murphy, David Nash, and John Tancock; Christine Speroni (Musée d'Art Moderne de Strasbourg); Anna Maria Staechelin; Louis Stern; Ms. Mikako Tsukada (Bridgestone Museum of Art, Tokyo); M. Roland Vasseur; Roger B. Ward (Nelson-Atkins Museum of Arts); Ted Weisman; Daniel Wildenstein; the staff of the Wildenstein Foundation, especially Thérèse Nanus in Paris and Mrs. Ay-Whang Hsia in New York; Eve Winson (Whitworth Art Gallery, Manchester); Dorit Yifat (Tel Aviv Museum of Art); Koji Yukiyama (National Museum of Western Art, Tokyo); Dr. Michael F. Zimmermann (Kunsthistorisches Institut der Freien Universität, Berlin).

Index